AN
ANGLO-INDIAN DICTIONARY

AN
ANGLO-INDIAN DICTIONARY

A GLOSSARY

OF INDIAN TERMS USED IN ENGLISH, AND OF SUCH ENGLISH OR OTHER NON-INDIAN TERMS AS HAVE OBTAINED SPECIAL MEANINGS IN INDIA

GEORGE CLIFFORD WHITWORTH

GYAN

Published by

Gyan Publishing House
5, Ansari Road
Daryaganj, New Delhi-110002
Phone: 011-47034999, 9811692060
E-mail: books@gyanbooks.com

Distribution Network
gyanbooks.com
India, USA, Canada, UK, Australia

ISBN: 978-93-6280-077-0 (HB)
First Published, 1885

2nd Impression 2024

Printed at: Gyan Press, Delhi.

AN ANGLO-INDIAN DICTIONARY
Author: GEORGE CLIFFORD WHITWORTH

AN

ANGLO-INDIAN DICTIONARY

AN

ANGLO-INDIAN DICTIONARY

A GLOSSARY

OF INDIAN TERMS USED IN ENGLISH, AND
OF SUCH ENGLISH OR OTHER NON-INDIAN TERMS AS
HAVE OBTAINED SPECIAL MEANINGS IN INDIA

BY

GEORGE CLIFFORD WHITWORTH

BOMBAY CIVIL SERVICE
FELLOW OF THE UNIVERSITY OF BOMBAY

LONDON

KEGAN PAUL, TRENCH & CO., 1, PATERNOSTER SQUARE

1885

CONTENTS OF THE PREFACE.

PREFACE.

Of the Scope of the Work.

IN calling this work an Anglo-Indian Dictionary, some apology is needed, first, for the name itself, and secondly, for giving it to this particular collection of words. The term 'Anglo-Indian' would properly designate something which, originally Indian, has been specially modified by something English; but popularly it is applied to English persons residing in India and to things pertaining to them. And, while the stricter meaning does not wholly disqualify it, this inaccurate but common use of the term makes it specially appropriate as the name of a book which is not the work of an Oriental scholar, but only a compilation made for popular use by an Anglo-Indian official.

In this sense, then, an Anglo-Indian Dictionary should contain all those words which English people in their relations with India have found it necessary or convenient to add to their own vernacular, and should give also any special significations which pure English words have acquired in India; or, briefly, it should be an Indian supplement to the English dictionary. The words of Indian origin will be by far the most numerous, as it is usual, when new objects and ideas are met with to call them by the names they already possess. But this is not always done, and no one can make much acquaintance with India without hearing of alienated and unalienated land, permanent and annual settlements, inferior and superior holders, twice-born classes, right-hand and left-hand castes, village headmen and village accountants, governors and district officers; then references are frequently made to the solar race, the lunar race, the serpent race; even such words as 'month' and 'year' have different meanings in

India and in England; and there are many names which, though their component parts are familiar English, yet express things, unknown in England, such as 'bell music,' 'black buck,' 'carpet snake,' 'dancing-girl,' 'egg-plant,' 'fire-temple,' 'prayer-wheel,' 'slave-king,' 'sacred thread.' Again, there are several words which the Portuguese in their period of power introduced, and which are still current, such as 'ayah,' 'caste,' 'compound,' 'gram,' 'oart.'

But the present compilation falls far short of such a work as I have suggested above, and the title 'Anglo-Indian Dictionary' must be taken rather as denoting what it may possibly at some future time, with the help of fellow-workers in different parts of India, become, than as properly befitting it now. Still, I have reason to believe that, even in its present imperfect form, it will be found to be of considerable use; and having now devoted to it such spare time as I have been able to find in a period of ten years, I take the opportunity of my present furlough to have it published.

2. The scope of the work, as regards range of subject, is, as already shown, very wide; it remains to show how within each subject the range is limited. It seems to have been the usual practice, in compiling a glossary upon any Indian subject, to take and define every native word relating to the subject. But it is no part of the object of this glossary to serve the purpose, in any subject, of a Hindi or Bengali dictionary. I exclude such terms as are not commonly used in documents which purport to be written in English. As a rule, I exclude words which have adequate English equivalents. For example, I give no place to *farz*, duty; *farmaish*, an order; *farosh*, sale; *farzand*, offspring; *fasad*, vice; all taken from one page of Professor Wilson's glossary. And my reason is that persons who meet with any such word are those only who have knowledge of the native language to which it belongs, or at least have at hand a dictionary of that language. If, however, the word, unnecessary though it be, have yet forced its way into common use in English, it is inserted. Such words are **bundobust,** arrangement; **chit,** a letter; **kárkun,** a clerk. And if, though the word have a fair English equivalent, yet there is some special information to be given about it which it would be beyond the province of the Hindi or other vernacular dictionary to give, that word also is inserted. Such words are **devi, fasl,**

id, mandir, Shiah, Śiwa. Or an illustration of the line I attempt to draw may be taken from the names of the months and of the days; **Paush** and **Magaram** are not identical with January, and therefore are included; *Itwár* and *Raviwár* are precisely identical with Sunday, and therefore are excluded.

3. The second great limitation which I have endeavoured to observe has been to exclude words of minute technical meaning or of very restricted use. The book by no means purports to give the information of an encyclopædia, but is meant only as a ready handbook for immediate and momentary reference. Thus, while all important tribes and castes are inserted, minute subdivisions of castes (of which, indeed, sometimes nothing but the separate name could be predicated) are omitted. The great harvests, as the **kharif** and the **rabi**, are mentioned, but not the local names of minor intermediate ones. The commonest names of the principal crops (not possessing, like rice and cotton, well-known English names) are given, as **jawár** and **bájri** among cereals, and **arhar** and **chaná** among pulses; but not the names of the different varieties of these, nor the small occasional crops, nor any of the hundred different kinds of rice. So the main divisions of the land, according to its mode of cultivation, as the **ziráat, bágháyat,** and **kyári**, or according to the nature of the soil, as **khádar, kálibhui, bháṭhá**, are inserted, but not all the scores of names which natives find to distinguish every different quality and every possible mode of treatment. So the principal kinds of land tenure and of settlement, and the chief classes of the cultivators are described, as, for instance, under the words **inám, ryotwár, zamindár, paṭṭidári, khudkásht**, but not every peculiarity of relationship between landlord and tenant, nor any but the most important of the books and accounts kept in the management of land. So, again, some account is given of the more important divinities of the Hindu pantheon, as **Ganpati, Krishna, Jagannáth**, but not of every locally deified ghost.

However, it is much easier to point to salient examples upon each side than to uniformly follow the line of demarcation conceived; and I cannot hope that, in a work carried on so intermittingly as this of necessity has been, the question of selection or rejection has always been judiciously determined. Probably even strict impartiality has not been attained, but the information supplied will be found fuller in relation to parts of

India in which I have myself served, and scantier as more and more distant provinces are touched.

With regard to an important province of the work, namely, the definition of tribes and castes, information is still very incomplete; so much so that it is often doubtful to what extent different communities are allied. From time to time strange resemblances between distant peoples come to notice, as well as curious differences among tribes supposed to be closely allied. The whole subject deserves systematic treatment, and as one simple method of working in this field, especially on the borderland between Aryan and other races, I would suggest the recording of evidence under the following heads. They are restricted to matters upon which any one man of the tribe in question can furnish information:—

(1) Name of the caste or tribe.
(2) Specimens of personal names common among them.
(3) Language.
(4) Names of their chief gods.
(5) Occupation.
(6) Settled or wandering.
(7) Do they employ Bráhmans?
(8) Is marriage usually made in childhood or at full age?
(9) Is more than one wife allowed?
(10) Do widows remarry?
(11) Do they burn or bury their dead?
(12) Do they shave the head? or how do they wear the hair?
(13) What animals do they eat or refuse to eat?
(14) Do they drink spirits?

Of the Authority of the Work.

4. This work differs from most Indian glossaries in that it has not been prepared or published under the authority, or even with the countenance or encouragement, of any government. It, therefore, lacks such credit as would attach to a work carried out by an officer selected for his special competence. On the other hand, this absence of all official help has not been wholly without compensation, inasmuch as it has made the selection and definition of each word to be the work of a single hand; so that it will not, I think, be found in this glossary, as it too often is

in official ones, that the information given on one page has been written in obvious ignorance of what is recorded on another.

The work might have been more valuable if I had been able more frequently to quote authority for the statements made. With a few exceptions I have done this only when the whole of the information recorded has been taken in his own words from a single author. Where I have made even the slightest modification of an author's opinion I have usually omitted his name. And such cases are very numerous, because the system on which I have worked has been to read book after book, taking notes from each, and finally, from these notes under their several heads, and with the aid of the appropriate dictionaries, to frame the definitions. The preparation of the glossary has thus been subordinate to the study of general Indian questions; and I would suggest to possible workers in the same field that this is the most instructive, and perhaps the most effective, though it certainly is not the most rapid, mode of proceeding.

Though it is more than twenty years since I first began the study of Sanskrit, yet I never made much way in it, and my actual experience of India has been limited to a period of fifteen years. It will be readily understood, therefore, that, scarce as is the quotation of authorities in the following pages, yet little of the work, beyond the function of collecting, comparing, and selecting, is mine. In the comparatively few instances in which any opinion of my own has been advanced it has usually been done in qualifying terms indicating that the matter is suggested, not asserted.

Of the Arrangement.

5. It remains to give some account of the arrangement of the work, and this divides itself into three parts. First, there is the question of the system of transliteration of Indian words to be adopted. Next, the question of the amount of recognition to be given to forms which do not accord with that system, and the mode by which multiple forms of the same word are to be presented, and the correct shapes of corrupt forms indicated. Thirdly, some plan is necessary by which different and perhaps mutually distant definitions may be made to support and supplement one another.

6. With regard to the system of transliterating Indian words,

as there is now something like general agreement, and as in this work I abstain from all use of foreign characters, I will not present any table of equivalents, but it will be sufficient to say that the method adopted is that which was advocated by Sir William Jones, and is usually called by his name. That method, at least in its main principles, is now adopted by the Indian governments and by Oriental scholars, though a few variations of use in minor points remain. With regard to these a few remarks are necessary.

First, as to vowels. I have used no diacritical marks to distinguish the long and the short **i** or the long and the short **u**. Though the forms are distinct in print, yet natives of India do not observe the distinction in writing, and I have not thought it desirable to introduce special marks into English in order to do so. On the contrary, the length of the letter **a** can never be disregarded, and the two forms **a** and **á** are therefore used.

A difficulty remains as to the treatment of the short **a** so common at the end of Sanskrit nouns. Oriental scholars usually express it; the vernacular languages drop it. Sanskrit professors write amrita, veda, but the modern Indians say amrit, ved; and the popular god is Rám, not Ráma. If uniformity is to be attained, it must be by conforming to the vernacular practice, for many words are under that habit well established in English: such, for instance, as Bráhman and the name Sanskrit itself, which in their classical forms are *Bráhmana* and *Sanskrita*. But when the letter preceding the final **a** is either a semi-vowel or a double consonant, the **a** may well be expressed, for in these cases it is pronounced, though faintly, in modern speech, as **dewa** rather than *dev*, **śástra** not *śástr*. Meanwhile, the rule that I have adopted has been to follow the vernacular mode in the words which have entered English through modern speech, and to retain the Sanskrit form only in those which have come direct from Sanskrit literature.

Next, as to consonants. For the sake of persons who may use the book in India, I have distinguished between **ḍ**, which is pronounced with the tongue at the back of the palate, and the dental **d**; and so of **ṭ** and **t**, and the aspirated forms of the same letters; but English readers need pay no attention to these marks.

Professor Monier Williams's adoption of the otherwise idle

character **c** for the Indian **ch**, and of **ch** for the Indian **chh**, is very neat and attractive, but in a popular work of this kind I cannot ask English readers to pronounce **c** as **ch** in 'church,' and so I retain **ch** to represent the sixth consonant of the Sanskrit alphabet, and **chh** to represent the same letter aspirated.

I have not thought it necessary to introduce marks to distinguish the different letters corresponding to the English **n**; the variations of sound are not noticed by the English ear, and are in a majority of cases indicated to the Indian by the position of the letter or by the class of letter in connection with it.

So also the rare variety of the letter **l**, and the Sanskrit vowels which can be adequately represented by the combinations **ri** and **lri**, are not specially distinguished.

With regard to the representation of the sibilant which in sound holds a position between **s** and **sh**, a variety of use prevails. Some authorities give it as **sh**, which necessarily confuses it with another letter; others distinguish it by a dot placed beneath, which suggests that it belongs to the ḍ and ṭ class, while in fact it belongs to the **ch** and j class. I follow Sir William Jones and Professors Max Müller and Monier Williams in representing this letter as **ś**.

A difficulty remains as to the treatment of the letter which in English may be given either as **v** or **w**. Speaking in reference to Sanskrit only, Professor Monier Williams says it is pronounced as **w** after consonants, though for the sake of uniformity he uses always the form **v**. But to my ear there seems to be a decided difference in the native pronunciation of this letter in, for instance, such words as Varuna (Waruna) and Vishnu; and again just the same difference between dvápura (dwápura) and dvija, where a consonant precedes. And when we come to the corresponding letters of the Arabic alphabet, the distinction is very broad; the word for viceroy is certainly nawáb, not naváb. The best rule upon the point seems to me to be one which was prescribed by the Bombay government some years ago, namely, that the letter should be written as **w** before **a**, except **ai**; and as **v** in all other cases. This, then, is the rule which I have generally followed, making, however, many exceptions in the case of the Dravidian languages, which, judging by popular practice, make less use of the **w** sound.

Closely connected with the question of transliteration is that of the native form of the Indian word to be selected for representation. The rule I have adopted has been to reject terminations expressive of case, number, or gender (except when that is essential), and to use only root or oblique forms. The neglect of such a rule has led to some confusion, especially in the Madras presidency, where the English transliteration is sometimes from the nominative singular, as *Beḍan*, sometimes from the plural **Beḍar**, though treated in English as singular, and again sometimes from the oblique form, as *Beḍa*.

7. But whatever system of transliteration is approved, it is certain that, at least for many years to come, words will be introduced framed on other systems or even on no system. And the scope for variety in this way is almost unlimited. For instance, even such a short word as **wakil** may appear in as many as thirty-two forms; for the first letter of the original word may be given in English as **v** or **w**, the second as **a** or **u**, the third as **k**, **ck**, **q** or **qu**, and the fourth as **i** or **ee**. Obviously it would make this work very cumbrous if all such forms were inserted. The principles I have followed are these: (1) Where the irregular form has become familiar in English I have adopted it in preference to the correct one, indicating what the latter is in parentheses following, and, if necessary, inserting it also in its alphabetical place with a cross-reference to the more common orm. Thus—

Sepoy. [A corruption of the Persian *sipáhi.*]
Nautch. [A corruption of the Hindi *nách.*]
Nách. More commonly Nautch.

(2) Where the correct form of the word is preferred, other (inaccurate) forms are or are not inserted in their proper alphabetical places according to a combined consideration of the frequency of their use and the degree of their disguise. Though a form differ but slightly from the correct transliteration of the original, yet if it is of frequent occurrence it is inserted, as—

Beebee. See Bibi.

On the other hand, though a form be of rare occurrence, yet if it be difficult to recognize as identical with the form for which it is intended, it also is inserted, as—

Simrut. See Smriti.

This leaves an immense number of forms to be excluded as being neither of common use nor difficult to trace to their adopted forms. Readers acquainted with the system of transliteration will have little difficulty in determining under what form to look for any such word. For the sake of other readers I append a table by which the commoner corruptions can be got rid of and a word transformed to its proper shape (see page xvi.).

In writing irregular forms I do not use the diacritical marks belonging to systematic transliteration. The corrupt forms must be taken as attempts to represent Indian words by means of English characters as they are. Therefore I write **Bengali**, not *Bengáli*, the correct transliteration being *Bangáli*; **dacoity**, not *ḍácoity*, the correct form being *ḍákáiti*.

8. It remains to be explained next how I have attempted to make different parts of the dictionary supplement one another. This object is important, not only to save space, but also to facilitate comparison between different parts of India. For in a country of a hundred languages, as India is, there is often much of resemblance, or even identity, concealed under a difference of name. My plan has been to make frequent cross-references from one article to another, and sometimes to collect information, or even collect names, under one head, and refer to it when necessary. See, for instance, under the words Headman, Millet, Month. But besides the express references, I have intentionally throughout the work made frequent use of terms defined on other pages. So that any one using the dictionary can, if he desire, by looking out word after word, obtain more and more information upon the subject in hand.

Of Pronunciation.

9. The following letters should be pronounced as in the examples given :—

a	as in	mica	*ch*	as in	church
á	„	father	*g̱*	„	gun
ai	„	aisle	´	„	session
e	„	prey	*th*	„	ant-hill
o	„	cone			

For the rest the most natural English pronunciation will be sufficient for all English purposes.

RULES

FOR FINDING WORDS NOT GIVEN UNDER THE FORM FIRST LOOKED FOR.

(See section 7 of the Preface.)

For	*au*	substitute	*á*	as	ghaut—ghát.
„	*e*	„	*a*	„	dervish—darvesh.
„	*ee*	„	*i*	„	beebee—bibi.
„	*i*	„	*a*	„	sirkar—sarkár.
„	*o*	„	*a*	„	connaut—kanát.
			á	„	dol—dál.
			u	„	gomasta—gumáshta.
„	*oo*	„	*u*	„	gooroo—guru.
„	*ou*	„	*au*	„	chout—chauth.
„	*ow*	„	*au*	„	chowky—chauki.
„	*u*	„	*a*	„	guddee—gaddi.
„	*y*	„	*ai*	„	dyte—daitya.
„	*c*	„	*k*	„	cauzy—kázi.
			s	„	circar—sarkár.
„	*dg*	„	*j*	„	hedgra—hijra.
„	*f*	„	*ph*	„	phakeer—fakir.
„	*qu*	„	*k*	„	fuqueer—fakir.
„	*r*	„	*ḍ*	„	wara—wáḍa.
„	*sh*	„	*ś*	„	Sheev—Śiwa.
„	*v*	„	*w*	„	vuckeel—wakil.
„	*w*	„	*v*	„	Wishnoo—Vishnu.
„	*z*	„	*j*	„	Guzerattee—Gujaráti.

Strike out any consonant which is silent, or is used only, after the English manner, to modify the sound of a previous vowel, as chawbuck—chábuk, chudder—chadar.

ANGLO-INDIAN DICTIONARY.

Ábád. [Persian.] Populous, cultivated; applied to a village or tract of country which pays revenue; or, as a military phrase, to a place where supplies may be expected. The word is often affixed to a proper name to give a name to a city; as Murshidábád, the city of Murshid.

Ábádi. [Hindi, from *ábád.*] A place that is inhabited, or a place that is cultivated; a village site.

Aban. The name of the eighth month of the Pársi year. See Month.

Abar. [Assamese.] This name is applied by the Assamese to many frontier tribes, but belongs properly to one who call themselves Pádgam, and occupy a tract of country west of the Mishmi hills, east of the Miri hills, and north of the Lakhimpur district, but how far north their villages extend towards Thibet is not known. Their largest settlements are on the Dibang river. Formerly they used to make frequent raids upon the plains of Assam.

Abáshan. [Bengali.] The name of a low caste; they are cultivators and labourers.

Abd. [Arabic.] A slave. The word is much used in the composition of Muhammadan names; as Abdullah, the slave of God. Compare Ghulám.

Abdáli. [Hindustáni.] The name of a community of fakirs of the báshara order; they play the tambourine and chant hymns in aid of exorcists; when begging they play the one-end drum.

Ábdár. [Hindustáni, from the Persian *áb*, water, and *dár*, who holds.] A servant whose office it is to prepare water for domestic use.

Abdhut. [Hindi, from the Sanskrit *awadhuta*, from *awa*, off, and *dhuta*, from *dhu*, to shake.] One who has shaken off worldly feeling and obligation; the name of a sect of religious mendicants.

Abhidharma. [Sanskrit, from *abhi*, a prefix expressing intensity, and *dharma*, q.v.] The supreme truth; the name of one of the three piṭakas, that which treats of metaphysics.

Abhir. [Bengali, from the Sanskrit *abhira.*] The name of a caste more commonly called Áhir; they are cowherds and shepherds. Also the name of a dynasty supposed to have reigned in Magadha about 200 B.C.

Ábi. [Hindi, from the Persian *áb*, water.] A term applied to lands watered from ponds, tanks, or water-courses, in distinction to that which is watered from wells.

Ábkár. [Hindustáni, from the Persian *áb*, water, and *kár*, maker.] A maker of strong waters; a distiller.

Ábkári. [Hindustáni.] Revenue derived from duties on intoxicating liquors and drugs. The chief items are duties on distillation, fees for extracting juice from trees, and licences for the sale of liquors or drugs. In Bombay opium revenue is technically excluded from ábkári.

Abri. A variegated stone obtained from Kábul and used in building.

Ábukári. The Telugu form of Ábkár.

Abwáb. [Arabic, plural of *báb*, a section.] Heads or subjects of taxation, or the taxes which were imposed by the Muhammadan governments in addition to the regular assessment on the land; miscellaneous cesses, imposts, and charges, levied by zamindárs and public officers.

A. C. These letters stand for the words, 'after compliments,' an expression used in English translations in lieu of the adulatory phrases with which all Indian native letters commence.

Áchára. [Sanskrit, from *á*, to, and *char*, to go.] Established rules of conduct with regard to particular temporal duties. Finding no sufficient authority for these in the veda, some Indian writers have tried to prove that they are based on parts of the veda which no longer exist.

Áchári. A vernacular form of Áchárya.

Achárjya. [Bengali, from the Sanskrit *áchárya*, q.v.] The name of a caste in Bengal; they are astrologers and fortune-tellers, and generally resemble the Bháṭs. They claim to be of Bráhman origin.

Áchárya. [Sanskrit, from *áchára*, conduct.] A spiritual guide or teacher; the founder of a sect; or the conductor of a religious service. The word is affixed as a title to the name of any illustrious and learned man; as Śankaráchárya.

Achátur. [Kanarese.] The name of a caste of cultivators.

Achkát. [Kanarese.] The total area of land attached to a village, or the total area capable of being irrigated by a particular work.

Aḍad. The Gujaráti form of Urid.

Adálat. [Arabic, from *adl*, justice.] A court of justice. The adálats under the Muhammadan government were of four classes: the nizámat, the diwáni, the fauzdári, and the adálat-al-kázi (q.v.). Under the British government these courts were continued, with some modifications, until 1793, when the judicial and revenue departments were separated, and zillah and provincial courts were established, subordinate to one sadar or supreme adálat at the presidency (*H. H. Wilson*).

Adálat-al-kázi. [Arabic.] The court of the kázi, in which civil causes and questions regarding the Muhammadan religion were tried.

Adam. The name of one of the khels, or clans, of the Afridis.

Adar. The name of the ninth month of the Pársi year. See Month.

Áḍatiyá. [Gujaráti, from *áḍat*, agency, business carried on on behalf of another.] An agent, a broker.

Aḍatyá. [Maráṭhi, from *áḍat*, agency.] An agent, a broker.

Adbhutaśánti. [Sanskrit, *adbhuta*, wonderful, supernatural, and *śánti*, peace, from *sam*, to be calm.] An atharwa liturgy and burnt sacrifice used to avert misfortunes which would follow evil omens.

Áḍḍi. [Bengali.] A title or cognomen given to persons who are, or whose ancestors were, money weighers and changers.

Addika. [Kanarese, from the Sanskrit *adhyaksha*, from *adhi*, over, and *aksha*, the eye.] An officer employed to superintend cultivation and the division of the produce on behalf of government.

Adhela. [Hindi, from the Sanskrit *arddha*, half.] Half a pice, a copper coin worth three pies.

Adheli. [Hindi, from the Sanskrit *arddha*, half.] Half a rupee, a silver coin worth eight annas.

Adhiár. [Hindi, from *arddha*, half.] A cultivator who assists in cultivating land on condition of receiving half the crop.

Adhika. [Sanskrit.] Additional; a term applied especially to an intercalated tithi or month. See Tithi. A month is intercalated in the luni-solar year when two new moons occur in one solar month; the extra and the ordinary month receive the same name, distinguished by the additions adhika and nija. Thus in the solar month Eddavam 1052 Paraśuráma (which began May 13, 1877) the moon was twice in conjunction with the sun, and there were consequently two Jyeshṭhs in the luni-solar year. See Month.

Adhikári. [Sanskrit, from *adhi*, over and *kári*, a doer, an agent, from *kri*, to do.] A superintendent, a person having authority.

Adhipati. [Sanskrit, from *adhi*, over, and *pati*, a master.] A ruler, a king.

Adhiráj. [Sanskrit, from *adhi*, over, and *rája*.] A paramount ruler.

Adhwaryu. [From the Sanskrit *adhwara*, a sacrifice.] The name of the third class of priests required at a vedic sacrifice. They had to prepare the ground, procure and kill the animals, and do all the manual labour of the sacrifice. The yajurveda was for their use, the part called bráhmana prescribing every act they had to do, and the sanhita furnishing them, in right order, with the mantras they had to mutter.

Áḍi. The Tamil name of the solar month Karkatagam, corresponding most nearly to Śráwan. See Month.

Adigar. A Sinhalese form of Adhikári.

Ádi Granth. [Panjábi, *ádi*, the first, and *granth*, book, from the Sanskrit *granth*, to string together.] The first and principal scripture of the Sikhs, consisting of the sayings of the first four gurus, collected by Arjun, the fifth guru. Compositions by later gurus and various saints and singers have been added. The whole is metrical, and the language mostly Hindi, and in the gurumukhi characters.

Adil Sháhi. The name of a Musalmán dynasty, a branch of the Báhmani, which ruled at Bijápur from 1489 till 1672 or later. The Báhmani contests with Vijayanagar were continued by the Adil Sháhi sultáns, and that state was broken up in 1565 by a combination between Bijápur, Ahmádnagar, Golconda, and Bidar. The Adil Sháhis acquired much of the territories of Bidar and Ahmadnagar as those states successively fell, and were themselves extinguished by the Moguls in 1686.

Aḍima. [Malayálam, from *aḍi*, the bottom, the base.] The feudal dependency of a Nair upon some chief whom he selects for his protector or patron ; a grant of land on favourable terms from a superior to his vassal.

Ádináth. [Sanskrit, *ádi*, the beginning, and *nátha*, lord.] The name of the first arhat or jin of the Jains. It is fabled that before his time there was neither rain, nor fire, nor any thorny tree ; he introduced learning and the sciences of literature, government, and cultivation. He is called also Ádiśwara and Rishabhdewa.

Ádisamáj. [Sanskrit, *ádi*, the first, and *samája*, society.] The name of a religious community, a branch of the Brahmasamáj.

Ádiśwara. Another name of Ádináth.

Áditya. [Sanskrit, from *aditi*, that which is not tied, creative power.] The sun, the god of the sun. According to one vedic legend, Brahma from his feet created the earth, from his body the sky, and from his head the heaven, and then created Agni, Wáyu, and Áditya, as gods of those three regions. There are sometimes said to be seven, and again twelve, Ádityas, by which are meant the twelve diversified forms of the sun in the twelve months of the year.

Aḍiya. [Malayálam, from *aḍi*, the base, the foot.] A vassal, a bondman ; a predial slave attached hereditarily to land, and only transferable with it.

Ádlingadawar. [Kanarese.] The name of an agricultural caste.

Adoni. See Aḍima.

Advaita. [Sanskrit, *a* privative, and *dvaita*, q.v.] Non-duality ; the doctrine affirmed by the Smártas, that spiritual existence only is real, the human soul being one with the divine essence.

Advichinchi. [Kanarese.] The name of a cultivating caste.

Adyar. See Adhiár.

Adzan. See Azán.

Afái. [Hindi.] The snake echis carinata. See Fursá.

Afghán. The name of a particular tribe that gives its name to Afghánistán, and also the general name of all the tribes of that country. In the latter sense the term includes (1) the Afgháns proper, or Bani Israil, as they call themselves, and who are supposed to be of Jewish or Arab descent, and the chief branch of which is the Duráni ; (2) the Paṭhán tribes, considered to be of Indian origin ; (3) the Ghilzai tribe ; and (4) the Tájik and Hazára, two Persian-speaking tribes. See Pashṭo.

Afridi. A large Paṭhán tribe occupying the extensive hill region extending from the Cabul river round the spurs of the Safed Koh as far as Kohat. Their neighbours on the north are the Mahmands, and on the south the Arakzais. They have no connection with the Cabul government. The Afridis are the best-armed and the most warlike of all the border tribes, and they can muster about 20,000 fighting men. Through the northern portion of their country pass the Khybar and Tatarra routes between Peshawar and Cabul. On the south of the Khybar Pass their hills project eastwards towards the Indus, and very considerably indent the British border, thus separating, by a strip of independent hills, the two most important frontier garrisons of Peshawar and Kohat. There are two passes through these hills, the Galli and the Jawaki, but both are out of the direct control of the British, who pay the Afridis of the Galli Pass Rs. 13,700 a year for its use (*H. W. Bellew*). There are some Sikhs settled in the Tiráh valleys among the Afridis; they are called Tiráhi Sikhs or Tiráhi Afridi Sikhs. Some have enlisted in British regiments and the police.

Afrit. [Arabic, from *afr*, to roll in the dust.] A giant, a demon.

Áftábi. [Hindustáni, from the Persian *áftáb*, the sun.] A large flat circular or semicircular parasol, one of the Mogul insignia of high rank.

Aganhotri. A vernacular form of Agnihotri.

Agaram. A Tamil contraction of Agrahára.

Ágari. [Maráṭhi, from *ágar*, a tract of land on which salterns are established.] The name of a division of the race of Kolis who occupy themselves in the production of salt, in the cultivation of khárapáṭ lands, and as boatmen; some also are liquor-sellers. Their favourite deity is Khandoba of Jejuri.

Agarwálá. [Hindi, from *Agrohá*, the name of a place to the west of Delhi.] The name of a caste in the North-West Provinces and Central India; their profession is trade, and many are Jains by religion. They are reputed to be Vaiśyas, but claim in some parts to be Kshatriyas.

Agasa. [Kanarese.] The name of a caste; they are washermen, and seldom follow any other profession. Some few are engaged in agriculture or as labourers. Both men and women wash. Their proper beasts of burthen are asses. The Agasa is a member of the village corporation; the office is hereditary, and the duties, besides washing, include the bearing of a torch in public processions.

Agasála. [Kanarese.] The name of a subdivision of the Pánchálas; they are goldsmiths.

Agási. [Maráṭhi, from the Sanskrit *ákása*, the sky.] A verandah, or terrace, made of chunam, built on the top of a house or over some projecting portico, and open to the sky.

Agayadi. [Kanarese.] Small plots of land in which rice is first sown to be transplanted afterwards to the field.

Ágdán. [Hindustáni, from *ág*, the Sanskrit *agni*, fire, and the Persian *dán*, a receptacle.] A small vessel of metal with a wooden handle, for serving burning charcoal to light cigars with.

Agent. This word, with or without the prefix 'political,' is the usual official title of the chief representative of the British power in a native state over which a considerable degree of control is maintained. There are agents to the governor-general in Central India, Rájputáná, and Baroda, and agents to governors in many smaller states. Compare Resident.

Ágewán. [Gujaráti, from the Sanskrit *agra*, first.] A leader; the chief of a gang. The term is sometimes used to distinguish those of the sharers in a watan who render the services for which the watan was granted.

Aghan. [Hindi contraction of the Sanskrit *agrahâyana*, from *agra*, first, and *hâyana*, a year.] Another name of the month Márgaśirsha, which was at one time counted the first of the year.

Aghani. [Hindi.] The harvest of Aghan, the kharif or cold-season harvest.

Agharni. [Gujaráti.] A joyful celebration on the occasion of a woman's first pregnancy.

Agháṭ. [Gujaráti.] A deed of gift or sale of land engraved on stone and placed in the land to which it refers.

Agháṭiá. A term applied to land held on an agháṭ title.

Aghora, Aghori. [Hindi, from the Sanskrit *aghora*, a euphemistic name of Śiwa, from *a* privative, and *ghora*, terrible.] The name of an order of religious mendicants whose practices are designed to make them as terrible as possible in the eyes of the people. They usually go naked, with a human skull full of ordure in one hand and a pan of burning coals in the other. They pretend to be perfectly indifferent as to what they eat, be it ordinary food, carrion, ordure, or a human corpse; so also they will drink any liquid. Aghoris are found in many parts of India; at the gháṭs in Benares, in Tirhut, and in the wilder parts of Káṭhiáwár. An Aghori was lately convicted of offering an indignity to a human corpse, he having disinterred the body of a child and eaten a portion of it. Another was found with the hand and foot of a child only partially stripped of the flesh. (Aghori has been suggested as the possible origin of the word 'ogre.')

Aghormárg [Sanskrit *márga*, a way], **Aghorpanth** [Sanskrit *pantha*, a way]. Other names for Aghori.

Agiári. [Gujaráti, from the Sanskrit *agni*, fire, and *agár*, a place.] A Pársi temple in which a perpetual fire is maintained as an emblem of Hormazd.

Agni. [Sanskrit.] Fire; the god of fire. Agni is one of the principal vedic gods. He is sometimes called the lowest of the gods, inasmuch as, being the god of fire on the hearth, he is the nearest god who descends from his high station to befriend men, and who, in the form of the sacrificial fire, becomes the messenger and mediator between god and men. Agni is sometimes spoken of as being of triple form, namely, those of fire on the earth, lightning in the air, and the sun in heaven.

Agnihotra. [Sanskrit, from *agni*, q.v., and *hotra*, a sacrifice.] An oblation to Agni; the sacred fire; maintenance of it.

Agnihotri. [Sanskrit.] One who makes or maintains agnihotra.

Agnikula. [Hindi.] The pit for the sacrificial fire; several Rájput tribes, not pretending to be of the solar or lunar races, say they are sprung from progenitors created by a rishi from a fire-pit on mount Ábu; among these are the Parmár, Solanki and Chauhán; the Parihár is sometimes added, and sometimes the Ráṭhor and Jádav.

Agradána. [Bengali.] A Bráhman of inferior rank, who conducts funeral obsequies for hire.

Agrahára. [Sanskrit, from *agra*, first, and *hára*, taking.] Land granted to Bráhmans, either rent free or at a low rate. Also, in Tamil, a street or quarter occupied by Bráhmans.

Agrahayan. See Aghan.

Agrahri. The name of a trading class in Behar. They are Sikhs by descent.

Ágri. See Ágari.

Ágri. [Maráṭhi.] Salt bagáyat land.

Águri. [Bengali.] The name of a caste in Bengal; they are cultivators, and are deemed equal in rank to pure Śudras.

Agwa. [Hindi.] A village servant who acts as guide to travellers.

A. H. These letters stand for the words 'anno hijra.' See Hijra.

Ahádis. [The plural of *hadis*, q.v.] Traditions, especially those of the acts of Muhammad.

Aham. The name of the tribe which has given its name to Assam. They were of Shan origin, and are supposed to have entered the Brahmaputra valley from the north-east in the thirteenth century; they possessed a highly organized system of government, all the adult males being classified into regiments and brigades for civil as well as military purposes; they became converts to Hinduism about the year 1650, and their dynasty survived to the beginning of the present century.

Ahambadiyan. [Tamil.] The name of a caste; they resemble the Marawans, but are esteemed slightly inferior. They are chiefly cultivators, but many are employed by zamindárs as retainers and domestic servants, and some are shopkeepers.

Ahar. [Hindi.] The name of a tribe or caste extensively spread through Rohilkhand and other districts in the North-West Provinces, following pastoral occupations and claiming to be Jádon Rájputs. They smoke and drink with Játs and Gujars, but disclaim all connection with Áhirs.

Áhir. This name, which is a Hindi form of Abhir, belongs to a very large pastoral tribe found in many different parts of India; at the beginning of the Christian era the Áhirs were the ruling tribe in Nepal, and Ásirgarh in the Deccan is named after one Ásá, an Áhir; they are now most numerous in the North-West Provinces, but are found also under the same name in Kaṭhiáwár and Khándesh, while it is probable that the Goálás are only a subdivision of the tribe. Some Áhirs have been converted to islám.

Ahl-i-hadis. [Arabic.] People of

the hadis, or tradition, a name of the Wahhabi sect.

Ahl-i-kitáb. [Arabic.] People of the book, that is Muhammadans, Jews, and Christians.

Ahl-i-sunnat. [Arabic.] People of the sunnat, or sunnah, a name for the Sunni Muhammadans.

Ahl-ul-iltizal. [Arabic.] The people of separation, another name for the Mutazala sect.

Ahluwalia. See Alhuwáliá.

Ahmad Sháhi. The name of the branch of the Báhmani dynasty which, on the dismemberment of the latter in 1489 A.D., established itself in Berar. This dynasty lasted till 1574, when Berar was conquered and annexed to the Ahmadnagar state.

Ahom. See Aham.

Ahri. One of the gods of the Himálayan tribes; he is conceived as a mighty hunter armed with bows and arrows of steel, and is considered to preside over ordeals.

Ahriman. The name of the personified principle of evil in the Zoroastrian religion.

Ahun. The title of the chief of a clan among the Toungjynyas, corresponding to the diwán of the Chakmás.

Ahura Mazda. The Zoroastrian name of God; he is recognized as the creator, ruler, and preserver of the universe, without form and invisible; therefore no image of him is required for the purpose of worship; he is an immense light, from which all glory, bounty, and goodness flow; the adoration or worship of any other object is blasphemous. (*Dosábhái Frámji*).

Áil. [Bengali.] An earthen balk or ridge, dividing one plot of cultivated ground from another; it is generally very narrow, but sometimes broad enough for a trackway.

Aima. [Arabic.] Land granted by the Mogul government, either free of rent or subject to a small quit-rent, to learned and religious Muhammadans, or for religious and charitable uses.

Aimadár. [Persian *dár*, holder.] The holder of aima land.

Aimak. See Eimák.

Aimmokkalu. [Koḍagu, from *aiwattu*, fifty, and *wokkalu*, farmer.] The name of an agricultural caste the descendants of fifty families brought from the Mysore frontier into Coorg, in the reign of Vira Rajendra (1780–1809 A.D.). They conform generally to the habits of Koḍagas, but are Śri Vaishnawas in religion.

Ain. [Arabic.] Property actually existing. As a revenue term in the Bombay presidency, ain means actual, regular, or standard, as opposed to sáyer, or occasional. So the term is applied to regular regiments as opposed to irregular soldiery.

Áin. [Persian.] Secular as distinguished from sacred laws; regulations, as the ain Akbari, the regulations of Akbar (the third Timuride).

Áin. [Hindi.] The tree terminalia tomentosa; the wood is hard and durable, and is used both for building and for fuel; the bark is used in tanning, and the sap yields a gum which is largely eaten.

Ain-mokásá. [Maráṭhi, from the Arabic.] The share of sixty-six per cent. of the Maráṭhi chauth, which was given to the Maráṭhá jágirdárs for keeping up the troops.

Airi. The name of a subdivision of the Pánchála in Coorg; they are carpenters and iron-smiths, and are said to have come from Malayálam.

Aishmahal. [Hindi, from Arabic *aish*, pleasure, and *mahal*, a chamber.] The inner or female apartments of a palace.

Ajamán. A Telugu form of Jajmán.

Aka. [Assamese.] The name of a hill tribe on the Assam frontier. The Akas call themselves Hrusso, and are divided into two clans, called Hazárikhoa and Kapáschor, nicknames which mean 'eaters of a thousand hearths' and 'thieves that lurk in the cotton-fields' respectively. The latter clan has lately adopted a form of Hinduism.

Akábar. [Gujaráti, from the Arabic.] A term used among Pársis to denote a leader of their community.

Akáli. [Panjábi, from the Sanskrit, *a* privative, and *kála*, time.] Eternal or immortal; the name of a body of Sikh devotees, who claimed for themselves a direct institution by Govind Singh, the last guru. They professed to have sacrificed everything for the faith, and followed only the profession of arms.

Ákáśiá. [Gujaráti, from the Sanskrit *ákáśa*, the sky.] A term applied to rice-crops watered by rain only, and not from tanks.

Ákáśmukhi. [Sanskrit, *ákáśa*, the sky, and *mukha*, the face.] A Śaiwa ascetic who keeps his head always bent back and his face turned up to the sky.

Akháḍá. [Hindi.] A place for bodily exercises and games; also a place of resort for gambling or any improper practice; also the residence of a society of religious mendicants.

Ákhari - chárshambah. [Hindustáni.] The last Wednesday; the name of a lesser id held on the last Wednesday in Safar, in remembrance of the prophet's having in his last illness recovered a little on this day.

Akhat. See Akshata.

Akhátari. A Gujaráti corruption of Akshayatritiyá.

Akhbár. [Arabic, the plural of *khabar*, q.v.] News, intelligence, a newspaper; especially the written intelligence of the proceedings of native courts and princes circulated to other courts and princes by their appointed agents—a regular practice under the native administration.

Akhbárnavis. [Hindustáni, from *akhbár*, and *navis*, q.v.] A news-writer, the correspondent of a native state or of a newspaper.

Ákhun. [Persian.] A teacher or schoolmaster. In the Muhammadan villages of the south of India, the ákhun is a village officer paid by the community (*H. H. Wilson*). Ákhun is also the title of the ruler of Swát. He is a very powerful personage—saint and king combined—who entirely controls the actions of all the tribes between the Indus and Cabul, from the confines of Káshmir to those of Sindh, and who is extremely hostile to all infidels, especially Europeans (*H. W. Bellew*).

Akikiá. [Gujaráti, from the Arabic *akik*, a cornelian.] This is the name given to the master artificers in the cornelian and agate business in Cambay. There are five classes of persons who work upon these stones (besides the Bhils, who collect them), and the whole body is called the *Akikiá jamát*, the Akikiás being the chief of the five classes.

Akoukwoon. [Burmese, from *akouk*, custom duties, and *woon*, q.v.] A collector of customs.

Akrá. [Hindi.] A kind of vetch, vicia sativa; it injures crops, but is useful as fodder.

Akshata. [Sanskrit.] Literally, unbroken; applied to whole grains of rice placed on the forehead of an idol, or of a bride or bridegroom; also a name of the tilak.

Akshayatritiyá. [Sanskrit, from *a* privative, *kshaya*, decay, and *tritiya*, the third day.] The festival of the third Vaiśákh śudh; it is the first day of the satyayuga, and is supposed to secure permanency to actions then performed. It is the great day of omens; on the previous evening little model towns are made of grain outside the villages, and omens taken in the morning from the disturbance caused by the weather or animals.

Ál. [Hindi.] The name of a plant, the morinda citrifolia, the root of which yields a red dye. It is called also suranji and sorangi.

Alakhgir, Alakhnámi. [Hindi, from the Sanskrit *alakshya*, without attributes, and the Persian active affix *gir*, or the Sanskrit *náma*, a name.] The name of a sect founded in Bikanir by a Chamár; he denounced idolatry, and taught his followers to call only on the incomprehensible, and to practise charity and asceticism, which would bring their own reward in peace of mind.

Alcanna. [Through the Spanish, from the Arabic *al-hiná*, the shrub lawsonia inermis.] Another name for Henna.

Alhuwáliá. [Panjábi, from *Alhu*, a village on the left bank of the Bias.] The name of one of the Sikh misls and of the family now ruling in Kapurthála.

Aliá. [Gujaráti.] The name of a body of trading Vorás, who in 1624 refused to accept the successor appointed by their high priest, and made themselves a separate body under Ali, the son of the late high priest.

Alienated. This term means transferred in so far as the rights of government to payment of the rent or land revenue are concerned, wholly or partially, to the ownership of any person. Alienated land is usually surveyed and assessed by government like other land; if wholly alienated, the whole of the assessment belongs to the inámdár, but usually a small portion is received by government as quit-rent, salámi or joḍi, and the rest is called alienated revenue, nuksán, or loss. An alienated village (see Village) is one of which the whole revenue or some fixed proportion of the revenue has been transferred to a private owner.

Alienation. When the government right to receive revenue from any land has been transferred to any person, and when any periodical cash allowance has been made to any person or family, either permanently or for one or more lives, such land or cash allowance is termed an alienation.

Alifshái. [Hindustáni.] Another name for the Benawa fakirs, so called from their wearing a straight line, like the letter alif, down the brow and nose.

Ali-Iláhi. The name of a heterodox school of Muhammadans. They believe in incarnations of God, beginning with Adam and ending with Ali. They say that Allah took the form of Ali when he saw the defects of Muhammad as a prophet. They affirm that the koran was forged by the first three caliphs.

Alim. [Arabic.] A wise man; a doctor of the law.

Alkoran. This is the word 'koran' with the article prefixed.

Allah. [Arabic, from *al*, the, and *ilah*, God.] The highest of the hundred Moslem names of God.

Allah-ho-Akbar. [Arabic.] 'God is great!' the exclamation repeated at Musalmán funerals, while the bier is in the outer court of the mosque.

Almára. [A Hindi corruption of the Portuguese *almaria.*] A cupboard, a cabinet.

Almirah. See Almára.

Alpesee. See Arpasi.

Alsandi. [Kanarese.] The name of a pulse, the dolichos catjang.

Áltamghá. [From the Turkish *ál*, red, and *tamghá*, a stamp.] A royal grant under the seal of some of the former native princes of Hindustán, and recognized by the British government as conferring a title to rent-free land in perpetuity, hereditary and transferable (*H. M. Elliot*).

Alu. [Hindi.] The name of an esculent root, the colocasia antiquorum.

Alutá. [Maráṭhi.] This is an alliterative term derived from balutá, and is used to denote collectively various other village servants of less importance than the balutás.

Aluvar. See Álvár.

Álvár. [Tamil.] Rulers, the collective name of twelve teachers of the Vaishnawa faith in southern India; they lived in different times and different places, and translated portions of the veda into Tamil.

Amah. [Maráṭhi, *ámá*, the breast.] A term used in Anglo-Indian nurseries for wet-nurse.

Amaldár. [Hindustáni, from the Arabic *amal*, office, and Persian *dár*, holder.] An officer, a manager, an agent. In Mysore, the native head revenue officer of a táluka, corresponding to the tahsildár or mámlatdár of other provinces.

Amalnámah. [Hindustáni, from the Arabic *amal*, business, and Persian *námah*, a writing.] A document giving authority to manage property or to take possession.

Amáni. [Tamil.] A system of land revenue under which the government share of the produce is taken in kind. The term is also applied to the direct management of a village by government officers without the intervention of a zamindár.

Amanji. [Tamil.] Compulsory service without payment for a public purpose. Compare Veṭh.

Ámanth. [Bengali.] The name of a caste of whom there are many in Tirhut; they are employed chiefly as personal servants.

Amarapura Samágama. [Sinhalese, from *Amarapura*, the capital of Burma, and Sanskrit *samágama*, a society.] The name of a sect of Buddhists who were introduced from Burma into Ceylon at the beginning of the nineteenth century, and who maintain communion with Burma.

Amári. See Ambári.

Amás. A vernacular contraction of Amáwasi.

Amátya. [Sanskrit.] A counsellor, a minister; especially the title of one of the eight pradháns of the Maráṭhá state.

Amáwasi. [Sanskrit, from *amá*, together, and *was*, to dwell.] The day of conjunction of the sun and moon, the day of new moon; it is always the last day of the Krishnapaksha. See Month, Purnima, Tithi.

Amazai. A Paṭhán tribe settled on the mountains on the west of the Indus in that part of its length (between lat. 34° 20′ and 34° 40′ N.) in which it forms our frontier. Part of the tribe is settled on the Yusufzai plain within our border.

Ambá. [Sanskrit.] A mother; an epithet of Durgá or Bhawáni. Ambá is no doubt the same word as the Dravidian amma, but whether the latter is a corruption or the former an adoption is uncertain.

Ambáḍi. [Maráṭhi.] A plant, the hybiscus cannabinus, called also Bombay hemp. Oil is extracted from the seed, and ropes are made of the fibre, and the leaves are edible.

Ambala. [Tamil.] A place or shed where public affairs are discussed. In Malabar, a temple of the first class.

Ambalagár, Ambalakára. [Tamil, from *ambala*, and *kára*, agent.] The head of a village, a náṭṭánmaikára, a paṭel; especially in a Marawa or Kalla village.

Ambári. [Arabic.] A canopied seat on an elephant or camel.

Ambári. See Ambáḍi.

Ambashṭha. [Sanskrit.] The name of a caste said to be the offspring of a Bráhman father and Vaiśya mother; the occupation of the caste is medicine.

Ambaṭṭan. [Tamil.] The name of a caste; they are barbers, and many of them doctors and surgeons as well, and their women are commonly employed as midwives. Compare Hajám, Nápit, Nhávi.

Ambu. [Tamil.] The name of a division of the Paraiyans; their proper profession is hunting with the bow and arrow; they act as shikáris and beaters to zamindárs and others.

Ameen. See Amin.

Ameindaw. [Burmese.] A government order, or farmán.

Ámil. [Arabic.] The name of a high revenue officer under the Muhammadan government; he used to receive the revenue from the máliks, who collected it from the villages. In Sindh, the term is applied to all Hindus of the writer class.

Amildár. This title has arisen out of confusion between the Arabic words *amal*, or office, and *ámil*, a particular officer. The addition of the Persian *dár* to ámil is meaningless. The term is used to denote that particular amaldár who is ámil.

Amildári. The office or jurisdiction of an ámil.

Amin. [Hindustáni, from the Arabic *aman*, to trust.] An umpire, an arbitrator; a trustee, a confidential agent; a judge. In Gujarát formerly influential cultivators were appointed under this name to assist the revenue officers in estimating crops, assessing land, etc. This office was not hereditary.

Amin paṭel. [Gujaráti.] An officer appointed under the Maráṭhá government in Gujarát to aid the district officers in estimating crops, fixing the assessment upon waste lands, and in collecting the revenue. The office, unlike that of deśái and majmudár, was stipendiary, and not hereditary.

Aminsukhḍi. [Gujaráti, from *amin*, and *sukhḍi*, q.v.] The emoluments of amins appointed to assist in the revenue management of a táluká.

Amir. [Arabic, from *amar*, to command.] A commander, a nobleman, a Muhammadan of high rank. Amir is the hereditary title of the ruler of Afghánistán, and was also that of the chieftains of Sindh. The plural is *amrá*, or *umrá*, which in English sometimes appears as *omrah*.

Amir-al-mumanin. [Arabic, *munin*, faithful.] Commander of the faithful, a title adopted by the second caliph Omar, and thence applied to his successors.

Amir-al-umra. [Arabic.] Chief of the nobles; a title conferred by the sovereign at his pleasure, sometimes designating the commander-in-chief.

Ámla. [Arabic, plural of *ámil*.] A collective name for the officers of a court or office.

Amma. [Kanarese.] A mother; especially Máramma, the village goddess, and, in Coorg, the river goddess, mother Káveri. The Amma Koḍagas are a small and exclusive sect, supposed to have been the indigenous priesthood, but now ousted from their position by Bráhmans. They do not eat or intermarry with the other Koḍagas, nor do they use flesh or fermented liquor.

Ampadda. See Ambaṭṭan.

Amrita. [Sanskrit, *a* negative, and *mrita*, dead, from *mri*, to die.] Immortality, the nectar conferring immortality, the soma juice. It is fabled that when the daityas became too strong for the gods, by a device of Vishnu's the ocean was churned, mount Mandara serving as the stick, and the serpent Wásuki as the rope, and the amrita produced, by drinking which the gods renewed their strength and drove the daityas to pátála. The apsarás, the moon, Wáruni, and many other valuable things were produced on the same occasion, and served to distract the daityas' attention from the precious amrita, and among the products was also some poison which Śiwa, or, as some say, the Nágas, appropriated.

Amshom. See Ansam.

Áná. More commonly Anna.

Anákálabhrita. [Sanksrit, *anákála*, an unseasonable time, and *bhrita*, supported.] One who has voluntarily become a slave in consideration of maintenance in a time of scarcity.

Ananás. The name of a species of bromelia; the pine-apple. Webster says the word is Malay, and marks the second syllable as long; but the word spelt as above exists in Hindustáni, Maráṭhi, and Gujaráti.

Anant. [Sanskrit, from *an* privative, and *anta*, end.] The endless, a name applied to Vishnu, to Śeshnág, and other gods; also a cord of silk and gold lace, which is tied round the arm on the anant ċhaturdaśi, or festival of the 14th Bhádra śudh, held in honour of Vishnu. The cord is worn in token of a vow made to Anant.

Anchatra. See Annachhatra.

Ancheyawa. [Koḍagu, from *anche*, post.] A postal runner.

Andala. [Koḍagu.] A kind of palanquin used by gurus and at marriages.

Andhra. [Sanskrit.] The name of a country supposed to be the modern Telingana or Telugu country; also the name of a caste of Bráhmans; and of a dynasty reigning at Magadha, and also in the Deccan and Konkan, about the beginning of the Christian era.

Andhyáru. [Gujaráti.] The Pársi priest who tends the agiári.

Ánḍi. [Tamil.] A Śaiwa mendicant.

Andra. The name of a Buddhist dynasty considered to have reigned in Central India from 31 B.C. to 429 A.D.

Angarkhá. [Hindi, from the Sanskrit *anga*, the body, and *rakshana*, protecting.] A long coat worn both by Hindus and Musalmáns.

Anglo-Indian. A term applied to an Englishman residing in India, or anything pertaining to the English in India.

Angrej. [A vernacular corruption of *English.*] An Englishman.

Angreji. English, or the English language, or the English rule.

Áni. The Tamil name of the month Mithunam, which corresponds most nearly with Ásháḍh.

Anicoody. See Anyakuḍi.

Anicut. [A corruption of the Kanarese *anekattu.*] A dam or embankment retaining the waters of a river for irrigation.

Anjali. [Hindi.] A handful; a handful of grain taken at the division of produce for an offering to the gods or as the perquisite of any person. Compare Dosili.

Anjaman. [Persian.] An assembly, a society; as the Anjaman-i-Panjáb, the name of a society in the Panjáb for the revival of Oriental learning and for discussion. Among the Pársis, a council to which disputes concerning their customs are referred.

Ánjná. [Gujaráti.] The name of a division of the Kanbi caste.

Ankuṭ. [Gujaráti, from *anna*, food, and *kuṭ*, a hillock.] A pile of food made to represent the mountain Gowardhan, and worshipped on the 1st Kártik śudh. Previously Indra was worshipped on this day, but Krishna is said to have substituted the mountain.

Anna. [A corruption of the Hindi *áná.*] The sixteenth part of a rupee, nominally equivalent to three halfpence. No coin of this dimension is current, but there are copper pieces representing the half and quarter anna (besides the pie, which is the twelfth part), and silver pieces of the value of two, four, and eight annas. The term 'anna' is used also to express the sixteenth part of any unit; thus an anna of land means the sixteenth part of the standard unit of land measurement in the locality; a four-anna share in an estate means a quarter of it.

Annachhatra. The Maráṭhi and Gujaráti form of Annasattra. Besides its use as the name of permanent charitable institutions, the term is applied also to occasional funds for the distribution of food in times of famine or other distress.

Annapráśana. [Sanskrit, from *anna*, food, and *práś*, to taste.] The sanskár or ceremony on the occasion of giving a child solid food for the first time.

Annapurná. [Hindi, from the Sanskrit *anna*, food, and *purna*, full, from *pur*, to fill.] A goddess to whom there is a temple at Benares, and who is supposed to feed all the inhabitants of that city.

Annasattra. [Kanarese, from the Sanskrit *anna*, food, and *sattra*, q.v.] An institution for the distribution of food to Bráhmans and mendicants, or to travellers; the building used for such purposes.

Annekat. More commonly Anicut.

Ansam. [Malayálam, from the Sanskrit *ansá*, a part.] A subdivision of a district; a táluk.

Ansári. A tribe of Shaikhs in the North-West Provinces who pretend to be descended from the original *ansár*, or auxiliaries of Muhammad, who adopted his faith at Medina. They appear to have come into India from Herat at the time of Firozsháh (*H. H. Wilson*).

Antyaja. [Sanskrit, from *antya*, last and *ja*, born.] The latest born, the lowest; the common name of seven low tribes—the Rajak, or washerman; the Chamár, or currier; the Naṭ, or player; the Baruḍ, or basketmaker; the Kaibartta, or fisherman; the Meda, or attendant on women; and the Bhil, or forester.

Anubhavam. [Malayálam, from the Sanskrit *anu*, according to, and *bhawa*, being.] Literally, enjoyment; a deed of gift of land as a reward for services performed. The right is hereditary, but purushántaram is paid on each succession, and on failure of heirs the land reverts to the janmi.

Anubhogam. [Sanskrit, *bhoga*, enjoyment.] Another name for Anubhavam.

Anukshetra. [Sanskrit, from *anu*, according to, and *kshetra*, a place of pilgrimage.] A charitable allowance made to the servants of certain temples in Orissa by the Maráṭhás and continued by the British government (*H. H. Wilson*).

Anwádidár. [Kanarese.] A re-mortgagee, as distinguished from the bogirnudár, who holds from the proprietor.

Anyakuḍi. [Tamil, from the Sanskrit *anya*, other, and *kuḍi*, a resident.] A cultivator who does not live in the village in which his land is.

Aonla. [Corruption of the Hindi *anolá.*] The myrobolan tree, phyllanthus emblica.

Aorja. [Uriya.] A revenue account showing the number, area, assessment, of each field of a village, together with the name of the occupant and the kind of cultivation.

Apásrá. [Gujaráti, from the Sanskrit *apáśraya*, from *apa*, away, and *áśraya*, an asylum.] A sacred building of the Jains, a chaitya ; also the residence of a gor.

Appanam. [Telugu.] Literally, tax or revenue, but applied especially to lands assessed beyond their value, but which the holder cannot resign without also resigning other lightly assessed land.

Apsará. [Sanskrit, from *ap*, water, or the air, and *sri*, to go.] The name of certain female divinities who were produced from the ocean and reside in the sky ; they are sometimes regarded as the wives of the Gandharwas.

Arabi. The name by which Musalmáns of Coimbatore call the Tamil language.

Arabic. This Semitic language is known in India chiefly as the language of the koran and Muhammadan law.

Aráin. The name of a tribe peculiar to the Panjáb ; they are market-gardeners, and a few are general cultivators; nearly all are Muhammadans.

Arakanese. The name of the people and of the language of Árákan. The people are a branch of the Mramma race. The language closely resembles the Burmese, except that the pronunciation is quite different.

Arakzai. A Paṭhán tribe, occupying the eastern and southern off-shoots of the Safed Koh. Their country adjoins the Afridi country near Kohat. They are not subject to the Cabul government. They can muster about 18,000 fighting men.

Áranyaka. [Sanskrit, from *áranya*, a forest.] A treatise deemed so holy that it should be read only in the solitude of a forest. This is the name of a part of the veda. The older áranyakas form portions of the bráhmanas, and so belong each to a particular veda, but others are esteemed distinct works, and some are even attributed to human authors. The most important part of the áranyakas are the philosophical chapters called upanishads.

Arasapalli. [Tamil.] The name of an insignificant and low caste, living by cultivation and cooly work (*Nelson*).

Arati. See Árti.

Arayan. The name of a hill tribe of Travancore, of good condition compared with that of other hill tribes ; they have fixed villages, and are as fair as high-caste Hindus, and some are rich ; they are great hunters, and averse to working for hire or carrying loads ; they worship the spirits of ancestors, Ayappan and local demons, and have some sacred groves; they bury their dead.

Arbáb. [The plural of the Arabic *rab*, a master.] This term is applied to persons employed by the Panjáb frontier officials as middlemen in their dealings with the tribes across the border. In Sindh, it means a great landholder or headman.

Archáka. [Kanarese.] The officiating priest of a pagoda.

Ardás. [Panjábi.] Any portion of the Sikh granth.

Ardhanáriśa. [Sanskrit, from *arddha*, half, *nári*, a woman, and *íśa*, lord.] The name of Śiwa in his form as half male, half female.

Ardheli. [Maráṭhi, from *arddha*, half.] A cultivator, usually a bádhekari, who pays his landlord half the produce of his land. His engagement is usually annual, and includes the condition of one day's service in eight.

Areca. [Through the Portuguese, from the Malayálam *arik*, or the Kanarese *aḍike*.] A genus of palms, one species of which produces the areca or betel-nut. See Betel.

Arghun. The name of a dynasty in Sindh that succeeded the Sama jáms in 1521 A.D.; it was a Muhammadan family tracing its descent from Changiz Khán.

Arhar. [Híndi.] A kind of pulse, the red grain cytisus cajan or cajanus indicus; it is otherwise called dál, togari, kandi, thuwarei, tuwar, and tur.

Arhat. [Sanskrit, from *arh*, to deserve.] Deserving, worthy; among Buddhists the title of those who have reached the fourth stage in their progress to nirwána. Also a synonym for jin or tirthakar.

Arhaṭ. [Hindi.] A large wheel with pendent buckets on its circumference, which fill themselves as the lower rim of the wheel passes through a trough of water, and empty themselves into a channel at a higher level as they come to the top of the wheel; a Persian wheel.

Arhatiya. Another form of Aḍatyá.

Ariá. [Uriya.] The name of a low caste; they are salt-makers.

Arippukáran. [Tamil.] The name of a division of the Paraiyans; they wash sand for gold.

Árjá. [A vernacular form of the Sanskrit *áryá*, the feminine of *árya*, noble, venerable.] A female mendicant.

Arpasi. The Tamil name of the solar month Tulam, which begins about the middle of October, and corresponds most nearly to Kártik. See Month.

Arrack. [A corruption of the Hindustáni *arak*, the Tamil *araku*, or the Maráṭhi *ark*.] A fermented liquor made from the juice of the palm, or from rice. See Toddy.

Arrian. See Arayan.

Árti. [Hindi, from the Sanskrit *árátrika*, the light which is waved before an idol at night.] A vessel containing burning wicks which is waved before an idol, a bridegroom, or other person whom it is intended to honour.

Arudikarai. [Tamil, from *arudi*, fixed, and *karai*, boundary.] A tenure under which each occupant has a defined portion of the village lands, which he may dispose of as he wills.

Aruwa. [Uriya.] Rice that has been husked without having been heated.

Aruwa. [Kanarese.] One who knows, a man of experience; the title of the particular friend and adviser, of which every family among the Koḍagas has one. The aruwa acts as the representative of a family in negotiating marriages and other great occasions of life.

Aryan. [Sanskrit, *árya*, of good family, noble.] The name of that primeval family who spoke a language the common source of Sanskrit, Prákrit, Zand, Persian, and Armenian in Asia; and of the Hellenic, Italic, Celtic, Teutonic, and Slavonic languages in Europe. Starting at a later period than the primitive Turanian races, but like them from some part of the table-land of Central Asia, they separated into distinct nationalities, and peopled Europe, Persia, and India. The Hindu Aryans, after detaching themselves from the Persian branch of the family, settled themselves down as agriculturists (probably at some period between 2000 and 1500 years B.C.), in the districts surrounding the Indus, the five rivers of the Panjáb and the Saraswati, and thence in time spread over the whole of Áryáwarta (*Monier Williams*). But these Aryans do not appear to have been a single tribe or to have arrived all at one time; there is a marked distinction between the peaceful and pastoral solar race of the Rámáyana and the fighting lunar race of the Mahábhárata seven hundred years later.

Áryasamáj. [Sanskrit, *árya*, noble, Aryan, and *samáj*, a society.] The name of a religious society founded in the present century by Dayánand Saraswati an Odich Bráhman and Śaiwa of Káṭhiáwár. The society holds the veda to be fully and literally inspired.

Áryáwarta. [Sanskrit *warta*, living, dwelling.] The abode of the Aryans. This is the classical name for the region between the Himálaya and Vindhya mountains north and south, and the two seas east and west.

Arzál. [Hindustáni, plural of *razl*, vile.] Low-caste dependents on a zamindár's estate. Compare Aḍiya, Háli.

Arzi. [Hindustáni.] A petition, a memorial.

Asábardár. [Hindustáni, from the Arabic *asá*, a staff, and Persian *bardár*, a bearer.] A mace-bearer.

Asaga. Another form of Agasa.

Asahr. See Ásárh.

Asaljamá. [Hindustáni, from the Arabic *asal*, root, origin, and *jamá*, total.] The original revenue of an estate, village, or district, without extra cesses; also the amount taken as the basis of a revenue settlement.

Asámi. [Hindi, from *asám*, the plural of the Arabic *ism*, a name.] This word now commonly means a man, a person, an individual; also sometimes a cultivator, a tenant, but this use is chiefly in composition as asámi-maurusi, an hereditary tenant; asámi-paikásht, a tenant-at-will; páhi-asámi, a non-resident cultivator; asámi-mustakall, a tenant whom his landlord has no right to dispossess.

Asámiwár. [Hindi.] According to names, or persons; dealing with each individually; ryotwar.

Asan. The Hindustáni form of Áśvin.

Ásani. [Sanskrit, from *ás*, to sit.] A small seat; but now applied to a woollen carpet used at prayers by Hindus.

Asapinḍa. [Sanskrit, from *a* privative, and *sapinḍa*, q.v.] One who is not connected by offerings of the funeral cake to the same ancestors.

Asaputra. [Sanskrit, from *a* privative, *sa*, with, and *putra*, a son.] A son adopted from a different family, not descended from a common ancestor.

Ásárh. The Bengali name of Áshádh.

Aśáśwat. [*A* privative.] See Śáśwat.

Áshádh. [Sanskrit.] The name of the Hindu month most nearly corresponding under the śukladi reckoning with July; it is so called from *ashádhá*, invincible, the name of the nakshatra (in Sagittarius) in which the moon is at full in this month.

Ashrafi. [Hindi, from the Arabic *sharif*, noble.] A gold coin, a mohur.

Ashtarani. A small Paṭhán tribe occupying the Saleman range from a little south of the Takht to the Korah Pass.

Ashurah. [Arabic, from *asharah*, ten.] The fast of the first ten days of the month of Muharram.

Ashurkhánah. [Hindustáni, from *ashurah*, and *khánah*, a house.] A house appointed for the mourning ceremonies at the Muharram.

Ashwin. See Áśvin.

Áśirwád. [Hindi, from the Sanskrit *áśis*, a blessing, and *wáda*, speech.] The benedictive address or salutation of a Bráhman or of a superior to his inferior. See Namaskára. Áśirwád is also the name of part of the marriage ceremony among Pársis.

Asmáni. [Hindustáni, from the Persian *asmán*, heaven.] Derived from heaven. This word is often used in deeds, together with sultáni, to express causes over which the parties have no control—causes which are the act of God or of the sultán. It is also the name by which the Musalmáns of Coimbatore call their own language, in contradistinction to the Tamil, which they call Arabi.

Asni. See Ásani.

Áśrama. [Sanskrit.] An order or stage of life. Manu prescribes that a Bráhman's life should consist of four áśramas: in the first of which he is a student; in the second a householder; in the third an anchorite; and in the last a mendicant. See Bhikshu, Brahmachári, Grihastha, Wánaprastha.

Assamese. The name of the people and language of Assam. There is no distinct Assamese nationality; the population consists of the Aham and Chutiyá tribes, both of which formerly ruled the country; many aboriginal tribes, as the Nágá, Khásiá, Gáro, and Mikir; a large number of Kochs, Chandáls, and Kaibarttas; and the offspring of various mixed marriages. Most of the tribes have adopted a form of Hinduism. The language is akin to the Bengali, and the characters a variety of the Dewanágari.

Assassin. See Hashishin.

Assigned Districts. The name of a province, otherwise called Berar, consisting of six districts, made over to the British administration by the nizám of Haidarábád for the maintenance of the Haidarábád contingent, which he was bound by treaty to maintain, and in discharge of other obligations (*W. W. Hunter*).

Assin. The Bengali form of Áśvin.

Assistant-Collector. The name of a class of officers, of which there are several grades, who are usually members of the covenanted civil service, and who, under the control of a collector, exercise most of that officer's powers, each within a portion of the district assigned to him. In Bengal and the North-Western Provinces the highest officer so subordinate to a collector is termed the deputy-collector, and those junior to him assistant-collectors; in Madras and Bombay, all are termed assistants, the deputy-collector in those presidencies being an officer of a distinct class.

Assistant-Commissioner. An officer, usually a member of the covenanted civil service, who bears the same relation to the deputy-commissioner in a non-regulation district as the assistant-collector bears to the collector in a regulation district.

Assistant-Magistrate. This term is unknown to the law, but is popularly used in Bengal to designate the officer who is an assistant-collector and a magistrate.

Asthal. [Hindi, from the Sanskrit *sthala*, a place.] A place of residence, a monastery; a temple.

Asura. [Sanskrit, from *asu*, breath, from *as*, to be.] A spirit; an evil spirit, an enemy of the gods; a daitya.

Aśvin. [From the Sanskrit *aśwa*, horse.] The name of two vedic divinities, imagined as two rays of light preceding the dawn; also the name of a lunar mansion part of the sign Aries.

Áśvin. [Sanskrit, *áśvina*, from *aśvin.*] The name of the Hindu month most nearly corresponding, under the śukladi reckoning, with October. See Month.

Aśwamedha. [Sanskrit, from *aśwa*, a horse, and *medha*, sacrifice.] The actual or typical sacrifice of a horse, a ceremony of vedic times. Any one claiming to be a supreme ruler would turn loose a horse, which any one disputing his title would endeavour to seize; the armed attendants would fight, and if the horse returned untaken it was sacrificed, and the title then deemed established.

Áṭa. [Koḍagu.] A dance, of which the Koḍagas have several kinds, as kombáṭa, the horn-dance, in which each man wears the horns of a deer on his head; piliáṭa, in which peacock's feathers are worn; and chauriáṭa, in which the performers swing yák-tails (*L. Rice*).

Atash Adaran. A Pársi fire-temple.

Atash Behram. A principal fire-temple of the Pársis.

Aṭasil. [Sinhalese, from Sanskrit *ashṭan*, eight, and Sinhalese *sil*, a precept.] The eight precepts binding on an upásaka: they forbid (1) the taking of life; (2) theft; (3) sexual intercourse; (4) lying; (5) the use of intoxicating drinks; (6) eating solid food after midday; (7) being present at places of amusement, adorning or perfuming the body; and (8) the use of seats or couches above a prescribed height.

Atharwa. [Sanskrit, said to be from an old root, *athar*, fire.] The name of the fourth veda. The songs of the atharwa-veda were not at first considered to be part of the veda, but were intended to counteract the influence of any untoward event that might happen during the sacrifice. Now, the supervision of the whole sacrifice, and the remedying of any mistake that might have happened, belonged not to the Hotri, Adhwaryu, or Udgátri priest, but to the Bráhman, whence the atharwa came to be called the veda of the Bráhman (*Max Müller*).

Aṭhávisi. [Gujaráti, from *aṭhávis*, twenty-eight.] A collocation of twenty-eight villages. See Bárah.

Atheewoon. [Burmese.] The title of an official sitting on the hlootdau, apparently to represent the classes other than those in the royal service.

Atit. [Sanskrit, *atita*, passed away.] One who has given up all consideration of worldly affairs—the name of a class of wandering mendicants. They are supposed not to marry, but some in Káṭhiáwár do.

Atprahari. [Bengali.] A village peon who attends and receives orders at the zamindár's kacheri.

Atta. [Corruption of the Hindi *átá*.] Flour, meal.

Attar. [A vernacular corruption of the Arabic *itr*, perfume.] A perfume, particularly the essential oil extracted from the petals of roses. Attar is obtained by skimming off the essential oil from rose-water which has been exposed to the air all night in large open vessels. It is said to take 200,000 roses to produce an ounce of attar. This is one of the various things presented to a guest on bidding him farewell. See Rukhsat.

Attár. [Hindi.] A maker of attar, a perfumer.

Atwenwoon. [Burmese, from *atwen*, interior, and *woon*, q.v.] The title of the officials whose business relates to the palace, and who form a sort of privy council called byadeit.

Audi. See Áḍi.

Aukamma. The name of a village goddess. See Amma.

Auni. See Áni.

Aurang. [Hindustáni.] A place where any article of trade is manufactured and collected for wholesale disposal or export. During the Company's commerce it was applied to the factories for piece-goods, etc. (*H. H. Wilson*).

Áutbandi. [Maráṭhi, from *áut*, a plough, and *bandi*, settlement.] Assessment of land revenue according to the number of ploughs used.

Avastá. [Zand, from *vid*, to know; compare Veda.] Literally, knowledge, information, word; the name of the Zoroastrian scriptures; these, as originally delivered by the prophet, consisted of twenty-one nusk or volumes, but the greater part was destroyed either on the Greek invasion or upon the conquest of Persia by the Arabs.

Awadhi. The dialect of Hindi spoken in Awadh or Oudh and eastern Rohilkhand.

Awadhuta. See Abdhut.

Awal. [Gujaráti, from the Arabic *avl*, first.] First, the best; a term applied to land of the highest quality. An awal kárkun is the first kárkun in a mámlatdár's office; he supervises the accounts, and is usually a magistrate of the third class.

Awán. The name of a tribe in the Panjáb who trace their descent from Kutb Sháh of Ghazni, a descendant of Ali the son-in-law of Muhammad by a wife other than Fátima. Their true origin is uncertain, but probably Aryan. They employ Bráhmans as family priests. They are chiefly husbandmen.

Áwani. The Tamil name of the solar month Chingam, or Bhádra, which begins in August and corresponds to parts of the luni-solar Śráwan and Bhádra. See Month.

Áwáre. [Kanarese.] A kind of pulse, the cow-gram, dolichos lablab; other names in different parts of India are anamalu, mocchei, bullar, wál.

Awatár. [Sanskrit, from *awatri*, to descend.] The descent of a deity upon earth and his incarnation as a man or animal. Vishnu, the pervader, who can infuse his essence into anything, is the god with whom the notion of awatár is chiefly associated. His principal incarnations —but many others are described— are the following: (1) Matsya, the fish; (2) Karma, the turtle; (3) Waráh, the boar; (4) Narsinh, half man, half lion; (5) Wáman, the dwarf; (6) Parśurám, a Bráhman; (7) Ráma, the hero of the Rámáyana; (8) Krishna; (9) Buddha; and (10) Kalki. The number is sometimes extended to twenty-four, but Kalki is always the last.

Áya. [Tamil, from the Sanskrit *árya*, venerable.] A common adjunct in the south of India to the names of Bráhmans, especially the religious teachers of the Lingáits.

Ayah. [Probably the Portuguese *aya*, a governess.] A nurse for children, or a lady's-maid.

Ayaing. This term, which means wild, is applied in British Burma to all hill-men who are not tributary.

Ayappan. [Malayálam.] The hunting god of the Arayan tribe; tigers are regarded as his dogs. Also the forest-god of the Koḍagas.

Ayeen. See Áin.

Ayenar. The name of a god of the south of India who is supposed to ride about the fields and guard them from demons. Huge clay horses are placed about his shrine.

Azád. [Persian, *azád*, solitary.] The name of an order of fakirs. They shave their beards, whiskers, mustachios, eyebrows, and eyelashes, and take vows of continence, and live on alms. They consider their sanctity such as to exempt them from observing the koran.

Ázam. [Arabic.] A title prefixed to names; officially it is used to denote a lower rank than that indicated by mehrbán.

Azán. [Arabic.] The Muhammadan call to prayer, chanted by the mulla or muezzin from the minaret of the mosque. The call is: 'God is great; I bear witness there is no God but one God; I bear witness that Muhammad is His prophet; come to pray; come to salvation; prayer is better than sleep; God is great; there is no God but one.'

Azgar. See Rock-snake.

B.

Bábá. [Hindustáni, from the Turkish.] A father, but commonly addressed as a term of kindness to children, whence bábálok is the usual name for children among domestic servants.

Bábáshábi. The name of the Baroda currency. A bábáshábi rupee is worth thirteen annas eleven pies.

Bábhan. [Bengali.] Another name for Bhuinhár. Bábhan is a corruption of Bráhman, the corruption of the name betokening that of the caste.

Baboo. [Bengali, *bábu*, perhaps from the Sanskrit *pitri*, a father.] A term of respect formerly applied in upper India to the younger sons of a rájá; in a Bengal village it is the usual title of the zamindár; it is also appended to a proper name as an equivalent to 'mister;' but among the English it is chiefly used to denote a native clerk or manager.

Bábriá. The name of a tribe in Peninsular Gujarát, who have given their name to a district on the south coast. The Bábriás are more haughty and warlike than the Áhirs, with whom, however, they intermarry. There are seventy-two tribes of Bábriás, the first of which is the Kotilá tribe, said to be of mixed Bráhman and Áhir descent. The term Bábriá itself is said to be derived from a word *bábar*, meaning 'mixed,' and, according to one tradition, the tribe is the offspring of a body of famine emigrants.

Bábul. [Sanskrit *babbul.*] The gum arabic tree, the acacia arabica or mimosa arabica; the timber is crooked, but valuable on account of its toughness, especially for wheels, and is also much used as firewood and to make charcoal; the smaller branches, with their long, sharp thorns, are used for fencing.

Badaga. [Kanarese; literally, a northman. Compare the Tamil Waduga.] The name of a group of Aryanized Dravidian castes settled on the middle plateau of the Nilgiri hills; they are chiefly workers with the hoe; they are very industrious, and are much employed in the coffee plantations. In religion they are Śaiwas, and some of them Lingáits. See Wodea, Konga, Kanaka. They burn their dead.

Baḍagi. [Kanarese.] A carpenter. See Pánchála.

Badakshání. A native of Badakshán, the mountainous principality of Turkistán lying to the north of Afghánistán, between 69° and 73° E. long., and 36° and 38° N. lat.

Badhak. [Hindi, from the Sanskrit *badha*, killing.] A robber of a particular tribe associated with thugs, and, like them, murdering those they rob, residing chiefly on the borders of Oudh, but carrying on their depredations usually at a distance (*H. H. Wilson*).

Bádhekari. [Maráṭhi, from *bádhen*, which is said to mean lands without a proprietor, and the affix *kari*, which means master, dealer in, worker.] One who, having no land of his own, undertakes the temporary cultivation of waste land either in his own or any other village. Bádhekaris usually pay the khot half or some other fixed portion of the crop.

Badi. See Wadi.

Baḍiga. [Kanarese.] One who gives water to travellers.

Badikari. See Bádhekari.

Badmásh. [Hindustáni, from the Persian *bad*, bad, and *máash*, livelihood.] A bad character, a disreputable person.

Bádsháh. [Persian.] A king.

Bádsháhi. [Persian.] Royal; held under a royal grant.

Badragga. The Pashṭo form of Badrakah.

Badrakah. [Arabic.] Safe conduct under armed protection; a guide, an escort.

Baer. [Hindi.] The tree zizyphus jujuba.

Báfta. [Hindustáni, from Persian *báftan*, to weave.] A kind of cotton cloth; sometimes applied to a mixture of cotton and silk.

Bag. See Bágh.

Bágáit. Another form of Bágháyat.

Bagalá. [Gujaráti.] A trading-vessel used on the west coast of India. They go also to the Persian Gulf and Red Sea, and are largely used as transports in expeditions from Bombay.

Bágdi. The name of a low caste in Bengal and Cuttack; they are a numerous caste, and by occupation are cultivators, day-labourers, and fishermen.

Bágh. [Persian.] A garden, an orchard, a plantation; more particularly a pleasure garden with a summer house or palace, or báradari, in it. Compare Wáḍi.

Bágháyat. [Hindi, from the Persian *bágh*, a garden.] Land which is artificially watered—usually by means of a well, from which the water is raised by bullock-power and distributed by channels cut for it in the field—and rendered fit for the growth of vegetables, fruit trees, and superior crops of grain.

Baghel. See Bhagela.

Bagla. See Bagalá.

Bágri. The language of the Bágar or Bikaner prairie; it is the northern form of the western or Márwári type of the dialects of Rájputáná, spoken to the west of the Arawalli range. It is a pure Hindi dialect, but is very distinct from the Hindustáni of Delhi, from which it differs almost as much as it does from Panjábi, both in inflection and in vocabulary (*D. C. J. Ibbetson*). Also an inhabitant of the Bágar country, which lies between the south-west borders of Hariána and the Satlaj. Also another form of Wághri.

Bahádur. [Persian.] A hero, a warrior; a title of honour given to nobles under the Muhammadan government, and now to distinguished native officials.

Bahangi. [Bengali.] A bamboo furnished with cords at each end, by means of which luggage is carried slung across the shoulder. Hence the parcels post is termed the bahangi or banghy post, and a parcel itself a banghy.

Bahárwaṭiá. [Gujaráti, *bahár*, out, and *waṭ*, to withdraw.] A voluntary outlaw; one who, failing to obtain redress from his government, takes to the hills and jungles, collects a band of robbers, and seizes every opportunity of making raids upon or otherwise harassing the state to which he belonged, in the hope of forcing it to come to terms with him. The practice belongs particularly to the small states of Káṭhiáwár.

Báheliá. The name of a semi-Hinduised tribe of Bengal; they are day-labourers, cultivators, swine-keepers, and bird-catchers.

Bahi. The Hindustáni form of Wahi.

Bahir. [Hindustáni.] A camp-follower; also the baggage and incumbrances of an army.

Bahli. [Hindi.] A two-wheeled carriage drawn by bullocks.

Báhmani. [A corruption of Bráhman.] The name of a Muhammadan dynasty which ruled in the Deccan from 1347 to 1489 A.D. It was founded by Zafir Khán, an Afghán, who adopted this title in compliment to his patron, a Bráhman, who had aided his advancement. Zafir Khán first became a jágirdár, and then became the head of a successful rebellion against the emperor Muhammad Tughlak. He took the title of Alauddin Husen Kangu Báhmani, and made Kulbarga his capital. In 1417 the capital was changed to Bidar. There was a long succession of wars and alliances between this kingdom and that of Vijayanagar. The Báhmani dynasty, though it nominally ended in 1489, continued under different names in the five states of Bijápur (see Adil Sháhi), Golconda, Berar, Ahmadnagar, and Bidar.

Bahti. Another name of the Ghirth caste.

Bahu. [Hindi.] A wife, but usually used to designate a son's wife.

Bahucharáji. [Gujaráti.] The name of a modern goddess much worshipped in Gujarát. She is the deified form of a Cháran woman Bahuchará, who committed suicide; no image is used in her temples, but the object of worship is a square panel covered with pieces of tinsel, and placed in a niche which fronts the rising sun; animals and flesh and liquor are offered to her (*A. K. Forbes*).

Bahurupia. [Hindi, from the Sanskrit *bahu*, many, and *rupa*, form.]

The name of a caste; they are actors and ventriloquists, and have a special knack of dressing one side of the face like a man, and the other like a woman, and moving the head about so sharply as to appear to be two persons. Some have adopted islám.

Bahutá. [Panjábi.] An amulet to be worn on the arm. Worshippers of Nársingh wear silver bahutás containing pictures of him in the form of a man.

Bái. [Maráṭhi.] A lady; madam. The word is used as a respectful way of addressing an elderly woman. It is also used as the title of the wives of reigning chiefs not of the highest rank, such as ṭhákors. In this way it is applied both to Hindu and Muhammadan princesses lower in rank than ránis (Hindu) or begams (Muhammadan). In northern India the term means a dancing-girl.

Baid. A shortened form of Baidya.

Baider. See Beḍar.

Baidni. [Hindi.] A woman of the Baidya caste; also a woman engaged in the practice of medicine.

Baidya. [Hindi, from the Sanskrit *vaidya*, a learned man.] The name of a caste, called by Manu Ambashṭa, and supposed to be the offspring of a Bráhman father and Vaiśya mother; their hereditary profession is medicine, but many are now landowners.

Baiga. [Hindi.] The name of one of the Gonḍ tribes; they hold themselves superior to the others, for whom they act as priests, sorcerers, and medicine-men. They are distinguished by an extraordinary reverence for mother earth.

Baikunṭh. The Bengali form of Vaikunṭha.

Bail. [Hindi, from the Sanskrit *baliwarda.*] A bull or bullock. Often used in composition as *bail-gári*, a bullock-carriage.

Baili. [Hindi.] A bullock-carriage, a bahli.

Baira. [Bengali.] The name of a low caste; they are cultivators and labourers.

Bairági. Another form of Vairági.

Bais. A vernacular form of Vaiśya. Also the name of a numerous tribe of Rájputs in Oudh and the North-West Provinces; they are esteemed of high rank, and regard themselves as of the same lineage as Sáliwáhana, the author of the śaka era.

Baiśákh. The Bengali name of the month Vaiśákh.

Baisbaniyá. The name of a caste; they are general traders.

Baisnav. See Vaishnawa.

Baiṭhak. [Hindi, from *baiṭh*, to sit.] Anything placed to sit upon; a stool, a bench; an idol's stand; a mendicant's customary seat. Also an assembly or company, or their session. Also the right of sitting, as of holding a stall in a market, or the fee paid for that right; a verá on shops.

Baiṭhakhánah. [Bengali, from *baiṭha*, sitting, and Persian *khánah*, a place.] The sitting-room or public portion of a native dwelling-house.

Baithán. [Hindi.] A homestead, a farm; a farmer's residence and the ground adjacent.

Báiti. The name of a semi-Hinduised tribe in Bengal; they are mat-makers, musicians, and dancers. They are called also Bájuár.

Bait-ul-mál. [Arabic, *bait*, place, *mál*, property.] The public treasury, the office into which all taxes and property taken in war are sent.

Baiyá. [Hindi.] A person appointed in bazárs to measure grain.

Baiyá. [Hindi, from *bais*, twenty-two.] A collocation of twenty-two villages. There are baiyás of Játs in the Firozpur and Hoshiarpur districts. See Bárah.

Bajániá. A wandering tribe who are rope-dancers and jugglers. They are found in Gujarát. Some are Hindus, and other classes of them are Muhammadans.

Bájantari. [Hindi, from *bájá*, a musical instrument.] A village musician.

Bajara. More commonly Budgerow.

Bajauri. An inhabitant of Bajaur or Bajawar, a piece of independent territory lying south of the Káfirs' and north of the Mahmands' country. They number 15,000 fighting men.

Bájri. [Hindi.] The name of a cereal, the penicillaria spicata, holcus spicatus, or panicum spicatum; it is called in different languages kambu, matári, sajje, and sazza.

Bájuár. Another name of the Báiti tribe.

Bakán. [Hindi.] A species of nim tree, the melia sempervirens; it bears long bunches of small, purple, sweet-smelling flowers.

Bakhshi. [From the Persian *bakhshidan*, to give.] A paymaster. Under the Mogul government, a general, a commander-in-chief. In Mysore, a superior magistrate or revenue officer.

Bakhshish. [From the Persian *bakhshidan*, to give.] A gift, a present. This is the common word for miscellaneous gratuities, and it has been suggested that it may be the origin of Christmas *box*, that festival being a great occasion of bakhshish in India.

Bakr-id. [Arabic, *bakr*, a bull.] The Muhammadan festival of the 10th Zilhijjah, held in honour of Abraham's purposed sacrifice of his son Ishmael.

Balabhadra. [Sanskrit, from *bala*, strong, and *bhadra*, propitious.] A name of the third Ráma, the elder brother of Krishna.

Balabhi. The name of a dynasty of northern India that reigned from 465 to 712 A.D.; and of an era called after them which dates from 319 A.D.

Balagai. [Kanarese, from *bala*, eight, and *gai*, hand.] The right-hand castes; they include the Banajiga, Wokkaliga, some of the Gániga, the Kuruba, Kumbár, Agasa, Besta, some of the Golla, the Nainda, Appar, and other castes, and the Holaya. See Yeḍagai, Left-hand.

Balái. [Bengali.] The name of a caste of Śudras; they are cultivators.

Balaji. [Telugu.] The name of a caste; they are tradesmen chiefly, but some are cultivators.

Balál. [Gujaráti.] The name of a devi, sister to Bahucharáji.

Balám. [Gujaráti.] A canoe used as a ship's boat.

Balarám. [Sanskrit, from *bala*, strong, and *ráma*, q.v.] The name of the third Ráma. He is usually the elder brother of Krishna, but sometimes an independent incarnation of Vishnu. He is called also Balabhadra.

Bálá Sháh. The name of one of the gurus of the Chuhrás; he either is or is confounded with Bálmikji or Wálmiki. Again he is sometimes said to be identical with Lál Beg.

Bálbodh. [Maráṭhi, from *bála*, a child, and *buddhi*, understanding.] A name of the simple Dewanágari character as distinguished from the more difficult Moḍ.

Balegár. [Kanarese, from *bale*, a glass ring, and *gár*, maker.] The name of a division of the Banajiga caste; they are makers of glass bangles. They do not use animal food or spirits, and claim to be superior to the other Banajigas.

Balev. [Gujaráti, from the Sanskrit *bali*, an oblation.] Another name for cocoa-nut day, or the nárali purnimá.

Balhára. The name of a dynasty that was paramount in western India in the ninth century A.D. They are sometimes said to be of the solar race, at others a branch of the Parmárs.

Bali. [Sanskrit.] The name of a daitya and king sent to pátál by Vishnu incarnate as a dwarf. See Wáman. Bali is worshipped on the 1st Kártik śudh, and Vishnu the dwarf on the 12th Bhádra śudh. Also the name of anything offered to an idol.

Baliyá. A Gujaráti name of the small-pox goddess Śitalá. Her husband is called Káká Baliyá.

Bálmikji. Another form of Wálmiki. According to one legend, Bálmikji was the original sweeper who swept the stairs of heaven; one day God gave him a bride's bodice, and from the bodice was born a babe which God declared to be for a guru to Bálmíkji, and which was called Lál Beg or Bálá Sháh.

Balolikára. [Kanarese.] The name of an agricultural caste of South Kanara.

Baluchi. [Hindustáni.] An inhabitant of Biluchistán; the descendants of Baluchi immigrants settled in India. Many settled in Sindh, when the Tálpur government succeeded that of the Kalhoras, and received lands there. They are now found also in Gujarát, chiefly as messengers and village watchmen. They are Sunni Musalmáns. See Biluch.

Balutá. [Maráṭhi.] A collective name of the chief village servants, such as the carpenter, the blacksmith, the potter, the astrologer; they are nominally twelve in number, but the enumeration differs in different parts; the headman and accountant are sometimes included in the term and sometimes not. Compare Waswáyá.

Baman. See Bábhan.

Bambetiyá. [Bengali.] A river-pirate.

Bamboo. [According to Webster, this word is of Malay origin. It now exists in Kanarese, Maráṭhi, and Gujaráti, but may be of late introduction, as country-people usually use another name, *bans*, *wanś* or *wánś*, from the Sanskrit *wanśa*.] A reed that grows to the height of forty or fifty feet. It is very strong and hard, and is used for building and many other purposes. The seed also is eaten as corn.

Bamon. See Bráhman.

Banajiga. The Kanarese form of Banyá. The Banajigas are much subdivided. Besides their proper occupation, trade, they engage in agriculture and labour. They are also bricklayers, carpenters, and lime-burners, musicians, and dancers. Many of the dancing-girls belonging to the temples are of this caste. The caste are permitted to eat meat and drink spirits. They are Śudras, and do not, like the Wániás, claim to be Vaiśyas. Some are Vaishnawas, and some Lingáits. Their gurus are certain chiefs of the Śrivaishnawa Bráhmans and pancháṅgis of the Smárta Bráhmans. The Linga Banajigas are very strict in their observances, and abstain from flesh and spirits. A large division call themselves Adi Banajiga.

Banana. The musa paradisiaca, or its fruit; it closely resembles the plantain.

Bánaprasth. A vernacular form of Wánaprastha.

Bandá. [Hindi, from Persian *bandah*, bound.] A bondman, a slave; an hereditary bondman descended from a female slave.

Bandapanthi. [Panjábi: Sanskrit *pantha*, a way.] The followers of Banda, a sect of Sikhs who revere Banda, the temporal successor of the last guru.

Bandáwat. The name of a cultivating class of high rank who claim to be Rájputs.

Bándhar. [Maráṭhi.] A guard sent into a village, the chief of which had come to terms with the Maráṭhás, to protect it from plunder by the mulukgiri army.

Bandhára. [Gujaráti.] The name of a caste in Gujarát. Their occupation is dyeing clothes in a particular manner, namely, by tying up portions of the cloth with cord so that the colour is not applied to them, and then dipping the cloth into the dye-stuff. When the colour is fixed the knots are unfastened, and the portions kept uncoloured form a pattern. The Bandháras also are washers of silk and embroidered clothes. There is a separate community of Sunni Musalmán converts from this caste.

Bandhu. [Sanskrit, from *bandh*, to bind.] A relation; but the term is usually confined to distant kindred of another gotra, that is, to others than sapiṇḍas and samánodakas; or, in other words, to distant kindred not connected wholly through males.

Bandy. [Tamil *wanḍi*.] A two-wheeled chaise; a cart.

Bang. See Bhang.

Bangala. The name of a wandering tribe of Bengal; they live in tents, and are tattooers.

Bangáli. More commonly Bengali.

Bangáli. [Tamil.] A shareholder of village lands under a tenure by the terms of which the fields are divided by lot every six years.

Bangash. The name of an Afghán tribe settled partly within the British border near Kohat and partly in the Kuram valley.

Banghy. See Bahangi.

Bangi. Another name for Banjogi.

Bangle. [A corruption of the Hindustáni *bangri.*] A bracelet.

Bangu. The river-thug of Bengal; these inveigle people into their boats, and, after strangling, cast them into the water (*H. H. Wilson*).

Banian. See Banyá or Banyan.

Bani Israil. [Arabic, *ibn*, a son.] The children of Israel, the name by which the Afgháns proper call themselves, and also the name of a small tribe in the Konkan. See Beni Israel.

Banik. [Hindi.] A trader, a banker, a money-changer, a banyá.

Bániyá. The Bengali and Panjábi form of Banyá. It is said that the Bániyás of the Panjáb are a subdivision of the despised Chamár caste, and that they still privately worship the rámpi, the symbol of their original occupation. The Panjáb Bániyás are some Vaishnawas and some Jains.

Banjárá. [Hindi, from Sanskrit *banij*, a trader.] The name of a class of traders who travel over the country with numerous pack-bullocks, carrying grain, salt, etc., from market to market. Some are Hindus and some Musalmáns. Their origin is obscure. Lambánis and Sukális are often spoken of by this name.

Banjátrá. [Hindi, from *ban*, a forest, and *játrá*, q.v.] The perambulation of the groves sacred to Krishna at Gowardhan, near Ágrá, made by pilgrims in Bhádrapad.

Banjiga. See Banajiga.

Banjogi. The name of one of the Toungthá tribes. They generally resemble the Lushais, but affirm that they are sprung from the Shans of Burma. They acknowledge a supreme god called Patyen, but all their reverence and sacrificial rites are directed towards Khozing, the patron deity of their nation. Unlike the Lushais, they bury their dead without first drying the body, and they wear their knot of hair on the forehead like the Shendus and Kumis (*T. H. Lewin*).

Bankar. [Bengali, from *ban*, Sanskrit, *wana*, a forest, and *kar*, revenue.] Forest produce, such as timber, brushwood, gum, honey; also the privilege of cutting wood, hunting, and fishing.

Bánkot Knees. Curved teak logs from Bánkot, highly prized for shipbuilding.

Bankśál. [Bengali, from the Sanskrit *banik*, trade, and *śála*, a house.] The office where harbour dues and tolls are paid.

Bánsái. [Bengali, from *bans*, a bamboo.] A frame of bamboo-work used as a harrow for breaking clods after ploughing.

Bansáj. [Bengali, Sanskrit *wanśája*, from *wanśa*, race, and *ja*, born.] Of good family; the title given to the third and last class of Gauḍa (subdivision) Bráhmans.

Bánsphor. [Hindi, from *bans*, a bamboo, and *phor*, to split.] The name of a caste who make baskets.

Banṭar. [Tulu.] The name of an agricultural caste. Many have migrated into Coorg. They correspond to the Tamil Vellálans and Malayálam Nairs.

Bantariá. [Hindi.] A class of wood-rangers formerly holding rent-free land in quittance of police duties, in the northern parganas of Gorakhpur (*H. H. Wilson*).

Banṭrotu. [Telugu.] A peon, a policeman.

Banyá. [Hindi, from the Sanskrit *banik*, a merchant.] A Hindu trader, shopkeeper, or money-changer. In Bengal it is commonly applied to the native cashier, or man of business in the service of Europeans. In the west of India it ordinarily denotes Hindu merchants, settled either as agents or principals at the chief places of traffic in the Persian Gulf or Red Sea (*H. H. Wilson*). See Wáni.

Banyan. A corruption of Banyá.

Banyan. The name given in English to the Indian fig tree—ficus indica—known in Sanskrit as *waṭa*, and in the vernaculars as *waḍ* or *bar*, whence the other English name *burr*.

Báoḍi. [Maráṭhi.] A well, either with or without a flight of steps leading to the water.

Báoli, Báori. [Hindi, from the Sanskrit *wápi*, a large oblong pond; intermediate forms are found in *wáo*, *wáoḍi*, and *báoḍi*.] A well with a flight of steps leading down to the surface of the water; these are often elaborate constructions, with landing-places and chambers at different levels. Also the well-room of a palace.

Báori. [Hindi.] A vagrant tribe in the Bhatti country and west of Delhi, and in Tonk and Jáipur, who are professional thieves and very bold and skilful; they go armed to commit open raids on villages, and use disguises, especially that of the jogi, to effect secret thefts. They enter houses by digging a hole in the wall near the bar of the door, and so opening it.

Bár. [Panjábi.] Desert or forest land; especially the central table-land of the Chaj Jetch doáb.

Báradari. [Hindustáni, from *bárah*, twelve, and the Persian *dar*, a door.] A house with many doors, a summer-house or summer-palace. Báradaris were often converted into mausoleums on the death of the owner.

Bárah. [Hindi.] Literally, twelve; a collocation of twelve villages. The villages so grouped are generally the settlement of one tribe or caste, and the name often remains after the number of villages has changed. There are bárahs of Awáns, of Játs, of Rájputs, and of Paṭháns in the Hoshiarpur district. Compare Aṭhávisi, Baiyá, Báwani, Chaubisa, Chaurási.

Baráhan. [Hindi.] The name of a goddess who is supposed to cure swelled hands and feet. There is a temple to her at Benares.

Bárah Wafát. [Hindustáni.] The

12th of Rabi-al-awal, called also Bari Wafát.

Baraichi. A tribe occupying Shorábak, a country about sixty miles square between the Khojah Amran range and Pishin.

Barakzai. The name of the Afghán tribe to which the family of Shir Ali, the late ruler of Afghánistán, belonged. Shir Ali's grandfather, Fattah Khán, was wazir to Mahmud (the last ruler but one of the previous dynasty of the Saddozais), and in this capacity appointed his sons to the principal provincial governments. On the murder of Fattah Khán, in 1818, the country was generally convulsed, and much of it was lost to the Sikhs; the sons of Fattah Khán made themselves independent, one of them, Dost Muhammad, holding Cabul and Ghazni. On the final expulsion of the Saddozais, Dost Muhammad became ruler of all that remained of the country, *i.e.* the territory now called Afghánistán.

Báráni. [Hindustáni, from *bárán*, rain.] A term applied to land which is watered by rain, not by irrigation. It is also the name of a cloak for keeping off rain, commonly corrupted by Europeans to 'brandy' (*H. H. Wilson*).

Barasinga. [Hindi.] The swamp deer, rucervus duvaucellii.

Barat. [Hindi.] The leather rope used for drawing up a bucket from a well.

Barát. [Hindi, from the Sanskrit *wara*, a bridegroom, and *rátri*, night.] A bridal procession, the final ceremony of a marriage. Among Rájputs the second half of the dower is paid on the day of barát. See Lagan.

Barát. [Arabic.] See Shab-i-barát.

Bardá. The name of a small tribe in the hills in the north-west of Khándesh. They are skilful cultivators and basket-weavers. They are called also Dorepis.

Bardásht. [Hindustáni.] Stores, supplies; also the furnishing of porters and provisions to troops or travellers.

Bardáshtkhánah. A temporary storehouse for supplies for troops or travellers.

Bargá. [Bengali.] An agreement by which the cultivator engages to pay the landlord half the produce, the latter providing half the seed and paying the whole revenue.

Bargáit. [Bengali.] A cultivator on bargá tenure.

Bárgir. [Persian.] A trooper whose horse is not his own, but the state's; a págádár as distinguished from a silahdár.

Bargujur. The name of a division of the Rájputs, accounted one of the thirty-six royal races, and claiming descent from Ráma's second son; they are numerous in Rohilkhand. A branch of the tribe adopted islám in the time of Alauddin Khilji, but retains many Hindu customs. The name has been adopted also by subdivisions of Bráhmans, Bhuksás, and Meos.

Bárhah Sádát. The name of a powerful tribe of Saids in the eastern part of the Muzaffarnagar district, where they seem to have been established since the time of Shamsuddin Altamash (*H. M. Elliot*).

Barhái. The name of a caste numerous in Behar; they are carpenters.

Bári. A caste of the North-West Provinces. Their special occupation is to stitch together large leaves by the insertion of small wooden pegs, to serve as dishes; they are employed also as torch-bearers and barbers (*M. A. Sherring*).

Bári. The Hindi and Bengali form of Wáḍi. An enclosed piece of ground; a homestead, a dwelling-house. The Bengali bári is erected upon bhiti land, the house and farm buildings standing along the sides of a rectangle, and so more or less enclosing the uthán in the centre.

Barid Sháhi. The name of the branch of the Báhmani dynasty which, on the dismemberment of the latter in 1489 A.D., established itself at Bidar. This, though it retained the ancient Báhmani capital, was the weakest of the five states about this time established, and was the first to fall. Most of its territory was annexed to Bijápur.

Bárikudu. [Telugu.] The name of a low caste; they are village scavengers and watchmen.

Bari Wafát. [Hindustáni *bari*, great, and Arabic *wafát*, death.] The fast of the prophet's death, observed by Sunnis on the 12th, and by Shiahs on the 28th Rabi-al-awal.

Barkandáz. [Hindustáni, from the Persian *bark*, lightning, and *andáz*, who throws.] A match-lock man, an armed guard, a constable.

Bárkhali. [Gujaráti.] Alienated or rent-free land. See Alienated.

Barnawár. The name of a trading caste in the Gayá and Patna districts.

Bárnis. [Maráṭhi *nis*, from the Persian *navis*, a writer.] A clerk whose duty it is to enter the contents of a document in a register, and notify his having done so by writing the word 'bár' (the origin of which is unknown) on the original.

Bárnisi. [Maráṭhi, from *bárnis*.] The work of registering correspondence, that is, of noting the substance of each letter or document in a book kept for the purpose, in lieu of making duplicates of each despatch. See Tumár.

Bároṭ. [Gujaráti.] The name of a class of the Bháṭs.

Barothi. [Hindi.] A subdivision of the Áhir tribe.

Baru. [Maráṭhi.] The reed of which kalams are usually made.

Barudiá. [Gujaráti, from the Sanskrit *waruḍa*, but probably connected with *baru*.] The name of a caste, the same as the Buruḍ; they are basket-makers.

Bárui. [Bengali.] The name of a caste; they are growers and sellers of the betel, and are considered to be pure Śudras.

Barwá. The hereditary wise man and exorcist among Bhils.

Barwáik. [Hindi.] A class of hereditary chaukidárs.

Barwár. [Hindi.] The name of a caste; they are rice-cleaners. Compare Golá. Also the name of a tribe of Rájputs in Gorakhpur.

Barwatiya. See Bahárwaṭiá.

Basant. A Hindi form of Wasant.

Basavi. [Maráṭhi.] A woman dedicated to a god; a prostitute.

Basawá. [Maráṭhi.] The sacred bull, the wáhan of Śiwa.

Básbanyá. [Hindi, from *bás*, scent, and *banyá*, q.v.] A dealer in scents, a perfumer.

Báshara. [Hindustáni, from the Persian *bah*, according to, and the Arabic *shara*, the law.] The word signifies 'according to the law,' and is applied to those classes of fakirs who observe the koran, as distinguished from the beshara, without the law, who deem themselves of such sanctity as to be above the necessity of observing the law. The báshara fakirs usually marry and have fixed homes; the beshara are mostly celibates and live wandering lives.

Báśing. [Maráṭhi.] A sort of diadem made of gilded paper or tinsel, worn by the bride and bridegroom at a wedding.

Baśiniá. [Hindi.] The headman of a village in Rangpur. See Headman.

Basti. [Hindi, from the Sanskrit *wasa*, to dwell.] An inhabited place, an abode; in Bengal, a block of native huts generally the property of one owner, crowded together, with often a tank in the centre; in the south of India basti is the name also of the ordinary Jain temple. See Beṭṭa.

Batáni. The name of an Afghán tribe within our border near Dera Ismail Khán.

Bátar. The name of a semi-Hinduised tribe from the Nepal hills; they are day-labourers.

Batelá. [Maráṭhi.] A particular kind of vessel used in the coasting trade; it is from fifty to four hundred candies burthen.

Batta. [A corruption of the Hindi *bhatah*, or Maráṭhi *bhaṭṭá*.] An allowance to a public servant in addition to his regular pay, to meet some special cause of expense, such as service in the field in the case of a soldier, travelling, temporary dearness of the staple food-grain; an allowance paid by a creditor for the subsistence of a debtor detained in prison; an allowance to witnesses summoned to court.

Baṭṭá. [Hindi.] Rate of exchange; used particularly, in the time when numerous independent mints were issuing money, for the amount to be added to, or deducted from, any payment according to the currency in which it was paid; also, discount on debased or uncurrent coins.

Batty. [A corruption of the Kanarese *batta*.] Rice in the husk, paddy.

Batty. [A corruption of the Maráṭhi *bháṭi*.] Rich alluvial loam along the bank of a river.

Baṭwárá. [Hindi, from Sanskrit *waṭ*, to divide.] The division of an estate among the co-owners so that each receives a separate portion, of which the revenue is separately assessed.

Bau. [Bengali.] A wife; but in a family the term is usually applied to a son's wife.

Bauddha. [Sanskrit.] Relating to Buddha; a follower of the religion of Siddhárta the Buddha. The English form Buddhist is more common.

Baugh. See Bágh.

Bauli. [Hindi.] A settlement made with the cultivators direct; a ryotwár or khás settlement. See Settlement.

Báuri. [Bengali.] The name of a semi-Hinduised tribe of Bengal and Orissa; they are cultivators, labourers, swine-keepers, fishermen, salt-makers, and palanquin-bearers.

Báwani. [Hindi, from *báwan*, fifty-two.] A collocation of fifty-two villages. See Bárah.

Bawari. See Báori.

Bawarij. The name of a class of pirates whose head-quarters used to be at Somnáth and the Cutch coast.

Bayadere. [A corruption of the Portuguese *bailadeira*.] A dancing-girl. See Dancing-girl.

Bázár. [Persian.] A market, or a market-place; any street which is composed chiefly of shops. Compare Ganj, Háṭ, Melá.

Bázigar. [Hindustáni, from the Persian *bázi*, play, and *gar*, the active affix.] A juggler, a tumbler; the name of a caste of jugglers.

Báznámah. [Hindi, from the Persian *báz*, back, and *námah*, a writing.] A deed of relinquishment.

Bazoti. The name of an independent Afghán tribe beyond the border to the north-west of Kohat.

Bazzáz. [Hindustáni.] A cloth-merchant, a draper.

Bearer. A common name in Bengal for a body-servant; perhaps a corruption of *Behárá*, the name of the caste to which such servants usually belong.

Beastie. See Bhisti.

Bebartta. [Uriya.] The head officer of a tributary rájá.

Bechoba. [Hindustáni, from the Persian *be*, without, and *chob*, a staff.] A small kind of tent made without any pole; the roof is in the form of a square umbrella, the ribs of bamboo being fixed together at the peak and the lower ends resting on the four walls.

Beḍar. [Kanarese *Beḍaru*, the plural of *Beḍa*.] The name of a caste of which there are two divisions, the Karnáta and the Telinga, who neither eat together nor intermarry. Formerly they were hunters and soldiers by profession; now they are employed in agriculture, labour, and as peons and village policemen. Most of the Mysore pálegárs are of this caste. They are chiefly Vaishnawas. See Rámosi.

Bedar ware. See Bidri.

Bediyá. The name of a wandering tribe of Bengal; in some parts, as Nadiya, they are of predatory habits; in others, as Bogra, they are peaceful, and live by bird-catching, juggling, etc. They are mostly Muhammadans.

Beebee. See Bibi.

Beega. See Bighá.

Beegotee. See Vighoṭi.

Beer. See Bir.

Begam. [Hindustáni.] A Musalmán lady of rank. Among Saïds the title is commonly affixed to all women's names.

Begári. [Hindustáni, from the Persian *be*, without, and *gár*, the Sanskrit *kára*, worker.] Forced labour or a forced labourer; in modern times a labourer for hire; also, in the south, a village servant remunerated by fees in grain or inám land. Compare Veṭh, Veṭhiá.

Behárá. [Bengali.] The name of a low caste; they are palanquin-bearers and domestic servants.

Behdi. The name of the subdivision of the Khatri caste to which Nának, the first guru of the Sikhs, belonged; thence also the name of a separate sect of the Sikhs founded by Lakshmi Dás, a younger son of Nának, when the succession passed from Nának to Angad, who was of the Tihan subdivision.

Behdin. A Pársi who is not of the hereditary class of priests; a layman.

Behri. [Hindustáni.] A proportionate rate, or subscription, or distribution. Compare Phálá. Also a large division of a village including many paṭṭis.

Bel. The Hindi form of Bilwa, the tree ægle marmelos. Bel is also a Hindi form of the Sanskrit *walli*, a creeper.

Bela. [Sindhi.] A block of forest formed as a preserve for game.

Belbhanḍár. [Maráṭhi, from *bel* and *bhanḍár*, turmeric powder.] The bel leaves and turmeric placed on an idol; a form of oath by taking the belbhanḍár off an idol and swearing by them.

Beldár. [Hindustáni, from the Persian *bel*, a spade, and *dár*, who holds.] The name of a low caste of Bengal; they are tank-diggers and day-labourers. In the Deccan, Beldárs are stone-cutters and quarry-workers.

Bell music. A mode of music practised by the Sánáns. A bow seven or eight feet long is fitted with a cord of strong leather, on which are strung a number of bells; the singers sit down on the floor with the bow before them and strike on the cord with short sticks (*S. Mateer*).

Beloochistani. See Biluch.

Belwa. See Bilwa.

Benámi. [Hindustáni, from the Persian *be*, without, and *nám*, a name.] Nameless, fictitious, but not necessarily fraudulent; a term applied to transactions in which the name of one of the real parties does not appear, but some third person's name is substituted. Compare Farzi.

Benámidár. [Persian *dár*, holder.] One whose name appears in a benámi transaction, but who is not the real proprietor of the right indicated. A benámidár may be either a stranger whose name is used in order to conceal the real owner, or he may be a relative for the sake of whose reputation a nominal assignment of property is made.

Benawá. [Hindustáni.] The name of a community of fakirs of the beshara order. They are Sunnis. They do nothing but beg. Their patron saint is Saïd Abdul Kádir Jiláni the pir-pirán.

Bendy. See Bhendi.

Bengali. [Corruption of *bangáli.*] The language of Bengal; it is spoken by about thirty-six millions of persons, and is one of the principal languages derived from the Sanskrit; the character is a modification of the Dewanágari.

Beni Israel. [From *benu*, the plural of the Arabic *ibn*, a son.] The children of Israel, the name of a race of people, numbering only a few thousands, found in the Konkan. Their ancestors, they say, came to the coast of India from a country to the northward about 1600 years ago. They were in number seven men and seven women, saved from a shipwreck on the Colaba coast. The Beni Israel in their physiognomy resemble the Arabian Jews. They are fairer than the other natives of India of the same rank of life, but are not much to be distinguished from them with regard to dress. They have no shendi like the Hindus, but they preserve a tuft of hair above each of their ears. Their turbans, angarkhás, and shoes are like those of the Hindus, and their trousers like those of the Musalmáns. The vernacular language of the Beni Israel is Maráṭhi, and each of them has generally two names—one Hebrew, which is conferred at the time of circumcision, and the other Hindu, which is given about a month after birth. They use the Hebrew liturgy of the Sephardim. The Beni Israel chiefly occupy themselves in agriculture and in manufacturing oil, and some are artisans, particularly masons and carpenters. A few are blacksmiths, goldsmiths, and tailors, and there are several of them in the native army (*J. Wilson*).

Beohara. See Bohrá.

Ber. See Baer.

Berá. [Hindustáni.] A boat decorated and illuminated in honour of Khizr.

Berad. [Maráṭhi.] The name of a hill tribe resembling the Rámosis; they worship Ganpati and the cobra; their headman is called gauḍa.

Berak. [Gujaráti, from the Arabic.] An Arab drum-and-fife band; as many Arab mercenaries as go with one band; a battalion.

Berár. The name in Baitul of the village accountant. See Village accountant.

Beri. [Kanarese, from *bera*, trade.] The name of a branch of the Siwáchár Nagartas; they are traders.

Besar. [Gujaráti.] A black soil of character intermediate between kálibhoy and goráṭ. It is especially suited to rice, juwár, and sugar-cane.

Beshara. [Hindustáni, from Persian *be*, without, and Arabic *shara*, the law.] Without or above the law; the common name of those classes of fakirs which hold themselves above the law, as distinguished from the báshara. See Báshara.

Besta. [Kanarese.] The name of a caste, perhaps the same as the Telugu Boïs, and allied to the Kahárs of Bengal. They are fishermen and palanquin-bearers specially, but many are engaged as husbandmen, labourers, weavers of cloth, and lime-burners. Many of the women are cotton-spinners. They are accounted pure Śudras, and worship all the Hindu deities, but especially Gangamma, mother Ganges.

Betel. This word, which exists in the same form in Spanish, Portuguese, and French, and is perhaps connected with the Sanskrit *patra,* a leaf, is the name of a creeping plant, the chavica betle, which is a species of pepper, but grows something like the kidney-bean. It bears no nut, but the leaves are used to wrap up, and are chewed with, the nut of the areca palm; whence that nut is often called betel-nut, it being the nut that is wrapped up in betel. The vernacular name for the leaf is pán, and for the nut supári.

Beṭhiá. The Uriya form of Veṭhiá.

Beṭṭa. [Kanarese.] Literally, a hill; also the name of an inferior sort of rice-land, situated on high ground, and bearing only one crop a year; also the name of a kind of Jain temple, different from the basti, and consisting of only a court-yard, usually on the top of a hill, surrounding a colossal image of Gomaṭeśwara. A subdivision of the Kurubas is called Beṭṭa; they are a diminutive race, but very active and enduring. Their principal business is felling timber, at which they are very expert; they work also on coffee estates. See Káḍu.

Beyrupia. See Bahurupia.

Beyshurra. See Beshara.

Bezanjoi. [Corrupt form.] The name of a tribe of Biluchistán; their head-quarters is Nal, in lat. 27° 20′ N., long. 66° E.

Bhaḍariá. [Hindi.] A tribe of mendicant astrologers of Bráhman descent.

Bhadauriá. A branch of the Chauhán Rájputs.

Bháḍbhunjá. [Gujaráti, from *bháḍ,* a parching-stove, and *bhunj,* to dry.] The name of a caste; they are grain-parchers. Some have been converted to islám. Compare Kándu.

Bhádon. The Urdu name of the month Bhádrapad, or September. See Month.

Bhádra. A shortened form of Bhádrapad.

Bhádralog. [Bengali, from the Sanskrit *bhadra,* good, and *loka,* people.] Respectable, well-to-do people.

Bhádrapad. [Sanskrit.] The Hindu month most nearly corresponding, under the śukladi reckoning, with September; it is so called from *bhádrapadá,* auspicious steps, the name of the nakshatra (in the constellation Pegasus) in which the moon is at full in this month. See Month.

Bhádu. [Uriya.] The name of a degraded class of Uriya Bráhmans; they prepare tobacco.

Bhadun. See Bhádon.

Bhagat. [Hindi, from the Sanskrit *bhakta,* devoted to, from *bhaj,* to assign.] A follower, a worshipper; a saint.

Bhagawad-gita. [Sanskrit.] The

song of the adorable. This is the name of a poem inserted in the Mahábhárata. It attempts to reconcile the conflicting views of different philosophical systems by engrafting the sánkhya and yoga upon vedánta doctrines. It inculcates also the doctrine of faith in Krishna, and stern devotion to caste duties (*Monier Williams*).

Bhágbaṭái. [Hindi, from the Sanskrit *bhága*, a share, and *wanṭa*, a share.] A system of collecting land revenue by taking a fixed share in kind of the produce of each field each season. The quantity of grain to be made over to government was determined by appraisement (see Kaltar) while the crops were standing.

Bhágdár. [Sanskrit *bhága*, share, and Persian *dár*, who holds.] A sharer in a bhágdári village.

Bhágdári. Another name for the narwa system of land tenure.

Bhagela. The name of a branch of the Solanki Rájputs; they have given their name to Bhagelkhand or Rewa, where they are the ruling family. Some have adopted islám. The rájá of Barrah is also of the Bhagela clan.

Bhagtá. The name of a branch of the Áhir tribe.

Bhagwán. [Sanskrit *bhagawan*, from *bhaj*, to adore.] The holy one, the revered; an epithet of Vishnu, also of Śiwa; a general name for God.

Bhagwat. [Sanskrit *bhagawat*, from *bhaj*, to adore.] Revered, adorable; a name for God.

Bhái. [Hindi.] Literally, brother; the ordinary title of Sikhs who have acquired a name for holiness.

Bháiband. [Hindi, from *bhái*, brother, and *band*, to tie.] One closely associated with another either by blood or by friendship and community of interest.

Bhairavi. [Sanskrit.] The terrible; a name of the wife of Bhairawa.

Bhairawa. [Sanskrit, from *bhiru*, fearful, from *bhi*, to fear.] Terrible; a name of Śiwa, in his character as a destroyer.

Bhairawanáth. [Sanskrit *nátha*, lord.] A name of Śiwa. The god of the temple of Bhairawanáth at Benares is in public estimation the deified koṭwál of the city, which he supervises under the orders of Bisheśwar.

Bhairon. A shortened form of Bhaironáth. He is worshipped under many names, as Kál Bhairon, who frightens death; Bhut Bhairon, who drives away evil spirits; Bhattuk Bhairon, the child Bhairon; Láth Bhairon, or Bhairon with the club; Nand Bhairon; Bhairon Jati, or the ascetic Bhairon.

Bhaironáth. A Hindi form of Bhairawanáth.

Bhákta. [Sanskrit, from *bhakt*, devoted to, from *bhaj*, to adore.] A devotee, a follower, a member of a religious sect; especially a dakshinácházri sákta.

Bhakti-márg. [Hindi, from the Sanskrit *bhakti*, devotion, from *bhaj*, to adore, and *márga*, a road, from *márg*, to follow.] The way of love or faith, the way to salvation through devotion to personal deities. See Hinduism.

Bhál. [Hindi.] The name of a tribe of Rájputs.

Bhámṭyá. [Maráṭhi.] The name of a caste said to have come to the Deccan from the Telugu country; they are professional thieves; they never commit burglary or violent crime, but are most expert pick-pockets; they carry in their mouths a minute curved knife for cutting open bags and pockets; the gum and the inside of the cheek are hardened with salt to make a receptacle for the knife.

Bhánḍ. [Hindi, from the Sanskrit *bhanḍa.*] A jester, a buffoon. Originally Hindus, the Bhánḍs are now mostly Musalmáns, some Sunni and some Shiah.

Bhandári. [Maráṭhi.] The name of a caste; they extract and distil the sap from cocoa and other palm trees. Some also are sailors, and a few trade, and some enlist in the army or the police. There are four divisions of them, called Kitte, More, Gauḍ, and Sinde, who do not eat together or intermarry. The Bhandári's still consists of two earthen pots, connected together by a hollow piece of wood; the larger of the pots is the boiler, and contains the toddy, the steam from which passes through the tube into the other pot or condenser, which is partly buried underground, and is every now and then sprinkled with water. The Bhandáris seldom partake of the liquor they make; drinking of toddy before it is fermented is also not allowed by the caste rules.

Bhanḍári. [Gujaráti, from the Sanskrit *bhánḍa*, goods.] A treasurer, especially the treasurer of a religious establishment. His is an important post, as he has not only charge of the treasure, but is also general manager of the whole establishment, and representative of the whole body of resident sádhus. It is the sádhus who elect the bhanḍári, and they usually choose a perfect stranger, so that their head may have no local interests.

Bhang, Bháng. [Hindi.] An intoxicating drink prepared from the leaves of the cannabis sativa; the plant with female flowers only is used for this purpose. See Gánjá.

Bhanga. [Bengali.] A term used to denote a Kulin who has taken to wife the daughter of a Bansáj.

Bhangi. [Hindi.] The name of a very low caste; they are sweepers and scavengers, and are known also as Chuhrá, Mehtar, and Halálkhor. Bhangi was also the name of one of the Sikh misls, and that which for a time was the most powerful of all; they occupied the country containing the cities of Lahore and Amritsar, and extending thence northwards to the Jhilam.

Bhansáli. The name of a caste in Cutch; they are of Rájput origin, Vaishnawas in religion, husbandmen and shopkeepers by occupation; they are called also Vegu.

Bhaoli. [Bengali.] A term applied to land for which the zamindár receives his rent in kind, as distinguished from nakdi land.

Bhar. The name of an aboriginal tribe, and perhaps the origin of Bhárata, the old name of India; they were once a powerful people about Oudh, but are now in a broken condition and occupied chiefly as swineherds.

Bháradár. [Nepalese.] A minister.

Bháradár Sabhá. The great council of state in Nepal.

Bhárata [Sanskrit], **Bháratkhand, Bháratwarsh.** The country of Bharata the son of Dushyanta; the classical name for India. The terms *khand* and *warsh* both mean division.

Bharbhunjá. [Hindi; see *bháḍbhunjá.*] A grain-parcher; the name of a separate caste, and also of a branch of the Káyath caste, following the occupation of parching grain.

Bharwáḍ. [Gujaráti.] The name of a caste; they are shepherds. See Rabári.

Bharwatiya. See Bahárwaṭiá.

Bháshá. [Sanskrit.] Speech, language; but the name especially, among natives, of that form of Hindustáni which the English call Hindi.

Bháskar. [Bengali.] The name of a low caste; they are stonemasons.

Bhaṭ. A vernacular form of Bhaṭṭa. The term is especially applied to mendicant Bráhmans. It is also the name of a particular tribe of Bráhmans in the district of Benares.

Bháṭ. [Hindi, from the Sanskrit *bhaṭṭa.*] The name of a caste supposed to be sprung from a Kshatriya father and Vaiśya mother. They are by hereditary profession bards, chroniclers, and genealogists; but they are now message-bearers and beggars, and some are cultivators. What was called Bháṭ security used to be common in Gujarát; its peculiar efficacy arose from the Bháṭ's readiness to put himself to death if default was made in an engagement for the fulfilment of which he was surety, and the supposition that his blood would in such case be on the head of the defaulter. See Dharná, Trágá.

Bhata, Bhátá. More commonly Batta.

Bháṭhá. [Gujaráti.] Rich alluvial loam along the banks or in the bed of a river.

Bháṭhelá. [Gujaráti.] A caste of Bráhmans belonging to the Surat collectorate. They came originally from the village of Anáwal, whence they are called sometimes Anáwalás. Another name they go by is Mástán. They are distinguished from other Bráhmans by never begging; they are industrious and expert cultivators and a prosperous class; they are also very cunning and very litigious.

Bhaṭi. The Maráṭhi form of Bháṭhá or another form of Bhaṭṭi.

Bháṭiá. The name of a caste in Sindh, Cutch, and Gujarát, connected with the Bhaṭṭis. In Sindh, they are fishermen; in Gujarát, shopkeepers and milksellers; in Cutch, they are traders, clerks, shopkeepers, husbandmen, and labourers. The Cutch Bháṭiás were converted to the Wallabhacháryan religion about the end of the fifteenth century.

Bhaṭṭa. [Sanskrit.] A title used in addressing, or affixed to the name of, a learned Bráhman. In Tamil it denotes the officiating priest in a pagoda.

Bhaṭṭamánya. [Sanskrit *mána*, honour.] Lands given rent free or on favourable terms to Bráhmans in honour of their learning.

Bhaṭṭi. The name of a branch of the Yadu, Yádawa, or Jádon tribe of Rájputs. The ruler of Jáisalmir of this branch. Many of them are now Muhammadans.

Bhattuturaka. The name of a caste in North Arcot. They are intelligent and educated, can speak several languages and personate any caste.

Bhavaiá. [Gujaráti.] A strolling actor and dancer. Some have adopted islám, and form a distinct community; they are Sunnis.

Bhávin. [Maráṭhi, from the Sanskrit *bháwa*, in its sense of attachment, devotion.] A woman who has been given in childhood by her parents, or who devotes herself, to service in a temple. A woman so dedicates herself by taking oil from a lamp burning before the idol and putting it on her head. A bhávin's connection with the temple is never broken; if she is allowed to live away from the temple she has to send presents to it. She is usually a prostitute, but not a public dancing-girl. Still her position is lower than that of a náikan.

Bhávsár. [Gujaráti.] The name of a caste; they are calico-printers.

Bhawan. [Hindi.] A house built round a quadrangle; a palace.

Bhawáni. [Sanskrit.] The wife of Bhawa. Bhawa, which means being, existence, is a name of Śiwa's.

Bhawbij. The Gujaráti form of Bhrátridvitiya.

Bháyád. [Gujaráti, from *bhái*, a brother.] Brotherhood, kinsmen. The word is specially used in Káṭhiáwár to express the body of nobles connected by blood with the reigning family.

Bheestee. See Bhisti.

Bhekrá. [Hindi.] A kind of deer, the cervulus aureus. It is commonly called the rib-faced deer, but in Bengal it is known as the barking deer, and in Madras as the jungle sheep.

Bhenḍi. [Maráṭhi.] The name of a tree, the thespesia populnea, commonly called bendy; it was introduced by the Portuguese from the Eastern Archipelago; it is found in the coast forests; the wood is used for wheels and boat-timbers, and the shoots as rafters (*G. Birdwood*). Also the name of a vegetable, the hibiscus esculentus.

Bher. See Baer.

Bhihar. [Hindi.] A tribe which, according to tradition, was one of the primitive tribes of the upper doáb. They were expelled from Nirauli and the neighbouring districts by the Bargujar Rájputs. In Rohilkhand they are called Bihar.

Bhikhári. The Bengali form of Bhikshu.

Bhikhu. The Hindi form of Bhikshu.

Bhikshu. [Sanskrit, from *bhiksh*, to beg.] A beggar, a religious mendicant, especially a Bráhman in the fourth áśrama. Among Buddhists, one who has undertaken to be bound by the dasasil, a member of the sangha.

Bhil. [Sanskrit *bhilla.*] The name of an aboriginal race found in Máłwá, Mewár, Khándesh, the most northern parts of the Deccan, and scattered among the villages of Gujarát. Dr. Wilson considers them to be of Scythian origin, and derives their name from the Dravidian *billu*, a bow. Bowmen they are to the present day. 'The true race of Bhil,' says Captain James Rose, 'is easily distinguished by the dark colour, diminutive size, prominent cheek-bones, large nostrils, activity, power of enduring fatigue, and rare qualifications for the chase, of those who belong to it.' A Bhil corps of militia has been established in Khándesh, and in Gujarát Bhils are much employed as wartaniás. Some also are in the regular district police. Bhils have always subsisted partly by cultivation, and are now settling down more than formerly to that occupation. They now profess Hinduism, and employ Bráhmans to some extent; they worship Mátá and Wágheśwar.

Bhilálá. The name of a tribe found in Khándesh and the native dales to the north-west of it. They are supposed to be a mixture of the Rájput and Bhil races. They live by husbandry and are industrious. They are Hindus by religion.

Bhimsen. [Hindi, from the Sanskrit *bhima*, terrible, and *sena*, army.] Having a terrible army; the name of (among others) the second Páṇḍawa, but considered to be only the reputed son of Páṇḍu and really the son of the wind-god Wáyu. He is represented by a huge recumbent human figure at Benares, and by a post with a knob at the top at Bastar in the Central Provinces, where he is one of the principal deities.

Bhisti. [Hindustáni, from the Persian *bihisht*, paradise.] A water-carrier, one who carries water for domestic use, or waters the roads or trees. Strictly the bhisti uses a leather bag called a masak, which he carries on his back, while the pakháli uses a double bag called a pakhál, which is carried by a buffalo or bullock.

Bhiṭi. [Bengali.] High ground which is suitable or has been used for the site of a homestead.

Bhogajásti. [Telugu, from *bhoga*, enjoyment, use, and *jásti*, additional.] An extra assessment on account of a second crop raised on land that usually bears only one crop in the year.

Bhogtá. A semi-Hinduised tribe of Bengal and Chutiá Nágpur; they are labourers, and are also employed to exorcise demons.

Bhoï. The Maráṭhi form of Boï.

Bhoï. [Uriya.] A village accountant. See Village accountant.

Bhojah. [Gujaráti.] The name of a class of Bráhmans who are employed chiefly in Jain temples.

Bhojpatra. [Hindi.] A manuscript written on a leaf or the bark of a birch tree.

Bhojpuri. A dialect of Hindi used in western Behar, and the conterminous districts of the North-West Provinces (*C. J. Lyall*).

Bholánáth. [Sanskrit *nátha*, a lord; the meaning of *bholá* is unknown.] An epithet of Śiwá. Also in Kumáun, a demon who is ruler or guide of the spirits of the dead.

Bhonslá. [Maráṭhi.] The name of the

family, claiming descent from the ráná of Udáipur, to which Śiwaji, the founder of the Maráṭhá kingdom, belonged; a branch of the family rose to independent power at Nágpur, and levied chauth from Bengal, but was conquered by the British in 1817 A.D. Bhonslá is also the name of the wild dogs of the Himálaya, considered to be Bhagwán's hounds.

Bhopá. Another name for Rabári.

Bhopi. [Maráṭhi]. The priest of a village temple, generally a Śudra.

Bhorpi. [Maráṭhi.] A contraction of Bahurupia.

Bhrátridvitiya. [Sanskrit, *bhrátri*, brother, and *dvitiya*, the second day.] The brother's second, namely, the 2nd of Kártik śudh, on which day men are entertained by their sisters, in commemoration of Yamuna's entertaining her brother Yama.

Bhu. [Sanskrit.] The earth; the earth-goddess is generally worshipped by the wilder tribes of southern and central India.

Bhudki. See Buḍki.

Bhuimáli. The name of a semi-Hinduised tribe of eastern Bengal; they are scavengers, manure-spreaders, and gardeners.

Bhuinhár. [Hindi, from the Sanskrit *bhumi*, land, and *hár*, holder.] A tribe of Hindus settled in great numbers in the districts of Gorakhpur, Azimgarh, and Benares, the rájá of which last is a member of the clan. They claim to have been originally Bráhmans; and, although they admit that the distinction is impaired by their having become cultivators, which pure Bráhmans should not be, they do not wholly abandon their pretensions, and style themselves ṭhákurs, a title common to both Bráhman and Rájput tribes (*H. H. Wilson*).

Bhuiyá. The name of an aboriginal tribe of Chutiá Nágpur, now semi-Hinduised and numerous in Bengal and Behar. Their favourite god is Hanuman, and they are supposed to be the race described as monkeys in the Rámáyana. They are cultivators and labourers.

Bhujári. [Bengali, from *bhuj*, to parch.] Another name of the Kándu or Bharbhunjá caste.

Bhujki. The name of a caste in the Kángrá valley; they are the hereditary priests of the country.

Bhuksá. The name of a tribe claiming descent from the Parmár Rájputs; being expelled from Dhár, they took refuge first in Oudh, and finally in the hills bordering on Kumáun. They are cultivators, but do not usually remain more than two years on the same ground.

Bhulle. [Corrupt form.] The name of the subdivision of the Khatri caste to which Amar Dás, the third Sikh guru, belonged; also the name of the sect of Sikhs founded by the son of Amar Dás when the succession passed not to him but to Rám Dás of the Sodhi subdivision. See Tihan.

Bhumiá. [Hindi, from the Sanskrit *bhumi*, land.] A landlord, a proprietor of the soil; among the Bhils, a guide; among the Gonḍs, a priest. The sons of a Rájput ṭhákor in Gujarát are called indifferently by this name or garásiá.

Bhumij. [Hindi, from the Sanskrit

bhumi, the earth, and *ja*, born.] The name of a low caste resembling the Chuyárs and allied to the Mundas; they are numerous in Orissa.

Bhunga. See Bungá.

Bhungee. See Bhangi.

Bhunhar. See Bhuinhár.

Bhuniyá. [Hindi.] The head of a village. See Headman.

Bhur. [Hindi.] An unproductive soil, consisting for the most part of seven-tenths of sand and the rest of clay.

Bhurtanea. See Wartaniá.

Bhusá. [Hindi, Sanskrit *busa*.] The husk or chaff of corn; bran; sometimes also the straw.

Bhusár. [Maráṭhi, from *bhusá*.] A generic name for the grains, grasses, and esculent culms (*J. T. Molesworth*).

Bhusári. [Maráṭhi.] A grain-dealer, a corn-chandler; also one that husks and sifts and cleans rice, and splits pulse for sale.

Bhut. [Hindi, from Sanskrit *bhuta*, past participle of *bhu*, to be.] The spirit of a dead person; a goblin, a fiend. Bhuts, and especially those of murdered or notoriously evil-lived persons, are worshipped throughout India, and are the origins of most village divinities; for example, Bahucharáji, Tejaji. Bhut is also the name of a higher order of demons, of whom Śiwa is the lord. Bhut is also the name of an element, of which, according to the Hindus, there are five—earth, water, fire, air, and ether.

Bhuta. The classical form of Bhut.

Bhuṭá. Another form of Bhuṭṭá.

Bhute. See Bhutyá.

Bhuteśwara. [Sanskrit, from *bhuta*, a fiend, and *iśwara*, lord.] The lord of demons, a name of Śiwa in his lower aspect as a mere destroyer.

Bhutiá. An inhabitant of Thibet, or an inhabitant of Bhután of Thibetan origin. All the Bhutiás are Mongolian by race and Buddhists by religion. The Bhután Bhutiás build good houses, and have superior crops of the ordinary grains, and raise also cotton, hemp, and flax.

Bhuṭṭá. [Hindi.] The cereal, zea mays, commonly called Indian corn, though it is a native of America. A bhuṭṭá means a single head of the corn.

Bhutyá. [Maráṭhi, from *bhut*, a goblin.] The name of a class of devotees of Bhawáni. They go about begging, decorated with shells, with their clothes soiled with oil, and a torch in their hand (*J. T. Molesworth*).

Bhuwá. [Gujaráti.] A class of persons, of any caste, who are considered to be the favourites of some one or other local goddess, and who are employed to cast out evil spirits or to cause rain to fall.

Bhuwarlok. [Sanskrit, from *bhuwas*, the atmosphere, and *loka*, space.] The space between the earth and swarga, and which is the abode of various spirits, good and evil.

Bhuyniar. A tribe of mountaineers inhabiting the forests of Sarguja. They frequent the highest spots and deepest forests, neglect husbandry, and employ themselves in gathering the produce of the woods, especially the resin of the sál, which they exchange for grain and other necessaries of life.

Bhye. See Bái or Bahi.

Bibi. [Hindustáni.] A Musalmán lady. Among Shaikhs the title is commonly affixed to all women's names.

Bichári. [Nepalese.] A judge. Two preside in each principal court, and all are subject to the superintendence of the ditha.

Bichháiti. [Maráṭhi, from *bichhánà*, a mat.] A trader who does not keep a shop, but hawks his wares and spreads them on a mat for sale.

Bid. See Bir.

Bidi. See Biri.

Bidri. A kind of damascene work invented at Bidar in the nizám's dominions in the time of Hindu rule there. The material used is a composition of copper, lead, and tin, on which gold and silver are inlaid.

Biggah. See Bighá.

Bighá. [Hindi.] A measure of land varying in different places, but usually between half and three quarters of an acre; in Hindustán generally equal to 3025, in Bombay to 2844, and in Bengal to 1600 square yards. In British India the acre is now the ordinary standard of measurement.

Bighati. [Hindi.] According to bighás.

Bijogi. A vernacular form of Viyogi.

Bilimagga. The name of a Kanarese caste of weavers. They claim to be Banajigas. They are Śaiwas.

Biluch. The collective name of several tribes who give their name to Biluchistán; they are divided into Kheláti, Persian, and Panjábi Biluches; the first are spread over 80,000 square miles of country, and number about 400,000 persons; the second occupy 60,000 square miles, and number 110,000; the Panjábi Biluches include the Bozdar, Khetran, Kasrani, Gurcháni, and Laghári tribes. Biluches settled in India are generally called Baluchi.

Biluchi. The language of the Biluch tribes; it is of Aryan origin.

Bilwa. The name of a wild tribe in Mysore; they collect forest produce and also draw toddy from the palm tree.

Bilwa. [Sanskrit.] The bel tree or wood-apple, ægle marmelos. It is held sacred to Śiwa, and its leaves are used in his worship; the fruit is eaten. The triple leaf is also held to be typical of the three gods of the trimurti.

Bin. [A vernacular corruption of the Arabic *ibn*, son.] A term inserted, like walad, or the English Fitz, between the name of a person and his father's name.

Bind. [Bengali.] The name of a semi-Hinduised tribe of Bengal; they are cultivators, fishers, and labourers.

Bindrában. [Hindi, a popular corruption of *brindában*, from *brindá*, the Sanskrit *vrindá*, q.v., and *ban*, a forest.] The tulsi grove in which Krishna is fabled to have been brought up as a cowherd. The spot is also called Nidhban, and is now surrounded on all sides by the streets of the modern town of Bindrában. See Braj.

Bine Battar. The name of a class of persons in Coorg, emigrants from Malabar, who were formerly musical mendicants, but now engage in agriculture; they also prepare the parched rice for the Koḍagas on their festive occasions.

Bir. [Hindi.] A tract of grass-land reserved for hay.

Birgujar. See Bargujar.

Biri. [Hindi.] A small parcel of areca-nut, catechu, spice and chunam rolled up in betel leaf, to be chewed. Biris are presented to guests as a mark of courtesy. Biri is also the name for a cigar.

Birjuntry. See Bájantari.

Birt. [Hindi, from the Sanskrit *vritti*, maintenance.] A grant or endowment for maintenance; as jiwan-birt, an assignment to a younger son for his maintenance; márwat-birt, compensation to one killed in service; birt-jajmán, the emoluments received by a family priest from his jajmáns.

Birtiá. [Hindi.] One holding a birt.

Bisáti. [Hindi.] A pedlar, a trader who carries his goods about; a bichháiti.

Bisheśwar. [Hindi, from the Sanskrit *vish*, poison, and *iśwara*, q.v.] The poison-god, a name of Śiwa, from his having swallowed the poison when the gods and demons churned the ocean. See Amrita. The principal temple at Benares is dedicated to Bisheśwar, and so also was the older temple, which was destroyed by Aurangzib and replaced by the existing mosque.

Bishnavi. [Hindi.] The name of a caste said to derive their name from one Bishnu, a Tagá Bráhman, but the pupil of a Musalmán fakir. They consider themselves rather Hindu than Musalmán, but generally call themselves Shaikhs, adding that title to a Hindu name, or adding sometimes a Hindu title to a Musalmán name; they sometimes bury and sometimes burn their dead, and observe both Hindu and Musalmán ceremonies.

Bismillah. [Arabic.] The name of the formula, 'In the name of God the most merciful,' with which all letters and public documents, among Musalmáns, are inscribed; which is repeated on the killing of any animal for food; and which is worn as a talisman against evil spirits. Bismillah is also the name of the ceremony held when a child reaches the age of four years four months and four days, when it is made to repeat the first chapter of the koran.

Biswá. [Hindi, from *bis*, the Sanskrit *vinśati*, twenty.] A twentieth, but applied especially to the twentieth part of a bighá. The biswá is divided into twenty biswánsis.

Biswánsi. [Hindi, from *biswá*, q.v., and the Sanskrit *anśa*, a portion.] The twentieth part of a biswá.

Black buck. The antelope bezoartica. The full-grown male is black on the back and sides and white underneath, it has twisted horns in the general shape of the letter V and about twenty inches long; the female is hornless and of a pale fawn colour, white below. The buck stands about thirty-two inches high at the shoulder; the doe is rather smaller. The Hindi name is harna or hiran.

Black crop. See Dáluá.

Black gram. See Urid.

Black soil. See Kálibhui.

Blackwood. The timber of the dalbergia latifolia, Hindi śisam, Panjábi táli; much used for furniture and cabinet-work.

Blister-fly. This is the common Anglo-Indian name of the cantharis vesicatoria, or Spanish fly, which is a great pest in the rainy season. The insect is attracted by lamps, and wherever it touches the body it raises a blister if roughly handled in being brushed away.

Boa, or Boath. A kind of temple, a conical-roofed building surrounded by a wall, used by the Todas, but supposed to belong properly to some earlier race.

Board of Revenue. The name of a permanent committee in the Madras presidency that exercises authority intermediate between that of the government and the collectors of the different districts. See Commissioner.

Bobbery. This term is used as an equivalent of 'uproar,' and may be a corruption of the common exclamation of dismay, *Báp re!* O father!

Bodo. The name of a non-Aryan tribe on the Bhutan frontier. They are cultivators, especially of cotton; and the women spin, weave, and dye, and make beer of rice or millet. They have no fixed villages. They eat animal food, but not oxen. They worship the sun and moon and the terrene elements, and especially the rivers. As the natures of these gods are deemed benevolent, the religion is free from savage or cruel rites. The Bodos buy their wives, and women are esteemed among them. They bury their dead. Their character is very amiable and devoid of violence (*Hodgson*).

Bogadaw. [Burmese.] A dancing-girl.

Bogar. The name of a class of Jains who are dealers in brass and copper vessels and glass bangles.

Bogár. Another name for Kanchugár.

Bogsa. The name of a tribe of the low tarái adjoining Rohilkhand.

Bohmong. [Arakanese, from *boh*, a head, and *mong*, leader.] The title of a chief, otherwise called the Poang rájá, whose residence is at Bandrában, on the Langu river, and to whom the Kumis, Mros, and other tribes pay tribute.

Bohrá. [Hindi, from the Sanskrit *vyawahára*, business.] A trader, a banker. See Vorá.

Boï. [Telugu.] The name of a caste; they are fresh-water fishermen and palanquin-bearers, but are much used in Madras as domestic servants.

Boïdu. [Telugu.] A man of the cowherd or shepherd caste.

Boishnob. See Vaishnawa.

Boitakhana. See Baiṭhakhánah.

Bojá. [Hindi.] A load: two dokarás of cotton make one bojá.

Boládár. [Hindi, from *bola*, speech, and the Persian *dár*, holder.] A tenant under a verbal agreement.

Bombay duck. A nickname for a resident in Bombay, possibly in allusion to the extreme moisture of the climate. Also a name for the bommelow fish when dried.

Bombay hemp. See Ambáḍi.

Bommelow. [A corruption of the Maráṭhi *bombil.*] The name of a small salt-water edible fish; when dried it is known as the Bombay duck.

Bonti. [Bengali.] A broad, sickle-shaped knife-blade, fixed vertically into a heavy wooden stand. In use the stand is held firm by the feet, and the fish, vegetable, straw, or other article to be cleaned, sliced, or cut up, is with the hand duly worked against the concave cutting edge thus made fast (*J. B. Phear*).

Boolee. See Báoli.

Bor. See Baer.

Borah. See Bohrá.

Bose. [An English corruption of the Bengali *basu*, from the Sanskrit *wasu*, wealthy.] An adjunct to names borne by families of the Káyath caste.

Bo-tree. [Sanskrit and Páli *bodhi*, Sinhalese *bogaha.*] The ficus religiosa or pipal. Siddhártha is believed to have become Buddha while seated under a bo-tree at Gayá, in Behar, and the tree is believed still to exist. The bo-tree now growing at Anurádhapura, in Ceylon, is said to be a branch of that at Gayá.

Boṭṭu. [Telugu.] The sectarial mark made with pigment on the forehead; the tilak.

Botwa. The name of a very wild tribe, found in the forests of Távunád, in Coorg; they live by the chase and seldom work for hire. They frequently change their huts.

Boucheraji. See Bahucharáji.

Boudh. See Bauddha.

Bowley. See Báoli.

Bowry. See Báori.

Boy. This word may be a corruption of the Telugu *boï* (q.v.), or perhaps in some instances of the Hindi *bhái*, a brother, which is a common compellation among natives. It is now used both as a compellation and a common name for the higher domestic servants.

Brab. [The Portuguese *brav*, wild.] A name of the fan-leaved palm, borassus flabelliformis.

Brahma. [Sanskrit, from *brih*, to grow.] The supreme being, the first cause of all things. In the rig-veda it is said that in the beginning there was nothing else: there was neither sky, atmosphere, time, light, darkness, life, or death; and this spirit by its own volition formed everything out of itself. Brahma is regarded as impersonal, and the name itself is neuter. Some English writers use the form Brahman.

Brahmá. [Sanskrit.] The first person of the Hindu triad—the creator. See Trimurti. Brahmá (the final *a* long) is, like everything else, an emanation from, or form of, Brahma (the final *a* short): Brahmá is Brahma appearing as creator, or is that part of the divine essence which creates. The notion of the essence Brahma is rather confined to philosophers, while Brahmá and the other personal gods are more in the minds of the people. The notion of Brahma, Professor Monier Williams considers, grew out of that of the vedic Agni, the god of fire and generative heat. He was also regarded as the personification of all manifested matter, in connection with which aspect his wáhan or vehicle is a winged animal, the swan or goose. Brahmá is represented with four faces as the utterer of the four vedas. It seems to be under this character of the god that Saraswati is made his śakti or, popularly, wife. Pashkara, near Ajmir, and Idar are said to be the only places where Brahmá is now worshipped.

Brahmachári. A Bráhman in his first, or brahmacharya, áśrama, in which he learns the veda in the house of a preceptor. A brahmachári, instead of passing on into the other áśramas, may bind himself to remain a student for life, and such persons now constitute a numerous order. Colebrooke remarks of them that they seem to hold the austerities as more essential than the studies connected with the brahmacharya discipline, and that many of them appear to be wholly illiterate.

Brahmacharya. [Sanskrit *charya*, practice.] The first of the four áśramas into which the Brahman's life is divided, the period to be spent in religious study. This period lasted twelve years if the student wished to become a grihastha; if not, it might go on for forty-eight years.

Bráhman. [Sanskrit *bráhmana*, from *bráhman*, religious devotion.] The name of the first of the four castes into which, according to their own scriptures, Hindus were originally divided. A hymn in the rig-veda states that the Bráhman was the creator's mouth, the Kshatriya his arms, the Vaiśya his thighs, and the Śudra his feet. The allegory of the Bráhman being the mouth of the creator denotes his office as the possessor and imparter of knowledge. For the orthodox manner of a Bráhman's life in early times, see under Áśrama. Besides acting as priests to almost every caste of Hindus, the Bráhmans now fill a large part of every profession requiring education; they are also landholders and cultivators, and many take service as soldiers. The office of prime minister and adviser to the Kshatriya king belonged from the beginning to Bráhmans, and some (notably the peshwás) have acquired sovereign power. Bráhmans are subdivided almost beyond calculation; see Gauḍa and Dráviḍa. But it is not supposed that all were originally of one race: no doubt they from time to time admitted the higher ranks of the aborigines to their order; this is borne out both by existing race-differences and by the legends of the fabrication of Bráhmans.

Bráhmana. [Sanskrit.] The name given to the second division of the veda-ritualistic precept. The bráhmanas are intended, as their name implies, for the Bráhmans, and especially for their use in conducting the complicated sacrificial ceremonies. Their chief aim is to serve as guides or directories for the employment of mantras at sacrifices. But they also speculate as to the meaning and effect of using particular verses and metres. Their central doctrine is the need of expiation through the immolation of animals. The bráhmana period of Hinduism lasted probably from 800 to 500 B.C. It succeeded the mantra or physiolatrous period, and was followed in turn, when humanity rebelled against its sacerdotalism, by the pantheistic doctrine contained in the upanishads (*Monier Williams*).

Bráhmani. A woman of a Bráhman caste.

Bráhmasamáj. [Sanskrit *bráhma*, adjective from *brahma*, the supreme spirit, and *samája*, society.] The society of God, the name of a theistical sect founded in Bengal by Rammohan Roy, in the beginning of the nineteenth century. The doctrines of this sect are founded on the veda purified from the corruptions of polytheism and the use of idols.

Brahmchhatri. The name of a caste in Gujarát; they are writers by profession, and very intelligent. They claim to be of Rájput descent.

Brahmosomaj. See Bráhmasamáj.

Bráhmottara. [Bengali.] Land granted rent free to Bráhmans for their support.

Brahui. A tribe belonging to Khelát. General Jacob describes them as being faithless and untrustworthy as soldiers, as being quarrelsome, unruly, and murderous, and as given to the most detestable vices. The Brahui language is partly Dravidian.

Brain-oil. See Mumiái.

Braj. [Hindi, from the Sanskrit *vraja*, pasture-land.] The tract of country round about Mathurá, and including Gowardhan, Bindrában, and Gokal, all sacred to Hindus as the scenes of Krishna's boyhood and his gambols with the Gopis.

Brajbási. [Hindi *bási*, inhabitant.] An inhabitant of Braj; an armed attendant, escort, or door-keeper.

Brajbhákhá. [*Bhákhá*, the Sanskrit *bháshá*, speech.] The language of Braj; it is a variety of Hindi, and is much used in literature, even outside of its local limits.

Brajmandal. [Hindi.] The mandal or circle of Braj. According to Hindu topography, this consists of a circuit of eighty-four kos, with the town of Mathurá as the centre. This would make it include the Muhammadan capitals of Delhi and Agra, and indeed Brajbhákhá is the speech of the Hindu residents in and around those cities.

Bramin. See Bráhman.

Brandy. See Báráni.

Brihaspati. See Vrihaspati. The Brihaspati chakra is a cycle of sixty years, each with a separate name.

Brij. See Braj.

Brijman. This word is a corruption of the English word 'prisoner;' it is used in the Bengal army to denote a sepoy placed in the guard-room.

Brinjal. The name of a vegetable, called also the egg-plant; it is the solanum melongena.

Brinjarrie. See Banjárá.

British Burma. The name of one of the eight provinces into which British India is divided. It consists of a long narrow strip of territory, 87,220 square miles in extent, on the eastern shore of Bengal. It was annexed partly in 1825 and partly in 1852. The population is now 3,736,771, or about equal to that of Scotland. It is administered by a chief commissioner. There are no native states under this province.

British India, British Territory. These names are applied in India to that part of the country which is not under the jurisdiction of any native chief, but is directly administered by British officials. It contains about three quarters of the area and four-fifths of the population of the whole country, and is divided into eight principal provinces, namely, Bengal, Madras, Bombay, the North-West Provinces, the Panjáb, the Central Provinces, British Burma, and Assam, each under a separate local government, subordinate to the governor-general in council.

Broto. [A corruption of the Sanskrit *vrata.*] A self-imposed exercise of a devotional character, an obligation, a vow.

Bruj. See Braj.

Buddha. [Sanskrit, from *budh*, to observe, to perceive, to know.] Conscious, enlightened, wise; one who by perfect knowledge of the truth is liberated from existence; especially Siddhártha, the son of Suddhodana, of the family of Śákya, the tribe of Gautama and the caste of Kshatriya. He lived in the sixth century B.C., in the province of Behar, and founded the religion called after his name. His teaching was founded on Bráhmanism, and he has been regarded as an incarnation of Vishnu. There have been Buddhists in India who rejected Siddhártha and worshipped an earlier Buddha. Buddhists generally hold that one Buddha more, called Maitreya, is yet to appear.

Buddha-warshe. [Sinhalese.] The Buddhist era; it is reckoned from the death of the Buddha, 543 B.C.

Buddhism. The religion founded by Siddhártha the Buddha. He had lived in the world as a king's son, he had studied Hindu philosophy with Bráhman hermits, and he had practised austerity. Then, finding all these things vain, and conceiving that he understood the cause of their insufficiency, he began to teach. He did not seek to explain the primary origin of the world, or to define or treat of God, but he accepted the world as it was, and only sought to teach men how they might become free from the evil which he had found in every form of life until he became enlightened. He did not set himself in opposition to the Bráhmanical religion, but, accepting it as part of the existing order of things, he explained its words and customs in a new spiritual sense; associating them also with earlier pre-Aryan ideas. Assuming the doctrine of the transmigration of souls, and recognizing the progress of events from cause to effect, he held that the condition of each man in this present life was the consequence of his actions in a previous state, and that his actions in this life would determine his future condition. He perceived that what was necessary was not austerity or anything outward, but a purification of the heart; he required no temples, or priests, or prayers, but self-renunciation. To secure this, the means he indicated were companionship with the good, the hearing of the law, enlightened reflection, and the practice of virtue. Thenceforward the disciple's course towards nirwána, or perfect holiness, was fancifully divided into four stages, in which he gradually got rid of the delusion of self, doubt, dependence on rites, sensuality, malevolence, the love of life, pride, self-righteousness, and lastly ignorance. Every Buddhist was bound by the panchasilaya, and any who thought it would help him might take the further vows appropriate to an upasaka or to a bhikshu, but the great object of one and all was to pass through the four stages into nirwána. In course of time, Buddhism and Bráhmanism became antagonistic, and, after long rivalry, the former was eventually, in the sixth century A.D., exterminated in India. Out of India the religion became greatly transformed; the Buddha became a god and the bhikshus priests; temples and idols came into vogue, and even a trinity was invented, consisting of the Buddha, Dharma or his precepts, and Sangha the assembly.

Buddhist. A votary of Buddhism, a Bauddha. Buddhists are numerous in Ceylon and Burma, but there are hardly any in India proper.

Buddick. See Badhak.

Budgerow. [Bengali *bajará.*] A heavy spoon-shaped boat, formerly much used for river travelling in Bengal; it had two or three cabins at the stern, and above them a higher deck; it had a mast and topmast carrying two large square sails, and, when these did not serve, was either rowed or dragged by the crew by a long track-rope from the shore.

Budibudaki. [Kanarese *budi*, ashes.] A religious mendicant who covers his body with ashes.

Buḍki. [Maráṭhi.] A well sunk for irrigation at the edge of a river or watercourse; a ḍhekuḍi.

Budrukh. This is a Persian word, signifying great or venerable. It and 'khurd' are added respectively to the names of two neighbouring towns or villages bearing the same name, to distinguish them.

Buggalow. See Bagalá.

Buggy. [A corruption of the Gujaráti *bagi.*] Any kind of horse-carriage, but used in English particularly to denote a light two-wheeled one-horse carriage with a hood.

Bugti. The name of an independent tribe beyond the frontier near Dera Gházi Khán.

Bulbul. [Hindustáni, from the Persian.] The name of three kinds of birds, distinguished as the *kálá*, the *sháh*, and the *sipáhi*, which are respectively the common bulbul, pycnonotus pygæus; the paradise fly-catcher, chitrea paradisi; and the red-whiskered bulbul, otocompsa jocosa.

Buná. The name of a labouring class in Bengal, employed chiefly in the indigo plantations. In some parts the Bunás are a separate caste.

Bund. [A corruption of the Hindi *band*, from the Sanskrit *bandh*, to bind.] A dam, an embankment; usually of masonry, built across a river or the course of a stream so as to retain a supply of water above it. Sometimes used laxly to denote the sheet of water itself.

Bundela. A spurious tribe of Rájputs who have given their name to Bundelkhand, but are now settled chiefly about Agra, Benares, and Cawnpore; they differ from Rájputs in the practice of marrying among themselves as if they were a caste and not a clan. The rulers of the small states of Urchah, or Tehri, and Datiá are of this tribe. The Bundelas work in the field with their own hands.

Bunder. [A corruption of the Hindustáni *bandar*.] A harbour, a landing-place; also a port town; and in Bengal also a market.

Bundobust. [A corruption of the Hindustáni *band-o-bast*, tying and binding, both words being derived from the Persian *bastan*, to bind.] Arrangement, settlement; especially a land revenue settlement. Proverb: *Bandobast naram, tahsil garm*, 'Light assessment, brisk collection.' The word is often used by Anglo-Indians to express the planning, preparation, or arrangement of any undertaking great or small.

Bungá. [Panjábi.] A block of houses built round a sacred tank; a palace.

Bungáh. [Hindustáni.] The followers, suttlers, and baggage of an army.

Bungalow. [Corruption of the Bengali *bánglá*.] A thatched cottage of one floor. The term is now extended to any house that stands apart in its own grounds.

Bunia. See Banyá or Banyan.

Bunny. [Corrupt form.] A name given in Berar to the ordinary kharif cotton crop as distinguished from the jári or jerry crop.

Buraj. [Persian.] A tower or bastion.

Buresingh. [Panjábi.] Another name of Nársingh.

Burhá. [Hindi.] An old man, an elder; in Kumáun, the headman of a village.

Burhá Deo. A common name for the great god among the Goṇḍs and other tribes.

Burj. The same as Buraj.

Burki. See Buḍki.

Burkundaz. See Barkandáz.

Burman. A native of Burma, a Burmese; especially one of the Burmese proper, or Mrammá.

Burmese. The name of the people and of the language of Burma. The name is sometimes used to include all the different tribes of Burma, as the Karens, Chins, Shans, and at others to denote only the one race distinguished by some writers as Burman instead of Burmese, and named by themselves as Mran-ma or Mrammá, of which name Burma is a corruption. These people are of short, stout, active form, and are remarkable for good temper and cheerfulness; they are Buddhists. The language is monosyllabic, related both to Chinese and Thibetan; the character is of Indian origin. The people themselves claim to be of western origin, and of the solar race.

Burr. See Banyan.

Buruḍ. [Maráṭhi, from the Sanskrit *waruḍa.*] The name of a caste, one of the antyaja; their occupation is splitting canes and making baskets.

But. [Gujaráti.] The name of a devi, sister to Bahucharáji.

Buteela. See Batelá.

Butler. This is presumably the English word, but is used in the Bombay presidency to denote the head servant in a household; he is not specially connected with the wine-cellar, but performs all the duties of the Bengal khánsamán and the sardár-bearer.

Butty. [Hindi *batti.*] Properly, a wick, but popularly used for any sort of lamp or candle.

Buxees. See Bakhshish.

Buzote. See Bazoti.

Byadeit. [Burmese.] The privy council of independent Burma; it consists of four atwenwoons, and is supposed to advise the king privately, and to discuss all questions before they are submitted to the hloot-dau.

Bye. See Bái.

Byheree. [A corrupt form.] Another name of the Nizám Sháhi dynasty. Nizám ul mulk was so surnamed from his having had charge of the royal falconry before his rise to power. He is said to have been the son of a Bráhman, the kulkarni of Pathri, and to have been taken prisoner as a boy and brought as a slave to the Báhmani court, where he was made a Musalmán.

Bylee. See Bahli.

Byragee. See Vairági.

Byse. See Bais.

Byshak. See Baiśákh.

Bythuk. See Baiṭhak.

C.

Caaba. See Kaabah.

Cachari. See Káchári.

Cadjan. A term used by Europeans for the leaves of the fan-palm, or cocoa-nut, on which the natives write with an iron style; the letters are sometimes blackened with ink. The word is used also for huts made of palm leaves, and is said to be the Javanese word for 'mat.'

Cajan pea. See Arhar.

Calabash. [From the Portuguese *calabaça*, from the Arabic *garah*, a gourd, and *aibasah*, dry.] The dry rind of a gourd used as a bottle or float.

Calingulah. See Kalingu.

Caliph. [English corruption of the Arabic *khalifah*, a successor.] This title was first given to Abubakr, who was elected successor to Muhammad on the death of the latter. Then followed Omar, Usman, and Ali. These four form a class by themselves, as they were all relations of the prophet; they led the prayers and preached in the mosque, and resided at Medina. Then followed nine caliphs of the Ommiad family, whose capital was Damascus, and then thirty-seven Abbaside caliphs, whose capital was Bagdad. All these were kings and not priests. They were of the same tribe as the prophet, but not of his family, and the office under them was hereditary. When Bagdad was destroyed by the Mongols in 1258 A.D., the survivors of the Abbas family went to Cairo, and there maintained for 260 years a succession of titular caliphs without any temporal power. When Selim, the Sultan of Turkey, took Cairo in 1517, he carried away the last caliph prisoner to Constantinople, and made him cede to him the title and privileges of his office. Thus the name caliph at different periods is the designation of four distinct classes of real or nominal rulers. Besides these, during the reign of the Abbasides rival caliphs set themselves up in Egypt and in Spain.

Caliphate. [Corruption of the Arabic *khiláfat.*] The office of caliph, the head of islám according to the Sunnis. The Shiahs do not recognize the caliphate, but substitute the office of imám.

Canarese. See Kanarese.

Candy. [Tamil *kaṇḍi*, or Maráṭhi *khaṇḍi.*] A measure of weight; it varies at different places from 480 to 720 pounds; at Madras it is 500, at Bombay 560 pounds.

Cape gooseberry. The fruit of the physalis peruviana, called in Hindustáni *tipári*; it is used for making tarts and preserves.

Caranchie. [Corrupt form.] A kind of carriage used by natives in Calcutta.

Carcoon. See Kárkun.

Carpet snake. This term is loosely applied to any kind of snake found in a dwelling-house, other than a cobra or a dháman, but is most commonly used of the lycodon aulicus, which enters houses in pursuit of skinks and geckos. Though fierce and active, it is perfectly harmless, and is usually nocturnal in its habits. It bears a bad reputation, owing to its resemblance to the really dangerous krait. It grows to a length of two feet, of which the tail measures one-sixth. The eye of the lycodon is small and very black, with a vertical pupil, whereas the krait has a round pupil (*G. W. Vidal*).

Cash. See Káśa.

Cashew. [Through the French *acajou*, from the Brazilian *acajaiba.*] The anacardium occidentale; it bears an apple-like fruit, at the end of which grows a nut, the juice of which is used as a flux for soldering metals. The Maráṭhi name is *káju*, no doubt a corruption of some of the forms above, for the tree is not indigenous.

Cassid. See Kásid.

Caste. [From the Portuguese *casta*

race, lineage.] The various classes into which Hindus are by birth divided are called castes. As different castes cannot intermarry, it follows that every legitimate child born belongs to one caste. A Hindu can never change his caste, but he may, for offending against its rules, be excommunicated by his caste-fellows, and become an outcaste. The usual recourse in such a case, if the offence admits not of expiation, is to join some religious sect which disregards caste ; or, if the number of persons expelled is considerable, they form themselves into a new caste. As to the origin of caste, little can be said but that the distinction was sometimes a difference of race and sometimes of occupation ; why persons following different occupations should have been so rigidly separated has never been explained. The learned caste, which had the making of the scriptures, have greatly exalted themselves, taking precedence even of the royal families, or Kshatriyas ; the Vaiśyas, whom they place third, probably included all the free men other than the priestly and military castes ; and the fourth class, or Śudras, all the conquered tribes. And it seems to have been the fashion, as new communities were met with or formed themselves, to describe them as the offspring of some combination of the four declared to be original. The use of the term 'caste' is still unsettled, but it is most usually accepted as denoting a community of persons who can marry only among themselves ; in this sense the Bráhmans are not of one caste, but constitute a countless number of castes ; the subdivisions of Rájputs are not castes, for they marry usually one clan with another, and not within their own body ; and communities converted to islám cease to be castes in this sense, though often called so. See Warna.

Catamaran. [Tamil *kattumaram*, or Sinhalese *káthámárán*.] A raft made of three palm logs lashed together and propelled by a sail or paddle. They are used in Ceylon and on the Madras coast.

Catanar. A priest of the Syrian Church in southern India.

Catechu. See Kát.

Catty. See Káṭhi.

Causy. See Kázi.

Cawn. See Khán.

Central India. The name of a group of native states politically connected only by the fact that their relations with the government of India pass through one agent. The two most important states of the group are Gwalior the territory of Sindia, and Indore the territory of Holkar. The area of central India is 89,000 square miles, and the population 8,000,000. See Native State, Agent.

Central Provinces. The name of one of the eight provinces into which British India is divided. See Province. This province was formed in 1861 out of territory taken from the North-West Provinces and Madras. It is administered by a chief commissioner. The area of the province is 84,000 square miles, and the population is nearly 10,000,000, or about twice that of Sweden. The native states in political connection with the provincial government contain an area of 29,000 square miles, and a population of 1,700,000, or nearly equal to that of Norway. See Native State, Political.

Chábuksawár. [Hindi, from *chábuk*, a whip, from the Persian *chábuk*, alert, and *sawár*, q.v.] A rough rider.

Chabutarah. [Hindustáni.] A police station; the public hall of a village. Also a platform of masonry or earth serving as a meeting-place for the residents of a village.

Cháchá. [Hindustáni.] Properly a paternal uncle, but used to designate a father-in-law, many natives of India objecting to the mention of a father-in-law as they do to that of a wife.

Chadar. [Hindustáni, from the Persian.] A sheet, a cloth, a shawl.

Chaghurzai. The name of a clan of the Yusufzai tribe.

Chagul. [Persian *chaghal.*] This is the name, in the Bombay presidency, of a leather bag used for carrying a small quantity of drinking-water; it is something in the shape of a satchel with a spout added, and has a leather cord by which it is carried.

Chain. The name of a low caste of Bengal and Behar; they are cultivators and market-gardeners.

Chait. A shortened form of Chaitra.

Chaitanya. [Sanskrit, literally, perception.] The name of a Vaishnawa sect in Bengal and Orissa. It was founded early in the sixteenth century by Chaitanya, who was regarded as an incarnation of Krishna. The Chaitanyas hold that Krishna is the supreme being, and that faith in him is more efficacious than knowledge, subjugation of the passions, meditation, or anything else. All castes become by such faith equally pure, and all are equally admissible into the sect. Their chief ritual consists in constantly repeating the name Krishna (*Monier Williams*).

Chaitra. [Sanskrit.] The Hindu month most nearly corresponding with April; it is so called from *chitrá*, bright, the name of the nakshatra (in the sign Virgo) in which the moon is at full in this month. See Month.

Chaitya. [Sanskrit, from *chitá*, a funeral pile, from *chi*, to pile up.] A monument, a tombstone; a place of sacrifice or worship; a Buddhist church (distinct from the vihára), a Jain temple or apáśrá.

Chákarán. [Hindi, from *chákar*, a servant.] Lands held rent free or at a reduced rent in remuneration of service, but especially that of village servants such as the kánungo, paṭwári, the peons, and chaukidárs.

Chákariá. The Maráṭhi form of Chákarán. Páṭils and kulkarnis and the lower village servants usually hold such land.

Chaki. [Hindi, from *chakra*, q.v.] The steel disc which Sikh soldiers wear in the turban as a badge.

Chakkara. [Malayálam.] Coarse sugar made from the juice of the cocoa-nut and other palms. See Jaggery.

Chakkili. [Tamil.] The name of a low caste; they are dressers of leather and makers of harness and shoes, and correspond to the Chamárs, Máḍigas, and Mochis of other parts. In Madura the men are left-hand

and the women right-hand. See Idangai.

Chaklá. [Hindi, from the Sanskrit *chakra*, a wheel, a circle.] A large division of a country, comprehending a number of parganas.

Chakledár. [Persian *dár*, holder.] The superintendent or renter of a chaklá.

Chakmá. The name of a tribe living in the Chittagong Hill tracts. They generally resemble the Khyoungthás, but have adopted a corrupt form of Bengali speech, though their written alphabet is derived from the Arakanese; they have also added some elements of the Bráhman religion to their Buddhism. The Chakmás do not change the sites of their villages. They are divided into clans called gozas, each of which has an hereditary head called diwán. In a large goza the diwán appoints officers to assist him, called khejas.

Chakora. [Sanskrit.] A fairy bird said to subsist upon moonbeams; identified with the bartavelle or Greek partridge.

Chakra. [Sanskrit.] The wheel of a carriage, the wheel of the sun's chariot, the wheel of time; a potter's wheel; a discus, the weapon of Vishnu.

Chakrawartti. [Sanskrit, from *chakra*, a wheel, and *wartin*, turning.] One the wheels of whose chariot roll everywhere, a universal sovereign, an emperor.

Chakwand. [Hindi.] A common weed, the chenopodium viride, bearing a long legume, growing from eight inches to two feet high, used by the poor as a pot-herb.

Chalan. [Hindi, from *chal*, to go.] A document sent with treasure and recorded as a voucher of the sum received.

Chalier. [Probably identical with the Malayálam *cháliyan*, a weaver.] The name of a caste in Ceylon; some are weavers and others cinnamon-peelers.

Cháliyar. Another name of the Sále caste; apparently identical with Chalier.

Chálukya. The name of one of the agnikula tribes of Rájputs who ruled in Oudh in the early years of the Christian era, and in the fourth century entered the Deccan, where they encountered the Kalachuryas, the Raṭṭas, the Kadambas, and the Pallawas. The first three were reduced to the condition of feudatories, but the Pallawas in the first instance drove off the invader; his successor, however, defeated them, and then formed an alliance with them, marrying a Pallawa princess. The Chálukya capital was established at Kalyán, which is still known by that name, and lies about one hundred miles west of Hyderabad; and their country was called Kuntala deśa and Karnata deśa. Early in the seventh century the Chálukyas separated into two branches, one of which continued to rule at Kalyán, while the others made Vengi, taken from the Pallawas, their capital. In the middle of the eighth century the Raṭṭas regained an ascendancy, and the Chálukya power was for some time obscured; but at the end of the tenth century their authority was restored, and they reigned with increased glory to the middle of the twelfth, when they were subverted by the Kalachuryas (*L. Rice*).

Chalwádi. [Kanarese.] An hereditary officer among the Lingáits who bears their insignia on public occasions; he is remunerated by voluntary gratuities.

Cháma. The Malayálam name of Chenna.

Chamár. [Hindi, from the Sanskrit *charma*, skin, and *kára*, worker.] The name of a low caste; they are tanners, leather-dealers, and shoemakers. The Chamár is often the village crier, and his wife the village midwife. Other forms of the name are Chámár, Chámaḍiyá, Chámbhár, and Chámhár.

Chámar. [Bengali, Sanskrit, *chámara.*] A fly-flap or fan made of a yak's tail, peacock's feathers, or horse-hair, a chowry; it is one of the insignia of royalty, and is also used in temples to fan the idol.

Chamárjuláhá. [Panjábi.] A division of the Chamár caste who have given up their hereditary calling and have taken to weaving. They have given up also the habit of eating cattle that have died a natural death.

Chamármaimár. [Panjábi.] A recent division of the Chamár caste; they are masons, and live as vegetarians.

Chammar. Another form of Chámar.

Champaka. [Sanskrit.] The tree michelia champaka; it bears fragrant white and yellow flowers, which are offered to idols, especially on the 14th Jyeshṭh.

Chámpáwat. [Gujaráti.] The family name of a branch of the Ráṭhors, so called from its ancestor Chámpá.

Chámtha. The name of a small tribe in Káṭhiáwár and Gujarát; they wander about with asses, and sell handmills and dance; and some of them cultivate. Some are Hindu and others Musalmán.

Chámundi. [Kanarese.] A goddess, sometimes regarded as a form of Durgi, sometimes as the first of the five bhutas, or mother Earth. She is the principal of the kulis worshipped by the Koḍagas.

Chaná. [Hindi, from the Sanskrit *chanaka.*] The pulse cicer arietinum, or chick-pea. See Gram.

Chanan. See Sánan.

Chanappan. See Sanappan.

Chancharu. [Kanarese.] A tribe of savage people tenanting the forests in the south of India.

Chánchiá. [Gujaráti, from *chánch*, a beak.] The name of a caste in Gujarát, Cutch, and Sindh, so called from the form of their turbans. Also a pirate.

Chandai. [Tamil.] An annual fair; a melá.

Chanḍál. [Sanskrit.] The name of a caste said to be sprung from the union of a Śudra man and a Bráhman woman. Such a union being in the eyes of a Hindu the grossest pollution, the Chanḍál is utterly despised. Manu calls him the lowest of mortals, and ordains that he must live out of the town, his sole wealth being dogs and asses, his dishes broken pots, his clothes those of dead men, and his ornaments rusty iron.

The Chanḍáls of Bengal are now very numerous, and in some parts, as Rájsháhi, are becoming well-to-do. They are cultivators, boatmen, grass-cutters, gardeners, palanquin-bearers, and labourers. Their real origin is unknown, nor has it been determined to what other tribes they are related.

Chandan. [Sanskrit *chandana*, from *chand*, to shine.] The sandal tree—sirium myrtifolium ; also the wood, and especially the paste obtained by grinding the wood on a stone made for the purpose ; it is used for marking the forehead or an idol. See Tilak.

Chandel. The name of a Rájput tribe which claims to be of the lunar race, but does not hold a high rank among Rájputs ; they formerly ruled at Mahoba, in Bundelkhand, but were conquered by the Chauháns. They are now numerous in Sháhjahánpur and the North-West Provinces.

Chandeli. [Hindi.] A very fine sort of cotton cloth, originally fabricated at Chanderi.

Chándlá. [Hindi, from *chánd*, the moon.] A small wafer-like ornament of mica, talc, or other metal, worn on the forehead between the eyes. Also the round mark made on the forehead with chandan, kanku, or other unguent, on occasions of betrothal, investiture with the janeo, agharni, and the like.

Chandrawanśa. [Sanskrit, from *chandra*, the moon, and *wanśa*, lineage.] The race of the moon ; the name of a tribe supposed to have entered India about the twelfth century B.C., and to have superseded the more peaceable solar race which had entered seven or eight hundred years before. Later the Kshatriya dynasties were divided into two branches, called the solar and the lunar races. The lunar race ruled in Benares, Magadha, and near the modern Delhi ; it had two chief branches, one called Yadu, in which Krishna was born, and the other Puru, to which the Pánḍawas, the heroes of the Mahábhárata, belonged. The Yadus are now represented by the Jáḍejas of Cutch and the Bhaṭṭis of Jaisalmir ; and some say that the Tomars also were of the Yadu race.

Chándráyana. [Sanskrit.] An expiatory penance prescribed by Manu for sins which degrade to a mixed class, for stealing a person, for seizing a field or horse, and some other sins. 'If he diminish his food by one mouthful each day during the dark fortnight, eating fifteen mouthfuls on the day of the full moon, and increase it in the same proportion during the bright fortnight, fasting entirely on the day of the conjunction, and performing an ablution regularly at sunrise, noon, and sunset, this is the chándráyana or lunar penance' (*Manu*).

Chanḍul. [Gujaráti.] A preparation of opium for smoking.

Chang. Another name of the Ghirth caste.

Chánk. [Hindi.] A ceremony on the occasion of forming the winnowed corn into a heap at the threshing-floor.

Chapáti. [Hindi.] A thin flat cake ; especially one of flour and water, without leaven, baked on a griddle.

Chappar. [Kanarese.] A thatched

roof, a shed; the Hindi chhappar; also a maṇḍap.

Chappar. [Kásmiri.] The oar or paddle used to propel the kishti; the blade is heart-shaped.

Chappategár. [Kanarese.] The name of a subdivision of the Pánchála in Coorg; they are carpenters.

Chaprás. [Hindustáni.] The brass plate which a messenger wears on his paṭṭá, or shoulder-belt, as a badge of office. On the chaprás is engraved the name of the office to which the messenger belongs (or, in the case of a private chaprási, his master's name).

Chaprási. A servant wearing a paṭṭá and chaprás. He is called also paṭáwálá, sepoy, or peon.

Char. [Hindi.] New land formed in the bed of a river.

Charak. [Bengali, from the Sanskrit *chakra*, a wheel.] A wheel, a mill; also the ceremony of swinging a person suspended in the air by hooks passed under the skin above each blade-bone.

Charaki. [Bengali.] A small wheel, a charkh.

Charakpujá. [Sanskrit *pujá*, worship.] The swinging festival held on the day when the sun enters the sign Mesha, or Aries.

Charan. [Literally, a foot, a section; thence a sect.] A number of men who are pledged to the reading of a certain śákhá of the veda, and who have in this manner become one body (*Jagaddhara*).

Cháran. [Hindi, from the Sanskrit *chárana*, a pilgrim, a bard, a panegyrist of the gods.] The name of a caste analogous to, or identical with, the Bháṭ. Besides their proper function as bards and genealogists, many tend cattle, and engage in trade, especially the carrying of grain.

Charas. [Hindi.] The exudation of the flowers of the gánjá plant; it is collected by persons running through a field of gánjá with leathern aprons, to which the exudation sticks.

Chárdiá. [Gujaráti.] The name of a class of persons who carried on the trade of common informers, and extorted money by threatening innocent persons with false charges (*A. K. Forbes*).

Charkh. [Persian *charkh*, a wheel.] A machine for removing the seed from cotton. The principle of it is that two solid cylinders, placed one over the other, are made to revolve in opposite directions, the double friction dragging the soft cotton through, while the space between the cylinders is too small to let the seeds pass. It takes two persons to work the charkh, one turning each cylinder. Also, in Sindh, a water-wheel.

Charkhá. The Gujaráti form of Charkh.

Charkhi. [Hindustáni, from the Persian *charkh*, a wheel.] A pulley for raising water from a well; a spinning-wheel.

Charpoy. [Corruption of the Hindi *chárpái*, from *chár*, four, and *pái*, a foot.] A bedstead consisting of a plain frame of wood set on four short legs; broad tapes are folded along and across the frame to form the bed.

Charra. See Chora.

Chásá. [Bengali.] A cultivator, a ploughman. The word is sometimes prefixed to the name of a caste to indicate the branch of it employed in agriculture, as Chásá Kaibartta, the cultivating as distinguished from the fishing Kaibarttas. In Orissa, the common caste of cultivators is called Chásá simply.

Chasam. A kind of refuse from silk cocoons. One sort is distinguished in the trade as waste chasam or gudhar.

Chastán. A small shrine, usually a pyramid surmounted by an urn.

Chátánulu. [Telugu.] The name of a caste; they are Vaishnawas, and sell flowers.

Chátlá. [Gujaráti.] The name of a poor wandering tribe of woodcutters. They call themselves Musalmáns.

Chatra, Chattah. See Chhatra.

Chattah. The name of a Muhammadan dynasty at Rámnagar on the Chenáb, conquered by Ranjit Singh.

Chattiram. [Tamil.] An institution for the free distribution of food to the poor, especially to Bráhmans. The word would seem to be only another form of Sattram. The same form is sometimes used for Chhatra.

Chattiriyan. The Tamil form of Kshatriya.

Chattiskula. [Hindi, from *chattis*, thirty-six, and *kula*, family.] The thirty-six royal tribes of Rájputs; the list begins with the Suryawanśi, the Chandrawanśi, the Gahlot, Yadu, Tomar, Ráṭhor, Kachhwáha, Parmar, Chauhán, Chálukya, and Parihár, but includes also some, such as the Ját and Ṭák, which are not recognized as Rájputs.

Chattri. See Chhatri.

Chattur. [Bengali.] A consecrated cake of cow-dung.

Chaṭty. [Corrupt form.] An earthenware pot.

Chaubári. [Bengali.] A school or college, especially one in which Sanskrit is taught by a paṇḍit.

Chaubi. [Hindi, from *chatur*, four, and *veda*.] A Bráhman learned in the four vedas. The term is now applied to a class of Bráhmans who are not always men of literary habits; in the upper provinces they are usually boxers, wrestlers, and the like (*H. H. Wilson*).

Chaubisa. [Hindi, from *chatur*, four, and *visa*, twenty.] A collocation of twenty-four villages. See Bárah.

Chaudhari. See Chodhri.

Chaudhri. [Hindustáni, literally, the holder of four, perhaps shares or profits.] The headman of a profession or trade in towns; the headman of a village; a holder of landed property classed with the zamindár and tálukdár (*H. H. Wilson*). A Meo speaks of his wife's father as chaudhri.

Chaughalá. [Maráṭhi.] An hereditary officer of a village; he is an assistant to the páṭil.

Chauhán. The name of one of the agnikula tribes of Rájputs; they founded Ajmir about 800 A.D., and in 1153 conquered the Tomars of Delhi; the Chauhán prince married a daughter of the Tomar king, and their son was Prithi Ráj, who was conquered by the Musalmáns in 1191. Different branches of the Chauháns are known by the names of Hárá, Deora, and Khichi. There are few Chauháns now at Ajmir, but the chief of Nimrana and the ráo of Kusalgarh are of this family.

Chauk. [Hindi.] A square or open space in a city.

Chauki. [Hindi.] A police-station or any place where a watch is posted; a customs station.

Chaukidár. [Persian *dár*, who holds.] Any one in charge of a chauki; a watchman, especially a village watchman.

Chaukutiyá. A tabular stone altar on four low pillars; they are used for sacrifices, and are common in Kumáun.

Chauli. See Chawali.

Chaumása. [Hindi, from *chau*, the Sanskrit *chatur*, four, and *mása*, month.] A period of four months, but especially the rainy season, consisting of the two ritus warsha and śarad.

Chaunro. [Sindhi.] A domed building made of brushwood and thatched with grass, the ordinary dwellings of the people in the Thar and Parkar district.

Chaupál. [Hindi.] A shed in which the village community meet for public business, a chabutarah, a chorá.

Chaura. The name of a dynasty that ruled over Gujarát from 746 to 942 A.D. Their capital was Anhilpor, and they are accounted one of the Chattiskula, though it is not known to what branch of the Rájputs they belonged; but they must have given daughters to the Solankis, as the prince of that clan who succeeded the last Chowra ruler was his nephew.

Chaurási. [Hindi.] Literally, eighty-four; a collocation of eighty-four villages. See Bárah. Groups of eighty-four are common, but they are often only administrative subdivisions, and not tribal collocations. There is a tribal chaurási of Chauháns in Ambálá.

Chauri. More commonly Chowry.

Chausinga. [Hindi, from *chau*, four, and *singa*, horn.] The four-horned antelope, tetraceros quadricornis. It is brownish-bay in colour, lighter beneath the four legs, the muzzle and edge of the ear dark, and inside the legs and ears white. The longer pair of horns are about five inches, and the little ones in front about an inch long (*R. A. Sterndale*).

Chauth. [Maráṭhi, an abbreviation of *chauthai*, one-fourth.] An assessment equal to one-fourth of the original standard assessment (or to one-fourth of the actual government collections) demanded by the Maráṭhás from the Muhammadan and Hindu princes of Hindustán, as the price of forbearing to ravage their countries.

Chavalan. [Malayálam.] A low caste of Náirs; they are fishermen.

Chavudái. [Telugu.] Land held on payment of one-fourth of the nett produce to the state.

Cháwaḍi. [Telugu.] A public office;

a lodging-place for travellers; also the pillared hall built in front of a vimána.

Chawali. [Maráṭhi.] The pulse dolichos sinensis, or Chinese dolichos.

Chawali. [Maráṭhi.] A silver coin worth two annas.

Chawara. See Chaura.

Cháwaṭi. The Malayálam form of Cháwaḍi.

Chawl. [Maráṭhi *chál.*] A long narrow building divided into several compartments suitable for being let separately; a lodging-house.

Chayroot. [A corruption of the Telugu *chiruveru.*] The name of a plant, the oldenlandia or hedyotis umbellata, the root of which forms the red dye of commerce, known as Indian madder.

Cheetah. [Hindi *chíta.*] The hunting leopard, felis jubata. This animal, which is possessed of extraordinary speed for two or three hundred yards, is trained to hunt the antelope.

Cheetail. See Chital.

Chelá. [Hindi, said to be from the Sanskrit *cheṭa*, a servant.] A disciple, a pupil; especially the disciple of a guru or a mahanta. In Kángrá, also a magician.

Chelan. See Chalan.

Chenchu. [Telugu.] The name of a wild tribe; they are hunters, and breed cattle, sheep, and goats, and collect forest produce, but never cultivate. They build small huts about a yard high in clusters of ten or twelve, and each such village has a headman. They speak a dialect of Telugu.

Chendi. [Telugu.] The fermented juice of the date tree.

Chenna. [Hindi.] A kind of millet, the panicum miliaceum, or small millet. It is known also as barag, cháma, chini, chiná, sámli, sáme, sáve, sáwá, and wari. The form chenna is sometimes wrongly used for chana. Barag and wari are, perhaps, rather the panicum miliare.

Chera. The name of a Dravidian dynasty that ruled in Kongu and other parts of the south-west of the peninsula. In the second century they abandoned the Jain faith for that of Śiwa, and in the ninth they were subdued by the Cholas.

Cheru. The name of a tribe who appear to be the aborigines of Gházipur, a part of Gorakhpur, the southern portion of Benares and Mirzápur, and of Behar. They are sometimes said to be a branch of the Bhar tribe, and sometimes to be identical with the Seori, and again with the Kol tribe. They declare themselves to be descended from the great serpent, and may therefore be a remnant of the Nágbansi dynasty of Magadha (*H. M. Elliot*). The Cherus wear the janeo and claim to be Rájputs; they formerly ruled in Kumáun and at Palamon.

Chetan. [Malayálam.] The name of a caste; they are weavers.

Chetram. The Malayálam form of Kshetra.

Cheṭṭi. [Malayálam.] The name of a caste; they are weavers. The form cheṭṭi is also used for chiṭṭi, which appears more commonly in English as chitty.

Chhandas. [Sanskrit, from *chhad*, to please.] Delight; a sacred hymn; metrical science, prosody; the name of one of the vedángas or doctrines necessary for a proper use of the veda. Some parts of the veda itself treat of the subject of metre, and in the sutras the subject is dealt with systematically. Chhandas is also the name given to the earliest period of Sanskrit literature.

Chhandoga. [From the Sanskrit *chhandas*, metre, and *gai*, to chant.] Another name for the udgátri priest.

Chháoni. [Hindustáni.] Cantonments, stations for troops.

Chhappar. [Hindi.] A thatched roof, a hut.

Chhárá. [Gujaráti.] Broken bricks and mortar, used for road-making. A layer of chhárá is placed over the kankar to bind the surface. See Rorá.

Chhárá. [Hindustáni.] The name of a wandering tribe said to live by begging and stealing. They are Musalmáns, and wear the hair and beard long.

Chhatra. [Sanskrit, from *chhad*, to cover.] An umbrella; it is regarded as an ensign of royalty. Also a monumental structure in the form of an umbrella, a mausoleum; in the south of India, also a sarái. The word in the last sense is perhaps a corrupt form of Sattra.

Chhatra-pati. [Sanskrit *pati*, lord.] One entitled to have an umbrella, a king. Śiwaji's coin is known by this name, which was stamped upon it.

Chhatri. [Hindi.] A small chhatra. Some chhatris, however, as at Gowardhan, are large buildings.

Chhatri. [A Bengali abbreviation of *Kshatriya.*] The name of a class of Rájputs settled in Bengal; they are landowners and cultivators, and some in military or police service.

Chhetra. A vernacular form of Kshetra.

Chhi-chhi. A name given to the *patois* of English spoken by persons of mixed English and Indian blood.

Chhint. [Hindi, from the Sanskrit *chitra*, variegated.] A kind of cloth with a spotted pattern, the English word 'chintz.'

Chhipá. The Gujaráti form of Chhipi. Some Chhipás have been converted to islám. Some are itinerant dealers bartering cloth for grain.

Chhipi. [Hindi.] The name of a caste; their business is to stamp patterns on cloths.

Chhola. A Hindi name of the Bengal gram, cicer arietinum. See Gram.

Chhuṭ. [Hindi.] Relinquishment, remission; the term used for the remission of revenue.

Chhutár. A Bengali form of Sutradhár or Sutár.

Chibár. [Gujaráti.] A kind of boat used for carrying wood.

Chick. See Chik.

Chief Commissioner. The title of the ruler, under the immediate control of the Supreme Government, of three of the provinces of British India, namely, the Central Provinces,

British Burma, and Assam. See Province.

Chief Court. This is the title of the highest judicial authority, civil and criminal, in the Panjáb; it is not established like the High Courts by royal charter, but is modelled on the plan of those tribunals.

Chihái. [Hindi.] A place where dead bodies are burned, a masán.

Chik. [Bengali.] The name of a semi-Hinduised tribe of weavers belonging to Chutiá Nágpur.

Chik. [Hindustáni.] A hanging screen or curtain made of narrow thin slips of bambu fastened together horizontally by perpendicular strings, and painted. The chik serves to moderate the glare of the sun and exclude the view from outside, while (the slips of bambu not fitting closely together) it admits air and light.

Chikandoz. [Hindustáni, from *chikan*, embroidering, and the Persian *doz*, sewer.] An embroiderer.

Chikandozi. [Hindustáni.] Hand embroidery in cotton.

Chikárá. The Indian gazelle, the gazella bennettii.

Chikdoree. A term used to designate an assistant-planter on a coffee estate.

Chikli. A ryot who cultivates in one village while he resides in another. Compare Páikásht.

Chikṭi. [Maráṭhi.] The name of a disease affecting grain crops; its cause appears to be want of moisture, and crops suffering from it in October or November often recover under the influence of the latter rain.

Chilam. [Hindustáni.] The part of the hukka in which the tobacco or gánjá burns; thence used also for the whole pipe.

Chilamchi. [Hindi, from the Turkish.] A wash-hand basin of metal, a gindi.

Chillah. [Hindustáni, from the Persian *chhil*, forty.] A forty-days' fast; the period during which a Musalmán woman after child-birth may not pray or touch the koran. Also a cenotaph raised in honour of a saint.

Chillan. See Chalan.

Chilli. [Spanish *chili*.] The pod of the plant capsicum annum, largely used as a condiment both in the green and the ripe state.

Chin. The name of a hill tribe of Burma less civilized than the Karens, and of which the different clans are continually at feud with one another. The name is written also Khyen or Khyin.

Chingam. [Malayálam, the Sanskrit *sinha*, a lion.] The month during which the sun is in the sign Leo, coinciding most nearly with August and Śráwan (in Bengal, Bhádra). See Month.

Chini. [Hindustáni.] The juice of the sugar-cane after it has been boiled and solidified (goor) and again broken up, the molasses extracted, and again dried. It requires a still further process to convert the chini into sugar. Chini is also another name of the pulse chenna.

Chinka. An apparatus for crossing mountain streams, consisting of a basket drawn by ropes along a cable which is laid across the stream and fixed to trees on either side.

Chippiga. The Kanarese form of Chhipi.

Chir. [Malayálam.] A dam, a bank, a bund.

Chirḍá. [Gujaráti.] Originally a commission allowed by garásiás to their agents who collected the garás, and for some reason continued after government undertook the payment of garás.

Chiriá-Már. The name of a low caste in Orissa; they are bird-catchers.

Chiṭ. [An abbreviation of *chiṭi* or *chiṭṭhi*, one of which is found in every vernacular.] A note, a short letter, a written message or order.

Chita. More commonly Cheetah.

Chital. [Hindi.] The spotted deer, the axis maculatus.

Chitárá. The Gujaráti form of Chitári.

Chitári. [Hindi, from the Sanskrit *chitrakára; chitra*, a picture, *kára*, maker.] A painter.

Chiṭnis. [Hindi, from *chiṭ*, a letter, and the Persian *navís*, a writer.] The word originally designated an officer of state who wrote despatches. In British India it means the head clerk in the vernacular division of an office.

Chitpáwan. [Maráṭhi, from the Sanskrit *chitta*, heart, and *páwana*, pure.] The name of a subdivision of the Mahárásḥṭra Bráhmaṇs; they are most numerous in the northern part of the Ratnágiri district. Up to the time of the peshwás they were thought very little of, and were employed chiefly as harkárás or spies, but they are now very largely engaged in the native civil service; also in cultivation and trade; and many villages are held by them as khots.

Chitragupta. [Sanskrit.] The name of the first of the ministers of Yama; he records the good and evil deeds of men.

Chitrakár. [Sanskrit *chitrakáṛa*, a painter.] The name of a low caste; they paint and dye. See Chitári.

Chitrali. An inhabitant of Chitral, a rich and fertile territory lying beween the Hindu Kush and Swát on the north and south, Cashmere and Káfiristán on the east and west. The Chitralis are Muhammadans, mostly of the Sunni, but some of the Shiah, division.

Chitrini. [Sanskrit.] Literally, variegated; the name of one of the four classes of women. She is described as of a pleasing height, neither too stout nor too thin, with a small waist, bright eyes, black hair, and the voice of a peacock, disposed to fun and amusement, but not too voluptuous. The other classes are the padmini, the śankhini, and hastini.

Chiṭṭha. [Bengali.] An account, a memorandum; a banker's acknowledgment of accountability for money deposited. Also the name of a business-book used in the management of a zamindár's property; it is a register of all the fields, showing the measurement of each, its situation, the quality of the land, the ryot who cultivates it, and so on.

Chiṭṭhi. [Hindi.] A note, a short letter.

Chitty. [A corruption of *chiṭṭi*, the

Telugu form of *śeṭh*, q.v.] A tradesman, a shopkeeper; also the common name for a sirastedár in the Madras presidency.

Chiváti. [Malayálam.] A small vessel, a kind of pattemár.

Chobdár. [Hindustáni, from *chob*, a stick, and the Persian *dár*, holder.] An attendant who carries a silver stick or mace before a chief or an officer of rank, as an ensign of authority.

Chodhri. [Gujaráti.] The name of one of the Káliparaj races, and the most intelligent of them; they sometimes burn and sometimes bury their dead; they use no Bráhmans.

Choga. [Sindhi.] A long cloak with arms, made of camel's hair.

Chohar. See Chuyár.

Chokiyát. [Gujaráti, *choki* is another form of chauki.] A village watchman; he is usually in the employ of a caste or class, and not of government, as the jiwáidár is.

Choky. See Chauki.

Chola. The name of a Dravidian dynasty that overcame the Cheras at the end of the ninth century. Their territory lay to the south of the Chálukyas. In 1023 A.D. the Chola king, having married into the family of the eastern Chálukyas, succeeded to their kingdom. The name Coromandel is said to be the Chola manḍal, or circle.

Cholipanth. [Hindi, from *choli*, a woman's bodice, and *panth*, q.v.] A new free sect of Panjábis who permit promiscuous intercourse of the sexes.

Chollu. [Telugu.] A grain, the cynosurus corocánus. See Náchni.

Chonṭi. [Hindi.] The tuft of hair left growing on the top of a Hindu's head, the chuḍá.

Choora. See Chuhrá.

Chopaṭ. [Gujaráti.] A game played by moving pieces on a board according to the throws of dice.

Chopper. See Chhappar.

Chora. [Pashṭo.] A long straight knife used by Afgháns.

Chorá. [Gujaráti.] A house used for public purposes in a village. Nearly every village in Gujarát has a chorá; the building is usually the property of government, and the paṭel receives a small allowance for maintaining it, lighting it, etc. The chorá is the place where the paṭel inquires into offences, where arrested persons are temporarily confined, where the taláti receives the revenue, where government sales take place, and generally where all public business is enacted.

Chorákharach. [Gujaráti *kharach*, expense.] An allowance paid from the government treasury to paṭels for the maintenance of chorás.

Chori. [Gujaráti.] A marriage-hall; the place, usually distinct from the manḍap, where the fire sacrifice (homa) is made, and at the corners of which water-vessels are set up one above another.

Chota. [Hindustáni *chhoṭá*.] Little, small. The word is often used in English with an Indian noun; as chota háziri, a light early breakfast; chota sáheb, the younger gentleman;

chota barsát, the little rain, a fall that usually precedes the heavy fall of the monsoon.

Choṭali. [Gujaráti, the feminine form of *choṭalá*, a woman's hair; the masculine is used to denote that which is great in quantity, the feminine that which is less.] The tuft of hair which is allowed to grow on the top of a man's head when the rest is shaved. See Chuḍá.

Choti. See Chonṭi.

Choultry. A corruption of Cháwaḍi.

Chousinga. See Chausinga.

Chout. See Chauth.

Chowdry. See Chaudhri.

Chowky. See Chauki.

Chowpatty. See Chapáti.

Chowput. See Chopaṭ.

Chowra. See Chaura.

Chowry. [Sanskrit *chámara*, Hindustáni *chaunri*, Maráṭhi *chauri*.] The bushy tail of the yak made into a brush to drive away flies; or a fly-waver made of any other material, as of feathers or ivory shavings.

Chronogram. A sentence or passage by which, each letter having a certain numerical value, a date is expressed. The sum total of the values of all the letters used gives the date Hijra. Inscriptions in the Tughra or ornamental Arabic alphabet were a common form of decoration with Muhammadan builders, and a chronogram denoting the date of erection was usually a part of the inscription. It was part of the art to make the chronogram appropriate in meaning as well as indicative of the date. For example, the date of Akbar's mosque at Fathepur Sikri is given by the chronogram: 'This mosque is the duplicate of the holy place.'

Chuokerbutty. See Chakrawartti.

Chuckler. A corruption of Chakkili, but in vogue in the Kanarese as well as the Tamil country.

Chuḍá. [Sanskrit.] The lock of hair left on the crown of a Hindu boy's head when the rest of the head is shaved. It is called also choṭi, chonṭi, choṭali.

Chudder. See Chadar.

Chuḍel. [Gujaráti.] The bhut or spirit of a woman who has died in travail; the Hindi churel. Also the name of a Rájput tribe, a branch of the Jáḍus, said to be descended from a woman who died in child-birth.

Chuḍigár. [Gujaráti, from *chuḍi*, a bracelet, and the active affix *gár*.] A maker of bracelets and armlets.

Chuḍiwálá. [Hindustáni.] A class of Sunni Musalmáns who make bracelets of glass and lac or tin.

Chughatai. Another name for the Mogul dynasty.

Chuhá Sháh. [Hindi *chuhá*, a rat, and *sháh*, q.v.] The sháh's rats, a name given to a class of idiots dedicated to a pir named Sháh Daulá, who is said to have been originally a Gujar, and a native of Gujrát in the Panjáb. The Chuhá Sháhs are of stunted growth, with flattened heads and pinched features, and it is suspected that they are not congenital idiots, but that they have been subject to maltreatment as infants; the superstition is that the pir confers children on condition that the first child born is given up to him.

Chuhrá. [Hindi.] The name of a very low caste or depressed tribe; they are scavengers, and correspond to the Bhangi and Mehtar of other parts. They worship as gurus or gods Bálá Sháh and Lál Beg.

Chukáni. [Bengali.] An under-tenant.

Chula. [Hindi.] A fireplace, a semi-circular erection of earth to contain the fire in its cavity, and support the cooking-vessel on its rim.

Chuliá. [Uriya.] A salt-boiler. Chuliá is also the name given to Muhammadans in Malabár.

Chunam. [A corruption of the Tamil *channam* or the Hindi *chuná*, from the Sanskrit *churna*, lime.] Quick-lime, whether obtained from lime-stone or from shells. A very fine kind made from oyster-shells is eaten with pán. Chunam is also the common name of a plaster of which quicklime and sand are the chief ingredients, and which is largely used in building; the finest kinds are very white, and take a high polish.

Chunárá. The Gujaráti form of Chunári. There is a separate community of Sunni Musalmán converts from the Chunárá caste.

Chunári. [Hindi form of the Sanskrit *churna-kára*, a lime-maker.] The name of a low caste; they are lime-burners, plasterers, and bricklayers.

Chundadigirá. [Hindustáni.] A class of Sunni Musalmáns who claim to be of Arab descent. Their occupation is making patterns in silk cloth by gathering the silk in puckers and rosettes and knotting it.

Chundail. See Chandel.

Chunna. See Chaná.

Chur. See Char.

Chur, or **Churá.** [Hindi, from the Sanskrit *chuḍá*, q.v.] A top-knot; also the bracelet put on the bride's arm as part of the marriage ceremony.

Churel. [Hindi.] A hobgoblin in the form of a hideous woman, and supposed to embody the spirit of a woman who has died in child-birth.

Churruchpuja. See Charakpujá.

Chuta. The name of one of the numerous divisions of the Numria tribe. They inhabit the banks of the river Hubb, in Sindh. The Chutas do not usually cultivate the land or live in permanent villages, but wander about with their herds of goats, and live in huts made of matting or coarse cloths drawn over a rough frame-work of sticks. They are badly reputed for pilfering and quarrelsomeness.

Chuteescula. See Chattiskula.

Chuttriah. See Kshatriya.

Chuyár. [Bengali.] The name of a tribe of mountaineers inhabiting the mountains bordering Bengal on the west, in Rámgarh and the neighbouring districts (*H. H. Wilson*).

C. I. These letters stand for Crown of India. See Order.

C. I. E. These letters stand for Companion of the Indian Empire. See Order.

Circar. See Sarkar.

Clashee. See Khalási.

Classer. [English.] One who is employed to test the quality of land by an examination of the soil. Sixteen, the number of annas in a rupee, is usually taken as the symbol of quality of the best land in the area to be classed, and inferior fields are placed in classes of fifteen annas, fourteen, and so on.

Cobra. See Nág.

Cocum. See Kokamb.

Coel. See Koil.

Coffle. See Káfilah.

Coir. [From the Tamil *káyaru*, rope.] Rope made of cocoa-nut fibre. The term is in Bombay applied also to the fibre itself. The substance is used to make a coarse and durable kind of matting, and also for bedding.

Colamb. See Kulang.

Cole. See Kol.

Collector. The officer charged with the administration of a zillah or district. The name comes from early times, when the chief duties of the servants of the East India Company were connected with the collection of revenue. The person holding the office of collector is invariably invested also with that of district magistrate, whence he is sometimes called collector-magistrate. The corresponding officer in a non-regulation district is the deputy-commissioner.

Collerie. A corruption of Kallaru, also of Khálári.

Colly. See Káli.

Commissioner. This term, when not qualified by the addition of the name of some special department, as customs, police, survey, and the like, designates an officer who exercises supervision and appellate authority over the executive heads of districts, whether termed collectors or deputy-commissioners, and whose office is the usual channel of communication between the executive district officers and the government. For the purpose of this supervision most of the provinces are parcelled into divisions, each under a commissioner; Bengal has eight such divisions, Bombay four, the North-West Provinces seven, the Panjáb twelve, the Central Provinces and Burma four each. In Madras a permanent committee, called the Board of Revenue, takes the place of the commissioners.

Compound. [A corruption of the Portuguese *campaña.*] The ground enclosed round about a house and pertaining to it. The compound may include a paddock, or even agricultural land, as well as yard, gardens, etc.

Comptum. See Kamata.

Congee. See Kánji.

Conicopoly. See Kanakku-pillai.

Connaut. See Kanát.

Cooja. See Kujá.

Coolty. See Kulthi.

Cooly. [Tamil *kuli.*] A day-labourer. This word exists in all the Dravidian languages, and also in Bengali and Hindustáni, but not in Hindi, Maráṭhi, or Gujaráti.

Coour. See Kunwar.

Corah. [A corruption of the Hindi *korá*, new, fresh, unbleached.] Plain, undyed silk cloth (*H. M. Elliot*). Unbleached or undressed cotton cloth (*H. H. Wilson*).

Coran. See Koran.

Coss. See Kos.

Cossid. See Kásid.

Cossyah. See Khásia.

Cost. See Káyasth.

Cottah. [A corruption of the Hindi *kaṭṭhá*.] A measure of land of eighty square yards, or the twentieth part of a Bengal bighá.

Council of India. Before the passing of the act of 1858 for the better government of India (21 & 22 Vict., c. 106), this was the name of the council of the governor-general in India. Since the passing of that act, it is the name of the council of fifteen members appointed in England to conduct, under the direction of the secretary of state, the business transacted in the United Kingdom in relation to the government of India and the correspondence with India.

Council of the Governor-General of India. By statute 24 & 25 Vict, c. 67, it was enacted that the council of the governor-general should be composed of five ordinary members, three of whom should be appointed by the secretary of state from among Indian public servants, and the remaining two, one of whom should be a barrister or advocate, by her Majesty. The commander-in-chief in India might be made an extraordinary member. And by statute 37 & 38 Vict., c. 91, it was enacted that a sixth ordinary member, to be called the Member of Council for Public Works purposes, might be appointed by her Majesty. So that the council now usually consists of seven members besides the governor-general himself.

Cow-gram. See Áwáre.

Cowle. See Kaul.

Cowry. [Hindi *kauri*.] A small shell, the cypræa moneta, still used as money in northern India; about 6500 go to the rupee.

Cowry. A corruption of Kavaḍi.

Cowtell. [Corrupt form.] A kind of ferry-boat used in Sindh.

Crambo. See Karambu.

Cranny. See Karáni.

Crore. [Hindi *kror*, from the Sanskrit *koṭi*.] A hundred lákhs, or ten millions.

C. S. These letters affixed to a name denote that the person named is a member of the covenanted civil service.

Cshatriya. See Kshatriya.

C. S. I. These letters stand for Companion of the Star of India. See Order.

Cubalat. See Kabuliyat.

Cullum. See Kulam or Kulang.

Cumba. See Kambu.

Cumbly. See Kamli.

Cummerbund. See Kamarband.

Curnum. See Karnam.

Curry. [A corruption of the Malayálam *kari*, or the Kanarese and Gujaráti *kaḍi*, from the Sanskrit *kaṭu*, pungent.] A dish made originally of sour milk, with salt, pepper, turmeric, and other spices, and eaten with rice or pulse; as now prepared for Anglo-Indians, meat or vegetables are used instead of the sour milk.

Cuscus. See Khaskhas.

Custard-apple. The fruit of the anona squamosa, or sweet-sop; it is about the size of an orange, full of black seeds, each of which is covered with a yellow edible pulp.

Cutch. See Kát.

Cutcha. See Kachchá.

Cutcherry. See Kachahri.

Cuttean. See Khatiyán.

Cutwal. See Koṭwál.

D.

Ḍáb. A vernacular form of Darbha.

Ḍábá. [Bengali.] A large vessel to receive the juice of the sugar-cane from the mill.

Ḍabaḍá. [Gujaráti.] A vessel made by stretching fresh skins over a mould of clay till they become hard and retain the shape; they are used for holding ghi or oil.

Dábaḍá. [Gujaráti.] A large covered vessel either of metal or wood, and of any shape.

Dabba. [Hindi.] A kind of leathern vessel made at Rámnagar on the Chenáb.

Dabbi. [Telugu.] A small box, a cash-box; the treasury of a temple.

Ḍabḍá. [Maráṭhi.] A leathern bottle.

Dacoit. [Bengali *ḍákáit*, from *ḍáká*, an attack by a gang of robbers.] A member of a gang of robbers. Dacoits were formerly robbers by profession, and brought up their children to the same occupation; they were banditti with strongholds to retire to, and committed raids on a large scale, a gang often numbering several hundreds.

Dacoity. [Corruption of the Hindi *ḍákáiti*.] A robbery committed by dacoits, a gang robbery. Technically, under the present criminal law of India, any robbery in which as many as five persons take part is a dacoity.

Dádá. [Hindustáni.] A paternal grandfather, but applied to any elderly person.

Dádupanthi. [Hindi, Sanskrit *pantha*, a road.] Followers of Dádu, a Vaishnawa sect, founded by Dádu, a cotton-cleaner of Ahmedabad at the beginning of the seventeenth century; they are monotheistic, and resemble the Kabirpanthis both in doctrine and practice.

Dafadár. [Persian.] The head of a number of persons, whether soldiers, police, peons, or labourers. In the native cavalry the dafadár corresponds to the English sergeant, and the kote dafadár to the troop sergeant-major. See Risáldár.

Ḍafgar. The name of a caste; they are workers in leather.

Daftar. [Persian.] A record, a register, the whole body of papers pertaining to an office; the record of a case. Chháltá daftar means the papers required for current business, as distinguished from records not immediately or constantly required.

Daftardár. [Persian *dár*, who holds.] A record-keeper; but, in the Bombay presidency, a member of the collector's establishment, and the highest in rank of those actually serving in the collector's office; his function is to advise on revenue questions.

Daftari. [Hindi.] An office servant who prepares writing materials, arranges books, etc.

Daftarkhánah. [Persian *khánah*, a place.] A house or room in which records are kept; an office.

Dág. [Bengali.] A lot or portion of an estate that has been measured.

Dágḍi. A slender climbing plant, the cocculus villosus, found in nearly every part of western India; the leaves are eaten as a vegetable by poor persons; cattle feed on it, and it is given in particular to milch cows to increase the yield of milk.

Dágoba. [Sinhalese, from *dá*, relics, and *geba*, the Sanskrit *garbha*, a womb, a receptacle.] A solid dome-shaped structure built over relics of the Buddha or a saint.

Dah. See Dáo.

Ḍahia. The name of a tribe of Jats in the Delhi district.

Dahlan. The name of a tribe of Tagás in the upper Doáb.

Dahya. [Hindi.] Cultivation by clearing a spot in the jungles, which after a season or two is abandoned for another. It is called in the south kumari.

Dái. [Persian, or from the Sanskrit *dhátri.*] A nurse, a wet-nurse, a midwife.

Ḍáin. [Bengali, from the Sanskrit *ḍákini*, q.v.] A witch, a female malignant being.

Daingnet. A tribe of Assam connected with Nepál; they dress in white, and gather the hair together at the back of the head.

Dáirah. [Arabic.] A circle, a round enclosure; a monastery. Also another name of the Mahdavi sect.

Dáirahdár. [Persian *dár*, holder.] The head of a Muhammadan monastery.

Daitya. [Sanskrit, from *diti*, which is a name formed as an opposite to *aditi*, the mother of the ádityas; so *diti* is made the mother of the daityas.] A demon, an order of beings who are the implacable enemies of the ádityas, or gods.

Daiwaka. [Hindi.] The name of a caste; they are astrologers and almanac-makers.

Daiwatapka. The betrothal ceremony among Pársis.

Dajjal. [Arabic.] The Shiah antichrist; a power that is to appear and work for evil for forty years till the reappearance of the Mahdi, by whom he will be slain.

Ḍák. [Hindi.] Post, relays of palanquins or other carriage along a road; post-office. A ḍák bungalow is a traveller's rest-house at the end of a ḍák stage; a ḍák chauki a stage where a relay is posted; a ḍák ghar, a post-office; a ḍák gári is a stage-carriage; a ḍákwálá, a postman.

Daka. [Sindhi.] A water-wheel for irrigation; the cultivation by means of it.

Ḍakaut. [Hindi.] A tribe of mendicants of Bráhman descent practising astrology, fortune-telling, and the like. Compare Dákochá.

Dakhni. The name of the Hindustáni language as spoken in the Dakkhan, or Deccan; though also written in the Persian character, this variety of Urdu retains a much larger proportion of Indian, as opposed to Persian, words, and is altogether more archaic in its grammatical forms than the language of the north; a certain proportion of its peculiarities must be ascribed to its separate development as the tongue of Muhammadan colonies severed for some centuries from their original country (*C. J. Lyall*).

Ḍákini. [Sanskrit.] A female imp attending upon Káli, and feeding on human flesh. In the modern languages the term means a witch or a female goblin.

Dákochá, or Dákotá. [Maráṭhi.] The name of a caste professing to be descended from a Bráhman father and a Gauli mother; they are fortune-tellers and almanac-makers, and followers of a Śudra astrologer called Sahdev. Some deal in cows and buffaloes. Compare Ḍakaut.

Dakshiná. [Sanskrit, from *daksha*, able.] A good and prolific cow suitable to be given to a Bráhman; thence, any present to a Bráhman; alms.

Dakshinácharí. [Hindi, from the Sanskrit *dakshina*, right, from *daksha*, able, and *áchára*, conduct.] A member of a right-hand caste. See Right-hand.

Dakshináyana. [Sanskrit, from *dakshina*, south, from *daksha*, able, right, the south being to the right hand of the worshipper facing the east; and *ayana*, going.] The passage of the sun to the south from his entrance of Cancer to his leaving Sagittarius; the unlucky half of the year preceding the makarsankránti.

Dál. [Hindi, from the Sanskrit *dal*, to split.] Split pulse. When the kind of pulse is not specified, arhar dál is usually meant.

Dalál. See Dallál. Also the name of a tribe of Jats.

Dalaway. [Tamil.] The title of an officer holding the combined offices of prime minister and commander-in-chief.

Dalayat. A Tamil form of Ḍhaláit.

Dalbeherá. [Uriya.] The chief or head of the Gwálá and other castes. Also an officer in command of páiks. Also, formerly, a feudal chief holding lands for military service.

Dálbhyeśwar. [Hindi.] The name of a god supposed to exercise great power over the clouds in procuring rain. In the temple to this god at

Benares the image is in a cistern and is kept drenched with water.

Dáldi. [Maráṭhi.] The name of a class of Sunni Musalmáns dwelling on the Konkan coast; they are sailors, fishermen, and cultivators, and make and sell nets and ropes.

Dalhi. Another name for Dahya.

Ḍáli. [Hindi.] A tray, or a couple of trays, fastened by slings to each end of a pole, carried over the shoulders. Also complimentary presents so carried.

Dallál. [Hindustáni.] An agent between buyer and seller, a broker.

Dalláli. Brokerage, commission.

Dáluá. [Uriya.] Light crops of rice grown in the dry hot weather in moist situations, commonly called the black crop (*H. H. Wilson*).

Dámdupaṭ. [Maráṭhi, *dám*, cash, and *dupaṭ*, double.] The name of the rule of law that the interest on a debt may not exceed the amount of the principal. The rule will be found in Manu, viii. 151.

Dammer. [A corruption of the Hindi *ḍámar*.] Rezin, pitch. Colebrooke describes how the Bhuyniars extract dammer from the sál tree: in the beginning of the rainy season they take off a ring of bark six or eight inches in breadth and about two feet above the ground; the rezin exudes with the descending sap and accumulates in this ring; it is gathered in the winter, and the tree perishes in the same season.

Dánawa. [Sanskrit.] A kind of demon or Titan.

Dancing-girl. The common name of various classes of women whose profession it is to dance, either in temples or for the amusement of spectators in private houses. Different classes of them are called Basvi, Bhávin, Kanchani, Máhári, Náikan, and Rámjani.

Danḍi. [Hindi, from the Sanskrit *danḍa*, a stick.] Any one who bears a staff; applied especially to a numerous order of religious mendicants, founded by Śankaráchárya, many of whom have been eminent as writers on various subjects, especially on the vedánta philosophy. They are divided into ten classes, each of which is distinguished by a peculiar name, as Tirtha (a shrine), Áśrama (an order), Gir (a hill), which is added to the proper name of the individual, as Purushottamgir. They are hence known collectively as the Daśnámi, or ten-named gosains (*H. H. Wilson*).

Dánḍi. An oarsman, a boatman. Also the name of an inferior kind of dooly, consisting of a bag hung from a pole; the person carried sits in the bag.

Danḍpán. [Hindi, from the Sanskrit *danḍa*, a stick.] The name of the deified truncheon of Bhairawanáth.

Ḍáng. [Maráṭhi.] A tract of hilly and jungly country.

Dáng. The name of a division of the Sama tribe, settled in Cutch. They are of the same stock as the Jáḍejás, but are rougher, poorer, and retain more traces of the Muhammadan religion.

Ḍangá. A decked sailing-vessel used in coasting between Gujarát and Káṭhiáwár.

Dángohi. The name of a class of Bhils living below the Sahyádris. They call themselves rájás, are idle and drunken, and too proud to work.

Dangi. [Sindhi.] A kind of trading-vessel.

Dántghusai. [Maráṭhi.] An extra tax levied by the Maráṭhás for delay in paying the ordinary taxes. The word literally means 'teeth-grinding,' the tax being imposed on the ground that, while they were kept waiting, they were needlessly wearing their teeth away.

Danuv. See Dánawa.

Dáo. The knife universally used by the hill-men in eastern India. The ordinary dáo is a blade about eighteen inches long, narrow at the haft, square and broad at the tip, pointless, sharpened on one side only, and set in a handle of wood; it is generally stuck naked into the waistband. The fighting dáo is a long, heavy, pointless sword, and is generally worn at the waist in a scabbard.

Darbár. [Hindi.] A court, the court of a king or chief. Also a levee or audience. The word is very often used also as equivalent to the local government of a native state: the chief and his officers, as distinguished from the British agent and his officers. See Agent.

Darbha. [Sanskrit.] Another name for the kuśa grass.

Dare. See Dheḍ.

Dargáh. [Persian.] A Muhammadan shrine; the tomb of a saint. But in the original the word means a royal court.

Dariapanthi. The name of a new sect, followers of Dariá Sáheb of Shahabad, near Dumraon; they are monotheists, and are regarded as a branch of the Kabirpanthis. They do not allow caste distinctions.

Darkhást. [Hindustáni.] An application, a proposal; especially an application to a court as distinguished from the filing of a suit, such as an application for the execution of a decree. Also, in Madras, an application to take up land for cultivation.

Darma. [Bengali.] A kind of long grass, the arundo bengalensis; it is used for making mats, and the mats are used for making fences and the walls of huts.

Dárogá. [Persian.] A manager, a superintendent, an overseer; particularly the head of a custom or excise station, or of a distillery. Previously to 1861 the officer in charge of a police tháná in Bengal was called dárogá.

Darśan. [Sanskrit, from *driś*, to see.] Seeing, especially seeing a god, visiting a temple. The word is commonly used in this sense to the present day. It is also applied to the systems of Hindu philosophy which are commonly called the six darśans. These are the two mimánsás which are allied, the nyáya and vaiśeshika which are allied, and the sánkhya and yoga which are allied. Each of these systems purports to teach how the soul which is associated with any human body may finally emancipate itself from liability to be again associated with any body.

Dár-ul-harb. [Arabic.] A country

under a government that is not Muhammadan.

Dár-ul-islám. [Arabic.] A country under a Muhammadan government.

Darvesh. [Persian, literally, poor.] A Muhammadan religious mendicant, a fakir.

Darwán. [Hindi.] A janitor, a door-keeper.

Darwáza bund. [Hindustáni *darwáza*, door, and *band*, closed.] Literally, doors closed, an expression equivalent to 'not at home.'

Darzi. [Persian.] A tailor. In Orissa and Midnápur there is a caste known by this name, who are tailors. Elsewhere darzis are usually of the Śimpi caste.

Dása. [Sanskrit.] A slave. Often used in composition to form a name, as Bhagwan-dás, the slave of god. Compare the use of the Musalmán ghulám. Also the name of a class of devotees; it is recruited from all castes by men or women vowing themselves to the deity in some contingency, or women so vowing their firstborn; their duty is to sing hymns in the temples, and at weddings and funerals.

Daśa. [Hindi.] A prefix to the name of a caste denoting a branch of impure descent; the full blood is represented by the number twenty, visa, and the half blood by ten, daśa. Bráhmans, Rájputs, and Wániás all have daśa branches.

Dasara. [Hindi, from the Sanskrit *daśahará*, from *daśa*, ten, and *hara*, taking away, from *hri*, to carry.] An epithet of Ganga, or the Ganges, as the taker-away of ten sins. A festival was formerly held in her honour on the 10th Jyeshṭh śudh. But the name is now given to the festival on the 10th Áśvin śudh in honour of Durgá, and supposed to relate to the autumnal equinox. The day is kept in commemoration of three distinct events. (1) Durgá's conquest of the demon Mahishásur, whence her image, after being worshipped for nine days, is committed to the water; (2) Ráma's worship of Durgá before setting out to invade Ceylon, whence Kshatriyas and Maráṭhás worship their arms on this day, and formerly made it the occasion of resuming military or plundering operations after the rains; and (3) the commencement of the mahábhárata, or great war, when Arjun the Pánḍawa washed and decorated his favourite horses, whence grooms now put garlands on their horses and expect presents from their masters on this day.

Dásara. A Dravidian form of Dása.

Dásarapada. [Kanarese, from *dásara*, and *pada*, a foot.] A song of the dásaras attached to a temple.

Dasasil. [Sinhalese, from the Sanskrit *daśan*, ten, and Sinhalese *sil*, precept.] The ten precepts to be observed by Buddhist bhikshus: they forbid (1) the taking of life; (2) theft; (3) sexual intercourse; (4) lying; (5) the use of intoxicating drinks; (6) the eating of solid food after midday; (7) being present at places of amusement; (8) adorning or perfuming the body; (9) the use of seats or couches above a prescribed height; (10) the receiving of gold or silver.

Daśáśwamedh. [Hindi, from *das*,

ten, and *aśwamedha*, q.v.] A sacrifice of ten horses. Brahmá is said to have made such a sacrifice on the bank of the Ganges at Benares.

Dási. [The feminine of *dása.*] A female slave; a woman dedicated to a temple.

Dasnámi. See under Danḍi.

Dastur. [Arabic.] Custom, usage; also a customary fee, a commission. For their constant appeal to dastur the natives of India have the authority of Manu, who says, 'Immemorial custom is transcendent law, approved in the sacred scripture, and in the codes of divine legislators: let every man, therefore, . . . diligently and constantly observe immemorial custom. A man of the priestly, military, or commercial class who deviates from immemorial usage tastes not the fruit of the veda; but by an exact observance of it he gathers that fruit in perfection' (i. 108).

Dastur. [Persian.] A high priest or bishop among the Pársis; the office passes from father to son.

Dasturi. A customary fee, a commission, a perquisite.

Daswa Pádsháhká Granth. [Panjábi.] The book of the tenth king, the name of the second of the two books composing the Sikh scriptures. It is the work of Govind Singh, the tenth guru, and of scribes who assisted him; it is metrical, and written in Hindi, except the collection of tales at the end, which are in Persian, but, like the rest, in the gurumukhi characters. See Ádi Granth, Vichitr Náṭak.

Dasyu. [Sanskrit.] The name of a class of evil beings or demons, the enemies of gods and men; also one of the opprobrious names by which the Aryans called the unfortunate races whom they drove to the hills; thence used as a synonym for the pre-Dravidian races.

Datta. The name of a subdivision of the Káyasht caste.

Dattaka. [Sanskrit, from *datta*, given.] An adopted son.

Datura. [Hindustáni *dhaturá*, from the Arabic *táturah.*] The plant datura stramonium; it is very common in India, and is often used as an instrument of poisoning. The plant grows to the height of six or seven feet, and has an oval, lanceolate leaf, and a trumpet-shaped flower of a purplish white colour.

Daudi. [Gujaráti.] The name of the main body of the city or trading Vorás. They are the richest, best-organized, and most widely spread class of Gujarát Musalmáns, and are settled at many places out of the Bombay presidency, and even out of India. They are merchants, local traders, and especially shopkeepers. They are noted for their taste for large and airy houses, and for their fondness for display in house ornaments and furniture. They dress mostly in white. They are religious, and pay great respect to their chief mulla, who is secular as well as spiritual head.

Daudputra. [Hindi *daud*, the name David, and *putra*, son.] Sons of Daud; the name of a tribe, probably of Biluch origin, who migrated from Sindh to the Satluj in the middle of the eighteenth century, to avoid being carried off to Ghazni by Nádir Sháh. They founded the state of Baháwalpur, the present nawáb of which is a lineal descendant of the leader of the refugees.

Davy. See Devi.

Dawari. A native of Dawar, the upper valley of the Tochi, which rises in the Jadrán hills and, flowing eastward, joins the Kuram a little before that river joins the Indus.

Dawk. See Ḍák.

Dáyabhága. [Sanskrit, from *dáya*, share, portion, inheritance, and *bhága*, division.] The partition of inheritance.

Deb. See Dewa.

Debater. See Dewottara.

Deccan. [Hindi *dakhan*, from the Sanskrit *dakshina*, the right hand, or the south.] The south of India, the peninsula south of the Vindhya range. The Deccan, it has been conjectured, partly from appearances and partly from tradition, was formerly an island, the Vindhya range being its northern shore, and the sea flowing over Hindustán to the foot of the Himálayas.

Decoity. See Dacoity.

Deftori. [Corrupt form, perhaps for *daftari*, that which is recorded.] A term used to distinguish the regular Afghán troops from the unorganized fighting men.

Deitya. See Daitya.

Deloyet. See Ḍhaláit.

Demáno. The oracular priest of the Rájmahál hills; on his death his body is not buried nor burnt, but exposed in the jungles.

Deo. See Dewa.

Deora. The name of a branch of the Chauháns, descended from Deoráj, a descendant of Prithi Ráj, the King of Delhi. The Deoras drove the Parmars out of the country about Abu in the thirteenth century; they are a ruling family at Sirohi.

Deorhi. [Bengali.] A threshold, a porch; the anteroom at the entrance door or gateway of a house, where the daftarkhánah usually is. Also an enclosure containing several buildings.

Deostan. See Dewasthán.

Deotar. See Dewottara.

Depálá. The name of a branch of the Lohánás; they are house-servants, labourers, and traders.

Deputy-Collector. In Bengal and the North-West Provinces this is the name of the officer next in grade below the collector, and occupying the rank from which collectors are appointed; in Madras and Bombay it is the name of an officer of a distinct branch of the public service, and occupying the highest rank in that branch. See District Deputy-Collector, Huzur Deputy-Collector.

Deputy-Commissioner. The officer charged with the administration of a district in a non-regulation province; he corresponds to the collector in a regulation province.

Deputy-Magistrate. A term loosely used for a magistrate who is also deputy-collector.

Ḍerá. [Hindi.] A tent, a temporary dwelling; an encampment; a hermitage.

Derájat. [Arabic plural of *derá.*] The name given to the strip of territory which lies on the western bank of the Indus, and contains the two towns called Derá, distinguished as Ismail Khán and Gházi Khán.

Dervish. See Darvesh.

Deśái. [Maráṭhi, from the Sanskrit *deśa*, country, and *adhi*, over.] One who is placed over a country or province, the principal revenue officer of a district under the native government; the office was hereditary, and frequently recompensed by grants of land, so that the deśái often became a kind of petty chief in the south of India.

Deśáigiri. The office of a deśái and its emoluments.

Deśasth. [Maráṭhi, from the Sanskrit *deśa*, country, which in Maráṭhi means the Deccan country in particular, and *stha*, who is.] The name of a subdivision of the Mahárásh̤ṭra Bráhmans; those belonging originally to the Deccan.

Deshi. [Hindi *deśi*, from the Sanskrit *deśa*, country.] Native, belonging to the country, local. Often used in contradistinction to Viláyati.

Deśmukh. [Maráṭhi, from the Sanskrit *deśa*, country, and *mukha*, chief.] An hereditary native officer under the former governments, exercising chief police and revenue authority over a district containing a certain number of villages, and responsible for the revenue; holding for compensation lands rent free, and being entitled to various fees and allowances, corresponding generally to the zamindárs of Bengal (*H. H. Wilson*). Under the Muhammadan government the deśmukh was the superintendent over a certain number of village paṭels (as the deśpáṇḍe was over the kulkarnis of the same villages). The Maráṭhá government used hereditary district officers less and appointed stipendiary officers. Under the English government the duties of deśmukhs and deśpáṇḍes became less and less, and in 1863 they were given the option (which nearly all of them accepted) of being freed from all liability for service on condition of their paying a certain fixed assessment on their holdings.

Deśpáṇḍe. [Maráṭhi.] An hereditary revenue accountant to whom the kulkarnis of his district were subordinate. See under Deśmukh.

Dev. See Dewa.

Devi. [Sanskrit, the feminine form of *dewa*. There is but one letter in Sanskrit corresponding to the English *v* and *w*; it takes the sound of the former before *i*, and of the latter before *a*.] A goddess; especially Durgá.

Devli. [Maráṭhi, from the Sanskrit *dewa*, a god.] A small building made for an idol only, not admitting worshippers; a small shrine within a temple. Also the name of the descendants of Bhávins; they are players.

Devrukhá. [Maráṭhi.] The name of a tribe of Konkani Bráhmans. Their head-quarters are in the Ratnágiri táluká, and especially on and near the Sangameshwar river, where many villages are owned by them. There they are mostly occupied in agriculture, but a good many enter the government service, and some engage in trade (*A. K. Nairne*).

Devrukhi. [Maráṭhi.] The innermost room in a temple, that in which the idol is fixed.

Dewa. [Sanskrit.] A deity, a god; also his representation, an idol. Also a divine man, a god among men, a king. Also an inhabitant of heaven, whence 'to become a dewa' is a euphemism for 'to die.' Dewa is added to the name of a god to form a human name, as Wásudewa, one who has Wásu, or Vishnu, for his god.

Dewadáya. [Tamil, from the Sanskrit *dewa*, a god, and *dáya*, a gift.] Lands or allowances for the support of a temple; dewasthán.

Dewanágari. [From the Sanskrit *dewa*, god, and *nagar*, a city.] The name of the Sanskrit character.

Dewánga. [Kanarese, from the Sanskrit *dewa*, a god, and *anga*, the body.] One who wears the emblem of Śiwa on his person; a lingáit. This name has been assumed by a caste of Kanarese weavers. There is also a caste of Telugu weavers called by this name, though they do not wear the linga, and one sect of whom are not Śaiwas, but Vaishnawas.

Dewani. See Diwáni.

Dewasthán. [Hindi, from the Sanskrit *dewa*, a god, and *sthána*, a place.] A temple; also cash allowances for the support of a temple.

Dewatá. [Hindi, from *dewa*.] A deity, a divine being; an idol. In the Kunáwar hills the dewatás are considered to be spirits that mediate between men and the gods.

Dewitter. See Dewottara.

Dewottara. [Hindi, from the Sanskrit *dewa*, god, and *uttara*, which, as the second part of a compound word, has the force of 'attended by' or 'characterized by.'] A religious endowment, land granted rent free for the support of a temple.

Dewotthána. [Hindi, from the Sanskrit *dewa*, god, and *utthána*, rising.] A festival in connection with the sun's entrance of the sign Scorpio. Vishnu is supposed now to rise up from his four-months' sleep during the rains.

Dewri. See Diárá.

Dha. See Dáo.

Dhádi. [Hindustáni.] A Musalmán bard.

Dháhima. A tribe of Rájputs reckoned one of the chattiskula. There are also divisions of the Áhirs and Jats so called.

Ḍhák. The Hindustáni name of the paláśa tree.

Dhal. See Dál.

Ḍhaláit. [Hindi.] An armed attendant, or peon.

Dháman. [Hindi.] The ptyas mucosus, or rat snake; it grows to a length of seven or eight feet, and is usually found in grassy places, in pairs; it is not venomous, but with its powerful jaws and sharp teeth it can inflict a painful bite. It feeds on rats, mice, frogs, and young birds, and often comes into houses in search of its prey. It is commonly exhibited by snake-charmers, but is never tamed by captivity.

Dhang. The name given among the Bábriá Kolis of Káṭhiáwár to an assemblage of robbers or marauders.

Dhangar. [Maráṭhi.] The name of a caste; they are shepherds, and also weave wool; they are less settled than the Gaulis, and live chiefly in the hills.

Dhángar. [Hindi.] The name of a tribe in Chutiá Nágpur; they are labourers, and the name is said to be derived from *dhan*, grain, their wages being paid in grain. Some or all are supposed to be of the Uráon tribe.

Dhaniál. The name of a tribe found near Ráwal Pindi; they claim to be of Arab descent.

Dhansár. The name of the fourth of the four principal courts in Nepál. It is presided over by two bicháris, who decide minor cases themselves, and report important ones for the orders of the ditha.

Dhanu. [Malayálam, the Sanskrit *dhanus*, a bow.] The month during which the sun is in Sagittarius, corresponding most nearly to December and Márgaśirsh (in Bengal Paush). See Month. Also the name of a bow used for cleaning cotton.

Dhánuk. [Bengali form of the Sanskrit *dhánushka*, a bowman.] The name of a low caste formerly archers and fowlers, but now following agriculture, and largely employed as personal servants by the higher castes. Also the name of a bow used for cleaning cotton.

Dhárekari. [Maráṭhi, from the Sanskrit *dhárá*, custom, from *dhára*, a stream, and the affix *kari*, a maker, a worker.] A permanent inhabitant of a village, possessing rights of cultivation by inheritance. Compare Khudkásht.

Dhárhi. [Bengali.] The name of a low caste; they are musicians and dancers.

Dháriá. [Gujaráti.] An implement consisting of a bamboo about ten feet long, with a short curved blade, sharpened on the inner edge, fixed at one end. It is used for lopping trees. Also a globe-shaped metal pot with a narrow neck, and holding about seven gallons, used by spirit-distillers for carrying spirit.

Dharichá. [Hindustáni.] The practice of karáo; or the second husband of a widow.

Dharma. [Sanskrit, from *dhri*, to hold.] That which holds man in the right path, religion, law; or, subjectively, the observance of law, virtue, morality, duty; a general duty, as charity, or one specially enjoined for a particular class, as justice for kings, courage for soldiers.

Dharmádhikári. [Sanskrit, from *dharma*, duty, and *adhikára*, who presides over.] A judge, a magistrate; especially one appointed to punish violations of caste. The title is still used in Nepál as that of a judge who sits with the ordinary bicháris only when a caste question is involved in the case. Also a judge in a contest between bards or literary disputants.

Dharmakarttá. [Sanskrit *karttá*, maker.] A judge, a magistrate; also, in Madras, the manager of a temple.

Dharmasabhá. A society instituted on account of any dharma. Thus it may be a society for upholding religion, a society for the collection and distribution of alms, or any other purpose covered by any meaning of dharma.

Dharmaśástra. [Sanskrit: see *śástra*.] A law-book, especially the laws of an inspired lawgiver.

Dharmśálá. [Hindi, from the Sanskrit *dharma*, q.v., and *śála*, a hall.] A building for the object of any dharma, a place of religious assembly, a court of justice, etc. But the word is most commonly used to denote a rest-house, the establishment of such houses having been a favourite form of the dharma of charity. Besides the dharmśálás of private charity, many are now erected and supported out of local public funds. There is usually a well within the enclosure, and as the native traveller carries his cooking implements with him, the shelter and water of the dharmśálá is all he requires in the way of hotel accommodation. Among the Sikhs the term denotes a place of worship.

Dharná. [Hindi, from the Sanskrit *dhri*, to hold, to have in the hand.] The sitting at the door of a house in order to enforce the performance of an engagement on the part of the resident—as the payment of a debt or the like. The person who sits dharná neither eats nor drinks, and the notion is that if he dies there the guilt of his death is on the head of the man who failed to fulfil his engagement. It was practised especially by Bháṭs. An instance occurred in 1835 of a regiment of sibandi sitting dharná at the residence of Suraj Mal, a ṭhákur in Máhi Kántá, for their pay. And Colebrooke mentions an instance of a fakir remaining for several years near Cawnpore, buried up to the chest in the ground, until the sum which he required was contributed by a battalion of native infantry.

Dhatura. See Datura.

Dhavda. See Dhawaḍ.

Dháwá. [Bengali.] The name of a low caste; they are personal servants and labourers.

Dhawaḍ, or Dháwaḍ. [Maráṭhi.] The name of a caste; they are smelters of iron, and blacksmiths; they have high cheek-bones, large lips, small eyes, and wear beards; they speak Maráṭhi with a large admixture of Hindustáni.

Dheḍ. The name of a depressed aboriginal tribe in Gujarát. They are village watchmen and messengers, and do other menial service. They eat the flesh of animals that die, and by village custom the flesh of such animals is theirs by right. They are not allowed to live among the general population of a village, but have a separate quarter outside or just at the entrance. This fact, and the contempt Dheḍs are held in, are exemplified in the Gujaráti proverb, *Gám tyán Dheḍwaḍo hoy*, which is used to imply that there are usually some disreputable members in every body. Having no caste prejudices to prevent them, many Dheḍs have become domestic servants to Europeans, and a class of them from the city of Surat, commonly called Suratis, form a large portion of the servants, high as well as low, of the Europeans in Bombay.

Ḍhekuḍi. [Gujaráti.] A contrivance for drawing water from the bed of a river to irrigate fields upon the bank; it consists of the common apparatus of a well built at the edge of the bank, where it rises perpendicularly from the water; a buḍki.

Ḍhenki. [Bengali.] An instrument for husking rice, and which, in its essential parts, is a pestle and mortar; the mortar is commonly a vessel excavated out of a log of wood, and is sunk in the ground; the pestle is the hammer-head (also wood) of a horizontal lever bar which works on a low post or support, and the other arm of which is depressed by one or two women applying their weight to it; upon their relieving this arm, the hammer falling pounds the paddy in the mortar and rubs the husk off (*J. B. Phear*).

Ḍhenkli. [Hindi.] A machine for raising water, a horizontal lever resting on an upright, having a weight at one end and a string (pulled by a man) with a bucket attached to it at the other. The word is no doubt the same as ḍhekuḍi and ḍhenki, but the ḍhekuḍi is on a larger scale, usually worked by bullocks, and the purpose of the ḍhenki is different.

Dher. See Dheḍ.

Dhimál. The name of a tribe very closely resembling the Bodos, but now almost extinct.

Dhimar. [Hindi, from the Sanskrit *dhivara*, a fisher.] The name of a caste; they are fishermen and bearers, and said to be a branch of the Kahár caste.

Dhirmali. [Panjábi.] The name of a sect of Sikh dissenters, followers of Prithi Chand or Dhirmal, the brother and opponent of Arjun, the fifth guru.

Dhobi. [Hindustáni.] Another, and more common, form of Dhopá. A washerman.

Dhol. [Bengali.] The name of a low caste; they are weavers and cultivators.

Dhoni. See Ḍoni.

Dhopá. [Bengali, perhaps from the Sanskrit *dháv*, to wash.] The name of a caste in Bengal; they are washermen. But some have taken to agriculture and are called Chásá Dhopá.

Dhotar. The Maráṭhi form of Dhoti.

Dhoti. [Hindi.] A cloth worn by Hindus round the waist, passed between the legs and tucked in behind the back, and falling to the knee.

Dhotra. The Kanarese form of Dhoti.

Dhow. See Dow.

Dhuḍia. See Donḍiá.

Dhuldhoyá. [Gujaráti, from *dhul*, Sanskrit *dhuli*, dust, and *dho*, Sanskrit *dháv*, to wash.] A class of Sunni Musalmáns, said to be converts from the Khatri caste, who buy dust and rubbish from the houses of goldsmiths, wash it, and pick out the particles of gold and silver. The women spin. They are a distinct community, marrying only among themselves.

Dhund. The name of a tribe found near Ráwal Pindi; they claim to be of Arab descent.

Ḍhunḍiá. [Gujaráti, from *ḍhunḍ*, to search.] The name of a sect of Jain ascetics of dirty habits. See Tapá. They revere the tirthankars, but do not use images.

Dhuti. See Dhoti.

Diárá. [Hindi.] Alluvial land formed in the bed of a river.

Didár. [Hindustáni.] An overseer, an inspector.

Digambar. [Sanskrit *diś*, space, and *ambara*, clothing.] One clothed in space, that is, naked. This is the name of one of the two divisions of the Jains. They do not, however, go naked, but wear coloured clothes in opposition to the śvetámbars, who wear white. There seems to be no really important difference between the two divisions.

Dighi. [Hindi, from the Sanskrit *dirgha*, long.] A long or large tank or pond.

Digojy. [Corrupt form.] A cloth worn about the loins.

Dihdár. [Hindustáni, from the Persian *dih*, a village, and *dár*, holder.] A village overseer or superintendent on the part of a zamindár or the government.

Din. [Arabic.] The practical part of islám, consisting of recital of the kalimah, prayer and ablution, and fasting, which are incumbent upon all Musalmáns; and alms and haj, which are enjoined upon those who can afford them. 'Din' is the party cry of Musalmáns in quarrels with those of other beliefs.

Dinghy. [Bengali *ḍingi*.] A small rowing-boat belonging to a larger vessel.

Dipáli. More commonly Diwáli.

Dipdán. [Hindi, from the Sanskrit *dipa*, a lamp, and *dán*, giving.] The offering of a lamp to an idol; setting a lamp afloat on a river and watching whether it passes lighted out of sight, which is a favourable omen, or is extinguished, which is unfavourable; a lamp-stand.

Dipmál. [Hindi, from the Sanskrit *dipa*, a lamp, and *málá*, a garland.] A row of lamps; the name of a Sikh festival held on 14th Kártik wadi. Also the domed tower or pillar for lamps in front of a temple.

Dirgast. See Darkhást.

Dirvesh. See Darvesh.

District. As an official term, this word usually denotes a zillah or a collectorate. A district officer is one who is stationed up country, not at the presidency or provincial head-quarters; again, a district officer may be one whose duties are in relation to a whole district, as opposed to a táluk, or a village officer. In the plural the term 'districts' is often used as equivalent to the country, as opposed to the town; for example, a collector is directed to spend a certain part of the year in the districts, *i.e.* travelling about the country away from the chief town of his district. From this use the adjective 'district' gets a third meaning, namely, the opposite to huzur.

District Deputy-Collector. An officer of the uncovenanted civil service in Bombay who discharges the same functions as an assistant-collector.

Ditha. The title of the highest judicial officer in Nepál. He sits personally with two bicháris in the Kot Linga, where all cases are decided by the three officers jointly. He receives reports from the other principal courts, and instructs the bicháris as to their decisions in serious cases.

Diṭṭhwan. A vernacular corruption of Dewotthána.

Divan. This form of the Persian word *diwán* has come into English probably through Turkey and not through India, and means, not a council, but a council-chamber, or any room or saloon fitted up in an Oriental manner. Thence it is used also to denote the kind of seat appropriate to such a room, an ottoman.

Division. This term, when used without special modification (as division of a district) and without special relation to a particular department (as a division for the purposes of the educational department), means the division of a presidency or province placed under the supervision of a commissioner. See Commissioner.

Divisional. This word is used (1) in relation to the division of a province, and (2) in relation to the division of a district; a divisional officer in the first sense is a commissioner, in the second an assistant or deputy collector, or an assistant-commissioner.

Diwáli. [Hindi, from the Sanskrit *dipáwali*, from *dipa*, a lamp, and *áwali*, a row.] The festival of the row of lights, held originally in honour of Kárttikeya on the last day of Áśvin (śukladi reckoning), but now extended so as to include several festivals; the 13th Áśvin wadi is sacred to Lakshmi, when money and all forms of wealth are worshipped; the 14th is the anniversary of Vishnu's conquest of Narakásur, after which he was received with illuminations; and the next day, the 30th, or amáwasi, is sacred to Saraswati, when the account-books are worshipped; the next day, 1st Kártik śudh, is the first day of the samwat year, when the new account-books are opened.

Diwán. [Persian.] A royal court, a council of state, a tribunal of revenue or justice. A minister, a chief officer of state. Under the Muhammadan government it was especially applied to the head financial minister, whether of the state or of a province, being charged, in the latter, with the collection of the revenue, the remittance of it to the imperial treasury, and invested with extensive judicial powers in all civil and financial causes. Under the Maráṭhá government the diwán was the chief minister after the pradhán. The title also denoted the head officer of any revenue or financial department, as the diwán of the mint, of the jewel office, and the like; in which sense it is retained under the British government as the diwán of the mint, of the bank, of the salt-agency, and formerly of a collectorate, and is even applied to the managers of zamindáris for native proprietors, and to native servants entrusted with the management of the financial interests of a house of business, or of any responsible individual. The title of diwán, or office of diwáni, equivalent to the right of collecting the whole revenues of Bengal, Behar, and Orissa, was conferred upon the East India Company by the nominal emperor of Hindustán, Shah Aálum, in 1765. The word also signifies a record or account-book; and in Muhammadan law the bags in which the kázi's records are kept (*H. H. Wilson*). Diwán is also the title of the ruler of the Páhlanpur state. Among the Chakmás it is the title of the head of each clan.

Diwáni. Of or relating to a diwán, civil, as opposed to criminal. The office, jurisdiction, emoluments, etc., of a diwán. The right to receive the collections of Bengal, Behar, and Orissa, conferred on the East India Company by the titular Mogul. It is used also in the early reports for the territory of which the revenue was receivable under the grant in Bengal (*H. H. Wilson*).

Diwán-i-aám. [Arabic *aám*, all or common persons.] The large general audience-chamber where the Mogul emperor sat on a raised seat, resembling a pulpit, to which he had access by a private passage.

Diwáni Adálat. A court of civil and revenue jurisdiction. See Adálat.

Diwán-i-khás. [Arabic *khás*, select.] The private audience-chamber of the Mogul emperors, and always one of the most beautiful features of their palaces.

Diwar. [Tulu.] The name of a caste; they are toddy-drawers, and also work as labourers.

Diwár. [Hindi.] The tutelary divinity of a village, for whom a portion of grain is set apart at each harvest.

Dnán-márg. See Jnán-márg.

Doáb. [From the Persian *du*, two, and *áb*, water.] The land which lies between two rivers above their junction. The land between the Ganges and Jamná is known pre-eminently as the Doáb.

Dobash. See Dubháshi.

Dobe. [Hindi, from *do*, two, and *be* for *veda*.] A Bráhman who has studied two of the four vedas.

Dodia. See Donḍiá.

Dogar. The name of a pastoral and agricultural tribe in the Panjáb; they are nearly all followers of islám, but claim to be of Chauhán or Punwar descent; they generally resemble the Gujars in their habits.

Dogra. See Dogar.

Doingnak. [Arakanese.] The name of a section of the Chakmá tribe, which separated about 1782 A.D. They call themselves Khimbanago.

Dokará. [Gujaráti *dokaḍá*.] A bale of cotton; also the hundredth part of a rupee. See Bojá.

Dokhmá. [Gujaráti.] A low round building without a roof, in which the Pársis expose their dead to be devoured by vultures; the bones fall through an iron grating into a pit beneath. The dokhmá is built in as secluded a spot as possible, and is commonly called in English a tower of silence.

Dol. See Dál.

Doláyátrá. [Sanskrit *dolá*, swinging.] The swing festival. See Holi.

Dom. [Hindustáni.] The name of a low caste, apparently one of the aboriginal races. In Hindustán they are usually by avocation makers of ropes, mats, fans, and baskets. In Oudh they are sweepers, and in some places perform the lowest offices, as carrying dead bodies and skeletons. The Dom is often a musician, and the female Domni is an actress and singer, who performs in the inner apartments before the women of the family (*H. H. Wilson*). See Mir.

Dombaru. The Kanarese name of the Dommara caste.

Dommara. [Telugu.] The name of a wandering tribe, perhaps the same as the Doms. Both the men and women are singers and gymnastic performers. They usually possess cattle and asses, but do not seem to engage in the carrying trade; they traffic in pigs and asses, and sell mats, baskets, and combs. They travel with portable huts resembling the top of a country cart. They eat all sorts of flesh, and usually wear heavy clothes (*Stokes*).

Domunhá. Another name for the Dutonḍá.

Ḍon. [Maráṭhi.] A long flat-bottomed boat made of unḍi wood fastened with oiled and dammered coir yarn.

Donḍiá. [Gujaráti.] The name of one of the Káliparaj tribes; besides cultivating they make date matting; they burn their dead and use Náikás for religious ceremonies.

Done. [Telugu.] A coasting-vessel, usually one-masted.

Ḍongarkoli. [Maráṭhi, *ḍongar*, a hill, and *koli*, q.v.] A tribe of hill Kolis.

Ḍongi. [Bengali.] A canoe made of sheaths of plantain leaves.

Ḍoni. [Kanarese.] A canoe hollowed from a log.

Donigar. The name of a class of Musalmán shepherds and blanket-weavers in the south.

Donwár. A tribe of zamindárs of mixed origin, partly Bráhmans and partly Rájputs.

Doob. See Dub.

Dooly. [A corruption of the Sanskrit *ḍoli*, Hindustani *duli*.] A swinging litter for carrying women or sick persons.

Doombah. [Sindhi *dumbá*.] A kind of sheep with a very broad tail.

Doondah. [Corruption of the Sindhi *ḍunḍi*.] The name of the common cargo-boat of the Indus from Bukkur to the sea. Compare Zohrak.

Dopatra. [Hindi, from *do*, two, and *patra*, Sanskrit *pátra*, a bowl.] A musical instrument made of two tumbás connected by a bamboo rod, along which a wire runs; the music is produced by twanging the wire.

Dopaṭṭah. [Hindi, from *do*, two, and *paṭṭah*, a strip.] A piece of cloth of two breadths, forming the principal or only garment of women of the lower orders.

Dosádh. [Bengali.] The name of a low caste; they cultivate, and will do any sort of work. In Behar nearly all the chaukidárs are of this caste. They are worshippers of Ráhu.

Dosili. [Telugu.] A handful, as much as can be held in two hands; a small quantity of grain as a perquisite; an anjili.

Doura. Another name for chenna or small millet, the panicum miliaceum.

Douri. See Dawari.

Dow. [Maráṭhi *ḍáv.*] A two-masted Arabian boat, of from seventy-five to one hundred and fifty tons burthen.

Dragoman. [A corruption of *tarjamán*, from the Arabic *tarjama*, translation.] An interpreter.

Drávida. [Sanskrit.] The name of the country roughly defined by the coast-line from Madras to Cape Comorin, and lines drawn from those two places to the Nilgiri mountains; this is the country of the Tamil language. Also the name of the second of the two great divisions of the Bráhmans; also that of the third subdivision of this division. The five subdivisions are the Mahárāshṭra or Maráṭhi, the Tailinga or Telugu, the Drávida or Tamil, the Karnáṭa or Kanarese, and the Gurjara or Gujaráti.

Dravidian. An English adjective formation from Drávida, pertaining to Drávida; a collective name of the Tamil, Telugu, Kanarese, Malayáḷam, Tulu, and Koḍagu languages. The Dravidian races form a fifth part of the whole population of India. They are generally described as Turanian, and sometimes more particularly as Western or Scythian Turanian. It is not known when or how they entered India, but it is generally agreed that they came later than the Dasyas or Kolarian races, and before the Aryans. The Dravidian elements in the Brahui language suggest that these tribes came by the lower Indus. It is remarkable that, though later comers, their position is to the south of that of the Kolarians.

Dren. [Panjábi.] An inflated bullock's hide, used as a float in crossing rivers.

Droog. [Corrupted from the Sanskrit *durga*, difficult of access.] A place difficult of access, an isolated rock; a hill-fort, a fortress.

Dub. A vernacular form of Durwá.

Dubáru. [Bengali.] The name of a caste; they are divers and fishermen.

Dubber. This term, a corruption of some one or other of the forms ḍabaḍa, dábaḍá, ḍabba, dabbi, or ḍabḍá, is used in English to denote such vessels, usually of tin, as are used for preserving provisions.

Dubháshi. [Maráṭhi, from *du*, two, and *bhāshá*, language.] One who speaks two languages, an interpreter.

Dublá. [Gujaráti, perhaps from *dur*, without, and *bala*, strength.] The name of a tribe sometimes classed among Bhils, sometimes among the Káliparaj, but they differ from both, especially the latter, in that they are never found occupying villages of their own, but are always in the service of other cultivators, or in the employment of government as wartaniás. They are transferred from one master to another almost as slaves. The Dublás use Bráhmans (generally of the Odich caste) for their religious ceremonies, and burn their dead. The tribe is divided into Taláviá and Mádaviá Dublás.

Dudhkháná. [Hindi, from *dudh*,

milk, from the Sanskrit *duh*, to milk, and the Persian *khánah*, a place.] An establishment opened in times of famine for the maintenance of young children.

Dudhwálá. [Hindustáni, from *dudh*, milk, from the Sanskrit *duh*, to milk, and *wálá*, q.v.] A milk-seller. Also another name of the Musalmán Gaulis.

Duffedar. See Dafadár.

Duftur. See Daftar.

Ḍugḍugiwálá. [Imitative: see *wálá.*] A man with a small drum, who on the march of a regiment accompanied the camp colour-men, going in advance to mark out the ground for the new camp, and who, when the ground was fixed upon, went a little way back, and, sitting down, beat his drum to announce to the regiment and camp-followers as they came up that camp was close at hand (*T. Seaton*).

Duggah. A boat used on the higher Indus, above Mithun and on as far as Attok. Compare Zohrak.

Duhágin. [Gujaráti, from the Sanskrit *du*, evil, and *bhága*, lot.] A wife who is not the sauhágin, or favourite wife.

Dulanḍi. [Maráṭhi.] A man who has no land in his own village, but cultivates gáwik or other inferior land wherever he can get it.

Dulbera. See Dalbeherá.

Dulhá Deo. [Hindi *dulhá*, a bridegroom.] One of the gods of the Gonḍs; he is the apotheosis of a bridegroom who died in the marriage procession.

Dulicha. A kind of cotton carpet made at Mirzápur.

Duliya. [From the Hindustáni *duli*, a litter.] The name of a low caste in Bengal, whose occupation is to carry doolies or other burdens. Some of them are fishermen.

Dullehwala. [Corrupt form.] The name of a Sikh misl, occupying the right bank of the upper Satluj.

Dumálá. [Maráṭhi.] A term applied to a village or lands temporarily alienated; also used loosely for inámi.

Dumbki. The name of a tribe on the frontier of Sindh and Khelát. Their habits are predatory. They are not hill-men like the Bugtis, but live in the plain and use horses. They recognize the Khán of Khelát as their sovereign. General Jacob, who did much to lead these people into civilization, wrote of them in 1855 thus: 'The quietest, best-behaved, and best-disposed people on the border are these Dumbkis, who have completely adopted our principles, and abandoned their lawless pursuits, trusting entirely to our power and will to protect them.' At the same time, he describes them as one of the most manly and war-like tribes in the whole country.

Dund. See Dhund.

Dungah. [Corrupt form, perhaps for *ḍangá.*] A river-boat used in Cashmere.

Dungari. A coarse cotton fabric, different kinds of which are used for clothing by the poorer classes, for tents and for sails. It is generally woven with two or more threads together in the web and woof.

Dungkang. A tomb erected over the ashes of a lama.

Dupada. A resin that exudes from the vateria indica and is used as incense in temples. Also a solid oil prepared from the seeds and used for lamps, and suitable also for soaps and candles (*E. Balfour*).

Dupaṭi. The Telugu form of Dopaṭṭah.

Duráni. The name of a tribe, a branch of the Afgháns and the most important as well as the most civilized and tolerant tribe of Afghánistán. They were formerly called Abdáli, but their name was changed by Ahmad Sháh when he took the title of Dur-i-durán. The Duráni territory lies in the south-west between Kandahar and the Persian frontier. By religion they are Sunni Muhammadans, and their language is Pashṭo. The Sadozai and Barakzai are clans of the Duráni tribe.

Durbar. See Darbár.

Durgá. [Sanskrit, from *dus*, difficult.] The difficult of access, a name of the daughter of Himawat and wife of Śiwa in his character as the malignant destroyer. Durgá is imagined as of terrible form and irascible temper.

Durgápujá. [See *pujá*.] The worship of Durgá, a festival now included in the Dasara.

Duria. See Donḍiá.

Durra. Another name of Jawár.

Durry. [Hindi *dari*.] The name of various fabrics: a kind of rug made of cotton; striped cotton cloth; also a plain silk cloth made at Derá Gházi Khán.

Durum. See Dharma.

Durwá. [Sanskrit.] The grass cynodon dactylon; it is highly esteemed for fodder.

Dusatti. A kind of cloth, woven sometimes with single, sometimes with double, threads.

Dusrah. See Dasara.

Dussa. See Daśa.

Dussera. See Dasara.

Dustoor. See Dastur.

Dutonḍá. [Maráṭhi, from *du*, two, and *tonḍ*, mouth.] This name is applied to all snakes with thick tails, but especially to the eryx johnii. It is found in dry stony fields, where it preys on mice. It is of a reddish-brown colour, irregularly dotted with black. It is thick, heavy, and very slow in its movements. Snake-charmers often mutilate its short, thick, rounded tail to give it the appearance of a second head. The real head is covered with scales instead of shields, and is not distinct from the neck. The dutonḍá grows to a length of four feet, and is perfectly inoffensive (*G. W. Vidal*).

Dutt. See Datta.

Dvaita. [Sanskrit, from *dvi*, two.] Duality; the doctrine affirmed by the Madhwácháryas that matter and spirit are separate existences. See Advaita, Viśishtádvaita.

Dvija. [Sanskrit, from *dvi*, two, and *ja*, born.] Twice-born. The first three, namely Bráhmans, Kshatriyas, and Vaiśyas, of the four castes into which Hindus were, according to the Bráhmans, originally divided were called by this name, the investiture with the sacrificial cord being deemed to constitute a second birth. See Upanayana, Janeo.

Dwáparayuga. [Sanskrit.] The name of the third yuga or age of the world. See Yuga.

Dwárapála. [Sanskrit, from *dwára*, a door, and *pála*, a guard.] A door-keeper, a warder; also a painted or modelled figure set up at a doorway.

Dwária. [Nepálese.] A judicial and revenue officer who, with the assistance of four local pradháns, manages a village or community.

Dyte. See Daitya.

Dzul-caada. See Zilkadah.

Dzul-hijja. See Zilhijjah.

E.

Eahtimam. See Ihtimám.

Edagai. See Yeḍagai.

Eddavam. [Malayálam, from *eddu*, an ox.] The name of the month during which the sun is in the sign Taurus, most nearly coincident with May and Vaiśákh (in Bengal Jyeshṭh). See Month.

Eedgah. See Idgáh.

Egáli. [Tamil.] The name of a low caste; they are washermen.

Egg-plant. See Brinjal.

Eimák. [Pashṭo.] A sept or section of a tribe: the name is applied especially to some nomadic or semi-nomadic tribes to the west of the Hazáras; they are Sunnis, and some of them are subject to Persia.

Ejamanen. See Yajmán.

Ekka. [Hindi.] A small light two-wheeled carriage made chiefly of bambu; it is drawn by a single horse or pony, the shafts meeting on the animal's back; it has no seat in the European sense, and is used only by natives.

Ekrar. See Ikrár.

Ekwál. [Bengali.] A general account of a village or estate, showing, under the name of each cultivator, the quantity and description of the land held by him.

Elakeh. See Iláqah.

Elchi. [Persian.] An envoy, an ambassador.

Elephant-apple. The fruit of the tree feronia elephantum; among its Indian names are kawanṭh, koṭh. See Kawtha.

Ellaqah. See Iláqah.

Ellaváḍu. [Telugu.] A village servant; he looks after the village boundaries.

Emaum. See Imám.

Emir. See Amir.

Empress of India. A title assumed by her Majesty the Queen under the authority of statute 39 Vict., cap. 10.

Enam. See Inám.

Eri. [Tamil.] A large reservoir or piece of water, partly artificial, constructed for purposes of irrigation.

Eria. See Inḍi.

Ervad. A title given to Pársi priests and prefixed to their names.

Eshamán. A Tamil form of Yajmán.

Etlanama. See Itláanámah.

Etmaum. See Ihtimám.

Eurasian. This word, a combination of *European* and *Asian*, is used to denote persons of mixed English and Indian origin.

Evil-eye. See Nazar.

Extra Assistant-Commissioner. An officer of the uncovenanted civil service, in non-regulation districts, who corresponds to the deputy-collector of Madras and Bombay.

Ezhuwan. The name of a caste in Cochin; they are agricultural labourers.

F.

Faisal. [Tamil, from the Hindustáni *faisal*, a decision.] The settled rate, the assessment fixed at the time of the original survey in Madras.

Faisal-patrak. [Hindi: *faisal*, a decision, and *patrak*, a document.] The final survey paper showing the area and assessment of each survey number.

Faizullapuria. [Panjábi.] The name of one of the Sikh misls; they occupied tracts on the right bank of the Bias and Satluj. They were otherwise called the Singhpuria misl.

Fakir. [Arabic, from *fakr*, poverty.] A Muhammadan religious mendicant. They are divided first into báshara, or with the law, and beshara, without the law, and under each head are various distinct brotherhoods, each having its own office-bearers and special practices. Every new-comer is admitted first as a murid or disciple, and may afterwards become a murshid or teacher.

Fala. See Phálá.

Fanam. [A corruption of the Hindi *phalam*.] A name applied at different times and places to several different coins, but most commonly to a small silver coin of which 12¼ made a rupee. In the Deccan the phalam was a gold coin.

Faquir. See Fakir.

Farangi. More commonly Firangi.

Farásh. [Arabic *farsh*, spreading.] A servant whose duty it is to spread carpets, etc. Now usually a servant who sweeps an office.

Faráshkhánah. [Persian *khánah*, a house.] The place where carpets, tents, etc., are kept.

Farázi. [Hindustáni, from the Persian *faráz*, above.] The name of a sect of Muhammadan reformers, established in Dacca in 1828 A.D., by a man named Sharkatullah.

Farid. [Persian.] A Muhammadan saint.

Fárighkhatti. [Arabic, from *fárigh*, free, discharged, and *khat*, a writing.] A written receipt and acquittance, a release; a deed of dissolution of partnership, or of partition of property; a written divorce.

Fársi. The Arabic name of the Persian language.

Farughuttei. A corrupt form of Fárighkhatti.

Fáruki. The name of an Arab dynasty founded by Malik Rája Fáruki, to whom the districts of Thálner and Karanda were assigned by the Emperor of Delhi in 1370 A.D. His son and successor captured Asirgaḍ from the Áhir chief then holding it, and became ruler of Khándesh. The dynasty, tributary sometimes to Delhi and sometimes to the kings of Gujarát, lasted till 1599 A.D., when Asirgaḍ was taken by the Moguls and Khándesh became part of the Delhi empire.

Farzi. [Hindustáni.] A term used, like benámi, of a transaction which is partly fictitious.

Fasl. [Hindustáni, from the Arabic *fasl*, to divide.] A division of the year, a season; a harvest, a crop. The principal crops are divided into kharif and rabi, according to the time of their harvests.

Fasli. [From *fasl.*] The name of an era instituted by Akbar, who made the samwat year agree with that of the hijra by arbitrarily cutting 649 years off from the former. This was done in the year 963 of the hijra, which year was therefore also 963 fasli; but the fasli or harvest year was necessarily counted according to the seasons, while that of the hijra is the lunar year of only 354 days; thus a difference of about eight years has already arisen, the current year 1302 hijra being the year 1294 fasli. See Year.

Fatáwá. [Arabic, the plural of *fatwá.*] A collection or digest of judicial decisions. The best known is the fatáwá Alamgiri, compiled by order of Aurangzib.

Fatemari. See Pattemár.

Fátihah. [Arabic, from *fatah*, to open.] The opening surat or chapter of the koran; it is read for dying persons, whence the word has come to mean prayers offered up for a deceased person.

Fatwá. More commonly Fetwah.

Faujdár. [Hindustáni, from the Arabic *fauj*, an army, a body of troops, and Persian *dár*, holder.] The chief of a body of troops; under the Mogul government, an officer who was head of the police and also a magistrate; under the British government, the head police officer of a city or táluká; in some places, a village constable. In Bengal there were, till 1781 A.D., hereditary faujdárs, who had both police and magisterial powers.

Faujdári. [Hindustáni.] Criminal, as opposed to diwáni or civil.

Faujdári Adálat. A criminal court. Under the Muhammadan government this was the title of a district criminal court, subordinate to the central one called the nizámat adálat; and this use of the term was retained in Bengal, while in the other presidencies the name fauzdári adálat was given to the highest criminal court.

Fazendar. A superior landholder under the Portuguese government. He paid a small quit-rent, and levied from the cultivators a fixed proportion of the produce.

Fehrist. [Persian.] A list, a table.

Feringhi. See Firangi.

Fetwah. [Corruption of the Arabic *fatwá.*] A judicial decision, a written opinion on a point of law; especially that delivered by the mufti to the kázi.

Firangi. [Said to be a corruption of Frank.] This is the name by which the Portuguese, who settled on the west coast of India, were known to the natives. It was also applied to natives converted by the Portuguese. It is now used to denote any European.

Fire-temple. See Agiári.

Fire-worshipper. A term sometimes ignorantly applied to Pársis from the regard they have for fire as an emblem of good, and their maintenance of a perpetual fire in their temples. See Zoroastrian.

Firman. [Persian *farmán.*] A royal mandate, an edict, a charter.

Fiswa. [Bengali.] The trade name for silk reel-pickings. The price of fiswa is about half that of good chasam, and double that of gudhar.

Fitr. [Arabic.] Breaking a fast, especially the meal taken after sunset every day in the month of Ramazán, or the id-al-fitr when that month is complete.

Flying-fox. An animal of the fruit-eating order of bats, the pteropus edwardsii. They live together in great numbers, hanging all day to the branches of trees. Their general colour is brown, with long hair of an orange tint about the shoulders and chest. They measure as much as four feet and a half from tip to tip of the wings. The Hindi name is warbagul.

Foras. [From the Portuguese.] The name of the tenure on which the lands reclaimed from the sea, or inter-insular channels about the island of Bombay, used to be held before the settlement made by Act No. vi. of 1851. These lands were reclaimed chiefly by the erection of vellards, and being originally very salt, they were let out at very low rents to induce people to cultivate them. In process of time they improved and became valuable, and it was a question much discussed in 1844 whether the foras quit-rent could be raised or not.

Fotadar. More commonly Poddár.

Foujdar. See Faujdár.

Four-horned antelope. See Chausinga.

Fuqueer. See Fakir.

Furnavees. See Phadnis.

Fursá. [Maráṭhi *phursá.*] A small snake of the viper class, the echis carinata; it is seldom more than twelve or eighteen inches long; the body colour is in various shades of brown, with a connected chain of white arches or semicircles on each side, cutting into a median or vertebral row of white spots. The bite is often fatal, but not usually for several days. The pángla is used as a remedy.

Fusly. See Fasli.

Fysul. See Faisal.

G.

Gábdi. See Gábid.

Gábhárá. [Maráṭhi, from *gábh*, Sanskrit *garbha*, the womb.] The inmost apartment of a temple; that in which the idol stands.

Gábid. [Maráṭhi.] The name of a caste; they are sea-fishers and sailors, cultivators and labourers; they also dry fish.

Gaḍ. [Maráṭhi.] A fort, especially the fortified summit of a hill, such as Śiwaji used so much.

Gaḍariá. [Hindi, from *gáḍar*, a sheep.] The name of a caste; they are shepherds. There are several subdivisions. They allow karao.

Gaddi. A common name for a hill shepherd, but especially the name of a Hindu tribe of the Panjáb who are supposed to be of Khatri origin, and of a class of Musalmán milkmen in Delhi, Karnál, and Ambála.

Gaddi. [Hindi.] A cushion to sit upon, the ordinary Indian seat; but especially a king's cushion, a throne.

Gaddi-nashin. [Persian *nashin*, who sits.] One who sits upon the gaddi, a ruler, a king; but sometimes an heir-apparent.

Gaḍhavi. [Gujaráti.] Another name of the Cháran caste.

Gáḍi. [Bengali.] A carriage or cart. In some of the vernaculars a masculine or a neuter form, gádá, is used to denote a cart for carrying goods, and the feminine, gáḍi, one to carry persons.

Gádi. The Maráṭhi form of Gaddi, a throne.

Gádipati. [Bengali, from *gádi*, a bench, and *pati*, a lord.] The chief of a body of religious mendicants.

Gáḍit. [Gujaráti, from *gáḍa*, a cart.] A cart-man; another name of the Musalmán Gaulis.

Gaḍkari. [Maráṭhi, from *gaḍ*, q.v., and *kari*, active affix from the Sanskrit *kri*, to do.] A soldier serving in a hill fort, or holding land on condition of his so serving when required; or the descendant of such a soldier.

Gadun. A Paṭhán tribe settled on the southern slopes of the Mahaban mountain overlooking the Yusufzai plain, and allied to the Kákars.

Gáekwár. The family name of one of the four Maráṭhá leaders who became independent as the peshwá's power waned, whence it is commonly used as the title of the ruler of the Baroda state. The state has an area of 4399 square miles, and a population of over two millions.

Gágrá. [Hindi.] A subdivision of the Bhangi or sweeper caste.

Gaharwár. A tribe of Rájputs, one of the Chattiskula ; they are numerous in the North-West Provinces.

Gahlot. The name of a Rájput tribe, who claim to be of the solar race, and are reckoned the first in rank of all the Rájputs ; they are usually said to be of two clans, the Aharya and Sisodia, but the Gohil clan also seem to be Gahlot. The name is variously derived : by themselves from *goha*, a cave, one of their ancestors having been born in a cave during the flight of his mother ; by their enemies from *gahla*, a slave-girl ; and from *guhila*, the name of the second king of the Udáipur dynasty. The Sisodia Gahlots still reign at Udáipur, and are the oldest dynasty in India.

Gaita. [Telugu.] The name of an aboriginal tribe.

Gaitree. See Gáyatri.

Gaj. See Gaz.

Gakkhar. The name of a tribe numerous along the plateaus at the foot of the lower Himálayas in the Ráwalpindi, Jhelum, and Hazára districts. They are Shiah Musalmáns and claim to be of Mughal descent, but are rated as later Turanian.

Galbat. A name generally used in India for large foreign vessels, such as English ships and steamers. The word seems to be the Amharic or Abyssinian *jalbah*, the Arabic *jim* being pronounced hard in Yemen, and the final *h* being interchangeable with *t* (*J. S. King*).

Gáli. [Sanskrit.] Abuse. The commonest form of abuse among Hindus is to address one another by some name signifying relation by affinity, in order to imply that the speaker has had such intimacy with a female relation of the person addressed as the term used would indicate ; but the practice of using terms of such significance is so common that they are often applied where no insult, but merely an expression of irritation, is intended, and even a mother will call her child sálá. At the same time, gáli seems to be what is meant by Manu as the twelfth principal title of law in his eighth chapter, where it is coupled with assault, and placed between boundary disputes and larceny.

Galiárá. [Gujaráti, from *gali*, indigo.] One who dyes cloth with indigo.

Gallias. A kind of vessel used by the Portuguese pirates of Arákán ; perhaps the same as the gallivat.

Gallivat. [Perhaps from the Portuguese *galeota*, a vessel.] A large row-boat used in war in the last century ; it was of about seventy tons, with one main and one small mast, and carried six or eight three or four pounder guns, and was generally used to tow the grab (*J. M. Campbell*).

Gámit. Another form of Gámtá.

Gamlá. [Bengali.] An open earthen vessel.

Gámlá. [Gujaráti.] The name of a caste ; they are employed in the preparation of cloth.

Gamot. More commonly Ghámoṭ.

Gámtá. [Gujaráti.] The name of

one of the Káliparaj tribes; besides cultivating, they work under Golás at rice-cleaning; married women among them wear very large necklaces of shells, which are broken off when they become widows. The Gámtás use no Bráhmans; they bury their dead.

Ganak. [Bengali, from the Sanskrit *ganaka*, from *gan*, to count.] An arithmetician, an astrologer. The Ganaks of Bengal and Orissa are a degraded class of Bráhmans, who calculate horoscopes and make and decorate idols.

Gándá. [Bengali.] The name of a semi-Hinduised tribe of Chutiá Nágpur; they are weavers.

Gaṇḍá. [Hindi.] A string worn round the neck, the wrist, or the ankle, to avert evil influences.

Gandapur. A Paṭhán tribe who have abandoned Afghánistán and settled in the Derájat as cultivators. They are Sunni Muhammadans, frank and hospitable, and free from the vices and treachery of the Afgháns of the frontier (*Meadows Taylor*).

Gandharwa. [Sanskrit.] A class of beings supposed to live in the sky under the rule of Waruna, and to be the guardians of the soma. In epic poetry they are the celestial singers who attend the banquets of the gods. Also, in the vernaculars, a gandhrap. Also a form of marriage in former times depending solely on the mutual consent of the parties; in modern times the name given sometimes to an inferior kind of marriage which gives the wife less than full rights, and sometimes to a marriage between persons of full age.

Gandhbanik. [Bengali, from the Sanskrit *gandha*, fragrance, and *banij*, a trader.] The name of a caste; they are spice-dealers and grocers.

Gandhel. The grass andropogon calamus aromaticus, from which a fragrant oil is distilled.

Gandhrap. [Gujaráti, from the Sanskrit *gandharwa*, q.v.] A class of persons, originally Hindu, now many of them Sunni Musalmáns. They are by profession singers, but some are cultivators also.

Gandrupin. [Hindi.] A dancing-girl.

Ganeśa. [Sanskrit, from *gana*, a flock, a troop, and *íśa*, a lord.] The name of a god, the son of Śiwa and Párwati, or, according to another legend, of Párwati alone; and so called as being the master of the troops of demi-gods attendant upon Śiwa. Ganeśa is the god of wisdom, and so is represented with the head of an elephant. He is also the god of obstacles, and is therefore worshipped at the commencement of every undertaking. His wáhan is the rat.

Ganeśa. [Bengali.] The name of a caste; they are cultivators and weavers.

Ganeśachaturthi. [Sanskrit *chatur*, four.] The festival of Ganeśa on the 4th of Bhádrapad śudh; clay images of the god are made, decorated, worshipped, and finally committed to the water.

Gangá. [Sanskrit.] The river Ganges, personified as the daughter of Himawat, the king of mountains; also the Godáwari, or any river.

Gángaunta. [Bengali.] The name of a semi-Hinduised tribe; they are fishermen and cultivators of river-lands.

Gániga. [Kanarese.] The name of a Śudra caste; their principal occupation is making and selling oil; some are engaged in agriculture and labour. They are known by different names according to the customs of the sects in following their trade, such as Heggánigas, those who yoke two oxen to the stone oil-mill; Kirgánigas, those who make oil in wooden mills; Onṭiyettu, who yoke only one animal to the mill; and Yenne Telugaru, those who clarify oil. They are known collectively as Jotipans, and are found scattered all over Mysore. They are both Vaishnawas and Śaiwas, but worship their oil-mills principally (*Rice*).

Ganj. [Hindi.] A market, a market town.

Gánjá. [Hindi.] A name for both the cannabis sativa and cannabis indica, also for a preparation made from either of these for smoking. From the former a drink called bhang is also made.

Ganjeli. [Hindi.] A kind of coarse sacking or canvas made from the fibres of the gánjá plant.

Ganjifah. [Persian.] The game of cards, or the pack; there are eight suits, and twelve cards in each.

Ganotiá. [Gujaráti, from *ganot*, rent.] A tenant, one who holds land, not directly under government, but under a superior holder.

Ganpati. [Hindi, from the Sanskrit *gana*, a troop, and *pati*, lord.] Another name of Ganeśa.

Gánrár. [Bengali.] The name of a Śudra caste of middle rank; their occupation is to prepare the parched rice which Hindus eat when they cannot cook a meal.

Ganṭhá. Another form of Gaṭhá.

Gánṭhidár. [Bengali.] An occupant of lands under a landlord at a fixed rent and by heritable tenure (*H. H. Wilson*).

Gánṭi-chhárá. [Bengali.] The ceremony of tying a bride and bridegroom together.

Gaolee. See Gauli.

Gárá. [Hindi.] A convert from Hinduism to islám. The same name was given to the issue of the slave-girls of the royal palace of Delhi.

Garabi. The name of a sect who say that Ali was the real prophet to whom Gabriel was sent, but that the angel, misled by the family likeness, went to Muhammad instead.

Garás. [Gujaráti, from the Sanskrit *grása*, a mouthful, food, from *gras*, to eat.] An assignment of land or cash for maintenance; the earliest grants under this name were religious endowments; but the same name was given to grants made by a ruler for the support of his younger sons; and, thirdly, to a kind of black mail levied by Rájputs and Kolis in purchase of exemption from marauding.

Garásiá. [Gujaráti.] A holder of garás land or of a garás cash allowance. Garásiás are now of two kinds: (1) the descendants of cadets of Rájput ruling families, so called from the grants of land made to their ancestors; and (2) the descendants of the recipients of garás in the sense of black mail.

Garbhagriha. [Sanskrit, from *garbha*, the womb, and *griha*, a house.] An inner apartment, especially the sanctuary or adytum of a temple. See Mandir.

Garbhsuti. [Maráṭhi, from *garbh*, a fœtus, the pith or marrow of anything, and *sut*, cotton thread.] A cloth of which the texture is half silk and half cotton.

Gáre. [Kanarese.] Lime-plaster, mortar, chunam. Also the name of a thorny shrub, the fruit of which is used as medicine.

Gáreri. [Bengali.] The name of a Śudra caste of middle rank in Bengal; they are a pastoral people, and make and sell blankets. It is customary among them, when an elder brother dies, for the next brother to marry his widow.

Garhi. [Hindi, diminutive of *garh* or *gaḍ*, q.v.] A fort, a hill fort, a mud fort in a village.

Garhiband. [Hindi *band*, closed.] The name of a tenure in Bundelkhand, so called from the practice of ṭhákurs shutting themselves up in their garhis to resist the government demand of revenue; in this way they secured very favourable terms both from the Mogul and Maráṭhá governments.

Gári. The Hindustáni form of *Gáḍi*, a cart or carriage.

Gáriá. [Uriya.] A small tank or reservoir of water.

Gáribán, or **Gáriwán.** [Hindi.] A coachman, a cart-driver.

Garjantail. [Bengali.] Wood-oil, an oil that exudes from incisions in the bark of several species of dipterocarpus (*H. H. Wilson*).

Garkari. See Gaḍkari.

Gáro. The name of an aboriginal tribe of the hills in Assam to the north of the Maimansinh district of Bengal; they are strong and hard-working, but very uncleanly, and will eat anything; they cultivate jungle-land, and make and drink pachwái.

Garuḍa. [Sanskrit.] A mythical bird, the king of birds and the great enemy of serpents; he is also an attendant on and the wáhan of Vishnu.

Garuḍá. [Gujaráti.] A family priest of the Dheḍs. In northern India a priest of the Chamárs.

Gáruḍi. [Maráṭhi, from the Sanskrit *gáruḍa*, a charm against poison.] A snake-charmer, a juggler. Some are Mángs, but the greater number are Muhammadans. See Madári. The snakes most commonly kept are the cobra, python, and rat-snake (dhá-man), with occasionally the so-called two-headed snake (dutonḍá). Some common harmless snakes, such as the checkered water-snake (pándi-wad) and the fasciolated cowry snake, are also kept to be sacrificed to show the skill of the mongoose. The Máng Gáruḍis have a bad reputation for stealing, and especially cattle-lifting.

Garwárá. [Bengali.] The name of a low caste belonging to Dacca; they spear alligators, porpoises, turtles, and otters, for the sake of their oil or skins.

Gaswallah. [A misuse of the English word *gas*, and *wallah*, q.v.] A name used in Bombay to designate a seller of petroleum.

Gaṭhá. [Hindi.] The twentieth part of a jarib.

Gatkul. [Hindi, from the Sanskrit *gata*, gone, and *kula*, a family.] Deserted, unclaimed.

Gaṭṭu. [Telugu.] A bank, a dam, a bund.

Gauḍa. [Sanskrit.] The name of the country forming the central part of the present Bengal; thence the name of the first great division of the Bráhmans; also the name of one of the five subdivisions of this division. The five subdivisions are Kánya-kubja, Saraswata, Gauḍa, Maithila, and Utkala. The Gauḍa subdivision is again divided into the Wárendriya, Rádhiya, Sáṭshati, and Vaidika. The Gauḍa subdivision was in the eleventh century otherwise classified by the rájá of Bengal into Kulin, Śrotriya, and Bansáj. The same name, generally under the vernacular form Gaur, is taken also by divisions of other castes and classes, as the Gaur Káyath, the Gaur-Rájput.

Gauḍa. [Kanarese.] The headman of a village in the Karnatic; also the headman of certain castes. Also the name of an agricultural caste in Mysore and the Tulu country.

Gauḍá. [Maráṭhi.] The name of a caste; they were formerly headmen of villages, but are now cultivators, cart-men, and salt-workers.

Gaudian. A term, derived from Gaur or Gauḍa, the old name of Bengal, and sometimes used to designate collectively all the north Indian vernaculars of Sanskrit affinity.

Gauli. [Hindi, from the Sanskrit *go*, a cow.] The name of a caste; they are cowherds and milk-sellers, and live chiefly in towns and large villages. There are also Musalmán converts from this caste.

Gaunḍi. [Maráṭhi.] A mason, a bricklayer.

Gaur. The name of a caste in Orissa; they are cowherds and shepherds, and correspond to the Goálás of Bengal.

Gaur. A vernacular form of Gauḍa.

Gaur. The Indian bison, the gavæus gaurus; it differs from the American bison particularly in the fineness of the leg below the knee, and its pointed deer-like hoofs. The Hindi name is bodá.

Gauriga. Another name of the Meda tribe.

Gaur-Rájput. [Hindi, from *gauḍa*, q.v.] A Rájput tribe numerous in the districts of Agra and Cawnpore; they are of three divisions, called Chamár-Gaur, Bhaṭ-Gaur, and Báhman-Gaur, from some intercourse, it is supposed, with the Chamár, Bhaṭ, and Bráhman castes. The first class ranks highest, and prefers to call itself Chaunhar-Gaur; it is again divided into Rajas and Rais.

Gautama. The name of a tribe rated among the Chandrawanśa, but not of the Chattiskula; they were formerly a very powerful clan in the lower Doáb, where their representative is still called rájá; they are now numerous in Fatahpur, Cawnpore, and Gorakhpur. Many of them have become Muhammadans. Siddhártha, the last Buddha, was of this tribe, whence he is often called Gautama.

Gavial. The slender-snouted alligator; it lives exclusively on fish, and though it grows to a greater size than the magar, it is comparatively harmless.

Gávit. Another name of the Mauchi tribe.

Gawali. The Maráṭhi form of Gauli.

Gawanḍi. Another form of Gaunḍi.

Gawár. [Gujaráti.] The name of a pulse, the cyamopsis psoraloides or dolichos fabæformis; it is a kharif crop, and is often sown with bájri and kodrá; the grain is given cooked to cattle, the stalks are used as fuel and the thinner parts as fodder.

Gáwik. [Maráṭhi, from *gánv*, a village.] This is an adjective meaning common to the whole village. It is applied especially, in khoti villages, to those lands which are not held by the khot's family or by kardás, but are either not under cultivation at all, or are let out by the khot to bádhekaris or dulanḍis. Compare Kamata, Pannai.

Gayál. Another form of Gayári.

Gayáli. Another form of Gayáwál.

Gayálli. [Maráṭhi, from *gayál*, deserted.] Land which, being deserted by the kardá, comes under the management of the khot, and is treated as gáwik land.

Gayálu. [Telugu.] Land unfit for cultivation.

Gayári. [Hindi.] Unclaimed land left by a deceased shareholder, and which comes under the management of the málguzár.

Gáyatri. [Sanskrit, from *gáya*, a song.] The name of a metre, and especially a particular verse in that metre, from the rig-veda. The verse is, *Tat savitur varenyam bhargo devasya dhimahi: dhiyo yo nah prachodayat.* 'We meditate on that excellent light of the divine sun: may he enlighten our minds.'

Gayáwál. [Hindi.] The name of a class of Bráhmans who act as conductors of pilgrims at Gayá.

Gaz. [Persian.] A measure of length, about a yard, but it varies in different places and different trades, and is sometimes only two feet. The iláhi gaz fixed by Akbar is now taken as having been thirty-three inches.

G. C. S. I. These letters stand for (Knight) Grand Commander of the Star of India. See Order.

Gelarpatta. See Gillarpattar.

Gentoo. [From the Portuguese *gentio*, a gentile, a heathen.] This was formerly a common name for a Hindu, but is now never used.

Gentry-book. [Corruption of the Hindi *jantri*, an almanack.] An almanack and directory with civil and army lists, formerly published in India.

Gesta. A Kanarese form of Grihastha.

Ghádi. [Maráṭhi.] The name of a caste; they are temple servants, and some have taken to agriculture.

Ghadir. See Id-i-ghadar.

Ghaḍsi. [Maráṭhi.] The name of a caste; they are village musicians and singers.

Ghairmahdi. [Hindustáni, from the

Arabic *ghair*, without, and *mahdi*, q.v.] A sect of Shiah Musalmáns who hold that the Mahdi has already come, in the person of Muhammad Mahdi, who was born at Jaunpur, near Benares, in 1443 A.D. They are peasants.

Ghámoṭ. [Gujaráti, from *gám*, the Sanskrit *gráma*, a village, and *bhaṭ*, q.v.] A Bráhman settled in a village to perform general services to the community, and remunerated by pasáetá land. 'A ghámoṭ's mare' is a proverbial expression for a person of extreme meekness, as a ghámoṭ usually keeps a wretched pony, which all the village borrow, and which becomes so inured to work that it is said to open its mouth for the bridle on the mere approach of any person.

Ghanas. [Sanskrit.] A particular kind of snake. It is very venomous, and it is a proverb with the Maráṭhás that a charm has no effect on a ghanas.

Ghánchá. [Gujaráti.] The name of a class of persons who make bamboo baskets and mats. They may be identical with the Buruḍ or Wánsphoḍá caste.

Ghánchi. [Gujaráti.] The name of a caste; they express and sell oil, and some are vegetable-sellers. There are also Musalmán Ghánchis, converts from this and the Pinjárá caste; they are Sunnis.

Ghara. [Bengali, from the Sanskrit *ghaṭa*, a jar, from *ghaṭ*, to fashion.] A necked, narrow-mouthed, earthen vessel.

Gharámi. [Bengali.] A thatcher, or maker of mat houses.

Ghari. [Hindi.] A term of twenty-four minutes, but sometimes used for an English hour.

Ghariál. [Hindi.] A gong on which to strike the hours; thence used for a clock or watch.

Gharib-parwar. [From the Arabic *gharib*, poor, and the Persian *parwar*, who protects.] Protector of the poor. A common form of address to a superior, both orally and as a heading to petitions.

Gharry. A corrupt form of Gári or of Ghari.

Gharui. [Bengali.] The name of a Śudra caste of middle rank in Bengal; they are cultivators.

Ghásdáná. [Maráṭhi, from *ghás*, grass, and *dáná*, grain.] A contribution levied nominally for the grass and grain required for the horses of the mulukgiri force.

Ghási. [Bengali.] The name of a low caste; they are cultivators and labourers.

Gháṭ. [Hindi.] A landing-place, steps on the bank of a river for bathing on, a wharf. Also a mountain pass; or mountains themselves, especially the ranges of southern India known as the Western and Eastern Gháṭs.

Ghaṭaka. [Sanskrit, from *ghaṭ*, to be busy, to exert one's self.] An agent, a negotiator; especially, in Bengal, a professional go-between who arranges marriages between Hindu families; a genealogist.

Ghaṭasphoṭa. [Maráṭhi, from *ghaṭ*, a water-pot, and *sphoṭa*, breaking.] The ceremony of ejecting a person from caste or of repudiating a wife, typically expressed by the actual breaking of a pitcher.

Ghaṭi. [Bengali.] A brass gong on which the hours are struck.

Gháṭi. [Uriya, from *ghát*, q.v.] A watchman in charge of a pass or of a landing-place.

Gháṭi. [Maráṭhi, from *ghát*, q.v.] Belonging to the country above the Western Gháṭs.

Gháṭiyá. [Hindi, from *ghát*.] A Bráhman who attends where pilgrims bathe, to exact fees and perquisites.

Gháttá. [Panjábi.] A caste formed of persons outcasted from the Bániyá caste and of their descendants. There is a further subdivision called Ghátteká - Gháttá, formed similarly of outcastes from the Ghát(ás.

Gháṭwál. [Hindi, from *ghát*, q.v., and *wálá*, q.v.] The name of a class of landholders in Bengal. Some are of Afghán and some of Rájput descent. They were granted their lands originally for guarding passes (gháṭs) in the hills, and it is still their duty in some parts to keep the wild jungle people in order; in other parts they constitute a rural police.

Ghaus. [Arabic.] A fakir of the very highest sanctity; such as the Akhund of Swat. The ardour of devotion of a ghaus, according to vulgar tradition, is such that in the act of worship his head and limbs fall asunder.

Ghaut. See Gháṭ.

Ghautee. See Gháṭi.

Ghází. [Arabic.] One who takes part in a *ghazu*, which originally meant a plundering raid, but in the time of Muhammad came to mean an expedition against infidels; one who fights for the faith; a champion ready to fall fighting without hope of victory.

Ghee. [Hindi *ghi*, from the Sanskrit *ghrita*, from *ghri*, to sprinkle.] Butter clarified by being gently boiled and then allowed to cool; it is used both for religious and for culinary purposes.

Gheianee. [Corrupt form, perhaps for *jnáni*, from the Sanskrit *jnána*, knowledge.] The name of a class of Sikhs reckoned both learned and pious.

Gherwal. See Gaharwár.

Ghi. More commonly Ghee.

Ghilzai. [Pashṭo *zoe*, son.] The most important, after the Duránis, of the tribes of Afghánistán. They occupy the high mountainous territory extending from a little north of Kandahar up to Kábul, and along the Kábul river as far as Jalálabád. They are Sunni Muhammadans and their language is Pashṭo. They number about 15,000 fighting men.

Ghirth. The name of a Śudra caste found chiefly in the Kángrá hills; they are hardworking cultivators and labourers.

Ghisáḍi. [Maráṭhi.] The name of a caste; they are blacksmiths for coarse rough work.

Ghoghári. [Gujaráti.] A man of Ghoghá, or Gogo; but especially one of the hereditary seamen of that port; they are Kolis by race, but some have adopted islám. Many lascars on British steamers are of this caste.

Ghol. [Maráṭhi.] The plant portulaca quadrifida, or the plant portulaca oleracea, both of which are used as pot-herbs, especially in times of scarcity.

Ghoráwálá. [Hindustáni, from *ghorá*, a horse, and *wálá*, q.v.] A horseman, a groom.

Ghorcharhá. [Hindustáni, from *ghorá*, a horse, and *charhná*, to mount.] A horseman, a trooper.

Ghori. The name of a succession of dynasties, called also the Afghán or the Paṭhán dynasties, which reigned at Delhi from the beginning of the thirteenth century till they were overthrown by the Moguls in the middle of the sixteenth. They take their name from Ghor, the capital of the first Afghán invader, Shahab-ud-din, or Muhammad, and the dynasty was founded by his viceroy, Kutab-ud-din. The several Ghori dynasties are called severally the Slave-Kings, the Khilji, the Tughlak, the Saïd, and the Lodi dynasties.

Ghose. See Ghosh.

Ghosh. [Bengali.] The name of a subdivision of the Káyath caste.

Ghosi. A pastoral tribe in the Panjáb, allied to the Áhirs.

Ghulám. [Arabic.] The son of a female slave, a slave. The word is often used in composition to form a Muhammadan proper name, as Ghulám Hussein, *i.e.* slave of Hussein. Compare the Hindu use of dása.

Ghurree. See Garhi.

Ghurrial. See Gavial.

Ghuslkháná. [Hindustáni, from *ghusl*, bathing, and the Persian *khánah*, a house.] A bathing-room; that part of a palace, often consisting of many elaborately ornamented chambers and passages, used for bathing.

Gidia. [Hindi.] The name of a vagrant class.

Gillarpattar. [Panjábi.] A kind of seaweed used in the earliest stage of goître.

Gingal. See Jinjal.

Gingelly. [Tamil *ellu.*] The sesamum indicum and sesamum orientale. It is grown in the Káru season, cut down when ripe, and stacked for seven days; it is then exposed to the sun for three days, but at night collected again into a heap, and between every two days' drying in the sun it is kept a day in the heap; by this means the capsules burst of themselves and the seed falls to the ground. The cultivators sell the greater part of the seed to the oil-makers. The oil is in common use both for the table and for unction. The seed is also made into flour, which is mixed with jaggery and formed into a variety of sweet cakes. The straw is used for fuel and for manure (*Buchanan*).

Giras. See Garás.

Girike. [Kanarese.] A machine for removing the seed from cotton.

Girth. See Ghirth.

Goálá. A Bengali form of Gopál.

Goanese. A resident of Goa, but used especially to designate the community, originally the offspring of Portuguese fathers and Indian mothers, but now marrying only among themselves. They speak Maraṭhi and Portuguese, and observe the Roman Catholic religion. They are much employed as domestic servants, and also as clerks.

Goa potatoe. A name in Bombay of the dioscurea aculeata or prickly-stemmed yam; the tuber is used as a vegetable (*G. Birdwood*).

Godown. [A corruption of the Bengali *gudám*, from the Dravidian *giddangi.*] A storehouse, a warehouse.

Gohil. The name of a Rájput tribe; they appear to be identical in name and origin with the Gahlots; they were driven from the north by the Ráṭhors at the end of the twelfth century, and came into Káṭhiáwár, where for a long time they held Piram and Gogo; they are still the ruling family at Bhaunagar and also in Rájpipla.

Gokhá. [Uriya.] The name of a caste; they are fishermen, and are not allowed to enter the temple of Jagannáth.

Gokhru. [Hindi.] The herb tribulus terrestris or the tribulus lanuginosus; they are used medicinally for colic, and both the leaves and the pounded seed are eaten in times of dearth. Also the name of the iron crows' feet thrown on the ground to impede cavalry.

Gokuláshṭami. [Sanskrit.] Another name for the Janmáshṭami, Krishna's birthday, he having been removed to Gokul the day after his birth, to save him from Kans. As Krishna was brought up among cowherds at Gokul, and used to dance with the Gopis, cowkeepers celebrate this day with dancing.

Golá. [Hindustáni, from *gol*, round.] A granary consisting of a circular mud wall placed on a base of masonry or wood, that again being supported on posts or stone pillars about three feet in height, and the whole covered with a movable conical thatched roof.

Golá. [Gujaráti.] The name of a caste; they are cleaners of rice and other grain. Also a zanánah servant. Also one who has bound himself to serve for life. Also another name for khawás.

Golam. See Ghulám.

Golandáz. [From the Persian *gol*, a ball, and *andáz*, who throws.] An artilleryman.

Gold mohur. A gold coin of the value of about fifteen rupees. Also a corruption of *gulmuhr*, the tree poinciana regia.

Golkár. [Kanarese.] The sons of female slaves or bondwomen.

Golla. The name of the Kanarese caste corresponding to the Gop and Gauli of other parts of India. The Gollas were formerly largely employed in transporting money, both public and private, from one part of the country to another, and were famed for their integrity in such matters. Their chief occupations now are tending cattle, agriculture, and labour. The sub-sects called Kilári and Kawáḍiga are milk-sellers. The same caste in Chitaldrug and Kolar are called Yákula.

Gomasta. See Gumáshta.

Gomedha. [Sanskrit, from *go*, a cow, and *medha*, a victim, from *medh*, to kill.] The sacrifice of a cow. It does not appear at what period such sacrifices were ever made, but the feeding and worship of the cow at modern weddings is said to be in remembrance of the old rite of gomedha.

Gonḍ. An aboriginal tribe belonging to the Central Provinces, and also found in small numbers in the forests and hills of the Narbadá as it enters the Bombay territories. The Gonḍs in their social position resemble the Bhils, but their language is decidedly Dravidian, and closely approximates to the Telugu when its purity is not interfered with by infusions of Hindi and Maráṭhi (*J. Wilson*). There are many tribes of Gonḍs, and some are not Dravidian but Kolarian. The Gonḍ language has lately been systematized and expressed in Dewanágari characters. Marriages between first cousins are most approved among the Gonḍs.

Gondhal. [Maráṭhi, literally, tumult.] A tumultuous festivity held in honour of Devi.

Gondhali. [Maráṭhi.] The name of a caste; they are actors and musicians, and perform the gondhal.

Goniga. [Kanarese, from *goni*, the popular *gunny*, q.v.] The name of a caste; they are sack-weavers, and some are husbandmen. They are divided into Janaba, Sanapa, and Sádu Wamsasta, and are found chiefly in the Nandidrug division of Mysore. They are mostly Vaishnawas.

Gonrhi. [Bengali.] The name of a low caste; they are boatmen, fishermen, and lime-burners.

Gonṭiá. [Hindi.] The headman of a village. See Headman.

Goollar. See Gulaḍ.

Goontha. See Gunta.

Goor. [Hindi *gur*, from the Sanskrit *guḍa*.] The juice of the sugar-cane boiled and solidified into cakes.

Goorchar. See Ghorcharhá.

Goorkha. See Gurkha.

Gooroo. See Guru.

Gop. [Sanskrit *gopa*, from *go*, a cow, and *pá*, to keep.] The name of a caste of Śudras of intermediate rank; they are cowherds, and sell milk.

Gopál. [Sanskrit *gopála*, from *go*, a cow, and *pála*, a keeper.] Another name for Gop. In the Konkan there is a class of Gopáls who are singers and acrobats.

Gopi. [Sanskrit.] A cowherd's wife, or a woman of the Gop caste; applied especially to the cowherdesses of Brindában with whom the youthful Krishna played.

Gopura. [Sanskrit.] A building over the gate of a city or temple. In the south of India the gopura, consisting of pyramidal towers, is often the loftiest and most imposing feature in the temple.

Gorá. [Hindi, Sanskrit *gaura*.] White, fair; a white man, a European; especially a white soldier.

Goráḍu. [Gujaráti.] A light-coloured soil resembling goráṭ, but more sandy.

Gorait. See Goret.

Gorakhnáth. [Hindi, from the Sanskrit *go*, a cow; *raksh*, to preserve; and *nátha*, lord.] A name of Śiwa; also of the guru of Rukmini, wife of Krishna. One or other of these Gorakhnáths is much worshipped by yogis.

Gorát. [Gujaráti.] The red soil of southern Gujarát. It contains more clay than the goráḍu of the northern districts. It is more valuable than the black soil, and almost any crop except wheat can be raised in it. It is used especially for bájri and for horticulture.

Goret. [Hindi.] A village watchman and messenger. Compare Chaukidár, Wartaniá.

Gorkhodiá. [Hindustani, from the Persian *gur*, a grave, and *khod*, to dig.] The name of a class of Sunni Musalmáns; the men are grave-diggers and the women spin.

Gosain. [A vernacular corruption of *goswámi*, from the Sanskrit *go*, passion, and *swámi*, master.] One who subdues his passions, an ascetic; a mendicant. The name is applied to the Daśnámi Danḍis, the Wallabhácháryas, and other classes of mendicants. There are some classes of gosains who marry and engage in trade or agriculture. (The true derivation may be, in the case of some, from *go*, a cow.) Gosains are recruited from almost all castes.

Goshanashin. [Hindustáni, from *gosha*, a corner, and *nashin*, who sits.] A Muhammadan ascetic. The term is also sometimes used for pardanashin.

Got. A vernacular form of Gotra.

Gotama. The Páli form of Gautama.

Gotra. [From the Sanskrit *go*, cow, and *tra*, protection.] Literally, a cow-pen, an enclosure, a hurdle; thence the family enclosed by the hurdle; family, lineage, kin; a caste, a tribe claiming to be sprung from a particular progenitor.

Gotraja. [Sanskrit *ja*, born.] One born in the same family, that is, related as sapinḍa or samánodaka, but not a bandhu. Marriage between gotrajas is not allowed.

Goung. [Burmese.] An officer appointed to superintend a village; he is subordinate to the thugyi of the circle.

Gounghpo. [Arakanese, from *goung*, a head, and *hpo*, price.] A demand for composition for the ḍeath of a relative.

Gour. See Gaur or Gauḍa.

Goutam. See Gautama.

Government of India. See Supreme Government.

Governor-in-Council. This is the denomination of the governments of Madras and Bombay, each of which consists of the governor as president, and three members, namely, the commander-in-chief of the presidency, and two members appointed by the secretary of state from the covenanted civil service.

Govindasingh. The name of a Sikh sect.

Grab. [A corruption of the Arabic *gharáb*.] A sailing-vessel formerly used on the Malabar coast and in the Arabian Gulf, especially for piracy. A grab had two or three masts, and was of as much as 300 tons burthen, and carried guns.

Graha. [Sanskrit, from *grah*, to seize.] The power that seizes and obscures the sun and moon, and causes eclipses, Ráhu; a planet; also an evil spirit that takes possession of the body and mind of man.

Grahilot. See Gahlot.

Gram. [From the Portuguese *grao*, which is both the general name for grain, and also the name of a sort of pease much used in Spain and Portugal, whereof there are none in England (*A. Vieyra*).] The name of several kinds of pulse, but especially the cicer arietinum or Bengal gram; among its vernacular names are chana, harbhará, kaḍale. Other kinds are distinguished, as Black gram, Cow-gram, Green gram, Horse-gram, Red gram.

Grámadewatá. [Hindi, from *gráma*, a village, and *dewatá*, a god.] The tutelary deity of a village.

Grámádhipati. [Malayálam, from *gráma*, a village, *adhi*, over, and *pati*, a lord.] The headman of a village. See Headman.

Gramani. [Tamil, from *gráma*, a village.] A village headman. See Headman.

Grandhavari. [Malayálam, from the Sanskrit *grantha*, a book.] A book formed of the leaves of the talipot tree, in which janmis register their agreements respecting land with their tenants or mortgagees (*Graeme*).

Granth. [Panjábi, from the Sanskrit *granth*, to string together.] A book, but especially the holy book of the Sikhs. See Ádi Granth.

Granthi. [Panjábi, from *granth*.] A reader of the Sikh scriptures. One or more granthis were appointed to each Sikh regiment.

Gras. See Garás.

Grassia. See Garásiá.

Grass matting. See Madurkati. But there are also many other kinds.

Green gram. See Mung.

Griffin. A slang term used among Anglo-Indians to denote one who has lately arrived from England, and is still unacquainted with the peculiarities of life in India.

Grihadewa. [Sanskrit, from *griha*, a house, and *dewa*, a god.] The tutelary god of a house; he is often represented by the sálagrám, the tulsi plant, or even a water-pot.

Grihastha. [Sanskrit, from *griha*, a house, and *stha*, to stay.] A householder; a Bráhman in the second áśrama. The term is now the common word for gentleman. Compare Korta.

Grihini. [Hindi, from *griha*, a house.] The wife of a householder, the mistress of a house.

Grishma. [Sanskrit, literally, hot.] The season during which the sun is in the signs Taurus and Gemini; where the luni-solar year is observed, the season is defined either as Vaiśákh and Jyeshṭh, or as Jyeshṭh and Áshádh. See Ritu, Year.

Guaranteed railway. A railway constructed and worked by a private company to which government guarantees a certain rate of interest. The first and principal railways made in India are of this character. Besides guaranteeing interest at 5 per cent., government gave the land free. Profits in excess of the guaranteed rate are divided between government and the company, and a right is reserved to the former of purchasing the whole property under certain conditions. In later years the state has itself constructed railways.

Guḍamu. The Telugu form of Goor.

Guddee. See Gaddi.

Guḍhi. [Maráṭhi.] A pole erected in front of a house on the first day of the year (1st Chaitra śudh) to represent the banner of Indra; thence the festival of the new year.

Guḍikár. [Kanarese.] The name of a caste, nearly all of whom are settled in the Sorab táluká of Shimoga, in Mysore, but who are supposed to have come from the Deccan; they speak a mixed dialect between Kanarese and Maráṭhi; they are by trade turners and carvers in wood, horn, and ivory. They do all the sandal-wood carving for which Mysore is famous.

Gudu. The name of a tribute paid in grain which the Toḍas receive from the Kotas, Irulas, and Badagas.

Guebre. [A corruption of the Persian *gabar.*] An infidel, especially a reputed fire-worshipper or Pársi.

Guga. [Panjábi.] The name of a pir or saint to whom offerings are made to avert danger from snakes. By his shrines are erected, right and left, smaller shrines to Nársingh his diwán, and Gorakhnáth his guru.

Guikwar. See Gáekwár.

Guj. See Gaz.

Gujar. The name of a tribe supposed to have come from eastern Tartary and to have settled about Peshäwar about 100 B.C. Some centuries later they moved further south, and gave their name to the district of Gujrát in the Panjáb, and also to the province of Gujarát on the west coast. They are now a numerous body of cultivators and cowherds in the Panjáb and the North-West Provinces, and generally resemble the Játs and Áhirs, but are far inferior to the former as cultivators and in industry. The Gujars of the Kángrá hills keep herds of buffaloes and cultivate scarcely at all. As the Gujars have given their name to Gujarát, so again persons of any caste who have migrated from that province are called elsewhere Gujars; such emigrants are usually traders. The name is rendered into Sanskrit as Gurjara.

Gujaráti. The language of the people of Gujarát; it is derived from the Sanskrit, and closely allied to Hindi and Maráṭhi, and the character is a modification of the Dewanágari. Gujaráti is spoken by over nine millions of persons.

Gujesta. See Guzásht.

Gujri. [Telugu.] A market or market-place.

Guláb. [Persian, from *gul*, a rose, and *áb*, water.] Rose-water. Guláb is of two kinds—that from which the essential oil has been skimmed to make attar, and that which retains its cream. Guláb is one of the things given to a visitor on his taking leave. See Rukhsat.

Gulaḍ. [Maráṭhi.] The name of the tree ficus glomerata. It is moderately shady, rapid in growth, and hardy.

Gulál. [Hindi.] A red powder which is thrown about at the Holi festival.

Guldastah. A shaft with a cupola on the top erected at the corner of a building.

Gulika. [Koḍagu.] The name of a divinity, an invisible star, to whom the Koḍagas make offerings.

Gully. [Hindustáni *galli.*] A lane, an alley.

Gulmuhr. More commonly Gold mohur.

Gumáshta. [Hindustáni, from the Persian.] An agent, a steward; a collector of rents under a zamindár or málik; an accountant. In Madras, the tahsildár's clerks are called by this name. The gumáshta-kánungo is an agent or deputy of the kánungo.

Gumbara. A Kanarese form of Kumbhár.

Gundarve. See Gandharwa.

Gunesh. See Ganeśa.

Gunge. See Ganj.

Gunja. [Sanskrit.] The shrub abrus precatorius or its seed, which is black and red with a speck of white, and which was formerly used as a jeweller's weight; but the jeweller's standard gunja is heavier, and weighs two grains and three-sixteenths.

Gunny. [Hindustáni *ganni*, from the Sanskrit *goni.*] A coarse kind of canvas made from the fibre of two plants of the genus corchorus.

Gunta. A measuring-chain eleven yards long, or the superficial measure of this length squared, that is, the fortieth part of the acre. The word is placed by Professor Wilson as of Telugu origin, but as it is an exact measure of the English acre, and (at least in Gujarát) was introduced with the use of the acre (in supersession of the bighá and its subdivisions), it seems possible that the word is nothing but the English Gunter; the gunta is exactly half a Gunter's chain in length.

Gunwutteea. See Ganotiá.

Gup. [Hindustani *gap.*] Common report, popular talk, news. Also, in English, gossip, scandal.

Gupta. [Sanskrit, literally, protected.] The name of a Vaiśya dynasty that ruled in the north of India for many generations, and ended in the fourth or fifth century A.D. The Guptas were Buddhists, but Bráhmanism began to recover in their time.

Gur. More commonly Goor.

Gurav. [Maráṭhi.] The name of a caste of Śudras; they are employed in temples, sweeping them and decking the idols. Some are Lingáits, and the others call themselves Bhávik, or faithful; of the latter some have taken to agriculture.

Gurchání. The name of a Biluch tribe; some of them are independent hill-men, and others are settled in the lowlands within the British border.

Gurjara. [Sanskrit.] The name of a district, the modern Gujarát; thence the name of the subdivision of Drávida Bráhmans residing there. These are again subdivided into eighty-four classes, among the principal of which are the Nágar, the Kheḍáwal, the Moḍ, and the Odich.

Gurkhá. [From the Sanskrit *go*, a cow, and *raksha*, to preserve, a cow-herd.] The name of one of the principal races of Nepál. They are of Rájput origin, and claim descent from the Udáipur family. They conquered Nepál in 1768. They are small men, but very brave and hardy, and make excellent soldiers.

Guru. [Sanskrit, literally heavy, weighty.] A religious teacher, a spiritual guide. Particularly the instructor who imparts the veda to a student. 'Him who confers on a man the benefit of sacred learning, little or much, let him know to be here named guru in consequence of that heavenly benefit' (*Manu*, ii. 149). Some tribes speak of their gods as gurus, and among the Sikhs the name denotes their founders and spiritual leaders, of whom there was a succession of ten, lasting through the sixteenth and seventeenth centuries.

Gurumata. [Panjábi, from *guru*, and *mata*, doctrine, opinion, advice.] The advice of the guru; the name of the diet or conclave of the Sikh leaders, held annually at Amritsar in times subsequent to the gurus.

Gurumukhi. [Hindi, from *guru*, and the Sanskrit *mukha*, mouth.] The language of the Sikh gurus, but applied most commonly to the modification of the Dewanágari alphabet which they used.

Gurung. The name of a tribe in Nepál; they are breeders of sheep. They have to some extent adopted Buddhism, but are not in the least Hinduised.

Gurzmár. [Hindustáni, from the Persian *gurz*, a mace, and the Hindustáni *már*, to strike.] Another name of the Rafái fakirs, who beat themselves with a spiked mace.

Gussulcan. See Ghuslkháná.

Guttinae. [Tulu.] A village headman. See Headman.

Guz. See Gaz.

Guzásht. [Persian.] Past, gone by; applied to land sub-let by the proprietor; also to accounts or transactions of a past year.

Guzerattee. See Gujaráti.

Gwálá. A Hindi form of Gopál.

Gwallah. A corrupt form of Gwálá.

Gwárá. Another form of Gwálá.

Gyan-marg. See Jnán-márg.

Gymkhana. The origin of this Anglo-Indian word is unknown; the latter part appears to be the Persian *khánah*, a house, which is so much used in composition, as in kárkhánah, and the first syllable is often said to stand for the word 'gymnasium;' but it is difficult to see how such a combination could have come into popular use. A gymkhana in western India is a club for all kinds of sports, and the name is given also to the house or pavilion and the grounds where the sports are held; in northern India the name is given rather to a particular celebration of sports than to a permanent club and ground.

H.

Habshi. [Arabic, from *habs*, imprisonment.] Now another name for Sidi, but formerly a slave brought from Africa. Also the name of an African coast dialect spoken by the Sidis. The nawáb of Janjira, as the chief Sidi, is sometimes called the Habshi.

Hackery. A native bullock-cart. The derivation of this word is unknown; it has been suggested that it is a corruption of the Hindustáni *chhakrá*, the Sanskrit *śakaṭ;* and again that it is from the Portuguese *acarretai*, to carry. Niebuhr, writing in 1764, says he went from Dumas to Surat in a peasant's hakkri.

Hádi. [Bengali, from the Santáli *hád*, a man.] The name of a helot race in Bengal.

Háḍiá. [Gujaráti.] Land assigned to the heirs of a person killed in defending any place.

Hádi Hotri. [Bengali.] The name of a tribe, numerous in Maimansah, but little Hinduised as yet; they are cultivators and labourers.

Hádikáth. [Bengali.] A fetter or stock by which the landholder used to confine his serfs until they agreed to his terms; also the log used to fasten the victim in human sacrifices.

Hadis. [Arabic.] The traditional sayings and doings of Muhammad, on which the sunnah is founded.

Hadji. See Háji.

Hafta. [Persian *haftah*, from *haft*, seven.] A week; also a fixed period at which any money is to be paid; especially the time for paying government revenue; thence the portion of revenue paid, a kist, an instalment.

Haj. [Arabic.] Pilgrimage; especially the pilgrimage to Mecca, sometimes called hajj-al-farz, the ordained haj (*farz*, to command), as it is enjoined upon every Musalmán who has the means to perform it. The haj is to the Kaabah, round which the pilgrim walks seven times, kissing each time the black stone which is imbedded in the north-east corner of the wall, and which is said to have been given by an angel to Abraham.

Hajám. [Arabic.] A barber; they act as surgeons also, and their women as midwives and nurses. They are Sunnis.

Háji. [Hindustáni, from *haj*.] One who has performed the haj.

Hajj. More commonly Haj.

Hajjám. More commonly Hajám.

Hak. [Arabic *haq*.] A right, a title to a share. Used especially of the dues of hereditary officers.

Hakár. [Bengali.] The name of a low agricultural caste; some are boatmen.

Hakdár. [Persian *dár*, who holds.] One who possesses a hak, one entitled to a share.

Hakim. [Arabic.] A sage, a physician.

Hákim. [Arabic.] A governor; a judge.

Halálkhor. [From the Persian *halál*, lawful, and *khordan*, to eat.] A name given to sweepers, who are considered so vile that, eat what they like, they cannot be further defiled, so that it is lawful for them to eat anything.

Halbá. The name of a non-Aryan tribe in Bastar in the Central Provinces. They distill spirits. Their deities are called Náráyan Gosáin, Burhá Deo, Sati, and Ratná.

Halbandi. [Hindi, from *hal*, a plough, and *bandi*, settlement.] Assessment according to the number of ploughs used.

Halbani. The name of a sect who say that Muhammad usurped the office of prophet, which belonged to Ali.

Halcarra. See Harkára.

Háldár. [Hindi.] A village officer next to the paṭwári, an assistant-accountant. A name borne by some Bengal families of the trading castes.

Haldi. [Hindi, from the Sanskrit *haridra*.] Turmeric; or the ceremony of anointing a bride and bridegroom with turmeric.

Half fowl. A term used by Indian cooks to denote a fowl of intermediate growth between a chicken and the full-grown bird.

Halhallia. The snake more commonly called Ráth.

Háli. [Hindi.] Present, actual; as applied to coin, current.

Háli. [Gujaráti.] The name of a class of hereditary field-servants belonging chiefly to Anaula landholders. A háli often has a plot of land of his own.

Hallam. The name of a tribe in Hill Tipperah; they are said to be of Lushái origin, but to resemble the Tipperahs in their habits.

Hálui. The Bengali form of Halvái.

Háluya. [Uriya, from the Sanskrit *hala*, a plough.] The name of a degraded class of Uriya Bráhmans who plough with their own hands.

Halvái. [Hindustáni.] A maker of halwá, a confectioner. In some places, as the Doáb, the Halváis form a caste.

Halvirá. [Maráṭhi, from *hal*, a plough, and *vira*, a cess.] A tax on ploughs. The name of a system of land revenue under which the cultivator was taxed according to the number of cattle he had, or according to any other circumstances which might show how much land he could cultivate. The unit of estimation was the area of land a man could cultivate with a plough and one yoke of oxen.

Halwá. [Hindustáni, from the Arabic *halu*, sweet.] A sweetmeat made of flour, ghi, and sugar, or sometimes of other ingredients.

Hamaku. [Bengali.] The name of a plant resembling tobacco, but smaller in size and stronger in its narcotic effects.

Hamál. [Hindustáni.] A porter, a

palanquin-bearer. Also, in Bombay, a subordinate house-servant; a bearer.

Hambali. The name of the fourth of the four orthodox schools of Sunnis. It has few followers now and none in India.

Hammam. [Arabic.] A Turkish bath.

Hamsáya. [Pashṭo.] A retainer, a person living under the protection of a náik.

Hanbalite. See Hambali.

Hanefi. The first of the four Sunni schools, that founded by Abu Hanifa. Most of the Sunnis of northern and western India are of this school, and so are the Turks. It is the most conservative of all, and permits no modification of old doctrine to adapt it to modern life.

Hans. The name of a cultivating tribe in the Panjáb; they are Musalmáns, and claim to be of Qureshi origin.

Hansi. [Bengali.] The name of a low caste; they are weavers and cultivators.

Hapta. See Hafta.

Har. [Hindi, Sanskrit *hara*, from *hri*, to seize.] A name of Śiwa.

Hárá. The name of a branch of the Chauhán Rájputs; they give their name to the province of Háráwati, and two chiefs of the clan rule at Kota and Bundi.

Haragolu. See Harigolu.

Harámi. [Hindi, from the Arabic *harám*, forbidden.] Unlawful, improper; base-born; used as a term of abuse.

Harámzáda. [Arabic *harám*, forbidden, and *záda*, born.] Base-born, a bastard. Also used to mean a rogue or scoundrel.

Harat. See Arhat.

Harbhará. [Maráṭhi, from *har*, Śiwa, and *bhar*, full of.] The name of the pulse cicer arietinum, or chaná. See Gram.

Hardá. A Mahár priest.

Hardaur. [Hindi.] The name given to oblong mounds, raised in villages, and studded with flags, for the purpose of averting epidemic diseases (*H. M. Elliot*).

Harem. [Hindustáni *harim*, from the Arabic *haram*, sacred, forbidden.] The portion of a house which is reserved for the women of a family; thence the women themselves, the wives and concubines of a Musalmán collectively.

Hari. [Sanskrit, literally, green.] A name of Vishnu.

Hari. [Hindi.] Compulsory contribution of assistance by ryots in ploughing the fields of zamindárs; also, sometimes, voluntary mutual assistance of cultivators among themselves (*H. H. Wilson*).

Hari. [Gujaráti.] A third crop, raised by irrigation after the kharif and rabi; it is sown in the beginning of the hot weather, *i.e.* in March or April, and the produce is gathered just before the monsoon.

Hári. [Bengali *háḍi*.] The name of a very low caste; they are sweepers and swine-keepers, and, in some districts, drum-players.

Hári. [Sindhi, from *har*, a plough.] A cultivator, a peasant.

Haridás. [Hindi, from *hari*, a name of Vishnu, and *dása*, q.v.] A servant of Hari; one who sings hymns and relates legends.

Harigolu. [Kanarese.] A circular basket of stout wicker-work, eight or ten feet in diameter, composed of interlaced bamboo laths and covered with buffalo hides, used for crossing rivers; a coracle.

Harik. [Maráṭhi.] The cereal paspalum frumentaceum or scrobiculatum; it is a kharif crop grown on flat uplands or on hill slopes, and is one of the cheaper grains. See Millet.

Hárka. The cereal panicum semiverticillatum.

Harkára. [From the Persian *har*, every, and the Hindustáni *kár*, business.] A messenger, a courier; a spy.

Harpuji. [Hindi, from *har*, a plough, and *pujá*, worship.] The worship of the plough on the day which closes the season of ploughing and sowing; the plough is washed and decorated with garlands, and to use it or lend it after this day is deemed unlucky (*H. M. Elliot*).

Harwáhá. [Hindi, from *har*, a plough.] A ploughman, an agricultural bondsman, a háli.

Hashishin. [Arabic.] One who has drunk of *hashhish*, or hemp; the name of a Nazarian sect called in English Assassins. They ceased to be of importance after the fall of the Bagdad caliphate in the thirteenth century.

Hásil. [Hindustáni, from the Arabic *hásal*.] Produce, especially produce accruing to government; thence revenue, tax.

Hásilkhálári. [Bengali.] Produce of salt-works.

Hassanzai. The name of a Paṭhán tribe settled in the mountains east of the Indus but west of our frontier, in lat. about 34° 50′ N., long. 73° 20′ E. They number about 8000 fighting men.

Hastini. [Sanskrit.] Literally, an elephant; the name of one of the four classes of women according to Hindu writers, and the only one of which an unfavourable description is given; the hastini is short, thickset, of dark complexion and libidinous disposition. The other classes are the padmini, chitrini, and śankhini.

Hasular. [Kanarese.] The name of a wild tribe met with along the gháṭs on the north-western frontier of Mysore. They are a short, thickset race, very dark in colour, and with curled hair. Their chief employment is felling timber, but they sometimes work in areca-nut gardens, and gather wild cardamoms, pepper, etc. They speak a dialect of Kanarese (*L. Rice*).

Hát. [Hindi, from the Sanskrit *hasta*, a hand.] A cubit measured from the elbow to the tip of the middle finger; a foot and a half.

Háṭ. [Hindi, Sanskrit *haṭṭa*.] A fair, a market; especially the regular market held on a fixed day of the week, or in some places twice a week, in a particular town or village. Many dealers have no fixed shop, but move in a round from háṭ to háṭ. In Bengal the háṭ is often made a source of revenue to the zamindár, each stall-holder paying him a fee. Compare Melá.

Haṭṭi. [Kanarese.] A fold for cattle; a herdsman's residence; a house-yard; a cattle-pound; a cluster of huts.

Haut. See Háṭ.

Haveli. [Arabic.] A house, a mansion, a palace; also lands attached to a capital town or administered from head-quarters.

Havildár. See Hawáldár.

Hawáḍá. [Gujaráti.] A trough made of masonry and chunam at the side of a well for cattle to drink from.

Hawálá. [Hindi.] Charge, care, custody, trust; consignment of any property, duty, or liability. Also a description of tenure in eastern Bengal, an intermediate holding of a part of an estate, or of a farm under a zamindár or tálukdár, to whom a stipulated portion of the rents collected from the ryots is paid (*Taylor*).

Hawáldár. [Hindi, from the Persian *hawálah*, charge, and *dár*, holder.] Any one holding a charge or trust; a steward. In the native army (infantry) the hawáldár is a non-commissioned officer ranking between the jamádár and náik and corresponding with sergeant; in the police he is a third-class head-constable; the head of a small body of peons is sometimes called by this name; there is also a village officer called hawáldár, who assists the paṭel both in police and revenue matters.

Hayobans. [Hindi, from the Sanskrit *haihaya*, under which name the tribe is mentioned in the puráns; and *wanśa*, race.] The name of a Ráj-put tribe of the lunar race; they once held large dominions on the banks of the Narbadá.

Hazárá. [From the Persian *hazár*, a thousand, the tribe being said to be the descendants of a thousand slaves purchased by a king of Balkh.] A large Persian-speaking Shiah tribe of Afghánistán, settled in the hilly country between Kábul and Herát. They are of good disposition, and are much oppressed by their neighbours, to whom (says Burnes) they are hewers of wood and drawers of water. They also keep sheep and make carpets. They have no paramount head.

Hazári. [Urdu, from the Persian *hazár*, a thousand.] A commander of a thousand either actually or nominally as an honorary title.

Háziri. [Hindustáni, from the Arabic *házir*, present.] Presence; a muster-roll. Also the name of breakfast.

Hazrat. [Arabic.] Presence, dignity; a title of honour.

Headman. The member of the village community who acts as its representative in dealing with external authorities, and who is the head of the village establishment. The office is usually hereditary, subject to the approval of government on each succession. In some cases the practice is to select a suitable person from one or more families which have a prescriptive right to furnish candidates. The remuneration is usually in the form of inám land. The duties are multifarious, and are sometimes shared between two headmen, one undertaking the revenue and the other the police business. It is the revenue headman's work to collect the revenue, to look after the boundary marks, to prevent encroachments, and generally execute the orders of the tahsildár or mámlatdár regarding waste lands, trees, and the farming or selling of privileges. The police headman has to inquire into offences, hold inquests, and watch the predatory classes and bad characters of his village; he has also limited magisterial authority to try cases of abuse, trifling assaults, and petty theft, and in the Madras presidency he is competent also to try suits in which the property involved does not exceed ten rupees. How wide is the practice of having a representative head of the village community may be judged from the number of names there are for this officer. Among them are Ambalagár, Baśiniá, Bhuniyá, Burhá, Chaudhri, Gauḍa, Gonṭiá, Grámádhipati, Gramani, Heggaḍe, Jethryot, Kápu, Lambardár, Málik, Manḍal, Mánjhi, Mukaddam, Mukhi, Náṭṭánmaikára, Paṭel, Páṭil, Purseṭh, Raulia, Reḍḍi, Roaja, Takka.

Hebahnamah. See Hibánámah.

Hedgra. See Hijra.

Heggaḍe. [Kanarese.] The headman of a village or town. It is sometimes affixed to the name of a caste to denote a chief, as Kuruba-heggaḍe, a chief shepherd; it is also affixed to proper names as an honorific title. Heggaḍe is also the name of a division of the Wokkaligas in Coorg, whither they are said to have come from Malayálam.

Heggániga. See under Gániga.

Hejaz. [Arabic.] The name of that province of Arabia in which the holy cities of Mecca and Medina stand, thence called the holy land of the Muhammadans. See Haj.

Hejira. See Hijra.

Hell. The name of a custom in the Kotáhá hills similar to that of the 'bee' in America. When a man wants to build a house or break a fresh patch of cultivation, or do any other work which requires the assistance of his neighbours, he has a drum beaten on the surrounding hills, and collects as many men as may be necessary. These he feeds liberally till the work is finished.

Hemant. [Sanskrit, from *hima*, cold.] The season of the two solar months during which the sun is passing through the signs Scorpio and Sagittarius; where the luni-solar year is observed, hemant consists either of Kártik and Márgaśirsh, or of Márgaśirsh and Paush. See Ritu, Year.

Henna. [A corruption of the Arabic *hiná*.] The shrub lawsonia inermis, from the leaves of which a red dye is prepared. This is used to stain the palms of the hands and the soles of the feet, and the tips of the fingers and toes. Musalmáns use it also to dye their beards, the orange colour being afterwards turned to a deep black by the application of indigo. The Hindustáni name is *menhdi.*

Heri. [Hindi.] A tribe of Muhammadan Rájputs, chiefly found in Jaspur, a parganá of Morádábád, where they are hereditary chaukidárs (*H. M. Elliot*).

Heṭkari. [Maráṭhi, from *heṭ*, which

means down, to the south, or down the coast, and is applied especially to that part of the Konkan which is south of the river Savitri; and the affix *kari*, q.v.] An inhabitant of the southern Konkan, especially Málwan; they were much employed as soldiers by Śiwaji.

Hibánámah. [Hindustáni.] A deed of gift.

High Court. This is the title of the highest judicial authority, civil and criminal, in each of the three presidencies and in the North-Western Provinces. The four High Courts are located at Calcutta, Madras, Bombay, and Allahabad, and take their names from those cities respectively. They have been established by royal charter, and possess original and appellate jurisdiction. Appeal from a High Court lies to the Judicial Committee of the Privy Council in England.

Hijra. [Arabic *hijrah*, departure, from *hajara*, to forsake.] The name of the Muhammadan era which dates from Muhammad's departure from Mecca, which took place on the night of the 15th July, 622 A.D. The Muhammadan year is lunar, and therefore about eleven days shorter than the Christian year. The year 1303 Hijra will begin on the 10th October, 1885.

Hiná. More commonly Henna.

Hindi. [A relative adjective from *Hind*, India.] The name given by Europeans to that form of Hindustáni which employs the Dewanágari character or varieties of it, and is used chiefly by Hindus. There are many varieties of this language. The following types are the most important: (1) the so-called High Hindi, which agrees in its grammatical structure with Urdu, but, where the latter recruits its vocabulary from Persian, prefers to borrow from Sanskrit; (2) Braj-bhákhá; (3) Kanauji; (4) Márwári; (5) Mewári; (6) and (7) the hill dialects of Garhwál and Kumáun; (8) Nepáli; (9) Awadhi or Baiswári; (10) the dialects of Rewah and Baghelkhand, south of Allahabad and the united Ganges and Jumna as far east as the Son; (11) Bhojpuri; (12) Maithili.

Hindki. A tribe of Hindu descent settled in Afghánistán.

Hindu. [A corruption of the Sanskrit *sindhu*, a river, but adopted in the vernaculars.] The river Indus, among other rivers, being called sindhu, that name was applied also to the country about it and the people living on its banks, and was then further extended by Europeans to the whole country beyond and all its inhabitants. Thus Indus, Sindh, India, Hindu, are all European formations from the Sanskrit *sindhu*. Hindu, therefore, primarily means any inhabitant of India, but as an ethnical term it is confined to the Dravidian and Aryan races, to the exclusion of the earlier Kolarian or aboriginal; and, as a religious name, it is restricted to followers of the veda.

Hindui. A name used by some European writers to include the old extinct dialects of Hindi.

Hinduism. The religious system of the Hindus. It is a creed based on an original, simple, pantheistic doctrine, but branching out into an endless variety of polytheistic superstitions. The formula of its leading dogma is *Ekam eva advitiyam*, 'There is but one being, no second;' that is, nothing really exists but the one universal spirit, and whatever appears to exist independently is identical with that spirit. This is the severe, uncompromising creed of true Bráhmanism. This, according to the orthodox Hindu philosophy, is the only true veda. This, at least according to the belief of the generality of educated Hindus, is the only true knowledge to which the veda leads. Popular Hinduism, on the other hand, though supposed to accept this creed as the way of true knowledge, jnán-márg, which it admits to be the highest way of salvation, adds to it two other inferior ways, karm-márg and bhakti-márg (*Monier Williams*).

Hindustán. [Sanskrit *sthána*, a place.] The abode of the Hindus. This name is given to the country bound on the north and west by the Satluj and Indus, and on the south by the Vindhya mountains, and extending to the east as far as Benares. But the name is often used in a wider sense, and sometimes even as coextensive with India.

Hindustáni. The language of Hindustán; the name given by Europeans to the most generally spoken and understood of the modern Aryan languages of India. Various forms of the language are by native authors called by different names: the dialect written in the Persian character, largely stocked with Persian words and phrases, and spoken chiefly in towns and by Musalmáns or Hindus imbued with Persian culture, is known as Urdu; the same language when used in poetry is called Rekhtah; and when the poems are written in the special dialect of the zanánah, which has a vocabulary of its own, it is named Rekhti; in the region to the south of the Narmadá, the same language is called Dakhni; while that form of the language which employs the Dewanágari character or varieties of it, and is used chiefly by Hindus, is denominated by Europeans Hindi, and by the natives generally (in its literary form) Bháshá or the language *par excellence* (*C. J. Lyall*). Also a resident of Hindustán. And Hindustáni, as the name of a school of architecture, denotes the system which was formed by the adaptation of the old Paṭhán forms and requirements to the habits of Hindu workmen. It began under the Ghori dynasty in the thirteenth century, but made its most rapid progress in the latter half of the sixteenth under Akbar, by whom Hindu ideas were not merely suffered, but welcomed. The most famous buildings of this school were erected by Akbar's grandson, Sháh Jahán, in the time of Cromwell. See Jáli, Manabhatkári, Mogul, Saracenic.

Hircarrah. See Harkára.

Hirḍá. [Maráṭhi, from the Sanskrit *haritaki*.] The yellow myrobolan tree, terminalia chebula; the galls are used for dyeing and for making ink, the bark for tanning.

Hissadár. [Hindustáni, from the Arabic *hissah*, a share, and Persian *dár*, holder.] A shareholder, a coparcener, one who pays his share of the revenue to the state or to a zamindár.

Hissa-hákimi. [Hindustáni, from the Arabic *hissah*, a share, and *hákim*, q.v.] The share of the produce of the land or revenue to which the king or government is entitled. Compare Melváram.

Hissa-raiyati. [Hindustáni.] The ryot's share of the produce. Compare Kudiwáram.

Hloot-dau. [Burmese.] The public council of independent Burma; it consists of the four woongyees or ministers and many officers of lower grade, with the king or crown prince as president, and is at once a legislative assembly, executive council, and court of justice and appeal.

Hnan. [Burmese.] The common boat of burden of the Irrawaddy, resembling in shape the old galley of the Mediterranean. The stern rises to a great height, the bow not so high; the keel-piece is a single tree hollowed out, whence ribs and planking are carried up. Nearer the stern than amidships is the cabin, which forms a sort of deck-house; it is of fantastic woodwork, with a perch on the top of it for the steersman. The mast is, in fact, two masts; it is a pair of shears bolted and lashed to two posts rising out of the keel-piece, and can be let down or unshipped almost instantaneously. Wooden ratlines link and bind together the two spars, and form a ladder for going aloft. The yard is a bamboo, or line of spliced bamboos of enormous length, suspended from the masthead by numerous halyards, and from a rope running along this yard depends the huge mainsail, running on rings outward from the mast. These vessels, from their vast spread of canvas, can only sail due before the wind; when the wind is unfavourable they are rowed or punted along on the shallow water near the edge of the river. They often take four months to ascend the Irrawaddy from Prome to Mandalay.

Ho. See under Mundá.

Hobali. [Malayálam.] A division of a district, a subdivision of a táluk.

Hoḍi. [Gujaráti.] Properly, a small boat with only one, if any, mast, and used only on rivers and kháḍis; but the sailors of Gujarát give the name also to a two-masted coasting-vessel.

Holár. [Maráṭhi.] A subdivision of the Mahár tribe; they are village musicians.

Holder. See Háldár.

Holeya. [Kanarese.] An outcaste; there are in Coorg four kinds of Holeyas, the Kembatti and Máringi from Malabar, the Kukka from Tuluwa, and the Badaga from Mysore; in Mysore they are distinguished only as Telugu and Kanarese Holeyas. They belong to the right-hand faction. See Balagai. The Holeyas were for ages held in slavery by the Koḍagas, but have been legally freemen since 1836. They still hold a very low position. Some have become Christians.

Holeyaru. The plural form of Holeya.

Holi. [Sanskrit *holáká.*] This most popular festival is supposed by Sir W. Jones to relate to the vernal equinox, and to be similar to the Persian Naoroz. It commences fifteen days before the full moon of Phálgun, on which day the ceremonies are terminated, and is held in honour of Krishna's sportive swinging. It is kept as a complete saturnalia. Red powders are daubed upon the image of the god, and thrown and squirted by his worshippers on each other, while females are insulted by exclamations and jests of the most ribald and impure description, persons are sent on bootless errands, and the dance of drunken devotees in commemoration of Krishna dancing with the Gopis, or female cowherds, crowns the scene. The wheaten cake, which is placed on the pile lighted in every village at the close of the festival on the 1st of Phálgun wadi, is called poli, and the right of first offering it is considered as an honorary privilege. Neither the origin of this festival, nor the obscene manner in which it is observed in western India, can be described. Nor is the observation of it confined to the lower classes of the native community—the highest join in it with the same zest as the lowest. This festival nominally continues from the new to the full moon; but only a few of the last days are practically and openly devoted to it. The festival is called also by the names dolá-yátrá, hutáśani, and śimgá (*Times of India Calendar*).

Holia. See Holeya.

Holkar. [Maráṭhi, from *Hol*, the name of a village on the Nira, and the affix *kar*, resident of.] The family name of one of the four Maráṭhá leaders who made themselves independent as the power of the peshwá declined; thence, popularly, the title of the ruler for the time being of the native state of Indor, which was founded by that leader and is still ruled by his descendants. Indor has an area of 8000 square miles and a population of 635,000 persons.

Homa. [Sanskrit, from *hu*, to offer.] The act of making an oblation by pouring clarified butter on fire; an oblation, a sacrifice.

Hookah. [Arabic *huqqah*.] An apparatus for smoking, consisting of a box in which the tobacco burns, a vessel of water through which the smoke passes, and a long pliant pipe through which it is conveyed to the mouth.

Hooly. See Holi.

Hoon. [Hindi *hun*, from the Kanarese *honnu*, gold.] A gold coin, the star pagoda.

Hoondy. See Hunḍi.

Hormazd. A popular corruption of Ahura Mazda.

Horse-gram. The gram distinguished by this name is not the chaná, though that is a very common food for horses, but the kulthi, or dolichos uniflorus; it is known also as kollu, huruli, and vuluva.

Hotri. [Sanskrit, from *hu*, to offer.] The name of the highest of the three classes of priests employed in the ceremonial of a vedic sacrifice. They had to recite the sacrificial hymns of the rig-veda. Distinct from the three classes of adhwaryu, udgátri, and hotri was the superintending Bráhman, who superintended all and performed the whole sacrifice mentally.

Houri. [Arabic *huri*, the plural of *ahwar*, beautiful-eyed.] A nymph of the paradise of islám. 'Theirs shall be the houris with large dark eyes like close-kept pearls, a recompense for their labours past' (Koran, 56. 10).

Howdah. [Corrupted from the Arabic *hauda.*] This word originally denoted a litter fixed on the back of an elephant or camel for ladies to travel in. But in India it denotes the seat fixed on the elephant. (The camel carries a double-seated saddle with two pairs of stirrups, not a howdah.) The ordinary native howdah is a kind of box with low sides and no top, and holds several persons. For the European mode of sitting, the howdah is made more in the shape of a carriage-seat.

Howlong. [Corrupt form.] The name of a tribe on the Chittagong frontier. See Lusháí.

Hoysala Balláła. The name of a dynasty which ruled from the beginning of the eleventh century till their overthrow by the Musalmáns early in the fourteenth. Their capital was at Dorasamudra (now Halebid, in Mysore), and at the height of their power they ruled over all Karnaṭaka up to the Krishna, Tuluwa, Draviḍa, and part of Telingana. The earlier kings were Jains, but the fourth was brought over to the Vaishnawa faith by Rámánuja.

Huck. See Hak.

Hudees. See Ahádis.

Hujra. An Afghán institution, described as a sort of club where the male inhabitants of a village assemble to smoke and gossip. The spot chosen is generally the foot of a large tree in a central position, with water at hand. Here travellers are received and entertained, and there is a regular attendant to keep the place in order (*E. Clarke*).

Hukamnámá. [Hindi, from *hukam*, an order, from the Arabic *hukm*, command, and *námá*, the Persian *námah*, a writing.] A written order, a written award or judgment; the decree of a civil court. Among the Sikhs, the guru's requisition for contributions was so called.

Hulgá. [Maráṭhi.] The pulse dolichos biflorus.

Hunḍábandi. [Gujaráti, from *hunḍá*, which appears to have the general meaning of a disposal for a fixed sum of the right of realizing some variable amount; and *bandi*, settlement.] A settlement by which the government revenue of a village is sold for a permanent fixed sum to one or more proprietors.

Hunḍi. [Hindi.] A written order purchased from a saukár in one place for the payment by a specified saukar in another place of a specified sum of money; a bill of exchange.

Husaini Bráhman. [Hindustáni.] The name of a community of fakirs of the beshara order. They follow the atharwa veda, but adopt all the doctrines of islám that are not contrary to it. The men dress like Musalmáns, the women like Hindus. Most of their customs are Muhammadan, and they observe the Ramazán fast, but they wear the tila. Their patron saint is Khája Moin-ud-din Chishti of Ajmir. They practise astrology and palmistry.

Hutáśana. [Sanskrit, from *huta*, offered, from *hu*, to offer, and *aśana*, food.] That which eats the oblation, that is, the sacrificial fire; the god Agni; also an epithet of Śiwa.

Hutáśani. [Sanskrit, from *hutá-śana.*] The pile for the holi fire; the holi ceremony or festival.

Huttari. [Koḍagu, from the Malayálam *pudi-ari*, new rice.] The name of the great national festival of the Koḍagas and Holeyas, held in honour of the rice-harvest.

Huzur. [Arabic.] The presence, the royal presence, the presence of a superior authority, as of a judge or collector, and, by metonymy, the person of the prince or functionary; also the place where he presides, the hall of audience, the court; also abstractedly, the state, the government (*H. H. Wilson*).

Huzur Deputy-Collector. An officer of the uncovenanted civil service in Madras and Bombay, who resides permanently at the head-quarter station and is the head of the collector's account department, treasury officer, and the authority to whom the táluka accounts are rendered. He is usually also a magistrate of the first class.

I.

Ibádat. [Arabic.] Religious worship.

Ibádatkhánah. [Persian *khánah*, a house.] A room used for religious controversy.

Id. [Hindustáni, from the Arabic *aid.*] A general name for a Muhammadan festival. The two principal ones are the Id-al-fitr and the Bakr-id.

Idagai. See Yeḍagai.

Idaiyan. [Tamil, perhaps from *idai*, the middle, as being the occupants of the grazing lands lying midway between the hills and the arable lands.] The name of a caste; their proper occupation is tending cattle and sheep, but they are also cultivators, gardeners, and traders on a small scale. They commonly bury their dead (*J. H. Nelson*). They correspond to the Golla and Gop castes of other parts, and themselves assume the title of Konan.

Id-al-fitr. [Arabic.] The festival of breaking fast, the great Muhammadan holiday held on the 1st day of Shawál, when the Ramazán fast is broken.

Id-al-zoha. [Arabic *zoha*, sacrifice.] Another name for what is now generally known as the Bakr-id.

Idangai. The Tamil equivalent of Yeḍagai. See Walangai. The Vellalans belong to neither faction.

Id-as-saghir. [Arabic.] This is another name of the Id-al-fitr. It means the lesser festival, but the holiday is now the greatest of all.

Idgáh. [Arabic *gáh*, a place.] A place where Musalmáns meet for prayer on holy days. It is a stone or chunam pavement, raised three or four feet above the level of the ground and screened by a wall on the west side. An idgáh is generally built a little way outside a town.

Idiga. [Kanarese.] The name of a caste; they are toddy-drawers and palanquin-bearers.

Id-i-ghadar. [Persian.] The festival of the lake, held by Shiahs on the 18th Zilhijjah, as on that day the prophet by the side of a lake proclaimed that Ali was his own flesh and body.

Id-i-kurbán. [Persian *kurbán*, a sacrifice.] Another name for what is more popularly called the Bakr-id.

Ihrám. [Arabic.] A name given to the confines of Mecca, on arrival at which the pilgrim throws away his clothes and puts on two special cloths, which he may not wash or change till the haj is completed.

Ihtimám. [Arabic.] Care, charge; thence, sometimes, the local charge of a zamindár.

Ihtimámdár. [Persian *dár*, holder.] The holder of a trust, the person charged with the realization of a stipulated revenue for a certain district under the Muhammadan government, a zamindár; also a zamindár's agent (*H. H. Wilson*).

Ijárá. [Arabic.] A lease or farm of land, or of the public revenue, or of customs or the like. In former times these farms were made on a very large scale; for instance, the Peshwá in 1800 farmed his share of Ahmedabad to the Gáekwár at the rate of Rs. 5,00,000 a year.

Ijárádár, or **Ijárdár.** [Hindi, from the Arabic *ijárá*, q.v., and the Persian *dár*, who holds.] A farmer of the public revenue, whether of a single village or a large area, or of customs, excise or other source.

Ijmáa. [Arabic.] An assemblage, a court; a dogmatic opinion delivered by a council of doctors.

Ijmáli. [Arabic.] Held in common, unpartitioned.

Ijman. See Jajmán.

Ikrár. [Arabic.] Agreement, assent; a settlement.

Ikrár-námá. [Hindi, from *ikrár*, and the Persian *námah*, a deed.] A deed of assent or acknowledgment in general. In the North-West Provinces it applies especially to the engagement entered into with government by the málguzar and coparceners of a village: it is to specify the mode of paying the revenue; how the shares are to be distributed; the shares whether held in common or in severalty; the number, functions, and privileges of the lambardárs; the items of sáyar; rights of irrigation; extent and appropriation of waste culturable land; and the number, duties, and pay of the village servants; it is to be signed by all the lambardárs and as many paṭṭidárs as possible, to be attested by the paṭwári and kanungos, and finally confirmed by the signature of the settlement officer, after being read out before him in open court in the presence of the subscribing parties (*H. H. Wilson*).

Iláhi. [Arabic, from *ilah*, God.] Divine, the name of the era beginning with the first year of the reign of Akbar, 963 of the Hijra and 1556 A.D.

Iláhi-gaz. [Hindi.] The standard gaz fixed by Akbar at forty-one fingers, and by the British government at thirty-three inches.

Ilaka. See Iláqah.

Ilambádi. The Tamil name for Banjárá.

Iláqah. [Arabic.] Dependency, connection; a property, an estate, a district, a jurisdiction; thence commonly used in the vernaculars for presidency.

Ilavan. [Malayálam.] Another name for the Tiyar tribe.

Ilayathu. The name of a caste in Travancore; they serve as priests to Śudras.

Iluwakan. [Tamil.] The name of a caste; their occupation is distilling arrack. (Perhaps the same as the Ilavan of Malabar.)

Imám. [Arabic, from *ammia*, to preside.] The priest who officiates in a mosque. Also, among the Shiahs, their spiritual and temporal head; they recognize a succession of twelve imáms, beginning with Ali the son-in-law of the prophet, who was followed by his two sons Hásan and Husain, after whom came Husain's son Zain-al-Ábidin, and eight descendants of his, the last of whom, Abul Karem Muhammad, is supposed to be still alive. See Mahdi. The Sunnis give the title to the founders of their four schools, namely, Sháfai, Abu Hanifa, Málik, and Hambal. In the koran Abraham, Isaac, and Jacob are called imáms.

Imámat. The office of imám.

Imámbárah. [Persian *bárah*, a house.] A building in which the festival of the muharram is celebrated, and service in commemoration of the deaths of Ali and his sons Hásan and Husain is performed at that season; at other times their taziahs or shrines are preserved in it; sometimes it is used as the mausoleum for the family of the founder (*H. H. Wilson*).

Imámia. A follower of the imáms, a Shiah.

Imán. [Arabic.] Faith, as distinguished from din, practice. The two together constitute islám.

Imlák. [Hindi.] Land held rent free which has fallen to the zamindár for want of an owner (*H. H. Wilson*).

Immanu. [Kanarese.] Lands yielding two crops of rice in a year.

Inám. [Hindi, from the Arabic *inâam*.] A gift, especially a grant of land. Inám grants were originally rent free and perpetual, and were given for services previously rendered. Later, grants partially rent free and grants for services to be rendered (for instance, the paṭel's service land) have also been called inám.

Inámdár. [Persian *dár*, who holds.] The holder of an inám.

Inámi. Relating to an inám. Alienated as opposed to government (revenue). See Alienated.

Inámpatra. [Maráṭhi.] A deed of inám.

Inámsarpao. [Gujaráti: see Inám and Sarpao.] A cash allowance drawn by paṭels and deśáis. Originally this sarpao was given in recognition of assistance given in collection of the revenue, and came to be called inám probably when it became an annual charge.

Indi. [Assamese.] A variety of silk commonly known as eria silk; it is soft and of strong fibre, but difficult to reel off the cocoon.

Indian corn. The grain zea mais; it is a native of America, but is much grown in India. Native names of it are maká, makai, makka-cholam, makka-jonna; and the head is called bhuṭá or bhuṭṭá.

Indian cuckoo. See Koïl.

Indian hemp. See Śan. Also the name of a medicinal preparation from the root of the common hemp.

Indian madder. See Munjeet.

Indian roller. The name of a bird, often called the jay; it is the coracias indica (*S. B. Fairbank*).

Indo-Briton. A person of mixed Indian and British blood.

Indra. [Sanskrit.] One of the vedic gods, the ruler over the deities of the atmosphere (not of heaven). He is represented as the strongest of the vedic gods. He afterwards came to be considered the lord of all the gods (but not with such marked supremacy as that of Zeus, or Jupiter), and retained that place until the notion of the trimurti came into being. Indra also was considered to be one of the twelve ádityas. Indra's vehicle is the elephant, and the water-spout is said to be the trunk of that animal.

Indrawáḍu. [Telugu.] The name of a caste; they resemble the Iḍiga.

Inferior holder. When land is not held directly by the cultivator under government, but some intermediate person collects the revenue either for government, or, if government have assigned it to him, for himself, then that intermediate person is commonly termed a superior holder, and the cultivator an inferior holder. An inferior holder may be a mere tenant or may have the highest occupancy rights; a superior holder may be an ordinary ryot who has let some of his land to another person, or he may be an inámdár or a zamindár. Or one and the same person may be an inferior holder in relation to one person and superior holder in relation to another.

Ingár-tuppa. [Kanarese.] A tax on the Tálwárs in Mysore, in lieu of a ram and a pot of ghi annually contributed by them to the pálegárs in former times (*H. H. Wilson*).

Ingrez. [Corruption of *English.*] An Englishman.

Ingrezi. The adjective English; or, as a substantive, the English language or the English rule or dominion.

Inta Chapli. [Nepáli.] The name of a court subordinate to the Kot Linga, but which tries the most serious criminal cases.

Iraliga. [Kanarese.] The name of a wild tribe who live by the collection of forest produce.

Iráni. Of or belonging to Irán, or Persia.

Iravan. See Ilavan.

Iriká. [Uriya.] The name of a caste; they are salt-workers.

Irlá. [Maráṭhi.] A covering made of basket-work with leaves intersewn, used by cultivators in the Konkan to protect them from rain while working in the fields. One end of it is narrowed into a shape like a hood, and this resting on the head, the hands and arms are left free for work.

Irula. [Tamil, from *irul*, blackness.] The name of an aboriginal tribe on the slopes of the Nilgiris and supposed to be allied to the Beḍar. They are superior in physique to the Kurumbas. They are very dark and their hair is straight; the men shave the head and wear the kudumi. They grow rági and tenne, plantains and lime trees; and they collect jungle produce to take to market. Unlike the other Nilgiri tribes, they profess to worship Vishnu, but they bury their dead.

Ishá-namáz. [Hindustáni.] Prayer at sunset.

Ishrák-namáz. [Hindustáni.] Prayer at sunrise.

Ishṭadewa. [Sanskrit, from *ishṭa*, sought, desired, and *dewa*, q.v.] A chosen or tutelary deity, a favourite god, one particularly worshipped.

Islám. [Arabic.] Submission to the will of God, peace, salvation; the name of the Muhammadan religion. Islám is divided into imán, or faith, and din, practice. The principal tenets are that there is only one God; that Muhammad is his last and greatest prophet; that there is a paradise of bliss for the faithful and a terrible hell for the ungodly. Adam, Noah, Abraham, Moses, and Jesus are recognized as prophets who brought in succession new laws and revelations, till all were finally superseded by those of Muhammad. The din, or practice, is of five kinds: recital of the kalimáh, prayer and ablution, fasting, alms, and pilgrimage. See Din, Haj, Koran, Muhammadan.

Ismaili, or Ismailian. See under Shiah.

Istáwá. [Maráṭhi, from the Arabic.] The practice of letting out inferior land at a low assessment to be gradually raised to the full rate of the district as the land is improved.

Iśwara. [Sanskrit, from *iś*, to own.] A master, a lord; god; the supreme being. Also a name of Śiwa, and as such much used in composition, as Iśwardás, Mahábleshwar.

Itláanámah. [Hindustáni, from the Arabic *itláa*, making known, and Persian *námah*, a writing.] A proclamation addressed generally to the chiefs of any country or the residents of any district.

Iyawan. [Tamil.] The name of a low caste; they are workers in leather.

Iyen. See Ain.

J.

Jack. An English corruption of *chakka*, the Malayálam name of the fruit of the artocarpus integrifolia. The name is in English extended to the tree itself also.

Jádar. The name of a caste of weavers in Malabar, allied to the Telugu Dewángas. Some are Lingáits and some Vaishnawas, but they intermarry.

Jaḍebille. [Kanarese, from *jaḍe*, braided hair, and *bille*, anything made in plate form.] An ornament worn by women over their braided hair.

Jáḍeja. The name of the Rájput clan now ruling in Cutch; they claim to be of the lunar race, and intermarry with the Wághela, Shoḍá, Jhálá, Ráṭhor, and Gohil clans. They were at some former time converted to islám, but afterwards reverted to Hinduism.

Jádon. [Hindi, from the Sanskrit *yádawa*, a descendant of Yadu.] A tribe of Rájputs who are found in considerable numbers about Agra and Mathura, in the central Doáb, and in eastern Málwá, as landholders and cultivators. The rájá of Karaoli is of this tribe (*H. H. Wilson*). It has been suggested that some of this tribe settled also in the Deccan, and, mixing with the previous inhabitants, produced a part of the race now called Maráṭhás, among whom Jádav is a common surname.

Jádran. [Pashṭo.] A Shiah tribe of Afghánistán, occupying the mountain range, called after their name, running nearly north and south about 69° 10′ E. long., and 33° to 33° 30′ N. lat.

Jadu. More commonly Jádon.

Jádu. [Persian.] Magic, incantation, fortune-telling, the use of a mantra to bring about some desired end; conjuring.

Jádugar. [Hindi, from *jádu*, q.v., and *gar*, maker.] A magician, a conjurer.

Jáduṭona. [Maráṭhi.] A general term for all acts in the nature of incantation.

Jáfari. [Gujaráti.] The name of a body of city Vorás converted from the Shiah to the Sunni faith at the close of the fifteenth century. Their pir is Saïd Ahmad Jáfar. A few are merchants, but most keep hardware and glass shops, and some are pedlars, and, in Ahmedabad and Patan, silk-weavers.

Jág. [Maráṭhi, from the Sanskrit *jágri*, to be awake.] The riotous vigil or wake kept by Śudras on the tenth night after a sudden death, in order to summon the spirit of the deceased into the body of his son or other person and reveal the cause of death, the place his treasures are hid, or other matter desired to be known (*J. T. Molesworth*).

Jagannáth. [Sanskrit, from *jagat*, the world, and *nátha*, lord.] The lord of the world, a name of Vishnu or Krishna, whose chief temple under this name is at Puri on the coast of Orissa. This temple was built in the last years of the twelfth century, but the idol called Jagannáth had then existed for many centuries. Besides the principal idol, the temple contains idols of Balabhadra and Sabhadra, the brother and sister of Krishna. The wide catholicism of those who have taught in the name of Jagannáth has made Puri a great place of pilgrimage: the chief occasion of assembly is at the annual car festival, when the three idols are placed on three enormous carriages and dragged by thousands of persons from the temple to a country-house about a mile distant. It used frequently to happen that some persons were trampled to death in the crowd, and instances have occurred of frenzied persons throwing themselves under the wheels of the cars. See Mahåprasåd.

Jágariá. See Ráwaliá.

Jaggery. [A corruption of the Malayálam *chakkara*, identical perhaps with the Sanskrit *śarkará* and the English *sugar*.] Sugar in its unrefined state, or the juice inspissated by boiling and poured into moulds where it is allowed to dry in pyramidal balls; clayed or candied sugar; also an inferior kind of sugar made from the inspissated juice of the date and other palms.

Jaghdal. The name by which the Biluchis call the Játs.

Jágir. [Hindi, from the Persian *já*, a place, and *gir*, taking.] A village or district assigned to any person for the internal government and the enjoyment of the revenue thereof. Jágirs were usually given for some service to be rendered, especially for the maintenance of troops, and thus differed from ináms, which were more properly presents; jágirs also had not usually the perpetuity of the inám, but were given for specified terms. But these distinctions have ceased, and existing jágirs are hereditary and free of service.

Jágirdár. [Persian *dár*, who holds.] The holder of a jágir.

Jáglyá. [Maráṭhi, from *jágá*, awake.] A village servant appointed to keep watch at night.

Jagni. [Hindi.] A kind of dwarf sunflower, from the seeds of which oil is expressed.

Jágri. See Jaggery.

Jágria. The name of a caste; they are braid-weavers.

Jah. [Hindustáni.] A title of very high rank among Muhammadans.

Jahannam. [Hindi, from the Arabic.] The Muhammadan hell, consisting of seven divisions, allotted respectively to wicked Muhammadans, to Christians, Jews, Sabaeans, Guebres, idolaters, and hypocrites.

Jáidád. [Persian, from *jái*, place, and *dád*, that gives.] The capabilities of a district in respect of revenue; an assignment of territory for the maintenance of troops.

Jain. [Sanskrit *jaina*, an adjective formed from *jin*, and meaning relating to *jin*.] The name of the heterodox Hindu religion, of which the most striking features are the exaltation of saints called jins above the ordinary Hindu gods, and the denial of the divine authority of the vedas. In its earlier stages the Jain religion, like Buddhism, with which it has much in common, disregarded caste, and received converts from any class. Now there are among them different castes which do not eat together or intermarry. Apart from these distinctions all Jains are either yatis or śráwaks, and either digambars or śvetámbars. A Jain believes the world to be uncreated and imperishable but deteriorating. The golden age, when there was no sin and when man's stature and his age were immeasurably greater than they are now, is gone, and this is the time of decrease; but worse times are to come. Now a good man goes to heaven and a bad man to hell, while one of intermediate merit undergoes transmigration until his merit or demerit be accomplished. In the third and last age all will go to hell. In each age appear twenty-four jins or tirthankars. These are now regarded as gods, and it is to them that Jain temples are erected.

Jáji. [Pashṭo.] A Shiah tribe of Afghánistán occupying the mountain tracts about the Kuram valley as far west as Hazardarakt, where the Ghilzai country begins.

Jajmán. [Hindi, Sanskrit *yajamána*, from *yaj*, to worship with sacrifice.] One who employs Bráhmans to perform a sacrifice for him; a patron, a client; a rich man, the head of a house or of a caste. Family priests call all the families to whom they are priests their jajmáns. Jajmán and purohit, or gor, are relative terms.

Jajmánwarti. See Yajmánvritti.

Jakát. The vernacular form of Zakát; now commonly applied to import, export, and other dues.

Jalakára. [Kanarese.] One who searches in goldsmiths' sweepings for gold; a subdivision of the Pánchála.

Jáli. [Hindustáni, from *jál*, Sanskrit *jála*, a net.] The pierced screen-work in marble or sandstone which is such a conspicuous feature in later Hindustáni architecture. Whole windows are made of this fine filigree carved out of large slabs. The effect from a little distance is as of lace. Also a door or window made of thin slats like a Venetian blind.

Jáliyá. [Bengali, from the Sanskrit *jála*, a net.] The name of a low caste; they are fishermen and trappers of animals.

Jalkar. [Bengali, from the Sanskrit *jala*, water, and *kara*, revenue.] Revenue derived from lakes and ponds; the right of fishing.

Jalkarwálá. [Bengali: see *wálá*.] One who has rights of fishing.

Jam. A vernacular form of Yama.

Jám. The title formerly borne by the Sama rulers of Sindh, and now by the Jáḍeja rulers of Cutch and Nawanagar. It is also a title among the Játs and Mochis of Derá Ghází Khán.

Jamá. [Arabic.] Amount, total; the whole revenue of a village or estate.

Jamábandi. [Hindi, from *jamá*, and the Persian *band*, a binding, bond, settlement.] The settlement of the amount of revenue assessed on a village or district. Under the ryotwári system the jamábandi is made annually; it declares what each khátedár has to pay, and also classifies the revenue under various heads. In Bengal, the name is given to an account-book, which is an assessment-paper made up for each year, showing for each ryot each piece of his land, the rate, the total due, and the instalments in which it is to be paid.

Jamádár. [Hindi, from the Persian *jamát*, a troop, *dár*, who holds.] The chief or leader of a band of persons; particularly, in the native army, a subaltern officer next in rank below the subahdár (of infantry) or the russaidár or the náib risáldár (of cavalry); in the police, a head-constable of the first or second class; in the customs, an officer below the dároga; the head of a staff of peons.

Jamádi. [Arabic.] The name of the fifth and of the sixth month of the Muhammadan year (following Rabia), distinguished as Jamádi-al-awal, the first, and Jamádi-al-ákhir, the last Jamádi. See Month.

Jámáityá. The name of the fighting caste of the Tipperahs.

Jáma-masjid. [Hindi, from the Arabic.] The principal mosque in a city.

Jamát. [Gujaráti.] A band or company of persons; a body of persons who may eat together; a society, a caste.

Jamáti. [Maráṭhi.] A general name for all Konkani Musalmáns except the Dáldis, who are held to be inferior.

Jamátkhána. [Hindustáni.] A place of assembly.

Jamá-wasul-báki. [Hindi, from the Arabic *jamá*, total, *wasul*, collection, and *báki*, remainder.] An account, showing the revenue demand, payments, and balances.

Jámbu. [Gujaráti.] The fruit of the jámun tree.

Jambudvipa. [Sanskrit, from *jambu*, a rose-apple, and *dvipa*, a division of the earth.] The name of that division of the earth which contains India. The name is used in poetry and by Buddhists for India.

Jambukuṭiga. [Kanarese.] The name of a subdivision of the Pánchála in Coorg; they work in copper.

Jámdáni. [Persian.] A kind of cloth in which flowers are woven in, not worked; coats are made of it.

Jamdut. See Yamdut.

Jamedar. See Jamádár.

Jamidar. See Zamindár.

Jamkhána. [Kanarese.] A tent-carpet, a dari; a sitting-carpet, a rug.

Jamkhánwálá. [Kanarese.] The name of a caste in Mysore; they are immigrants from the Madras presidency, where they are known as Paṭnulwálás. They make a superior kind of woollen carpet, and a few are engaged in cotton and silk weaving. They are Vaishnawas, and speak a language peculiar to themselves (*L. Rice*).

Jampaun. See Jhámpán.

Jampti. [Sindhi.] A large decked boat used on the Indus.

Jámun. [Hindi, from the Sanskrit *jambu*.] The rose-apple tree, eugenia jambolana. It bears an edible plum; the wood is brittle, the leaf aromatic.

Janána. A vernacular form of Zanánah.

Janaswár. [Gujaráti, from *janas*, Persian *jins*, a thing, an article, goods; and *wár*, according to.] A system of revenue under which the assessment was made annually according to the kind of crop sown, the rate for each kind being fixed; so that the laborious appraisement necessary under the bhágbaṭái system was got rid of.

Jánbáz. [Pashṭo, from *ján*, life, and *báz*, wager.] Afghán cavalry.

Janeo. [Hindi, from the Sanskrit *yajnopavita: yajna*, a devotional act, and *upavita*, investiture.] The sacred triple thread to be worn by Bráhmans, Kshatriyas, and Vaiśyas across the left shoulder and hanging down to the right hip, the investiture with which is considered to be a second birth. See Dvija, Upanayana. The Bráhman's janeo should be made of cotton, the Kshatriya's of hemp, and the Vaiśya's of wool. It is now worn by many of the mixed castes also.

Jangama. [Sanskrit, usually *jangam* in the vernaculars; the common meaning is 'movable.'] The name of a sect, a division of the Lingáits. See Lingáit. Jangamas are again divided into Sámánya or ordinary, and Viśesha or extraordinary, the latter professing greater purity of manners. The Jangama division, it appears, furnishes priests for all the Lingáits. In Coorg there is a class of mendicants called by this name.

Janjirá. [Maráṭhi, from the Arabic *jarra*, an island.] A fortified rock wholly or partially surrounded by the sea.

Janmáshṭami. [Sanskrit *janma*, birth, and *ashṭami*, the eighth.] The birthday of Krishna, the 8th Bhádra wadi in Bengal and Márwár, the 8th Śráwan wadi in southern India. Some Vaishnawas observe the birthday and some the following day, the Gokuláshṭami, when the infant was removed from Mathura to Gokul. They abstain from their ordinary food, eating only particular prescribed kinds till midnight, when they worship the image of the infant and then eat.

Janmi. [Malayálam, from the Sanskrit *janma*, birth, birthright.] A landed proprietor.

Janoi. The Gujaráti form of Janeo.

Jánwá. The Maráṭhi form of Janeo.

Japji. [Panjábi, from the Sanskrit *jap*, to repeat, and *ji*, q.v.] The name of two Sikh prayers, the first, called also guru mantra, was composed by Nának, and the second by Govind Singh; they are contained respectively in the ádi granth and the daswa pádsháhká granth.

Japti. The Gujaráti form of Zabti. Japti kheḍuts are those permanently settled, as distinguished from those who cultivate now in one village and now in another.

Jaráyat. The Gujaráti form of Jiráit.

Jári. [Arabic.] Literally, flowing, current; cultivated for a second or subsequent crop; applied to the cotton sown after the rains, in contradistinction to the ordinary kharif or bunny crop.

Jarib. [Arabic.] A measuring-chain or rope, twenty gaṭhás or sixty gaz in length; the square of the jarib is the bighá.

Jariph. [Gujaráti, from *jarib.*] A measure, first of capacity, then of land, the standard being the area sown with a jarib of seed; thence, a survey.

Jartosti. The name by which the Pársis call their own, the Zoroastrian, religion.

Jasáwar. The name of a branch of the Kurmi caste settled in Behar; their occupation is agriculture.

Jasgam. The name of a tribe in the Panjáb; they claim to be of Arab descent.

Ját. [Hindi.] The name of a very numerous race of people in the North-West Provinces, the Panjáb, and Sindh; their origin is not well determined, some authorities saying they are descended from the White Huns, others that they are a mixture of the Rájputs and the Getæ. The name is also written Jat. There are many different clans of them, and they seem to have entered India at many periods far apart, but all from the region of Ghazni and the west of it. The Játs are counted among the Chattiskula, but are not admitted to intermarriage with Rájputs. Some have adopted islám and very many of them sikhism; they are in general industrious and enterprising cultivators, and a brave and hardy race. The rájás of Bhartpur, Dholpur, Patiálá, Jind, and Nábhá are of the tribe. Ját is also the name of a pastoral tribe in Bengal. Also that of a tribe holding a low social position in Afghánistán; these are mostly farm-servants, sweepers, and musicians; they speak a dialect of Hindustáni.

Jaṭá. [Sanskrit, from *jaṭ*, to clot, to be matted together.] The hair worn long and braided as by Śaiwa ascetics. In Gujaráti poetry it is often compared with the hanging roots (also jaṭá) of the banyan tree; it is also the subject of a proverb: 'He has only just become a jogi, and already his jaṭá reaches to his knees.'

Játaka. [Sanskrit, from *játa*, born, from *jan*, to beget.] The astrological casting of a nativity. Also the name of a Páli book, part of the second piṭaka, a collection of 550 birth-stories of Gautama the Buddha in the various stages of existence.

Játamále. [Kanarese.] The name of a class of outcastes in Mysore.

Jati. A vernacular form of Yati.

Játrá. [Sanskrit *yátrá*, from *yá*, to travel.] A pilgrimage to a holy place, particularly a pilgrimage on a fixed day recurring annually or at longer intervals. Játrás are usually made the occasions of fairs and various amusements, as well as of visiting the temple, bathing in the holy water, etc.

Játri. [Hindi.] A pilgrim.

Játuá. [Hindi.] One of the seven branches of the Chamár tribe, located chiefly in the upper Doáb.

Jauhar. [Hindi.] The putting to death of women and children to prevent their falling into the hands of an enemy. One of the tanks at Gwalior is still called by this name from the jauhar that took place there when Altamsh took the fort in 1232 A.D.

Jauhari. [Hindi.] A jeweller. See Johari.

Jaurak. [Sindhi.] A boat used on the upper Indus. See Zohruk.

Jawáb. [Hindustáni.] An answer; the term is applied to a building erected to correspond to, or balance, another, as for instance the false mosque on the east of the táj.

Jawal-Bráhman. [Maráṭhi.] A small sect in the Dápuli táluká of Ratnágiri. They live entirely by agriculture and have the appearance of well-to-do Kunbis. They are said to be the descendants of the crew of a vessel wrecked at Burundi (their chief village) in a storm (*jawal*) (*A. K. Nairne*).

Jawár. [Hindi.] The millet, holcus sorghum, or sorghum vulgare. It is one of the principal dry crops and one of the staple food-grains in western India. It grows to a height of eight to twelve feet, and the heads of some kinds are so heavy that three or four stems have to be tied together near the top for mutual support.

Jawári. The Maráṭhi form of Jawár.

Jawása. [Hindi.] A kind of shrubby grass, the hedysarum alhagi, on which cattle, and especially camels, browse.

Jay. [Sanskrit, from *ji*, to win.] Victory; used as an exclamation either by itself or with a name. 'Rám rájá jay!' is a war-cry of the Hindu soldier. Pilgrims, when they come in sight of the temple at Dakor, exclaim repeatedly, 'Ranchod raiji jay!' Jay is also often put before the name, as 'Jay-mahárájá!'

Jazárchi. More commonly Juzailchi.

Jaziah. [Arabic.] A capitation tax levied on all who refused to become Muhammadans. It was abolished in India by Akbar, but reimposed by Aurangzib.

Jeel. See Jhil.

Jehad. See Jihád.

Jekráni. The name of a tribe of predatory horsemen on the frontier of Sindh and Khelát. They generally resemble the Dumbkis. Under the influence of General Jacob they were got to settle down to agriculture, and proved industrious and well-behaved.

Jelabi. [Gujaráti.] A sort of sweetmeat.

Jellikattu. [Tamil.] A kind of bull-baiting practised by the Maravar and other castes; the object is to get possession of a prize which is tied to the bull's horns.

Jemedar. See Jamádár.

Jenmcar. See Janmi.

Jenu Kuruba. [Kanarese *jenu*, honey.] A subdivision of the Kurubas; they are a wild hill tribe chiefly engaged in collecting honey and bees-wax. They are said to be inferior to the Beṭṭa Kuruba and much darker in colour. Their language is peculiar, but allied to Kanarese. They worship Káli and pronounce her name over their food.

Jenwa. See Janeo.

Jerry. See Jári.

Jeṭh. [Hindi.] The name of the month nearly corresponding with June. See Jyeshṭh.

Jethryot. [Hindi, from the Sanskrit *jyeshṭha*, best, and *ryot*, q.v.] A village headman in Behar. He is hereditary and independent of the landowner.

Jewcotte. See Jiwakoṭhi.

Jezail. See Juzail.

Jezia. See Jaziah.

Jhál. Another form of Jáliyá.

Jhálá. The name of a Rájput clan claiming to be a branch of the Solankis; they were formerly settled at Patri and then at Halwad, and give their name to Jhaláwár. In Cutch they are called Makwána.

Jhámpán. A sedan used in travelling in the Himálaya. It is borne by two cross poles, not by a pole in the line of its length, as a palanquin.

Jharaja. See Jáḍeja.

Jharal. [Nepáli.] The goat hemitragus jemlaicus.

Jhil. [Hindi.] A swamp or morass, often in the rains becoming a lake.

Jhinwar. [Hindi.] The name of a caste; they are fishermen and bearers.

Jhirga. See Jirgah.

Jhojhá. [Hindi.] The name of a Muhammadan tribe converted from Hinduism, considered as of base origin, but good cultivators, found in parts of the Doáb and Bundelkhand (*H. H. Wilson*).

Jhul. [Hindustáni.] A horse-cloth.

Jhulá. [Hindi.] A sort of basket suspended between two poles, on which people are swung at festivals; a wooden swinging seat suspended from the ceiling; a hanging cradle pulled horizontally by a cord. Also, in the Panjáb, a rope bridge for crossing rivers; it consists of three ropes, one to walk on and the other two as hand-ropes on either side.

Ji. [Hindi, from the Sanskrit *jaya*, conquering.] A particle of respect added to names and titles, as Raghunáthji, Sáhebji. It also forms the termination of most Pársi names, as Jamsetji, Káwasji; and is used by the Sikhs in the personification of their church as Khálsaji, and of their chief prayer as Japji. It is also used in conversation as equivalent to the English 'sir;' also as the affirmative 'yes.'

Jihád. [Arabic.] Mutual effort, a general effort such as Muhammad preached to exterminate unbelievers; a holy war, a war against infidels. The Sunnis say a jihád should be entered on only when there is probability of success; the Shiahs add that the army must be led by the rightful imám.

Jijman. See Jajmán.

Jilá. The Bengali form of Zilá.

Jilláyat. [Gujaráti, from the Arabic *zila*, a share.] One holding land for military service under a paṭṭáwat, and bearing to him the same relation as the paṭṭáwat bore to the rájá.

Jin. [Sanskrit *jina*, victorious.] A term applied to a chief saint both among Buddhists and Jains. The Jain jin is called also tirthakar and is worshipped as a god.

Jin. [Hindi, from the Arabic.] An evil being, a goblin.

Jineśwar. [Sanskrit, from *jina* and *íśwara*, q.v.] A supreme jin; another name for an arhat.

Jingar. [Maráṭhi, from the Persian *zin*, a saddle.] A class of persons in the Deccan who make saddles and bridles and also little images of Ganpati. Some of them have settled in Mysore, where they retain their native Maráṭhi speech.

Jinjal. [Kanarese *janjáli.*] A small portable piece of ordnance mounted on a swivel.

Jinjira. See Janjirá.

Jinnaswár. The Maráṭhi form of Janaswár.

Jiráit. [Maráṭhi, from the Arabic *zirát*, agriculture.] Land that is cultivated without artificial irrigation as distinguished from bágáit or garden land. From jiráit, as a revenue term, is excluded also rice-land, tari or kyári.

Jiráyat. Another form of Jiráit.

Jirgah. [Pashṭo.] The council of headmen which governs each Afghán tribe.

Jiwagár. [Tamil.] A Buddhist ascetic.

Jiwáidár. [Gujaráti *jiwái*, subsistence allowance, from Sanskrit *jiwa*, life, and Persian *dár*, holder.] A village watchman remunerated by a small grant of land.

Jiwakoṭhi. [Hindi, from *jiwa*, life, and *koṭhi*, a house.] A hospital for outworn or useless animals, a pánjrápol.

Jiyyaru. [Telugu.] The head of the Vaishnawa Bráhmans in the south of India (*H. H. Wilson*).

Jnándewa-panthi. [Hindi *panthi*, a follower, from *panth*, q.v.] A follower of Jnándewa or Jnánoba, a Bráhman of Alandi, near Poona, and supposed to be an incarnation of Vishnu. His views were those of the bhágwadgitá, of which he composed a paraphrase.

Jnán-márg. [Hindi, from the Sanskrit *jnána*, knowledge, and *márga*, a road.] The way of knowledge, the way to salvation through the knowledge that nothing exists but one universal spirit. See Hinduism.

Joar. See Jauhar or Jawár.

Joḍi. [Telugu.] A quit-rent, a small payment made to government on account of land held in inám.

Jog. The Hindi form of Yoga. Also clairvoyance, mesmerism.

Jogi. The Hindi form of Yogi.

Jogi. [Hindi.] The name of a low caste; their primal occupation is weaving, but they occupy themselves in different places in many ways: in parts of Bengal they rear silkworms; in the Sundarbands they are money-lenders; in Kuch Behar they prepare lime from shells and make shell bracelets; in Gujarát they make bags, carry grain on donkeys, and play musical instruments in marriage processions; in Káṭhiáwár they make tape and pads to wear on the head beneath a burden, and are musicians and snake-catchers.

Jográ. [Arakanese.] A sweet fermented liquor made from rice.

Johari. [Maráṭhi, from the Arabic *johar*, a jewel.] A jeweller; a pedlar who buys up old brocade and lace. They are reckoned a distinct caste in the Deccan, whither they have come from Hindustán.

John Company. A slang personification of the authority of the East India Company. When in 1858 the rule of India passed from the Company to the Crown, the same imagination that had created John regarded the queen as his widow and successor.

Joint Magistrate. This term is not now used by the law, but only popularly in Bengal and the North-Western Provinces, to denote the officer who is deputy-collector and who is also a magistrate.

Jokiá. A pastoral tribe in Sindh. They claim to be of Rájput origin, and their aquiline features, courage, and martial bearing certainly tend to support their claims. They are held in high repute, not only in Sindh, but throughout Káṭhiáwár and Gujarát, and even in the nizám's territory, for their courage and fidelity (*Official Report*, 1856).

Jolá. The Bengali form of Julaha.

Jonángi. [Telugu.] Another name for Labbay.

Joodee. See Joḍi.

Joshi. [Hindi, from the Sanskrit *jyotisha.*] An astronomer, an astrologer. The joshi is often a village servant remunerated by inám land. He is a Bráhman by caste, and his duties are to prepare the calendar, cast nativities, and announce the time propitious for any act; he is also the Hindu artist and paints the idols and pictures of the gods. Joshi is also the name, in upper India, of a Bráhman caste, and in the Deccan of a Śudra caste of fortune-tellers.

Jot. [Bengali.] Cultivation, tenure; the holding of a ryot or of a body of co-sharers; a khátá.

Jotdár. [Hindi, Persian *dár*, holder.] A small landholder.

Jotipan. See under Gániga.

Jowaki. A clan of the Afridi tribe. Their country projects into British territory on the north-east of Kohat.

Jowari. See Jawári.

Jowly. [Maráṭhi *jáhwali.*] A branch of a palm tree or a screen made of matted palm leaves to protect windows in stormy weather.

Juang. The name of a wild tribe in the Central Provinces and Orissa; their language is Kolarian. Till lately they wore nothing but leaves.

Juddabillay. See Jaḍebille.

Juggernauth. See Jagannáth.

Jugi. The Assamese form of Jogi (the caste).

Jujman. See Jajmán.

Julaha. [Hindi.] The name of a Muhammadan tribe of weavers.

Julam. A vernacular form of Zulm.

Jum. [Arakanese.] The method of cultivation practised by the hill-men of Chittagong, which consists of clearing the hillside with the dáo, burning the cuttings after they have become dry, and then sowing with mixed seed. Compare Kumari, Dahya.

Jumáh. A cultivator on the jum system. The term is sometimes used to embrace all friendly hill-men, as distinguished from the wilder Kukis.

Jumah. [Hindustáni, from the Arabic.] The Muhammadan Friday, the day of public prayer.

Jumarát. [Hindustáni *jumah*, Friday, and *rát*, from the Sanskrit *rátri*, night.] The Muhammadan Thursday, so called as being the eve of the great day Friday.

Jumiá. Another form of Jumáh.

Jumiá Magh. Another name of the Khyoungthá tribe.

Jummabundy. See Jamábandi.

Jumma-Musjeed. See Jáma-masjid.

Jumptee. See Jampti.

Jungle. [Hindi *jangal*, from the Sanskrit *jangala.*] A wild or uninhabited country, a desert; a forest.

Jungly. [Hindi *jangali.*] Wild, rough, untrained, boorish.

Junwa. See Janeo.

Juptee. See Japti.

Jute. [Bengali *jut.*] The fibre of a plant, corchorus olitorius, used for making mats and gunny-bags.

Jutee. See Jati.

Juttra. A corruption of *jatrá*, which is the Maráṭhi form of Játrá.

Juwár. The Gujaráti form of Jawár.

Juzail. [Pashṭo, corrupt form.] The large heavy rifle, with an iron forked rest, used by Afgháns; it carries generally an ounce ball, which is put into the barrel naked and requires to be hammered a good deal to get it home.

Juzailchi. A man armed with a juzail.

Juzia. See Jaziah.

Jydad. See Jáidád.

Jye. See Jay.

Jyeshṭh. [Sanskrit.] The month nearly corresponding with June; it is so called from *jyaishṭha*, best, the name of the nakshatra (part of the sign Scorpio) in which the moon is at full in this month. See Month.

Jyn. See Jain or Jin.

Jyotisha. [Sanskrit, from *jyotis*, light.] Astronomy. See Vedánga.

Jyzeyeh. See Jaziah.

K.

Kaabah. [Arabic, from *kaab*, a cube.] A square building; especially the small cubical oratory within the temple at Mecca said to have been built by Abraham and Ishmael, and which was made by Muhammad the kiblah for all his followers all over the world. The kaabah is the object of the haj.

Kábá. [Maráṭhi.] A description of people to the north of the Maráṭha provinces, said to be a piratical tribe in the Gulf of Cutch (*H. H. Wilson*).

Kabábi. A term used by Indian servants for a very large fowl. Compare Kharcha.

Kabála. [Hindustáni.] A deed of conveyance, a written stipulation.

Kábiráj. [Bengali.] A physician; he is generally of the Vaidya caste.

Kabir-panthi. [Hindi *panthi*, a follower, from *panth*, q.v.] Followers of Kabir, a Vaishnawa sect. Kabir, the weaver, was one of twelve reputed disciples of Rámánanda, and (the name being Arabic) is supposed by some to have been originally a Muhammadan. He flourished in the fifteenth century. His books contain many anti-polytheistic, anti-idolatrous, and anti-caste passages, but they are often very parabolic and mystical. They have procured for him a great many followers from all castes of Hindus who have really some claim to the character of reformers (*J. Wilson*). Kabir promulgated a high moral code, declaring that life was a sacred gift of God, and that the blood of men or animals ought never to be shed by his creatures. He laid great stress on truthfulness (*Monier Williams*).

Kabob. [Persian *kabáb.*] Small pieces of meat roasted on a skewer and highly seasoned with assafœtida and garlic.

Kabulát. The Maráṭhi form of Kabuliyat.

Kábuli. [Hindustáni.] Relating to Kábul, the capital of Afghánistán. Afghán settlers from Kábul are known by this name. They are Sunnis, and form to a great extent a distinct community, marrying only among themselves. Horse-dealing is their chief employment.

Kabuliyat. [Hindi, from the Arabic *qabul*, consent.] A written agreement, but especially a one-sided one, a written promise; the counterpart of a paṭṭá.

Káchá. The Gujaráti form of Kachchá.

Kachahri. [Hindi.] A court, a public office.

Kachár. [Hindi.] Low-lying land that can be easily irrigated.

Káchári. The name of a tribe who have given their name to the district of Káchár, but the great majority of whom are found in the Brahmaputra valley of Assam, where they were once dominant; they remain in a state of primitive barbarism, except one class, called Barman, which has adopted Hinduism.

Kácháru. [Bengali, from the Sanskrit *kácha*, glass.] The name of a low caste whose occupation is making glass.

Kachchá. [Hindi.] Unripe, raw; rough, unfinished; the opposite of pakká. Thus a well which is merely dug and not lined with brickwork is called kachchá; so is a house made of mud or unbaked bricks; so is a person deficient in skill and experience; and when there are different measures or weights of the same name, the smaller is distinguished as kachchá.

Kacheli. [Telugu.] A court, a public office.

Kacheri. [Maráṭhi.] A court, a public office.

Káchhi. [Hindi.] The name of a caste; they are cultivators and especially market-gardeners.

Káchhiá. The Gujaráti form of Káchhi; they are divided into two branches, called Pádariá and Sagáriá Káchhiás.

Kachhwáhá. The name of a tribe of Rájputs usually called of the solar race; they derive their name from Kasha, a son of Ráma, but Kachhapagháta, tortoise-killer, has been suggested as the probable origin, the race being mentioned by that name in old inscriptions. The Kachhwáhás formerly ruled at Gwalior and still rule at Jáipur; they are numerous in the Jáipur state and in Alwar.

Kachin. The name of a Burmese tribe, called also Singpho. They are a turbulent, quarrelsome race, apparently; and, though small in stature and utterly devoid of any civilization but what is implied by a rudimentary knowledge of agriculture and metallurgy, they are yet hardy and, at all events in their vendettas, persevering (*R. H. Pilcher*).

Kádala. Another name of the Botwa tribe.

Kadambá. The name of a royal line ruling in the west of Mysore and in Kanara at the commencement of the Christian era. In the fifth century they were reduced by the Chálukyas to the condition of feudatories.

Kadapá. [Telugu.] The counterpart of a revenue lease; a kabuliyat.

Kaḍata. [Kanarese.] A cloth covered with a composition of charcoal and gum, and used instead of a slate for writing (*D. Sanderson*).

Kaḍiá. [Gujaráti.] The name of a caste; they are bricklayers and chunam-workers. There is a distinct community of Sunni Musalmán converts from this caste.

Kadmi. The name of that division of the Pársis who reformed their calendar when a priest named Jamasp, arriving from Persia, pointed out that a month had been lost in the Pársi reckoning. The Kadmi year thus begins a month earlier than the Śehersai or Rasami.

Káḍu. [Kanarese.] A thicket, a forest. Another name of the Beṭṭa Kurubas. They have rather high and prominent cheek-bones, a short and flat nose, large lips, small, dark, deep-set eyes, and curly hair which through neglect becomes matted. They are middle-sized, well-proportioned, nimble, and enduring. They excel in making mats, baskets, umbrellas, and boxes and cradles of bamboo and cane (*L. Rice*).

Kaesta. See Káyasth.

Kaffir. See Káfir.

Káfilah. [Arabic.] A caravan. Merchants from Khelat and Kandahár enter India with káfilahs of camels bearing their merchandise.

Káfir. [Arabic.] An unbeliever, one who does not accept the teaching of Muhammad. In western India the word is a common term of abuse. Káfir is also the name, among themselves as well as with their Muhammadan neighbours, of a tribe inhabiting the mountain region north-east of Kábul, the angle between the Hindu Kush and the western Himálayas, called after them Káfiristán. The origin of this tribe is uncertain. Some say they are descended from Greek soldiers left behind by Alexander, others that they are of Persian descent. Their language is Aryan; writing is unknown among them. The Chinese pilgrim Sung Yun speaks of them as Buddhists in the sixth century A.D., and as suffering persecution under the Tartars. They have now an intense hatred of all Musalmáns, and think it very creditable to slay any of that religion. The Káfirs neither bury nor burn their dead, but expose them on the top of a hill. They sacrifice cows and goats to their god Doghán.

Káfiri. The language of the Káfirs; it is an Aryan language.

Kághazi. [Hindustáni, from the Arabic *kághaz*, paper.] A paper-maker; the name of a class of Sunni Musalmáns who make paper. They are a distinct body, marrying only among themselves. Also the name of a kind of pottery made at Tánk, and so called from its very thin consistency.

Kahár. [Bengali.] The name of a

low caste belonging chiefly to Behar; they are partly agricultural, but are principally employed in domestic service and as palanquin-bearers. They are divided into Rawáni and Kharwárá Kahárs.

Kaibartta. [Bengali form of the Sanskrit *kaiwarta*, a fisherman.] The name of a numerous Śudra caste in the Bengal presidency. They are divided into Jáliá Kaibartta, who are still fishermen and despised as a low caste, and Chásá Kaibartta, who have taken to agriculture and hold a middle rank.

Kaidu. See Kedu.

Kaifiyat. [Hindi.] Statement, description; especially a statement of facts which cannot be disposed of by the ordinary routine, but require the special decision of a superior officer.

Kaikári. A wandering tribe of the southern Maráṭhá country. They have, like the Lambánis, a bad reputation for thieving.

Kaikola. [Telugu.] The name of a caste; they are weavers.

Kailása. [Sanskrit.] The heaven of Śiwa and of Kubera. See Swarga. The name is given to a particular rock-cut temple at Ellora.

Kailmurta. [Koḍagu.] A festival held on a day fixed by the astrologer after the heavy work of ploughing and sowing is over and there is a lull in the monsoon. The holiday is devoted to athletic games and hunting.

Kaimaṭṭa. [Koḍagu.] A small building, erected near a Koḍaga's house, for the use of the ghosts of his ancestors. Figures of the káranas in metal or stone are placed inside, and offerings of food are made on special occasions.

Káimkháni. The name of a class of Muhammadans in Rájputáná, who are converts from the Chauhán clan.

Kaisar-i-Hind. [Persian *kaisar*, the Latin Cæsar and Greek Kaisar; *i*, of, and *Hind*, India.] Emperor or Empress of India; a title assumed by the Queen of England in 1876.

Kaista. See Káyasth.

Káit. The Bengali form of Káyasth.

Kaivert. See Kaibartta.

Kájal. [Hindi, Sanskrit *kajjala*.] Lampblack considered as a collyrium, and applied by Hindus to the eyelids medicinally or to avert the evil eye. See Nazar, Surmá.

Kájári. The Maráṭhi form of Kácháru.

Kákar. The name of a Paṭhán tribe occupying territory between 67° 30′ and 70° E. long., 30° 10′ and 30° 30′ N. lat.; they are nominal subjects of Kábul, and are always at feud with the Maris and other Biluch tribes; they number about 14,000 fighting men. The Kákars are divided into seven clans quite independent of one another. They are both agricultural and pastoral and also engage in trade.

Kákhyan. The name of a Burmese tribe.

Kala. [Kanarese.] A threshing-floor, a place where grain is beaten or trodden out of the husk.

Kalachurya. The name of a dynasty that ruled over the province of Kalyán (now part of the nizám's dominions); they were reduced by the Chálukyas in the fifth century, but again subverted the latter in the twelfth. Their restoration was for but a short time, and their territories were absorbed by the Hoysala Ballálas and the Yádawas as those dynasties became powerful.

Kalaigar. [Hindi, from *kalai*, tin, and the affix *gar*, agent.] A tinman; one who coats copper vessels with tin.

Kalál. [Hindi, from the Sanskrit *kalyapála*, a distiller.] The name of a low caste; they distil and sell spirits. Many of them are now Muhammadans.

Kalálkhánah. [Persian *khánah*, a house.] A liquor-shop or a distillery.

Kalam. [Hindi, Sanskrit *kalama*: compare the Arabic *qalm*, and the Greek *kalamos*.] A reed used for writing with. The kalam is cut with a broad undivided nib, which will freely pass over paper in the due line of its length as well as in any other direction, and thus allows those greater extremes of broad and narrow lines which both the Arabic and the Dewanágari characters require for their perfect delineation. Kalam is also the word used for paragraph. And tázá kalam, or fresh pen, means a postscript.

Kalamdán. [Hindi *kalam*, and the Persian *dán*, a receptacle.] A stand for holding kalams, ink, and sand.

Kalán. [Persian.] Great. Kalán and khurd are added to the names of neighbouring places of the same name to distinguish them, as Dhaka Kalán, Dhaka Khurd.

Kalandar. [Hindustáni, from the Arabic.] The name of a community of beshara Sunni fakirs. They shave the whole body, including the eyebrows.

Kálápáni. [Bengali *kálá*, black, *páni*, water.] The sea; transportation beyond sea.

Kalár. Another form of Kalál.

Kalasi. See Khalási.

Kalatri. [Sindhi.] The headman of a caste or trade.

Kaláwant. [Hindi, from the Sanskrit *kalá*, an art.] One who is skilled; a singer or dancer.

Kaláwantin. [Hindi.] A female kaláwant, a dancing-girl, a courtesan.

Kálesingh. Another name of Nársingh.

Kalhora. The name of a Muhammadan dynasty that ruled in Sindh previously to the Tálpurs, by whom they were succeeded in 1783 A.D.

Kali. [Sanskrit.] The name of the last and worst of the four yugas, the present iron age, considered to have begun on the 18th February, 3102 B.C., and to last 432,000 years.

Káli. [Sanskrit.] A goddess, the wife of Śiwa, so called from Śiwa's epithet of *kála*, black.

Kálibhoy, or Kálibhui. [Hindi *káli*, black, and *bhoy* or *bhui*, earth.] The common black alluvial soil of Gujarát. Its principal crops are juwár, cotton, rice, and wheat. See Regur.

Kalimah. [Arabic.] The Muhammadan confession of faith: 'There is but one God, and Muhammad is the prophet of God.' The Shiahs add, 'Ali is the caliph of God.'

Kalingu. [Tamil.] A dam, a stone bank or dyke, a sluice.

Káliparaj. [Gujaráti, from *kála*, black, and *paraj*, probably a corruption of *parat* or *prat*, signifying class, kind.] A general name for certain tribes of darker colour than, and reckoned inferior to, the Kanbis and the general cultivating classes, who are contradistinguished as the Ujliparaj, or fair people. The Káliparaj are settled chiefly by themselves in the poorer soils; they are a simple people, with few faults except fondness for liquor. Many have learnt to read and write, and some officiate as paṭels and schoolmasters in their own villages. The Káliparaj include the Chodhri, Gámit, Konkona, Donḍiá, and Náiká tribes.

Kalita. More commonly Kulta.

Kálive. [Kanarese.] A channel by which water is drawn from above an anicut for irrigating the lands below.

Kalki. [Sanskrit.] The name of Vishnu in his tenth and last awatár, which is to take place at the end of the present, or kali, age, when he will destroy the wicked and inaugurate a new age of purity. The Sikhs represent Kalki as having already come, and as having been destroyed by the Musalmán mahdi.

Kallan. [Tamil.] The name of a tribe formerly predatory, now agricultural. Their favourite weapon was the boomerang. They call themselves Śaiwas, but worship chiefly peculiar deities of their own, and have adopted little of Hinduism. They consider marriages between first cousins and other near relations the most appropriate. They allow polyandry, divorce, and the remarriage of widows. In Ceylon they are chiefly coolies.

Kallar rori. [Panjábi.] A substance of the nature of ammonia found among old ruins; just before sunrise it is seen to glisten on the ground, and is immediately swept up and spread as a top-dressing over wheat crops; it is found of great efficacy in counteracting the effect of brackish water (*D. Ross*).

Kallaru. A plural form of Kallan.

Kallukuṭika. [Kanarese, from *kallu*, stone, and Sanskrit *kuṭṭ*, to cut.] A stonemason; one of the subdivisions of the Pánchála.

Kalpa. [Sanskrit.] Literally, practicable, possible; the name of one of the vedángas. Also a fabulous period of time, 1000 yugas or 432,000,000 years. At the end of each kalpa the world is annihilated; hence kalpa means also the destruction of the world.

Kalpadruma, Kalpataru, or Kalpavriksha. [Sanskrit.] A fabulous tree that can satisfy all desires.

Kaltar. [Gujaráti.] The appraisement of the crops under the bhágbaṭái revenue system. It was the duty of the táluká officers, with the aid of the matádárs and taláṭi, to make the kaltar from the appearance of the crop as it was growing. If the cultivator agreed to the kaltar made, the assessment was complete; but if he did not, it was necessary to set a guard upon the crop and determine the government share by actual measurement when the crop was reaped.

Kalu. [Bengali.] The name of a low caste; they express and sell oil.

Kalwár. Another form of Kalál.

Kamál. [Arabic.] Entire, perfect, complete; as a revenue term, the total assessment before any reduction, allowance, or remission is made.

Kamáliá. [Gujaráti.] A class of persons who profess islám, but nevertheless worship Bahucharáji, and serve as musicians in her temples, and receive a portion of the revenues, and also wander about with Pavais.

Kamángar. The name of a class of Musalmáns who make shields out of rhinoceros and elephant hides which they import from Zanzibar.

Kámár. [Bengali form of the Sanskrit *karmakára*, a blacksmith.] The name of a caste; they are blacksmiths, but some have of late taken to work in gold and silver. They are deemed a high caste among Śudras.

Kamarband. [Hindi, from *kamar*, the loins, and *band*, to bind.] A shawl or cloth worn round the waist.

Kamarkusa. [Pashṭo.] The Afghán soldier's ammunition-pouch.

Kamarpaṭia. [Hindi, from *kamar*, the loins, and *paṭṭa*, q.v.] The name of a small sect of Hindus founded in the Central Provinces in 1864; they are ascetics, and wear nothing but a bark rope round the waist.

Kámárthi. [Hindi.] A person who carries the water of the Ganges to distant places in vessels cased in basket-work (*H. H. Wilson*).

Kámat. [Hindi.] Lands held by a non-resident tenant. The word seems to be identical with the kamata of the south; those lands which the zamindár has upon his own hands are those which he would employ outsiders to cultivate. See Páhi, Parakuḍi.

Kamata. [Telugu.] Land which a zamindár or other proprietor has cultivated by his own labourers or by tenants-at-will, as distinguished from the land in possession of his hereditary tenants. See Kámat, Pannai, Parakuḍi, Ulkuḍi.

Kámáṭhi. The name of a caste, numerous in the city of Bombay, and found also in the Deccan and Kanara, but whose vernacular is Telugu; they are an industrious class, engaged in household, outdoor, factory, and building work, also as shop-keepers, rice-cleaners, corn-grinders, and lascars.

Kamávisdár. [Maráṭhi, from the Sanskrit *karmma*, work, *visá*, to engage, and the Persian *dár*, who holds.] A manager; especially the head officer of a district; often under the Maráṭhá government he was merely a farmer of the revenue and not resident in his district. Later, the head officer of a táluká, a mámlatdár.

Kambam. [Malayálam, the Sanskrit *kumbha*, a water-pot.] The name of the month during which the sun is in the sign Aquarius, corresponding most nearly to February and Mágh (in Bengal, Phálgun). See Month.

Kamboh. The name of a cultivating

caste in the Panjáb; they are as industrious and skilful as the Aráins, whom they generally resemble. A good many Kambohs have adopted sikhism and a few islám. There is a branch of them devoted, not to agriculture, but to military, mercantile, and clerkly pursuits.

Kambu. The Telugu name of the cereal panicum spicatum. See Bájri.

Kamdar. [Uriya, from the Persian *kam*, less, and *dar*, rate.] Land of inferior quality.

Kámdár. [Hindustáni, from *kám*, work, and *dár*, holder.] A man of business, a steward, an agent.

Kami. The name of one clan of a tribe consisting of two clans, the other being the Kumi.

Kamiá. [Hindi.] An agricultural labourer of low class, a harwáhá.

Kámil. Another form of Kamál.

Kamin. [Hindi, from the Persian *kam*, little, less.] Inferior; applied in the North-West Provinces to the artificers and servants of a village, who, besides allowances of grain, receive small allotments of land, and are therefore minor or inferior cultivators (*H. H. Wilson*).

Kamli. [Hindi, from the Sanskrit *kambala*.] A coarse woollen blanket or wrapper.

Kammálan. [Tamil.] The caste of artificers corresponding to the Kanarese Pánchála. The Tamil names of the five classes are Taṭṭán, Tajen, Karumán, Kaltajen, and Kannan.

Kammára. [Kanarese.] A blacksmith. See Pánchála.

Kammari. The Telugu form of Kámár or Kammára.

Kammawan. [Telugu.] The name of a caste; they are a division of the Toṭṭiyans.

Kana. A geometrical design worked in dry colours on the threshold of a dwelling-house.

Kánaḍá. [Kanarese, the Sanskrit *karnáṭa*.] The ancient name of the central districts of the Indian peninsula, and the name of the language of that region, or Kanarese. In later times the name, under the corrupt form Carnatic, has been transferred to a coast district. Kánaḍá is also the name of a peculiar race of drovers, probably of Dravidian origin. Their pastures are in the north-west corner of the Deccan. They are more civilized and respectable than most wandering herdsmen, and in parts of Násik they have taken entirely to agriculture. They have a peculiar breed of black-and-white cattle, called hatkar, which, though not large, are much prized for their strength and spirit. Krishna is their favourite god.

Kanaka. [Kanarese.] The name of one of the Badaga castes; they are accountants, physicians, and exorcists.

Kanakku-pillai. [Tamil *kanakku*, account, *pillai*, son.] A village accountant.

Kánam. [Malayálam.] The thing or consideration for which a mortgage or pledge is given.

Kanarese. [An English formation from *kánaḍá*.] A Dravidian language spoken by about nine millions of persons in Kanara, Mysore, and the southern part of the Bombay presidency. It is closely allied to Telugu and uses almost the same characters.

Kanát. [Arabic.] The walls of a tent.

Kanauji. The language of the central Doáb; it holds a middle place between High Hindi and Brajbhákhá (*C. J. Lyall*).

Kanaujiá. The Hindi form of Kanyakubja.

Kanbi. [Gujaráti.] The name of an agricultural caste, identical with the Kurmis of Hindustán and the Kunbis of the Deccan. The Kanbis of Gujarát are divided into three sections, called Lewá, Kaḍwá, and Ánjná, which do not intermarry; and besides these are the Matiá Kanbis, who have been half converted to islám.

Kanchani. [Hindustáni.] A Muhammadan dancing-girl.

Kanchari. [Maráṭhi.] The name of a caste; they are workers in glass and crystal.

Kanchugár. [Kanarese, from *kanchu*, the Sanskrit *kánsya*, mixed metal, and *gár*, worker.] A worker in mixed metal. See Pánchála.

Kandáchára. [Kanarese.] An armed peon, a militia soldier.

Kandárá. [Uriya.] The name of a semi-Hinduised tribe of Orissa; they are fishermen, labourers, cultivators, salt-makers, and village watchmen.

Kandh. The name of a Dravidian tribe occupying the hills to the west and north-west of Orissa. There are 73,000 of them in Kalahundi alone. They are chiefly husbandmen and hunters, and have no trade. They live in villages of well-built huts of timber and mud thatched with grass. They eat animal food when they can get it, and are prone to intoxication. They have many deities, the chief one being the earth-god, to whom human sacrifices used to be made. See Meria. The Kandhs are ruled by their headmen, manjhis, and councils of elders. They use oaths and ordeals.

Kandi. More commonly Candy.

Kandi. The Telugu name of Arhar.

Kandoi. [Gujaráti, perhaps from the Arabic *kand*, sugar.] A seller of sweetmeats, a confectioner.

Kándu. [Bengali, from the Sanskrit *kandu*, an oven.] The name of a Śudra caste of middle rank; they prepare the parched rice which Hindus eat when travelling and unable to procure a cooked meal. They also build mud walls, sow gunny-cloth into bags, dig, and thatch.

Kándur. The cowry snake, the daboia elegans. It is a viperine snake and very venomous, the bite being usually, if not always, fatal; it is from three to five feet long, of thick build and with a decided distinction between body and tail; it is of a rich brown colour, conspicuously marked with three rows of darker cowry-shaped rings edged with white; it is rather sluggish.

Kanet. [Panjábi.] A low cultivating class at the base of the Himálayas; they are divided into two branches called Khasia and Ráo; the former wear the janeo and the latter do not.

Káng, or **Kangni.** [Hindi, from the Sanskrit *kangu.*] The cereal panicum italicum. Other names of it are kora, navane, tene.

Kángu. [Telugu.] Coarse blue cotton cloth.

Kani. [Malayálam, the Sanskrit *kanya*, a virgin.] The month during which the sun is in Virgo, coinciding most nearly with September and Bhádrapad. See Month.

Kánikáran. [Tamil.] An hereditary proprietor or hereditary coparcener in village lands held in common (*H. H. Wilson*).

Kaniya. [Koḍagu.] The name of a class of mendicants and conjurers in Coorg, said to be the descendants of a Malayálam Bráhman and a low-caste woman.

Kániyáṭchi. [Tamil, from *káni*, property, and *áṭchi*, power.] That which is held in free and hereditary property; mirási.

Kanjar. [Hindi.] The name of a wandering class; they make strings of hemp and cotton.

Kánji. [Sanskrit.] Rice-water; gruel; starch.

Kankar. [Hindi, from the Sanskrit *kana*, a piece.] A coarse kind of limestone; gravel: the smaller kind is much used in road-making.

Kankari. [Another form of *kankar.*] Gravel.

Kanku. [Gujaráti, from the Sanskrit *kunkuma*, the saffron plant.] A red powder composed of turmeric, borax, and other ingredients, and used for marking persons and things by way of good omen and as an expression of rejoicing. See Chándlá, Holi, Kunku.

Kankut. [Hindi.] The appraisement of standing crops; kaltar.

Kannaḍa. See Kanarese.

Kánphaṭá. [From *kán*, ear, and *phaṭ*, split.] The name of an order of mendicants whose head-quarters are at Gorakhmadi, in Káṭhiáwár, and who worship Gorakhnáth, the guru of Rukmibai the wife of Krishna. Kánphaṭás are so called from the practice at initiation of slitting open both the ears. They wear large metal ear-rings, which they consider the symbol and stay of their faith, and the loss of which they will not survive. The Kánphaṭás are under vows of celibacy, with the exception of their báwá, or head, who marries to keep up the succession. They are under no restraint in matters of food, excepting the cow, which is held sacred, and the hog, which is unclean. It is part of their code to receive travellers hospitably (*G. Le G. Jacob*).

Kans. See Káśa.

Kansa. [Sanskrit.] The name of a king of Mathurá, slain by Krishna, and treated in later times as a demon capable of assuming any form.

Kansáli. [Telugu.] The name of a caste; they are workers in the precious metals, and are one of the chief left-hand castes at Madras.

Kánsár [Maráṭhi,] **Kansárá** [Gujaráti], **Kánsári** [Bengali; all from the Sanskrit *kansya*, a mixture of copper and zinc or of copper and tin]. The name of a high Śudra caste; they are workers in brass and bell-metal, and cover copper vessels with tin. See Panchál.

Kántári. [Maráṭhi, from *kát*, to turn.] The name of a caste in the Konkan. They work with the lathe in wood and ivory.

Kánungo. [Hindustáni, from the Arabic *qánun*, a rule, and the Persian *go*, who speaks.] An expounder of the laws, but applied in Hindustán especially to village and district revenue officers.

Kanwa. The name of a Buddhist dynasty considered to have succeeded the Sungas, and to have reigned till 31 B.C.

Kanwar. The name of a non-Aryan hill tribe in the Central Provinces; they worship the sword.

Kanyakubja. [Sanskrit, from *kanyá*, a virgin, and *kubja*, crooked.] The ancient name of Kanauj. Also the name of the first subdivision of the Gauḍa Bráhmans; they are again divided into the Sarjupári, or Sarwaria, the Jijhautia, the Sanauḍhiya, and the Bhuinhár.

Káorá. [Bengali.] The name of a low caste; they are swine-keepers.

Kápaḍi. [Gujaráti.] A devotee of the temple of Áshápura Mátá at Madh, fifty miles from Bhuj; they do not marry, but recruit chiefly from the Loháná caste; their high priest is called rájá. Also the name of a class of mendicants in the Deccan who go about with a red flag, selling rosaries, janeos, etc.

Kápála. The name of a small class of persons supposed to be descendants of the Sidi body-guard of the Coorg rájás; they possess landed property which was given by the rájás, and also work as day-labourers with the Koḍagas (*L. Rice*).

Kapáli. [Bengali.] The name of a low caste; they spin jute and cotton and weave sackcloth.

Kapar. The Sindhi name of the fursá snake.

Kapás. [Gujaráti, from the Sanskrit *karpása*.] The cotton plant, gossypium herbaceum; also raw cotton. It is a kharif crop.

Kapásiá. [Gujaráti, from *kapás*.] Cotton seed.

Kápu. [Telugu.] A cultivator, a ryot; sometimes used for reḍḍi, or headman.

Karai. [Tamil.] A share. A karai village is one divided into shares, which are or ought to be periodically reallotted. Compare Bhágdári.

Kárakat. [Tamil.] A branch of the Vellálans living on the Palani mountains, less strict than most of the Vellálans, and associating with the Kunnuvans.

Karáliá. [Gujaráti.] The name of a class of Sunni Musalmáns converted from the Kumbhár caste. They sell, but do not make, pots; they work also as labourers and house-servants. They intermarry with the Kaṭhiárás.

Karambu. [Tamil.] Waste or uncultivated land.

Karan. [Sanskrit *karana*, from *kri*, to do.] The name of a caste in Orissa; they are writers, and correspond to the Káyasths of Bengal. Some Karans are cultivators.

Kárana. [Kanarese.] A hero, the head of a family; also the spirit of an ancestor. To ascertain the wishes of a kárana, a ceremony called kárana kola is performed, in which the spirit is represented by a living person, who dances and sings and is supposed to become possessed by the spirit.

Karáni. [Hindustáni form of *karan*, q.v.] A clerk, a scribe. The word, sometimes corrupted into *cranny*, is used to denote the whole class of writers or their profession.

Karáo. [Hindi.] The practice of marrying a widow to her deceased husband's younger brother; it is common among the Ját, Gujar, and Áhir tribes. The same practice is known in different parts as urhari, bathi, and dharichá.

Káratiá. The name of a class of Bráhmans who assist in funeral obsequies of other than Bráhman castes.

Karbala. The meeting-place of the táziahs at the Muharram festival, so called after Karbala, in Turkish Arabia, the burial-place of Husain.

Kárbári, or **Kárbhári.** [Hindi, from the Persian *kár*, Sanskrit *kárya*, business, and the Persian *bár*, or Sanskrit *bhára*, a burden.] A minister, an agent; particularly a native ruler's ministers.

Karbi. [Gujaráti *kaḍbi.*] The stalks of jawár or other grain, used as fodder.

Karḍá. [Maráṭhi.] A cultivator under a khot. A karḍá holds an intermediate position between that of a dhárekari and that of a bádhekari.

Kárdár. [Sindhi, from the Sanskrit *kárya*, business, and the Persian *dár*, holder.] An agent; the title of a former revenue and magisterial officer, since replaced by the mukhtyárkár; also the title of an officer under the Sikh government.

Karḍi. [Maráṭhi.] An annual plant, the carthamus tinctorius, or safflower. Oil is extracted from the seed and the flowers are used as a dye.

Karen. The name of a group of several hill tribes of Burma, speaking many distinct dialects, but all monosyllabic and tonic. They are considered to be later immigrants than the Mrammá, Talaing, or Shan tribes. They cultivate on the jum system. Some of the principal tribes are the Sgaw, Pwo, and Bweh Karens.

Karenni. A division of the Karen, sometimes called the Red Karens.

Karewa. See Karáo.

Kárez. [Persian.] A watercourse, especially one constructed for irrigation underneath the surface of the ground.

Karháḍá. [Maráṭhi.] The name of a subdivision of the Mahárásḥṭra Bráhmans; they are most numerous in the Ratnágiri district; they engage much in trade; many enter the civil service, and some are khots of villages.

Kari. [Maráṭhi, from *kar*, Sanskrit *kri*, to do.] An affix to nouns, implying, like *wálá*, master, doer, dealer in, bearer of, belonging to; as *ghar-kari*, master of the house; *kápad-kari*, dealer in cloth; *paṭṭekari*, a paṭáwálá, a messenger wearing a belt.

Karikallu. [Kanarese.] Slabs of stone set up at the foundation of a village. They are generally painted in broad vertical stripes of red and white, and are objects of worship. All the cattle of the village are presented before them annually as a means of averting the cattle disease (*L. Rice*).

Karinda. [Hindustáni *karandah.*] An agent, a clerk, a manager.

Karisal. [Tamil.] Punjey black soil of the first quality.

Karkatagam. [Malayálam, the Sanskrit *karka*, a crab.] The month during which the sun is in Cancer, coinciding most nearly with July and Áshádh (in Bengal, Śrában). See Month.

Kárkhánah. [Hindustáni, from the Persian *kár*, work, and *khánah*, a house.] A workshop, a manufactory.

Kárkun. [Hindustáni, from the Persian *kár*, work, and *kun*, making.] A clerk, a writer. The word is usually confined to writers in the vernacular as distinguished from English-writing clerks.

Karm-márg. [Hindi, from the Sanskrit *karma*, work, and *márga*, a way.] The way of works, the way to salvation through the efficacy of rites, ceremonies, and virtuous actions. See Hinduism.

Karnam. [Telugu.] A village accountant. In Mysore the office is hereditary. See Village accountant.

Karnáṭa. [Sanskrit.] The name of a country, not the English Karnatic, but the central part of the peninsula, including Mysore, the district of the Kanarese language; thence the name of the subdivision of Dráviḍa Bráhmans residing there.

Karniji. The name of a goddess much worshipped in Bikaner; she is the devi or spirit of a Cháran woman whose supernatural power secured the country to Bika the Ráṭhor.

Kartá. [Sanskrit, from *kri*, to do.] A maker; an epithet of Brahmá, Vishnu, and of Śiwa; any agent; especially the member of an undivided family who manages the family property; he is usually the eldest man of the eldest branch.

Kártik. [Sanskrit *kárttika*, from *krittika*, the Pleiades.] The Hindu month most nearly coincident with November. See Month.

Kárttikeya. [Sanskrit.] The name of the god of war, the son of Śiwa. He is fabled to have been reared by the Pleiades, the nakshatra from which the month Kártik, the first suitable after the rains for military operations, is named. The god is otherwise called Skanda.

Karu. [Malayálam.] A stake for impaling criminals.

Káru. [Kanarese.] The rainy season; warsha; the kharif crops.

Karwant. [Maráṭhi.] The name of a small sect of Bráhmans found at Alibág and a few other places in that district. They have grown rich by money-lending, and some of them have therefore been allowed to intermarry with Chitpáwans.

Káśa. [Sanskrit.] The grass saccharum spontaneum; it grows to a height of six or eight feet and has a white feathery head. It is used for making mats, ropes, and roofs.

Kasab. [Gujaráti, from the Arabic, in which the word means business, art, skill.] Cloth woven of silk and gold or silver thread.

Kasáb. Another form of Kasái.

Kasái. [Hindustáni.] A butcher. Kasáis are a distinct class, marrying only among themselves. They are Sunni Musalmáns.

Kasár. The Hindi form of Kánsár.

Kasarwáni. The name of a trading caste in Bengal.

Kasbah. [Hindustáni, from the Arabic.] A small town, especially the head-quarter town of a mahál or parganá.

Kasbáti. [Hindustáni, from *kasbah*, a town.] The owner of a town; the name of a class of Sunni Musalmáns in northern Gujarát who hold large grants of land. They are of several classes—Náiks, Bhaṭṭis, Menás, Rehens, and Parmárs, and are descended partly from Biluch and Paṭhán mercenaries, and partly from converted Rájputs. They sometimes take Hindu wives, but give their daughters only to Musalmáns. They used to command the services of a number of horsemen, whom they let out to states requiring them.

Kásdár. [Corruption of *qaezah*, a cleaning rein, and *dár*, holder.] A groom.

Káshi. [Panjábi, perhaps a shortened form of *nakáshi*, from the Arabic *nakshah*, a picture.] A system of fresco painting used in the time of Sháh Jahán, especially at Lahore, where there was no marble with which to face the brickwork in the ordinary Saracenic manner.

Kásid. [Arabic.] A courier, a messenger.

Kaskas. See Khaskhas.

Kásmiri. The language of Cashmere; it is of the Aryan family.

Kassibeh. See Kasbah.

Kástá. [Bengali.] The name of a low caste; they are cultivators and labourers.

Kasti. [Gujaráti.] A cincture of woollen cord, which all Pársis, women as well as men, wear round the waist as a religious emblem.

Kasturi Manjal. A kind of wild turmeric which has a smell somewhat resembling musk. It is mixed with the powder of sandal-wood, with which Hindu women of rank rub their skins (*Buchanan*).

Kásu. [Telugu.] A small copper coin of which sixty-four make a rupee. In Tamil the word is used for coin or money in general.

Kasumbá. Another form of Kusumbha.

Kát. [Maráṭhi.] A gummy resin extracted from the khair and some other trees. It is the substance called catechu, cutch, or terra japonica. The Kátkaris in the Konkan, and hill tribes in other parts of India, extract it. It is used in making mortar. It is also eaten with the betel leaf and areca nut, and is astringent in its action.

Kaṭai. [Maráṭhi.] The name of a small caste of workers in leather.

Kataki. [Assamese.] The name of a caste; they were employed by the Aham dynasty as ambassadors, and are still used for communication between government officials and the independent tribes, but most of them have now taken to agriculture.

Káṭama Ráya. [Kanarese.] The name of a sylvan god worshipped under the form of an acute conical mound of mud, erected on a circular base also of mud (*L. Rice*).

Kataoni. The Tamil form of Khatauni.

Kathak. [Bengali, from the Sanskrit *kathá*, a story.] A professional story-teller, a reciter of traditional poems.

Káṭhi. The name of a tribe inhabiting the central part of the Gujarát peninsula, which is now after them called Káṭhiawár, or, corruptly, Kattywar. They were formerly a marauding race, and trained a hardy breed of horses to aid them in their excursions. Dr. Hore, who travelled in Gujarát in 1787, describes how all the villages on the borders of Káṭhiáwár were surrounded by mud walls with loopholes for musketry, and had each a high observatory, in which watch was kept night and day, and from which a gun was fired on the approach of the Káṭhis, as a signal to the villagers to drive in their cattle. And he was told that the cattle themselves had so much experience of this that they also understood the signal.

Kaṭhiárá. [Gujaráti.] A wood-cutter; the name of a class of Sunni Musalmáns. They intermarry with Karáliás.

Káthuriyá, or **Káṭhuyá.** [Bengali, from the Sanskrit *káshṭha*, timber.] A wood-cutter, a wood-seller.

Kátkari. [Maráṭhi.] An aboriginal tribe found in the Konkan. They have a tradition that they are descended from the wild tribe—called in the legend monkeys—which Ráma took as allies in his expedition against Ceylon. It is perhaps in accordance with this that they say the brown-faced monkey has a human soul, and that they will not eat it, though they do eat other monkeys, and almost all other animals except the cow. The Kátkaris are a small, hardy race, of dark complexion and with very low foreheads. The men wear shendis like the Hindus, but do not use turbans. The women are more on an equality with the men than is the case among Hindus, and marriage takes place at the adult age, not in childhood. The name Kátkari is derived from *kát*, catechu, which these people extract from the khair tree. Kátkaris also cultivate land on the slopes of the hills, cut firewood, and make charcoal. They also eke out their living by thieving, especially from the government salt-fields (*W. M. Hearn*).

Katkhudá. [Persian.] The head of a family; sometimes applied to a village headman.

Katodi. Another name for Kátkari.

Kaṭora. [Hindi.] A semi-spherical dish, a bowl.

Katra. [Hindi.] A market-place, a suburb.

Kaṭṭe. [Kanarese.] A basin or small pond, a tank; a basin round the trunk of a tree for irrigation. Also a dam, a dike.

Katti. [Kanarese.] A knife, a sword, especially that used by toddy-drawers.

Katti. See Káṭhi.

Kaṭṭubaḍi. [Telugu.] A subordinate village servant remunerated by rent-free land.

Katuka. [Hindi.] The snake daboia elegans. See Kándur.

Kaul. [Hindustáni, from the Arabic.] A promise, an agreement on the part of a superior, especially a document granted by a superior to an inferior holder of land, specifying the terms of the tenure; a paṭṭá. Also a safe-guard.

Kaulige. [Kanarese.] A village accountant or karnam under a pálegar.

Kauri. More commonly Cowry.

Kauribhágiá. [Uriya.] A village accountant.

Kavaḍi. [Telugu.] A couple of baskets or boxes, suspended one on each end of a yoke borne on the shoulder. Compare Bahangi.

Káveri. The name of the river (Cauvery) which rises in Coorg, and is there deified under the title of Amma. The Káveri feast is celebrated every autumn, when pilgrims resort to the source of the river, and, at the moment of the sun's entering Libra, bathe in the tank.

Kavile. [Telugu.] An account-book made of slips of palm leaves.

Kavulu. The Telugu form of Kaul.

Káwaḍi. [Kanarese.] A split bamboo which rests on the shoulder, and to the two ends of which burdens are tied. Also the name of a division of the Wokkaligas in Coorg.

Kawáḍiga. See under Golla.

Káwaḍigár. [Kanarese.] One who carries burdens on a káwaḍi.

Káwalál. [Toda, from *káwal*, guard, and *ál*, a person.] The attendant on a pálál; he serves for a time only, and is for the time an ascetic.

Káwalgár, or **Káwalkára.** [Tamil, from *káwal*, guard, and *kára*, doer.] A village watchman; his duty is to watch the crops, and he is usually paid by the ryots themselves. He acts also as a messenger and guide for travellers. In Nellore, leaders of robber-gangs, who acquired black-mail privileges (káwali) over single villages or clusters of villages, were formerly known as men káwalgárs, and robbers on a smaller scale as káwalgárs.

Káwarei. [Tamil.] The name of a caste called also Nayakka; they are most commonly manufacturers and sellers of bangles made of a particular kind of earth. Others are spinners, dyers, painters, and the like.

Kawtha. [Hindi.] The feronia elephantum, or Indian elephant apple; the fruit is used as a drug, the gum forms a part of the gum-gattie and East India gum of commerce, and the wood is used in building (*G. Birdwood*).

Kayáni. [Persian, from *kai*, a king.] Royal; the name of a dynasty of Persian kings; also that of a branch of the Gakkhars who claim descent from the Persian kings.

Káyasth, Káyat, or **Káyath.** [Sanskrit *káyastha*.] The name of a caste, said to be the offspring of a Kshatriya father and Śudra mother; their occupation is writing, and all paṭwáris in Bengal are of this caste. Káyasths are the competitors of Bráhmans in all the higher professions, but they have themselves suffered of late from the competition of lower castes, to whom education has spread. Káyasth is also the name of a division of the Parbhus—the writer caste of southern and western India.

Káyati. Pertaining to a Káyat or writer; applied to the scribe's running hand as opposed to the square Dewanágari character.

Kázi. [Arabic.] A judge. Under the Muhammadan empire the kázi was a civil and criminal judge. Under British rule he became an adviser to the courts on points of Muhammadan law. He still holds a high place in Musalmán communities, and leads the public prayers on great festivities. He is also registrar of marriages and divorces, for which he receives fees; he has also usually some endowment.

K.C.S.I. These letters stand for Knight Commander of the Star of India. See Order.

Keblah. See Kiblah.

Kedárnáth. [Hindi, from *kedár*, the name of a peak in the Himálayas, and *nátha*, lord.] The lord of Kedár, a name of Śiwa.

Keddah. See Khedá.

Kedgeree. See Khichri.

Kedu. [Toda, from *ked*, a dead body.] A burial mand. Also a funeral, of which there are two kinds, the háse kedu, or green funeral, which is special for each Toda, and takes place as soon as possible after death, and the bara kedu, or dry funeral, which takes place some months later, and may include all the members of the tribe who have died during the year. The skull and bones collected after the burning of the body at the green funeral are kept to be burnt at the dry. Buffaloes are slaughtered at both. The bara kedu is an elaborate ceremony lasting three days. The carcases of the buffaloes are the perquisites of the Kotas who attend as musicians.

Keflat. See Kaifiyat.

Kei-kolan. See Kaikola.

Kelassy. See Khalási.

Ker. The name of a class of Sunni cultivators and cattle-breeders found at Pálanpur.

Kerri. [Pashṭo.] The tent, made of black blanket, of a Povindah.

Ketu. [Ṣanskrit.] The dragon's tail, or the point where the moon in its southward course cuts the ecliptic. See Ráhu.

Keut. [Uriya.] The name of a low caste; they are fishermen, boatmen, and salt-makers.

Kewat. See Keut.

Kewaṭi. [Maráṭhi.] A retail dealer, a huckster.

Khabar. More commonly Khubber.

Khádál. [Bengali.] The name of a low caste formerly engaged in making salt, but now boatmen and fishermen.

Khádar. [Hindi.] Low land of easy irrigation suitable for rice; also kyári land, rice-beds.

Khádi. [Maráṭhi.] An arm of the sea, a creek, the portion of a river which is tidal; also a deep trench cut to carry off water.

Khádim. [Hindustáni.] A mosque servant, or one who has charge of a religious endowment.

Khagga. A cultivating Muhammadan caste of the Panjáb, claiming to be of Qureshi origin.

Khair. [Hindi, from the Sanskrit *khadira.*] The tree mimosa catechu, or acacia catechu, from which kát is extracted; the wood is used for uprights for houses.

Khairát. [Arabic.] Inám land granted for the support of the dumb, cripples, and others unable to support themselves.

Khájan. [Maráṭhi.] Salt marsh; land that is from time to time flooded by sea-water.

Khajawah. [Persian.] A camel-saddle.

Khajur. [Hindi.] The date tree, phœnix dactylifera or sylvestris; toddy is extracted from it.

Khákhara. Another name of the paláśa tree.

Kháki. [Hindustáni, from the Persian *khák*, ashes.] Relating to dust or ashes; of the colour of dust or ashes. A mendicant who smears his body with ashes.

Khákrob. [Hindustáni.] A sweeper, a menial servant of the lowest class; also the sweeper of a village, acting at times as a watchman, a guide, or a police spy; one of the village establishment (*H. H. Wilson*).

Khala. [Bengali, from the Sanskrit.] A threshing-floor, a place either in the field or a shed where the grain is trodden or beaten out of the husk. Also a granary. In the Dravidian languages the form is kala.

Khalapunji. [Maráṭhi, from *khala*, q.v., and *punji*, a heap.] Small heaps of grain taken from each larger pile at the time of measurement, and, under the Maráṭhá government, considered as the perquisite of the state (*H. H. Wilson*).

Khálári. [Bengali.] A place where salt is manufactured, a salt bed or pan.

Khalása. The name of a division of the Sikhs who followed the teaching of the first guru, the peaceful Nának, but would not enrol themselves as the singhs or soldiers of Govind, the tenth guru.

Khalási. [Hindustáni.] A sailor; a tent-pitcher; an artilleryman.

Khalawáḍi. [Maráṭhi.] A wáḍi or enclosure containing the khalas or threshing-floors, and the stacks of grain of several independent cultivators (*J. T. Molesworth*).

Khali. [Gujaráti, from the Sanskrit *khala.*] A threshing-floor; either the general threshing-floor of the village or a private one. Formerly all the produce used to be brought to the khali and guarded there till the government share was taken; this is what is meant by the khali system.

Khalif. More commonly Caliph.

Khalita. See Kharitah.

Khálkuwá. [Gujaráti.] A very deep pit dug underneath a house to collect all the drainage and every kind of refuse.

Khálpá. [Gujaráti.] The name of a caste; they are workers in leather, and identical with the Chamárs.

Khálsá. [Hindi, from the Arabic *khális*, pure.] This term is applied to lands or villages over which no intermediate landlord exercises any right, but the revenue of which belongs solely to the state. See Unalienated. Thence it came to be the name of the revenue department or the exchequer under the Mogul government. The same word, apparently as meaning free, not subject to any one else, was assumed as the name of the Sikhs when they became a distinct government and people. Their religion is pantheistic, but they speak of the khálsá as peculiarly the representation of god: the tenth guru says, 'The image of the almighty is the visible body of the immortal khálsá; the khálsá is everything; other divinities are as sand which slips through the fingers.'

Khámár. [Bengali.] A threshing-floor; also a farm, a farmyard. The term is applied also to lands which, originally waste, were retained by the zamindárs in their own hands and kept distinct from ryottee land.

Khámbi. [Gujaráti.] A structure of stone like a cairn, built in memory of one who has died a sudden death.

Khámti. The name of a tribe settled in Assam; they are of the same origin as the Aham and Shan tribes.

Khan. [Corruption of the Persian *khánah*, a house.] An inn, a caravansary.

Khán. [Persian.] A prince, a chief. Paṭháns usually add this title to their names. See Khátu.

Kháná. [Hindustáni.] Eating, food; among Anglo-Indians, dinner.

Khánabári. [Bengali, from the Persian *khánah*, a house, and *bári*, q.v.] A house with the grounds about it; a patch of ground exempt from revenue, near a ryot's house.

Khánahdámád. [Panjábi, from the Persian *khánah*, a house, and Hindi *dámád*, a daughter's husband.] A son-in-law who resides with his father-in-law.

Khánam. [Persian.] The wife of a khán; any lady of rank. Among Moguls the title is commonly added to the names of all women.

Khánáwal. [Maráṭhi.] The cost of living at another person's house; board; an eating-house. For a monthly payment of four or five rupees a Hindu in Bombay can have all his meals in a khánáwal.

Khánazád. [Bengali, from the Persian *khánah*, a house, and *zád*, born.] The children of slave-girls born to their master.

Khán Bahádur. [Persian *khán*, chief, *bahádur*, brave.] A title of honour bestowed by government as a personal distinction. The Hindu equivalent is ráo bahádur, and these titles are higher than khán sáheb and ráo sáheb.

Khanḍ. [Maráṭhi.] A fine, a cess levied for any licence or privilege; a contribution levied by an enemy. Under the khoti system, the agreement as to what the tenant is to pay the khot.

Khanḍáit. [Uriya, from *khanḍá*, a sword.] A swordsman; the name of a class of persons now, but not formerly, constituting a separate caste. They were originally military landholders, or mere soldiers under the rájás of Orissa; they are now cultivators, policemen, and messengers. They are very differently esteemed in different districts; in some they rank next after Rájputs.

Khanḍeráo. [Maráṭhi.] The name of an incarnation of Śiwa. There is a class of persons mentioned by Colebrooke called the dogs of Khanḍeráo. These are firstborn children dedicated to the temple of Khanḍeráo, near Poona, by persons who have, in the hope of obtaining progeny, made vows so to dedicate their first children.

Khandi. More commonly Candy.

Khanḍikar. [Bengali.] The name of a low caste; they are workers in horn.

Khanḍni. [Maráṭhi.] Tribute; a fine; a cess; a contribution levied from a village as revenue for the paramount power.

Khanḍobá. A familiar appellation of Khanḍeráo.

Khánkáh. [Hindustáni.] A Muhammadan monastery; also a rest-house.

Khánsámán. [Hindustáni, from *khán*, chief, and *sámán*, effects.] One of the head-servants in a European household in Bengal; he purchases the daily supplies in the bázár, and is chief table-servant.

Khánzádah. [From *khán*, q.v., and the Persian *zád*, born.] The son of a khán, a title assumed by the Mewátis.

Khár. [Hindi, from the Sanskrit *kshára*, salt.] Saline land; land recovered from the sea.

Kharábá. [Hindi.] Land that is wholly unculturable.

Kharádi. [Gujaráti, from *kharád*, a lathe.] The name of a caste; they turn wood, ivory, and metal. There is a distinct community of Sunni Musalmán converts from this caste.

Khárapáṭ. [From the Maráṭhi *khár*, salt.] This is the name given to land that has originally been submerged by the sea and afterwards recovered for cultivation. It is usually used for rice, and commonly called salt batty land.

Kharcha. A term used by servants in the north of India for a fowl not full-grown but large enough for the table. See Half fowl.

Kharia. The name of a small tribe in the district of Singhbhum, in Bengal; their language is Kolarian.

Kharif. [Arabic.] The season of autumn; the autumnal harvest; the crops that are reaped in the cold season. Among the principal kharif crops are rice, cotton, jawár.

Kharitah. [Arabic.] A bag, the ornamental bag used as an envelope for a letter from or to a person of high rank; thence the letter itself.

Khária. [Panjábi.] A tent made of camel's hair.

Khárji. [Arabic.] The name of a Muhammadan sect who exclude Ali from the number of the caliphs.

Khár-páṭil. [Maráṭhi, from *khár*, land recovered from the sea, and *páṭil*, q.v.] The name of a small caste of the Konkan.

Kharral. The name of a Panjáb tribe, Muhammadan in religion, but with many Hindu customs; they are reputed a turbulent, savage, and thievish people, and bad cultivators.

Khárvi. [Maráṭhi.] The name of a caste, whose occupation is much the same as that of the Khárwás, namely, boating, fishing, and tile-turning. Some also cultivate, and a few trade.

Khárwá. [Gujaráti, from *khár*, salt.] A class composed chiefly of Kolis who are salt-workers, sailors, and fishermen. They are also cultivators and layers and turners of tiles. They eat fish and flesh, except that of the cow.

Khárwá. [Gujaráti.] A particular kind of strong cloth, dark red in colour.

Kharwár. The name of an aboriginal tribe.

Khás. [Arabic.] Select, private; any high officer of state. See Khawás. As a revenue term, it means the management of an estate directly by government without middle-men.

Khásia. The name of a Hindu tribe inhabiting the hill country of Garhwál, Kumáun, and Dehra Dun. They claim to be of Rájput descent, and are scrupulous in their eating and drinking, but do not wear the janeo. They descend from the mountains yearly to cultivate in the forest.

Khásia. The name of an Indo-Chinese tribe settled on the Khási hills in Assam; they have a peculiar language, which has been described as monosyllabic in the agglutinative stage, and which has no written characters. The Khásias are divided into twenty-five small states, each ruled by an elective chief. Property descends in the female line, and the woman is regarded as the head of the household. The Khásias cultivate on the jum system, and smelt iron and keep cattle, though they do not drink milk. They erect cromlechs over the ashes of their dead.

Khaśia. [Gujaráti, from *khas*, the name of a village in Káṭhiáwár.] The name of a tribe said to be of mixed Rájput (Gohil) and Mhair blood.

Khaskhas. [Hindustáni.] The fragrant grass, andropagon muricatum, with the roots of which tatties are made.

Khásmahal. [Hindustáni, from the Arabic *khás*, private, and *mahal*, a place.] The women's apartments in a Muhammadan palace.

Khátá. [Hindi, perhaps from the Arabic *khat*, a note of hand.] An account; an account kept with one individual, or an account of the receipts and outlay pertaining to one particular subject. Where a general day-book is kept, the items of the different khátás or heads of account are extracted from it; and if, instead of being taken on separate pieces of paper, they are recorded under their appropriate heads in a book, that book constitutes a ledger. See Khátáwahi. The word khátá, being thus associated with the idea of classification, has come to be used as the equivalent of the business term 'department,' the revenue department, the public works, the judicial, and all the other departments being separate khátás in the government accounts. In the Bombay presidency khátá, as applied to a ryot's land, means the land standing in his name in the government books, as distinguished from land which he may hold under another khátedár; his khátá land corresponds with his khátá in the village ledger.

Khátábahi. [Hindi, from *khátá*, q.v., and *bahi*, a book.] A book of khátás, an account-book in which the transactions are not recorded in the order of occurrence, but under classified heads; a ledger.

Khátábandi. [Gujaráti, from *khátá*, q.v., and *band*, a binding.] A system of land assessment in which the land taken into account was assessed beyond its real value, the khátedárs making good their position by cultivating or letting to ganotiás other lands not counted in their khátás. Each sharer's khátá, *i.e.* the amount of vetá land assigned to him, was fixed by the community so as to make up the lump sum they had to pay to government.

Khatauni. [Hindi, from *khátá*, q.v.] A ledger, or the act of posting items from the day-book to the ledger.

Khátáwahi. The Gujaráti form of Khátábahi.

Khatba. [Bengali.] The name of a low caste; they are weavers.

Khátedár. [Maráṭhi, from *khátá*, q.v., and Persian *dár*, holder.] One who has a khátá, especially, in the Bombay land revenue system, one who has a khátá in the government accounts, that is, one whose name is registered in the village books as the occupant of certain specified land.

Khatib. [Hindustáni.] The officer who preaches in the mosque on Fridays and feast days.

Khatiyán. The Bengali form of Khatauni.

Kháṭki. [Hindi, from the Sanskrit *khattika.*] The name of a caste; they are mutton-butchers. There are also Musalmán Kháṭkis; they are butchers and tanners, and are of the Sunni division.

Khatri. [A Hindi abbreviation of *kshatriya*, q.v.] The name of the great trading class of northern India; different divisions of them are called Khanna, Kupur, and Marotra. Also the name of a caste in Gujarát called otherwise *Gámlá*, q.v. Also the name of a caste in the Konkan and Mysore who are silk-weavers. Some of these claim to be descended from the Kshatriyas.

Khattá. [Maráṭhi.] A preparation of opium, alum, turmeric, lemon-juice, etc., levigated together in a copper vessel and heated; it is applied to the eyes in ophthalmia; to the head in headaches; to sprains, etc. (*J. T. Molesworth*).

Khattak. The name of a Paṭhán tribe settled within our frontier near Kohát. They are identified with the Sattagyda of Herodotus, and were originally settled on the Sulemán range and its great western offshoot the Koh Sanwál and the plain country down to the Indus, but were driven out by the Waziris about six hundred years ago. Under British rule the Khattaks have proved well-conducted and loyal. The salt-mines of Kalabagh are in their hands, and many of them are employed as travelling merchants and salt-carriers (*H. W. Bellew*).

Khattar. The name of a tribe in the

Panjáb claiming kinship with the Awáns.

Khátu. [Hindustáni.] A title commonly added to the name of Paṭhán women.

Khawás. [Arabic, the plural of *khás*, q.v.] Nobles, grandees; the personal attendants on a king or chief. Also the offspring of a domestic slave-girl; they form a separate community in Cutch, where they are employed as personal servants of chiefs, as soldiers, and also as husbandmen and labourers.

Kháwind. [Persian.] An honorific title of address; lord, master.

Khayrath. See Khairát.

Khedá. [Hindustáni.] An enclosure for catching wild elephants. A khedá is made in thick jungle near an elephant cover; it is about a hundred yards in diameter, surrounded by a ditch except at one point, where a chain-and-log gate is suspended between two trees. Two guiding trenches converge from the cover to this entrance.

Kheḍut. [Gujaráti, from *kheḍ*, to cultivate.] A cultivator.

Kheir. See Khair.

Khejá. [Arakanese.] An officer subordinate to the diwán in a Chakmá clan.

Khel. [Arabic.] A company, a troop, a party; affixed to a man's name to designate his adherents or the clan sprung from him. The term is used chiefly in Pashṭo and in Assamese.

Kherwar. [Corrupt form.] The name of a tribe inhabiting the forests of Sarguja, and who prepare starch from the root of the tikhur.

Kheryaut. See Khairát.

Khetrpál. The Hindi form of Kshetrapála.

Khetwál. The name of a tribe in the Panjáb claiming to be of Greek descent.

Khewaṭ. [Hindustáni.] Assigned quotas of revenue; a record of village shares.

Khewaṭdár. [Persian *dár*, holder.] One who is responsible for a khewaṭ, a sharer.

Khichaḍi. The Maráṭhi form of Khichri. The term is applied to villages which are partly khoti, but in which there are also some dhárás.

Khichi. The name of a branch of the Chauhán Rájputs, now found in the North-West Provinces, Raghugarh, and Jaisalmir.

Khichri. [Hindi, from the Sanskrit *kriśara.*] A dish composed of rice and dál boiled together with spices; any medley; miscellaneous charges or taxes.

Khiddar. See Khizr.

Khidmatgár. [Hindustáni, from the Arabic *khidmat*, service.] A servant, a personal attendant.

Khil. [Bengali.] Land that is waste but not unculturable.

Khiláfat. More commonly Caliphate.

Khilári. [Maráṭhi.] The name of a tribe of herdsmen and shepherds who wander about the west of Khándesh and down as far as the Tungabhadra. They keep a special breed of cattle, which is known by their name. The Khilári bullocks are rather small and of slender build, but strong and hardy, fast-trotting, and very teachable, though of fierce temper. They are generally white, with long and nearly straight horns and small hump. The cows are used only for breeding purposes, and the whole of the milk is given to the young stock.

Khilat. [Arabic.] A dress of honour presented as a mark of distinction. It may include jewels, arms, or a horse or elephant.

Khilji. The name of the second of the Ghori dynasties. It began with Jalál-ud-din of Khilji in 1290 A.D., and lasted thirty years.

Khiong. [Arakanese.] A Khyoung-thá temple; there is one in each village; it is a bamboo structure raised some six feet from the ground, and contains an image of Gautama. The boys of the village usually sleep in the khiong, under the supervision of their goung or leader.

Khiráj. [Arabic.] Tax, tribute; applied originally especially to the tribute levied by Muhammadans upon infidels after conquest, afterwards to the general land revenue.

Khirakasi. The name of a sect of Hindus in Ráwal Pindi who repudiate idolatry and Bráhmanism.

Khisári. [Hindustáni.] The pulse lathyrus sativus.

Khist. The Maráṭhi form of Kist.

Khizr. A mythological personage, made up of different rabbinical fables concerning Eliezer the servant of Abraham, and the prophet Elijah, on which are engrafted the chivalrous legends concerning St. George. He is held in great veneration by the Musalmáns of Dacca (*R. Heber*).

Khodiár. [Gujaráti, from *khodiá*, lame.] The name of a popular goddess, the devi or spirit of one of seven sisters of the Cháran caste.

Khojá. [A Gujaráti corruption of the Persian *khwájah*, q.v.] The name of a numerous body of Musalmáns settled in Sindh, Cutch, Gujarát, and Bombay. They claim a Persian origin, but are mostly the descendants of Hindus, chiefly, it is said, carpenters, bricklayers, and oil-pressers, who were converted to islám by Sadir Din, a pir who came from Persia about 1430 A.D., and preached the koran first at Multán and afterwards at Karáchi; their customs, too, are mostly Hindu. The early converts were Nazarian Ismaili Shiahs, but under the rule of the Sunnis it was not safe to make open profession of that faith, so some of the Khojás declared themselves to be Sunnis; these are now a separate sect. The religious head or imám of the Shiah Khojás lives in Bombay, and claims descent from Nazár, the grandson of Jáfir the sixth imám of the Shiahs (from whom also were descended the Hashishins, or Assassins). The Khojás are chiefly traders, either wholesale or retail, but some are cultivators.

Khokhar. The name of a Panjáb tribe of doubtful origin, some claiming to be Rájputs, others Játs, and others to be descended, like the Awáns, from Kutb Sháh of Ghazni.

Kholbandi. [Hindustáni, from *khol*,

to loose, and *band*, to bind.] The operation of taking off the shoes of a horse and replacing them after paring the hoofs.

Khombhátri. The name of a caste; they are dyers. Some have been converted to islám.

Khond. See Kandh.

Khordah Avastá. [Persian *khurd*, short.] The name of a shortened form of the avastá, containing only the portions necessary for the laity.

Khosá. The name of a tribe of marauders who used to frequent the Runn of Cutch and the sandy tract between Sindh and Hindustán.

Khostwal. A Shiah tribe of Afghánistán situated between the Mangals on the west and the Waziris on the east, and having the Turis next them on the north.

Khot. [Maráṭhi.] A revenue contractor or farmer. In the Konkan are many hereditary khots who have by degrees assumed many of the rights of proprietors of the land.

Khoti. An adjective formed from khot, and applied to the system of farming the revenue to khots.

Khoṭiá. [Gujaráti.] The name given to the land other than the vetá land of each sharer in a khátábandi village. The khoṭiá being very lightly assessed, its possession was advantageous, and the community frequently sold portions of such land to individual members; hence the claim to consider such land alienated.

Khotil. The name of a small class of Bhils, generally resembling the Naháls, and regarded by the pure Bhil as degraded because they eat carrion and will touch the dead body of the cow. They are great huntsmen, and some worship the tiger-god.

Khozing. [Arakanese.] The name of the patron deity of the Khyeng, Pankho, and Banjogi tribes. He is supposed to have a village somewhere in the Chittagong hills, but no mortal can enter it. The tiger is his watch-dog. The Shendus also recognize this god.

Khubber. [Hindustáni *khabar*.] News, information.

Khudáwand. [Persian.] An honorific title of address; master, lord, husband.

Khudkásht. [Hindi, from the Persian *khud*, self, and *kásht*, cultivation.] A term applied to a ryot who cultivates his own hereditary land; and also to the land which only the resident ryots may cultivate, as opposed to páhikásht. The word thus corresponds to the ulkuḍi of the south. It is also applied in the north-west to lands which a proprietor cultivates himself or by tenants-at-will, and in this sense corresponds to the pannai or kamata of the south.

Khurd. [Persian.] Little, small. This word is added or prefixed to the name of the smaller of two places of the same name, as Khurd Khyber, the little Khyber pass.

Khurreeta. See Kharitah.

Khutbah. [Arabic.] A public prayer or discourse pronounced in a mosque at a Friday service.

Khwábgah. [Hindustáni.] A sleeping-apartment in a palace.

Khwájah. [Persian.] A rich or respectable man, a holy man.

Khyberi. The common name of the tribes occupying the Khyber pass, the Afridis, the Shinwaris, and others.

Khyen. [Bengali.] The name of a semi-Hinduised tribe numerous in Rangpur and Kuch Behar. They seem to be connected with the Rájbansis, but are more respected. They are employed in agriculture and as labourers and domestic servants; in Dinájpur also as oilmen; and in Kuch Behar many are clerks.

Khyeng. The name of a Toungthá tribe considered to be of common origin with the Mro.

Khyoungthá. [Arakanese, from *khyoung*, a river, and *thá*, a son.] The children of the river, the generic name of those tribes of the Chittagong hill tracts who dwell upon the banks of the mountain streams, as distinguished from the wilder Toungthá who live higher on the hills. The different Khyoungthá tribes or clans take their names mostly from the streams on which they live. They speak a dialect of Arakanese; the written character is the same as the Burmese. They are Buddhists by religion, and burn their dead. They cultivate on the jum system, and change the sites of their villages. See Khiong, Roaja, Shiang.

Khyr. See Khair.

Kiári. The Uriya form of Kyári.

Kiás. [Arabic.] Reasoning, inference; a conclusion not expressed in, but deduced from, the koran or the sunnah.

Kiblah. [Arabic, from *kibl*, what is placed opposite.] The point to which Muhammadans look when they pray. Muhammad first made the temple at Jerusalem the kiblah, as he wished to conciliate the Jews and professed to be restoring the religion of Abraham. He afterwards changed it to the kaabah, which is still the kiblah.

Kikar. [Hindi.] The acacia arabica, or bábul.

Kilári. See under Golla.

Kilidár. [Gujaráti, from the Sanskrit *kila*, a key, and the Persian *dár*, holder.] A merchant's treasurer, who pays or receives money upon the munim's voucher.

Killá. [Bengali, from the Arabic *kalah*.] A fort, a castle; also, in some provinces, the territory under the protection of a fort.

Killádár. [Persian *dár*, holder.] The governor of a fort.

Killádári. The office and emoluments of a killádár; or the revenues to be collected by him; or a tract of country formerly under a killádár.

Kincob. [An English corruption of the Persian *kimkhwáb*.] Cloth interwoven with gold or silver thread; brocade.

Kinḍan. [Tamil.] A kind of cotton cloth, commonly called gingham (*H. H. Wilson*).

King-crow. The drongo shrike, the dicrurus macrocercus, a very graceful bird with a pleasing note. Though only the size of a blackbird, it attacks much larger birds, especially crows. The Hindi name is bhojanga.

Kir. The name of a small caste in Rájputáná; they cultivate melons.

Kirar. [Hindi.] A money-lender.

Kiráta. [Sanskrit.] The name of a wild hill tribe, of whom it is related that Arjun went to live with them in order to learn archery from Śiwa, who was their god. They are the Cirrhadæ or Kirrhadæ of ancient writers. The Kirátas of to-day are settled in the eastern part of Nepál, and are some of them Buddhists, and others Hinduised.

Kirttistambh. [Gujaráti, from the Sanskrit *kirtti*, renown, and *stambha*, a pillar.] A triumphal column, an ornamental pillar in front of a temple.

Kishti. [Káśmiri.] A flat-bottomed boat used on the lakes and rivers of Cashmere, and propelled by paddles called chappars. The kishti has a cabin in the centre and a high deck over it; the paddle-men, sometimes as many as forty, sit half of them in front and half behind the cabin, and face to the bow.

Kismat. [Arabic.] Share, distribution; fate, fortune; in law, partition of inheritance; in revenue matters, a portion of land detached from a larger division, as from a mauza.

Kist. [Hindi, from the Arabic.] An instalment; especially an instalment of government land revenue, and thence the period fixed for its payment.

Kiswah. [Arabic.] The black cloth with which the kaabah is covered.

Kitábi. [Arabic, from *kitáb*, a book.] A term applied by Muhammadans to Jews and Christians as persons recognizing the authority of the Old Testament.

Kizhdi. The Afghán tent. Kizhdis are made of black hair-cloth which is waterproof. They are sometimes large enough to shelter cattle and camels as well as men.

Kisilbáshi. A Persian-speaking Shiah tribe of Afghánistán, descended from the followers of Nádir Sháh; they are handsome men and good soldiers, and form the greater portion of the Afghán cavalry. Many of them are also to be found in our horse regiments. Numerically they are a small tribe.

Koavang. [Arakanese.] A person inspired by Khozing. Such persons are supposed to possess the gift of tongues and to be invulnerable. They are employed to make sacrifices and to interpret omens.

Koch. The name of a tribe, the origin of which is disputed, but which first rose into power about the end of the fifteenth century, and founded a kingdom on the ruins of the Hindu kingdom of Kámrup. Kuch Behar is still called after them, but most of the tribe have rejected the name of Koch or Kuch, and call themselves Rájbansi. The Koches are cultivators, weavers, and palanquin-bearers, and speak a dialect of Hindi.

Kod. The name of a small tribe in the Tháná and Násik districts, which may be identical with the Kota tribe of the Nilgiris. They hold a higher position than the Wárlis, and are esteemed about equal to Kolis. They eat animal food, except beef, and burn their dead.

Koḍaga. The name of the principal

tribe of Koḍagu, Kurg, or Coorg; they are a tall, hardy race of mountaineers, of frank and independent bearing, but ignorant and superstitious. Their religion consisted formerly of the worship of demons and of ancestors, but has now become to some extent Bráhmanized. They sometimes bury and sometimes burn their dead. Polygamy is allowed, but is not much practised. They eat all sorts of meat and drink spirits. See Amma, Aruwa, Kárana, Kuli.

Koḍagu. The language of Koḍagu, or Coorg; it stands about midway between old Kanarese and Tulu; the Kanarese alphabet is used. The language is spoken by the Koḍagas and their former slaves, the Holeyas.

Kodáli. [Hindi, from the Sanskrit *kuddála.*] A tool uniting the uses of spade, shovel, and hoe.

Kodmál. [Bengali.] The name of a low caste; they are cultivators and labourers.

Kodo [Hindi], **Kodrá** [Gujaráti], or **Kodru** [Maráṭhi; all from the Sanskrit *kodrawa*]. The cereal paspalum scrobiculatum or frumentaceum; it is a kharif crop, and is chiefly eaten by the poor, the husk and grain being ground up together. The grain freed from the husk is called kodri. See Millet.

Koeri. The name of a caste of Śudras of middle rank; they are cultivators and are excellent husbandmen. They are most numerous in south Behar, where they are the chief poppy-cultivators; they are quiet and hard-working. They are divided into two divisions, Dangi and Maghyá, which do not intermarry.

Koftgari. Inlaid ware of steel and gold; the pattern is drawn out on the surface of the steel and a wire of soft pure gold hammered in. The chief centre of the art is Gujrát in the Panjáb.

Kohistáni. A Paṭhán tribe, emigrants from Swát, and settled on our frontier, east of the Indus. They are called also Swátis.

Koi. The name of an aboriginal tribe in the northern part of the Godáwari district; they are allied to the Gonḍs.

Koïl. [Hindi, from Sanskrit *kokila.*] The bird eudynamis orientalis, or Indian cuckoo.

Koit. See Káyasth.

Kokamb. The Maráṭhi name of the garcinia gambogia, a variety of the mangosteen. An oil, commonly called cocum, is obtained from the seeds and is used as an adulterant of ghee.

Kokhni. See Konkani.

Kol. The name of one or more primitive tribes found in Benares, Behar, Bundelkhand, and Chutiá Nágpur. The name is loosely used, being sometimes applied to the Bhumij and Mundas, and sometimes even to the Uráons, who are a Dravidian tribe.

Kolarian. A collective name given to several languages of the type of that of the Kols, which is distinct both from the Aryan and Dravidian languages. The Kolarian races are regarded as aboriginal. See Turanian.

Koli. The name of an aboriginal tribe numerous in western India, and of several distinct classes. The Kolis of Gujarát were formerly a predatory tribe, but are now settled down to agriculture, and some take service as wartaniás. The Son Kolis of the coast are boatmen and fishermen; they wear red caps instead of turbans. Other divisions are called Malar, Marvi, and Mahádewa Kolis; the rájá of Jawár is of the last-named division, which is numerous above the Gháṭs. The Kolis have given their name to the coast district of Colaba and the island of the same name, which is now part of Bombay.

Koliya. [Tamil.] The name of a division of the Paraiyans; they weave coarse cloths.

Kollekallu. [Kanarese, from *kollu*, to kill, and *kallu*, stone.] Tombstones in honour of warriors slain in battle. See Virakallu.

Kollu. [Tamil.] The pulse dolichos uniflorus. See Horse-gram.

Komaṭi. [Kanarese.] The name of a caste who claim to be the only pure Vaiśyas; they are traders and shopkeepers. Some are Vaishnawas and some Śaiwas. The marriage of cousins is the established rule among them.

Komavishdar. See Kamávisdár.

Kond. See Kandh.

Konga. [Kanarese, from *kongu*, the name by which Coimbatore is known to the hill tribes.] The name of one of the Badaga castes.

Kongu. The name of the country ruled by the Cheras; it seems to have consisted of the territory now forming the Coimbatore, Malabar, and Salem districts.

Konkan. [Maráṭhi.] The name of a strip of country between the Western Gháṭs and the sea, about 320 miles in length, and varying from thirty to sixty miles in breadth; the parts near the coast are fertile, highly cultivated, and populous, and the inland parts rocky and rugged; north of Bombay the coast is sandy and shallow, containing in many places great expanse of salt swamp, and the harbours are few and small; south of Bombay the coast is bold, with many navigable rivers, commodious harbours, and in most parts with deep water near the shore.

Konkana. [Gujaráti.] One of the Káliparaj tribes; besides cultivating they are collectors of asindra leaves, which they tie in bundles and sell to the Wániás; they bury their dead, and use no Bráhmans for their religious ceremonies.

Konkanasth. [Maráṭhi, from *konkan*, and the Sanskrit *stha*, who is.] An inhabitant of the Konkan; another name for Chitpáwan.

Konkani. An inhabitant of the Konkan. In the southern half of the Konkan the inhabitants are Maráṭhás; the castes are few and very exactly defined; but in the north there are large tribes more or less aboriginal, several somewhat mixed castes, and, except for comparatively recent settlers, a total absence of pure Maráṭhás and Bráhmans. Until the accession of the British government, the population had always a distinctly warlike character, and the South Konkan still supplies a great number of recruits to the native army. The southern Konkanis also are much more in the habit of seeking their living abroad than other natives. The Peshwás were Konkani Bráhmans (*A. K. Nairne*). Konkani is also the name of a tribe in Khándesh; in appearance they resemble the Konkan Ṭhákurs, but are more settled and use the plough. They bury their dead, and in their memory raise square single-stone pillars sometimes as much as eight feet high.

Konyon. [Arakanese.] A game played by the hill tribes of Chittagong. The konyon is a seed resembling the horse-chestnut; each player has one; he propels it by placing it at the end of the middle finger of his right hand, drawing it and the finger back with the left hand and then letting go suddenly; the object is to strike the opponents' konyons.

Kookeri. See Kukuri.

Kootel. [A corruption of *koṭhi wálá*, one who has storehouses.] An indigo-planter (*C. P. Brown*).

Kopali. See Kapáli.

Kora. [Bengali.] The name of a low caste; they are earth-workers.

Korachar. [Kanarese.] The name of a wandering tribe who carry salt and grain from one market to another by means of large droves of cattle and asses, and also make bamboo mats and baskets. The men wear their hair tied in a large knot on one side of the top of the head in the manner seen in the sculptured figures on old stone monuments. The women wear numerous strings of small red and white glass beads and shells round the neck and falling over the bosom, which also accords with the ancient practice as seen in old bas-reliefs. The Korachars carry with them the framework of a rude description of hut, and while one part of the tribe proceeds with the baggage animals, the others settle for a time and employ themselves in making mats and baskets and in begging and stealing. They often commit burglaries and dacoities. They speak Telugu and Tamil, and also a peculiar dialect a mixture of the two (*L. Rice*).

Koramar. The name of a wandering tribe in Coorg; they are distinguished as Uppu and Káge Koramar; the former engage in traffic, and are held superior to the latter. They appear to be the same tribe as the Korachars of Mysore.

Koran. [English corruption of the Arabic *qurán*.] The sacred book of the Muhammadans, and considered by them to be the fountain-head of all science, knowledge, and law. It purports to consist of revelations made to Muhammad, and is divided into 114 surahs or chapters. A few of the earlier surahs are rhythmical, but the greater part prose; they are not arranged in the order of delivery or according to any method. The book was compiled after the prophet's death from various writings left by him on parchment, leather, palm leaves, and even bones and stones, and from the revelations known by heart to his followers. A revised edition was made under the third caliph Osmán. Muhammad himself often revoked revelations. In one place he says, 'We recall none of our verses or bring them to oblivion without supplying better ones, or at least some equally good.' In some places he is conciliatory towards Jews and Christians, and in others violently denounces them.

Korawa. The name of a tribe in Cutch detached from the Korachars of Mysore.

Kori. [Gujaráti.] A silver coin in Cutch equal to a third of a rupee.

Korta. A corruption of Kartá, q.v., and the term commonly used in a Bengali household to denote the master of the house.

Korumbar. The name of a class of persons in Wynaad; they pulverize quartz between two stones, wash off the mud in a wooden dish, and collect the gold dust by means of mercury. They may be a branch of the Kuruba or Kurumba tribe.

Korwa. See Korachar.

Kos. [Hindustáni, from the Sanskrit *krosá*, or the Persian *kroh*.] A measure of distance, varying in different places, but usually one and a half or two miles.

Koshṭi. [Maráṭhi.] The name of a caste; they are spinners and weavers.

Kos-minár. [See *Kos* and *Minar*.] A small obelisk or a pillar of brickwork set up to mark kos distances upon a high-road. Jahángir had them erected from Delhi to Peshá-war, and they still remain between Agra and Sikandra.

Koṭa. [Koḍagu.] A mud-bank made under a tree where a Koḍaga family's first house stood. Kárana sacrifices are made at the koṭa as at the kaimaṭṭa.

Kota. The name of an aboriginal tribe of the Nilgiri mountains; they are the artisans of the hills, and are necessary to all the other tribes as their blacksmiths, carpenters, tanners, rope-makers, umbrella-makers, potters, musicians, and workers in gold and silver. The Todas pay them in dead buffaloes and ghi, the Kurumbas in grain, and the Irulas in plantains and grain. They are held in contempt as eaters of carrion. They are also addicted to drinking and opium-eating. They are, however, intelligent and hard-working. They worship a god called Kámataráya and his wife, each of whom is represented by a silver plate. They burn their dead. Their language is a dialect of Kanarese (*Grigg*).

Kotal. A pass, a dip in a range of mountains, the highest point in a road crossing a mountain range.

Kotál. [Bengali.] The name of a low caste, formerly employed as watchmen, and still acting as village messengers in Kumáun, but usually engaged in weaving or agriculture.

Koter. See Kota.

Koṭhi. [Sanskrit *koshṭa*.] A factory, warehouse, or granary; usually applied only to a large building. Also a commercial house, or the office or place of business of a public officer. In Gujaráti koṭhi means also a large earthen jar used for storing grain.

Koṭiá. [Gujaráti.] A sailing-boat, smaller than the ḍanga, and without a deck.

Kot Linga. The name of the supreme court of law in Nepál. See Ditha.

Kottur. See Kota.

Koṭwal. [Hindi, from the Persian.] A chief officer of police in a city or town. Under the native governments the koṭwál sometimes exercised magisterial power. Also, in some places, a village watchman.

Koṭwál. The name of a Koli tribe in Gujarát and the Mahi Kántá.

Krishna. [Sanskrit, literally, black or dark blue.] The name Vishnu took in his eighth or full incarnation at the end of the dwápara age, when he was born on the 8th of Śráwan wadi as the eighth son of Wásudewa, a Kshatriya of the lunar race. Some say that Krishna was not an incarnation of Vishnu, but the god himself, and these make Balarám, Krishna's elder brother, to be the eighth awatár. Krishna's main exploit was the destruction of the tyrant Kansa, his mother's uncle and the representative of the principle of evil. Krishna is the most popular of the Hindu gods. The Holi and Janmáshṭami festivals are in his honour. In the Mahábhárata he appears as the friend of the Páṇḍawas. Modern poets delight to represent him as a little boy full of tricks and mischief.

Krishnadi. The mode of reckoning a month by beginning with the krishnapaksh, or dark half, making, that is, the day following the full moon to be the first day of the month, and the day of the full moon to be the thirtieth. See Month, Tithi. In using the names of the months the krishnadi mode precedes; thus Chaitra śudh is the same period of time under both methods, but it is the second half of Chaitra krishnadi and the first half śukladi; Chaitra wadi śukladi is Vaiśákh wadi krishnadi, and so on, the śuklapakshas bearing always the same name, and the krishnapakshas the different names of two consecutive months.

Krishnapaksh. [Sanskrit *krishna*, black, and *paksha*, a side, a part.] The dark half of the month, that is, the fortnight from the full moon to the new moon, in which period there is a daily lengthening time of darkness between the setting of the sun and the rising of the moon. See Śuklapaksh.

Krita. [Sanskrit, from *kri*, to do.] Accomplished, performed; the side of the die marked with four points, the first or golden age. See Yuga.

Kror. More commonly Crore.

Krorasinghia. The name of a Sikh misl, called after their third leader Krora Singh. Their lands were in the Jalandhar doáb (*J. D. Cunningham*).

Krori. [Hindi, from *kror*.] An officer under the Musalmán government who was a collector of revenue to the extent of a kror of dáms, or two and a half lákhs of rupees; a taxgatherer generally.

Kshatrap. [Persian.] A representative, an agent, a viceroy; the name of a dynasty from the north that ruled in Káṭhiáwár from 78 to 328 A.D., and which drove the Andhras out of the Deccan and Konkan at the beginning of that period.

Kshatriya. [Sanskrit, from *kshatra*, dominion.] The name of the second of the four original castes of Hindus, according to Manu. The Kshatriya is described as the arms of the creator, thus denoting his to be the military profession. In the oldest Hindu communities the king was always a Kshatriya, though no doubt his power was circumscribed and overshadowed by that of his Bráhman subjects. The Rájputs of the present day claim to be pure Kshatriyas.

Kshetra. [Sanskrit.] Land, a field; a sacred spot, a place of pilgrimage; thence, in Malayálam, a temple.

Kshetrapála. [Sanskrit *kshetra*, a field, and *pála*, a guard, from *pá*, to watch.] A protector of fields, an epithet of Bhairawanáth.

Kshowrakan. The name of a caste, numerous in Travancore; they are barbers.

Kuar. See Kunwar.

Kubera. [Sanskrit.] Originally the chief of the evil spirits; afterwards the god of riches. See Kailása, Yaksha.

Kucha. See Kachchá.

Kuchela. [Sanskrit, literally, badly clothed.] A proverbial name for a man suddenly raised from poverty to prosperity, like Kuchela, the early companion of Krishna, who from extreme penury was, in return for a handful of grain, raised by the latter to a condition of great magnificence.

Kudaga. See Koḍaga.

Kuḍi. [Tamil.] An inhabitant, a cultivator, a ryot.

Kuḍipillai. [Tamil.] The name of a division of the Paraiyans; they are barbers.

Kuḍiváram. [Tamil *váram*, a share.] The cultivator's share of the crop, the hissa-raiyati, as distinguished from the melváram.

Kudiya. A wild tribe of the forests of Coorg. They are cultivators, farm labourers, and toddy-drawers.

Kufi. See under Navaita.

Kujá. [Gujaráti.] A narrow-necked earthen bottle for water, a kuzah.

Kuká. A modern Sikh sect.

Kuki. The name of one of the khels, or clans, of the Afridis.

Kuki. Another name of the Lushái tribe. The Bengalis sometimes use the name to include all hill-men, except the friendly tribes near the border, whom they distinguish as Jumáhs.

Kukri. Another name of the bhuṭṭá plant, or Indian corn.

Kukuri. [Nepálese.] The national Gurkhá weapon, half bill-hook and half falchion.

Kula. [Kanarese.] One who pays land revenue to government, a ryot.

Kuláchárya. [Sanskrit, from *kula*, family, and *áchárya*, q.v.] A family priest, one who conducts the domestic ceremonies of a family; in Bengal, a person whose occupation it is to negotiate marriages, as acquainted with the pedigrees of families.

Kulam. [Tamil.] A tank, a reservoir, an artificial lake.

Kulang. [Gujaráti.] The grus cinerea or European crane; it visits the west of India in great flocks in the cold weather and feeds on the growing wheat; it is good eating. The kullam or colamb fowl of the Bombay market is not the crane, but a variety of the domestic fowl.

Kuli. More commonly Cooly.

Kuli. [Koḍagu.] An evil spirit, a demon. When any calamity is declared by the Kaniya to have been caused by a kuli, a ceremony called kuli kola is performed, in which the part of the spirit, as in the kárana kola, is played by one of the performers.

Kulin. [Bengali, Sanskrit *kulina*, from *kula*, race.] Of good family; a term applied to certain families supposed to have maintained their caste principles with greater strictness than the generality of their caste. The classification is said to have been made by the rájá of Bengal in the eleventh century. It applies especially to the Gauḍa subdivision of Bráhmans, of whom three classes were made—Kulin, Śrotriya, and Bansáj, the first including only eight Warendriya and six Rárhiya families. Later on the Kulins were divided into Mukhya the most pure, and Gauna the less pure, Kulins. So much are Kulins desired as sons-in-law that they make a profession of marriage, and are too often supported by their numerous wives; these wives pay usually one visit each to the husband's house and live thereafter with their parents.

Kulkarni. [Maráṭhi, perhaps from the Kanarese *kula*, a payer of revenue.] A village accountant in the Deccan. The office is hereditary, and has rent-free lands attached to it. See Village accountant.

Kulla Hazára. [Pashṭo.] The Hazára's cap, a small shrub about eighteen inches or two feet in diameter, growing into the shape of a skull-cap, and armed with spines fully two and a half inches long. It is used for fuel (*T. Seaton*).

Kullam. A corruption of Kulang.

Kully. See Khali.

Kulrujuwát. [Maráṭhi, from *kula*, a revenue-payer, and *rujuwát*, confronting.] The work of comparing ryots' receipt-books with their oral statements as to what they have paid, in order to see that they have not been cheated.

Kulta. [A corruption of *Kalita.*] An agricultural caste of good position in Sambalpur, Bonai, and Assam.

Kulthi. [Maráṭhi.] The pulse dolichos uniflorus, or horse-gram.

Kulwádi. Another name for Kunbi.

Kumár. The Bengali form of Kumbhár.

Kumára. [Sanskrit.] A young boy, an heir-apparent; also a name of the god of war, Kárttikeya.

Kumari. [Kanarese.] The cultivation of high or forest lands; it consists in the clearing and cultivating of spots in the jungles or forests, which after a season or two are again abandoned for other similar spots. Compare Jum, Dahya.

Kumári. [Sanskrit.] A maiden; an epithet of Durgá and others. Cape Comorin received its name from a temple erected there to Kumári.

Kumbár [Kanarese], or **Kumbhár** [Maráṭhi, from the Sanskrit *kumbhakára*, a water-jar maker]. The name of a caste; they are potters, and sometimes makers of tiles and bricks, and earthen idols also. In Kanara some are dyers. They rank high among Śudra castes. Some of the Gujarát Kumbhárs have given up their hereditary occupation altogether and follow agriculture. Some have become Sunni Musalmáns.

Kumi. The name of a tribe in Arákán and the Chittagong hills; they are savage and warlike, and live in fortified villages which have generally but one door. They wear their hair bound in a knot over their foreheads. Their religion is the same as that of the other Toungthá tribes; they burn their dead, first filling the mouth of the corpse with food. The tribe is also called Kweymi, and a division of it Kami.

Kumpanis. This corruption of the word 'company's' is sometimes used in the sense of government or public, as the Kumpanis bágh or park at Allahábád and at Morár.

Kumpáwat. [Gujaráti.] The common name of a branch of the Ráṭhors descended from one Kumpá.

Kunbi. [Maráṭhi.] The name of the chief agricultural caste of the Deccan and Konkan, identical with the Kurmis of northern India and the Kanbis of Gujarát. The Maráṭhás are considered to be a branch of this caste.

Kunḍ. [Hindi, Sanskrit *kunḍa.*] A basin, a pit, a hollow for containing water, a small tank.

Kunḍagolak. [Maráṭhi.] One who is the illegitimate offspring of a married woman.

Kuneia. [Panjábi, corrupt form.] The name of a Sikh misl, an offshoot of the Faizullapuria misl, and dwelling between Amritsar and the hills.

Kunku. [Maráṭhi, from the Sanskrit *kunkuma,* saffron.] A preparation of turmeric powder with oil. See Kanku, Pinjar.

Kunkutilá. [Maráṭhi.] Part of the ceremony of betrothal, consisting of the marking of the girl's forehead with kunku at her house by the man's relations, followed by a return visit of the girl's friends to the man's house to mark his forehead in like manner (*B. V. Śástri*).

Kunnuvan. [Tamil.] A branch of the Vellálans; they are employed in agriculture.

Kunwar. [Hindi, from the Sanskrit *kumára,* q.v.] A young prince or princess, especially an heir-apparent; the title is given to the eldest sons of ṭhákors as well as of rájás.

Kuppas. See Kapás.

Kur. The name of a Kolarian tribe of the Central Provinces.

Kurán. More commonly Koran.

Kurawan. [Tamil.] The name of a tribe who wander about with tents, hawking goods and telling fortunes. They deal largely in salt, which they carry from the salt-pans on the coast into the interior, returning with grain. Some make boxes and baskets of bamboo, twigs, and palmyra leaves; others breed pigs and donkeys; others collect honey and other jungle produce. They are perhaps the same as the Korachars of Mysore.

Kurḍu. [Maráṭhi.] A wild vegetable; it grows to the height of about six inches and bears a white flower; the leaves are the part eaten.

Kurfa. [Bengali.] A sub-tenant, an occupant holding under a khudkásht cultivator, and not, as a sháhprajá, direct from the zamindár.

Kuril. [Bengali.] The name of a low caste, variously employed as cultivators, labourers, leather-dealers, weavers, grooms, and musicians.

Kurma. [Sanskrit.] The turtle or tortoise, the name of the second awatár of Vishnu, when he descended in the form of a tortoise to support mount Mandara at the churning of the ocean. See under Amrita.

Kurmi. [Hindi.] The name of an agricultural caste. In Hindustán, Bengal, and Behar, where there are superior cultivating castes, the Kurmis do not usually hold so good a position as, under the names of Kanbi and Kunbi, they do in Gujurát and the Deccan.

Kuruba. [Kanarese, from *kuru*, a sheep.] A shepherd; the common name of two castes distinguished as Háṇḍe Kurubas and Kurubas proper. These have no intercourse with one another. There are many subdivisions of them. Besides sheep-breeding, they engage in agriculture, labour, and blanket-weaving. The women spin wool. See Beṭṭa, Jenu Kuruba.

Kurumba. The name of an aboriginal tribe occupying the slopes of the Nilgiris, and found also in the plains. They are mostly breeders of sheep and goats; some are cultivators, others collectors of jungle produce, and some take work on coffee-plantations. Kurumbas officiate as priests to the Badagas, and as musicians at weddings and funerals of other hill tribes. They are much dreaded as sorcerers. They are small in stature, very uncouth, and wild and squalid in appearance. Some profess to be Śaiwas. They burn their dead. Their language is Dravidian. In Ceylon they are blanket-weavers. The name may be identical with Kuruba.

Kurwa. See Khárwá.

Kuśa. [Sanskrit.] The sacred grass poa cynosuroides; it has long stalks and numerous pointed leaves, and is much used in religious ceremonies. See Mekhalá.

Kusawan. [Tamil.] The name of a low caste; they are potters.

Kushki. [Kanarese.] Land in which crops are raised without irrigation, as distinguished from tari and toṭa lands. Compare Jiráit.

Kusti. Another form of Kasti.

Kusumbha. [Sanskrit.] The name both of the saffron, crocus sativus, and of the bastard saffron, or safflower, carthamus tinctorius; from the flowers of the latter a red dye is made. Kusumbha is also the name of an intoxicating beverage prepared from hemp or opium, and sometimes translated 'red cup' by English writers.

Kutab Sháhi. The name of the branch of the Báhmani dynasty which, soon after the dismemberment of the latter in 1489 A.D., established itself at Golconda. The dynasty was founded by Kutab al Mulk, tarafdár of Telingana, who assumed the royal title in 1512; it lasted till 1687, when Golconda was taken by the Mogul emperor Aurangzib.

Kutcha. See Kachchá.

Kutril. The name of a tribe near Ráwal Pindi claiming to be of Arab descent.

Kuṭṭadamma. [Koḍagu, from *kuṭṭa*, and *amma*, mother.] The name of a female devil, who has no temple, but is represented by some stones in an enclosure under a tree in the forest at Kuṭṭa, on the borders of the Wainád. Many vows are paid to her, and many presents made to the pujári, who is a Wokkaliga (*L. Rice*).

Kutteeanee. See Khatauni.

Kutthádi. [Tamil.] The name of a caste of wandering actors and dancers.

Kuvera. See Kubera.

Kuvetar. [Hindi, from *kuwá*, a well.] Land that is dependent on a well for irrigation.

Kuzah. [Hindustáni.] An earthen bottle or ewer for holding water; being slightly porous, the contents are kept cooler than in an ordinary vessel.

Kweymi. [Arakanese, said to be from *kwey*, a dog, and *mi*, men.] Another name of the Kumi tribe, from their habit of eating dogs, or from the long end of their breech-cloth, which hangs down like a tail (*T. H. Lewin*).

Kyári. [Hindi, from the Sanskrit *kedára*.] A field or bed which can be laid under water; one of the embanked squares into which rice-land is divided for the purpose of irrigation; hence rice-land. Also the shallow beds or tanks used in the preparation of salt.

Kyaw. The name of a small tribe which appears to be a branch of the Kumi tribe, though they wear their knot of hair at the back of the head.

Kyburt. See Kaibartta.

Kyewurt. See Kaibartta.

Kyfyut. See Kaifiyat.

Kylas. See Kailása.

Kythee. See Káyati.

L.

Labbay. [Origin unknown.] The name of a race of Tamil-speaking Musalmáns resembling the Máppillas. They claim to be of common origin with the Navaitas, but the latter say that the Labbays are the descendants of their domestic slaves. The Labbays are smiths, fishermen, and boatmen, and many live by trade.

Lac. A corruption of Lákh.

Lac. [Hindi *lákh*, from the Sanskrit *lákshá*, probably a later form of *rákshá*, from *ranj*, to dye, or else from *laksha*, from the thousands of insects forming the dye.] A resinous substance produced by an insect, the coccus lacca, which fixes itself on the bark of a tree, chiefly the butea frondosa, and exudes from the margin of its body this resinous substance. As first gathered it is called stick-lac; when boiled down and freed from foreign matter, seed-lac; and when reduced to a thin crust, shell-lac.

Lack. See Lac, or Lákh.

Lackiras. See Lákhiráj.

Láḍar. [Kanarese.] The name of a trading caste in Mysore, said to have come from the Maráṭhá country; they worship Bhawáni chiefly; their priests are Sanyásis (*L. Rice*).

Lagan. [Hindi, from the Sanskrit *lagna*, the sun's entrance into a sign, from *lag*, to be joined to.] An auspicious moment; marriage, the marriage ceremony, or that part of it which precedes the barát. Half the dower is usually paid on this occasion. The tilak ceremony has preceded.

Lagi. [Hindi, from the Sanskrit *lag*, to stick.] A pole, especially one used for keeping a boat off shore as it is being dragged along by the track-rope; also a pole with a flag carried in procession.

Láheri. [Bengali.] Another name of the Nuri caste.

Lailat-al-miráj. [Arabic.] The night of Muhammad's ascent to heaven.

Lailat-al-qadir. [Arabic.] The night of power, the 27th Ramazán, when the koran is said to have descended from heaven.

Lákh. [Hindi, from the Sanskrit *laksha*.] A hundred thousand. The Indian method of writing and reading numbers expressed in figures is by thousands, lákhs, and crores: thus, 1,02,30,000; *i.e.* one crore, two lákhs, thirty thousand.

Lakhárá. [Gujaráti.] A maker of lac bangles.

Lákhiráj. [From the Arabic *lá*, without, and *khiráj*, tribute.] Rent-free land, or land of which a portion of the revenue is remitted.

Lakshmi. [Sanskrit.] The goddess of good luck, prosperity, and wealth; in the later mythology identified with Śri, and made the wife of Vishnu.

Lál. A Lushái chief. A lál must be of a particular clan called Aidey. It is usual for a lál's son to set up a village for himself. The men of one lál can transfer their allegiance to another at will; so a lál's village becomes large or small as he is successful in war or the reverse. A fugitive may take refuge in the house of a lál; he cannot be harmed, but he becomes the slave of the lál.

Lálá. [Persian.] A writer, a clerk; it is used as an address in speaking, especially to a Káyasth, and generally with ji added. Lálá Sáhib is a title by which a Banyá designates his father-in-law.

Lálagunda. [Kanarese.] The name of a division of the Wakligas; they are farmers, bullock-hirers, gardeners, builders of mud walls, and traders in straw. They deny being Śudras, and claim to be Linga Banajigas. They do not eat animal food or drink spirits. Some are Vaishnawas and some Lingáits.

Lálah. [Hindustáni.] A term for a respectable Hindu, such as a banker.

Lál Beg. The name of one of the gurus or gods of the Chuhrás. See Bálmikji. The name is altogether Muhammadan, *lál* being the Persian for red, and *beg* being a Mughal title. It has been suggested that the name should be Lál Bhekh, *i.e.*

bhikhu or bhikshu, a beggar or monk.

Lalita Vistára. [Sanskrit *lalita*, simple, from *lal*, to play, and *vistára*, spreading, detail, from *vistri*, to spread.] The name of a Sanskrit sutra work, partly verse, partly prose, relating the simple, natural acts of the life of Siddhártha the Buddha.

Lalla. See Lálá.

Lama. [Thibetan.] A Buddhist priest of Thibet.

Laman, or **Lamáni.** See Lambáḍi.

Lambáḍi. [Telugu.] A tribe who wander about as gipsies; their occupation is grain-carrying, and they are reputed also to be generally thieves. They speak a dialect of Hindustáni. The name is also sometimes applied to the Banjárás and sometimes to the Sukális.

Lambán. Another form of Lambáḍi.

Lambardár. [From the English word *number*, and the Persian *dár*, who has.] The cultivator who, either on his own account or as the representative of other members of the village, pays the government dues and is registered in the collector's roll according to his number (*H. H. Wilson*). It is in Bengal that the word is used in this sense. In the Panjáb and North-West Provinces it denotes the head of a village.

Lambári. See Lambáḍi.

Land Revenue Assignment. The grant by government to a private person of the right to enjoy rents due from a certain parcel of land. See Alienated, Inám, Jágir.

Langar. [Hindustáni.] The name of a festival peculiar to Hyderabad in the Deccan; it is celebrated in the month of Muharram in commemoration of the recovery in that season of a young prince who had been carried away to the jungles by the elephant he was riding; his mother made a vow that she would have a gold chain or langar put round the elephant's neck and take him in procession to the tomb called Husain-i-alam if he should bring her son safely back; the procession is still annually made.

Langar. [Persian.] An almshouse. In Maráṭhi any extensive establishment is called langarkháná.

Langar. More commonly Lungoor.

Langoṭi. [Hindustáni.] A piece of cloth worn round the loins and tucked between the legs.

Laonipatrak. [Gujaráti, from *lená*, that which is to be taken, and *patrak*, q.v.] The name of one of the village account-books under the Bombay land-revenue system; it is an annual rent-roll. Opposite the name of each holder appear in succeeding columns all the items of revenue, such as the rent of different kinds of land, water-rates, fines, for which he is liable.

Lapcha. A square pile of stones erected to the spirits of the hills or passes in Ladakh and Kunáwar.

Larin. The name of a coinage of the Adil Sháhi kings; the coins are sections of a wire. The name is referred to Laristan in Persia.

Lascar. [Hindustáni *lashkar.*] An army, a camp; also a band, a gang; a gang of labourers, the crew of a ship, etc. Thence it has come to be used also for a single member of such a gang, a sailor, a tent-pitcher, etc.

Lashkar. [Hindustáni.] An army, a camp. See Lascar. The new capital of Gwalior is called the lashkar from its having grown up round Sindhia's camp.

Láṭ. [Hindi.] A column, a pillar; especially the ancient inscribed single pillars found in northern India, such as Aśoka's pillar on the ridge at Delhi; others are at Firuzábád and Allahábád, and there is one called Bhimláṭ in the Bhálághát district; these are monoliths; there is a láṭ of wrought iron inscribed with Sanskrit near the Kutb minár.

Láṭhi. [Hindustáni.] A stick, a club, a bludgeon; often a bamboo heavily ringed and ferruled.

Láṭhiál. Another form of Láṭhiwálá.

Láṭhiwálá. [From *láṭhi* and *wálá*, q.v.] A man armed with a club; particularly such persons employed by landowners to support their cause in quarrels about crops, boundaries, etc.

Lattee. See Láṭhi.

Laukik. [Sanskrit *laukika*, from *lok*, q.v.] Worldly, secular; applied to some classes of Bráhman to denote their inferiority to others called Vaidik.

Laund. [Hindustáni.] An intercalary month. See Adhika.

Launḍi. [Hindustáni.] A slave-girl.

Lawád. [Maráṭhi.] An arbiter, an umpire; the name of some arbitration courts lately established in Poona and some other districts to decide civil claims without the expense of resorting to the courts established by government. The lawád courts are thus described in the Bombay Administration Report for 1876–77: 'A set of rules has been framed defining the constitution and function of the courts. The members are drawn for the most part from the class of pleaders, traders, and retired government officials. They agree to serve as arbiters in turn for a week at a time. They receive no remuneration. The arrangements of the court are in the hands of a secretary, who, in each week, chooses two members to act as umpires. Each court has a staff of clerks and messengers. To meet this expense fees are charged. But these are very moderate, amounting to not more than one-third of the cost in the ordinary subordinate civil courts.'

Lawáni. [Perhaps from the Persian *rawáni*, a traveller.] Another name of the travelling merchants called Povindahs.

Left-hand. The origin of the distinction between right-hand and left-hand castes is founded on fable, and is said to have taken place at Conjeveram, where the goddess Káli placed certain castes on her right and others on her left hand. The two parties have ever since disputed as to the relative honour accorded to each side. The division appears to be of comparatively modern origin, as it is not mentioned in any ancient work. It is, moreover, confined entirely to the south of India. Each party insists on its exclusive rights to certain privileges on all public festivals and ceremonies, and it not unfrequently happens that one side usurps the supposed rights of the other, when a faction fight is almost sure to ensue. Cases are recorded where the carrying of an umbrella, or wearing particular coloured flowers in the turban, has given rise to severe outbreaks, accompanied by bloodshed (*L. Rice*). See Yeḍagai.

Legislative Council. This is the popular name of four distinct legislative bodies in India. The first is the Council of the Governor-General of India, together with from six to twelve additional members summoned for purposes of legislation only. The additional members are nominated by the governor-general, and half of them must be non-official persons. The second and third legislative councils consist of the governor of Madras or of Bombay in council (see Governor-in-Council), together with the advocate-general, and from four to eight other additional members. These members are nominated by the governor, and half the number (including the advocate-general) must be non-official persons. The fourth legislative council consists of the lieutenant-governor of Bengal and persons nominated by him under the provisions of statute 24 and 25 Vict. c. 67, s. 45. The governor-general has power to establish similar councils in other provinces.

Lepchá. The name of a tribe, aborigines of Sikkim. They are Mongolian in feature and of short stature, and wear their hair collected in tails. They are timid and peaceful, but very indolent. They cultivate rice, and eat every kind of animal food. They believe in the existence of good and bad spirits, but pray only to the latter. Lepchás are settled in Nepál and Dárjiling (*Hooker*).

Limbu. The name of a tribe belonging to Sikkim and the hilly country in the east of Nepál. They intermarry with Kirátas and Lepchás. They cultivate grain, and keep cows, pigs, and poultry.

Linga. [Sanskrit.] The phallus or emblematic representation of Śiwa in his character as the reproductive power, or, it would seem, the supreme creative power. The symbol, made of stone and of double form to represent the blending of the male and female principles in creation, is set up in temples dedicated to Śiwa, and small representations of it are worn by some of his followers.

Lingáit. [Maráṭhi, from the Sanskrit *linga*, q.v.] The name of a sect of Śaiwas, so called from wearing a representation of the linga. They deny the sanctity of the Brahmanical order and the authority of the veda, and do not recognize caste. The sect belongs to the south of India, and was founded in the twelfth century by Basawa, the brother-in-law, chief minister, and general of Bijjala, a Kalachurya and Jain, who usurped the Chálukya throne 1157 A.D. Different sections of the Lingáits are called Silwant, Pancham, and Tiréle.

Lobán. [Arabic.] An odorous resin obtained from the boswellia thurifera and other trees, olibanum, frankincense.

Lobáná. A Hindu tribe of the Panjáb. They are farmers, traders, and carriers by occupation, and are peaceful and industrious.

Local Fund. This term, beyond its general and obvious meaning, is often used as another name of the one-anna cess, which is the chief factor of local or provincial, as distinguished from imperial, funds.

Local Government. This term is synonymous with Provincial Government.

Lodha. A class of Muhammadan thugs descended from, or grafted on, the Oudh stock, and found chiefly on the borders of that kingdom, or in the Tarái bordering on Nepál (*H. H. Wilson*).

Lodhá, or **Lodhi.** [Hindi.] The name of a low caste; they are cultivators in the North-West and Central Provinces, and labourers and personal servants in Bengal.

Lodi. The name of an Afghán dynasty, the last of those known under the general name of Ghori. It began with the long reigns of Bahlol Lodi and his son Sikandar, but in the third reign the Mogul conquest began.

Logue. A corruption of Lok.

Lohána. The name of the most numerous class of Hindus in Sindh. They claim to be Vaiśyas and wear the janeo, but they eat meat and drink spirits. Some are Vaishnawas, some Śaiwas, and some Sikhs. They are divided into two classes—the ámils, or government servants, and those whose avocation is trade or agriculture. The ámils have adopted the Musalmán costume and wear the cylindrical hat; they let their beards grow long, and only shave the crown of the head. The other Lohánás dress, some like the ámils, and others like ordinary Hindus; they shave the beard and crown and back of the head. Those who have come into Cutch are mostly of the Rámánuja sect. They are engaged in trade and agriculture, and some as clerks, and some are masons.

Lohánì. See Povindah.

Lohár. [Hindi form of the Sanskrit *lohakára*, from *loha*, iron.] The name of a caste; they are blacksmiths. Some have adopted islám. See Panchál. There are nomad Lohárs in northern India who claim to be descendants of the Ráṭhor Rájputs who left Chitor after its capture by Akbar.

Lok. [Hindi, Sanskrit *loka*.] The world; any division of the universe, as heaven, earth, or pátála; thence mankind, people.

Lombardy. See Lambáḍi.

Lonári. [Maráṭhi, from the Sanskrit *lawana*, salt.] The name of a caste; they prepare salt, lime, and charcoal, and are also wood-cutters.

Loot. [Of Sanskrit origin; in the vernaculars *luṭ*.] Robbing, plundering; also the booty carried away.

Lorrie. This word, as used in India, has not the exact meaning of any of the British provincial terms 'lorry,' 'lurrie,' 'rolly,' 'trolly,' but denotes a light carriage used on the ordinary railways, and propelled by two or more coolies running behind or at the sides. In Oudh, a bullock-cart is called by a similar name.

Loṭá. [Hindustáni.] A small metal pot of brass or copper.

Lower Provinces. The Bengal presidency was in 1853 divided into the Lower and the North-West Provinces, and each division placed under separate lieutenant-governors. The Lower Provinces retain the title of Bengal. They contain a population nearly double that of the United Kingdom.

Lubbee. See Labbay.

Luchchá. [Hindustáni.] A libertine, a vagabond, a swindler; a common term of abuse.

Luggun. See Lagan.

Luhár. Another form of Lohár.

Lukibidya. [Bengali.] A science by which a person is supposed to have the power of rendering himself invisible (*H. H. Wilson*).

Lukta. [Arabic.] In Muhammadan law, property which a person finds and takes charge of as a trust until claimed.

Lumberdar. A corrupt form of Numberdár.

Lunar day. The lunar day of the Hindu calendar is independent of sunrise or sunset, and means the time occupied by the moon in traversing a thirtieth part of its circuit. See Tithi.

Lunar mansion. See Nakshatra.

Lunar month. This term, as used both in the Hindu and Muhammadan calendars, means the synodical month, except that, in the former under the Krishnadi method, the period taken is from full moon to full moon, instead of from new moon to new moon, and in the latter the beginning of the month is counted, not from the day of conjunction, but from the day that the moon is visible. See Month.

Lunar race. See Chandrawanśa.

Lungi. [Hindustáni.] A coloured check worn by Muhammadans as a dhoti; also a turban with a check or gold border (*S. W. Fallon*). In Bengali, a petticoat.

Lungoor. [Hindi *langur.*] The monkey presbytis entellus; it grows as tall as five feet, is grey, with black face and grey whiskers, and goes about in large herds.

Lusháí. The name of a powerful and independent people touching upon the borders of the Chittagong hill tracts, and extending in numberless hordes north and south-east until they reach Káchár on the one hand and Burma on the other. They cannot be considered as a nation, for they have no coherence of government or polity; but, with slight differences, they speak one language and follow the same customs. They have no distinctions of caste. Each village is a petty state under its own chief. The men chiefly employ themselves in making forays upon weaker tribes, or in hunting; the only home-work they do is to build the house, to clear the land for cultivation, and to help to gather the harvest. They work in iron, but are ignorant of pottery. The women fetch water, hew wood, cultivate and help to reap the crops, besides spinning and cooking. Both men and women are well made and wonderfully muscular, but of a sulky and forbidding cast of countenance. A Lusháí village is always situated on the top of a high hill; when the land within easy reach is exhausted the village is removed to a new site. The Lusháis used to make frequent raids across the frontier to carry off slaves. An expedition was sent to punish them in 1871. They are called by the Bengalis, Kuki, and by the Burmese, Lankhe. Those on the British frontier are divided into the Howlong, Lylu, and Ratan Poiya clans. Some of the Lusháis dry the bodies of their dead and keep them for months before burying them (*T. H. Lewin*).

Lutteeal. See Láṭhiál.

Luwana. See Loháná.

M.

Mábáp. [Hindustáni.] Literally, mother and father; but applied as an appellation to any one when invoking pity or protection.

Máchán. [Bengali, from the Sanskrit *mancha.*] A stage or platform supported on columns; a raised platform for spectators; a little shed erected on poles for the watchman of a field; an elevated frame to support a hay-stack out of the reach of cattle, or on which to expose grain to dry.

Machchhardáni. [Gujaráti, from *machchhar*, a mosquito.] A light curtain of lace or muslin hung completely round and over a bed to exclude mosquitoes.

Máchhi. [Gujaráti, from the Sanskrit *matsya*, a fish.] A fisherman. The name also of a caste who are fishermen and sailors. Some have been converted to islám (Sunni).

Machwá. [Maráṭhi, from *machchh*, a fish.] A fishing-boat, an undecked boat of from four to twelve candies. The machwás of different ports vary slightly in build. They are considered to be amongst the swiftest sailing-vessels known; they are very sharp in the bows, with hollow keel, well rounded in the stern, and the mast slopes a little forward; these vessels are chiefly made of teak, and cost from Rs. 300 to Rs. 400; they last about forty years.

Máḍ. [Maráṭhi.] The cocos nucifera, or cocoa-nut palm.

Madad. [Hindi, from the Sanskrit *mada*, intoxication.] An intoxicating pill or bolus made of betel leaf and opium.

Madaiyan. [Tamil.] A village servant who distributes water for irrigational purposes.

Madak. [Bengali.] The name of a caste, called also Mayrá; they are sweetmeat-makers, and hold a middle rank among the Śudra castes.

Madaka. [Hindi, from the Sanskrit *mada*, intoxication.] Anything stupefying or intoxicating; a pellet of opium or other drug for smoking.

Madári. [Hindustáni.] A juggler, a snake-charmer, a Muhammadan gáruḍi. They are mostly Sunni Musalmán converts from the Naṭs. Also the name of a community of beshara Sunni fakirs; their patron saint is Madár Sháh, supposed to be still alive in his tomb at Makanpur, in Oudh, where a festival in his honour is held on the 17th Jamádi-àl-awal; besides begging, Madáris are jugglers, bear and monkey leaders, and rope-dancers.

Madhwáchárya. [Sanskrit.] The name of a Vaishnawa sect founded by Madhwácharya (called also Sarwajna and by several other names), who lived early in the twelfth century, and is said to have been an incarnation of Hanumán. This sect identify Vishnu with the supreme spirit, whom they endow with real attributes. They distinguish between *paramátmá*, the supreme spirit, and *jíwátmá*, life, and consider each to be everlasting, and that there is no absorption of the latter after death. They are thus dualists, and opposed to the Smártas. They are divided into many parties, which, however, eat and intermarry with each other. They wear wrappers of an ochre colour, and go about bare-headed or covered by a simple cap. They add a central black line to the usual Vaishnawa frontal mark, which they make red. They are sometimes called Vir Vaishnawas.

Máḍi. [Maráṭhi, from *máḍ*, q.v.] Toddy extracted from the cocoa-palm, as distinguished from that taken from the palmyra or the date-palm.

Mádiga. [Kanarese.] The name of a large class of outcastes commonly called Chucklers by Europeans. They belong to the left-hand faction, and call themselves Yeḍagai in preference to their proper name. They are workers in leather. See Chakkili.

Madrasah. [Arabic.] A place for reading, a school, a college.

Madurkati. [Bengali.] The sedge papyrus pangorei, from which matting is largely made.

Máfi. [Hindustáni, properly *muáfi.*] Remitted, free; applied to lands exempt from the payment of revenue.

Mag. The Gujaráti name of Mung.

Mágadhi. [Sanskrit.] Pertaining to the country of Magadha or Behar; the name of an old prákrit resembling Páli; also the name of the modern vernacular of Behar.

Mágánam. [Tamil.] A division of a revenue district, usually consisting of six or seven villages under the management of one karnam.

Magar. [Hindi.] The name of both the crocodilus palustris and crocodilus porosus; they are smaller, but more dangerous than the gavial, and feed chiefly on animals that come to the water to drink.

Mágár. The name of a tribe in the lower levels of Nepál; their language is monosyllabic, but they use an alphabet of Indian origin; their religion is hybrid; they abstain from beef, but are otherwise unscrupulous in eating and drinking.

Magaram. [Malayálam, the Sanskrit *makara*, a sea-monster.] The name of the month during which the sun is in the sign Capricorn, corresponding most nearly to January and Paush (in Bengal, Mágh). See Month.

Magh. The name of a class of people the offspring of Bengali women by Burmans when the latter possessed Chittagong. The name is also applied by Bengalis to the Khyoungthá (*T. H. Lewin*).

Mágh. [Sanskrit.] The Hindu month most nearly corresponding with February; it is so called from *maghá*, the name of the nakshatra (part of the sign Leo) in which the moon is at full in this month. See Month.

Maghrabi. [Arabic.] Western, a native of the west; applied to natives of northern Africa.

Mahábhárata. [Sanskrit.] The great (war) of the Bháratas; the name of a collection of epic poems by different authors, but attributed to Vyása, the arranger of the vedas. The mahábhárata describes the contests between the descendants of Bhárata of the lunar race; on one side being the Pánḍawas, the five sons of the pale Pánḍu, and on the other their first cousins the Kaurawas, a hundred in number, sons of the blind Dhritaráshṭra. The Pánḍawas, and especially Arjun the third brother, are made the heroes. The whole work consists of over 200,000 lines.

Mahábráhman. Literally, a great Bráhman, but applied contemptuously in Bengal to a low-class Bráhman who officiates at funerals; also a Bráhman who performs religious ceremonies for Śudras and mixed castes (*H. H. Wilson*).

Mahádanda. [Bengali.] The name of a low caste of fishermen and boatmen.

Mahádeo. See Mahádewa.

Mahádevi. The wife of Mahádewa; Káli, Durgá.

Mahádewa. [Sanskrit.] The great god; a name of Śiwa.

Maháján. [Hindi, from the Sanskrit *mahá*, great, and *jana*, a person.] A great man; a term applied to merchants and bankers. In Bengal the mahájan is the village capitalist, who advances money to all the ryots of one or more mauzahs, receiving the return in grain at harvest; thence he becomes a grain-dealer also. In western India the leading Wániá, Kansárá, and Bháṭiá traders in Gujarát, Cutch, and Káṭhiáwár are spoken of collectively as the mahájans; they form a sort of trades-union and religious community combined. In some places the term means the head of a caste or the headman of a village.

Mahájanwádi. [Gujaráti: see *wádi*.] A place set apart for caste feasts and religious ceremonies.

Mahákála. [Sanskrit *mahá*, great, and *kála*, time, fate, death.] A name of Śiwa, in his aspect as the great destroyer.

Mahákáli. The wife of Mahákála.

Mahal. [Arabic.] A place, a house, an apartment, a seraglio; a palace, a báradari.

Mahál. [Hindi, properly the plural of *mahal*.] A province, a district, as the jungle Mahále on the west of Bengal, the Panch Mahále in Gujarát; also a division of a district, a parganá; an estate; also a branch or department of revenue. In the Bombay presidency mahál means particularly a part of a táluká placed under a separate officer, because the whole would be too large for the mámlatdár to manage. In Baroda a mahál is a táluká.

Mahálkari. [Affix *kari*, q.v.] An

officer in charge of a part of a táluká. He exercises most of the powers of the mámlatdár, but has a much smaller establishment, and usually no separate treasury.

Mahalla. [Hindi, a form of the Arabic *mahal*, a place, a district.] A ward of a town; sometimes especially the Muhammadan quarter.

Mahallá. The Bengali form of Mahalla.

Mahámandaleśwar. [Maráṭhi, from the Sanskrit *mahá*, great, *maṇḍal*, a circle, a province, and *iśwara*, q.v.] The ruler of a province, the title of great vassals resembling the páligars.

Mahánádu. [Tamil.] The great assembly, a sort of parliament or witenagemote of the leaders of agricultural castes.

Mahanta. [Sanskrit, from *mahá*, great.] The head of a body of sádhus, or religious mendicants; the superior of a monastery. According to the Mitakshara a mahanta is succeeded on his death by his virtuous disciple. If no such person is qualified, the mahantas of neighbouring maṭhs usually meet and elect a successor.

Maháprasád. [Sanskrit *mahá*, great, and *prasád*, q.v.] A great favour, a great distribution of prasád. The prasád of Jagannáth is generally called by this name, and the principle that all persons may partake of prasád has been most put in practice at his temple at Puri. In the Sambalpur district of the Central Provinces there is a practice of persons eating mahápraśád together in token that they are henceforth friends and brothers.

Mahár. [Maráṭhi.] The name of the low caste of the Deccan and Konkan corresponding to the Dheḍ, Holia, Mala, Pariah, and Poliyar of other parts of the south of India. The Mahárs are village scavengers, messengers, and watchmen; grass and wood cutters, and measurers of land under the supervision of kárkuns; and many enlist in the army. They eat the flesh of cattle that die, and live outside the Hindu villages; they worship some of the Hindu gods, but are not allowed to pass the threshold of the temples; they employ Bráhmans for marriages, but gosains or vairágis for other ceremonies. A Mahár prefers to be addressed as Parwári.

Mahárájá. [Sanskrit *mahá*, great, *rájá*, king.] A supreme king; applied in courtesy to every rájá, or to any person of high rank or deemed holy. The name is shortened to mahárája or maharáj when applied, not to a ruler, but to a man who sets himself up as holy. The religious heads of the Wallabhacháryas take this title. In Nepál it is the title, not of the ruler, but of the prime minister.

Mahárájadhiráj. [Sanskrit *adhi*, over, superior.] A compound of mahárája, or great king, and adhirája, or supreme king; a magniloquent title applied to some rulers, as those of Cutch, Dholpur, and Nepál.

Mahárání. [*Mahá*, great, and *ráni*, queen.] A queen, either in her own right or as wife of a rájá. The term is applied also in courtesy to Hindu ladies of lesser rank. It is the title commonly given in India to the Queen of England.

Maháráshṭra. [Sanskrit, according to the prevalent opinion, from *mahá*, great, and *ráshṭra*, kingdom, from *ráj*, to reign.] The great country; the land of the Maráṭhás. Thence the name of the subdivision of the Dráviḍa Bráhmans who occupied that region. Among the further divisions of the Maháráshṭras are the Chitpáwans, the Karháḍás, the Deśasths.

Máhári. [Uriya.] A dancing-girl attached to a temple.

Mahásankránti. [Sanskrit.] The great sankránti, another name for the makarsankránti, or the passage of the sun into Capricorn.

Mahasoy. [A corruption of the Bengali *mahásaya.*] A person of merit or respect. The word is used as a term of respectful address. A village schoolmaster is called guru mahasoy.

Mahat. [Bengali.] The name of a cultivating Śudra caste of middle rank in Midnápur.

Mahdavi. The Kanarese name of the Mahdiviyyah sect; they are settled at Channapatna, in Mysore, whither they withdrew when driven out of Hyderabad.

Mahdi. [Arabic.] A guide; especially the title of the twelfth imám according to the Shiahs, Abul Karem Muhammad by name, who disappeared A.D. 879, but who is supposed to be still alive, living in concealment. Muhammad is said to have prophesied that after a period of trouble the mahdi will reappear and establish peace. The Sikhs treat the mahdi as having come and gone, ineffectual like all other gods and prophets previous to the khálsa. See Kalki, Dajjal, Ghairmahdi.

Mahdiviyyah. The name of a sect of Shiahs who believe the mahdi came in the fifteenth century.

Maheśwar. [Sanskrit, from *mahá*, great, and *iśwara*, q.v.] The great lord, a name of Śiwa, or Mahádewa.

Máhili. [Bengali.] The name of a low caste; they are cultivators and labourers.

Mahishásur. [Sanskrit.] The Asura Mahisha, or demon buffalo, slain by Durgá. See Dasara. The name Mysore is a corruption of this word.

Mahometan. See Muhammadan.

Mahoul. The name of a creeping plant, bauhinea racemosa, or scandens. It is a gigantic plant, with tough woody stems.

Mahout. [A corruption of the Hindustáni *mahávat.*] An elephant-driver. The mahout sits on the neck of the elephant; he bids it move forward by applying the pointed end of his goad, stops it by the butt end, and turns it by pressing his leg to the neck.

Mahr. [Arabic.] A marriage settlement of property on the wife; it is a necessary concomitant of a contract of marriage; where no amount has been fixed, the wife is entitled to mahr-i-misl, or the dower of her equals, that is, the sum usual for persons of her rank.

Mahratta. See Maráṭhá.

Mahseer. [Hindi *mahásir*, from *mahá*, great, and *sir*, head.] A large fish of the carp species, common to all the mountain streams of upper India.

Mahsud. The name of a clan of Waziris. They occupy the eastern slopes of the Suláimán range north of the Gumal pass, and are divided from our frontier by the Batánis. They have proved a most incorrigible tribe. An expedition proceeded against them in 1860.

Mahtá. [Hindi.] A clerk, an agent; sometimes the headman of a caste or trade.

Mahtam. The name of a low vagrant caste in the Panjáb; some have been converted to islám and some to sikhism.

Máhuri. [Bengali.] The name of a trading caste in Gayá and Patná districts.

Mahwá. [Hindi.] The tree bassia latifolia. See Mowra.

Maidán. [Hindi, Arabic *medán.*] A plain, a level tract; any large open space, especially one covered with grass and maintained as a place for recreation or for the parade of troops.

Maind. [Maráṭhi.] A machine for smoothing a ploughed and sown field; a samár.

Maistree. See Mistry.

Maithila. [Sanskrit, from *mithila*, the name of a city the site of which is in the present district of Tirhut.] The name of the fourth subdivision of the Gauḍa Bráhmans.

Maithili. The language of Tirhut; it is a dialect of Hindi.

Maitreya. [Sanskrit, from *mitra*, a friend.] The name of the Buddha who is yet to appear.

Máji. [Hindi, from *má*, Sanskrit *mátá*, a mother, and *ji*, q.v.] A title of a woman in an exalted position, such as a queen-regent.

Majlis. [Arabic.] A party, a levee, an assembly, a court.

Majmudár. [Hindi, from the Arabic *majmua*, total, and Persian *dár*, holder.] A native revenue accountant either of a district or of a táluk, and remunerated either by inám land or by fees. In Gujarát the majmudárs were hereditary officers holding watans of very early date. Also the title of an auditor of accounts attached to a body of horse under the Maráṭhá government.

Majmun. [Gujaráti, from the Arabic *mazmum*, additional.] Under the narwá system the shares of the narwádárs did not comprise the whole of the village lands, but some portion was left common, to be let out to servants or given to persons to induce them to come and settle in the village; similarly within each principal share, when it was divided among subsharers, a portion was kept common; these common lands were called majmun. The village majmun was managed jointly by all the principal sharers, and the majmun of a particular share by the proprietor of that share.

Majum. [Hindustáni.] A decoction prepared from hemp leaves with water, ghi, sugar, and milk. Also a preparation of bhang, chillies, and sugar for chewing.

Majumdár. The Bengali form of Majmudár. Also the receiver and auditor of a zamindár's rents.

Majun. See Mahájan.

Majus. [Persian.] A magician; also a Pársi.

Maká. The cereal zea mais. See Indian corn.

Makara. [Sanskrit.] A fabulous sea-monster, the emblem of Kámadewa, and the tenth sign of the zodiac, corresponding to Capricorn. Though the name, in the vernacular form magar, is given to the alligator, the makara is represented in sculpture with the head and fore legs of an antelope, and the body and tail of a fish.

Makarsankránti. [Sanskrit *makara*, and *sankránti*, q.v.] The festival on the occasion of the passage of the sun into the sign Makara, or Capricorn; it occurs at the winter solstice, the first day of the solar month Magaram, called in Bengal Mágh, and introduces the lucky half of the year, uttaráyana.

Makráni. [Hindustáni.] An immigrant from the Makrán coast. They are Sunni Musalmáns, and serve as soldiers and watchmen.

Maktá. [Arabic *maqta*, cutting.] A contract, an agreement; in Telugu, rent, rate; in Maráṭhi, under the khoti system, a permanent fixed rent, a khanḍ.

Maktab. [Arabic.] A place for teaching writing; a Muhammadan school; applied now only to indigenous schools.

Makwáná. [Gujaráti.] The name of a division of the Koli tribe. Some have been converted to islám.

Mál. The name of a low caste or tribe most numerous in Murshidábád. The Máls of Bengal proper are closely allied to, if not identical with, the semi-aboriginal caste of Chanḍáls. On the other hand, the Márs or Máls who formerly ruled in Paláman, and are now settled chiefly in the tributary state of Sarguja, are thoroughly Hinduized in their habits, and appear from their features to be of Aryan extraction, with perhaps a slight admixture of Dravidian blood.

Mala. [Malayálam.] A hill; also the spirit of a hill; a hill-god.

Mala. The name in Telugu of the low caste corresponding to the Tamil Paraiyans, the Kanarese Holeyas, the Malayálam Poliyans, the Maráṭhi Mahárs, and Gujaráti Dheḍs.

Málá. [Bengali.] The name of a low caste very numerous in Tirhut; they are boatmen and fishermen.

Mala Arayan. See Arayan.

Malabár. The name of a class of pirates, so called as they chiefly infested the Malabár coast. They have given their name to a hill in Bombay, in the bay behind which they used to lie in wait.

Málair. The name of a division of the Paháriá tribe.

Malasir. The name of a rude tribe of Malabár speaking a mixture of Tamil and Malayálam. They collect forest produce, and cultivate small plots in the woods. They do not use Bráhmans, but worship a god called Mállang, who is represented by a stone encircled by a wall which serves for a temple. They burn their dead.

Mala Velan. Another name of the Arayan tribe.

Malayálam. A Dravidian language allied to Tamil, but employing a different alphabet. It is the language of nearly four millions of persons in Travancore and along the Malabár coast.

Malbá. [Hindi.] A collective term for the public expenses of a village community, such as the cost of entertaining visitors and of amusements, remuneration of such village servants as are not paid by government, fines imposed on the village, temple expenses, and the like.

Male. The name of a gipsy class in Coorg, said to have come from Malabár.

Malekite. See Máliki.

Malevar. [Kanarese, from *male*, a hill.] A tribe of hill-men in Mysore.

Málguzár. [Hindi, from *mál*, wealth, and *guzár*, payer.] A person who pays revenue either to government or a zamindár, either on his own account or as a representative of others.

Málguzári. [Hindi.] Revenue assessment, or land capable of paying assessment.

Máli. [Sanskrit, from *málá*, a wreath.] The name of a high Śudra caste; they are wreath-makers, florists, and gardeners. They are also workers in solá pith, firework-makers, and are often employed as inoculators or vaccinators.

Málik. [Hindustáni, from the Arabic *milk*, property.] A proprietor, an owner, a lord; a cultivator possessing hereditary rights; also a landlord, a zamindár; in the North-West Provinces the headman of a village. See Headman. Also the name of a tribe of Sunni Muhammadans found chiefly in Behar, but also in many other parts of India, and supposed to be of Rájput origin; their principal occupation is agriculture, but they serve also as village gumáshtas, and in the public service as messengers and constables.

Málikah. [Arabic.] A queen.

Malikana. [Tamil.] Subsistence allowance granted to zamindárs, poligars, and others dispossessed of their estates, usually at the rate of ten per cent. on the collections actually made from their estates (*J. H. Nelson*).

Máliki. The second Sunni school; that founded by Málik. It is puritanical, fierce in its dogma, severe in its morals, and those who profess it are undoubtedly the most fervent, the most fanatical, of believers. They represent more nearly than any other Musalmáns the ancient earnestness of the prophet's companions, and the sword in their hand is ever the sword of God (*W. S. Blunt*).

Málish. [Persian.] Rubbing; the hand-grooming of a horse; also the threshing and treading out of corn.

Málisthán. [Hindi.] The name of a god formerly worshipped at Multán. His idol was destroyed by the Muhammadans in the tenth century A.D., and again in the seventeenth.

Malla. [Sanskrit.] The name of a caste, the offspring of an outcaste Kshatriya by a Kshatriya woman; they are boxers and wrestlers.

Malláh. [Hindustáni.] A sailor, a boatman; also a salt-maker.

Mallee. See Máli.

Mallek. See Málik.

Malpan. The title of an ecclesiastic of certain rank in the Syrian Church in southern India, said to correspond to that of archdeacon.

Malvar. [Kanarese.] The name of a cultivating caste.

Málvi. [Maráṭhi.] Belonging to the country of Málwá. The name of a breed of cattle characterized by a mild temper; horns with a peculiar twist; broad, flat forehead, with an even ridge; large, quiet, full eyes; large, wide ears. The cow is a very good milker; the bullock is used as a draught animal, but is not fast-trotting like the Khilári.

Málwan. [Maráṭhi.] The name of a class of pirates whose head-quarters were on the Málwan coast in the Koṇkan.

Mamiyain. See Mumiái.

Mámlatdár. [Maráṭhi, from the Arabic *muadmalat*, business, and Persian *dár*, who holds.] The native officer at the head of a táluká in the Bombay presidency. The mámlatdár resides at the chief town of his táluká, where he has a treasury and a large establishment of kárkuns. He is directly subordinate to the assistant-collector, and his duties are multifarious. Through the village officers he collects the revenue of his táluká, and under orders disposes of lands that have been resigned by their holders, and sells annual usufructs. He receives accounts and statistical returns from every village, and thence prepares general statements for the táluká. From his treasury he pays his own and all the village establishments, and generally all the expenditure incurred by government within the táluká, and makes remittances to the district treasury. He supervises the smaller public works in progress, and ascertains the wants of every part of his táluká. He is also a magistrate, generally of the second, sometimes of the first, class, and his head kárkun has lower magisterial powers. The mámlatdár has also jurisdiction to try summarily cases of disturbed possession. His salary varies from 100 to 250 rupees a month.

Mamoty. [Corruption of the Tamil *manveṭṭi.*] A kind of hoe.

Mámuli. [Bengali, from the Arabic *mámul.*] Established, customary; according to routine.

Man. This word is used in Sanskrit and in all the vernaculars, but is originally Arabic. The common form of it in English is Maund.

Man. [Hindi, from the Sanskrit *mani.*] A jewel; particularly a jewel fabled to be found in the head of a cobra, or, as some say, a silky filament spat out by a cobra on a dark night, when it wants to see. It is reckoned a most valuable talisman.

Manabhat-kári. [Hindustáni, the past participle of the Arabic *nabt*, to plant, and *kári*, workmanship.] The Indian hard stone inlaying art. It is properly architectural rather than pictorial, and consists of the insertion of pieces of marble and other light-coloured stones into sandstone, or of that of jewels into white marble. The earlier patterns are geometrical; into the later leaves and flowers are introduced.

Manatappan. [Malayálam.] A caste

of Vellálans originally from Coimbatore, first settled in the Pálghát province, and intermixed and often confounded with the Náirs (*Graeme*).

Mánbhawa. The name of a Vaishnawa sect. They are devotees of Krishna, male and female. Their chief guru has his head-quarters at Karinja, in Berar. The Mánbhawas wear no tuft on the crown of their head, or moustachios, and do not let their beards grow to any length. Black is the favourite colour of their dress. Their favourite authority is the bhagwad-gita. They observe no festivals but the Gokuláshṭami and the Dattátreya (*J. Wilson*). Dattátreya was a sage deemed to be a portion of Vishnu, his father Atri having exacted this favour from the god by severe penance.

Manchial. [A Portuguese corruption of *manzil*, q.v.] A kind of litter much used in the Konkan, where roads for wheeled traffic are few; it has a thick roof and is open at the sides.

Mand. [Toḍa, from Kanarese *mane*, a house.] A Toḍa village. The express form *toḍamand* is also used. The village consists of a cluster of huts built of timber and bamboo, and thatched; the whole, and sometimes individual huts also, being surrounded with a wall of loose stones. Besides the dwelling-huts, each mand contains a páltchi, one or two huts for the calves, and a cattle-kraal.

Mandai. [Bengali.] The name of a semi-Hinduised tribe resembling the Gáros; they are cultivators and wood-cutters.

Mandal. [Bengali.] A village headman; the office is usually hereditary and without direct emoluments, but the other villagers help the manḍal in his cultivation. He and a few elders constitute the village panchâyat. See Headman.

Manḍal. [Maráṭhi.] The black sand-snake, commonly called the dutonḍá.

Manḍap. [Sanskrit.] A temporary building erected and decorated for wedding festivities. Also the porch in front of a mandir. Also, in Bengal, a permanent building for village gatherings and religious festivals.

Manḍapa. [Tamil.] A square or rectangular hall with a flat roof supported by pillars, generally open at the sides; the porch of a temple. See Vimána.

Mándátá. A division of the Kolis of Gujarát, allied to the Gohil Rájputs. They are sailors and cultivators, and of the Swámi-Náráyan sect.

Mandir. [Sanskrit, from *mand*, to be glad.] A house, a palace; and especially a temple. There are two distinct styles of Hindu temple, one peculiar to the south of India (see Vimána), and the other found in all other parts; the latter consists of the adytum or gábhárá, surmounted by a śikhar, and with a manḍap or porch in front of it.

Mánḍwá. Another form of Manḍap.

Maner. Another form of Manyár.

Máng. [Sanskrit *Mátang*.] A depressed aboriginal tribe. They are intermediate, says Dr. Wilson, between the Mahárs of the Maráṭhá country and the Pariahs of the Madras presidency. Strong antipathies exist between them and the Mahárs—they affecting to despise the Mahárs because they eat the flesh of the cow, and the Mahárs despising them because they eat the flesh of the sow. Mángs make ropes, mats, baskets, and muzzles for bullocks, and, when settled in the outskirts of villages, they act as village watchmen, guides, scavengers, and as executioners. They employ Bráhmans for their marriages, and they shave their beards as a sign of mourning. They bury their dead. See Gáruḍi.

Mangal. The name of a tribe of Turkish origin settled about the Pewár pass, Ali Khel, and at Zurmat; they number 5000 fighting men, and pay tribute to the amir of Kábul.

Mángela. [Maráṭhi.] A caste of the Konkan; they are fishers, coasting traders, and labourers.

Mango. [Malayálam *mángáy.*] The fruit of the tree mangifera indica, or the tree itself. The fruit is a solid oval in shape, three or four inches long, of a yellow or yellow-and-red colour when ripe, and contains a large stone; it is largely eaten by Europeans as well as natives. The tree grows to a height of forty feet, and is of a rounded form, with dense foliage.

Mango-bird. A little yellow bird, the oriolus kundoo, or Indian oriole.

Mango-fish. The polynemus risua; it is about fifteen inches long, resembles the perch in shape, and is found in the Bay of Bengal and the Indian Ocean.

Mangosteen. [Malay *mangusta.*] The garcinia mangostana, or the variety garcinea purpurea, or gambogia, or its fruit, which is of the size of a small apple. The tree grows to a height of twenty feet, and is a native of the Malay Archipelago. See Kokamb.

Mani. A pile of stones by the roadside on which are deposited slabs with sacred inscriptions in memory of deceased persons. Also a praying-machine, a small barrel-shaped instrument, two or three inches long, which is made to revolve round an axis, one end of which is held in the hand. In the mani are enclosed scraps of paper inscribed with sacred sentences (*Hutton*).

Mani. [Sanskrit.] A jewel. See Man.

Mániam. [Tamil.] Fee, grant, remuneration by occupancy of land rent-free. The Hindu word mániam appears to correspond pretty closely with the foreign word inám.

Mániamdár. [Tamil, Persian *dár*, holder.] The holder of a mániam.

Manihár. [Gujaráti.] The name of a caste; they sell bangles, beads, looking-glasses. There is a distinct community of Sunni Musalmán Manihárs, converts from this caste.

Manilla-man. [A corruption of the Telugu *maneláváḍu.*] An itinerant dealer in coral and gems.

Maniyakáran. [Tamil, from *maniyam*, management, and *kára*, agent.] A subordinate in charge of the revenues of one or more villages; a revenue inspector; auditor of accounts; supervisor (*J. H. Nelson*). Also the superintendent of a temple.

Mánjhá. [Panjábi, from the Sanskrit *madhya*, middle.] Land lying between the land in the immediate proximity of a village and that on the boundaries of its lands. Also the name of the upland region between the Satluj and the Bias on the one side, and the Rávi on the other; it is the original home of the Sikhs, and contains their capital Lahore and their sacred city Amritsar. Mánjhá is also the name of the dialect of Panjábi spoken in this district.

Mánjhi. [Bengali.] The steersman of a boat, usually of the Málá, Tíor, or Jáliyá caste. Also the title among some tribes, as the Kandhs and Santáls of their headmen. See Headman.

Manjholi. [Hindustáni.] A light cart for passengers.

Mánkari. [Maráṭhi, from *mán*, honour, and *kari*, the active affix.] A man of honour or dignity, especially the descendant of a mansabdár.

Mánki. The headman of a pir or group of villages among the Munḍás.

Mannan. The name of a hill tribe of Travancore; they are a wandering people, little, strange-looking mountain-men, hardy and very black, speaking bad Tamil, much employed by the sarkár to collect cardamoms, keep watch, etc.; they rarely cultivate anything but rági (*S. Mateer*).

Manori. An animal resembling the pole-cat, but usually inhabiting the space between the ceiling and roof of a bungalow.

Mansab. [Arabic.] Office, dignity. In Hyderabad the pension office is called the mansab.

Mansabdár. [Hindustáni, from *mansab*, and the Persian *dár*, who holds.] A title expressing rank, according to the number of horsemen the holder could bring into the field, under the Mogul government; as a mansabdár of 2000.

Manṭapa. The Kanarese form of Manḍapa. A manṭapa may be either the porch of a temple or a separate independent building. At Tirumala there is a manṭapa of a thousand pillars. See Vimána.

Mantra. [Sanskrit, from *man*, to conceive.] Prayer and praise embodied in the texts and metrical hymns that form the first and oldest portion of the veda. The word means literally the instrument of conveying thought, and is usually applied to those prayers, invocations, and hymns which are addressed to certain deifications of the forces of nature. The first forces deified seem to have been those manifested in the sky and air. Only a few of the hymns appear to contain the simple conception of one divine, self-existent being. The hymns contain no allusion to the doctrine of transmigration of souls, nor do they afford any sanction to the prohibition of widow-marriages, the encouragement of child-marriages, the iron rules of caste, and the interdiction of foreign travel. Nor is there in them any evidence of the use of idols. The hymns were probably composed by a succession of poets at different dates between 1500 and 1000 B.C. Mantras are of three classes, those of the rig-veda, which are metrical and meant for loud recitation; those of the yajur-veda, which are in prose for use at sacrifices; and those of the sáma-veda, which are metrical for chanting at the soma ceremonies (*Monier Williams*). In the present day every Hindu is taught a particular mantra by the guru of his family. Divine worship, as practised by a layman in person and at home, consists of reciting a mantra before the ṭhákur. The word is most commonly met with in English in its sense as a magical formula, an incantation, a charm. One way of getting the benefit of a mantra is to write it out on a pipal leaf, then to wash the leaf in water, and drink the water.

Mantri. [Sanskrit, from *mantra.*] One who is wise in counsel, an adviser, a minister.

Manu. [Sanskrit, from *man*, to think.] Thought; man. This, says Max Müller, is one of the oldest names for man, and was given in India, as elsewhere, to the supposed ancestor or ancestors of the human race; but the Bráhmans, like most Aryan nations, changed the appellative into a proper name. They believed in a real Manu, or in several real Manus, to whom they assigned various cognomina, and whom they counted among the earliest human rishis.—In the vedic legend of the flood the man saved by the fish is called Manu.—The name is most commonly met with now in connection with the Mánawadharmaśástra, which purports to have been uttered by the first Manu, the son of Brahmá. This work, commonly called the Code of Manu, is a compilation founded partly on the vedas and sutras, but admitting also rules and customs of a later age. The compilation was probably made about 500 B.C. It is written in ślokas. The author begins with the origin of the universe, which proceeded from the will of the self-existing power to produce a visible world; water was made, and a productive seed placed in it, from which sprang Brahmá in the form of an egg; the egg was divided into heaven and earth; and from Brahmá's mouth, his arm, his thigh, and his foot, proceeded respectively the Bráhman, the Kshatriya, the Vaiśya, and the Śudra. The other castes are as fancifully described as arising each from the intermixture of some two of these four original and subsequent mixed castes. The duties of all classes are prescribed with, in the case of Bráhmans, the elaborate system of áśramas. The vedas are spoken of as older than man, and immemorial custom is called transcendent law. Different parts of the work treat, with minute directions, of marriage, of private morals, of diet, and purification; of government and judicature; of penance and expiation; of transmigration and final beatitude.

Manyár. [Maráṭhi, from *mani,* a jewel, and *kára*, maker.] The name of a caste; they are lapidaries, and makers of beads and bracelets. The name also of several distinct snakes, of which only one, the bungarus fasciatus, is venomous. See Carpet snake.

Manzil. [Hindustáni.] A stage, a station; thence the Goanese word *manchial*, a litter. Also a house, a palace.

Mapárá. [Gujaráti, from *máp*, measure, from the Sanskrit *má*, to measure.] The name of a class of persons whose occupation is testing and weighing grain. They are sometimes wholesale dealers also. Some have adopted islám.

Mápári. [Maráṭhi, from *máp*, measure.] An officer in large towns whose duty it is to measure the grain brought to market.

Maphrian. The title of an archbishop of the Syrian Church in southern India. There is yet a higher rank, that of patriarch.

Mápile. The Kanarese form of Máppilla.

Máppilla. [Malayálam, said to be from *má*, mother, and *pilla*, son—the son of his mother, so called as sprung from the intercourse of foreign colonists, who were persons unknown, with Malabár women.] The name of a numerous class of Musalmáns in Malabár and South Kanara. They are chiefly Sunnis of the Sháfai school.

Maqbarah. [Arabic.] A tomb, a burial-place.

Marabou. A kind of stork, leptoptilos javanica, which in general appearance resembles the common adjutant, but has twelve feathers under the tail of much value. The Hindi name is *chuniári*.

Marabout. [Corrupt form.] A Muhammadan saint or mendicant.

Máramma. [Kanarese.] The village goddess; she seems to correspond, in some of her attributes, to Durgá or Káli, and is explained to be one of the furies attendant on that goddess. She is feared and propitiated as the source of calamity, rather than loved as the bestower of blessings. She is supposed to inflict small-pox, cholera, and other epidemics upon those who have incurred her wrath. She is appeased only by the shedding of blood, and therefore animal sacrifices are made to her.

Márán. The name of a caste in Travancore; they are drummers and musicians in temples.

Máráng Buru. [Santáli.] The great mountain; the name of the national god of the Santáls. As the Santáls and Hindus came into contact, the character of Máráng Buru, or that of Śiwa (as Śiwa was then conceived), or perhaps both, underwent a process of adaptation until the two gods became almost identical.

Marani. [Bengali.] The name of a low caste; they are weavers.

Maráṭhá. [Maráṭhi.] The name of a caste of Hindus of south-western India, who claim to be descended from the Kshatriyas. The pure Maráṭhás are chiefly found in the immediate neighbourhood of the Gháṭs, both above and below. They are a strong, active race, well-made and intelligent, and quite different in appearance from the ordinary cultivators. They formed the best part of the Maráṭhá armies, and are still much given to military service. They are distinguished by the affix 'rao' to their names. The term is sometimes applied more widely so as to include Kunbis, Bhandáris, and others. The Maráṭhás first became a political power about the middle of the seventeenth century, and their ascendancy lasted into the nineteenth. Of the original dynasty founded by Śiwaji there were two branches, one reigning at Satárá, and the other at Kolhapur, but early in the eighteenth century the real power passed into the hands of the Bráhman ministers called peshwás. There was a succession of seven peshwás reigning at Poona, but the later ones failed to maintain their influence over the whole state, and four Maráṭhá chieftains became severally independent of him at Nágpur, Gwalior, Indor, and Baroda. See Gáekwár, Holkar, Peshwá, Sindhia.

Maráṭhi. The language of the Deccan and Konkan; it is the vernacular of more than sixteen millions of persons, and is thus, after Hindustáni (in its various forms), Bengali, and Telugu, the language most widely spoken in India. Maráṭhi is perhaps, of all the hundred languages of India, the one most closely allied to Sanskrit; the vocabulary is recruited chiefly from Sanskrit, and the Dewanágari character is adopted unchanged, but a broken or modified form, called Moḍ, is used in business. There is a considerable Maráṭhi literature, both of verse and prose.

Maravar. [Tamil.] The name of a caste; they live almost entirely by cultivation, and are considered to be one of the lowest of the respectable castes. They are nominally Śaiwas, but worship chiefly peculiar deities of their own. They eat flesh and drink liquor, and differ a good deal from ordinary Hindus. They permit widows to remarry and wives to obtain divorce.

Márgali. The Tamil name of the solar month Dhanu, corresponding most nearly to December, Márgaśirsh, and, in Bengal, to Paush. See Month.

Márgaśirsh. [Sanskrit.] The Hindu month most nearly corresponding with December; it is so called from *mriga-śiras*, the antelope-head, the name of the nakshatra (part of the constellation Orion) in which the moon is at full in this month. See Month.

Marhatta. See Maráṭhá.

Marhi. [Hindi.] A hill temple.

Marhum. [Arabic.] Literally, one who has found mercy; one who is dead, as marhum nawáb, the late nawáb.

Mari. The name of a tribe on the borders of Afghánistán and Biluchistán in partial allegiance to the khán of Khelát. Also the name of a wild tribe resembling the Kandhs.

Mariamma. See Máramma.

Maricha-vesh. The guise of Maricha, a proverbial name for dissimulation like that of Maricha, the friend of Ráwana, who, in the form of a golden gazelle, drew Ráma in pursuit of him, and then, assuming the voice of Ráma, called Lakshman also to follow, by which Sitá was left unprotected to be carried off by Ráwana. See Rámáyana.

Mari Mai. [Panjábi.] The goddess of cholera. She is propitiated in the Kángrá district by the pachbalá and the satbalá ceremonies (*R. C. Temple*). Compare Máramma.

Marjádi. [Gujaráti, from the Sanskrit *maryádá*, a limit.] A name given to certain of the Wallabhácháryas, said to be more devoted in their observance of the tenet of pushṭimárg than are others.

Márka. [Kanarese, said to be derived

from *ma* privative, and *arka*, the sun, in allusion to their not worshipping the sun as Bráhmans do.] The name of a caste claiming to be Bráhmans, but not recognized as such. They worship the Hindu triad, but are chiefly Vaishnawas, and wear the náma. They call themselves Hale Karnáṭaka, the name Márka being considered as one of reproach. Their chief occupations are agriculture and government service as shánbhogs (*L. Rice*).

Marocha. The name of a tax on marriages levied by the Muhammadan government in Bengal.

Marsiah. [Arabic.] An elegy; especially one recounting the circumstances of the death of Husain, the third imám.

Marsiahkhán. [Hindustáni.] The officer in a Shiah community who chants the marsiah.

Marta. The name of a caste in Malabár; they are much employed as labourers on coffee-estates.

Maruta. [Sanskrit.] Wind, a god of the wind. The Marutas are vedic gods or demigods; they are described as being the sons and brothers of Indra, also as children of the ocean, sons of heaven, armed with lightnings and thunderbolts.

Máruta. [Sanskrit.] Belonging to the Marutas, a prince of the Marutas, the god of the wind.

Márwári. A native of Márwár, but especially those settled in other parts of India as bankers, merchants, or traders. The Márwáris have taken a higher position in northern than in southern India. In Maráṭhi the name is applied to any money-lender or corn-dealer. Márwári is also the name of the language of Márwár; it is a form of Hindi, and on the south slides into Gujaráti.

Masak. The Maráṭhi form of Mashak.

Masál. The Gujaráti form of Mashal. In Gujaráti, and thence also in Bombay English, masál is often used for Masálchi.

Masálchi. [Gujaráti.] A torch-bearer; also the domestic servants who supply the place of housemaids in England.

Masán. [Hindi, from the Sanskrit *śmasán.*] A place, usually on the bank of a river, where dead bodies are burnt.

Mashak. [Persian *mashk.*] A leather bag for carrying water. The bhisti carries it on his back. The name distinguishes it from the double skin used by the pakháli.

Mashal. [Arabic.] A torch, a lamp.

Mashálchi. A torch-bearer; also a house-servant.

Masháta. A waiting-woman.

Mashrua. [Arabic.] Literally, legal; a mixed stuff of silk and cotton which Muhammadans may wear at prayers, a pure silk garment being prohibited. The mashrua of trade is a mixed cloth, the warp being native-wound silk and the woof a fine European-made cotton.

Mási. The Tamil name of the solar month Kambam, corresponding most nearly to February, Mágh, and in Bengal Phálgun. See Month.

Masjid. [Arabic, from *sajada*, to bow.] A Muhammadan church. The first masjid was built on the spot where Muhammad's camel of its own accord stopped on his arrival at Medina after his flight from Mecca.

Masnad. [Arabic.] A cushion, a seat; a throne. Compare Gaddi.

Massoola. See Masula.

Mastán. [Uriya.] A Bráhman following the practice of agriculture (*H. H. Wilson*).

Mastán. [Hindustáni, from *mast*, puffed up, mad.] Another name of the Rasulsháhi fakirs.

Mastikallu. [Kanarese, from *maha*, great, *sati*, a virtuous wife, and *kallu*, stone.] A slab of stone about four feet high, bearing the sculpture of a pillar or post with a human arm projecting from it, and underneath a rude sculpture of a man and his wife. These stones mark the spots where widows became sati. Compare Páliá.

Mastisa. [A corruption of the Portuguese *mestiço*.] A person of mixed Indian and European descent.

Masula. A boat used for crossing the surf on the Madras coast; it is made of bended planks sewn together with rope-yarn and caulked with dammer, as the bar would break to pieces an inflexible boat; it has about ten rowers, and carries as many passengers.

Masur. [Gujaráti, Sanskrit *masura*.] The name both of the ervum lens or lentil, and ervum hirsutum or ervum bispennum, the tare.

Mátá. [Sanskrit.] The mother, a name applied to various goddesses, most often to Devi or Durgá, but also to the mother earth, and to the personified energy or wife of any god. But the mátá is often of earlier date than the arrival of the Aryans in India; she was the aboriginal village goddess in many parts, and it was probably in the attempt to make Hinduism swallow up the earlier creeds that the mátá was identified with Durgá and made the wife of Śiwa.

Matádár. [Gujaráti, perhaps from *mata*, a signature, or perhaps *matá*, property, and Persian *dár*, holder.] Under the narwá system the principal sharers were called matádárs, presumably because, as they were the persons directly responsible for the village revenue, they, and they only, signed the document setting forth the amount to be paid. In all village affairs each matádár was the representative of his sub-sharers, who equally with him were called pátidárs, but not matádárs. The matádárs have survived where the narwá system has been abolished. It is from among them that paṭels are selected; they are assistants to the paṭel, and usually hold smaller portions of the watan emoluments.

Maṭh. [Hindi, Sanskrit *maṭha*.] The cell, chamber, or hut of an ascetic; the house of a devotee and his disciples; a monastery; a college for young Bráhmans; an endowed temple or shrine with a dwelling-place for the mahanta and his disciples.

Maṭh. [Maráṭhi, Sanskrit *makushṭhaka*.] The pulse phaseolus aconitifolius; it is a kharif crop, often sown with bájri or jawár. It is eaten with kodrá by men, and is much used as food for camels, elephants, horses, and cattle.

Máṭh. [Bengali.] The open arable plain which forms the cultivated land of a village.

Máthábáná. A white linen cloth worn by Pársens over their hair and completely concealing it; the hair is tied with the ends of the cloth into a knot at the back of the head.

Mathwádi. A native of Mathwád. The name is also applied to the Panáris of Khándesh and sometimes to the Pávrás, both of which tribes are said to have come from Mathwád. The Mathwádi language is a mixture of Gujaráti and Rángdi Nemádi.

Matiá. [Gujaráti, from *mat*, opinion.] One holding an opinion, a believer; the name of that branch of the Lewa Kanbis which has adopted islám. They are followers of Imám Sháh, the saint of Piráṇa near Ahmedabad, but the only Musalmán custom they have adopted is that of burying the dead.

Mátiá. [Bengali.] The name of a low caste; they sell fish and vegetables.

Matiál. [Bengali.] The name of a low caste; they are day-labourers and earth-workers.

Matki. Another Maráṭhi name for Maṭh.

Maṭká. [Hindustáni.] An earthen pot of a round shape and of various size.

Matsya. [Sanskrit.] The fish, the name of the first principal awatár of Vishnu. This incarnation is differently described as being to recover the vedas which a sea-demon had stolen from Brahmá, and as a legend corresponding with the Hebrew account of Noah and the flood, the office of the fish being to support the ark.

Maty. [Presumably the English word *mate;* but see *meṭṭi.*] A term used in Madras for menial servant. In Bombay a cook usually has an assistant and apprentice whom he calls his mate.

Mau. [Gujaráti.] One who has left home and become a vagrant in consequence of a famine or other distress.

Mauchi. [Maráṭhi.] The name of a small tribe in Khándesh; they are quiet, well-behaved people, living chiefly by agriculture. They are not so industrious as the Pávrás, and move about instead of living in settled homes. They worship deities called Astamba and Gavli, as well as Wághdewa and Parmeśwar, and bury their dead.

Maujawár. The Maráṭhi form of Mauzáwár.

Maujawár Terij. [Terij, an abstract.] The name of one of the táluká account-books under the Bombay system; it is an abstract according to villages of the ṭharaobands of all the villages in the táluká, and gives the same particulars for the táluká as the ṭharaoband gives for each village.

Mauláná. [Arabic.] A learned Musalmán, a teacher, a doctor; in the Maráṭhá countries the master of a Musalmán school.

Maulud. [Arabic.] A hymn in honour of Muhammad's birth. Mauluds are chanted on the first eleven nights of Rajab, the month in which the prophet was born, and also at funerals.

Maulvi. [Arabic.] A learned Musalmán, a law doctor, a teacher of Arabic. Some maulvis are pirzádáhs also, and travel about preaching to their followers.

Maund. [The old English word for basket, applied as an equivalent of the Hindustáni *man.*] A measure of weight, containing 40 sers. The Bengal maund weighs 82$\frac{2}{7}$ lbs.; that of Surat, 41 lbs.; of Bombay, 28 lbs.; of Madras, 25 lbs.

Maurya. [Sanskrit, a metronymic from *Murá.*] The name of a dynasty which began with Chandragupta, the Sandracottus of the Greeks, about three centuries before Christ, and included Aśoka, the patron of the Buddhists. Their capital was Palibothra, the present Patná, and they were paramount over many states. The Maurya was a branch of the Parmár tribe; it is met with also in the south, and succeeded the Chálukya in power in the Konkan.

Mauzá. [Arabic.] A village and the whole area of land belonging to it, whether that land be contiguous or intermixed with that of other villages.

Mauzáwár. [Hindustáni, from *mauzá*, q.v., and the Persian affix *wár*, according to.] By villages; said of a settlement made, not with a zamindár, and not with the individual ryot, but with each village as a unit. See Settlement.

Máyá. [Sanskrit.] That which is not real, but only apparent, illusion; the visible world regarded as only a phantom; the vanities of the world that lead men astray.

Mayan. [Burmese.] A kind of acid plum.

Mayrá. [Bengali.] The name of a caste, called also Madak.

Mazhabi. [Hindi, from the Arabic *mazhab*, religion.] A name given to Sikh converts from islám; in some places especially to a Sikh of the sweeper caste.

Mech. Another name of the Bodo tribe.

Meda. [Sanskrit.] The name of a low mixed caste whose occupation was hunting, and who were not allowed to live within the town (*Manu*, x. 36 and 48). In the present day there is a caste of Medas in the south who are makers of mats, baskets, umbrellas, and sieves; they speak Kanarese and Telugu, and worship Káli; they are also called Gaurigas. There is also a later Turanian tribe of Medas in the Panjáb.

Medam. [Malayálam, the Sanskrit *mesha*, a ram.] The month during which the sun is in Aries; it begins on the 12th April and is the first month of the Paraśuráma year; it coincides with the Bengali Baiśákh; the most nearly corresponding śukladi luni-solar month is Chaitra. See Month.

Meer. See Mir.

Meeyana. See Miáni.

Meghwál. The name of a low caste found in Sindh, Cutch, and the Ganges provinces; they are shoemakers and weavers.

Mehmon. See Memán.

Mehra. The name of a tribe in the Central Provinces.

Mehráb. [Arabic.] An arch; an

alcove; the principal place in a mosque where the priest prays before the people with his face turned towards Mecca; also the royal closet or chamber (*S. B. Fallon*).

Mehrbán. [Persian.] Friendly, gracious; a title prefixed to names and technically regarded as equivalent to 'esquire.' Compare Ázam, Rájaśri.

Mehtá. [Gujaráti.] A writer, a clerk. Among Bráhmans, a householder as distinguished from a mendicant.

Mehtar. This is a Persian word meaning 'prince,' and is applied, no doubt originally ironically, but now as a common title, to Bhangis. It is usually used and accepted as a more agreeable appellation than Bhangi. In northern India, Mehtar or Mihtar is the name of a semi-Hinduised tribe who are sweepers.

Mehtar. This is a Maráṭhi word, and is used to designate any hereditary village officer, as the páṭil, kulkarni, or chaughalá.

Mehtráni. The feminine form of Mehtar; a woman of the Mehtar caste.

Meirinho. A superintendent of police under the Portuguese government of Bassein in the sixteenth and seventeenth centuries.

Mejar. [Gujaráti.] A memorial signed by a whole village or a great number of persons.

Mekhalá. [Sanskrit.] A girdle or waist-belt to be worn by the twice-born classes. It is distinct from the janeo, which is worn over the shoulder. The Bráhman's mekhalá should be of munja, or, failing that, kuśa grass, the Kshatriya's of murwá, and the Vaiśya's of hemp.

Melá. [Hindi, Sanskrit *mela*, from *mil*, to meet.] A fair, especially one held on an annual festival, as distinguished from a háṭ, which has no connection with religion. Where the religious element predominates the melá is called játrá.

Melváram. [Tamil, from *mel*, upper, and *váram*, share.] The landlord's share of the crop, as distinguished from the kuḍiváram.

Memán. [A Gujaráti corruption of the Arabic *mumin*, a believer.] A tribe of Sunni Musalmáns of the Hanefi school, found in Sindh, Cutch, and Gujarát. There are two divisions of them—the Cutchi Memáns, who are chiefly traders, and the Háláì, who are peasants. They do not intermarry. The former are descendants from converts of the Lohání caste, and the latter from Lohánás and Kachhiás. Compare Momná.

Member of Council. Members of council are either ordinary, extraordinary, or additional. The functions of the first two are administrative, of the third legislative. An ordinary member of council is either one of the six members of the Council of the Governor-General of India (q.v.), or one of the three members of the council of the governor of Madras or of Bombay. See Governor-in-Council. The term 'extraordinary member of council' pertains only to the Council of the Governor-General of India; the commander-in-chief in India may be so appointed during his term of office, and the governor of Madras or of Bombay becomes an extraordinary member of that council when it assembles within his presidency. An additional member of council exercises legislative functions only. See Legislative Council. Such members are appointed for two years at a time.

Memsáheb. [The English *madam*, and *sáheb*, q.v.] The appellation among Indian servants of an English married lady.

Menhdi. The common name of the hiná plant or dye. See Henna.

Menon. [Malayálam.] A village accountant.

Meo. The name of a people after whom the hill country of Alwar, Gurgaon, and Bhartpur is called Mewát; they claim to be Rájputs, and are sometimes included with the Rájputs of the same district under the name Mewáti, but they are really of the same origin or allied to the Minas. They are Muhammadans in name, but retain their Hindu village gods, employ Bráhmans as well as the Kázi, and observe the festivals of both the creeds. They are now settled to agriculture, and some are fishermen.

Mera. [Telugu.] Fees in kind paid to village servants.

Merchant. In the early days of the East India companies their servants were divided into five classes, called (1) residents; (2) senior or first merchants; (3) junior or sub-merchants; (4) factors; and (5) sub-factors or writers.

Meria. [Uriya.] A human victim; the rite among the Kandhs of sacrificing human beings to the earth-god. The victims were usually kidnapped from the plains, Bráhmans and Kandhs only being exempt, and were kindly treated and well fed till the day of sacrifice. Their flesh and blood were then distributed among the village lands. The practice was put a stop to in 1836. A similar custom is said to be still secretly practised amongst the Kois of the upper Godáwari.

Mesari. [Gujaráti.] A name given in Gujarát to Wániás who are not Jains but Vaishnawas.

Metikoru. [Telugu *meti*, chief.] The landlord's share of the crop. Compare Melváram.

Metran. A bishop of the Syrian Church in southern India.

Meṭṭi. [Malayálam.] An inferior domestic servant.

Mewári. The language of Mewár or eastern Rájputáná; it is a form of Hindi.

Mewási. [Gujaráti, from *Mahi*, and *was*, to dwell.] A native of Mewás, that is, of the country about the river Mahi. From the character of the inhabitants, Bhils and Kolis, the word has obtained the secondary meaning of freebooter or robber. A mewási village meant one in which a force of sibandi was required in order to collect the revenue. See Rásti.

Mewáti. The name of a branch of the Jádon Rájputs; they are now Muhammadans and are more usually called Khánzádah; they rule in Alwar, and are connected with the Meo tribe of the same country.

Mhair. The name of a tribe occupying the Mhairwara hills near Ajmir; they are nominally Musalmáns; they have no scruples as to kinds of food; they are of fine physique, and were formerly robbers by profession. A police battalion was formed from them in 1822, and this was converted after the Mutiny into a local battalion of regular troops.

Mhángiri. [A corruption of the Maráṭhi *mahágiri.*] A vessel of burden of various size up to 300 candies.

Mhátárá. [Maráṭhi.] An elder. The Portuguese government appointed village officers under this name in respect of lands not held by Portuguese landholders. Their duties corresponded to those of revenue páṭil.

Miáná. [Hindi.] A kind of palanquin.

Miáná, or **Miáni.** The name of a tribe in Cutch and Káṭhiáwár; they were formerly freebooters, and are now employed as soldiers and sailors, and some have taken to agriculture. They are Sunni Musalmáns, but have many Hindu customs.

Mihrab. See Mehráb.

Mihtar. Another form of Mehtar (Persian).

Mijlas. See Majlis.

Mikir. The name of an aboriginal tribe of Assam.

Milk bush. The euphorbia tirucalli, or Indian tree spurge; it is grown as hedges, and also to bind the side slopes of roads.

Millet. Though this name is not very commonly used in India, it will serve to bring together several cereals which are commonly called by their native names. The great millet is jawár, jonna, or cholum; the small millet, chenna, sáme, sáve, or wari; the common millet, kodrá harik, arike, or waragu; the spiked millet, bájri, sazza, or kambu; the Indian millet, banṭi; the Italian millet, káng, korra, or nawane. Some of the above English names cover different varieties, which will be found distinguished under the native names.

Mimánsá. [Sanskrit.] This word, which means literally 'reflection,' 'consideration,' is the name of one of the three great divisions of orthodox Hindu philosophy. It has two branches—the purwa mimánsá, so called from its being founded on the first or ritual part of the veda, and the uttara mimánsá, so called as being founded on the later or philosophical portion. The latter branch, however, is usually called the vedánta, and the name mimánsá confined to the purwa mimánsá. The purwa mimánsá was founded by Jaimini. Though it is classed as one of the six systems of philosophy, it does not concern itself, like the others, with the nature of soul, mind, and matter, but rather with a correct interpretation of the ritual of the veda (*Monier Williams*).

Mina. More commonly Myna.

Miná. The name of a tribe in Rájputáná, some of them claiming irregular descent from the Rájputs, while others are connected with the Bhils; they inhabit the outlying tracts and the skirts of the open country; some are industrious cultivators, while others are predatory.

Mináksbi. [Sanskrit, from *mina*, a fish, and *aksha*, the eye.] The name of a goddess worshipped in Madura and regarded as a form of Párwati.

Minam. [Malayálam, the Sanskrit *mina*, a fish.] The month during which the sun is in the sign Pisces, most nearly coincident with March and Phálgun (in Bengal, Chaitra). See Month.

Minár. [Arabic.] A minaret, the balconied tower of a mosque, or an isolated tower, as the Kutb Minár, which is 240 feet high. Also a small obelisk used to mark distance, a kos-minár.

Mingyee. [Burmese.] Another name of the high officer called Woongyee.

Minhá. [Arabic.] A deduction made from assessed revenue; thence laxly used for alienated or partially alienated land.

Minor. The minority of a Hindu extends, according to different authorities, to the beginning or to the end of the sixteenth year of age; and a Muhammadan is a minor till the expiration of the sixteenth year, unless symptoms of puberty appear earlier. But the British government has extended the period of minority to the end of the eighteenth year.

Mir. [Arabic.] A chief, a head, the head of a department. Saïds usually prefix this title to their names. It is also the name of a class of Musalmán singers and drum-players, said to be descended from Bháṭs and Doms.

Mir Akhor. [Arabic.] Master of the horse.

Mirás. [Arabic, from *waras*, to inherit.] Inheritance, inherited property; land held by hereditary right, as distinguished from that held by a tenant-at-will.

Mirásdár. [Hindi, from the Arabic *mirás*, and Persian *dár*, holder.] One who is proprietor of his estate, subject to the payment of a fixed land-tax to government.

Mirási. [Hindi.] Hereditary. The name also of a class of singers, called also Mirs. Mahárs sometimes call themselves Mirásis.

Mirbái. The name of a Vaishnawa sect founded by Mirbái, the wife of the ráná of Udáipur. The Mirbáis are a subdivision of the Wallabhácháryas.

Mirdhá. [Hindi.] The head peon or messenger of a zamindár; a village overseer; a headman. In Maráṭhi, the head of a body-guard of spearmen. In Gujaráti, the name of a class of Musalmáns who were formerly spies, and are now employed as messengers and policemen.

Mir-i-adl. [Persian, from the Arabic *mir*, and *adl*, justice.] Lord of justice, the title of the chief judicial authority of a subah under the Mogul government; he was assisted by a kázi, who conducted the trial and stated the law; the mir-i-adl gave judgment.

Mirzá. [Hindustáni, from the Arabic *mir*, and *zádah*, born.] A prince. Moguls prefix this title to their names and add Beg after them, as Mirzá Muhammad Beg; Mirzá, when affixed to a name, means prince.

Mirzái. A short jacket worn by Hindu shopkeepers in Behar.

Misal. The Hindi form of Misl.

Misl. [Arabic.] Similitude; an assembly, a corporation, an assemblage of persons of the same or like station and occupations; a collection of like or similar documents forming the body of public proceedings in judicial or in revenue matters; whence the instructions to the officers employed to assess the lands in the North-West Provinces are called the settlement misl; the term is also applied to a suit or proceedings at law, as misl diwáni, a civil suit, misl faujdári, a criminal case (*H. H. Wilson*). Misl is also the name of the different parties, generally called confederacies, into which the Sikhs were divided in the period intermediate between the rule of the gurus and the supremacy of Ranjit Singh. The misls, which were some large and some small, were distinguished by titles, either local or derived from the name of a distinguished sardár, or from some peculiarity of custom.

Miśr. [Sanskrit *miśra*, mixed.] A name given to the Kanaujia Bráhmans. Misrji is the title under which a man of this caste refers to his father-in-law. Compare the use of Paṇḍit.

Mistry. [A corruption of *mister*, or of the French *maistre*.] A head smith or head armourer, or head workman of any kind. The word is also used among Europeans and their servants to designate the cook.

Mita. Another form of Mutta.

Mitákshara. [Sanskrit, from *mita*, meted, and *akshara*, syllables.] The name of a commentary by Vijnáneśwara on the code of Yájnawalkya. This work is the chief authority of the Benares school of law, which is the prevailing one in middle India. The Mitákshara is implicitly followed in the city and province of Benares, and retains much authority also in the south and in the west of India, but less in the east.

Mitat. Another name for Mutah.

Miṭhágari. [Maráṭhi, from *miṭh*, salt, and *ágar*, a salt-pan.] The name of a caste; they are salt-workers.

Miṭhgauḍa. [Maráṭhi.] A Gauḍa salt-worker.

Mithunam. [Malayálam, the Sanskrit *mithuna*, twins.] The month during which the sun is in Gemini, coincident most nearly with June and Jyeshṭh (in Bengal, Ásárh). See Month.

Mitra. [Sanskrit.] An associate, a friend; the name of one of the vedic gods who is usually associated with Waruna; he presides over the day, as Waruna over the night. Also one of the twelve ádityas.

Miṭṭá. [Tamil.] The subdivision of a district, an estate forming such a division.

Mlechchha. [Sanskrit.] A foreigner, one who is not a Hindu. The term is as old as the Mahábhárata, in which the tribes of southern India are called by this name, and also Nisháda.

Mobed. [Gujaráti.] A priest of the Pársis; he is a family priest, and performs ceremonies.

Mocassa. See Mukhásah.

Mochi. [Hindustáni.] The name of a low caste; they are shoemakers and workers in leather generally. One class, called Multáni Mochis, are Sunni Musalmáns.

Mocurry. See Mukarrari.

Moḍ. [Maráṭhi, from *moḍ*, to break.] The broken or cursive form of the Dewanágari character, commonly used in writing Maráṭhi.

Modalayar. See Mudaliyár.

Modali. [Kanarese.] The name of a caste from the Madras presidency; they are generally well educated, and many are employed under government; they also engage in trade of all kinds, and as contractors for buildings, etc. A fair proportion of their females are able to read and write. They worship the Hindu triad, and have Bráhmans as their priests (*L. Rice*).

Moḍan. [Malayálam.] High land on which a particular kind of rice is cultivated. The ground is ploughed, manured with dung and ashes, and again ploughed, and then the seed is sown broadcast; again the ground is ploughed to cover the seed, and then the clods are broken with a large stick.

Modi. [Hindi.] A grain-dealer and grocer; a village shopkeeper. In Bengal the mahájan is chiefly the wholesale and the modi the retail dealer.

Mofussil. [A corruption of the Arabic *mufassal.*] This word means separate, distinct; thence a separate or subordinate district; the country, the provinces, as opposed to the sadar station or town; or the country in general, including large towns, as distinct from the capital of a province.

Mogara. [Hindi.] A kind of jasmine, jasminum zambac.

Mogari. [Hindi.] Arabian jasmine, jasminum sambæ.

Moger. [Kanarese.] The name of a fishing caste.

Moghal. More commonly Mogul.

Mogláí. [Hindi, from *mogal* or *mughal.*] The empire or government of the Moguls. The word is often used to denote great state or magnificence, and sometimes as equivalent to tyranny, as 'The English imperialism is slowly drifting into the old mogláí' (*Native Newspaper*). A mogláí hak in Gujarát is now the right to receive a cash payment from the government treasury in lieu of an item of revenue formerly levied by the Moguls, and which, as the Mogul power decayed, became the private property of the nawáb of Surat and other persons.

Mogul. [Corruption of the Hindustáni *Mughal.*] The name given by Hindus to the great Muhammadan dynasty founded by Baber in 1526, and made paramount in India by his grandson Akbar. The race to which these conquerors belonged was of mixed Mongolian and Caucasian origin, Baber's ancestor Tamerlane having in the thirteenth century united with his own Calmuck (Mongolian) subjects the Tartar and Turkish (Caucasian) tribes conquered by Changez Khán. The present Moguls or Mughals are generally poor; they are Sunnis. The name is also given to the descendants of some Persian refugees in western India; they are well-to-do, engaged chiefly in trade and the public service; these Mughals are

Shiahs. Mogul, as the name of a period of the Hindustáni school of architecture, is applied only to the time of Akbar and Jahángir. It is distinguished by a freer acceptance of the Hindu element, a larger introduction of colour, and the use of variegated marbles instead of the encaustic tiles of the earlier period. See Hindustáni, Saracenic.

Mohammedan. See Muhammadan.

Mohant. See Mahanta.

Mohil. The name of a branch of the Chauhán Rájputs.

Mohomati. [Gujaráti.] A cloth worn over the mouth by Jain jatis to prevent insects from entering.

Mohosul. See Muhassil.

Mohout. See Mahout.

Mohr, or Mohur. [Persian *muhr.*] A seal, a seal ring ; a gold coin of the value of fifteen rupees.

Mohurána. [Panjábi.] Stamp duties levied by the Sikh government.

Mohurram. See Muharram.

Moksha. [Sanskrit, from *much*, to loose.] Emancipation, deliverance; release from worldly existence ; exemption of the soul from further transmigration.

Molavi. See Maulvi.

Molesalám. [Gujaráti, from *mehel*, a palace, and *salám;* one who has bowed to the palace of the sultán.] The name of a community, including several ṭhákors, which, originally Rájputs, were in the fifteenth century partly converted to islám. They marry either among themselves or with Musalmáns, but in dress and appearance they rather resemble Hindus.

Mollah. See Mullá.

Molly. See Máli.

Momand. [Pashṭo.] The name of a Paṭhán tribe, the independent portion of which, numbering 12,000 fighting men, occupies the hills beyond our frontier between Peshá-war and Kohát; another part is settled in the plains within our frontier. Their chief town is Lálpura, on the left bank of the Kábul river, opposite the western entrance of the Khyber pass. They are nominally subjects of Kábul.

Momná. [A Gujaráti corruption of the Arabic *mumin*, a believer.] A class of Shiah Musalmáns descendants from converts of many castes. They still retain much of their Hindu customs, most of them shaving the beard, and many of them employing Bráhmans as well as Saïds for their birth and marriage ceremonies. In Cutch they are husbandmen and labourers ; in Gujarát their principal occupation is weaving, but some are dyers, cloth-dealers, and husbandmen. Compare Memán.

Momroghan. [Persian *mom*, bees-wax, *roghan*, oil.] A polish made of wax and oil.

Momyai. See Mumiái.

Mon. Another name of the Talaing tribe. Some authorities consider that the Talaings came after the Mons, and mixed with them.

Mongoose. See Mungoose.

Mong Rájá. The title of the chief of one of the Chittagong hill tracts.

Monigar. See Maniyakáran.

Monsoon. [Hindi *mausam*, from the Arabic *mausim*, season.] A division of the year according to the prevailing wind; but applied more particularly to the period of the south-west wind which blows from June to September, and brings the heavy rains. See Ritu.

Month. The months used in Indian chronometry are (1) the synodical month, or the interval between one new moon and another, and (2) the solar month, or the time which the sun takes to pass through a sign of the zodiac. The first or synodical month, which has a mean length of 29 dys. 12 hrs. 44 min., is used in the samwat, śaka, and hijra years. The solar month, with a mean length of 30 dys. 10 hrs. 29 min., is used in the Bengali san and in the Paraśuráma years. The synodical months are named after the nakshatra in which the full moon is observed; the solar months have either the same names, or (as in Malabár) are called after the signs which the sun traverses in each. Thus November may be either Virchigam, from vriśchika, the sign Scorpio, where the sun is, or Kártik, from krittiká the nakshatra of the Pleiades in the opposite sign Taurus, where the moon is at full. The commonest vernacular names of the months are given below, each preceded by the English month with which, under the śukladi method, it most nearly coincides (under the krishnadi method the month begins a fortnight earlier): January, Paush; February, Mágh; March, Phálgun; April, Chaitra; May, Vaiśákh; June, Jyeshṭh; July, Áshádh; August, Śráwan; September, Bhádrapad; October, Áśvin; November, Kártik; December, Márgaśirsh. The corresponding solar months of the Paraśuráma era are Magaram, Kambam, Minom, Medom, Eddavam, Methunam, Karkatagam, Chingam, Kani, Tulam, Virchigam, and Dhanu. The Bengali solar months have the same names as the Hindi synodical months, but with a precession of one month in the use of the names (perhaps from their having been borrowed from a krishnadi system); thus the Malabár Medam or Chaitra is the Bengali Baiśákh, and so on. See Year, Tithi.

Moodelier. See Mudaliyár.

Moog. See Mung.

Mookteer. See Mukhtár.

Moollah. See Mullá.

Mooluckgeery. See Mulkgiri.

Moolvy. See Maulvi.

Moondah. See Munḍá.

Moonga. [A corruption of the Bengali *mugá*.] A kind of silk called from the name of the worm—antheræa assama (Helfer), saturnia assama (Westwood)—which produces it. The silk is ordinarily fawn-coloured, but by feeding the worm on particular trees it can be obtained nearly white. The Moonga silk industry is confined to Assam and some Tipperah villages, but the silk is used in India for making various fabrics and garments.

Moor. This term, which properly means a Mauritanian, was formerly commonly used for Musalmán. The people called Moormen in Ceylon are believed to be descended from Arab merchants and native women;

they are traders, and deal especially in gems.

Moorum. See Murum.

Mootsuddy. See Mutasaddi.

Moozumdar. See Majmudár.

Mopla. See Máppilla.

Moral. A corruption of *moḍal*, which is another form of Manḍal.

Morang. The name of a branch of the Mech tribe.

Morchah. [Persian.] An entrenchment, the embrasures of a fort.

Morchál. A fan made of peacock's feathers, one of the insignia of rank.

Morhá. [Hindustáni.] A low stool or seat, a footstool.

Morlidar. See Murlidhar.

Moslem. See Muslim.

Mosque. [An English form derived through the Spanish *mezquita* from the Arabic *masjid.*] A Muhammadan church.

Motálá. A caste of Bráhmans, so called from Motá, a village in the Surat district.

Motarfa. See Muhtarafah.

Mothá. [Hindi, from the Sanskrit *mustá.*] The grass cyperus rotundus; the root is used in medicine.

Moullah. See Mulla.

Moulvie. See Maulvi.

Mouse-deer. The smallest of the deer tribe, the memimna indica; it is only ten or twelve inches high, and little heavier than a hare; it is brownish in colour, with the sides streaked and spotted with yellowish white; it belongs to the hornless family of musk-deer. The Hindi name is tur-i-mau (*R. A. Sterndale*).

Mow. See Mau.

Mowra. [A corruption of the Gujaráti *mahuḍá*, the Hindi *mohwá*, perhaps from the Sanskrit *moha*, frenzy.] The tree bassia latifolia, from the corolla of the flower of which a spirit is distilled; the dried flower is also eaten by poor people. The tree is a fine one, resembling the oak in appearance; the wood is worthless; an oil is extracted from the seeds.

Mrammá. The name by which the Burmese call their own race.

Mrigaśiras. [Sanskrit *mriga*, antelope, *śiras*, head.] The name of one of the nakshatras, called after the constellation of the antelope's head, which is part of Orion.

Mrigsál. [Maráṭhi, from the Sanskrit *mriga*, antelope, and *sál*, a year.] A name formerly used in the Bombay presidency for the harvest, or fasli, year, commencing about the 6th June.

Mro. The name of a tribe in the Chittagong hill tracts. They are tall, powerful men, but peaceful and timid. They weave their own clothes from cotton grown by themselves. The men wear only a strip of cloth, and the women only a short petticoat. They have slaves of two sorts —captives in war and debtors. They bury their dead. They have three gods—Turai, the great father; Sung Tung, the hill spirit; and Oreng, the deity of the rivers. They pay tribute to the Bohmong (*T. H. Lewin*).

Mru. See Mro.

Mrung. Another name of the Tipperah tribe, or of descendants from Tipperahs.

Muocadam. See Mukaddam.

Muchalká. [Hindi.] A written obligation or agreement; especially, in Madras, the counterpart of a revenue lease. See Paṭṭá. Also a recognizance or surety bond.

Muchche. The Telugu form of Mochi. Besides working in leather, the Muchche makes furniture and paints portraits, and is employed in public offices as a daftari and bookbinder.

Muchi. Another form of Mochi.

Mucqua. See Mukkuvar.

Mudaliyár. [From the Tamil *mudal*, chief.] A common title of respect in the Tamil provinces; a native magistrate in Ceylon.

Muezzin. [Arabic, from *azzana*, to inform.] The officer who chants the azán.

Mufti. [Arabic, from *fata*, to decide.] An officer whose duty it was to expound the law for the kázi. The word is commonly used also to denote the civilian dress worn by a military or naval officer when off duty.

Mug. [Hindi.] The pulse phaseolus mungo or radiatus; it is both a kharif and a rabi crop, and is sometimes called green gram.

Mugger. See Magar.

Mughal. More commonly Mogul.

Mughal Paṭhán. [Hindustáni.] A game like draughts, played with sixteen shells or pebbles on a diagram sketched on the ground, or on a board.

Muhammadan. [An English formation from the Arabic *muhammad*, praised, the past participle of *hamida*, to praise, and the name of the founder of islám.] A follower of Muhammad, a Musalmán.

Muhar. See Mohr.

Muharram. [Arabic.] Sacred, unlawful, prohibited; the first month of the Musalmán year, in which war was prohibited. Also the name of the great Shiah mourning, held on the first ten days of this month, in commemoration of the death of Husain, the third imám, at Karbala, A.H. 61. Passion-plays representing the events of the fatal day, Husain going forth to fight, his taking leave of his children, his sister's prediction of disaster, and finally the bringing home of his headless body, are acted at this season. Processions also are made through the streets with tábuts. The Sunnis, in ridicule of the other sect, turn the mourning into a farce, but they observe the tenth day as sacred in commemoration of the creation of Adam and Eve. See Month.

Muharrir. [Arabic.] A clerk, a writer.

Muhassil. [Arabic.] A tax-gatherer, a bailiff, but applied especially to messengers formerly sent to collect arrears of revenue, and to live at the expense of the defaulter till the arrear was paid.

Muhtarafah. [Arabic.] A tax on trades and professions, or on artificers.

Mujáwar. [Arabic.] A servant who takes charge of mosques and grave-yards. See Mullá.

Mujtahid. [Arabic.] A Muhammadan jurist of the highest authority; one competent to enunciate new doctrine.

Mujumdár. The Tamil form of Majmudár, and also a common corruption of that word in other than Tamil districts.

Mukaddam. [Arabic.] A chief, a leader; the headman of a village or of a caste. In Gujaráti any kind of overseer is called a mukaddam, and it is in this sense that the word is most commonly met with in English. In the mouth of a Meo it means his wife's father.

Mukarrari. [Arabic.] Fixed; said of rent or revenue the rate of which is permanently fixed.

Mukbara. See Maqbarah.

Mukhásah. [Hindustáni.] Private; said either of land retained under the direct management of the state, khás; or of land assigned as private property.

Mukhi. [Gujaráti, from the Sanskrit *mukhya*, chief, principal.] The chief of a body of persons, the head of a village, a paṭel.

Mukhtár, or **Mukhtyár.** [Hindi, from the Arabic.] An agent, a representative. The word in the original Arabic means absolute, free, at liberty to act. Taking advantage of a provision of the Code of Criminal Procedure, that with the permission of the court any person may be allowed to assist an accused person in his defence, men who were formerly merely petition-writers, or worse, now appear as legal practitioners, and are sometimes allowed, by mistake, to exercise all the functions of a wakil, appearing for complainants as well as defendants.

Mukhtyárkár. [Sindhi.] A revenue and magisterial officer corresponding to the tahsildár or mámlatdár of other provinces.

Mukhtyárnámah. [Hindi, Persian *námah*, a deed.] A written authority to act, a power of attorney.

Mukkuvar. [Malayálam, from *mukkuka*, to dip, to plunge.] A tribe of fishermen in Malabar whom Europeans call Mucqua; their number, according to an account taken in 1807, was 12,369 (*Graeme*). They are said to be immigrants from Ceylon with the Ilavan (*Gundert*).

Mukláwa. [Panjábi.] The ceremony previous to cohabitation in the case of a wife married in childhood.

Mukri. [Hindustáni, from *mukar*, to deny.] A kind of riddle in verse, consisting of a description which suggests one object while another is meant.

Mukti. [Sanskrit, from *much*, to loose.] Loosing, liberation; the final delivery of the soul from the body and exemption from further transmigration.

Mukuta. A head-dress resembling a pope's tiara and used for idols.

Mulha. See Malláh.

Mulkgiri. [From the Arabic *mulq*, a kingdom, and Persian *giri*, taking.] The taking possession of a country, the periodical incursion of a military force for the collection of tribute or revenue. Dr. Hove, under date 2nd July, 1788, writes, 'Within a mile of the town (Limri) I met with Fatehsing's army, consisting chiefly of horse, which collected the revenue from this district and the Cattyware country. . . . I understand that Fatehsing sends yearly an army of 20,000 horse to the inland districts, without which he could not obtain a single badam.'

Mulki. [Hindi, from the Arabic *mulq*, a kingdom.] Native, indigenous; the name of an era one month in advance of the fasli. When two headmen are appointed to a village in Gujarát, the one whose duty is in connection with the revenue is called the mulki paṭel, and the other the mukhi or police paṭel.

Mullá. [Arabic.] A learned Musalmán. Also the name of a mosque officer whose duty it is to call to prayers, and on ordinary occasions to lead the prayers. He is sometimes mujáwar also, and sometimes schoolmaster, and deals in charms. Among the Vorás the mullá is of much higher rank, the head of each separate settlement having that title, and the chief mullá of all is spiritual and temporal head of the whole community.

Mullagatawny. [A corruption of the Tamil *milagutannir.*] A kind of pungent soup.

Multáni. The name of a dialect of Panjábi; that spoken in the country about Multán.

Mumiái. A substance sold as brain-oil, or an extract from the human brain, but in reality a mineral pitch.

Muṇḍá. The name of a Kolarian tribe, also called Ho, or Laka Kol, and allied to the Bhumij; they are numerous in Chutiá Nágpur and Singbhum, and are thriving and industrious cultivators; they are divided into different clans, and no man may marry in his own clan; their women hold a good position; they burn their dead.

Muṇḍphoḍá. [Gujaráti, from *muṇḍ*, the head, and *phoḍ*, to break.] Another name of the Rafái or Gurzmár fakirs, from their practice of beating their heads till they bleed, in order to extort charity.

Mung. [Hindi.] The pulse phaseolus mungo, or green gram; it is called also hesaru, pesara, pachu-payaru, mag, and mug.

Mungoose. A name applied to several species of the herpestes, as the h. griseus of Madras, the h. malaccensis of Bengal. It is an extremely active animal, about thirty inches in length including the tail, and is carried about by snake-charmers to fight with snakes.

Muni. [Sanskrit, perhaps from *man*, to think.] A holy sage, an ascetic, a monk, a recluse.

Munib. [Arabic.] A master, a principal, one who employs an agent.

Munib-gumáshtah. [Hindustáni.] A head clerk or manager.

Munim. [The Maráṭhi and Gujaráti form of *munib.*] An agent or manager; particularly the head manager in a mercantile or banking business under a seṭh; on the munim's order only will the kilidár pay or receive cash.

Munja. [Sanskrit.] The rush or grass saccharum munja; it grows to a height of ten feet, and is used for basket-work; also for making the Bráhman's mekhalá, whence the investiture with that girdle is sometimes called the munja ceremony; and the same name is often applied incorrectly to the upanayana or investiture with the janeo.

Munjeet. [Hindi *manjiṭ* or *majiṭh*, from the Sanskrit *manjishṭhá*.] The root of the plant rubia munjista, which is used for dyeing, and called Indian madder.

Munshi. [Persian.] A writer, a secretary. The word is very commonly used among Europeans to denote a teacher of Arabic, Persian, or Urdu. It is sometimes applied also to a native officer appointed to administer a town.

Munsif. [Arabic.] Just; an arbitrator, a judge. Under the British government the term is applied to the native judge of lowest rank. In Madras there were formerly village munsifs.

Murdafarásh. [Bengali, from the Persian *murdah*, a dead body, and *farásh*, q.v.] The name of a low caste who remove dead bodies.

Murghi. [Hindustáni.] A fowl, a hen. See Kharcha.

Murid. [Arabic.] A disciple, a scholar; a member of the junior order in a brotherhood of fakirs. See Murshid.

Murlidhar. [Hindi, from the Sanskrit *murali*, a flute, and *dhara*, bearing.] The flute-bearer, a name of Krishna.

Murmi. The name of a tribe of Thibetan origin in central and eastern Nepál. They are a pastoral and agricultural people, inhabiting elevations of from four to six thousand feet, and living in stone houses thatched with grass. They are a large, powerful, and active race, grave, very plain in features, with little hair on the face (*Hooker*). This form is almost identical with the Arakanese pronunciation of Mrammá, the race to which the Burmese and Arakanese belong.

Murree. See Marhi.

Murshid. [Arabic.] A teacher, a spiritual guide; a member of the higher order in a brotherhood of fakirs. See Murid.

Murum. [Maráṭhi.] A kind of fissile gravel, much used in road-making.

Murwá. [Sanskrit.] The creeping plant sanseviera zeylanica, from the fibre of which bowstrings and the warrior's mekhalá are made.

Musaddi. The title of a class of Muhammadan devotees who have adopted the jap of Nának as their rule of faith.

Musáfirkhánah. [Hindustáni *musáfir*, a traveller, and *khánah*, a house.] A rest-house for travellers, a sarái. The name among Hindus is dharmśálá.

Musáhar. [Bengali.] The name of a low caste or tribe; they are cultivators, labourers, and fishermen, and resemble the Bhuiyás.

Musáheb. [Arabic.] A companion, an associate; a confidential servant, who is often also a relative, appointed as companion to a youth.

Musalmán. [The plural of *muslim*, q.v., but used in the Indian vernaculars and in English as a noun singular and as an adjective.] A follower of islám. According to religion, Musalmáns are divided into Sunnis and Shiahs, besides a few minor sects. The division dates from the death of Muhammad, though the leadership of both parties was for a short time united in the hands of Ali, who was fourth caliph of the Sunnis and first imám of the Shiahs. According to origin, Indian Musalmáns are of three classes : (1) the descendants of foreign Musalmáns, who came with their families into India, such as the Saïds, Shaikhs, Moguls, and Paṭháns ; (2) the descendants of Arabs and Persians, who came by sea and settled on the coast and took Hindu wives, such as the Máppillas of Madras ; and (3) the descendants of converts from Hinduism, such as the Khojás, Memáns, Momnás, Vorás, and many others, for there is hardly a Hindu caste from which converts were not made. And as a Musalmán of even the highest stock may take a wife from any other class, there are now few, if any, Musalmáns who are not at least in part of Hindu descent. The Musalmáns of India number about 50,000,000.

Musáni. The name of a tribe, a branch of or allied to the Brahui.

Musá Sohág. [Hindustáni.] The name of a small body of beshara Sunni fakirs, who dress as women. Their patron saint Musá, who lived at the close of the fifteenth century, is said to have adopted this dress as a symbol that he was devoted to God as a wife to her husband.

Mushṭigár. [Kanarese, from *mushṭi*, the fist.] The name of a caste ; the word means 'boxer,' but the caste is now agricultural.

Musjeed. See Masjid.

Musk-rat. A small species of rat, the sorex cærulescens, that infests Indian houses and emits an extremely powerful musk smell when frightened.

Muslim. [Arabic, from *salama*, to submit to the will of God.] The common name of all who profess islám ; a Musalmán or Muhammadan.

Mussalman. See Musalmán.

Mussoola. See Masula.

Mussoor. See Masur.

Mussuk. See Masak.

Mussundee. [Corrupt form.] The name of a subdivision of the Sikhs who were opposed to Govind, the last guru, and with whom he forbad his followers to have any intercourse.

Mustáli, or **Mustálian.** See under Shiah.

Mustámin. [Arabic.] Literally, one who seeks protection ; applied to any person who lives under a government of a different religion to his own.

Mustaufi. [Arabic.] An auditor of accounts ; an officer deputed to inquire locally into any matter.

Mustiger. See Mushṭigár.

Musty. [Hindustáni *masti*, from the Persian *mast*, puffed up, inflated.] Exhilarated, violent through high spirits; applied chiefly to horses and elephants.

Mutah. [Arabic.] A temporary marriage; a left-handed marriage, allowed by the Shiahs, but considered illegal by the Sunnis (*S. W. Fallon*).

Mutasaddi. [Arabic.] A writer, a clerk.

Mutawalli. [Hindustáni.] The warden of a mosque or of an endowment.

Mutazala. The name of an independent Muhammadan school, an offshoot of the Shiahs, and founded by Wásil bin Ata, a contemporary of Abu Hanifa. The Mutazalas maintain that the divine ordinances which regulate human conduct are the fruits of individual and collective development, and that the law has always grown with the growth of the human mind. They are called also Ahl-ul-Iltizal.

Muth. See Maṭh.

Muthali. [Tamil, literally, a leading or principal man.] The name of a small but highly respectable and influential agricultural caste. They are supposed to be an offshoot of the Vellálans, whom they generally resemble. They are Sáiwas (*J. H. Nelson*).

Mutira. The Malayálam name of the pulse kollu, or horse-gram.

Mutta. [Tamil.] A small estate. The word is loosely used as equivalent to pálaiya or zamindári.

Muttadár. [Tamil, Persian *dár*, holder.] The holder of a mutta.

Muwallad. [Arabic.] Literally, begotten; an Indian-born Arab whether of the whole or the half blood.

Muyairi. [Kanarese.] The name of a subdivision of the Pánchála in Coorg; they work in brass.

Myamma. Another form or pronunciation of Mrammá, and which is pronounced by the Arakanese Murma.

Myinzoogyee Woon. [Burmese.] The title of a military officer, a member of the Hloot-dau.

Myna. [The Maráṭhi *maina.*] The name of a very common Indian bird, a kind of starling, the acridotheres tristis. Other varieties are the dusky myna (acridotheres fuscus) and the Bráhmani myna (temenuchus pagodarum). The eggs of all three are glossy blue or greenish blue, and holes are used for nests (*S. B. Fairbank*).

Myo-uk. [Burmese *myo*, a town.] The governor of a town or district; in British Burma a revenue and judicial officer subordinate to the deputy-commissioner.

Myrobalan. This word (meaning ointment-acorn) is of Latin origin, but is used in English chiefly as the name of an Indian product. There are five kinds of myrobalans, the several fruits of five varieties of the terminalia known in Hindi as the *baddm*, the *bauri*, the *haritaki*, the *hilká*, and the *jaindl.* The fruit varies in size from that of an olive to a gall-nut, and is used in dyeing and tanning, calico-printing, and medicine. See Hirḍá.

N.

Nabob. A corruption of Nawáb.

Nách. More commonly Nautch.

Náchni. [Maráṭhi.] The grain cynosurus corocanus; it is one of the warkas crops of the Konkan, and one of the cheapest grains. It is the rágí of upper India.

Nacodah. See Nákhudá.

Náḍavár. The name of an agricultural hill tribe in Mysore.

Naḍi. [Bengali.] The name of a caste; they make lac ornaments for Muhammadans.

Nádiyá. [Hindi.] A bull bearing some mark, which is taken to indicate that it is sacred and therefore not to be put to work.

Náḍodá. [Gujaráti.] The name of an agricultural caste of partly Rájput descent and generally following Rájput customs.

Nág, or **Nága.** [Sanskrit.] A snake, particularly the naia tripudiens, or cobra di capello. Its bite is identified by two small punctured wounds about an inch apart. Also the name of fabulous serpent-demons with human faces, supposed to reside in pátál. Also the name of a Scythian tribe that spread over much of India. See Serpent race.

Nágá. [Hindustáni.] Literally, naked; the name of a class of heretical Hindu ascetics, who go naked and carry arms. Hordes of them have sometimes been engaged as mercenary soldiers by Indian princes, and have sometimes laid whole countries under contribution on their own account. There is also a class of Sikh mendicants of the same name.

Nágabhushana. [Sanskrit.] Snake-adorned, a title of Śiwa, expressive of compromise with the old serpent-worship of the Kolarian tribes.

Nágar. [Gujaráti, literally, belonging to a *nagar*, or town; thence keen, clever.] The name of a very prominent and very exclusive caste of Ḅráhmans in Gujarát.

Nágar. [Bengali.] The name of a low caste; they are agricultural labourers.

Nágari. [From the Sanskrit *nagar*, a town.] Relating to a town. This, or Dewanágari, is the name of the Sanskrit alphabet, which with more or less of modification is used also for the Hindi, Bengali, Maráṭhi, and other Aryan languages.

Nagarśeṭh. [Gujaráti, from *nagar*, a town, and *śeṭh*, q.v.] The principal merchant of a town, a title bestowed by the merchants upon one of their number and allowed to pass hereditarily.

Nagarta. [Kanarese.] The name of a class who claim to be Vaiśyas. They are traders and some are farmers, but they never till the ground with their own hands. They are divided into two sects—the Námadhári, who worship Vishnu, and the Śiwáchár, who are Śaiwas.

Nágavalli. [Telugu.] The betel vine; also a biri.

Nágbansi. [Hindi, from *nága*, q.v., and *wans*, race.] A tribe of Rájputs of Gorakhpur, and supposed to be partly descended from the Nága race. See Serpent race.

Nagdi. Another form of Nakdi.

Nágeśwaraswámi. [See *nága*, *iśwara*, and *swámi.*] A deified personification of the serpent in southern India.

Nághori. [Gujaráti.] The name of a class of Sunni Musalmáns; they are cart-drivers. Before railway times they used to carry goods between Málwá and Gujarát.

Nágin. The name of a snake, the zamenis fasciolatus, popularly but erroneously supposed to be the female of the cobra. It is an active reptile, of slender form and olive-brown colour. It grows to a length of forty inches, of which the tail covers nine. It is harmless, but popularly thought venomous (*G. W. Vidal*).

Nágli. Another form of Náchni.

Nagole. See Nágavalli.

Nagośi. [Gujaráti, from *na* privative, and *gos*, meat.] The name of a small body who seceded from the Aliá Vorás in the eighteenth century and adopted some new views, the chief of which was that to eat meat was a sin.

Nágpanchmi. [Gujaráti *panchmi*, fifth.] The fifth day of Śráwan śudh, on which day Śeshnág and the nágas in general are worshipped. In the south, offerings of food are made to snakes. This is the day also on which, according to Hindu practice, royal yearly grants should be paid.

Nahál. The name of a division of the Bhils. They are very dark, small, and harsh-featured, and are the most savage of the race, living chiefly on roots, fruit, and berries, and being seldom seen beyond the limits of their native forests. Some, however, raise a little grain or barter forest produce for cloth. Some of them are Musalmáns, but most have no noticeable religion. They live chiefly on the north side of the Sátpuras.

Náiatá. The Gujaráti form of Navaita.

Náïb. [Arabic.] A deputy. The word is prefixed, like the English 'sub-,' to the titles of officers, as náïb-risáldár, a lower grade of risáldár; náïb-diwán, a sub-treasurer.

Náïb-názim. The title of an officer nominally under the nawáb of Bengal, but appointed by the British authority to superintend the administration of criminal justice; the plan was adopted in 1755, but the office was abolished and courts of circuit substituted in 1790 (*H. H. Wilson*).

Náïk. [Sanskrit *náyaka.*] A leader, a chief; the chief of a tribe; the head of a body of persons. In poetry, náïk is the term for hero, and the feminine náyiká for heroine. In the Indian army, the corporal, whether of cavalry or infantry, is termed náïk. In the police, the náïk is a fourth-class head-constable. And náïk affixed to the name of a Bráhman denotes that he is a money-dealer. Náïk is also the name of a low agricultural caste in Bengal, and is another name for the Beḍar caste.

Náiká. [Gujaráti.] The name of one of the Káliparaj tribes; they seem to be distinct from the Naikras of the Panch Mahåls, and claim to be of the same stock as the Anáwala Bráhmans, among whom Náik is a very common surname, and they say they use the same Bráhmans as do the Anáwalas, while the Náikás themselves act as Bráhmans to the Donḍiás.

Náïkan. A dancing-girl. This word is the feminine form of náïk, and so means either the wife of a náïk or a mistress. But náïk and náïkan (or the other feminine form náyiká) are used to denote the hero and heroine—the lover and his mistress—in plays and poems, and it seems to be through this meaning of the word that náïkan has come to be used euphemistically for dancing-girl or courtesan.

Naikra (or, properly, *Náyakaḍa*). An aboriginal tribe residing in the jungles of the Panch Mahåls; they have been described as exceeding even the Bhils in predatory and lawless habits, and as great objects of terror to their more peaceable neighbours. They eat the cow without scruple, and do not employ Bráhmans at all; they worship Mátá, the mother, and Wágheśwar, the lord of tigers.

Naique. See Náïk.

Náir. [Malayálam *náyar.*] A caste of Śudras in Malabár, and the ruling caste there. With the exception that nephews and not sons succeed to property, they follow Hindu law.

Najib. [Arabic.] This term, signifying originally 'noble,' is applied among Muhammadans to irregular infantry. Ranjit Singh, the Sikh ruler, had a regiment of najibs consisting of Musalmáns, who joined him from Samru Begam on her death. The British government also retained some najib corps chiefly as a kind of militia.

Náká. [Maráṭhi.] Any salient or prominent point, as the junction of two roads or of a road and the ford of a river; a place selected for the taking of toll or customs.

Nakdi. [Bengali, from the Arabic *naqd*, cash.] Paid or to be paid in cash; the term is applied to land for which the zamindár receives his rent in cash per bighá, as distinguished from bhaoli land.

Nákedár. [Maráṭhi, from *náká*, q.v., and Persian *dár*, holder.] A receiver of tolls or customs.

Nákhudá. [Persian.] The captain of a ship.

Nakshatra. [Sanskrit, from *naksh*, to come near.] A lunar mansion, that is, one of the signs or asterisms into which the moon's path is divided. These were at first twenty-seven, but in the later astrology a division into twenty-eight mansions is made. Those nakshatras in which the moon is when in opposition to the sun give their names to the months. See Month.

Nakshbandiá. [Hindustáni.] The name of a community of fakirs of the báshara order, followers of the saint Khwájah Bahá-ud-din of

Nakshband; they are Sunnis; they beg at night, carrying a brass lamp, with the oil of which they mark the foreheads of those who give them anything (whence, some say, their name, mark-maker).

Nala. More commonly Nullah.

Nálband. [Hindustáni, from *nál*, a horse-shoe, and *band*, to fasten.] A farrier.

Náma. [Kanarese.] A sectarian mark worn on the forehead by followers of Vishnu; it is in the form of a trident, the middle line being yellow or red and the rest white. Compare Tilak.

Námadári. [Kanarese.] One who wears the náma; a Vaishnawa.

Namaskára. [Sanskrit, from *namas*, bowing, from *nam*, to bow; and *kára*, doing, from *kri*, to do.] Uttering the exclamation *namas*, and bending down in respectful salutation; bowing with the two hands raised to the forehead. Namaskára, though appropriate also to a deity, is considered the proper mode of salutation between equals, while an inferior should make pranáma, which a superior will acknowledge by áśirwád.

Namázgáh. [Hindusṭáni, from the Persian *namáz*, prayer, and *gáh*, a place.] A place of prayer, the part of a mosque where the prayers are said.

Namáz-i-janázah. [Persian, Arabic *janázah*, a bier.] The funeral service of the Muhammadans.

Namáz-i-shám. [Persian *namáz*, prayer, *i*, of, *shám*, evening.] Evening prayer; the fourth prayer of the five appointed for each day. See Sulátu'l maghrib.

Nambiyar. [Malayálam.] The title of a division of the Náirs.

Namburi. The name of a caste of Bráhmans in Malabár. The same name seems to be applied both to a high caste and also to a fishing caste said to have been changed into Bráhmans, but who are despised by the others.

Nának-panthi. [Sanskrit *pantha*, a way.] A follower of Nának Sháh, the founder of the Sikh religion; a Sikh.

Nánaksh//áhi. [Panjábi, from *Nának Sháh*, the name of the founder of the Sikhs.] A follower of Nának Sháh, a Sikh. The Sikh currency also was known by this name, as the rulers subsequent to Bábá Nának struck coins in his name and not in their own.

Nandá Devi. A name of Durgá from the cowherd Nanda, her foster-father. She is propitiated under this name in the Himálaya mountains.

Nandi. [Sanskrit, from *nand*, to be joyful.] The name of the bull, the wáhan or vehicle of Śiwa. A figure of Nandi usually stands in front of a temple to Śiwa.

Nándi. [Sanskrit, from *nand*, to be joyful.] Joy, satisfaction; eulogium or praise of a deity, benedictory verses at the opening of a ceremony or drama.

Nandrook. [A corruption of the Maráṭhi *nándurki*.] The tree ficus benjamina.

Náneti. The Maráṭhi name of the Ráth snake.

Nánewaṭi. [Maráṭhi, from the Sanskrit *nánaka*, money, and the Maráṭhi *watáv*, to exchange.] A money-dealer, a money-changer.

Nanjey. [Tamil, from *nal*, good, and *sey*, cultivation.] Land capable of being irrigated sufficiently for the growth of rice with water supplied by government (*J. H. Nelson*). See Kyári, Punjey.

Nánkár. [Hindustáni, from the Persian *nán*, bread, and *kár*, business.] An assignment of a portion of the land or revenue of an estate to the occupant or zamindár as an allowance for his subsistence (*H. H. Wilson*).

Nápit. [Sanskrit *nápita*.] The name of a high Śudra caste; they are barbers, and often act as village surgeons also, and take part in arranging marriage and funeral ceremonies. The caste is sometimes called by the Arabic name hajám, and in Orissa Nápits are commonly called Bhandári.

Narak. [Sanskrit.] Hell, a place of torment for souls. Manu (iv. 88–90) enumerates twenty-one naraks. They are supposed to be situated below the pátáls. The Buddhist naraks are 136 in number, and are situated in the interior of the earth. Under neither system is the narak a place of permanent residence. After a due measure of punishment there the soul has to return to earth with a new body. See Moksha.

Narakásur. [Sanskrit.] An asura or demon son of Bhumi, or the earth, and slain by Vishnu.

Náralipurnimá. [Maráṭhi *nárali*, a cocoa-nut, and Sanskrit *purnimá*, from *purna*, full, and *má*, for *mása*, the moon.] A name for the day of the full moon of Śráwan, on which day the stormy part of the monsoon is considered to be over, and flowers and cocoa-nuts are offered to the sea, which is then held to be fit again for navigation. Followers of the yajur-veda change the janeo on this day. See Balev.

Narangkár. The maker of men, the name of the chief god of the Doms; animals are offered up to him.

Náráyana. [Sanskrit.] The divine spirit moving on the waters. 'The waters are called *nárá*, because they were the production of *nara*, or the spirit of God; and since they were his first *ayana*, or place of motion, he thence is named Náráyana, or moving on the waters' (*Manu*, i. 10). After the notion of trimurti or the Hindu triad was formed, Vishnu was sometimes identified with Náráyana. The last name, however, is met with, in modern Hindu poetry, in its proper sense, namely, the impersonal spirit of God.

Nárjil. [Panjábi, from *náral*, a cocoa-nut.] A sacred cocoa-nut adorned with flowers, used in the worship of Nársingh.

Národá. [Gujaráti.] A semi-Rájput tribe; they are cultivators.

Nársingh. Another form of Narsinh. He is worshipped under this name in Kángrá, especially by women. Barren women worship him for offspring, and he is believed to cohabit with them in their dreams in the form of a Bráhman clothed in white (*Sardáru Balhári*).

Narsinh. [Sanskrit *narasinha*, from *nara*, man, and *sinha*, lion.] The form Vishnu took in his fourth awatár to destroy the demon Hiranyakaśipu, who had obtained the boon from Brahmá that he should be slain neither by man nor by animal.

Narwá. [Gujaráti.] The name of a particular system of land tenure, under which the principal sharers in a village are jointly responsible to government for the whole revenue of the village; if any principal sharer fail to pay his portion, his share lapses to the general body, who have to make good his default; so, within each principal share, if any sub-sharer fail to pay his quota, his land lapses to the principal sharer, who is responsible to the general body; thus under this system in its perfection each village managed itself and paid the government revenue in a lump sum. The same tenure is also called bhágdári. See Majmun, Páṭidár.

Narwádár. [Persian *dár*, holder.] A sharer in a narwá village.

Nasakchi. [Persian.] A chamberlain, an orderly; also an executioner.

Nasakchibáshi. A chief chamberlain or orderly. In Afghánistán the executioners are so called; they wear red jackets and fantastic caps.

Nasesalar. [Gujaráti.] A corpse-bearer among the Pársis; the name of a class of persons employed to carry dead bodies to the dokhmá.

Nassaukchibanshi. See Nasakchibáshi.

Nat. [Burmese.] A spirit credited with the power of warding off evil, and therefore worshipped.

Naṭ. [Hindi, Sanskrit *naṭa*, a dancer.] A tumbler, a rope-dancer. Also the name of a wandering tribe who go about with donkeys and goats and perform acrobatic feats. Different classes of them vary much in their customs. Some allow polygamy and others do not. Some worship Hanuman, some have adopted islám, and some are Kabir-panthis.

Náṭak. [Hindi.] Acting, dancing; a play, a drama.

Nátaru. [Gujaráti.] An inferior form of marriage entered into when there is some impediment to making a regular marriage (lagan), as when the woman is a widow or has a husband living from whom she is separated, or when the man has already a wife and the second is meant to be only an inferior wife. Compare Páṭ and the Musalmán Nikáh.

Náthgosain. [Hindi, from the Sanskrit *nátha*, lord, and *gosain*, q.v.] The name of a class of mendicants; they wear brick-coloured clothes and are distinguished by ear-rings of silver or pewter, called mudrá; few of them own houses, but some are settled, and live by fishing or making stone vessels or necklaces of glass and beads.

Native State. Politically India is divided into two parts, commonly known as British territory and the native states. The first portion alone is ruled directly by English officials, and its inhabitants alone are subjects of the Queen. The native states are sometimes called feudatory—a convenient term to express their vague relation to the British crown. To define that relation precisely would be impossible. It has arisen at different times and by different methods; it varies from semi-independence to complete subjection. Some chiefs are the representatives of those whom we found on our first arrival in the country; others owe their existence to our creation. Some are parties to treaties entered into as between equal powers; others have consented to receive patents from their suzerain recording their limited rights; with others, again, there are no written engagements at all. Some have fought with us and come out of the struggle without dishonour. Some pay tribute; others pay none. Their extent and power vary as greatly as their political status. The nizám of Haidarábád governs a kingdom of 80,000 square miles and 10,000,000 inhabitants. Some of the petty chieftains of Káṭhiáwár exercise authority over only a few acres (*J. S. Cotton*).

Nattambádiyan. [Tamil, from *nattam*, a village, and *pati*, master.] The name of an agricultural caste of good position. Many of them have been converted by Jesuit missionaries.

Náṭṭánmaikára. [Tamil, from *náṭṭánma*, the headship of a village, from *náḍu*, a country, a group of villages.] The headman of a district, but more commonly the headman of a single village.

Naṭṭuva. The Tamil form of Naṭ. Also the name of what appears to be a different caste in the south; some of them worship Vishnu, and are called Sátáni; others Śiwa, and are (it is said) called Pandaram; while others are Lingáits.

Naṭwá. The Kanarese form of Naṭ.

Naubat. [Hindustáni, from the Arabic *naubat*, succession.] A band of music stationed at the gateway of a palace and playing at fixed intervals.

Naubatkhánah. [Hindustáni, Persian *khánah*, a house.] A drum-stand; the chamber, usually over the palace gate, where the band plays.

Naugaji. [Hindi, from *nau*, nine, and *gaj*, q.v.] Nine gaj long, a name given to many very large tombs in Oudh, supposed to be the graves of giants. It has also been suggested that they are really the platforms of recumbent images of Buddha, turned in the course of time into Muhammadan tombs.

Nauniyár. [Bengali.] The name of a caste; they are traders, dealing especially in saltpetre.

Naurátri. [Hindi, from the Sanskrit *nawa*, nine, and *rátri*, night.] The period of the first nine days and nights of the śuklapaksh of Mágh, Chaitra, Ásháḍh, and Áśvin, but more especially those of the last-named month or the nine days before the daśara. All these periods are called the Mátá's days, and are sacred to Durgá.

Nautch. [A corruption of the Hindi *nách*.] Dancing, acting. A nautch is usually a combination of singing and slow dancing and gesticulating by one or more heavily dressed and decorated women, with an accompaniment of music played by two or three men sitting behind. See Dancing-girl.

Navaita. [Kanarese, perhaps from

nau, a ship. The fanciful derivation *nawa-ae-the*, those who have newly come, has also been suggested.] A class of Musalmáns, Sunnis of the Sháfai school, said to have been driven from Arabia in the eighth century. They were formerly known in Bombay as Kufis and in Gujarát as Náiatás. They were merchants and ship-captains, and famous for their skill as pilots.

Navar. [Gujaráti.] A priest of lower grade among the Pársis; he can officiate at kasti and marriage ceremonies, but cannot take part in the highest religious offices.

Navis. [Persian.] A writer, a scribe, a secretary.

Nawáb. [The plural of *náïb*, but used honorifically in the singular.] A viceroy, a governor of a province under the Mogul government; these often became independent, whence the term has become a common title for a Muhammadan sovereign. The title may also be conferred upon a person of high rank without any office being attached to it.

Nawárah. [Persian.] A large boat, a barge; the name of a flotilla formerly stationed at Dacca as a defence against the pirates of Árákan.

Náyadu. The Telugu form of Náyakka.

Náyakka. [Tamil, presumably the Sanskrit *náyaka*: see *náïk*.] The name of a caste who both cultivate and trade, and who were a ruling caste in Madura in the sixteenth and seventeenth centuries.

Náyar. More commonly Náir.

Náyinda. The Kanarese form of Nápit. The Náyindas speak both Kanarese and Telugu, and are generally employed as musicians as well as barbers. The Náyinda is a member of the village corporation.

Nazar. [Hindustáni.] A present, an offering; especially one made by an inferior on his presentation to a superior.

Nazar. [Hindi, the Arabic *nazr*, sight.] Seeing; the evil eye. The principle of the evil eye is thus explained by Mr. Gurdyal Singh: 'Anything beautiful and charming, when looked upon by a person bent on mischief, prompts him to do harm, just as a fat kid moves the hungry wolf. But anything in itself ugly is safe from the mischief of the eye, for it has no attraction in itself. Black being the colour of mourning, is looked upon as unlucky, and has no attraction to the native eye; hence anything beautiful is daubed with a little black so that the eye may fall, not on the thing itself, but on the black spot, and the mischief thus be averted.' For this reason writers blot their paper, cloth-workers introduce irregularities into their patterns, and builders will not let two doors or windows exactly correspond. It is not, however (says Mr. W. Cockburn), essential to nazar that the beholder should have any ill intention; the most benevolent person may produce the evil, and parents are particularly liable to cast it upon their children. To find complete satisfaction in looking at anything constitutes nazar; therefore everything beautiful requires, for its safety, some flaw or detraction, a disfigurement or an opprobrious name.

Nasári, or **Nasarian.** See under Shiah.

Nasarwattu. [Hindi, from *nazar*, and *watt*, to change, to move.] This term is applied to anything that averts the evil eye, especially to a small black stone with a hole in it, worn round the neck or on the shoulder; also, as a slang term, to any worthless fellow, implying that he is of no use but to serve as a foul speck to avert the evil eye (*Gurdyal Singh*).

Názim. [Arabic, from *nazm*, order.] An administrator, a governor, a government. Compare Nizám.

Názir. [Hindustáni, from the Arabic *nazr*, sight.] An inspector; but commonly the officer of a civil court who is charged with the serving of process and the execution of decrees. Also the warden of a mosque.

Nazránah. [Persian.] A present, especially one from an inferior to a superior; the offering made by a tributary chief on accession, or by an officer on succession to an hereditary appointment.

Nazrandáz. [Hindustáni, from the Arabic *nazr*, sight, and Persian *andáz*, estimate.] An estimate of the value of a crop, made by inspecting it.

Neem. [Hindi *nim*, from the Sanskrit *nimba*.] The tree azadirachta indica, or ash-leaved bead-tree; it is a fast-growing tree, and is much used for planting roadsides; the leaves, which are bitter, are chewed at funeral ceremonies.

Negli. A low-growing plant with a small yellow flower and round thorny fruit; it is used both as a vegetable and a medicine.

Nekdy. See Nakdi.

Nemináth. [Sanskrit *nemi*, a circle, and *nátha*, lord.] The name of the twenty-second arhat or jin of the Jains; he is also called Arishṭa-nemi, or the perfect Nemi; and Nemirájárshi, the rishi king Nemi.

Nepáli. An inhabitant of Nepál or an emigrant from that country. The principal Nepáli tribes are the Gurkhás, the Gurungs, the Newárs and Limbus, the Kirátis, the Bhutiás, the Lepchás. Also the name of the language of the country, which is a dialect of Hindi.

Nerrick. See Nirkh.

Nes. [Gujaráti.] A group of huts.

Nesakula. [Kanarese.] A class of fowlers and palanquin-bearers, speaking a corrupt dialect with a broad and curious accent (*D. Sanderson*).

Nesti. [Gujaráti.] A village modi, grocer, or general dealer.

Nevayat. Another form of Navaita.

Newár. The name of the aboriginal race of the central valley of Nepál. Both Buddhism and Hinduism have been partially engrafted on their primitive religion. The Newárs are the most civilized of all the Nepál tribes. Their agriculture is unrivalled; their towns, temples, and images of the gods are beautiful for materials and workmanship; and they are a steady, industrious people, equally skilled in handicrafts, commerce, and the tillage of the soil (*B. H. Hodgson*).

Ney. [Tamil.] Clarified butter, ghee.

Neyiga. [Kanarese, from *neyyu*, to weave.] A weaver. The name is common to many castes, such as the Sále, Seniga, Dewánga, Bilimagga.

Nga-pi. [Burmese.] Fish-paste.

Nhávi. [Maráṭhi, from *náh*, to bathe.] A barber. See Nápit.

Nigama. [Sanskrit, from *ni*, in, and *gam*, to go.] Insertion, especially of the name of a deity into a liturgical formula; a sacred precept; also a town, a market, or fair.

Nihang. The naked or pure; the name of a class of Sikhs.

Nija. [Sanskrit, from *ni*, in, and *jan*, to be born.] Innate, proper, ordinary; a term applied to the ordinary month, in connection with which another month is intercalated. See Adhika.

Nijjot. [Bengali, from the Sanskrit *nija*, and *jot*, cultivation.] Lands cultivated by the proprietors or revenue-payers by themselves and for their own benefit; also land allowed to be set apart for the private maintenance of a zamindár, on which, before the decennial settlement in Bengal, no revenue was assessed (*H. H. Wilson*).

Nikáh. [Arabic.] Marriage, the actual marriage bond. A wedding is usually called shádi. Hence the word nikáh is often used to designate a left-handed marriage, or one which for any reason is not celebrated with festivity; it is a nikáh, but not a shádi.

Nikáhmangná. [Hindustáni *mangná*, to ask.] A ceremony precedent to marriage, a betrothal.

Nikumbhawanshá. The name of a dynasty ruling the southern part of Khándesh in the eleventh and twelfth centuries.

Nilári. [Maráṭhi, from the Sanskrit *nila*, indigo.] The name of a caste in the Deccan; they are dyers in indigo. Compare Galiárá.

Nilgai. More commonly Nylghai.

Nim. More commonly Neem.

Nimbárka. The name of a Vaishnawa sect founded in the twelfth century. They worship Krishna and Rádhá conjointly, and their chief scriptural authority is the bhágwat purán (*Monier Williams*).

Nimchu. [Pashṭo.] A sheepskin coat; it is shorter than the poshteen, reaching only to mid-thigh.

Nimtáná. [Maráṭhi.] The process of estimating a crop by measuring the grain obtained from a few handfuls taken from different parts of the field; the testing of a subordinate's work by the examination of a certain percentage of his operations.

Nipáli. More commonly Nepáli.

Nirá. [Gujaráti.] The fresh unfermented juice of the date or other toddy-producing tree.

Nirdhi. The name of a tribe who, like the Tadvis, are of mixed Musalmán and Bhil descent. They live along the base of the Sátmálás in Khándesh, and generally resemble the Tadvis.

Nirganṭi. [Kanarese, from *niru*,

water.] A village servant who watches the tanks and channels, and distributes water for irrigation.

Nirkh. [Persian.] Market rate, price current; especially a rate of price fixed by authority. Also, in Bengal, the customary rate of rent for land.

Nirkh-dárogá. [Persian.] A clerk of the market, an officer who regulates the prices at which articles are sold in a public market.

Nirkhi. [Hindustáni.] An officer who fixes or records the prices of articles.

Nirmala. [Sanskrit, from *nis* privative, and *mala*, impurity.] The spotless, the name of a class of Sikhs; they are meditative celibates who do not live in colleges.

Nirwána. [Sanskrit, from *nirwá*, to be extinguished.] Extinguished, having the fire of life extinguished, liberated from existence; the name of that condition which is the ultimate object of a Buddhist's life, which is attained only when the consequences of all his past actions have been exhausted, when he has become perfectly holy, and no necessity remains for him to be born again. Compare Moksha.

Nisfkhiráj. [Hindustáni, from the Arabic *nisf*, half, and *khiráj*, tax.] Land of which half the revenue is remitted or alienated.

Nisháda. [Sanskrit.] One of a degraded tribe, an outcast. The word may mean either a settler or one who is afflicted. The name is applied in the Rámáyana to the wild forest tribes, and by Manu to the son of a Bráhman by a Śudra woman. Compare Mlechchha.

Nishánia. [Panjábi, from the Persian *nishán*, a sign, a flag.] The name of certain Sikhs who so called themselves as followers of the standard-bearers of the united army. They are sometimes spoken of as a separate misl.

Nizám. [Arabic, from *nazm*, order.] Administration; also an administrator, a viceroy; the title to the present day of the rulers of Hyderabad, the largest native state in India, who were formerly viceroys under the Mogul emperors.

Nizámat. [Arabic.] The office of nizám. As an adjective, nizámat means criminal, as opposed to diwáni or civil, as the nizám or governor exercised the highest criminal authority, leaving the adjudication of civil causes to his diwán.

Nizámat Adálat. [Arabic.] A criminal court. Under the Muhammadan government the highest criminal court was so called, and the district criminal court was called the Faujdári Adálat, but later this distinction was lost.

Nizám Sháhi. The name of the branch of the Báhmani dynasty which, on the dismemberment of the latter in 1489 A.D., established itself at Ahmadnagar, in the Deccan. The founder was Malek Ahmad Nizám-ul-Mulk Byheree, from whom it is sometimes called the Byheree dynasty. After the conquest of Berar in 1574, the Ahmadnagar kingdom included the greater part of it, Aurangabad, part of Khándesh, and the Konkan from Bassein to Bánkot. The dynasty lasted till 1637, when its territories were divided between the Moguls and Bijápur.

Nizám-ul-Mulk. [Arabic.] The administrator of the kingdom, the full title of the viceroy of the Deccan under the Mogul government.

Nmá-khám. The Pashṭo form of Namáz-i-shám.

Nobut. See Naubat.

Nolkol. A vegetable resembling the turnip; it was originally imported into India from the Cape.

Nonbar. [Kanarese.] The name of an agricultural caste.

Non-regulation. This term is applied to provinces or districts not sufficiently advanced for the regular action of the laws and regulations.

North-West Provinces. This is the title of one of the eight provinces into which British India is now divided. It dates from 1853, when it was separated from Bengal, of which it till then formed the north-west portion. In 1876 Oudh, which had previously been administered by a chief commissioner, was united with the North-West Provinces. The united province contains an area of over a million square miles, and a population of forty-four millions, or nearly equal to that of Germany. The native states under this provincial government are small: area, 5000 square miles; population, 745,000.

Noṭagára. [Kanarese, from *noṭa*, inspection, and *gára*, doer.] An officer who keeps the money accounts of a village; also a money-changer; a conjurer, a fortune-teller (*H. H. Wilson*).

Noṭṭakára. [Tamil, from *noṭṭam*, inspection, and *kára*, doer.] The village saráf, who examines the coins handed to him by the thandalkára and accounts for the same to the náṭṭánmaikára. He acts under the orders of the latter, and carries remittances to the táluka kacheri (*J. H. Nelson*). In Malabár, a money-changer.

Nuokdy. See Nakdi.

Nuḍiya. [Koḍagu.] The name of a caste, a division of the Waḍḍas; they sink wells and build mud houses.

Nujeeb. See Najib.

Nukeia. [Panjábi, corrupt form.] The name of the Sikh misl which occupied the country south of Lahore.

Nuliá. The name of a tribe in Orissa, but said to have come from the Telugu country; they are fishers and boatmen.

Nullah. [Corruption of the Hindi *nala.*] A ravine running down to a river or kháḍi; also a gutter, a drain.

Number. A common abbreviation of Survey number.

Numberdár. [The English word *number*, and the Persian *dár*, holder.] The person or persons in a village who represent the community in their financial dealings with the government, and who are registered in the collector's books by a number as well as by name. The word has been adopted in some languages as Lambardár.

Numria. A pastoral tribe in Sindh claiming descent from the Rájputs who ruled in Sindh in the eleventh century.

Nuniá. [Hindi, from *nun*, salt.] The name of a low caste, formerly salt-makers, but now chiefly employed as day-labourers. They are well-built and sturdy men, and make excellent excavators.

Nuri. [Hindi.] The name of a low caste; they are makers of lac ornaments.

Nuzzerana. See Nazránah.

Nyáya. [Sanskrit, literally, method.] The name of one of the six darśans or systems of Hindu philosophy. It was founded by Gotama. The object of the nyáya, as of the other systems, is to teach the method of obtaining final beatitude. The means of this is knowledge of the truth. The nyáya does not, like the mimánsa, assume that this knowledge can be obtained at once from the veda, but inquires into the process of reasoning and the nature of proof. It arrives at the conclusion that souls are distinct one from another and from the supreme soul, and that when a soul has perceived the evil attendant upon every desire it ceases to have need of, and is exempt from being associated with, any more bodies, and continues for ever to exist alone and free from pain. See Dvaita, Moksha. In Nepál, nyáya has the special meaning of trial by ordeal.

Nylghai. The plural and the feminine of Nylghau.

Nylghau. [English corruption of the Hindi *nilgau*, from the Sanskrit *nila*, dark blue; and *gau*, Sanskrit *go*, a cow or bull.] A large short-horned deer, the portax pictus. The males are slaty blue in colour, and the females rusty red. They may be as much as fourteen hands high, and in appearance are a mixture of antelope, bull, and horse.

O.

Oart. [From the Portuguese *horta*, Latin *hortus*.] A garden, an orchard, especially an enclosed and irrigated garden of cocoa-nut trees.

Occupancy right. This term is commonly used in reference to cultivators who have higher rights in the land they cultivate than mere tenants-at-will. The rights vary in different cases, but generally include right of transfer and of transmission by inheritance, with or without a nazránah, and undisturbed possession so long as the stipulated rent is paid.

Oḍ. [Gujaráti.] The name of a caste; they are tank-diggers and mud-wall makers, and usually use asses to carry the earth. Compare the Tamil Oṭṭa and Kanarese Waḍḍa.

Odich. [Gujaráti, from the Sanskrit *udichya*, northern.] The name of a Bráhman caste, said to have originated in the time of Mul Ráj, the first Solanki king of Anhilpur, towards the end of the tenth century A.D.

Oḍiya. More commonly Uriya.

Oghá. [Gujaráti.] The brush used

by Jain jatis to gently drive away insects before sitting down.

Olgana. See Walgániá.

One-anna cess. A tax of one anna in addition to every rupee of land revenue paid in the Bombay presidency. Two-thirds of the proceeds of this tax are devoted to the making of roads, bridges, and other means of communication, and to the improvement of water supply; the remaining one-third to education.

Om. [Sanskrit.] A mystic word made up of the three letters, *a*, *u*, *m*, which are said to be types of the three deities Brahmá, Vishnu, and Śiwa, and to have been milked out of the three vedas. The Buddhists also use it.

Omedwar. See Umedwár.

Omlah. See Ámla.

Omrah. See Amir.

Oondie. See Uṇḍi.

Ooprее. See Upari.

Ooreed. See Urid.

Or. [Uriya.] The name of an agricultural caste of Orissa.

Orakzai. See Arakzai.

Oraon. See Uráon.

Oras. The Gujaráti form of Uras.

Order. The following orders have been established by the Crown in India: the Star of India, instituted in 1861, of which there are three classes, called knights grand commanders, knights commanders, and companions; the Indian Empire; and the Crown of India; the last two were instituted in 1878, the last being for ladies.

Ore. See Ur.

Orhur. See Arhar.

Oriya. See Uriya.

Oswál. [Hindi, from Osia, a town in Márwár.] The name of a clan of Muhammadan Rájputs. Also the name of a division of the Wániá caste; they are mostly of the Jain religion, and are cultivators and traders, and some of those distinguished as Gujar Oswáls are merchants.

Oṭá. [Maráṭhi.] A terrace of mud or masonry in front of a house.

Otári. [Maráṭhi.] The name of a caste; they cast metal vessels and idols.

Oṭlá. [Gujaráti.] The raised platform or terrace in front of a house, or a low seat of mud or masonry running along the side of a room within.

Otmanzai. See Uthman.

Oṭṭa. [Tamil.] The name of an itinerant caste of tank-diggers and earth-workers. They are of Telugu origin, and are probably the same as the Waḍḍa caste.

Ottagakáran. [Tamil.] The name of a division of the Paraiyans; they are spinners of cotton thread, and some are cultivators.

Ottah. See Atta.

Otti. [Malayálam.] A form of mortgage which gives the mortgagee possession and the entire produce of the land, the landlord retaining merely the proprietary title and the right to redeem.

Otto. See Attar.

Outbundee. See Áutbandi.

Ouvidor. The title of a magistrate under the Portuguese government at Bassein.

Owdich. See Odich.

Owtar. See Awatár.

P.

Pachbalá. [Panjábi, from the Sanskrit *pancha*, five, and *bali*, an offering.] A sacrifice made to Mári Mái, consisting of a pumpkin, a male buffalo, a cock, a ram, and a he-goat. Compare Satbalá.

Pachwái. [Bengali.] An intoxicating drink prepared from fermented rice.

Padaiyátchi. [Tamil, from *padai*, a body of troops, and *atchi*, a ruler.] The name of a caste; they are now mostly cultivators.

Padamsáli. [Kanarese.] The name of a caste; they are weavers.

Padárti. The name of a class of persons employed as drummers in Hindu temples.

Paddy. [A Malay word.] Rice in the husk, whether growing or cut, before the grain is separated. It is a native of India and is found wild in some parts.

Paḍichára. [Kanarese.] A peon, a policeman.

Padma. [Sanskrit.] The lotus flower, nelumbium speciosum; an ornament in the shape of a lotus; a large number, a hundred crores.

Padmásana. [Sanskrit *ásana*, a seat.] A lotus seat, a throne in the shape of a lotus.

Padmawati. [Sanskrit, from *padma*, a lotus.] Possessing the lotus, abounding in lotus flowers.

Padmini. [Sanskrit.] Literally, a lotus plant; the name of the first and best of the four classes of women according to Hindu writers. The others are the chitrini, śankhini, and hastini.

Padow. More commonly Prow.

Padri. This is the Portuguese word *padre*, father, which has been adopted in all the Indian vernaculars as the common name for a clergyman, and is sometimes applied also to Bráhmans or other religious persons.

Padsáli. [Kanarese.] The name of a caste; they are weavers.

Pádsháh. [Persian.] A king.

Paḍtar. [Gujaráti.] Uncultivated land; either kharábá which is unculturable, or sir paḍtar which is assessed for cultivation and awaiting an occupant.

Padugai. [Tamil.] Land in the bed of a river and fit for rice-cultivation.

Páduká. [Hindi.] A mark attributed to the action of a god, as the charana páduká at Benares, supposed to be the impression of Vishnu's feet as he alighted there to worship Mahádewa; or that of Ráma, where he disappeared from earth at Faizábád.

Págá. [Maráṭhi.] Cavalry the horses of which belong to the state, as distinguished from śiledár cavalry, in which each trooper provides his own horse and arms. A single págá would consist of fifty or a hundred men; the commander was called págyá, or sarnaubat; under him was a hawáldár.

Págádár. [Persian *dár*, holder.] A trooper in a págá regiment.

Pagár. [Maráṭhi.] A canoe made of the trunk of a tree, usually the mango, hollowed out.

Pagár. [Portuguese *pagar*, to pay.] This word is commonly adopted in the Indian vernaculars for monthly salary.

Pagi. [Hindi, from *pag*, a foot.] The name of an aboriginal tribe whose profession is the tracing of thieves by following up their footmarks. Pagis are now often used as watchmen. Their skill in their original profession or in tracking animals is marvellous. General Jacob says, 'I have often followed them with astonishment, being unable to discern marks that satisfied them; a bent twig is a sign-post, a dent in the ground a book wherein they will read size, age, sex, and time of day.'

Pagoda. [According to Webster from the Persian *but*, an idol, and *kadah*, a house; but perhaps only a corruption of *dágoba*.] The European designation of a Hindu temple in the south of India. See Mandir.

Pagoda. A gold or silver coin, formerly coined at Madras, and worth about three and a half or four rupees. It used to be thought that the coin was so called from the device of a temple which it bore, but the name seems to be older than the device, and the derivation from Bhagawati (said to be a name of Párwati) is now generally accepted. The pagoda was divided into forty-five fanams.

Pagri. [Hindustáni.] A turban; also a poll-tax formerly levied in the Delhi districts.

Páhal. [Panjábi.] A gate; the name of the Sikh ceremony of initiation instituted by Govind, the tenth guru; it is performed by not less than five Sikhs, one of whom is usually a Nirmala, and consists of the sprinkling of the novitiate with sugar and water which have been stirred together with a dagger or other iron weapon.

Pahar. [Hindi, from the Sanskrit *prahara*.] A watch, or period of three hours.

Pahárá. [From the Sanskrit *prahara*, a watch, a space of three hours.] A watchman, a guard.

Pahári. [Hindi, from *pahár*, a mountain.] The name of a hill tribe in the district called Santál Parganás. They remained independent under the Muhammadans, and continued to be predatory until 1779, when they came to an understanding with Cleveland, the collector of Bhágalpur, under whom a corps of archers of this tribe was raised. The Paháris worship the sun as Bero Gosáin; they use idols and believe in the transmigration of souls; they bury their dead. Pahári is also a general name for any hill-men or their language. Thus the hill dialect of Panjábi is called Pahári.

Páhi. [Hindi.] A cultivator who does not live in the village to which the land he cultivates pertains. The páhi ryots are a migratory class, who take up land where they can get it on the best terms, while the regular or tháni ryots are most reluctant to forsake their hereditary holdings. See Páikásht.

Pahlavi. A language of Persia which was current in the Sassanian epoch, or that which followed the Parthian. Dr. Haug connects the name with Parthia. Pahlavi is the later of the two languages in which the sacred books of the Pársis are written; it is the language of the zand or commentary on the original avastá.

Páhn. A village priest among the Kols; he is remunerated by service land.

Pái. More commonly Pie. Also another form of Páhi.

Páijámá. [Persian.] Drawers, trousers, such as are worn by Musalmán men and women. Among Europeans, sleeping-drawers.

Páik. [Hindi, from *pái*, a foot.] A footman, an armed attendant, a courier; also a subordinate collector of rents; in Cuttack a local militia were formerly so called.

Páikári. [Telugu.] A cultivator without hereditary rights. The term is the equivalent of the Tamil parakuḍi and the Bengal páikásht.

Páikásht. [Hindi, from *páhi*, q.v., and *kásht*, cultivation.] A non-resident cultivator, or one without hereditary rights; the parakuḍi of Madras. See Khudkásht. The term is also applied in Bengal to the land which non-resident ryots may cultivate.

Páiphulla. [Hindustáni *pái*, foot, and *phul*, to swell.] The name of a new type of fever which appeared in Calcutta in the rains of 1878. It is so called from the puffy swelling of the feet which accompanies it, and which sometimes extends as far as the thighs, or even affects the face. When the disease once appears in any house it generally attacks all or nearly all of the inmates. The fever generally leaves on the third day, but the swellings may remain for a month or more.

Paitá. [Bengali, from the Sanskrit *pavitra*, from *pawa*, purification, from *pu*, to purify.] The sacred thread, the janeo.

Pajusan. A fast of the Jains in the rainy season; strictly it is of two months' duration, but is usually shortened; only the last day, the 5th Bhádrapad śudh, is universally observed.

Pakháli. [Hindi, from *pakhál*, a water-skin, from Sanskrit *payas*, water, and *khalla*, skin.] A waterman, one who carries water by means of a double bag borne by a bullock or buffalo. Some are Hindus and some Sunni Musalmáns.

Pákhmara. [Bengali.] The name of a semi-Hinduised tribe in Bengal; they are bird-catchers.

Pakká. [Hindi.] Ripe, mature; finished, full, perfect; the opposite of kachchá. A pakká ser is in most provinces about equivalent to two pounds.

Pakki. [Bengali.] A liquor distilled from rice.

Pal. [Hindi.] A measure of time consisting of twenty-four seconds.

Pál. [Hindi.] A place of shelter from the sun made by extending a piece of cloth across a transverse pole. Also a tent made on the same principle, the transverse pole being erected on two upright poles, but the roof, instead of being allowed to slope down to the ground, is cut short on each side by vertical walls of cloth stiffened with bamboos, and the gable ends are closed in with similar walls and the gables with cloths. By using two transverse poles and fixing the first two or three feet below the second, an outer roof can be formed parallel to the inner one. Pál means also a dam, or the ridge of earth made round a rice-plot to retain the water.

Pála. The name of a shepherd dynasty which ruled in Bengal from the ninth to the latter part of the eleventh century.

Pálaiya. The Tamil form of Péle. It denotes especially a military fief.

Pálaiyakára. [Tamil *kára*, doer.] Formerly a military chief seised of a pálaiya; thence any grantee of a pálaiya. The word is commonly spelt in English poligar.

Páláł. [Toḍa, from *pál*, milk, and *al*, a person.] The title of the highest kind of priest among the Toḍas; they live in isolated holy mands, and are believed to make known the divine will to those who come to them for counsel. Before entering on the office of pálál a candidate has to undergo a preparation of severe austerity, and while he holds it, which is usually for only a few years, to live an ascetic life. The milk of the sacred herd belongs to the pálál; it is too holy to be sold as milk, but is made into ghi and then sold.

Palankeen, or Palanquin. [Hindustáni *pálki.*] A long, low, closed carriage in which the occupant reclines at full length, and which is borne, by means of two projecting poles, one at each end, on the shoulders of men.

Paláśa. [Sanskrit.] The tree butea frondosa, called also ḍhak, khákhar, or khákhara; it bears a red flower. Leaves of this tree may be used to represent the deceased at the cremation ceremony when the body cannot be obtained. A strong rope is made from the root, an astringent exudation is obtained from the bark, and the leaves are used as dinner-plates. From this word is derived the name of the village Plassey.

Péle. [Kanarese.] A tract of country subject to a petty chieftain. In Maráṭhi, a hollow or confined spot surrounded by hills. Also the name of a small caste of Tulu-speaking farm-labourers.

Pálegár. The Maráṭhi form of Palaiyakára. He was usually a Koli or Maráṭhá employed in marauding from his inaccessible péle.

Paleya. The Kanarese form of Pálaiya. Also the name of a wild tribe in Coorg; they are distinguished as Maila and Achala Paleyas. They have Hindu features, are of middle stature, and have black straight hair. They have no idols, but, like the Tulus, call upon their gods Gulika, Khorti, and Kalurti when eating. See Pulayan.

Páli. This is the name of the ancient language of the Hindus, which as a spoken language developed into Prákrit, and as a written language was refined into Sanskrit. Páli is the sacred language of the Buddhists.

Páli. The name of a branch of the Koch tribe; they live much in the jungle, and mix as little as possible with the Bengali villagers.

Páliá. [Gujaráti.] A stone or monument of masonry erected in memory of distinguished warriors or of satis. Páliás usually bear the sign of a bloody hand if in memory of a sati, and that of a ship or a warrior on horseback if in commemoration of one who has fallen in defence of his village in war by sea or land; a dagger piercing the heart or throat of a man distinguishes the páliá of a Bháṭ who has killed himself in trágá. Compare Virakallu.

Pálki. More commonly Palankeen. Permission to use a pálki used to be a distinction conferred by sovereigns, and grants were sometimes made for the maintenance of the pálki.

Pálki-gári. [Hindustáni.] A kind of carriage resembling a palankeen on wheels; the shigram of Bombay.

Pálla. [Bengali.] A turn, as of enjoyment of property, or of the duty of officiating in a temple.

Pallan. [Tamil.] The name of a very numerous but most abject and despised caste, probably one of the aboriginal races of southern India. They are chiefly occupied as field-servants, and though nominally free they are usually slaves in almost every sense of the word. They are not allowed to live within the villages, but their huts form a detached hamlet at a distance. They bury their dead more commonly than they burn them. Their widows freely remarry, and divorces are most common (*J. H. Nelson*). See Pulayan.

Pallawa. The name of a dynasty that ruled over the eastern side of the peninsula from the Krishna to the Palar. They were repeatedly attacked by the Chálukyas and Cheras from the fourth to the seventh century, and finally made feudatories.

Palli. [Tamil.] A small town or village. The word is often used in combination, as Trisirá-palli (corruptly Trichinopoly). Also another name of the Tigala caste.

Palli. The name of a caste called also Vannia; they are agricultural, and were formerly predial slaves of the Vellálans.

Palliyan. [Tamil.] The name of a wild hill tribe of Madura. Perhaps the same as the caste known as Palli or Tigala, in Mysore. See Pulayan.

Paláá. [Maráṭhi.] The name of a caste whose head-quarters are at Bassein. They claim to be Bráhmans, and were for a long time the only officiating Bráhmans recognized by the British authorities (*A. K. Nairne*).

Páltchi. [Toḍa, from *pál*, milk.] A hut used as a dairy; there is one páltchi in each mand. Besides the ordinary dairy, there is in some villages a larger páltchi, in which relics are kept and which is looked on as a shrine.

Paltuna. [Hindi.] A reed which grows in water and has a soft woollen head used for stuffing pillows.

Palwár. A boat of burden, of from fifteen to twenty tons, employed for carrying goods, considered as originally of Dacca build (*H. H. Wilson*).

Palwári. [Bengali.] The name of a low caste; they are musicians.

Pán. [Uriya.] The name of an aboriginal tribe very numerous in Orissa; some are employed as labourers and musicians; they are not allowed to enter the temple of Jagannáth.

Pán. [Hindi, from the Sanskrit *parna*.] A leaf, especially the leaf of the piper betel. The word is used as an abbreviation of pán-supári.

Panári. The name of a tribe in Khándesh, called also Mathwádis. They live by agriculture, and some by grazing cattle and selling grass or fuel; they also deal in cattle. They formerly dressed as Hindus, but now rather as Bhils. They worship Wághdewa and the river Narbadá. They burn their dead.

Pancháit. More commonly Pancháyat.

Panchál. [Maráṭhi.] A collective name for five castes of artificers—the Sonár, Sutár, Lohár, Kánsár, and Pátharwaṭ. These five castes are distinct, and do not form one community as the same five classes of artificers do in the Kanarese, Telugu, and Tamil countries. See Pánchála, Kammálan. The term Panchál is seldom used. It is also the name of a small caste in Málwan, who claim to be of Bráhman descent and have priests of their own caste; they use flesh and spirits and are clever artisans.

Panchála. [Sanskrit, from *pancha*, five.] An ancient name for the Panjáb and the warrior tribe who inhabited it.

Pánchála. [Kanarese.] The name of a caste; they are artificers, and may follow any of the five professions of goldsmith, carpenter, blacksmith, mason, or mixed-metal worker. The Kanarese names of these five classes are Agasála, Baḍagi, Kammar, Kallukuṭika, and Bogára or Kanchugára. The Pánchála wear the janeo, and consider themselves as equal or superior to Bráhmans. The goldsmiths are admitted to be the head of the clan and have a caste jurisdiction over the rest. The various trades are not confined to particular families, but may be followed according to individual inclination. Some are Vaishnawas and some Śaiwas, but the two sections intermarry and eat together.

Panchamsáli. [Kanarese.] The name of a large agricultural caste.

Panchángi. [Kanarese, from *panchâng*, an almanac, from *panch*, five, and *anga*, members, from its five subdivisions.] An almanac-maker; he is usually a Bráhman, and the office is hereditary.

Panchasilaya. [Sinhalese, from the Sanskrit *pancha*, five.] The five precepts to be observed by all Buddhists; they forbid (1) the taking of life; (2) theft; (3) fornication and adultery; (4) lying; and (5) the use of intoxicating drinks. Compare Dasasil.

Pancháyat. [Hindi, from *panch*, five.] A committee or court of arbitration consisting of five persons. But the term is widely used irrespective of the number of persons, and may include all the elders of a caste assembled in council, or the two or three bystanders called by a policeman to witness a search.

Panchgavya. [Hindi, from the Sanskrit *pancha*, five, and *gavya*, belonging to the cow, from *gava*, a cow.] The five products of the cow, namely, milk, curds, ghee, urine, and dung, all of which are used in certain purificatory rites.

Pánchkalsi. [Maráṭhi.] The name of a small Hindu caste of the Konkan. Their proper occupation is carpentry, but they engage considerably in trade, take contracts, etc. (*A. K. Nairne*).

Panchkosi. [Hindi, from *panch*, five, and *kos*, q.v.] A circuit of five kos, especially that round Benares, which pilgrims are enjoined to make, and of which they get certificates at the temple of Sákshi Vináyak.

Pancholi. [Gujaráti.] The name of a small caste, who from their name and the diversity of their occupations appear to be connected with the Pánchála of the south; they are weavers, carpenters, and cotton-ginners. In Jodhpur the Káyath caste is called by this name.

Paṇḍá. [Hindi.] The proprietary or presiding priest of a temple, usually, though not invariably, a Bráhman; the office is hereditary.

Paṇḍal. [Tamil.] A shed, especially the temporary structure erected and decorated for a marriage ceremony.

Paṇḍala. [Malayálam.] The name of a Śudra caste of which the rájá of Calicut is a member.

Pándán. [Hindi, Persian *dán*, holding.] A box for holding pán and its accompaniments.

Paṇḍára. [Tamil.] The name of a Śaiwa sect in the south.

Pandaram. A hill tribe of Travancore, in a miserable condition, living in holes, rocks, or trees, and without clothing or implements; they bring wax, ivory, and other produce to the Arayans, and get salt from them (*H. Baker*).

Páṇḍawa. [Sanskrit.] A son of Páṇḍu; the five sons were Yudhishṭhira, Bhima, Arjuna, Nakula, and Sahadewa. See Mahábhárata.

Páṇḍharpeshá. [Maráṭhi, from *páṇḍhar*, the village community, and Persian *peshah*, practice.] A comprehensive term for the higher classes as distinguished from the mere cultivator — the Bráhman, Parbhu, goldsmith, blacksmith, etc. (*J. T. Molesworth*). These persons getting their lands at lower rates than the common cultivators, and being also exempt from many of the cesses, gave rise to what was called the páṇḍharpeshá tenure.

Pándikuri. [Malayálam.] An Arayan vault; each side and the top and bottom are made of a single slab of stone, and they are placed due north and south, with the opening to the south.

Panḍit. [Sanskrit *panḍita*, learned.] A learned man, a teacher. Some Bráhmans, objecting to the mention of a father-in-law, call that relative panḍitji. In Cashmere any clerk or native official is called a panḍit.

Pándiwad. [Maráṭhi.] The checkered water snake, the tropidonotus quincunciatus. It measures up to fifty-one inches; the colouration is very variable, ranging from blackish grey to greenish olive, with from three to seven rows of black spots down the body in quincuncial order. It is fierce and active, but not poisonous. It is abundant everywhere in or near rivers, pools, marshes, and canals, wherever frogs and fish are procurable. But it differs from the true fresh-water snakes in having the nostrils situated on the side instead of on the upper surface of the head (*G. W. Vidal*).

Pandy. A common name, among English soldiers, of the rebels in the Indian mutiny; they were so called from one Mangal Pande, a ringleader.

Pándyá. The name of a dynasty formerly ruling the Tamil country, and with their capital at Madura. These with the Chola and Chera constitute the three great Dravidian dynasties.

Panego. [Burmese.] A flat-bottomed barge used on the Irrawaddy, especially for the carriage of petroleum.

Pángla. [Maráṭhi.] The name of a plant of the labiate order, the pogostemon purpuricaulis, nearly allied to the patchouli shrub. The root is given both internally and as a paste for outward application to stop the hæmorrhage caused by the bite of the fursá.

Panguni. The Tamil name of the solar month Minam, corresponding most nearly to March, Phálgun, and the Bengal Chaitra. See Month.

Panika. The name of a class of mendicants in Coorg.

Pániká. [Bengali.] The name of a semi-Hinduised tribe of Chutiá Nágpur; they are weavers.

Páni-Koch. The name of a division of the Koch tribe, generally regarded as the original type of the whole tribe. They live in the woods and cultivate on the jum system. Women hold a high position among them, own all property, and do most of the work.

Pánipatrak. [Maráṭhi, from *pahâni*, inspection, and *patrak*, a list.] The name of one of the village account-books under the Bombay land-revenue system. In this book are recorded the number, the tenure, the holder's name, the area, and the assessment, of every field belonging to the village, and in subsequent columns is noted, after inspection each season, the crop or crops with which each field is sown, and the condition of the boundary-marks.

Panjáb. [Persian *panj*, five, and *áb*, water.] The country of the five rivers, the Jhelam, Chenáb, Rávi, Bias, and Satluj. It is now one of the eight provinces of British India; it has an area of 107,010 square miles, and a population of 18,794,260 persons, or more than half that of the United Kingdom. The native states politically connected with the Panjáb government have an area of 104,958 square miles, and a population of 4,852,360 persons.

Panjábi. The language of the Panjáb. It is of Sanskrit origin and is spoken by over fourteen millions of persons. There are many different dialects; among them the Mánjhá spoken in the Panjáb proper, the Multáni, and the Pahári. In order of extent of use Panjábi is the fifth Indian language.

Panjah. [Hindustáni, from the Persian *panj*, five.] A five-pronged mark made by smearing the hand with henna and clapping it against a wall or other object; the five prongs denote Muhammad, Ali, Fatimah, Hásan, and Husain. Also the figure of a hand carried in procession.

Pánjnigar. [Gujaráti, from *pánjni* starch.] The name of a caste; their occupation is stiffening cotton thread with starch made of wheat. There are also Sunni Musalmán converts of the same name, and some of these starch silk also, using a preparation of old leather boiled down with lime-juice.

Pánjrápol. [Gujaráti, from *pánjrá*, Sanskrit *pinjara*, a cage, and *pol*, an enclosed yard.] A hospital where broken-down, maimed, or useless animals are kept alive.

Panká. The name of a low caste in the Central Provinces; they were formerly of the Satnámi sect and then became Kabirpanthis.

Pankho. The name of a Toungthá tribe closely resembling the Banjogis. They bind their hair in a knot at the back of the head like the Tipperahs and Lusháis.

Pannai. [Tamil, literally, cultivation.] A term applied to land to which the proprietor has exclusive right, receiving the kuḍiváram as well as the melváram. It is identical with kamata, and is called pannai perhaps because it is the land which the proprietor has to cultivate, as distinguished from that which is held by his hereditary tenants.

Panniar. The name of a caste in Wynaad; they wash river-lands and surface soils for gold.

Pansári. [Hindi.] A druggist.

Pansi. [Bengali.] A boat, both rowing and sailing, with the aft part roofed in, used on the Hughli.

Pánsupári. [Hindi.] Pán and supári; slices of supári or areca nut, with chunam, spices, and sometimes catechu, are rolled up in the betel leaf, the whole making a little package of an ounce or two in weight. All classes of natives chew pánsupári, and it is always presented to visitors on occasions of ceremony. Pánsupári is also used as a euphemism for a small bribe.

Pant. [Maráṭhi, an abbreviation of *panḍit*.] A prefix to the titles of the eight pradháns of the Maráṭhá state.

Panth. [Hindi, from the Sanskrit *patha*, a path, a way.] A religious order or persuasion, a sect.

Panthi. [From *panth*, a way.] The follower of any particular sect or teacher.

Pantoji. [Maráṭhi.] A village schoolmaster.

Pao. Another name of the Toungthá tribes.

Paoṭá. [Maráṭhi.] Another name of the phaseolus radiatus or black gram. See Urid.

Papaw. [A corruption of the Bengali *papaya.*] The tree carica papaya; it grows to the height of twenty feet, with a soft herbaceous stem naked nearly to the top, where the leaves issue on every side on long foot-stalks, between which grow the flower and the fruit. Also the fruit, which is of the size of a melon, having an acrid and milky juice; it is sometimes eaten raw when ripe, but is more commonly cooked or pickled (*Loudon*).

Parab. [Gujaráti.] A place where vessels of water are placed ready for the use of persons who pass by.

Parabiá. A person appointed to supply water at a parab.

Paraḍ. [Maráṭhi.] The gongylophis conicus, one of the family of erycidæ, or sand-snakes. It is a very thick, clumsily made brown snake, marked on its back with large blotches, which frequently unite and form a broad zigzag band, and on each side is a row of smaller irregular brown spots. The tail is very short and tapering, and the head, which is scaled, not shielded, except at the lips and fore part of the snout, is flat, oblong, and scarcely distinct from the neck. The paraḍ has rudimentary hind limbs. Its maximum length is about two feet (*G. W. Vidal*).

Páradhi. [Gujaráti.] A hunter; also the name of a tribe in Cutch allied to the Meos, and who are half Hindu and half Musalmán; they are hunters and also weave mats of leaves. Compare Párdhi.

Parágar. [Bengali.] The name of a caste; they are labourers and menial servants.

Parai-cheri. More commonly Patchery.

Paraiyan. [Tamil.] This is the name, more commonly spelt Pariah, of a large class of persons generally considered as being lower than any caste. Their original occupation is said to have been beating the *parai*, or tom-tom, at funerals; but as they multiplied they were obliged to do indiscriminately all kinds of menial and degrading work. They are now employed as prædial slaves, scavengers, burners and buriers of corpses, musicians, and as domestic servants to Europeans. They are still theoretically loathed and despised by all but a few of the lowest classes of natives; their touch defiles, and their mere presence is believed to taint the air. They are obliged to live apart from their employers in separate quarters, called the parai-cheri, and must never come near a Bráhman or a Vellálan, or indeed any respectable man. But they are so numerous and so useful that they are gradually pushing their way into a better position. They are the principal supporters of the right-hand caste in the periodical disputes between the two hands (see Idangai), in which they always range themselves against the Pallans (*J. H. Nelson*). There are many subdivisions of the Paraiyans. See Ambu, Arippukáran, Egáli, Koliya, Kuḍipillai, Ottagakáran, Perum, Pola, Tamila, Tonda, Toṭṭi, Veṭṭiyán, Waduga.

Parakuḍi. [Tamil, from *para*, distant, foreign, and *kuḍi*, an inhabitant.] An outsider, a new-comer, a cultivator without hereditary rights, the páhi or páikásht of Bengal. See Ulkuḍi.

Paramahansa. [Sanskrit *parama*, best, and *hansa*, the first meaning of which is swan, but which also is a name of the supreme spirit.] The name of a sect of Śaiwa devotees.

Parámánik. A Bengali form of Pramánika.

Parasnath. See Párśwanáth.

Paraśuráma. [Sanskrit *parśu*, an axe.] Ráma with the axe, the name of Vishnu in his sixth awatár, when he was born as a Bráhman and destroyed the Kshatriya race. Also the name of a prince of Malayála in the twelfth century before Christ. The present Malabár era is called after him. It is reckoned in cycles of a thousand years, but instead of beginning afresh at the commencement of the present cycle in A.D. 1825, the first year was added to the previous cycle and called 1001; so the current year is called 1060 instead of 60. The year 1061 will begin on the 15th September, 1885. See Year.

Parawa. [Tamil.] The name of a caste; they are fishers. They are supposed to have been once a powerful race. Many have become Muhammadans and some Roman Catholics.

Parbat. [Hindi form of the Sanskrit *parwata*.] A mountain; about Oudh there are several mounds covered with broken brick-work, and which are called parbats.

Parbatiya. [Hindi, from *parbat*, q.v.] A mountaineer, a hill-man; particularly the hill-people of Nepál.

Parbhu. [Maráṭhi.] The name of the writer caste of western India; they correspond to the Káyasths of the north, and one division of them are so called; others are called Paṭanya. The Parbhus were employed as clerks by the Portuguese and English before the Bráhmans accepted such service, and the latter have been unable to oust them.

Parbutty. See Párwati.

Parcherry. [Perhaps the same word as *patcherry*, or from *para*, other, foreign.] The outskirts of a town, the quarter where the Paraiyans usually live.

Pardah. [Persian.] A veil, a screen, a curtain, especially one used to exclude women from public view.

Pardahnishin. [Persian *nishin*, who sits.] A woman who observes the practice of seclusion.

Pardeśi. [Hindi, from the Sanskrit *para*, other, and *deśa*, country.] A foreigner; but particularly, in the Bombay presidency, a Rájput from Hindustán.

Párdhi. [Maráṭhi, from *páradh*, hunting.] The name of a caste, whose profession is hunting and snaring wild animals. Many of them, especially those called Langoṭi and Phánsi Párdhis, are professional thieves, and are said to be a branch of the Báori tribe. Compare Páradhi.

Pardi. [Maráṭhi.] A small patch of

ground surrounding or adjoining a house, and usually free of assessment. When unduly large a limit is sometimes fixed, and pardi lands in excess of it are assessed.

Parganá, or **Parganah.** [Hindi.] A district, a province, but especially a subdivision of a zillah; a táluk.

Parheyá. An aboriginal tribe living in the hill ranges of Lohárdagá; they may be a branch of the Mundás, but have adopted Hindi speech, and their marriage and funeral ceremonies are according to Hindu custom.

Pari. [Persian.] A fabulous winged monster with the body of a horse and a human face. Also a beautiful woman, a fairy, a peri.

Pariah. A popular corruption of Paraiyan. Generally, one rejected and contemned by society; whence the term has been applied to the ownerless village dogs of India.

Parihar. The name of one of the agnikula tribes of Rájputs and the least distinguished of them; they were ruling in Márwár in 1194 A.D., when the Ráthors, themselves retreating from the Ghoris, drove them out; some of the Parihars established themselves at Idar, and there also they were eventually succeeded by the Ráthors.

Parishad. [From the Sanskrit *pari*, around, and *sad*, to sit.] An assembly or college of learned Bráhmans, competent by their collective knowledge to decide points of law.

Pariśishṭa. [From the Sanskrit *pari*, beyond, and *śish*, to leave.] A supplement, an appendix. This is the name of several works which may be considered as the very last outskirts of vedic literature. Their object was to supply information on theological and ceremonial points which had been passed over in the sutras. They differ much in style from the sutras, and treat everything in a popular and superficial manner. But they are still vedic in character, and contain no trace of the trimurti doctrine. They were composed probably in the third or second century B.C. (*Max Müller*).

Pariṭ. [Maráṭhi.] The name of a caste; they are washermen.

Parmár. The name of the first of the agnikula tribes of Rájputs; they were formerly settled in Málwá, and spread very widely over other parts of India, and are still numerous in the North-West Provinces. Among their branches are the Maurya, Shoḍá, Sankla, and the Umra and Sumra clans, the Balhára and the Rehár.

Parsál. [Gujaráti.] The front room or hall of a house.

Pársen. [Gujaráti.] A woman of the Pársi race.

Pársi. [Gujaráti, from *fárs*, the name of Persia.] An important community settled chiefly in western India, and especially in Surat, Naosári, and Bombay, the descendants of a body or successive bodies of refugees from Persia in the eighth century A.D. These Persians, in order to obtain sufferance at the hands of the Hindus, minimized their differences and adopted what they could of Hindu customs; and the present Pársis are still remarkable for the readiness with which they assume what is good in the manners and habits of other races. At the same time, they are a very distinct community, and persons of mixed blood, partly Pársi, are scarcely known. There are no different castes or sects among the Pársis, except that the priests are a separate hereditary class. There is, however, a nominal division of all Pársis into Śehersais and Kadmis, but the difference is confined to a question of chronology. They observe the Jartosti or Zoroastrian religion which their forefathers brought with them from Persia. They have adopted Gujaráti, the vernacular of the Hindus among whom they are settled, and very many of them have learnt English. The Pársis are an intelligent and enterprising race, with a special aptitude for trade either on a large scale or in the way of shopkeeping; they pay great attention to education, and occupy many posts in the public service and all the professions; but they have not given up agriculture, and there are a few villages of which all the principal cultivators are Pársis; these, however, show a tendency to add the business of distilling, or toddy-dealing, or toll-farming, or some kind of trade, to their original occupation. See Agiári, Ahura Mazda, Avastá, Dokhmá, Mobed.

Parsut. See Prasád.

Páréwanáth. [Sanskrit: *párśwa* means the region of the ribs; *nátha*, lord, is an affix to the names of most of the jins.] The name of the twenty-third arhat or tirthakar of the Jains.

Parṭin. A woman of the caste of Pariṭs, or washermen.]

Parwánah. [Persian.] A written pass or permit.

Parwári. Another and more acceptable name for Mahár.

Párwati. [Sanskrit, from *parwata*, a mountain.] A name of the wife of Śiwa in his character as a jovial mountain-god.

Pasáetá. [Gujaráti.] Rent-free lands assigned to village servants as remuneration for their service. Pasáetá was originally the name of a particular class of village servants, namely, the police. Compare Chákarán.

Pasári. [Hindi.] A druggist.

Pashmina. [Panjábi, from the Persian *pashm*, wool.] Woollen cloth.

Pashṭo. The name of the language of the Paṭhán tribes; it is of Aryan origin with an intermixture of Zand and Persian.

Pási. The name of an aboriginal tribe in the North-West Provinces; they are now in a very low condition, but were once powerful in Oudh; they tend pigs and labour in the fields, and are employed as watchmen to catch thieves (*M. A. Sherring*).

Páśi. [Bengali, from the Sanskrit *páśa*, a noose.] The name of a semi-Hinduised tribe who are toddy-drawers. They receive their name from the rope loop, encircling the man's body and the tree, they use in climbing. Compare Bhandári.

Páśupata. A follower of Paśupati. This is the name of a Śaiwa sect.

Paśupati. [Sanskrit *paśu*, an animal, and *pati*, lord.] The lord of living beings, a name of Śiwa.

Pát. A spot held sacred by the Gonḍs; it may be marked by a bamboo with a piece of rag tied to the end, or by a heap of stones, or only by a few pieces of rag tied to the branch of a tree. Offerings are made at the pát.

Páṭ. [Hindi.] An inferior sort of marriage. See Nátaru.

Paṭá. Another form of Paṭṭá, a belt, or of Paṭṭá, a lease.

Páṭá. Another form of Paṭṭá, a lease.

Pátál. [Sanskrit *pátála.*] The lower regions. It is fabled that there are fourteen regions resting one upon another; the lower seven are called pátáls and the upper seven (of which the earth is the lowest) are called worlds. Sometimes the name pátál is confined to the top one of the seven lower regions. The pátáls are not places of torment. See Wáman.

Paṭáwálá. [Gujaráti *paṭá* or *paṭṭá*, a belt, and the affix *wálá.*] A servant who wears a belt as a badge; particularly office attendants and messengers attached to the establishments of government officers; they are called also chaprási and peon.

Patcherry. [A corruption of the Tamil *paraicheri*, from *paraiyan*, q.v., and *cheri*, a village.] A Pariah village, or the Pariah quarter outside a village. In some native regiments the term denotes the married sepoys' quarters, possibly because Pariah sepoys had their families with them, while the higher castes left theirs at home.

Paṭel. [Gujaráti, from the Sanskrit *paṭa*, a piece of cloth for writing on, a register.] The headman of a village. The office is hereditary, sometimes in a single family and sometimes by rotation or selection in two or more. It is remunerated by land held either free of rent or at a reduced rate, and sometimes by cash allowances also. The duties of the office are of two distinct classes, one being connected with revenue and the other with police matters, and in some villages are divided between two persons, called respectively revenue-paṭel and police-paṭel. As revenue officer the paṭel, with the aid of the village accountant, collects the assessment due upon the village lands and remits it to the mámlatdár; he should insist upon the ryots duly maintaining the boundary-marks of their fields, and should report any matter, such as the unwarranted occupation of land, that calls for interference. As police officer the paṭel inquires into alleged offences and cases of sudden death; he has power of arrest, but when he finds an offence has been committed calls in the aid of the district police; the village watchmen are under his orders, and he keeps a roll and watches the movements of the bad characters of the village. The term paṭel is also applied to the head of a caste and as a title of courtesy to any Kanbi or Koli.

Paṭelá. [Hindi.] A large flat-bottomed boat used for merchandise on the Ganges.

Pateliya. [Gujaráti.] The name of a caste of Rájput descent; they are cultivators; they use animal food and worship Káli.

Páṭhaka. [Sanskrit, from *path*, to read.] A reader, a Bráhman who reads the sacred works in public.

Paṭhán. [Hindustáni, from the Pashṭo *pakhṭána*, the plural of *pakhtun*, the name of a people inhabiting the country called by Herodotus Pactiya.] This name as used in India includes all the natives of the country commonly called Afghánistán, and also the descendants of immigrants from that country into India. But in Afghánistán itself the name is confined to the Pashṭo-speaking tribes (excluding, therefore, the Hazárás and Tájiks), and as more strictly used it excludes the Afgháns proper and the Ghilzais. The Paṭháns (in the Indian sense) began a long course of invasions of India as early as the tenth century, and in 1206 Kutb-ud-din (at first viceroy of the Paṭhán ruler of Ghor and Ghazni) founded the Paṭhán dynasty, which reigned at Delhi for three centuries, till it was overthrown by the Moguls. The descendants of these old settlers have now, by intermixture with other classes, lost the peculiarities of feature and character which distinguish new-comers. All are Sunnis.

Páthariyá. [Bengali, from the Sanskrit *prastara*, a stone.] The name of a caste; they are stonemasons.

Pátharwaṭ. [Maráṭhi, from *páthar*, Sanskrit *prastara*, a stone.] The name of a caste; they are stonemasons. See Panchál.

Páthśálá. [Sanskrit *páṭha*, reading, from *paṭh*, to read, and *śálá*, a house.] A school, a college. In Bengal it generally means a petty indigenous school; in other parts, rather a college of some rank for the study of Sanskrit and the śástras.

Pati. [Sanskrit.] A lord, a master. Often used in composition, as *senápati*, a commander-in-chief; *jagpati*, the lord of the world.

Páṭi. [Bengali.] The part of a market occupied by dealers of one class.

Páṭi. [Bengali.] A mat of fine texture.

Páṭial. [Bengali, from *páṭi*, a mat.] The name of a low caste; they are labourers and mat-makers.

Páṭidár. The Gujaráti form of Paṭṭidár. This term seems to have been used first in connection with the narwá system, when it meant either a principal or a sub-sharer, as distinguished both from their tenants and from cultivators whose rights were confined to the majmu lands. The páṭidárs of the present day are the descendants of such original sharers. They are very careful of the distinction, and have become almost a separate caste among the Kanbis. A Kanbi páṭidár, when asked of what caste he is, will reply, not 'Kanbi,' but 'páṭidár;' nor will he readily take to wife the daughter of a common Kanbi. But the name is not confined exclusively to Kanbis; there are also Rájput, Vorá, and Koli páṭidárs.

Pátil. The Maráṭhi form of Paṭel. The Maráṭhás use it to designate the headman of a village, and also as a title of courtesy in addressing any member of a Śudra caste.

Patimar. See Paṭṭemár.

Patitábádi. [Bengali.] A term applied to leases of land which, from its being covered with jungle, is given free for a term of years and is afterwards subject to a progressive rate.

Pativrata. [Sanskrit, from *pati*, a husband, and *vrata*, a vow.] A chaste and virtuous wife.

Patni. See Paṭṭani.

Pátni. [Bengali.] The name of a branch of the Jáliyá caste, but deemed lower than other Jáliyás, because as ferrymen they for hire carry impure persons over holy rivers.

Pátrá. [Uriya.] The name of a caste; they are reckoned low, and are not allowed to enter the temple of Jagannáth; they are cloth-makers.

Patrak. [Maráṭhi, from the Sanskrit *pattra*, a leaf.] A sheet, a document; especially a tabular statement, a schedule.

Patshaing. [Burmese.] A particular musical instrument; it consists of a circular, tub-like frame about thirty inches high and about four feet six inches in diameter, formed of separate wooden staves fancifully carved, and fitting into a hoop which keeps them in place. Round the interior of this frame are hung vertically a number of drums or tom-toms graduated in tone as in size. The performer gets inside and squats down, and strikes the drum with his fingers and palms with great dexterity and surprising musical effect.

Paṭṭá. [Gujaráti.] A belt, a girdle; particularly a shoulder-belt or scarf, usually of a bright striking colour, worn as a distinguishing mark by peons or messengers.

Paṭṭá. [Hindi, perhaps the Sanskrit *paṭṭa*, a tablet.] A deed of lease. Among the Rájputs the word is applied also to the tract of land leased, and so comes to mean a division of a district, a group of villages. When a paṭṭá is given, a counterpart called muchalká or kabuliyat is usually taken.

Paṭṭádár. [Hindi, from *paṭṭá*, a lease, and Persian *dár*, holder.] One who holds a lease for his lands. The paṭṭádárs of Sindh are descendants of Afghán settlers who got from their governments deeds of reduced assessment on lands which they had purchased from Sindhi proprietors, or reclaimed from the waste.

Paṭṭanaseṭṭi. [Kanarese.] The chief merchant of a town, a nagarśeṭh.

Paṭṭani. [Bengali.] A tenure by which the occupant holds of a zamindár a portion of the zamindári in perpetuity, with the right of hereditary succession, and of letting or selling the whole or part as long as a stipulated amount of rent is paid to the zamindár, who retains the power of sale for arrears, and is entitled to a regulated fee or fine upon any transfer (*H. H. Wilson*). It has been otherwise described as a permanent tenure granted by a zamindár at a fixed rent, in consideration of a bonus, the holder being entitled to exercise all the powers of the grantor, but paying his land-tax through the zamindár.

Paṭṭanidár. [Persian *dár*, holder.] One who holds land on paṭṭani tenure. If a paṭṭanidár sublet land on the same tenure, the next holder is termed darpaṭṭanidár; and if the latter sublet on the same tenure, the third holder is called sehpaṭṭanidár.

Paṭṭáwat. [Gujaráti.] A minor chief who furnishes troops to a rájá, and holds land on that condition.

Paṭṭemár. [Malayálam.] A deep, narrow, fast-sailing vessel. The

Malabár paṭṭemár is from ten to eighty tons, and has one mast; that of the Konkan is larger, and has usually two masts.

Paṭṭi. [Hindustáni.] A share, a division of a village.

Paṭṭidár. [Persian *dár*, holder.] The holder of a share in a coparcenary village. Compare Bhágdár.

Paṭṭidári. The name of a coparcenary tenure in northern India, in which each sharer manages his own lands, but the general body is responsible for the default of any sharer.

Paṭṭunulkára. [Tamil, from *paṭṭu*, silk, *nul*, to spin, *kára*, doer.] The name of a caste of Surat silk-weavers whose ancestors were induced to settle in Madura by one of the earlier Náyakka kings; and who have thriven so well that they now form by far the most numerous of all the castes resident in the town of Madura. They are skilful and industrious workmen, and many of them have become very wealthy. They keep altogether aloof from other castes (*J. H. Nelson*). There are some also in Ceylon.

Patua. The name of a branch of the Jogi tribe; they make silk strings on which they thread beads.

Patuli. [Bengali.] A large boat used on the Ganges for carrying goods.

Patur. [Bengali.] The name of a caste; they are fishers and boatmen.

Paṭvegár. The name of a caste in Mysore who speak a language allied to Maráṭhi; they are silk-weavers. (Perhaps of the same stock as the Tamil Paṭṭunulkáras.)

Paṭwári. [Hindi, from the Sanskrit *paṭa*, a register.] A village registrar and accountant. In some parts of India he is a government servant, in others he is paid by the villagers, in others he is merely a zamindár's rent-collector. In Sindh the office of paṭwári was restored in 1856, and made stipendiary.

Patyen. The name of a god worshipped by the Banjogis and the Shendus.

Paunchway. See Pansi.

Paush. [Sanskrit.] The Hindu month most nearly corresponding with January; it is so called from *pushya*, a blossom, the name of the nakshatra in which the moon is at full in this month. See Month.

Pávai. [Gujaráti.] A class of eunuchs who worship Bahucharáji; they dress as women and wander about begging.

Pávrá. The name of a tribe found in Khándesh, said to be Rájputs who were driven by the Udáipur chiefs from their homes near the hill fort of Palagad. They are called Pávrá Bhils, Pávrá Náiks, and Pávrá Kolis indifferently. Their language is nearer Gujaráti than Maráṭhi. They are mostly husbandmen, and are much attached to their land. They build better houses than the Warlis, and grow mango and chároli trees about them. The women do not work in the fields, but gather mowra flowers for distillation and chároli nuts. They have neither priests, temples, nor idols, but near each village is a sacred tree to which offerings are made. They either burn or bury their dead.

Paweea. See Pávai.

Pawn. See Pán.

Pawnee. [Hindustáni *páni.*] Water.

Paycarry. See Páikári.

Pázand. [Persian *pá*, the foot, and *zand*, q.v.] Under the zand; the name of an explanation, written in mediæval Persian, of the zand or commentary on the Pahlavi edition of the avastá.

Pearl Mosque. A translation of *moti masjid.* A name given to a small private mosque, usually of white marble, attached to a Muhammadan emperor's palace. Pearl mosques may be seen at Agra, Aligarh, and Delhi.

Peg. A popular name in English for a glass of spirit and soda-water.

Pehlavi. See Pahlavi.

Peiki. [Toḍa.] The name of the division of the Toḍas which constitute the priesthood.

Peon. This word is a corruption of the Hindustáni *piyáda*, a foot-soldier. It is applied to policemen and paṭáwálás.

Pepper-vine. The piper nigrum. By a vine in the public accounts is meant as many vines as cling to one standard tree. The mango and the jack are most commonly used as standards. From eight to twelve vines are put to one tree. They begin to bear at six years of age; in four years more are in full perfection, and continue so for twenty years, when they die. The fruit is gathered green when intended for black pepper, but must become quite ripe for white pepper, and the ripening is apt to kill the vine.

Peri. [Persian *pari.*] A fairy, the descendant of a fallen angel; a beautiful woman.

Permanent Settlement. The name of the settlement made in 1793, by which government entered into an engagement with each zamindár in Bengal, Behar, and Orissa, by the terms of which, on the one hand, the zamindár became bound to pay a certain jamá or fixed amount of assessment, and on the other the government recognized him as hereditary proprietor of the land, and undertook never to alter his jamá. See Settlement.

Persian-wheel. See Arhat.

Perum. [Tamil.] The name of a division of the Paraiyans; they are employed chiefly as domestic servants.

Pesalu. [Telugu.] The pulse phaseolus mungo, or green gram.

Peshkár. [Hindustáni.] An agent, a deputy; the clerk next below the sarishtadár. Affixed to an officer's title to denote his deputy, as diwán peshkár.

Peshkash. [Persian.] First-fruits, fine, tax; but especially the quit-rent taken for lands which for any reason are exempt from full assessment.

Peshwá. [Maráṭhi *peśwá*, from the Persian *pesh*, esteemed, influential.] The title of the prime minister of the Maráṭhá kingdom; on the death of Sambhaji, the second king, in 1689 A.D., the sovereign power passed into the hands of the then peshwá, a Chitpáwan Bráhman named Báláji, and the office of head of the state, under the same title of peshwá, became hereditary in his family.

The peshwás continued to be real sovereigns till the battle of Pánipat in 1761, after which other Maráṭhá houses rose into power, and the peshwá's authority grew less. In 1817 the peshwá, in treaty with the Gáekwár, renounced his supremacy, and in the following year his territory was annexed to the Bombay presidency.

Peṭárá. [Maráṭhi, from the Sanskrit *peṭá*.] A large wicker box or basket.

Petbhátá. A rent-free tenure of Kuch Behar, granted by the rájá for the maintenance of his relatives; a petbhátá grant lapses on the death of the holder unless it be expressly renewed in favour of his heirs.

Peṭh. [Hindi.] A market, a bázár; the division of a city; or a separate subordinate town, a suburb.

Pettah. [Telugu *peta*.] A suburb, a village near a town.

Phaḍká. [Gujaráti.] A sowing-drill; it is drawn by a pair of bullocks like a plough; the driver carries the seed in a cloth bound round his waist, and, as he proceeds, with one hand keeps filling a wooden cup fixed in the upper part of the phaḍká; from the bottom of the cup proceed hollow bamboos the lower ends of which pass through the drill a little below the level of the soil; thus as the point of the drill is dragged through the soil the seed drops out behind it and is deposited in the earth before the soil disturbed by the passing of the drill falls back again.

Phaḍnis. [Maráṭhi, from *phaḍ*, an office, and the Persian *navis*, a writer.] The officer who kept the public registers under the Maráṭhá government; also, later, a collector's head clerk.

Phágan. The Hindustáni form of Phálgun.

Phakir. See Fakir.

Phálá. [Gujaráti.] Distribution, proportion, share; especially a subscription, collection, or tax assessed according to the quantity of land each contributor holds, or the amount of revenue he pays, or other such mode of distributing the burden according to the capacity of each.

Phálgun. [Sanskrit.] The Hindu month most nearly corresponding with March; it is so called from the nakshatra *phalguni* (part of the sign Leo) in which the moon is at full in this month. See Month.

Phárgati. The Gujaráti form of Fárighkhatti.

Pháridár. [Bengali.] A former police officer intermediate between the faujdár and the chaukidár.

Phárikhatu. The Kanarese form of Fárighkhatti.

Phárkhat. The Bengali form of Fárighkhatti.

Pharnavis. Another form of Phaḍnis. Commonly Furnavees.

Phatemári. The Maráṭhi form of Paṭṭemár.

Phera. [Panjábi.] The circumambulation of the sacred fire, an essential part of most Hindu marriages. See Saptapadi.

Phojdár. The Gujaráti form of Faujdár.

Phukeer. See Fakir.

Phulkári. [Panjábi.] A peasant woman's chadar or outer garment worked with sprigs of embroidery.

Phulkia. [Panjábi.] The name of a family of Ját Sikhs founded by one Phul, a village chaudhri, who died in 1652. This family gave their name to the Sikh misl which occupied the country south of the Satluj from near Delhi to Simla. The Phulkias formed no part of Ranjit Singh's kingdom, but received British protection in opposition to him. They sided with the British in the Sikh wars, and are still the rulers of the native states of Patiálá, Jind, and Nábhá.

Phuṭáyá. [Gujaráti, from *phuṭ*, to bud, to shoot.] A cadet of a ruling family; he may himself be an independent ruler, but the ṭiláyat of the family from which he sprang is his heir in the last resort.

Pial. A raised floor or terrace serving as a seat in front of a house.

Pice. [Maráṭhi *paisá.*] A copper coin of the value of three pies or the quarter of an anna. This division of the anna is not used in accounts, but it is the division in popular bázár use. Pice is sometimes used as a name for money generally.

Pichkor. [Gujaráti.] The weak liquor that issues last in the process of mowra distillation.

Picotah. [Tamil *pakota.*] A kind of pump used for raising water for irrigation.

Pie. [Bengali *pái.*] A copper coin, the twelfth part of an anna, or about the value of half a farthing.

Pie. A popular name in English of the pariah or unowned dogs of India.

Pilau. [Persian.] A dish consisting of boiled fowl with rice highly seasoned with cinnamon, cardamoms, mace, and ghee.

Pille. Another name of the Modali caste.

Pilu. [Hindi.] The fruit of the wán; it is an acrid red-and-white berry, and is eaten by poor people.

Pinḍa. [Sanskrit, literally, a lump.] A ball of rice, etc., offered at funeral ceremonies and śráddhas. The funeral pinḍa is supposed to be for the departed spirit to feed upon until it becomes a pitri; the śráddha pinḍas are offered to the pitris.

Pinḍári. [Maráṭhi, said to be from *pendhá*, a bundle of grass, and *hari*, who takes.] The marauders sent out from a mulkgiri army to plunder the country; a marauder in general. After the Mogul and Maráṭhá powers were broken, large armies of Pinḍáris became independent under their own chiefs; their head-quarters were in Málwá, but they carried their depredations as far as both coasts of the peninsula, and were finally suppressed only by a regular war in 1817. The Pinḍáris were of several castes—Maráṭhás, Játs, and Musalmáns.

Pinjar. [Maráṭhi.] Turmeric powder, kanku.

Pinjárá [Gujaráti], **Pinjári** [Maráṭhi; from the Sanskrit *pinja*, cotton]. A cotton-cleaner, one who extracts the seed from cotton.

Pinjni. [Gujaráti.] A cotton-cleaning machine; it is a hand-machine worked by a single person, and consists of a wooden bow which is affixed to the roof of the house, and a curved pole which hangs by a cord from the string of the bow; to the ends of the pole another cord is attached, and this, by striking with a mallet the pendent pole, is twitched through the cotton, and the latter is thrown into the air.

Pinjrápol. See Pánjrápol.

Pioni. The Sindhi name of the krait, the bungarus cærulens.

Pipal. [Hindi.] The ficus religiosa, or holy fig tree.

Pipari. [Maráṭhi.] The tree ficus tsicla.

Pir. [Persian.] A Muhammadan saint; a spiritual guide.

Pir. [Kolarian.] A group of villages.

Pirán-pir. The saint of saints; a name given to Saïd Abdul Kádir of Bagdad. The 11th of Rabias-sáni is held as a festival in his honour.

Pirzádah. [Persian *zádah*, son.] A spiritual guide, a murshid. Pirzádah and murid are relative terms.

Piśácha. [Sanskrit.] The name of a class of spirits always imagined as fierce and malignant.

Piṭaka. [Sanskrit, literally, a basket, thence a granary, a collection.] A division of the sacred books of the Buddhists; there are three piṭakas, named Sutra, Vinaya, and Abhidharma. They were compiled many years after the death of the Buddha, who himself left no writings.

Piṭárá. [Bengali, from the Sanskrit *peṭa.*] A wicker-work box.

Piṭhori. [Maráṭhi, from *piṭh*, flour.] The festival of the 30th Śráwan, when figures of yoginis are drawn in flour and worshipped. Women fast on this day to avert the evil of losing their children in infancy.

Pitpápadá. The plant glossocardia boswellia; it bears rose-coloured flowers; it is used as a remedy for fever and is eaten as a vegetable.

Pitri. [Sanskrit.] The deified soul of a deceased ancestor; the pitris of a particular person and those of the progenitors of mankind generally are both worshipped. See Pinḍa, Śráddha.

Pitrikárya. [Sanskrit *kárya*, to be done.] Obsequial rights, oblations to pitris.

Pitripaksh. [Sanskrit.] The fortnight sacred to pitris and especially appointed for their worship; it is always the krishnapaksh following the bright half of Bhádra; that is, it is either Bhádra wadi or Áśvin wadi. See Śukladi.

Plantain. [From the Latin *plantago.*] The musa sapientum, or its fruit; it has a soft herbaceous stalk, from which leaves of great length and breadth unfold themselves, and grows to a height of fifteen feet. Each plant bears a single cluster of fruit, consisting of a luscious pulp covered with a thick skin.

Poang Rájá. See Bohmong.

Pod. The name of a tribe considered to be of Turanian origin; they are divided into Chásá and Mechi Pods; the latter are mostly fishermen.

Poddár. [Hindustáni, from the Persian *fotah*, a bag, and *dár*, who holds.]

A cashier, a money-examiner. In Bengal, the name of a caste who are pawnbrokers and money-weighers.

Poita. See Paitá.

Pol. [Hindi.] A gate; also the enclosed space to which the gate admits; hence a courtyard, a square, an enclosed ward of a city.

Pol. [Maráṭhi.] A village stud bull. These animals are considered sacred to Śiwa, and are sometimes marked with a triśula and chakra; they are never confined or put to work, but are allowed to wander and eat what they like. See Sánḍ.

Pola. [Tamil.] The name of a division of the Paraiyans; they make baskets and mats.

Polá. [Maráṭhi, from *pol*, a bull.] A festival held on the new moon of Śráwan or Bhádrapad, on which day cattle are exempt from labour, decorated, and paraded about.

Polaiyan. [Tamil.] The name of an aboriginal tribe of the Palani hills; they are the prædial slaves of the Kunnuvans. They bury their dead. See Pulayan.

Poleramma. [See *amma.*] The name of a village goddess common in the Kistna district.

Poliá. [Gujaráti.] Literally, broad; the name by which the British currency of Bombay was formerly known, as distinguished from the Broach and Baroda currencies, of which the pieces were thicker and not so broad.

Poligar. A corruption of Pálaiyakára or of Pálegár. Also the name of a breed of dogs described as of a shining tawny colour, middle size, savage, fleet, and muscular.

Political. This name is applied in India to the diplomatic relations between the government and native states and to all the business transacted by British officials in native states. The political department of a local government is that branch of it to which all business in connection with native states is referred; and the British officials representing government at native courts, or taking part in the administration of a native state, are known as political officers. Where the native state is large and comparatively independent, the chief political officer is usually termed 'resident;' where British interference is greater, he is called 'agent.' In the former his duties are more those of an ambassador, in the latter more those of a controller. See Native State.

Poliyar. See Pulayan.

Pollam. See Pálaiya.

Pomelo. A kind of shaddock, the citrus decumana, sometimes called the forbidden fruit. The name appears not to be Indian; the fruit is called in Hindustáni batávi lemu, or the Batavian lemon.

Pomlá. [Gujaráti.] The name of a caste; they make baskets out of the leaves of the date palm.

Pon. [Tamil.] A coin worth nearly two rupees.

Pongal. [Tamil.] Boiling, the boiling of rice; the name of a festival held on the 1st of Tai and following days, and corresponding therefore to the Makarsankránti.

Ponwár. [Hindi.] The name of a caste in the Central Provinces; they are tall and fair, and skilful agriculturists.

Pooliar. See Pálaiya.

Poon. [Malayálam, corrupt form.] The tree calophyllum angustifolium.

Poonack. [Corruption of the Tamil *pinnakku*.] The substance that remains after oil has been expressed from seeds or cocoa-nut; oil-cake.

Poorbeeah. See Purbiya.

Pore. See Pur.

Portuguese. This term is applied in India not only to immigrants from Portugal, but also to the community of mixed Portuguese and Indian descent permanently settled in India. The latter are in western India called also Goanese.

Porya. [Nepáli.] The name of the lowest of all castes in Nepál.

Poshteen. A long Afghán coat made of sheep-skin with the wool worn inside. Compare Nimchu.

Potail. See Paṭel.

Potdár. Another form of Poddár.

Potkharábá. [Maráṭhi; *pot*, the belly, used as a prefix, denotes something comprised or included.] A small portion of kharábá within the limits of a survey number; if the occupant can render the kharábá culturable he may enjoy it without increase of assessment.

Pottah. See Paṭṭá.

Povindah. [Pashṭo, from the Persian *parvinda*, merchandise.] The name of the travelling soldier-merchants of Afghánistán who, since the time of Bábar (or of Henry VIII.), have carried on trade with India, fighting their way, when necessary, through the passes. They belong chiefly or wholly to different clans of the Ghilzai tribe, and are called also Lawáni or Loháni.

Powli. [A corruption of the Maráṭhi *páwali*, from *páw*, a quarter.] A silver coin worth a quarter of a rupee or four annas.

Powra. [A corruption of the Maráṭhi *pawḍá*.] A tool that combines the uses of the spade and shovel. The powra and the basket take the place of the English spade and wheelbarrow in ordinary road-making and excavation work. The powra is much shorter than a spade, and the head is not in the same line as the handle, but at an angle of about sixty degrees to it, so that in driving the tool into the soil the action is axe-like, not spade-like, and when driven in the head conveniently holds the loosened earth.

Poy. A name given to those tribes, such as the Shendus, Banjogis, and Kumis, who wear their hair in a high knot over the forehead.

Poyan. [Bengali.] A small channel used for artificial drainage.

Pradakshiná. [Sanskrit *pra*, before, forward, and *dakshina*, the right.] Reverential salutation by circumambulation with the right side towards the idol or person saluted.

Pradhán. [Sanskrit *pradhána*, from *pra*, before, and *dhá*, to place.] A principal person, either in a state or in a village; a minister, a prime minister; a principal cultivator, a headman. Śiwaji appointed eight officers, civil and military, under this common title in the Maráṭhá state. In Nepál four principal persons in each village or community are appointed under this title to assist the dwária in the judicial and revenue administration. Also the name of a tribe of the Gonḍs; they are bards and sometimes priests.

Pragana. See Parganah.

Prajápati. [Sanskrit, from *prajá*, progeny, creatures, and *pati*, lord.] Lord of creatures; a name applied to various gods, but in modern times chiefly identified with Brahmá. In Gujaráti the name is whimsically applied to Kumbhárs as the creators and lords of pots.

Prakásh. [Sanskrit *prakáśa*.] This word means 'light,' and, in conjunction with some other word, is often used to name a newspaper, book, etc., as Indu Prakásh, Moonlight; Dnyán Prakásh, Light of Knowledge; Buddhi Prakásh, Light of Reason.

Prákrit. [Hindi, Sanskrit *prákrita*, from *prakriti*, q.v.] That which has a prakriti, or original; anything derived; especially any vernacular language derived from Sanskrit.

Prakriti. [Sanskrit.] The original or natural form of anything; nature; the material world. In the Sánkhya philosophy, that unintelligent existence from which, when united with purusha or spirit, human souls and the visible world spring. In mythology, a goddess.

Pramánika. [Sanskrit, from *pramána*, measure, standard.] Forming a measure or standard, an authority; a trusty or upright man; among Santáls and other such tribes, often the title of the headman of a village or community; sometimes the deputy of the mánjhi. Also a village servant who assists the gumáshta and paṭwári; he is paid by the zamindár.

Pranáma. [Sanskrit, from *pra*, before, and *nam*, to bow down.] Prostration or respectful salutation before an idol or a superior. Compare Namaskára.

Pránt. [Sanskrit.] Edge, border, limit; a large division of a country, a province, a zillah.

Prárthnásamáj. [Sanskrit *prárthná*, prayer, and *samája*, society.] The name of a theistical sect lately founded in Bombay, and which has extended to Nariád, Kaira, and Ahmedabad.

Prasád. [Sanskrit *prasáda*, from *pra-sad*, to settle down, to become tranquil.] Tranquillity, repose, good humour, propitiousness, favour; a propitiatory offering; food offered to a god; the remnants of food presented to an idol or left by a spiritual teacher. All castes, and strangers, may eat prasád.

Pratinidhi. [Sanskrit.] A substitute, a representative; the title of an officer in the Maráṭhá state who was set above the eight pradháns.

Práyaschitta. [Sanskrit.] Penance, expiation by prescribed course of sin incurred. A man who for any forbidden act is put out of caste can re-enter only by práyaschitta.

Prayer-wheel. See Mani.

Presidency. This term belongs properly to the time when British India was divided between only three administrations, namely, those of Bengal, Madras, and Bombay, each of which was ruled by a president. Now British India consists of eight distinct provinces. See Province. In the case of Madras and Bombay the term 'presidency' still corresponds to a political division, but the Bengal presidency was in 1853 divided into two parts, the south-eastern portion retaining the name of Bengal, and the upper part of the plain receiving the title of the North-West Provinces. Again in 1874 Assam was separated from Bengal and made a separate province. The old division into three presidencies is still seen in the three distinct armies of Bengal, Madras, and Bombay; and in title the civil service is divided in the same way.

Pret. [Sanskrit *preta.*] Departed, deceased; the spirit of a dead person, a ghost. The pret is regarded as being in a happier condition than the bhut. Both have the power of assuming their previous forms, or of entering into a corpse or into the body of a living man.

Pretni. A female pret, the ghost of a deceased woman.

Prohit. See Purohit.

Province. British India is divided into eight provinces, each under a separate administration independent of each other and subordinate only to the supreme government. Two of these provinces, namely, Madras and Bombay, are ruled by governors and executive councils; three others, Bengal, the North-West Provinces, and the Panjáb, are ruled by lieutenant-governors; and the remaining three, the Central Provinces, British Burma, and Assam, by chief commissioners. Three of these provinces, Madras, Bombay, and Bengal, have legislative powers; for the remaining five laws can be enacted only by the Council of the Governor-General of India. See Central Provinces, Legislative Council, North-West Provinces, Panjáb, Presidency. Apart from the eight provinces, there remain the principalities of Ajmir and Coorg, the assigned districts, or Berar, and the Andaman islands; all these are administered by the Governor-General in Council.

Provincial Government. The government of a province (see Province) as distinguished from the government of India or the Governor-General in Council. A provincial government consists either of a governor in council, or of a lieutenant-governor alone, or of a chief commissioner alone.

Prow. [A Malay word, but found also in the Gujaráti as *paḍau.*] A one-masted sailing-boat, generally resembling a batelá, but smaller in size, not usually exceeding sixty khandis burden. A prow of twenty-five khandis carries four men, of fifty khandis seven men. These boats can stand heavy seas, and ply between Bombay and the ports in the Gulf of Cambay.

Puchwye. See Pachwái.

Pucka. See Pakká.

Puckalee. See Pakháli.

Puggee. See Pagi.

Puggree. See Pagri.

Pujá. [Sanskrit.] Worship, adoration; it consists chiefly in performing for the dewa such acts as a menial performs for his human master, such as ringing bells to awake him, washing and anointing him, clothing him in a manner suitable to the season, offering him sumptuous food, and placing flowers and waving lamps before him. Pujá as the name of a festival means the Durgápujá.

Pujári. [Hindi.] The priest who officiates in a temple. He is subordinate to the panḍá.

Pukhṭu. More commonly Pashṭo.

Pulayan. The name of an aboriginal tribe of Malabár. Presumably the Paleya, Pallan, Palliyan, and Polaiyan tribes are merely branches of this one. And some authorities consider that the Pariahs, Holias, Dheḍs, Mahárs, and Malas are also of the same race.

Pummalow. See Pomelo.

Punch. [Hindi *panch*, the Sanskrit *pancha*, five.] This word was first brought into English as the name of a drink consisting of five ingredients—water, tea, lemon-juice, sugar, and arrack. A writer in 1640 A.D. describes 'palepuntz' as a drink consisting of aqua vitæ, rose-water, juice of citrons, and sugar.—Punch is often used also as an abbreviation of Pancháyat.

Punḍari. [Bengali.] The name of a low caste; their proper occupation is the rearing of silkworms; they are also sellers of fish and vegetables.

Punḍarikáksha. [Sanskrit *punḍarika*, the lotus, and *aksha*, the eye.] Lotus-eyed; the name of a low caste in Bengal; they sell fish and vegetables. See Purá.

Punem. A vernacular form of Purnimá.

Punjey. [Tamil, from *pul*, inferior, and *sey*, cultivation.] Land which cannot be irrigated, and is therefore unfit for the growth of rice. Punjey garden or punjey bágháyat is punjey land irrigated by private wells or by streams in such a way as to admit of the growth of certain vegetables. Punjey-waravu-nanjey is punjey that has been converted into nanjey (*J. H. Nelson*).

Punkah. [Hindi *pankhá*, a fan, from the Sanskrit *paksha*, a wing, a pinion.] A large fan consisting either of a frame covered with canvas, or of a bar with a weighted curtain attached, suspended from the ceiling of a room and kept in motion by the pulling of a cord. Also a hand-fan.

Punyá. The annual settlement of the revenue in Bengal used to be called by this name.

Pur. [Hindi, from the Sanskrit *pura*.] A town, a city; much used in composition, as Kánhpur, commonly Cawnpore.

Purá. [Bengali.] The name of a low caste; they sell fish and vegetables.

Purab. [Hindi, from Sanskrit *purwa*, first, eastern.] The country to the east; the term is used in various provinces.

Purambok. [Tamil.] Lands reserved as being required for purposes other than those of cultivation, such as the sites of villages, beds of tanks, banks of channels (*J. H. Nelson*).

Purán. [Sanskrit *purána*, old.] This name was given in order to invest with a fictitious antiquity some books written after the doctrine of incarnation had received definite shape, and after strifes had arisen between the followers of different gods. The puráns are probably not really older than the sixth century A.D. They are eighteen in number, six relating more particularly to each of the three gods of the trimurti. They are named (1) Brahma, (2) Brahmánda, (3) Brahma-vaiwarta, (4) Márkandeya, (5) Bhavishya, (6) Wáman, (7) Vishnu, (8) Bhágwat, (9) Náradiya, (10) Garud, (11) Padma, (12) Waráh, (13) Śiwa, (14) Ling, (15) Skand, (16) Agni or Wáyu, (17) Matsya, (18) Kurma. Each purán is supposed to treat of the following five subjects: the creation of the universe, its destruction and re-creation, the genealogy of gods and heroes, the reigns of the Manus, and the history of the solar and lunar races of kings. But this character is not always maintained.

Purán. The name of a clan of the Tipperahs.

Puraṭṭási. The Tamil name of the solar month Kani, corresponding most nearly to September, Bhádrapad, and in Bengal to Áśvin. See Month.

Purbiya. [From the Sanskrit *purwa*, eastern.] A man from the eastern part of Bengal.

Purdhan. See Pradhán.

Puri. [Hindi.] A kind of cake fried in butter.

Purnimá. [Sanskrit, from *purni*, full, and *má*, for *mása*, the moon.] The day of full moon; it is always the fifteenth day of the Hindu synodical month when the śukladi mode is followed, and is always the last day under the krishnadi mode. See Month, Amáwasi.

Purodha. The Kanarese form of Purohit.

Purohit. [Sanskrit *purohita*, from *puras*, before, and *hita*, the past participle of *dhá*, to place.] An appointed priest, a family priest, one who conducts the domestic ceremonies of a tribe, a household, or family. The office is generally hereditary. One purohit usually serves several families; but families of distinction often have a separate purohit of higher rank and learning for periodic ceremonies, besides their ordinary one for the daily worship of the family idol. The guru, again, is distinct from both. See Ṭhákur.

Purokita. The Tamil form of Purohit.

Purseṭh. [Uriya, from the Sanskrit *pura*, a town, and *śreshṭha*, best.] The headman of a town or of a ward of a town; in Cuttack, the elected head and representative of the people of a village, who was admitted to engage with government for the rent of the ground on which the village was built.

Purusha. [Sanskrit.] Man; the human soul or spirit; the soul or spirit of the universe; god. In the Sánkhya philosophy, that passive soul which is neither a producer nor a production, which itself remains one, but the union of which with prakriti causes the creation of individual souls and the phenomenal world.

Purvoe. See Parbhu.

Purwaja. [Sanskrit, from *purwa*, before, and *ja*, born.] Elder, ancient; the deified progenitors of mankind. See Pitri.

Pus. The Hindustáni form of Paush.

Pushya. [Kanarese, from *pu*, to blossom.] The name of one of the nakshatras and of the month (the Hindi Paush) in which the moon is at full in that nakshatra. See Month.

Pykaust. See Páikásht.

Pyke. See Páik.

Python. See Rock-snake.

Q.

Qabr. [Arabic.] A grave, a tomb.

Qabuliyat. See Kabuliyat.

Qaitun. [Hindustáni.] A very narrow ribbon or braid woven of silk-and-gold thread.

Qazee. See Kázi.

Qibala. See Kabála.

Qiblah. More commonly Kiblah.

Qizilbásh. See Kizilbáshi.

Qui hye. This is a corruption of the Hindustáni *Koi hai?* literally, 'Is there any one?' the common exclamation to call a servant. It has become a nickname for an Englishman in Bengal.

Qurán. More commonly Koran.

Qureshi. The name of the family to which Muhammad the founder of islám belonged.

R.

Rá. [Gujaráti.] A title equivalent to rájá; it was borne by the ruler of Soreth.

Ráb. [Maráṭhi.] It is the practice in the Konkan to sow rice first closely in a small patch of land specially prepared by burning, and when the plants have shot up to transfer them to the field. The term ráb is used (1) for the grass, bushes, loppings of trees, etc., spread over the patch of ground and burnt upon it; (2) for the patch of ground itself; (3) for the crop thus raised.

Rabábi. [Panjábi, from *rabáb*, a particular musical instrument.] The name of a class of hereditary musicians among the Sikhs; they regard as their founder Mardána, a companion of the first guru.

Rabári. [Gujaráti.] The name of a caste. In some places this name and Bharwáḍ denote the same people; in others, Bharwáḍs are those who keep goats and sheep, and Rabáris those who keep cattle and camels.

Rabi. [Hindi, from the Arabic *rabia.*] The spring; the spring crop, which is sown at the beginning of the cold weather and reaped in the spring. It includes wheat, barley, indigo, gram, hemp, and vegetables.

Rabia. [Arabic.] The name of the third and fourth months of the Musalmán year (following Safar), distinguished as Rabial-awal, the first, and Rabial-ákhir or Rabias-sáni, the last Rabia. See Month.

Ráḍhiya. [Bengali, from the Sanskrit *ráḍhá.*] Belonging to Ráḍhá or Rarh, a district in western Bengal; the name of a branch of Gauḍa (subdivision) Bráhmans.

Rafái. The name of an order of fakirs, called also Gurzmárs, whose patron is Saïd Ahmad Kabir, son of the sister of the pirán-pir of Bagdad. They profess to be beshara fakirs, but have wives and children.

Rági. [Hindi.] The cereal cynosurus corocanus; called in southern India náchni, nágli, or chollu.

Rahat. See Arhat, or Arhaṭ. Among certain modern Buddhists a rahat is defined as an adept, or one who has developed his psychical powers to their fullest extent.

Ráhdári. [Hindi, from *ráh*, a road, and *dári*, keeping.] A passport, a permit; also, transit duties, tolls.

Rahim. [Arabic.] Merciful; an attribute of god in the bismillah, and thence used by the Sikhs as the name of the Musalmán god, as being conveniently alliterative with the Hindu god Ráma.

Rahirás. [Panjábi.] The evening prayer of the Sikhs; it was composed by Nának, but additions were made by succeeding gurus, and it was left in its present form by Govind Singh. It is sometimes called the sodar rahirás, from *so dar*, which are the first two words of the prayer, and which also have become the name of the metre in which it is written.

Rahitnámá. [Panjábi, from *rahit*, a rule, and *námá*, the Persian *námah*, a writing.] A code of rules, particularly that said to have been delivered by Govind Singh, the last Sikh guru.

Ráhu. [Sanskrit.] The dragon's head, the ascending node of the moon. It is fabled that a daitya, disguising himself, obtained some of the amrita when the gods churned the ocean; but the sun and moon detected him, and told Vishnu, who cut him in two, his head and arms forming Ráhu and the rest of him Ketu; in revenge he sometimes seizes the sun or moon and so causes eclipses. See Graha.

Rái. [Hindi.] A title equivalent to rájá or the ráya of the south, and in Bengal usually corrupted into roy.

Raiat. More commonly Ryot.

Raidási. [Panjábi.] Sikh converts from the Chamár caste.

Ráikat. Another name in some parts of Bengal, as Jalpigori, for zamindár.

Rainy season. See Monsoon.

Rais. [Arabic.] A prince or chief; often used in relation to raiyat or subject. It was the title of the Tálpur rulers of Sindh. In Bengal it is sometimes used for the manager of a religious endowment.

Rái Sáhib. A title used by a Káyasth to denote his father-in-law.

Raiyat. More commonly Ryot.

Ráj. [Sanskrit *rajyam.*] A kingdom; empire, rule; as the Mogul ráj, the British ráj, meaning the dominion in India of the power named.

Rájá. [Sanskrit.] A king, a prince; a common title for any Hindu ruler, and bestowed sometimes on private persons of high rank.

Rajab. [Arabic.] The seventh month of the Musalmán year; it follows Jamádi-al-ákhir. See Month.

Rajak. [Sanskrit *rajaka.*] The name of a low caste; they are washermen. Compare Dhopá.

Rájaśri. [Sanskrit, from *rájan*, a king, and *śri*, prosperity.] The fortune of a king, majesty; a term of address used in writing. Though rájaśri is often used as one of a string of complimentary titles, yet when used alone it expresses but the slightest degree of courtesy, equivalent to 'Mr.' as distinguished from 'Esq.'

Rájasthánik. The name of a particular court lately established in Káṭhiáwár. It is a tribunal for the adjudication of garás, or hereditary sharehold claims, which, as they are brought against their own revenues and estates, the chiefs cannot in fairness settle. The court consists of a president and two assessors. The president is an officer appointed by government; the assessors are chosen by government from a list of names submitted by the chiefs.

Rájasuya. [Sanskrit.] A great sacrifice or religious ceremony performed at the coronation of a supreme sovereign or universal monarch by the king himself and his tributary princes.

Rájbábti. [Maráṭhi.] Pertaining to the state; the state share of the chauth.

Rájbansi. [Bengali, from the Sanskrit *rájá*, a king, and *wansa*, race—of royal race.] The name of two branches of the Koch tribe, one of which adopted Hinduism and the other islám; the former were the families of higher condition, and the latter the bulk of the people despised by the Hindus. The Rájbansis are cultivators and weavers.

Rájbánsi. A name given to persons born of Burmese fathers and Bengali mothers; they speak Bengali and follow Hindu customs.

Rájbhar. Another name of the Bhar tribe.

Rájbhara. [Gujaráti.] The name of a small caste; they make the warp comb.

Rajeshri. See Rájaśri.

Rájgirá. [Maráṭhi.] The cereal amaranthus polygamus; the grain is small, round, and of a light yellow colour; it is eaten particularly on fast-days.

Rájgor. A class of Bráhmans, formerly the priests of the princes and chiefs of Káṭhiáwár.

Rájinámá. The Bengali form of Rázinámah.

Rájkumár. [Hindi, from *rájá*, and *kumár*, a youth.] The son of a king, a prince. This name has been given to a school in Káṭhiáwár established for the education of young chiefs. It is the name also of a numerous and opulent caste in the North-West Provinces, following agriculture, though claiming to be of the military or regal tribe.

Rájmaháli. The name of a tribe called also Pahári. Also the name of their language, which is Dravidian. These people call themselves Maler. Compare Male and Malevar.

Rájput. [Hindi, from the Sanskrit *rájá*, king, and *putra*, son.] The common name of many tribes claiming to be descended, some from the solar race of the Rámáyana, others from the lunar race of the Mahábhárata, others to be of agnikula origin, and all constituting the Kshatriya or military caste of Manu's code. The Bráhmans, however, have a legend that the Kshatriya race was exterminated, and some authorities consider the Rájputs to be of Scythian origin and to have entered India long after the Aryans. They differ from other Hindus in holding the practices of primogeniture, and of allowing marriages only between persons of different clans; also in their having no scruples as to the use of flesh, spirits, and opium. The Rájputs have from time immemorial furnished ruling families in all parts of India, but in no part at any time do they seem to have constituted the bulk of the inhabitants. The principal clans of Rájputs will be found under the main divisions of Suryawanśa, Chandrawanśa, and Agnikula. But in many instances Rájputs have mixed with lower races, and it is not always certain where the name is properly applicable. The Rájput is the most chivalrous of all Hindus, and when he cannot be a ruler or great landowner his taste leads him to military service, and the lower ranks seek employment as policemen, peons, and village watchmen.

Ráju. [Bengali.] The name of a Śudra caste of middle rank; they are cultivators.

Rájwár. [Bengali.] The name of a semi-Hinduised tribe in Behar; they were formerly employed in guarding the passes of the hills, but are now chiefly agricultural labourers.

Rákhaḍi. A Gujaráti form of Raksha. In the fifth or seventh month of pregnancy rákhaḍis are put on women for good luck.

Rákhi. [Panjábi, from the Sanskrit *rakshi*, protection.] Protection money levied by the Sikhs from tracts of country which they subdued but did not occupy. It varied from perhaps a fifth to a half of the rental or government share of the produce (*J. D. Cunningham*). Compare Chauth. Rákhi is also a Hindi form of Raksha (the bracelet).

Rakhwálá, Rakhwáldar, or **Rakhwar.** [Hindi, from the Sanskrit *rakshana*, protection.] A guard, a watch; especially one set to watch over standing crops to prevent depredation; a protector. In some places, as in Poona, they are hereditary village watchmen remunerated by inám holdings.

Raksha. [Sanskrit, from *raksh*, to

guard.] A bracelet worn as an amulet, especially the red or yellow silk or cotton bracelet put on at the Balev festival; the raksha is also worn by two persons as marks of mutual dependence, or is sent by a Rájput lady to any one whose protection she desires, and whom she thus adopts as a brother.

Rakshas. [Sanskrit, from *raksh*, to hurt.] An evil spirit, a demon, a goblin.

Rála. The cereal panicum italicum, or kangni. See Millet.

Rali. A goddess worshipped in Kángrá; she is the deified spirit of a Bráhman woman who drowned herself on being married to a child.

Ráma. [Sanskrit, literally, pleasing, from *ram*, to rejoice.] The name of the hero of the Rámáyana, considered to be the seventh awatár of Vishnu. The name repeated, *rám-rám*, is the common expression of salutation among the Hindus, at least in the Bombay presidency. The same name is used in the funeral cry, *Rám bolo bhái rám*, 'Say Rám, brother, Rám.' *Rámná ráj* is a proverbial expression in Gujaráti for a time of peace and prosperity. Ráma's festival is the 9th Chaitra śudh. This, the great Ráma, is called Rámachandra, in distinction from the other two, Paraśuráma and Balaráma.

Ramadhan. See Ramazán.

Rámánandi. The name of a sect of Vaishnawas, worshippers of Rámchandra and Sitá. They are ascetics and live in maṭhs, and admit disciples of any caste. Rámánand, the founder of the order, was originally a Rámánuja, and lived in Benares about the beginning of the fourteenth century. Rámánandis are called also *Rámwats* and, popularly, Bairágis. Their sectarial mark is similar to that of the Rámánujas.

Rámánuja. [Sanskrit, from *ráma*, and *anuja*, younger; the younger brother of Ráma.] The name of a Vaishnawa sect in the south of India, called after their founder, the great reformer Rámánuja, who lived in the twelfth century. The teachers are chiefly Bráhmans, but disciples are admitted of any caste not of impure birth. They are very careful about the sectarial marks—which they make in white, with an extra central line added in red to represent Lakshmi—and often have symbols of Vishnu branded on their arms, and they shave the upper lip. They hold the doctrine of viśishtádvaita. They are called also Śri Vaishnawas.

Rámáyana. [Sanskrit *ayana*, going, from *ay*, to go.] The deeds of Ráma; the name of the older of the two great Sanskrit epic poems. The hero is Ráma, an incarnation of Vishnu, as the son of Daśarath the king of Oudh. The poem describes the birth of Ráma, his marriage with Sitá, his banishment, their life in the forest, the carrying off of Sitá by Ráwana king of Ceylon, Ráma's alliance with Sugriwa the monkey-king, their invasion of Ceylon, and victory over Ráwana, the recovery of Sitá, and Ráma's return to Oudh and coronation there; subsequently his banishment of Sitá, his reunion with her, and his translation to heaven.

The work is attributed to Wálmiki, and was composed probably about 500 B.C. A modern rámáyana in Hindi was composed by Tulsidás in the sixteenth century; this later poem, which is very popular, inculcates faith in Ráma as a personal god.

Ramazán. [Arabic.] The ninth month of the Musalmán year, following Shabán. The year being lunar, each month occurs at all periods of the solar year. See Month. Ramazán is observed as a fast because the revelation of the koran began in it. Eating and drinking are absolutely forbidden from the earliest dawn till the stars are distinctly visible.

Ramban. The title of a priest of high grade, and who has to be celibate, in the Syrian Church of southern India. See Malpan, Maphrian.

Rámbán. [Maráṭhi, from *ráma*, and *bán*, an arrow.] The arrow of Ráma; anything as swift, as sure, or as certainly efficacious as the arrow of Ráma; said of promises, predictions, medicines, etc.

Ramdási. Another name of the Raidási or Sikh converts from the Chamár caste.

Rámdási. Sikh followers of Rámdas, the companion of Nának the first guru.

Rámgarhia. [Panjábi.] The name of a Sikh misl called after the fort of Rámgarh at Amritsar.

Rámjani. [Hindustáni, from the Sanskrit *ramá*, beautiful, and *jana*, person.] A Hindu dancing-girl; a courtesan.

Rámná. [Bengali.] A large grassy plain.

Rámosi. [Maráṭhi.] The name of a tribe resembling the Beḍars; they are found principally in the hilly district through which the Nira flows, and between the Bhima and Krishna, where are the territories lately occupied by the head of their body, the rájá of Shorapur; the Rámosis are devotees of the god Khanḍobá of Jejuri, about twenty-five miles to the south of Poona; they explain their name as Rámawanśi, of the lineage of Ráma; their language is a *patois* of Telugu. The Rámosis were formerly thieves, and are now employed chiefly as watchmen. They are divided into two main branches, with the Rájput names of Chauhán and Jádon.

Rámp. [Gujaráti.] An implement worked like a plough and used for clearing weeds and stubble from land being prepared for cultivation, and also for weeding between the furrows when the crop is up.

Rámpaḍi. [Gujaráti.] A small rámp.

Rámpi. [Hindi.] A knife for scraping skins and cutting leather.

Rám Rái. The denomination of Sikhs who adhered to Rám Rái, the son of Har Rái the seventh guru, when the succession passed, not to him, but to his great-uncle Tegh Bahádur.

Rámwat. See Rámánandi.

Ramzan. See Ramazán.

Ráná. [Hindi.] A title equivalent to rájá; it is used by the ruler of Udáipur (see Gahlot) and some chieftains in central India.

Rangani. [Bengali, from the Sanskrit *ranga*, colour.] A dyer. In Bengal it is the name of a caste who are weavers as well as dyers.

Rángarh. [Hindi.] A name given to the original issue of mixed marriages between Rájputs and Muhammadans. Also the name of a Rájput clan in Málwá and Mewár.

Rangári. The Kanarese form of Rangani.

Rangretha. The name of a class of Sikhs who were originally Chuhrás. They are sometimes called Mazhabi.

Rangrez, The Hindi form of Rangani.

Ráni. [Hindi, from the Sanskrit *rájni.*] The wife of a ráná or rájá, or a queen in her own right.

Ranwati. [Gujaráti.] A grant in compensation to the successor of a person murdered or killed in battle.

Ráo. [Hindi.] A chief, a prince, a king; also affixed to names as a title of honour, as Báláji Ráo.

Ráo Bahádur. A high title of honour bestowed on very distinguished Hindus.

Ráo Sáheb. A title of honour bestowed on distinguished Hindus and such officials as mámlatdárs. The equivalent among Muhammadans is Khán Sáheb.

Rarhi. See Rạḍhiya.

Rása. [Sanskrit.] A circular dance practised by cowherds, and that in which Krishna and the gopis engaged; any sportive game or festive amusement; a dramatic representation.

Rasáldár. The Gujaráti form of Risáldár.

Rasami. [Gujaráti, from *rasam*, custom.] One who follows the custom; another name of the Śehersai or Shensoy Pársis.

Rásti. [Gujaráti, from the Persian.] Literally, true, honest, but formerly applied to villages which were peaceable, and would pay their revenue without requiring the exercise of force, as did mewási villages. As the latter maintained a certain degree of independence, the term rásti, always used in contradistinction, came to be applied to villages held immediately and entirely by government. In the Baroda state the different maháls are classed as rásti and jungle mahàls.

Rásti-mewás. [Gujaráti.] A term implying a middling state of subordination between that of a rásti and a mewási village.

Rastogi. The name of a mercantile caste.

Rasul. [Arabic.] A messenger, especially applied to Muhammad as the messenger of God. Thence used to form proper names, as Ghulám Rasul, the slave of the prophet.

Rasulsháhi. [Hindustáni.] Followers of the prophet; the name of a community of beshara Sunni fakirs. They are dissipated and troublesome, and carry a large wooden club when they beg. They drink liquor. They are known also by the name of Mastán.

Rátabwálá. [Gujaráti.] An inferior servant paid by a daily allowance.

Rath. [Sanskrit.] A chariot, a car,

the vehicle of a god; in the vernaculars, also the car in which idols are conveyed; in the south of India certain rock-cut temples formed out of single boulders of rock lying on the sea-shore are known by this name. See Wáhan.

Ráth. The snake tropidonotus stolatus; its maximum length is two feet; it is of a brownish olive colour, with irregular pale-edged dark-brown cross-bars, and is easily distinguished by a pale buff streak running along each side of the back from neck to tail; at some seasons the head, neck, and sides acquire a bright red tinge. It is not venomous, though commonly believed to be so (*G. W. Vidal*).

Ráṭhor. The name of a Rájput tribe claiming to be of the solar race, but usually reckoned of the agnikula; they were ruling in Kanauj in 1194 A.D., when the Ghori Musalmáns drove them out; subsequently they established themselves at Jodhpur, where they rule to the present day; the chiefs of Bikánir and Ratlam also are of this tribe, and Raṭhors are numerous in those three states, Jaisalmir, and Kishengarh.

Rat-snake. See Dháman.

Rats of Sháh Daulá. See Chuhá Sháh.

Rául. [Maráṭhi.] The name of a tribe; they are tape-makers.

Raulia. A village headman in Kumáun. See Headman.

Rauniyár. [Bengali.] The name of a trading caste, chiefly petty dealers in country products.

Rawaja. See Roájá.

Ráwal. [Hindi.] A title borne by some Rájput rulers; it is reckoned inferior to rájá or rání, but superior to ṭhákor. Also the name of a tribe of Bráhmans in central India; and of a caste of salt-makers in Pálanpur. Compare Khárwá.

Ráwaliá. [Gujaráti.] The name of a low caste; they weave the broad tape used (by binding it lengthwise and cross-wise over and under an oblong wooden frame) for making bedsteads; and are also rope-makers. They also cut and sell dátans or tooth-sticks. They are otherwise called Jágariás. Ráwaliá is also the name of the Bhil priest.

Rawánah. [Persian.] A pass, a passport, a port-clearance.

Ráwana-sanyási. A proverbial name for one who conceals his evil character under a cloak of sanctity, like Ráwana, who presented himself before Sitá in the disguise of a sanyási. See Rámáyana.

Ráwaniá. [Gujaráti.] A village watchman. The ráwaniá of Kaira corresponds to the wartaniá of Broach and the jiwáidár of Ahmedabad. Ráwaniás are not usually remunerated by land, but receive cash wages, about three rupees a month. They are of various castes, and some even Musalmáns. They are armed with swords only.

Ráwat. The name of a wild tribe of Kumáun; of a caste in Gorakhpur; and of a small caste in Gujarát, who are chiefly cart-drivers.

Ráya. [Kanarese.] A king, a prince; the equivalent of rái or rájá.

Ráyadási. [Hindi.] The name of a sect founded by Ráyadása, a Chamár who lived in the fifteenth century; it is recruited chiefly from the lowest castes, but is said to be opposed to idolatry and the pretensions of Bráhmans. See Satnámi.

Ráyat. More commonly Ryot.

Razái. [Persian.] A quilt, a coverlet.

Rázinámah. [Hindustáni, from the Arabic *razá*, consent, permission, leave to depart, and the Persian *námáh*, a deed.] A deed of agreement or compromise; a written petition withdrawing a charge or plaint; a deed of relinquishment of land. See Kabuliyat.

Reḍḍi. [Telugu.] The name of a caste; they are purely agricultural, and are reputed to be excellent farmers, energetic, orderly in their behaviour, and of frugal habits (*J. H. Nelson*). Also the name of a division of the Wokkaliga caste. Also used as a title for headman.

Red gram. See Arhar.

Red soil. See Goráṭ.

Registered occupant. A ryot whose name is recorded as the holder of unalienated land, a khátedár.

Regulation. The name given to the legislative enactments of the councils under the company, and by which they are distinguished from the 'acts' of the later legislative councils. See Non-regulation.

Regur. [A corruption of the Kanarese *regaḍe*.] The black soil in which cotton is usually grown.

Reh. [Hindi.] A salt efflorescence which renders land quite unproductive. Glass can be made of it and caustic soda extracted from it. It is also called usar.

Rehar, or **Rehwar.** The name of a branch of the Parmár Rájputs.

Reihras. See Rahirás.

Reis. See Rais.

Rekhá. [Sanskrit.] Literally, a line, but used in Kanarese as the name of a settlement, the account of which was so arranged that the assessment of each field was shown on a separate line.

Rekhtah. Literally, crumbled or scattered; the name of the Hindustáni language when used in poetry, so called from the manner in which the vernacular is strewn with Persian importations (*C. J. Lyall*).

Rekhti. The feminine, in a diminutive sense, of Rekhtah, and the name of a special dialect of Rekhtah used in poems written for the zanánah (*C. J. Lyall*).

Reklá. [Gujaráti *renklá*.] A kind of bullock-cart.

Resáldár. The Bengali form of Risáldár.

Resident. The title of the representative of the British power in certain native states, namely, Hyderabad and Mysore. Until 1875 there was also a resident, at Baroda, but since then an agent. Residents are also appointed to the British possession of Aden and to the kingdom of Nepál.

Ressaidar. See Russaidar.

Rest-house. See Dharmsálá, Musáfirkhánah, Sarái.

Revenue-free. A term applied to land as to which the ruling power has assigned to any person its prerogative of receiving rent. See Alienated, Inámi, Jágir.

Reya. [Hindi.] A small caste found only in the Delhi district; they say they were Rájputs, but were excluded from the caste because they took to practising karewa; they are now quite separate; they eat and smoke with Játs and agricultural castes of similar standing, but will not marry with them except by karewa (*D. C. J. Ibbetson*).

Rezai. See Razái.

Rib-faced deer. Cervulus aureus; it is of a reddish chestnut colour and low in the fore quarters; from the mouth project two sharp little tusks which curve downwards; the skin between the eyes is puckered up into longitudinal ridges; on the brow are two bony pedicles, covered with skin and hair, to the height of three or four inches, and on each of these a short two-pronged horn. It is a very shy, solitary animal. The Hindi name is kákar (*R. A. Sterndale*).

Right-hand. See Balagai, Walangai. There is also a right and left hand division of Śakti worshippers, the rites of the former being principally magical, of the latter bloody and licentious. But there is no connection between this division and that of the Balagai and Yeḍagai.

Rig-veda. [Sanskrit, from *rich*, to praise.] See under Veda. The rig-veda consists of ten books: the first eight contain groups of hymns, each group ascribed to one author or to the members of one family; the ninth book contains the songs recited at the soma ceremonies; the tenth contains hymns of a very different character, composed by a greater variety of individual authors. In its wider sense the term rig-veda comprehends the bráhmanas and the sutra works on the ritual connected with the hymns (*Monier Williams*).

Rind. The name of a tribe in Sindh and Khelát.

Risálah. [Arabic.] A troop of horse; also a retinue, a suite.

Risáldár. [Hindustáni, from *risálah*, and the Persian *dár*, holder.] An officer commanding a troop of horse. The native officer of highest rank in the Indian cavalry was the risáldár major, who in the old irregular cavalry was called in English the native commandant. After him came the risáldárs and russaidars (grades of one rank, equal to that of subahdár in the infantry); then the wordie-major, or native adjutant; the náib risáldárs and jamádárs, who may be described as troop subalterns; the kote dafadár major, who is regimental sergeant-major; the kote dafadárs, or troop sergeant major; the dafadárs, or sergeants; and the náiks, or corporals. But under the new organization the native officers of a cavalry regiment (of six troops in three squadrons) are three risáldárs, three russaidars, one wordie-major, six jamádárs, six kote dafadárs, and forty-eight dafadárs.

Rishabhdewa. Another name of Ádináth.

Rishi. [Sanskrit.] A holy sage, one who has heard the eternal voice or seen the eternal words of revelation, and through whom the divine knowledge has been transmitted to the

Bráhmans. Hence the name has been held to be from *driś*, to see. The names of seven principal rishis have been given to the seven stars of Ursa major; their festival is the 5th Bhádra śudh. In later times the term rishi has been given to any Hindu ascetic of special sanctity.

Ritu. [Sanskrit.] A season. The year is variously divided into seasons, but most commonly into six of two months each: they are wasant and grishma which together make up the hot season, March to June; warsha and śarad which are the rainy season, July to October; and hemant and śiśira which are the cold season, November to February.

Roájá. [Arakanese.] The headman of a Khyoungthá village; he collects the revenue and receives fees for deciding petty cases and disputes. The office generally descends from father to son.

Rock-cut temple. The name of those temples, of which there are many in India, which are not structural but are carved out of the solid rock. The greater number of them and all the oldest are Buddhist; they date back as far as 200 B.C., and include both Viháras and Chaityas. These temples are excavations in the mountain-side, and consist of interiors only. Subsequently the Jains and Bráhmans both adopted to some extent the rock-cutting method. In later times the art was extended to the carving of exteriors as well as interiors, either as at Mahábalipur from single boulders of rock (see Rath), or, as in the case of the Kailása at Ellora, by cutting away the living rock from the outside as well as the inside of the temple, and leaving it standing in a cave. Buddhist rock-cut temples exist at Rájágrihá, Kárli, Kannari, Ajunta, and many other places; those of Elephanta are Hindu; at Ellora are specimens of the three religions.

Rock-snake. The python molurus; it inhabits thick jungles and groves, usually near water or swampy grounds, where it finds a regular supply of food in the animals which come to drink; after seizing its victim it smothers it by throwing several coils of the body over and round it. Indian pythons grow to a length of twenty feet. They incubate their eggs (*G. W. Vidal*).

Rohillá. [Pashṭo, from *roh*, a mountain.] The name of a highland clan of Paṭháns who early in the eighteenth century took possession of the district, now called after them Rohilkhand.

Roobcaree. See Rubakári.

Rootoo. See Ritu.

Ror. The name of a caste in the Panjáb; they are fine stalwart men of much the same type as the Játs, whom they almost equal as husbandmen.

Rorá. [Hindi.] Brickbats for road-making; chhárá. Rorá is also a name for the foot-and-mouth disease, or any other contagious or epidemic disease of cattle.

Rori. [Hindi.] The name of a caste; they are traders and shopkeepers.

Roshania. The name of a Muhammadan sect founded in the middle of the sixteenth century by Pir Roshan and his sons Jaláluddin and

Kamáluddin. They ignored the koran, and taught that nothing exists but God, of whom no formal worship is required.

Row. See Ráo.

Rowannah. See Rawánah.

Row Ras. See Rahirás.

Rowty. [A corruption of the Hindustáni *raoti.*] A small tent similar in construction to a pál, but of less size, usually not more than twelve feet long, and with the roof sloping down on two sides nearly to the ground.

Roy. See Rái.

Rozah. [Arabic.] A garden; but in India the term is applied to a Muhammadan tomb. Compare the use of báradari.

Rozah. [Persian.] A fast, especially the ramazán.

Roselle. The Indian hibiscus, or hibiscus sabdariffa; the calyx is used as a tart fruit, and a jelly is made from it.

Rozinah. [Hindustáni, from the Persian *roz*, a day.] A daily allowance, a pension.

Rubakári. [Hindustáni, from *ru*, the face, *bah*, to, and *kár*, business.] A document narrating the proceeding of a court or officer, the record of a case.

Rubbee. See Rabi.

Rudra. [Sanskrit, from *rud*, to roar.] A storm-god. The Rudras are vedic gods; they are sometimes identified with, and sometimes distinguished from, the Marutas. The Rudra, that is, the chief of the Rudras, afterwards became one of the elements which make up the compound character of Śiwa.

Rudráksha. [Sanskrit, from *rudra*, and *aksha*, the eye.] The tree eleocarpus lanceolatus; it is sacred to Śiwa, and the Śaiwa rosaries are made of its berries, either thirty-two or sixty-four being used.

Ruhur. See Arhar.

Rukhsat. [Arabic.] Leave, dismissal, the dismissal of a guest. It is usual among both Hindus and Muhammadans for the host, not the visitor, to close an interview. This act is called giving rukhsat, and is signalized by the host putting a garland of flowers round the guest's neck, and sometimes also bracelets of flowers on his wrists, and presenting him with bouquets and attar and pánsupári, and sprinkling rose-water on his handkerchief.

Rupee. [Hindustáni *rupiya*, from the Sanskrit *rupya*, silver.] A silver coin, the unit of the standard of value in India. The Indian government rupee in make and size resembles the English florin; it weighs 180 grains, of which 165 are pure silver; it used to exchange at the rate of ten to a sovereign, but its exchange value is now less by nearly a quarter. Rupees of many older coinages are still current in some parts of India. The rupee is divided for purposes of account into annas and pies, twelve pies making one anna and sixteen annas one rupee; the divisions coined are—(in silver) the half, the quarter, the eighth, (in copper) the thirty-second, the sixty-fourth, and the one hundred and ninety-second part, or pie.

Rushmi. See Rasami.

Russaidar. [Corrupt form, origin unknown.] The officer next in rank below the risáldár in a cavalry regiment.

Russaldar. See Risáldár.

Ryot. [A corruption of the Hindi *ráyat*, the Arabic *raiyat.*] A subject, but especially applied to the agricultural population, a peasant, a cultivator.

Ryottee. [A corruption of the Bengali *raiyati*, adjective formed from *raiyat.*] Belonging to a ryot. The term is applied to land held on the ordinary tenure, namely, with the right of permanent enjoyment on payment of a certain rent, and is thus distinguished from ziráat (in the special Bengal sense), khámár, nijjot, and sir lands which the zamindár may dispose of as he likes.

Ryotwár. An adjective meaning according to ryots. It is applied to that system of land revenue in which the government settlement is made directly with the ryot without the intervention of a zamindár or other middle-man.

S.

Sábaliá. [Gujaráti.] The name of a low caste; they tend cattle. Some are converts to islám.

Sabar. See Sawar.

Sabhá. [Sanskrit.] An assembly, a society. Also a council-chamber.

Sabhá-manḍap. [Maráṭhi.] The portico or vestibule of a temple; also the large open room in front of the gábhárá. See Mandir.

Sabsi. [Hindustáni, from the Persian *sabz*, green.] Vegetables, greens; the larger leaves and capsules of the hemp plant, or an intoxicating drink prepared from them.

Sabsifarosh. [Hindi, Persian *farosh*, sale, or a seller.] A vegetable-seller.

Sachidári. [Panjábi.] The true or pure, the title of a class of Sikhs.

Sachiwa. [Maráṭhi.] The title of one of the pradháns in the Maráṭhá state. See Sáhotra.

Sacred bull. See Pol, Sánḍ.

Sacred cord. See Janeo or Kasti.

Sacred shirt. See Sadrá.

Sacred thread. See Janeo.

Sadar. See Sadr.

Sádar. [Kanarese.] The name of an agricultural caste. They are mostly Śaiwas, but some are Námadáris, and a few are Jains. All eat together and intermarry, the wife adopting her husband's religion.

Sadáśiwa. [Sanskrit *sadá*, always.] A name of Śiwa in his character as the ever-blessed.

Sadáwarta. [Hindi, from *sadá*, ever, and *vrat*, a vow.] The distribution daily of food to all who come to take it. Sadáwartas were formerly especially for joshis and mendicants; now they are commonly established by well-to-do natives in time of famine for the benefit of all the poor. Compare Annachhatra.

Sadgop. [Bengali, from the Sanskrit *sat*, good, respectable, and *gop*, q.v.] The name of a caste in Bengal, originally a branch of the great Gop caste, but now engaged almost exclusively in agriculture. They are generally well-to-do, and are deemed the highest of the cultivating classes in Bengal.

Sadh Ját. A sect of Játs who use no idols or temples, but worship only the One God under the title *Sat*, or true.

Sádhu. [Sanskrit, from *sádh*, to complete.] One who is perfect, a saint, a sage; also a merchant, a money-lender. The Jains apply the term to their jins or deified saints. It is commonly used of all Hindu religious mendicants, whether sansári or tyági. Many persons become sádhus because they have first been turned out of caste. See Mahanta.

Sadiá. [Hindustáni.] The name of a class of Musalmáns in Cambay; they are carriers, plying between the landing-place and the town.

Sadr. [Arabic.] Eminence, superiority, chief, supreme; the chief seat of government, the presidency as opposed to the provinces or mofussil; but the term is most usually applied in India to denote establishments or individuals employed in the judicial and revenue administration of the state (*H. H. Wilson*).

Sadrá. [Gujaráti.] The sacred shirt worn by all Pársis, women as well as men; it is typical of the coat of mail with which Ahriman is to be withstood. See also Kasti.

Sadr Adálat. [Arabic.] The supreme court, the name of the highest court established under the East India Company in each presidency, and consisting each of two sides, known as the Sadr Diwáni Adálat, or chief civil court, and the Sadr Nizámat (or Faujdári) Adálat, the chief criminal court. The sadr adálats have been replaced by High Courts.

Sadr Amin. A chief commissioner or arbitrator, a native civil judge. Some of a higher grade are distinguished as Principal sadr amin.

Sadr Nizámat wa Diwáni Adálat. The supreme criminal and civil court, the title of a supreme court and court of final appeal established in Bengal in 1801.

Sadr Tálukdár. The title of an officer in the Hyderabad state corresponding to the commissioner of a division, and now usually called Subah.

Sadubá. [Gujaráti.] The name of a goddess, the bhut or devi of a Bháṭ woman killed in trágá by her husband.

Safar. [Arabic.] The second month of the Musalmán year; it follows Muharram. See Month.

Sáfi. A fabric composed of a cotton warp with a silk web.

Ság. [Maráṭhi, from the Sanskrit *śáka*.] The tree tectona grandis, or teak.

Sagáwálá. [Gujaráti *sagá*, from the Sanskrit *sagotra*, related to, and *wáhálá*, from the Sanskrit *wallabha*, beloved.] Relations and friends.

Ságnik. [Hindi, from the Sanskrit *sa*, with, and *agni*, q.v.] One whose family has preserved the fire consecrated by Manu, the first man after the deluge; or, commonly, one who maintains a perpetual household fire.

Sagotra. [Sanskrit, from *sa*, with, and *gotra*, q.v.] A kinsman, a gotraja.

Sáh. The name of a dynasty that appears to have come from Málwá and conquered the northern Deccan; they established a local seat of government at Násik and held that district and Khándesh in the second century A.D., and are found in Gujarát as late as 328 A.D.

Sáh. [Hindi, a shortened form of *sádhu*, q.v.] A merchant, a banker, a tradesman. The term is prefixed to the name of a Banyá in addressing him by letter. Sáhji is a term used as a substitute for father-in-law. See Cháchá, Panḍit.

Sáheb. [Arabic.] A lord, a master. The word is often affixed to titles expressive of rank, as Rájá Sáheb, Collector Sáheb. It is similarly affixed to proper names. It is also used by itself as a respectful appellation. Again, the word is often used as the peculiar designation of an English gentleman.

Sáheblok. [Sanskrit *loka*, people.] Gentlemen. Used especially to denote English gentlemen.

Sáhib. More commonly Sáheb.

Sáhibah. A lady, mistress, madam.

Sáhotra. [Maráṭhi, from *saha*, six, and *uttar*, above.] Six per cent., the name of the share of the chauth taken by the sachiwa.

Sáhu. A short form of Sáhukár. Also the name of a degraded class of Uriya Bráhmans occupied in trade.

Sáhukár. [Hindi, from the Sanskrit *sádhu*, q.v., and *kárya*, business.] A banker, a merchant; especially one whose dealings are on a large scale.

Saïd. [Arabic.] A lord; the designation of the descendants of Ali, the son-in-law of the prophet. There are Sunni as well as Shiah Saïds. Many are maulvis or pirs, but the poor follow all callings. Saïds usually give their daughters only to men of their own class, but they will take wives from the other classes of Musalmáns. There was a dynasty of Saïds at Delhi from 1414 to 1451 A.D. See Ghori.

Sailábi. [Hindustáni, from the Arabic *sail*, a flood, and *áb*, water.] Land watered by inundation.

Sáir. More commonly Sáyer.

Sáis. More commonly Syce.

Śaiwa. [Sanskrit.] A worshipper of the god Śiwa. The Hindus of the present day are divided generally into Vaishnawas and Śaiwas. The two classes do not hold opposite and incompatible creeds, but acquiesce to a certain extent in each other's views, while each lays an exaggerated stress on particular doctrines—the Śaiwa on the efficacy of works, penances, and austerities, and the Vaishnawa on faith in personal deities. The worship of Śiwa is prevalent throughout India, and no temples are so common as those which enshrine his symbol, the linga. See Lingáit, Smárta.

Saiyid. See Saïd.

Sajje. The Kanarese name of Bájri. See Millet.

Sajji. [Hindustáni.] An impure carbonate of soda extracted from the soil; also the alkaline produce of the coroxylon griffithii obtained from its ashes when burnt.

Śaka. [Sanskrit.] An era, especially that of the birth of Sáliwáhana, a king of southern India, whose capital was on the Godáwari, and who was born in 78 A.D. Śaka 1807 began on the 17th March, 1885.

Śakábda. [Sanskrit.] A year of the śaka era.

Śákhá. [Sanskrit.] A branch, a division or branch of a tribe, of a subject, etc. The word is used particularly with reference to the veda. Sometimes the three vedas are spoken of as the three śákhás of the veda tree, but more frequently śákhá is used to signify the various editions or traditions that branched off from each of the three original branches of the veda tree. Traditional text (recension) of the veda is perhaps the nearest approach to its real meaning (*Max Müller*).

Sakkili. See Chakkili.

Sákshi Vináyak. [Hindi, Sanskrit *sa*, with, *aksha*, the eye.] Vináyak the witness, at whose temple at Benares pilgrims of the pánch-kosi get certificates of their having made the round.

Śákta. [Sanskrit.] A worshipper of a śakti. The designation of a sect who worship the female principle according to the ritual of the tantras; there are two chief divisions of them—the Dakshináchári and Wámáchári, or right and left hand ritualists. The worship of the former is public, and no otherwise noticeable than as addressed to the goddesses. The worship of the left-hand division is private and unavowed, and is celebrated with impure practices; it is said to be most numerously followed, and branches into various subdivisions (*H. H. Wilson*). The Dakshinácháris observe the puráns and the Wámácháris the tantras as their peculiar veda (*Monier Williams*). In Bengal the Śáktas have come to be in great degree united with the Śaiwas (*J. B. Phear*).

Śakti. [Sanskrit.] Power; the energy or active power of a deity, personified, to meet the understanding of the people, as his wife.

Śákyamuni. [Sanskrit *śákya*, the name of the Buddha's family, and *muni*, q.v.] The saint of the Śákya family; an epithet of Siddhártha's.

Sál. [Sanskrit.] The shorea robusta, a magnificent tree yielding timber as much as sixty feet in length and with a girth of four and a half feet, much used for house and ship building. It is the holy tree of the Santáls, who make wheels of single slices of it.

Sálá. [Sanskrit *syála.*] A wife's brother. This is a very common form of abuse. See Gáli.

Śálagráma. More commonly Sálgrám.

Salám. [Arabic.] Peace; the common word of salutation among Musalmáns, and now in general use by all classes of persons; uttering the exclamation salám, bowing and raising the right hand to the forehead. The salám has to a great extent replaced the namaskára, except among Bráhmans. The English make a verb also of the word and speak of salám-ing, and also send saláms as equivalent to sending compliments.

Salámi. [Hindi, from *salám.*] A quit-rent, a joḍi, peshkash; lands paying only a quit-rent.

Salát. [Gujaráti.] The name of a caste; they are stonemasons. Some have become Sunni Musalmáns. Compare Pátharwaṭ.

Salátin. [The plural of *sultán.*] The younger members of a royal family.

Sále. [Kanarese.] The name of a caste of weavers said to be of Telugu origin, but perhaps identical with the Sáli and Sáliyan. They are divided into Śakunasále (*śakuna*, Sanskrit, an omen), who are Śaiwas, and Padmasále (*padma*, Sanskrit, a lotus), who are Vaishnawas.

Sálgrám. [Sanskrit *sa*, with, *ala*, a ring, and *gráma*, a multitude.] A black stone found in the river Ganḍak and considered to be a type of Vishnu. It is a kind of ammonite perforated by an animal of the snail kind. As Vishnu is represented by this stone, so is Mahádewa by a small oval agate, Ganeśa by a globular cornelian, and so on. A newly planted wood or orchard may be consecrated by the ceremony of marrying the sálgrám to a branch of the tulsi representing a nymph beloved by Krishna.

Sali. [Bengali.] Land which is wholly submerged during the period of the rains.

Sáli. [Maráṭhi.] The name of a caste; they weave silk and cotton.

Sáliánah. [Hindustáni, from the Persian *sál*, a year.] An annual pension. Compare Rozinah.

Salita. A bag of open rope network for packing camels' loads; a canvas sheet; a tent-bag, a canvas bag made for each separate part of a tent when travelling.

Sáliyan. [Tamil.] The name of a caste; they are weavers, chiefly of coarse coloured cloths for women's wear. See Khatri, Sále.

Sál-maháјani. [Hindi.] The year of the mahájans, or the mercantile year; it commences seven months earlier than the samwat year.

Salone. A tribe of sea-gipsies of Assam; they live in their boats except in the monsoon, when they take to huts.

Sálotari. [Hindi, from the Sanskrit *śálihotri*, a horse, from *śáli*, rice or corn, and *hotri*, sacrificing.] A farrier, a horse-doctor. The sálotari of a cavalry regiment ranks as a dafadár.

Saluppan. [Tamil.] The name of a caste; they weave gunny-bags and other coarse fabrics.

Sama. The name of a tribe in Sindh, and the ruling dynasty from 1351 to 1521 A.D.; they are believed to have been originally Rájputs, but to have early adopted islám; they have Rájput names, but their ceremonies are mostly Musalmán (Sunni); they are now cultivators and cattle-breeders; some are settled in Cutch. The Dángs and perhaps the Jáḍejas are branches of the Sama tribe. The Sama capital was Samni, three miles north-west of Tatta.

Sámádaskat. [Gujaráti, from *sámá*, opposite, the Sanskrit *sammukha*, confronting, from *sam*, with, and *mukha*, the face; and *daskat*, signature, from the Persian *dast*, hand, and *khat*, writing.] An account signed by the opposite party in a money-lender's book. This method is chiefly used in small transactions for which separate bonds are not deemed necessary.

Samádh. [Sanskrit *samádhi*, from *samá*, together, and *dhá*, to put.] Composing the mind, fixing the thoughts in profound contemplation until the connection between the body and soul is temporarily suspended, and the former remains apparently dead and independent of sustenance, but not subject to corruption. Many instances have occurred of mendicants having themselves enclosed in vaults for weeks or even longer periods, while they professed to be in a state of samádh, but it has sometimes been discovered that food was secretly conveyed to them. Samádh means also self-immolation by being voluntarily buried or burnt alive; a case occurred as lately as 1849 at the village of Serol in the Mahikánṭhá. Again, samádh is the name of the ceremony of burying or sinking in water the body of a deceased jogi or sannyási. Again, a tomb, with a tulsi plant growing on the top of it, built over the grave of a holy mendicant, is called a samádh. A mausoleum or a cremation-ground is also sometimes called a samádh.

Samaicha. The name of a branch of the Yadu or Jádon tribe; it is now represented by Muhammadan nobles in Sindh.

Samáj. [Sanskrit, from *sam*, together, and *aj*, to go.] A meeting, a congregation; a society, an association.

Samánodaka. [Sanskrit *samán*, equal, common, and *udaka*, water.] Lineal male ancestors or descendants of any man to any degree. They are so called as being the persons entitled to offer water at a śráddha to a deceased person. Samánodakas thus include sapiṇḍas.

Sámant. [Gujaráti, from the Sanskrit *sámanta*, bordering, neighbouring.] A feudatory prince, a military leader under a Rájput king.

Sámanta. [Bengali.] The name of a low agricultural caste.

Samár. [Gujaráti.] An implement for smoothing soil; it is a flat piece of wood, usually raen or bábul, drawn breadthwise by bullocks, the driver standing on it to increase the weight.

Sáma-veda. See under Veda.

Sámbar. [Hindi.] The deer rusa aristotelis; it grows to the height of fourteen hands, is dark brown in colour, has a massy neck clothed with bristling hair, and long antlers.

Śambhu. [Sanskrit, from *śam*, prosperity, *bhu*, being.] Being for happiness; a name of Śiwa.

Sáme. The Tamil name of Chenna. See Millet.

Śami. [Sanskrit.] The name of two plants, the śami tree or mimosa suma, and the serratula anthelmintica. The śami tree was worshipped by Arjun the Pándawa, and hence is still worshipped at the daśara, and is identified with Durgá under the title Aparájita, or the unconquered.

Samma. See Sama.

Samorin. See Zamorin.

Sampan. A Chinese boat used on the rivers of Burma, and remarkable for its swiftness both with sails and oars (*E. Balfour*).

Sampige. The Kanarese form of Champaka.

Śamprati. [Tamil.] A revenue accountant; an inspector or supervisor of a small tract of country.

Sámpri. [Hindi.] A snake-charmer.

Samputa. [Sanskrit, from *sam*, together, and *puṭa*, folded.] Two vessels tied together mouth to mouth; it is used at weddings, the vessels being filled with rice and presented to the bridegroom by the bride's mother.

Samra. See Sumrá.

Samvedi. [Maráṭhi.] The name of a caste; they belong to the northern Konkan; they are generally believed to be pure Bráhmans by race, but to have lost caste by their constant intercourse with Christians in the time of the Portuguese; they act as priests to the lower castes (*A. K. Nairne*).

Samwat. [Sanskrit.] A year, especially a year of the era of Vikramáditya, king of Málwá, who began to reign in 57 B.C. Samwat 1942 begins on the 7th November, 1885.

Samwatsara. Another form of Samwat.

San. [Arabic.] A year, especially a year of the era known as the Bengali san, established by Akbar. The year 1292 of this era began on the 12th April, 1885 A.D. The word san is also used in speaking of the Christian era, which is called isavi san, or the year of Jesus. See Year.

Śan. [Sanskrit *śana.*] A common name for both the cannabis sativa or hemp, and the crotolaria juncea or Indian hemp. See Bhang.

Sanad. [Arabic.] A written grant or patent; a deed by government assigning or acknowledging rights.

Sánan, or **Sánár.** [Tamil.] The name of a caste; their proper occupation is extracting the juice of the cocoa and palmyra palms. Many are petty traders. Some are found in Ceylon. They bury their dead.

Sanappan. [Tamil, from *śan*, hemp.] One who makes cloth or canvas of hemp. Compare Sangar.

Sánḍ. [Hindi.] A bull set at liberty as an act of piety and allowed to wander where it will, a pol.

Sandhi. [Sanskrit, from *sam*, with, and *dhá*, to put.] Junction, union; the euphonic junction of consecutive words in a sentence, peculiar to Sanskrit; or the same junction of the elements of compound words; as *gangodaka* for *ganga udaka*, or *sandhi* above for *sam-dhi*.

Sandhyá. [Sanskrit, from *sandhi*, a juncture.] Twilight personified as the daughter of Brahmá; a division of a day; morning, midday, or evening prayer.

Sand-snake. See Paraḍ, Dutonḍá.

Sanga. [Hindi.] A kind of bridge used in the Himálayas; a number of beams, laid side by side, project from each bank of the river, slightly pointing upwards, firmly secured by being built into the bank, and heavily laden at the shore end; another set of beams is made, in like manner, to project beyond these, and others again till the space left in mid-stream can be crossed by single timbers. Also a stockade or breastwork of stone, the Afghán sangu.

Sangama. [Sanskrit *sam*, together, *gam*, to go.] Meeting, the confluence of two rivers. Compare Triveni.

Sangar. [Maráṭhi, from *śan*, hemp.] The name of a caste; they weave coarse woollen cloth and blankets.

Sángḍa. [Kanarese.] A ferry-boat formed of two canoes secured together, with a platform or deck fastened upon them, and with sides, turning on hinges, which, let down, form a gangway for loading and unloading (*L. Rice*).

Sangha. [Sanskrit, from *samhan*, to join together.] An assembly, especially the Buddhist order of mendicants, called individually bhikshus.

Sangu. [Pashṭo.] A stone breastwork. Also the name of a khel of the Shinwáris.

Sanhitá. [Sanskrit.] A collection; used especially in connection with the collections made of the vedic hymns. The sanhitás of the hymns of the yajur and sáma vedas were made in the order that the hymns were required at the sacrifice, and so served as manuals for the adhwaryu and udgátri priests respectively. But the hotri priest was supposed to know all the hymns without the aid of a manual, and the rig-veda sanhitá is considered to have been made in earlier times without special reference to the order of the sacrifice. See Mantra.

Śankar. [Hindi, Sanskrit *śankara*, from *śam*, prosperity, *kara*, causing.] The causer of prosperity, a name of Śiwa; also the name of the áchárya who founded the sect of Smártas. Śankar is often used as a general name for god. There is a Gujaráti proverb: 'As many forms of Śankar as pebbles of Kankar.'

Śánkar. [Hindi, Sanskrit *śánkara*, an adjective from *śankar*.] A follower of Śankaráchárya; a Smárta.

Śankha. [Sanskrit.] The conch-shell, sacred to Vishnu, and used as a lamp and also blown as a horn in temples.

Śánkhári. [Bengali form of the Sanskrit *śankhakára*, a worker in shells.] The name of a high Śudra caste; they are shell-cutters and makers of shell bracelets.

Śankhini. [Sanskrit, from *śankha*, the conch-shell.] The name of one of the four classes into which Hindu writers divide women; the śankhini is described as tall, with long hair, and of an amorous and irascible disposition. The other classes are the padmini, the chitrini, and the hastini.

Sánkhya. [Sanskrit, from *sankhyá*, numbering.] The name of one of the six darśans, so called from its enumeration of the entities. It offers no explanation of the existence of the soul, but all other existences, including mind and intellect as well as the material world, it derives from a rootless germ called prakriti. This prakriti itself consists of three elements, namely, goodness, passion, and darkness. It is the misfortune of the soul to be united with prakriti, and the characters of men differ according to the predominance of one or other of the three elements of prakriti as united with their souls, but it is the object of all to break the union and get rid of every quality good as well as bad. And it seems to be assumed in this as in the other darśans that the desired end will follow a perfect perception of the truth. The sánkhya system, referring everything to soul and prakriti and recognizing no cause of either, makes no consideration of any supreme soul or god. It does not, indeed, deny the existence of a supreme god, but, as it looks upon all action as essentially bad, it cannot consistently allow that there can be any evidence of such existence; a perfect being would take no action and so would make no sign.

Sankla. The name of a branch of the Parmár Rájputs; they formerly ruled in Pugal, but were expelled by the Chauháns.

Sankránti. [Sanskrit, from *sam*, together, and *kram*, to go.] A meeting, a union; the passage of the sun from one sign into another.

Sannyási. [Sanskrit, from *samyam*, to control.] A Bráhman in his fourth áśrama or stage of life, a bhikshu, an ascetic. 'Having thus performed religious acts in a forest during the third portion of his life, let him become a sannyási for the fourth portion of it, abandoning all sensuous affections, and wholly reposing in the supreme spirit' (*Manu*, vi. 33). But the term 'sannyási' is applied now to a variety of religious mendicants; they are often persons who have lost their children or their property, or suffered some other calamity, against which they have not had resolution to bear up.

Sansári. [Sanskrit, from *sansára*, the world, from *sansri*, to revolve.] Worldly, mundane; engaged in secular life as opposed to tyági; a sádhu whose order permits him to marry. Compare Sanyogi.

Sanskár. [Sanskrit *sam*, with, and *kri*, to make.] That which perfects; a name given to certain ceremonies enjoined on the twice-born. The sanskárs are variously enumerated as ten, twelve, or more; but many of them are no longer observed. The first is celebrated as soon as there is indication that a child has been conceived. The most important is the upanayana, or investiture with the sacrificial thread.

Sanskrit. [From *sam*, with, and *kri*, to make.] The sacred language of the Hindus, so called as being perfectly constructed, polished, and refined. It is of the Aryan or Indo-European branch of the Caucasian, and akin therefore to the Pelasgic, Teutonic, and Sclavonian, whence Greek and Latin, German and English, Russian and Polish, are derived. See Aryan, Prákrit.

Sansthán. [Hindi, Sanskrit *sansthána*, from *sam*, together, and *sthá*, to stand.] A standing together, a common place of abode; a city; a royal town or capital; a place favoured by the manifestations of a god, or by the residence of saints. Sansthán is also the word used to denote a native state. See Darbár, Kárbári, Native State.

Santál. The name of an aboriginal tribe settled on the skirts of the Rájmahál hills and along the western frontier of lower Bengal. They are divided into different tribes, but the distinction is only by the father's side, as every Santál has to take his wife from one of the other tribes. The Santáls are described as brave, simple-minded, and honest; hospitable to strangers, and of a happy, sociable disposition. Their main occupation is agriculture, and very many are employed as agricultural day-labourers; those in the hills support themselves by collecting jungle produce, breeding buffaloes, and hunting. The Santáls worship Sing Bonga and Máráng Buru. They burn their dead.

Santáli. The language of the Santáls. It is of the Kolarian class, and has been described as a beautiful and elaborate language, though without literature or written character.

Sánwá. [Maráṭhi.] The cereal panicum frumentaceum, or miliaceum. See Millet.

Sanyasi. See Sannyási.

Sanyogi. [Sanskrit, from *sam*, together, and *yoga*, junction, from *yuj*, to join.] A religious man who leads the life of a householder and marries, as opposed to the viyogi. The two terms are equivalent to sansári and tyági.

Sáont. An aboriginal tribe of some of the native states of Orissa, said to be a branch of the Bhuiyás. There is also a tribe of the same name in Chutiá Nágpur; these have some Dravidian customs.

Sapiṇḍa. [Sanskrit *sa*, together, and *piṇḍa*, the sacrificial ball.] An ancestor or descendant in the male line, and of the first, second, or third generation. These kinsmen are so called because they, and they only, are entitled to offer the piṇḍa at a śráddha to a deceased person (*Manu*, v. 60). But according to Kulluka's commentary the sapiṇḍaship extends to the sixth degree of ascent or descent.

Sápsurali. [Maráṭhi.] The skink, or snake-lizard.

Saptapadi. [Sanskrit *sapta*, seven, and *pada*, a foot.] The pacing of seven steps round the sacred fire, an essential part of a Hindu marriage. See Lagan.

Sar. See Sawar.

Saracenic. This name is sometimes applied to the whole school of architecture referred to under the head Hindustáni. Again, it is sometimes confined to a late period of that school, namely, the time of Sháh Jahán (1628–1658 A.D.), under whom the Hindu practice encouraged by Akbar was to a great extent eliminated and Persian ideas predominated.

Śarad. [Sanskrit.] The season during which the sun is passing the signs Virgo and Libra; where the luni-solar year is followed the season is defined as the two months Bhádrapad and Áśvin or as Áśvin and Kártik. See Ritu, Year.

Saráf. More commonly Shroff.

Sarái. [Persian.] A large building, a rest-house for travellers. The word is compounded in the English caravansary. See Dharmśálá.

Śárak. [Bengali.] The name of a Śudra caste of middle rank; they are cultivators.

Sarákti. [Gujaráti, from the Arabic *sharik*, a partner.] The name of a tenure under which a share, commonly a third, of the revenue and the whole management of a village is given to a person who, for want of a more special name, is usually called jágirdár.

Sárangi. [Hindi.] A particular stringed instrument of music, used to accompany the voice.

Sarániá. [Gujaráti, from *sarán*, a whetstone.] The name of a caste who wander about Gujarát and Málwá, and whose avocation is the burnishing of arms and the sharpening of instruments.

Saranjám. [Persian.] This term as commonly used is equivalent to jágir, but was in earlier times confined chiefly to temporary assignments for the maintenance of troops or an officer of state.

Saráogi. [Panjábi.] A name of the Jain division of the Bániyás.

Sáras. [Hindi, from the Sanskrit *sarasa*, a pond.] A kind of crane, the grus antigone; it is found in pairs, and usually only one pair about the same piece of water.

Sáraswata. [Sanskrit.] Relating to Saraswati; the name of the second subdivision of the Gauḍa Bráhmans. They are again divided into ten classes, named Bháradwáji, Sipoli, Chaini, Sudhani, Bhárati, Khukaṭi, Rankhaṭi, Boli, Máli, and Grahani.

Saraswati. The name of a river in northern India which loses itself in the sands of the great desert and is supposed to reappear and join the Ganges and Jamná. This river, says Professor Monier Williams, was to the earlier Hindus what the Ganges was to the later; she was infused with divinity, and her influence permeated the writers of the vedic hymns. Hence she came to be invoked as the goddess of eloquence, letters, and arts, and was considered to be the śakti, the active power or wife of Brahmá the creator and author of the vedas. She is worshipped particularly on the Śri-panchmi, on which day books and writing implements are held sacred and not used.

Sárbán. [Persian.] A camel-driver.

Sardár. [Persian.] A chief, a prince; a military officer. Also, in Behar, the title of the hereditary head of a village pancháyat.

Sardár-bearer. The name given in Bengal to one of the two chief domestic servants in a European household. He has charge of the lamps, the linen, etc., and is responsible that the water-carriers, sweepers, and other subordinate servants do their duty; but he has nothing to do with the cuisine department, the head of which is the khánsámán. See Bearer.

Sardeśái. [Maráṭhi, from the Persian *sar*, the head, chief, and *deśái*, q.v.] This term is equivalent to sardeśmukh.

Sardeśmukh. [Persian *sar*, head,

and *deśmukh*, q.v.] A high officer to whom the deśmukhs were subordinate.

Sardeśmukhi. The office of sardeśmukh. Also the levy—ten per cent. beyond the chauth—by which the officer was maintained in the time of the Maráṭhá government.

Sardula. A mythical animal resembling the lion and represented in architecture.

Sarhang. More commonly Syrang.

Sári. [Hindi, from the Sanskrit *śáṭa*.] A Hindu woman's principal garment. It is a long piece of silk or cotton cloth which is wrapped round the middle of the body with one end falling nearly to the feet and the other thrown over the head.

Sarishtadár. [*Sarishta*, from the Persian *sar*, head, and *rishtah*, thread, means ordinary course, routine, practice, and *dár*, who holds.] A registrar, a record-keeper, a secretary. Particularly, in a court of justice, the clerk who administers oaths, records depositions, etc., and, in the office of an administrative officer, the head member of the native establishment; but the latter in some offices is called chiṭnis.

Sarkár. [Hindustáni, from the Persian *sar*, the head, and *kár*, business.] The government, the supreme authority in the state. The term is also applied as a complimentary title to any high officer. In Bengal, sarkár is the name also of a servant who keeps the household accounts, or of any accountant. Sarkár also signified an extensive division of country under the Muhammadan government, a subdivision of a subah.

Sarkhel. [Maráṭhi, from the Persian *sar*, head, and *khel*, clan.] A leader, a general; a title of rank bestowed by the peshwá.

Sarkil. The Tamil form of Sarkhel; a minister, a chamberlain, in Tanjore and Pudukottai.

Sarnaubat. [Persian *sar*, head, and *naubat*, a kettle-drum.] The highest military officer under the peshwá; also the governor of a fort or of a part of it; also the commander of a págá, or body of cavalry.

Saropá. [Hindi, from the Persian *sar-o-pá*, head and foot.] A dress of honour presented by a ruler or high officer on an occasion of rejoicing; a khilat.

Sarpanch. [Hindi.] The head or president of a panch or pancháyat.

Sarpech. [Hindustáni.] An ornament worn in the turban; it consists of square pieces of gold plates threaded together, each plate being set with precious stones. Also a band of silk or embroidery (*S. W. Fallon*).

Sarpṭoli. [Maráṭhi.] The green whip-snake, passerita mycterizans. It is of a bright grass-green colour, lighter beneath, with a yellow line along each side of the abdomen. Large specimens grow to six feet in length. It is found on trees, and its chief food consists of small birds and lizards. It is harmless (*G. W. Vidal*).

Sársut. Another form of Sáraswata.

Sáruya. [Uriya, from *sáru*, a sort of yam.] The name of a degraded class of Uriya Bráhmans who cultivate with their own hands and serve also as brickmakers and bricklayers.

Sarwadá. [Maráṭhi, literally, always.] Another name of the Dákochá caste, said to be given in allusion to their always predicting good fortune to those who consult them.

Sarwajanik. [Maráṭhi, from the Sanskrit *sarwa*, all, and *jana*, people.] Relating to all the people; public.

Śásana. [Sanskrit, from *śás*, to rule, to inform.] An order, an edict; a royal grant or charter, often inscribed on stone or copper.

Śástra. [Sanskrit, from *śás*, to rule, to direct.] A command, a precept, an institute; a religious or scientific treatise.

Śástri. One who is versed in the śástras, a learned man, a teacher.

Śáśwat. [Maráṭhi, Sanskrit *śáśwata*, perpetual.] A name given to certain offices, such as those of páṭil, kulkarni, deśmukh, deśpáṇḍe, which are perpetual, and therefore highly prized, though inferior in rank to some aśáśwat offices, as those of subhedár and mámlatdár.

Sátáni. [Tamil.] The name of a class of Vaishnawa Śudras; they are musicians and mendicants.

Satbalá. [Hindi *sat*, seven.] A sacrifice consisting of the five offerings of the pachbalá with a man and a woman added.

Sathwárá. The name of a small caste in Cutch; they are gardeners and husbandmen.

Sati. [Sanskrit, feminine of *sat*, virtuous.] A faithful, virtuous wife; especially one who burns herself with the corpse of her husband. But sati is commonly used in English to denote, not the wife, but her final act of suicide. Formerly some hundreds of widows burnt themselves every year. The practice was put a stop to in British India in 1829, but continued in some native states much longer. In 1834 seven wives and seven concubines of the rájá of Idar were burnt with his body as satis.

Sati. [Panjábi.] The name of an Early Turanian tribe; they claim to be of Persian descent.

Satin. [Bengali.] A wife who is not her husband's only wife; a co-wife; a saut or sok.

Sat-jug. A Hindi form of Satya-yuga.

Satnámi. [Hindi, from *sat*, true, and *nám*, name.] A worshipper of the true name; the name of a sect allied to the Ráyadásis.

Satra. The Maráṭhi form of Sattra.

Satraśálá. [Maráṭhi, from *satra*, and *śálá*, a hall.] A house or room for the distribution of alms to Bráhmans and mendicants, or for the gratuitous supply of food to travellers; an annasattra.

Sáṭshati. [Bengali.] The name of a branch of the Gauḍa (subdivision) Bráhmans.

Sáttáthavan. [Tamil.] An order of Vaishnawas who renounce caste; they are chiefly flower-sellers, minstrels, and vagrants.

Satti. The Telugu form of Śeṭh.

Sattra. [Sanskrit, from *sad*, to sit.] A sacrificial session; a sacrifice;

any oblation or offering; charity, the giving of alms; a place of refuge, an asylum. In southern India the word is now used especially to denote a place or institution for the distribution of alms to Bráhmans and mendicants or to travellers.

Sattram. The Tamil form of Sattra.

Saṭṭu. [Hindi.] Grain parched and ground to flour and made into a paste with water.

Satwái. [Maráṭhi.] A goddess who presides over the destinies of newborn children.

Satya-yuga. [Sanskrit *satya*, true, and *yuga*, q.v.] Another name of the first or krita age.

Saugata. [Sanskrit.] A follower of Sugata, the name of a formerly existing sect, resembling or identical with the Bauddhas or Buddhists.

Sauhágiá. Another name for Musá Sohág.

Sauhágin. [Hindi, from the Sanskrit *su*, good, and *bhága*, lot.] A woman whose husband is living; also a favourite wife as distinguished from a duhágin.

Saukan morá. [Hindi.] A piece of silver worn as a charm by a woman who marries a widower; it is meant as a preventive of evil caused by the dead woman's jealousy, and is treated with great respect as her representative.

Saukár. A Maráṭhi form of Sáhukár.

Saur. [A corruption of the Maráṭhi *sámwar*, the Sanskrit *śálmali.*] The red silk-cotton tree, the salmalia malabarica or bombax heptaphyllum.

Saura. [Sanskrit, from *sura*, the sun.] A worshipper of the sun; the name of a sect formerly numerous in the peninsula of Káṭhiáwár; they are said to have been of six classes, the first worshipping the rising sun as a type of Brahmá; the second the meridian sun as Iśwara; the third the setting sun as Vishnu; the fourth all the preceding three as Trimurti; the fifth the sun as a material body, and the marks on his surface, as his hair, beard, etc.; the sixth, in opposition to the last, meditated on a mental luminary, and stamped circular orbs upon their bodies with hot irons (*Anand Giri*).

Saura. The name of a tribe cognate with the Kandhs, and occupying with them the Eastern Gháṭs. Perhaps the same as the Sawar.

Saut. [Hindi, from the Sanskrit *sa*, with, *patni*, a wife.] A co-wife, a satin or sok.

Sáve. The Kanarese name of Chenna. See Millet.

Sávitri. [Sanskrit, from *savitá*, the generator, the sun, from *su*, to beget.] Relating to the sun; a name of the gáyatri because it was addressed to the sun; also of the janeo because the gáyatri is repeated at the investiture.

Sávitrivrata. [Sanskrit *vrata*, a religious act.] A fast kept by Hindu women on the 14th Jyeshṭh wadi to avert widowhood.

Sáwan. The Hindustáni form of Śráwan.

Sawar. [Uriya.] The name of an aboriginal or Kolarian tribe of Orissa; they are not allowed to enter the temple of Jagannáth.

Sawár. [Hindustáni.] A horseman; a horse-soldier; a mounted policeman; and particularly a mounted attendant or messenger of a chief or officer of state.

Sawári. A mounted retinue, a cavalcade. The application of the word is extended so as to include the whole body of the attendants of an officer in whatever way they may be travelling. A sawári horse or elephant means one used for riding.

Sawmy. See Swámi.

Sáya. [Hindi.] Shadow; possession by an evil spirit caused by the shadow of an evil person falling on any one.

Sáyar. The Maráṭhi form of Sáyer. The term is now applied in Bombay only to such ábkári revenue as is collected by village officers.

Sáyaru. The Telugu form of Sáyer.

Sáyer. [Bengali, from the Arabic *sair.*] This term, in its sense of balance or remainder, was applied to all the miscellaneous sources of revenue other than the land tax. What is included in sáyer revenue, therefore, varies both in time and place according to the taxation imposed. Some of the commoner items were customs, excise, and transit duties. The use of the term narrows as different items are made the subject of separate administration. See Sáyar.

Sáyerdár. [Persian *dár*, holder.] An officer who under the Sikh government collected transit duties.

Sayid. See Saïd.

Sassa. The Telugu name of Bájri. See Millet.

Sebáti. [Bengali, from the Sanskrit *sewaka*, a servant.] The manager or superintendent of a temple.

Sebundy. See Sibandi.

Secretary of State in Council. The act of 1858, for the better government of India (21 & 22 Vict., c. 106), provided that one of her Majesty's principal secretaries of state should have the powers and perform the duties which had previously been exercised and performed by the East India Company, or by the Court of Directors or Court of Proprietors of that Company, or by the commissioners for the affairs of India. A separate secretary of state is appointed for this purpose under section 6 of the act. He is assisted by a council of fifteen members, called the Council of India.

Seer. See Ser or Sir.

Śehersai. [Gujaráti, from *śeher*, a city.] The name of the division of the Pársis who reject Jamasp's reform of the calendar; they form a very large majority of the race, and are known also as Rasami. See Kadmi.

Sekera. [Bengali.] Another name for Sonár.

Selkhari. The Hindustáni name of the soapstone.

Sem. [Hindustáni.] The pulse dolichos lablab, cow-gram, or áwáre.

Semmán. [Tamil.] The name of a caste; they burn and sell lime for building purposes. See Chunári.

Senákhháskhel. [Maráṭhi, from *sená-khás*, the army of the state, from the Sanskrit *sená*, army, and the Arabic *khás*, select; and *sarkhel*, q.v., the first syllable being dropped.] The title of an officer second in rank only to the senápati in the Maráṭhá army.

Senápati. [Sanskrit, from *sená*, army, and *pati*, lord.] A general, a commander-in-chief. Under the Maráṭhá government the office became hereditary, even a minor succeeding to it. Compare Sipahsálár.

Śenḍi. [Maráṭhi.] The tuft or lock of hair left on the crown of a Hindu's head when the rest of the head is shaved; the chuḍá, or chonṭi.

Sendu Bir. The name of a spirit believed in by the people of Kángrá and Cashmere; he is supposed to appear in the form of a Gaddi, or hill shepherd, with a long beard and with a kira (long basket for carrying milk, etc.) on his back, and his appearance is preceded by a whistling sound. His chief shrine is at Basoli, in the territory of Jamman, and smaller ones are at Dhar, Bhangori, and Gungthá, in the Kángrá district. He is supposed to steal corn, milk, ghi, etc., from others to give to his special worshippers, and to burn down the houses of those with whom he is dissatisfied (*Sardáru Balhári*).

Seniga. [Kanarese.] The name of a wealthy caste of Kanarese weavers.

Śenvi. [Maráṭhi.] The name of a caste in the southern Konkan. They are not acknowledged as Bráhmans by the Chitpáwans, but are certainly higher in general estimation than some that are. They differ from Bráhmans chiefly in eating fish. They were first settled at Goa, and every family has still a private idol there. They hold a very leading position in Bombay, and engage in every profession and occupation in which wealth or distinction can be obtained (*A. K. Nairne*).

Sepoy. [A corruption of the Persian *sipáhi*.] A soldier, especially a native Indian, as distinguished from a British soldier. The term is also commonly applied to policemen and peons.

Ser. [Hindi.] A measure of weight, usually the fortieth part of a man or maund. A Bengal ser thus weighs just over two pounds.

Śerá. [Maráṭhi, from the Arabic *shara*.] An order, especially an order endorsed upon a report or petition.

Serang. See Syrang.

Serḍá. [Gujaráti.] A strip of land left uncultivated between two fields, to serve both as a boundary-mark and as a passage. The Bengali name is áil.

Serpent race. In many parts of India traces are found of an ancient race called by some name signifying serpent, either Takshak or Nága or some modification of one of those words. Mr. H. M. Elliot says they were a Scythian tribe, and Buddhists, and had the takshak, or serpent, as their national emblem; they extended their conquests in India from the time of the Mahábhárata to 500 B.C., and in one invasion under a leader named Śeshnág they penetrated as far as Magadha and established a dynasty which continued for ten generations. And Mr. J. A. C. Boswell, writing of the south of India, says the Nágas are found everywhere represented as worshipping Buddha, and Buddha as supported by the serpent's folds or shaded by his protecting hood. There is no doubt there was continued war between the Hindus and the Takshaks, and an attempt to exterminate the latter is often referred to. See Tagá. It is also certain that intermarriages sometimes took place, and some of the Takshaks have been reckoned to be of the Agnikula. A noble of the Hindu blood of the Takshak race, says Mr. A. K. Forbes, was viceroy of Gujarát in 1390 A.D. There is still a Takká tribe near Ráwal Pindi, and a Nága tribe on the hills to the south of Assam.

Śeruvegár. [Kanarese, from *śeruve*, a company, and *gár*, agent.] The head of a company of workmen. Also the name of a subdivision of the Wokkaligas in Coorg.

Śeshnág. [From the Sanskrit *śesha*, remaining, and *nága*, q.v.] The name of the fabulous thousand-headed serpent which supports the world; said to be so called from his being the only thing remaining beyond the world. He is king of the nágas, and is sometimes represented as forming the couch and canopy of Vishnu. He is worshipped on the nágpanchmi.

Set. [Bengali.] The name of a semi-Hinduised tribe; they are labourers.

Śeṭh. [Hindi, from the Sanskrit *śreshṭha*, best, excellent.] A merchant, banker, or trader; the head of a caste. The term used to be applied in Gujaráti only to a Wániá merchant, but is now used of any Hindu or Pársi tradesman; and in Maráṭhi it is extended also to Kánsár and Sonár artisans. In Birbhum it is the name of a caste of traders.

Śeṭhiá. [Gujaráti.] A wealthy merchant or banker, a sáhukár or śeṭh.

Sethupati. [Tamil.] The title of the head of the Marawans, the hereditary ruler of Rámnád.

Seṭṭi. A Tamil form of Śeṭh.

Settlement. From time immemorial the Indian cultivator has been accustomed to pay a portion of the produce of his fields to the government of the time being; the determination of the amount to be paid and the method of payment is termed the settlement. A settlement may be for a year or a term of years, or, as it is in Bengal, permanent—a term of thirty years is common. Again, a settlement may be with zamindárs, as in Bengal and Oudh; or with villages, as in the Panjáb and North-West and Central Provinces; or with individual holders, as in Madras and the greater part of Bombay. A settlement for a term of years is based upon a survey of the land, a classification of the soils, and a grouping of the villages. See Village. The villages are grouped according to their advantages in respect of communication and market, and a maximum rate is fixed for each group. The individual fields are assessed according to the quality of the soils, a faultless field receiving the maximum rate, and reductions in class being allowed for every deficiency. This settlement for a term of years does not, under the ryotwar system, preclude the necessity of an annual settlement (see Jamábandi) with each ryot, as both his holding may vary in extent from year to year and there are fluctuating items of revenue (see Sáyer) besides the fixed land assessment. See Bhágbaṭái, Chauth, Classer, Vighoṭi, Water-rate.—The term 'settlement' is used also to denote the arrangement come to between government and hereditary servants whose services have become useless, and who have agreed to accept a portion only of the hereditary emolument on condition that the service be no longer rendered.

Settlement Officer. This term is not applied to the officer who makes the annual settlement called jamábandi, but is restricted to him who makes an original or a new settlement based upon a new survey and classification of soils.

Śeṭyá. [Maraṭhi, from *śeṭh.*] A superintendent of traffic in a commercial town. The office is hereditary, but śeṭyás have ceased to render formal service. See Settlement.

Sevai. See Śaiwa.

Seyyid. See Saïd.

Shabán. [Arabic.] The eighth month of the Musalmán year, following Rajab. See Month.

Shab-i-barát. [Persian.] The night of record, a festival held on the 14th Shabán, when the fates of unborn souls are supposed to be registered.

Shádi. [Hindustáni, from the Persian.] A marriage, a wedding; the festive celebration of a proper nikáh.

Sháfai. The third of the Sunni schools; that founded by Sháfai. It is the Arabian school, and to it belong those numerous classes in southern India which are descended from Arab settlers or from Hindus converted to islám by the Arabs. Out of India this school is described as less bigoted than the others. See Labbay, Máppilla, Navaita.

Shafite. An English form of Sháfai.

Shágirdpeshá. [Uriya, from the Persian *shágird*, a disciple, and *peshah*, practice.] The name of a caste; they are menial servants.

Sháh. [Persian.] A sovereign ruler. The title is also given to eminent pirs or saints, and Saïds often affix it to their names.

Sháhá. [Bengali.] A name assumed by some of the Suri caste who have renounced their hereditary occupation of distilling and have become landholders and traders. Some Telis also call themselves by this name.

Sháhid. [Arabic.] A witness, a martyr; the name of one of the Sikh misls.

Sháhprajá. [Bengali.] A cultivator holding direct from the zamindár, as distinguished from a kurfa or sub-tenant.

Shaikh. [Arabic.] An elder; the designation of those Musalmáns who profess to be descended from the first or second caliphs or from the prophet's uncle Abbas. They follow all callings and are found in every grade of life. Also another name for Shaikhdá.

Shaikhdá. [Gujaráti.] A class of devotees followers of Bála Muhammad Sháh, but chiefly Hindu in their customs.

Shaikh Saddo. [Hindustáni.] A spirit who is supposed to enter into women and possess them, and to whom some Musalmáns pay vows.

Shaitán. [Arabic, from *shatan*, to rebel.] The devil, Satan.

Shámiána. [Persian *shámyánah.*] A canopy; an awning stretched from top to top of poles; a tent with no peak or central pole.

Shán. The name of a large group of tribes consisting of many principalities subject, some to Burma, some to China, and some to Siam. In build, face, and dress, as well as in their mode of life and industrious habits, the Sháns resemble the Chinese more than they do the Burmese. They are so fair that their faces are sometimes ruddy and sunburnt. Their eyes are set more obliquely, and the mouth and jaw are broader. Their stature is rather taller, too, than that of the Burmese. Their dress is the Chinese short wide jacket and baggy trousers, blue or white, by which they are easily distinguished. Though more industrious, they are rather less warlike than the Burmese, and they have hence long been subjugated and governed as feudatories by the latter. The Sháns, while Buddhists in religion like the Burmese, are less learned and know less about the rules of their religion. Among the people generally there are fewer who can read and write. The alphabet they use is imperfect and reading is necessarily difficult. The language is called Tai (*R. H. Pilcher*).

Shanar. See Sánár.

Shánbhog. [Kanarese *śánabhoga.*] A village accountant; he is paid by a grant of land and portions of the crop. See Village accountant.

Shandu. More commonly Shendu.

Shara. [Arabic.] The law, the precepts of the koran.

Sharáb. [Hindustáni, from the Arabic *shariba*, to drink.] Spirituous liquor; whence the English sherbet.

Sharábdár. [Persian *dár*, holder.] A butler.

Sharb. [From the Arabic *shariba*, to drink.] In Muhammadan law, the offence of drinking wine. Also the right to water, or to use the draw-wells or channels of irrigation.

Sharif. [Arabic.] Noble, exalted, a person of rank. The office of caliph passed, after Ali, from the family of Muhammad, but as the power of the caliphs waned the authority of the lineal representative of the prophet grew, and on him was conferred by one of the Abbasides the principality of Mecca, whence the title, sharif of Mecca, which still survives.

Sharki. [Hindustáni, from the Arabic *sharq*, rising, eastern.] The name of a dynasty that ruled at Jaunpur in the North-West Provinces during the greater part of the fifteenth century; it was founded by a Muhammadan, previously wazir of Delhi, who made himself independent, and took the title of sultán-us-shark.

Shaster. See Śástra.

Shastree. See Śástri.

Shátakarni. Another name of the Andhra dynasty.

Shatáwari. [Maráṭhi.] The plant asparagus racemosus; the leaves are eaten by the poor, and are given to milch cows to increase their yield of milk.

Shattiram. See Chattiram.

Shawál. [Arabic.] The tenth month of the Musalmán year, the first day of which, following Ramazán the month of fasting, is held as a festival, the id-al-fitr. See Month.

Shebunder. [A corruption of the Persian *sháh-i-bandar.*] The ruler of the bandar or port; a port-captain.

Sheeah. See Shiah.

Sheesham. See Śisam.

Shekh. See Shaikh.

Shekháwat. The name of a branch of the Kachhwáhá Rájputs; they are descended from Shekhji, the grandson of a former ruler of Jáipur, and give their name to a province of that state.

Shendi. See Śenḍi.

Shendu. The name of a Toungthá tribe inhabiting the country north-east and east of the Blue Mountain; they are taller than the other Toungthás, and wear more clothes, and are specially distinguished for the manufacture of a cotton cloth, black, with brilliant red-and-yellow stripes. The men bind their hair in a very high knot over the forehead and the women theirs in smooth bands on each side of the face, fastening it in a knot at the back. Their houses are built entirely of wood, and are raised from the ground. They are acquainted with terrace cultivation, and use a large hoe to break up the land. Women seldom do field-work. The Shendus make salt from brine springs and manufacture their own gunpowder. They also work in iron. They are of predatory habits and make slaves of their captives; a slave is valued at two gayals or eight muskets. They do not use money. Their chief gods are Sarpár, Patyen, Khozing, and Wanchang. They believe in a future life of idle enjoyment. They bury their dead in graves lined with stone. The Lusháis call them Lakheyr Poy.

Shensoy. A corruption of *śehenśáh*, itself an error for Śehersai.

Shenvi. See Śenvi.

Sheoráni. An independent Paṭhán tribe settled about the Takht-i-Suláimán mountain. They are Sunni Muhammadans, and by occupation graziers and cultivators. They can muster about 5000 fighting men. By descent they belong to the Bani Israil, or Afgháns proper.

Sher. See Ser.

Shera. See Śerá.

Sherbet. [Properly *sharbát*, from the Arabic *shariba*, to drink.] A drink made from the juice of fruit with water and sugar.

Sherebucha. [Corrupt form.] Literally, a lion-whelp; a name of the Afghán blunderbuss.

Sheristedar. See Sarishtadár.

Sherrif. See Sharif.

Sherugár. [Kanarese.] The name of an agricultural caste.

Shet. See Śeṭh.

Shetkari. [Maráṭhi *śet*, from the Sanskrit *kshetra*, a field, and the affix *kari*, q.v.] The owner of a field, a cultivator.

Shetsandi. [Maráṭhi, from *śet*, a field, and *sanad*, q.v.] One holding a grant of lands for military service; applied especially to a local militia acting also as police and as garrisons of forts. Shetsandis are now village police in the Deccan.

Shettia. See Śeṭyá.

Shiah. [Arabic.] A follower, meaning a follower of Ali, the son-in-law of Muhammad; the name of the second great division of the Muhammadans. The prime cause of separation was Ali's refusal to subscribe to the condition that, if elected to succeed Muhammad, he would govern according to the traditions (sunnah) of Arab society. His was the catholic as opposed to the national cause. The Shiahs do not acknowledge the prophet's actual successors, the caliphs Abubakr, Omar, and Usmán, but hold that Ali was the rightful head of islám from the date of Muhammad's death. Beginning with Ali, they recognize a succession of twelve imáms. They do not reject the sunnah wholly, but only those parts of it supposed not to have the approval of Ali. On the death of the sixth imám the majority of the Shiahs acknowledged his second son as imám, but a minority, following the eldest son's son Ismail, seceded and formed the Ismaili sect. These again, on a dispute as to succession between two brothers, Nazár and Mustáli, at the close of the eleventh century, divided into two branches—the Nazarian, represented in India by the Khojahs; and the Mustálian, represented in India by the Vorás.

Shiang. [Arakanese.] A religious ceremony or penance.

Shiangphrá. [Arakanese.] A Khyoungthá priest; they shave the head and wear saffron-coloured robes.

Shiangprahpo. [Arakanese.] A religious ceremony among the Khyoungthás, by which a boy or man assumes for a time the dress and manner of life of a priest.

Shiaposh. [Pashṭo, from *shia*, black, and *posh*, dress.] The name of a division of the Káfir tribe, so called from the black goat-skins which they wear.

Shigram. A carriage; in the city of Bombay, a carriage like the pálkigári of the north; in the country, a heavy carriage with a large removable roof and drawn either by a horse or a pair of bullocks.

Shiite. An English form of Shiah.

Shikár. [Persian.] Hunting; also game.

Shikári. A hunter, one engaged in, or whose profession is, the pursuit of game. In Bengal, the name also of a low caste.

Shikast. [Persian.] Broken; a broken or running handwriting.

Shikdár. [Hindustáni, from the Arabic *shaqq*, a division.] An officer appointed to collect the revenue of an estate or tract of country.

Shilwant. [Kanarese.] The name of a caste; they are traders and cultivators.

Shinda. See Śiṇḍá.

Shinwári. The name of a Paṭhán tribe living about the western end of the Khyber pass, and subsidized by the amir of Kábul; they number about 7000 fighting men. They engage in the carrying trade, and have a superior breed of mules and donkeys.

Shirpecha. See Sarpech.

Shishegar. [Hindustáni, from the Persian *shisha*, glass.] A class of Sunni Musalmáns; they are glass-makers, making bottles, rings, etc. They are a separate community with a headman called mukhi, and marry only among themselves.

Shivala. See Śiwálaya.

Shoḍá. The name of a branch of the Parmár Rájputs who formerly ruled a part of Sindh, and who are still found at Umerkot, but in poor condition, engaged chiefly as herdsmen.

Shri. See Śri.

Shroff. [Hindustáni *saráf*, from the Arabic *sarf*, expenditure, exchange.] A banker, a money-changer. Also, and more commonly, an expert employed in banks and treasuries to examine money.

Shroffage. The business of examining coins to detect the base ones.

Shuddh. See Śudh.

Shumee. See Śami.

Sial. [Uriya.] The name of a low caste; they are wine-sellers. Also the name of a class of Muhammadan Rájputs who ruled for centuries at Jhang till subdued by Ranjit Singh.

Śibáḍ. [Maráṭhi.] A large vessel of from one hundred to three hundred tons. Compare Mhángiri.

Sibandi. [Persian.] Irregular soldiery; a sort of militia or imperfectly disciplined troops maintained for the garrisons of forts and guards in towns and villages, and for the collection of revenue. See Mulkgiri.

Sicca. [Hindustáni *sikka*.] A seal, a stamp, a coining-die. Applied as an adjective especially to the silver currency of the Mogul emperors, whose sicca rupee was the general standard of value until superseded by the company's rupee. The sicca rupee as last coined weighed 192 grains, of which 176 were pure silver; its exchange value was about *2s. 2d.*

Siddha. [Sanskrit, from *sidh*, to be accomplished, fulfilled.] A semi-divine being of great purity and holiness; an inspired sage or seer, or a great saint. Also a magician, a necromancer.

Siddhártha. [Sanskrit, from *siddha*, accomplished, fulfilled, and *artha*, an object.] One who has accomplished his object; the name of the Buddha.

Siddhi. [Sanskrit.] Accomplishment, perfection; especially the acquisition of supernatural powers, of which eight are enumerated, such as the power of assuming a minute form, of transporting one's self from place to place at will, and so on.

Siḍi. [Telugu.] The swinging instrument or ceremony. See Charak.

Sidi. [Said to mean 'master.'] The name given in western India to settlers from Africa and their descendants. Some of them rose to high office in the Musalmán states in the Deccan, and they furnished the Mogul empire with the chief naval officers on the western coast.

They are still the ruling family in the small states of Janjira and Sachin. Elsewhere their condition is poor. They are all Sunnis, but their chief object of worship is Bábá Ghor, an Abyssinian saint and a great merchant, whose tomb is near Ratanpur, in Rájpipla.

Sihaśái. [Gujaráti.] A coinage of Baroda: 111 sihaśái rupees are equal in value to 100 government rupees.

Sijdah. [Arabic.] Adoration, prostration, an attitude in prayer. Several particular attitudes are prescribed.

Sijdahgáh. [Arabic *gáh*, a place.] A place for praying.

Śikalgár. [Maráṭhi.] One whose employment is the polishing or furbishing of weapons and tools.

Sikh. [Panjábi, from the Sanskrit *śikshaka*, a learner, a disciple, from *śiksh*, to learn.] The name of a religious sect founded in the Panjáb at the end of the fifteenth century by Nának Sháh, a Hindu reformer, of the Khatri caste. For the first two centuries of their existence they obeyed a succession of ten spiritual leaders called gurus. Nának Sháh, the founder and first guru, was a religious teacher only, and had in view to unite both Hindus and Musalmáns in his new faith (see Sikhism); but Har Govind, the sixth guru, was a military leader also, and served for a time with his followers under the Mogul government of Delhi. The ninth guru was put to death as a rebel by Aurangzeb, and there was never again peace between the Sikhs and the Moguls. Govind Singh, the tenth and last guru, made every man a soldier, calling them not Sikhs or disciples, but Singhs or lions, and giving the whole body, which was now a distinct political unity, the name of Khálsá. The succession of gurus closed with the death of Govind in 1708, and for the next hundred years misls or divisions of the khálsá or commonwealth managed their own affairs under their own sardárs. During the earlier part of this period (the eighteenth century) they suffered the severest persecution at the hands of the Mogul government, but on the downfall of that empire they became a territorial power, and early in the present century were formed into a kingdom by Ranjit Singh. They came into collision with the British power in 1845, and again in 1848, after which the Panjáb was annexed to British India. The bulk of the Sikhs were originally of the Ját race.

Śikhar. [Hindi.] A point, a peak; the narrow-peaked dome, or bell-shaped spire, that covers the adytum of a Hindu temple.

Sikhism. The religion of the Sikhs. The founder of this religion, himself a Hindu, was acquainted also with Muhammadan theology, and did not place himself in antagonism with either of the prevailing creeds, but, referring to all gods and prophets as having had their day and as having eventually failed, he urged all men to recognize the unity and spirituality of one supreme being, to be pure in mind and of good conduct. He had practised asceticism, but did not advocate it, extolling rather the virtues of the householder. He did not seek to make his followers a separate caste, and discountenanced rather than preached against the system of caste: 'God will not ask man of his birth; he will ask him what he has done' (*Ádi Granth*). He did not forbid the worship of idols and pilgrimages, but taught that these things in themselves were vain. The Sikhs believe the spirit of Nának to have been transmitted to the nine succeeding gurus. The teaching of the last was, however, very different; he suppressed the use of idols, and allowed men to bow to nothing visible but the granth; he did not permit his twice-born followers to wear the janeo, but said he would make the four races of one colour, and preached war against all religions but that of the khálsá.

Sikilkáran. [Tamil.] The name of a caste; they are wandering knife-grinders.

Sikilugár. [Kanarese.] The name of a subdivision of the Pánchála; they are cleaners and burnishers of swords and other weapons.

Sikra. See Śikhar.

Siláhára. The name of a dynasty, probably Dravidian, that ruled in the northern Konkan from about 810 to 1260 A.D.

Silahdár. [From the Arabic *silah*, arms, and Persian *dár*, who has.] One who wears arms; but particularly a horse-soldier who provides his own horse and arms, as distinguished from a bárgir.

Silahkhánah. [Hindustáni *khánah*, a house.] An arsenal, an armoury.

Śiláśásana. [Sanskrit *śilá*, a stone.] A śásana or grant inscribed on stone.

Śiledár. The Maráṭhi form of Silahdár.

Śilpi. [Sanskrit, from *śilpa*, art.] An artificer. In Mysore the name is applied more particularly to the Kallukuṭikas, which suggests another derivation from *śilá*, stone.

Simal. [Hindi, Sanskrit *śalmali.*] The silk-cotton tree, bombax heptaphyllum.

Śimgá. A Maráṭhi name for the month Phálgun and for the Holi festival.

Simperty. See Śamprati.

Śimpi. [Maráṭhi.] The name of a caste; they are tailors, and some are dyers and dealers in dying colours, also sellers of cloth, and they engage in other trades.

Simrut. See Smriti.

Simurgh. [Hindustáni.] A fabulous bird.

Śindá. [Maráṭhi.] The name of a tribe in the Konkan, said to be sprung from female slaves; they are cultivators, and generally resemble the Kunbis.

Sindhi. The language of Sindh. There are three dialects of it: the *Lári* of lower Sindh; the *Siraiki*, which is spoken to the north of Hyderabad; and the *Thareli*, the language of the desert. The Sindhi is a pure Sanskritical language, more free from foreign elements than any other of the north Indian vernaculars. It is beset with more intricacies and difficulties than any of its Prákrit sisters (*Trumpp*). Also an inhabitant of Sindh; and especially a particular division who are the descendants of the original Hindu population of the province, and were converted to islám during the rule of the Ummayide dynasty of khalifs; they are taller and more robust than the natives of India; they are quiet and inoffensive, but excessively indolent; they are Sunnis by religion, but some traces of the caste system remain among them (*Hughes*).

Sindhiá. The family name of one of the four Maráthá leaders who rose to independent power; thence the popular title of the ruler for the time being of the Gwalior state. Gwalior has an area of 33,119 square miles and a population of 2,500,000.

Sinduriyár. [Bengali, from *sindur*, red lead.] The name of a caste; they deal in red lead and grain.

Singh. [Hindi, from the Sanskrit *sinha*.] A lion; a usual adjunct to Rájput names; also to Sikh names, since Govind, the tenth guru, assumed it himself and gave it to all his followers, to signify that thenceforth all should be soldiers.

Singhárá. [Hindi.] The water-chestnut, trapa bispinosa; it is used as food in northern India and the Central Provinces.

Singhpuria. Another name of the Faizullapuria misl of the Sikhs.

Singpho. Another name of the Kachin tribe.

Sinhalese. The name of the people of the inner and southern parts of Ceylon; and of their language, which is of the Aryan family, but peculiar to the island. The Sinhalese are Buddhists and their sacred books are written in Páli.

Sipahsálár. [Persian *sipah*, an army, *sálár*, ruler.] A commander-in-chief. Compare Senápati.

Sir. [Hindi, from the Sanskrit *sira*, a plough.] A name applied to the lands in a village which are cultivated by the hereditary proprietors or village zamindárs themselves as their own especial share, either by their own labourers and at their own cost, or by tenants-at-will, not being let in lease or farm. The term is also sometimes applied to lands cultivated on account of the state, or to those in which the revenue is paid by the cultivators without any intermediate agent (*H. H. Wilson*). In Gujaráti the term 'sir,' or sometimes 'sir padtar,' is applied to land which has been assessed but is not held by any person.

Siraiki. See under Sindhi.

Sircar. See Sarkár.

Sirdar. See Sardár.

Siris. [Hindi.] The acacia elata, a tree used for shade.

Sir Punch. See Sarpanch.

Śisam. [Hindi.] The tree dalbergia latifolia. See Blackwood.

Śiśira. [Sanskrit, literally, cool.] The season of the two solar months Magaram and Kambam (in Bengal, Mágh and Phálgun) during which the sun is in Capricorn and Aquarius; where the luni-solar year is followed this season is defined as Paush and Mágh, or as Mágh and Phálgun. See Month, Ritu, Year.

Sisodia. A name assumed by the family of the rulers of Udáipur at the beginning of the thirteenth century, when an elder branch of the family, till then called Aharya, retired from Chitor and founded Dungarpur. The Sisodia is thus properly a branch of the Aharya, itself a branch of the Gahlot, but being the most prominent of all the Gahlots, the name is sometimes used to denote the whole tribe. See Suryawanśa.

Śitalá. [Sanskrit.] Literally, cool; the name of the goddess of small-pox. In Hindi she is also called Thandi, which also means cool; and the offerings made to her are of cold water and cold food. In Gujaráti she is called also Baliyá, and is regarded as the wife of a god Kákábaliyá or Saiyaḍ. Her festival is the 7th of Śráwan śudh, on which day she is supposed to wander about the cooking-stoves, and therefore no fire may be lighted.

Sitalpati. [Bengali.] A mat made from the split stems of the maranta dichotoma.

Śitalśimgá. [Maráṭhi, from the Sanskrit *śitala*, cold, and *simgá*, q.v.] The day after the full moon of Phálgun, on which day cold water is thrown on the burning embers of the Holi fires.

Sitana Wahábi. The name of a sect of Hindustáni fanatics settled among the Yusufzai clans.

Sitápadre. A term used by the natives of Gujarát to designate a Portuguese or an English priest; it is supposed that the Virgin Mary has been mistaken for Sitá.

Siula. The name of a low caste in Orissa; they are fishermen.

Siva. See Śiwa.

Sivism. See Śiwaism.

Sivite. An English form for Śaiwa.

Śiwa. [Sanskrit.] The third person of the Hindu triad—the destroyer. See Trimurti. Indra, Wáyu, the Maruts and Rudras of the vedas, appear to have been all forms and modifications of each other, and, with different names in the later mythology, to have been gathered into the one personification Śiwa. He has several distinct characters. In the first place, as Rudra or Mahákála he is the destroying and dissolving power of nature, when he is either a personification of all matter resolving itself into its constituent elements, or of *kála*, time, the great dissolver. His śakti or consort in this character is Káli. Secondly as Śiwa, Sadáśiwa, Śankar, or Śambhu, he is the eternally blessed one or the causer of blessings, the eternal reproductive power of nature, under which mysterious character he is often identified with the eternal creative essence, and even with the great impersonal eternal spirit as Mahádewa or Iśwara. In this character he is rather represented by a symbol—the linga with the yoni as śakti — than by any human personification; or when conceived of more as a person, his śakti becomes Jaganmátri, the mother of the world. Thirdly, he is Maháyogi and his śakti a yogini. In this character he teaches men by his own example the power to be acquired by mortification of the body, suppression of the passions, and abstract contemplation. This character was, perhaps, devised to meet the Buddhist movement and incorporate it in Brahmanism — just as the Vaishnawas made the Buddha an incarnation of Vishnu. Two other characters have been given to Śiwa apparently to satisfy the religious instincts of the aboriginal tribes. The first of these, Bhairawa, the terrible destroyer, or Bhuteśwara, the lord of demons, is a popular adaptation of the first conception of the destroyer. In this character the śakti, though now malignant, is still called Káli, or otherwise Bhairavi or Durgá. Fifthly, Śiwa is a wild, jovial god, living in the Himálaya mountains with his wife Párwati. Śiwa is usually represented with three eyes, perhaps referring to time, present, past, and future; and with a crescent moon on his forehead, which may refer to the measurement of time. His neck is blue from the stain of the poison he drank at the churning of the ocean. See Amrita. The Ganges flows from his hair. As Bhairawa he wears a necklace of skulls and garlands of serpents. His wáhan or vehicle is the bull (*Monier Williams*).

Siwai. A title of the mahárájá of Jáipur, and conferred also as a high distinction upon other rulers.

Śiwaism. That side of Hinduism which makes Śiwa the principal god. See Śaiwa, Vishnuvism.

Śiwálaya. [Sanskrit, from *śiwa*, q.v., and *álaya*, an abode.] A temple or shrine of Śiwa; especially a small shrine containing only the linga.

Śiwan. [Hindi.] A large and beautiful tree of the teak family, the gmelina arborea. It sheds its leaves in March and April, but becomes again covered with leaf in May; the wood is used for carriage panels.

Śiwarátri. [Sanskrit *rátri*, night.] The night of Śiwa, that is, the fourteenth of the krishnapaksh or dark fortnight of every month. The śiwarátri in Mágh is distinguished as the mahásiwarátri, or great śiwarátri; the previous day is a fast, and Śiwa is worshipped the whole night.

Siyam Samágama. [Sinhalese, from *siyam*, Siam, and Sanskrit *samágama*, society.] The name of a sect of Buddhists introduced from Siam into Ceylon in the middle of the eighteenth century.

Siyáná. [Panjábi.] An elder, a village wise man or exorcist.

Slave-king. The name of the first of the Ghori dynasties, so called from the fact of the first ruler, Kutab-ud-din, having been originally a slave. The slave-kings reigned at Delhi from 1206 to 1290 A.D.

Śloka. [Sanskrit.] The name of the Sanskrit common epic metre, or a verse written in that metre. A śloka consists of two lines of sixteen syllables. The first four syllables may be either long or short, the fifth is short, the sixth and seventh either both long or both short, and the eighth either long or short; the next four again are either long or short, the thirteenth short, the fourteenth long, the fifteenth short, and the last either long or short. The second line is similar.

Smárta. [Sanskrit, an adjective formed from *smriti*, q.v.] Based on smriti, relating to memory; thence post-vedic. The name of a numerous and influential sect of Bráhmans founded by Śankarácharya, whose expositions of the principle of unity, according to the vedánta doctrine, they professedly follow; Śiwa is nevertheless held by them in especial honour; they are distinguished by horizontal lines on the forehead made with the ashes of burnt cow-dung, and are treated with great veneration by the people in general.

Smriti. [Sanskrit, from *smri*, to remember.] That which is remembered, tradition. Under this term are included all the sacred Sanskrit writings which, though not directly revealed (sruti), have been founded on revelation and delivered by human authors. In its widest acceptation, smriti may be said to denote almost the whole of post-vedic literature (*Monier Williams*).

Snake-bird. A species of diver, the plotus melanogaster, which swims with its body under the water, only its long snake-like neck appearing above. The Hindi name is *banwá*.

Snake-gourd. The plant trichosanthes anguiana; the fruit is used as a vegetable.

Snake-stone. This name is given to small pieces of calcined bone, black, highly polished, and almond-shaped, which Gáruḍis provide. They have the property of absorbing liquid, and if applied to a wound will adhere and draw out the blood until saturation prevents further absorption. Besides the ordinary black snake-stones, Gáruḍis occasionally offer for sale as charms small transparent amber-coloured beads which they profess to have extracted from the palates of very old cobras. It is not known what these beads really are.

Soapstone. A species of steatite found in the Jáipur state; it is soft enough to be easily cut, but is tough and hardens by exposure; it is used for carving small models of buildings, making boxes, trays, or other ornaments. The colour is a warm grey.

Sodha. See Shoḍá.

Sodhi. The name of the subdivision of the Khatri caste to which belonged Rám Dás, the fourth guru of the Sikhs, in whose family succession to the office of guru became hereditary. See Bhulle.

Sohágá. [Hindi.] An implement for crushing clods in a field.

Sohágiá. See Sauhágiá.

Sohagin. See Sauhágin.

Sohalá. [Maráṭhi, perhaps from the Sanskrit *sobhá*, beauty.] A festive ceremony, a festive occasion.

Sok. [Gujaráti, said to be from the Sanskrit *sapatni*, from *sa*, with, and *patni*, a wife.] A woman who has the same husband with another woman; a fellow-wife. See Saut.

Solá. [Hindi.] A marsh plant, the æschynomene paludosa, or aspera, of which the pith is used for making sun-hats, thence called solá-ṭopis.

Solanki. Another name of the Chálukya tribe. Under this name they reigned at Anhilpur, in Gujarát, from 942 A.D. to 1215, and a branch of the same tribe, the Baghela or Wághela, continued in power there till 1299 A.D.

Solar race. See Suryawanśa.

Soliga. [Kanarese.] The name of a tribe almost entirely confined to the Biligirirangan hills on the south-east frontier of Mysore. They live in small communities of six or seven huts in the dense parts of the forests, and cultivate with the hoe small patches of ground, where they grow a coarse kind of plantain, vegetables, and a little rági; on these, together with edible roots and the flesh of any animal they may capture, they subsist. They avoid strangers as much as possible, and seldom visit the low country unless when they have occasion to procure supplies, when one of their number is sent to purchase what is required for the whole community (*L. Rice*).

Soma. [Sanskrit.] The moon-plant, asclepias acida, which is deified in the veda, and for the worship of which the arrangement of the veda known as the sáma-veda seems to have been made. The juice of the plant was regarded as a kind of amrita, conferring eternal life and vigour both on gods and men, and is represented as primeval and all-pervading, and finally identified with the supreme being himself. In later times Soma is the moon, the monarch of planets, plants, sacrifices, and penances. See Chándráyana.

Somaj. See Samáj.

Sonagar. The Kanarese form of Sonár.

Sonár. [Hindí, from the Sanskrit *suwarna*, gold, and *kára*, worker.] The name of a Śudra caste; they are goldsmiths. Sonárs are usually respected as Śudras of the middle rank, but in some places, as Behar, they are esteemed as pure Śudras; but the Sonárs of the Deccan deny their Śudra origin altogether, dispute the superiority of Bráhmans, and employed priests of their own caste. See Panchál.

Sondia. The name of a tribe numerous in Jhaláwár; they are of fair complexion and use Rájput clan names, and are reputed to have come from central and southern India; they were formerly freebooters, but are now settled to agriculture; they employ Bráhmans for wedding ceremonies.

Soni. The Gujaráti form of Sonár. Some in Cutch and northern Gujarát have adopted islám; they are Sunnis.

Son Koli. [Maráṭhi.] The division of the Koli tribe found on the coast from Surat downwards. Their chief employment is fishing, and they possess great numbers of boats. They put down great rows of stakes, in some places extending as much as twelve miles out to sea, to which are fastened bag-nets of great size and strength. The Kolis themselves generally grow the hemp, extract the fibre, prepare the string, and make the nets. They also build their own boats and dry the fish.

Sonnite. An English formation for Sunni, like Shiite for Shiah.

Sonthal. See Santál.

Sookree. See Sukhḍi.

Soonee. See Sunni.

Soor. See Sura.

Soor. [Hindustáni *suar.*] A pig; a vulgar term of abuse.

Soortee. See Surati.

Sorangi. [Gujaráti.] The name of a plant, the morinda citrifolia, from which is extracted the dye with which sádhus colour their clothes.

Sord. The name of a tribe allied to or resembling the Kolis; they were once a ruling race at Idar.

Sotá. [Hindi.] A channel, a watercourse.

Soṭábardár. [Hindustáni, from *soṭá*, a mace, and the Persian *bardár*, a bearer.] A mace-bearer.

Soubah. See Subah.

Soucar. See Sáhukár.

Soura. See Saura.

Sowar. See Sawár.

Spashṭha Dáyaka. The name of a sect, a branch of the Chaitanyas; they assert the spiritual independence of women, and some of their monks are women.

Spin. The name of one of the two divisions of Káfirs.

Spin Turin. The name of an agricultural tribe settled between Pishin and the Suláimán range.

Spotted deer. See Chital.

Śrában. A Bengali form of Śráwan.

Śráddha. [Sanskrit.] The ceremony of making an oblation to deceased ancestors, usually accompanied by much feasting of Bráhmans. Śráddhas are of many kinds, some general in respect of the sacrificer's deceased ancestors collectively, and some in respect of a particular person lately dead. Śráddhas are auspicious and not mournful occasions. The first śráddha in respect of a deceased person is performed the day after the ten days of mourning are over. It is usual to repeat it once a month for the first year and after that once a year. See Piṇḍa, Pitri.

Srauta. The adjective formed from *sruti*, and equivalent therefore in extent to vedic.

Sráwak. [Sanskrit, literally, a hearer.] A layman of the Jain religion. Also a Buddhist saint.

Śráwan. [Sanskrit.] The month most nearly corresponding with August; it is so called from *śrawaná*, the name of the nakshatra (three stars in Aquila representing three footsteps of Vishnu) in which the moon is at full in this month. See Month.

Śri. [Sanskrit.] Prosperity or the goddess of prosperity, Lakshmi, wife of Vishnu. The word is used also as a prefix of reverence to the names of deities, holy places, sacred books, spiritual teachers, etc. It is also written at the commencement of books, letters, and writings generally, elliptically for Śri Ganeśa (*J. T. Molesworth*).

Śrimáli. The name of a Bráhman caste in Gujarát; some follow the yajur and some the sáma veda.

Śri-Sampradáyá or **Śri-Vaishnawa.** Other names for the Rámánuja sect.

Śrotriya. [Sanskrit, from *śrotra*, conversancy with the veda, from *śru*, to hear.] One who is well read in the veda; the name of the second class of Gauḍa (subdivision) Bráhmans according to the classification made in the eleventh century.

Śruti. [Sanskrit, from *śru*, to hear.] That which has been heard, revelation. The Hindu sacred writings are divided into śruti and smriti, the first head comprising that which has been directly revealed, namely, the veda, and the second the post-vedic laws, founded indeed on the śruti, but delivered by human authors.

S.S. An abbreviation of Śaka Sáliwáhana.

Stambha. [Sanskrit.] A post, a pillar, a column, a láṭ; especially a pillar in a temple bearing an emblem or statue, or used as a dipdán. In some of the Jain temples in the south of India are seen elaborately carved monolith stambhas thirty or forty feet high.

State railway. A railway constructed by the state from its own resources. They are mostly made on the narrow or metre gauge, and are later in date than the broad-gauge trunk lines, which are of the kind known as guaranteed railways. The state lines are in some cases worked directly by *employés* of the state, and in others the working is entrusted to the company to whose line the state railway leads.

Sthamba. An error for Stambha.

Stháwara. [Sanskrit, from *sthá*, to stand firm.] Standing still, immovable; the opposite of jangama. Also the title of the chief devotee of the Jains.

Sthupa. An error for Stupa.

Stridhan. [Sanskrit, from *stri*, woman, and *dhana*, property.] The separate property of a wife: 'What was given before the nuptial fire, what was given at the bridal procession, what was given in token of love, and what was received from a mother, a brother, or a father, are considered as the sixfold separate property of a married woman' (*Manu*, ix. 194).

Stupa. [Sanskrit, from *stup*, to pile up.] A pile of earth, a mound; a monument erected over sacred relics of the Buddha, or on spots consecrated as the scenes of his acts.

Subah. [Arabic.] A province, a government; used also for subahdár. Akbar's empire was divided into fifteen subahs — twelve in Hindustán and three in the Deccan.

Subahdár. [Persian *dár*, who holds.] The governor of a province or district; a viceroy. Subahdár is also the name of an officer in the native army. The subahdár major used to be the native officer of highest rank in an infantry regiment; then came in order the subahdár, the jamádár, the hawáldár, and the náïk. For the corresponding officers of cavalry, see under Risáldár. Under the new organization each of the eight companies of an infantry regiment has one subahdár, one jamádár, five hawáldárs, and five náïks. See Subhedár.

Subarnabanik. [Bengali, from the Sanskrit *suwarna*, gold, and *banij*, a merchant.] The name of a caste; they are dealers in gold and silver and precious stones.

Sub-Deputy-Collector. A name used in some provinces to designate the officer elsewhere called mámlatdár, mukhtyárkár, or tahsildár.

Subedár. The Gujaráti form of Subahdár.

Subhadrá. [Sanskrit, from *su*, very, and *bhadra*, propitious.] The name of one of the idols in the temple of Jagannáth at Puri. Subhadrá was the sister of Krishna and wife of Arjun. See Mahábhárata.

Subhedár. The Maráṭhi form of Subahdár. Officers under this title were appointed by the Maráṭhá government in place of the deśmukhs, deśpáṇḍes, and sardeśáis of the previous Muhammadan government in Gujarát. It is still the title of the chief administrative officer of a district in the Baroda state.

Sud. [Bengali.] The name of a Śudra caste; they are cultivators, and reckoned of intermediate rank.

Sudder Court. See Sadr Adálat.

Śudh. [Hindi, from the Sanskrit *suddha*, pure, bright.] A term used after the name of a month to denote that the śuklapaksh, or bright half of the month, is meant; as 12 Mágh śudh, the 12th day of Mágh; 12 Mágh wadi would mean the twelfth of the second half or the 27th of the month. See Tithi.

Śudra. [Sanskrit, from *śuch*, to be afflicted.] The name of the last of the four classes into which, according to the arbitrary dictum of Manu, Hindus were originally divided. The Śudra is described as the feet of the creator, and his office was to serve the three others, the twice-born classes. Probably the first Śudras were really those of the aboriginals who lived in the plains, and were subdued by the Aryans, and incorporated into the Hindu system, while their brethren of the hills remained unconquered, and are still spoken of as aboriginals. Śudras were kept in a very abject condition in the time of Manu, but many of them have since risen to a position of respect in Hindu society. About a dozen Śudra castes, such as the Sadgops, the Mális, the Kánsáris, and the Kumárs—but the classification varies in different provinces—are considered to be pure Śudras, and rank highest among them; the Goálás, the Kaibarttas, and Sutárs represent an intermediate rank containing about two dozen castes; then come the low Śudra castes, as the Chámárs, the Dhobis, the Kahárs, not always distinguishable from aboriginal races which have become Hinduised. The name Śudra is also applied to a particular caste of Śudras in Bengal and Orissa; they are deemed pure, and are cultivators, boatmen, and domestic servants.

Sufi. [Arabic.] Wise; the name of a sect who outwardly conform to islám, but have adopted a mystical pantheism resembling the vedánta philosophy.

Suhi. The red colour produced from safflower, and worn by Hindu mendicants.

Suji. [Hindustáni.] The granulated portion of flour ground from the heart of the wheat; the Italian simola.

Sukáli. [Kanarese.] The name of a wandering tribe who, like the Yerukalas, are carriers of salt and grain. They speak a dialect of Maráṭhi and have some Hindu marriage ceremonies. They wear remarkably heavy clothes.

Sukarchakia. [Panjábi.] The name of a Sikh misl, that to which belonged Ranjit Singh, who reduced all the misls except the Phulkia under his sway as mahárájá. The Sukarchakias lived south of the Bhangis between the Chenáb and Rávi rivers.

Sukhḍi. [Gujaráti.] A kind of sweetmeat; the fee or perquisite which an agent or clerk expects from any seller when he pays a bill; the remuneration derived from villages by deśáis, majmudárs, or amin paṭels.

Śukladi. The mode of reckoning a month by beginning with the day following the conjunction of the sun and moon, so that the full moon falls on the fifteenth day of the month and the amáwasi on the thirtieth. See Krishnadi, Month, Tithi.

Śuklapaksh. [Sanskrit *śukla*, light, and *paksha*, a side.] The bright half of the month, the fortnight from the new to the full moon, in which period the early evening has the moonlight. Parties to a quarrel sometimes call themselves the śuklapaksh and their opponents the krishnapaksh.

Sukli. [Bengali.] The name of a low caste; they are cultivators and weavers.

Śukreśwar. [Hindi, from the Sanskrit *śukra*, the planet Venus, and *iśwara*, q.v.] The name of a god who is propitiated in the hope of obtaining well-favoured sons.

Śula. [Sanskrit.] A pike, a spear; also a stake for impaling criminals.

Sulátu'l maghrib. [Arabic *maghrib*, the west.] The prayer at sunset. This, the fourth prayer of the Musalmán day, is appointed to be said a few minutes after sunset. It is a tradition that the object of Muhammad in fixing the time was to avoid any suspicion of his followers holding the Sabian tenets and worshipping the sun, as also to remove from them all temptation to orientation, or sun-worship (*T. C. Plowden*).

Sulimáni. The name of a small division of the city Vorás who seceded from the general body in the sixteenth century, accepting as their high priest one Sulimán, sent from Yaman by some Vorás who had been previously converted to that faith by a missionary from Surat.

Sultán. [Arabic.] A sovereign, an emperor; first known in India as the title of Mahmud of Ghazni.

Sumrá. The name of a dynasty that ruled in Sindh from the eleventh century till 1351 A.D.; it was founded by Ibn Sumár, a governor of Multán under the ruler of Ghazni. Tatta was made the Sumrá capital. Descendants of the Sumrás are now settled in Cutch; they are soldiers, sailors, grass and wood cutters, and cultivators. They are Sunni Musalmáns.

Suna. [Bengali.] Land other than sali.

Sunar. See Sonár.

Sunderbunds. [A corruption of *sundariwana*, from *sundari*, the tree heritiera minor, and *wana*, a forest.] The name of a densely wooded tract forming the delta of the Ganges, and 6500 square miles in extent.

Sundullee. [Pashṭo, corrupt form.] A low four-legged stool or small table, eighteen inches high, under which is placed a pan of red-hot charcoal, with a thickly wadded cotton quilt of large size thrown over the whole; people sit round the sundullee and draw the quilt up, by which means no heat can escape before it comes in contact with the limbs (*T. Seaton*).

Sunga. The name of a Buddhist

dynasty held to have reigned from 188 to 76 B.C.

Sunguicar. A class of pirates formerly on the Konkan coast and so named from their station, Sangameśwar.

Sungum. See Sangama.

Suni. See Sunni.

Sunite. An English formation for Sunni.

Sunnah. [Arabic.] Traditional law, the name of a compilation of the sayings and practices of Muhammad, made about a hundred years after his death, to supplement the koran when that was found insufficient to regulate the affairs of the then greatly extended empire. The sunnah is invested with the force of law and some of the authority of inspiration. Changes were afterwards made in the collection, and the Sunnis have now six and the Shiahs four editions of it.

Sunni. [Arabic.] A follower of the sunnah; the name of the first great division of the Muhammadans. They hold that the sunnah, as left by their four imáms, is unalterable. There are four orthodox schools of Sunnis: (1) Hanefi, chiefly in Turkey and northern India; (2) Máliki, chiefly in Africa; (3) Sháfai, in Arabia and southern India; and (4) Hambali, in Arabia. Compare Shiah.

Sunnud. See Sanad.

Sunri. [Bengali.] The name of a caste, called also Kalál or Kalwár; they are by hereditary occupation distillers of spirits, and are usually deemed a low caste, but some have taken to trade or agriculture and rank higher; some of these have changed their caste name to Sháhá.

Śunyawádi. [Sanskrit, from *śunya*, naught, and *wáda*, assertion.] One who affirms that nothing exists; the name of a sect.

Supári. [Hindi.] The kernel of the fruit of the areca palm. See Pán.

Supreme Court. This term is sometimes used as a translation of Sadr Adálat, but it is more particularly applied to the courts established in the time of Warren Hastings to exercise jurisdiction only—except in the case of English-born subjects—in the presidency towns.

Supreme Government. This term, as used in India, denotes what is also called the 'government of India,' both names being in contradistinction to the local or provincial governments. The supreme government is composed of the governor-general and a council consisting of six ordinary members, with, usually, the commander-in-chief in India as an extraordinary member, and, when the council meet in the territory of Madras or Bombay, with the governor of the presidency also as an extraordinary member.

Sura. [Sanskrit, formed as an opposite to *asura*, as if the initial *a* were the *a* negative.] A deity, a god.

Surá. [Sanskrit, from *su*, to pour out or extract juice.] Wine or spirituous liquor, personified as a nymph produced at the churning of the ocean. See Amrita.

Surah. [Arabic.] A chapter of the koran, of which there are 114, each divided into verses.

Suráhi. [Persian.] A long-necked

bottle of metal or earthenware for holding water.

Surajbansi. A vernacular form of Suryawanśa.

Suranji. See under Ál.

Surati. A native of Surat; but adopted as a caste name by Dheḍs who have risen in social position.

Suri. Another form of Sunri.

Surinjam. See Saranjám.

Surkháb. [Hindi.] A kind of duck, the anas casarca.

Surla. [Pashṭo.] An instrument used by housebreakers.

Surmá. [Hindustáni.] Black sulphuret of antimony, used by Musalmáns as a collyrium. The Hindus use kájal.

Surpanakha. [Sanskrit.] A name applied to a woman who from careless conduct gives occasion to great disasters, as the original Surpanakha, the sister of Ráwana, by her light speech before Ráma, began the quarrel which led to the rape of Sitá and the consequent invasion of Lanka, as related in the Rámáyana.

Survey number. This term, under the Bombay revenue system, means any portion of land which has been separately demarcated and assessed by the survey department; as far as is practicable every distinct field is made a distinct survey number, but differences of tenure and the inconvenience that would result from having very small fields separately recorded produce exceptions.

Suryawanśa. [Sanskrit, from *surya*, the sun, and *wanśa*, lineage.] The race of the sun, the name of the dynasty of which Ráma, the hero of the Rámáyana, was a member; they ruled in Oudh and Tirhut, and are supposed to have entered India about 2000 years B.C. They are now represented by the Gahlot and Kachhwáhá dynasties, and the Ráṭhors also claim to be of the same origin. See Rájput.

Susi. [Panjábi.] A striped coloured fabric much used for making trousers for Muhammadans.

Sutár. [Hindi form of *sutradhár*, q.v.] The name of a Śudra caste; they are carpenters. They are looked upon as of intermediate Śudra rank in most places, but in some, as Midnápur, they are held to be a low caste. See Panchál.

Suthri. [Panjábi.] A Sikh sect founded by one Suchá, a Bráhman by birth, in the time of Har Rai, the seventh guru. They are called also Suthrasháhi. They beg in the name of Bábá Nának Sháh and are obstinate and troublesome.

Sutra. [Sanskrit, from *siv*, to sow.] A thread, a string of rules. A sutra should properly be expressed with the utmost possible brevity. It is frequently nothing but a few suggestive memorial words used like algebraic signs, and unintelligible without a key. In later times sutras are merely collections of formulated precepts, adapted to serve as manuals to particular systems of teaching, whether in ritual, philosophy, law, or grammar (*Monier Williams*). All the sutras are post-vedic, or, in other words, they are smriti and not sruti, but those of the kalpa vedanga are called srauta, as they relate to the vedic sacrifices. The sutras were composed probably between 600 and 200 B.C., and are intermediate between the vedic and the later Sanskrit. Sutra is also the name of one of the three piṭakas, that which prescribes rules for Buddhists in general.

Sutradhár. [Sanskrit *sutradhára*, from *sutra*, a thread, and *dhára*, holder.] A carpenter, so called from the thread with which he marks out his work. See Sutár.

Suttee. See Sati.

Suvusthan. See Sansthán.

Śuwálá. [Maráṭhi.] A boat resembling the paṭṭemár, but smaller.

Suwár. The Bengali form of Sawár.

Śvetámbar. [Sanskrit *śveta*, white, and *ambara*, clothing.] One clothed in white. The Jains are divided into śvetámbars and digambars.

Swámi. [Sanskrit, from *swa*, own.] An owner, a lord; a husband, a king; a name of Vishnu, of Śiwa, and of Kárttikeya. In the south, an idol.

Swámi-Náráyan. The name of a Vaishnawa sect founded in Gujarát, in the present century, by Swámi-Náráyan, or Sahájánand, a native of Oudh. Professor Monier Williams describes Swámi-Náráyan's teaching as a modern Puritan movement against the Wallabhácháryan corruption of the Vaishnawa faith, and says he made chastity and purity of life the key-note of all his teaching, and ended by boldly asserting that he himself, and not Wallabhácharya, was the true incarnation of Krishna. Swámi-Náráyan appointed his two nephews, Raghuvirji Mahárái and Ayodya Prasádji Mahárái, his successors, the one to preside at Waḍtál in Kaira, and the other at Ahmedabad.

Swarga. [Sanskrit.] The heaven of Indra and of the inferior gods. See Kailása, Vaikunṭha.

Swári. The Maráṭhi form of Sawári.

Swarnakár. See Sonár.

Swasti. [Sanskrit, from *su*, well, and *asti*, may it be.] A term of benediction often used at the commencement of a writing.

Swastik. [Sanskrit, from *swasti*, blessing, welfare.] A mystical mark made for good luck or in sign of rejoicing; it is in the form of a Greek cross, with additional limbs proceeding at right angles from the extremity of each of the four limbs. It has been suggested that the three-legged symbol of the Isle of Man and of Sicily is a debased form of the swastik.

Swáti. An inhabitant of Swát. There is a clan of Swátis, called also Kohistánis, settled on our frontier east of the Indus near the Hassanzais. See Ákhun.

Swayamwara. [Sanskrit, from *swayam*, one's self, and *wara*, choice.] A ceremony in ancient times by which a maiden chose her husband by putting a garland round his neck in public assembly.

Syce. [A corruption of the Arabic *sáis*.] A groom, a horse-keeper.

Syed. See Saïd.

Synteng. The name of a tribe settled on the Jáintia hills in Assam; they remain uninfluenced by Hinduism.

Syrang. [Corruption of the Persian *sarhang.*] A commander; the head of a crew or of a gang of labourers. Where the terms syrang and tindal are both used, as in a corps of store lascars, or in a light-house establishment, the syrang is the superior officer, and the tindal comes between him and the common lascars or khalásis.

Syud. See Saïd.

T.

Tábut. [Arabic.] A coffin, a bier; especially a model of the mausoleum of Husain, the third imám, at Karbala; tábuts made of light wood covered with paper and much ornamented are carried in the Muharram processions. Tábut is also the name of the ark of the covenant presented, according to Muhammadans, by God to Adam.

Tachariye. [Kanarese.] The name of a subdivision of the Pánchála in Coorg; they are carpenters.

Táḍ. The Maráṭhi form of Tár.

Táḍi. More commonly Toddy.

Tadvi. The name of a tribe in Khándesh, said to be descended from Musalmán men and Bhil women, and to date from Aurangzib's time. They live in villages at the foot of the Sátpura hills. They are tall and well made, and better-looking than the pure Bhil. They are poor cultivators, and live chiefly by wood and grass cutting, the women helping by carrying the loads. Tadvis make good soldiers and constables. They hold the Musalmán faith except as regards drinking. Some regard also certain Hindu deities.

Táfa. A float, a raft; often a charpoy floated on calabashes for crossing a river.

Taffeta. [Hindustáni *táftah*, from the Persian *táft*, to twist.] A silk cloth with a wavy lustre.

Tág. [Maráṭhi.] The plant crotolaria juncea; the fibre is used as hemp.

Tagá. [Hindi, said to be from the Sanskrit *tyága*, abandoning.] The name of a class of Bráhman husbandmen living between the Jamná and the Ganges. According to tradition they are the descendants of Bráhmans brought from Bengal by the rájá of Jind for the extermination of the Takshaks, or serpent race, and who abandoned their priestly character and took to agriculture.

Tagái. The Maráṭhi form of Takávi.

Tagore. See Ṭhákur.

Tahkhánah. [Hindustáni, from the Persian *tah*, under, and *khánah*, a house.] An apartment underground, or so situated as to be impervious to the sun.

Tahsil. [Arabic.] Collection of the revenue; also, in the south, the head-quarter station of a táluka.

Tahsildár. [Persian *dár*, holder.] A native officer who collects the revenue for a zamindár or under a collector. In the Madras presidency the tahsildár has charge of a táluka, is a magistrate, and corresponds generally to the Bombay mámlatdár. In the Central Provinces he is a civil judge also. See Tálukdár.

Tai. The Tamil name of the solar month Magaram, corresponding most nearly to January, Paush, and in Bengal to Mágh. See Month.

Tai. The name of the language of the Shán tribes; it is monosyllabic, and the same syllables are by difference of tone made to represent different meanings.

Tái. [Gujaráti.] The name of a community of Sunni Musalmáns; they are weavers, and some few money-lenders.

Tailinga. [Sanskrit.] The name of the country of the Telugu-speakers; thence the name of the subdivision of Drávida Bráhmans occupying that country.

Taipál. [Bengali.] A Śudra caste of intermediate rank; they are grocers.

Táj. [A vernacular form of the second syllable of *mumtáz*.] The popular name of the famous mausoleum of Arjmand Bánu, or Mumtáz Mahal, 'the chosen of the palace,' the favourite wife of Sháh Jahán, the fifth Mogul emperor.

Tájik. A tribe of Arabic descent settled in Afghánistán. They are industrious and peaceable, and skilful in agriculture, trade, and manufactures. They number nearly a million; some are Sunnis and some Shiahs. Some have taken service in our army. See Afghán.

Táj-ul-Mulk. [Arabic *táj*, a crown, *mulq*, country, kingdom.] The crown of the kingdom; a Muhammadan title of honour.

Tajvijdár. [Gujaráti, from the Arabic *tajvij*, investigation, and the Persian *dár*, holder.] A class of hereditary district officers formerly employed in Gujarát to make estimates, hold sales, and examine returns.

Ták. The name of a Rájput dynasty that ruled at Asirgaḍ and Khándesh from the ninth to the twelfth century A.D.

Ṭakári. [Maráṭhi, from *ṭánk*, to chisel.] The name of a caste; they are workers in stone. Many thieves assume the name, and make the repairing of stone-mills their ostensible occupation.

Takávi. [Hindustáni, from the Arabic.] An advance of money made by government to a cultivator at the time of sowing, to be repaid at the time of harvest.

Takenkar. See Ṭakári.

Takht. [Persian.] A throne. Takht-i-suláiman, or Throne of Suláiman, is the name of a mountain in the Suláimán range, and of another near Śrinagar.

Takhtaposh. [Hindustáni, from the Persian *takhtah*, a plank, a platform, and *poshid*, to cover.] A low platform or sitting-place, the seat in a baiṭhakhána.

Takhtnishin. [Persian *takht*, throne, *nishin*, who sits.] The reigning sovereign; or, sometimes, the heir-apparent.

Takht-rawán. [Hindustáni, from *takhtah*, a platform, and *rawán*, going.] A litter, especially one slung between two camels. Also the plank on which dancers are carried on men's heads in processions.

Takiyah. [Arabic.] Caution; outward conformity to prevailing religion in order to avoid persecution for opinions really held.

Takka. [Kanarese *takka*, worthy.] A headman, as uru takka, the headman of a village; náḍu takka, the head of a sub-district; dewa takka, the manager of a temple. The takka mukhyastaru in Coorg is a council of elders who are the moral censors and managers of social affairs, with power to fine and excommunicate.

Ṭakká. The name of a Scythian tribe formerly in the Panjáb, and who, according to tradition, were nearly exterminated by the rájá of Jind. Some remnants remain near Ráwal Pindi. See Serpent race.

Ṭáklá. [Maráṭhi.] The plant cassia tora; it is a small bush, growing to about two feet in height, with yellow flowers and pods; the young leaves are eaten as a vegetable, and the seed yields a blue dye.

Taksár. The name of the third of the four principal courts in Nepál; it is presided over by two bichàris, who decide minor cases and report serious ones to the ditha for orders.

Tákshá. [Panjábi.] A small plant bearing a pea-shaped flower of a pale rose-colour, the leaves of which are used for the curing of maggots in sheep.

Takshak. [Sanskrit.] The name of one of the nágas or serpents of pátál; also a name of the serpent race. See Serpent race.

Taksir. [Arabic, from *kasr*, to break.] A magic square, a set of numbers so arranged that the sum of each row or column or diagonal line is the same. They are worn as charms.

Takyah. [Hindustáni.] A pillow; also the abode of a fakir.

Tál. [Hindustáni.] A pond, a lake.

Talabdá. [Gujaráti, from the Sanskrit *sthalodbhawa*, from *sthala*, place, and *udbhawa*, production.] Produced in the country, indigenous; the name of the most numerous and respectable division of the Kolis of Gujarát. The name is applied also to the local breed of cattle, and to the cotton of the province.

Talaing. The Burmese name of a tribe deemed to be the oldest inhabitants of Burma. They are generally considered to be Dravidians from Telingana, but there is no trace of this in their speech, and they call themselves Mon; their language is monosyllabic, but distinct from Burmese.

Taláo. [Hindustáni.] A pond, a reservoir of water; especially one made by further deepening a natural hollow, and banking it on all sides but the one on which the flood comes in the rainy season. See Tank.

Talári. [Kanarese.] A village watchman. Compare Chaukidár, Jiwáidár, Wartaniá.

Taláṭi. [Gujaráti.] A village accountant in Gujarát; he is not an hereditary servant like the kulkarni of the Deccan, but a stipendiary on pay varying from ten to twenty rupees a month, and is liable to be transferred from one village to another. He is strictly subordinate to the paṭel, but sometimes, from the ignorance of the latter, the taláṭi appears rather as the collector of the revenue than the paṭel's assistant and accountant in that work. See Village accountant.

Ṭalávlá. The name of a division of the Dublá race; they worship chiefly a goddess called Kálka.

Talawára. [Kanarese.] A village watchman remunerated by a grant of land subject to a quit-rent only.

Táleband. [Maráṭhi, from *tálá*, agreement, correspondence, and *band*, binding.] A treasury account showing the correspondence between the balance in hand and that which should be left on a comparison of receipts and disbursements (*H. H. Wilson*). The term is commonly confined now to the jamábandi táleband; it corresponds for the táluká to the ṭharáoband of the village accounts, and is, in fact, an abstract, with the táluká as unit, of the maujawár terij, which again is a summary of the village ṭharáobands; but in the ṭáleband are included also such items of revenue (such as liquor licence sales) as do not come under village management, and so are not accounted for in the village books.

Táli. [Tamil.] A piece of gold, forming either the centre or the sole ornament of a necklace, which is tied on the neck of the bride by the bridegroom at the time of marriage; the term and practice are common to all the people of the peninsula (*H. H. Wilson*).

Taliari. See Talári.

Taline. See Talaing.

Tálipatra. More commonly Talipot.

Talipot. [A corruption of *tálipatra*, from the Sanskrit *táli*, the corypha talliera, and *patra*, a leaf.] The leaf of the corypha palm tree, especially when dried and used to form umbrellas, or when split into oblong pieces and used for writing upon; also the tree itself (*H. H. Wilson*).

Tallary. See Talári.

Talpad. [Gujaráti.] The name given to the government share of the lands of a village when the Muhammadans ruled in Gujarát; the talpad was normally three-fourths and the zamindár's wánṭá one-fourth of the whole.

Tálpur. The name of the dynasty that succeeded the Kalhora dynasty in Sindh; their title was rais, and the first ruler held the government under a firman from Kandahár. They are said to have been of a Biluch tribe.

Táluk. [Hindi, from the Arabic *taaluq*, from *aluq*, it belongs to.] Connection, dependence; possession, property; a dependency, a district, a division of a province; an estate. The two commonest uses of the word are to denote a subdivision of a zillah, and an estate resembling the holding of a zamindár.

Táluka. The Telugu form of Táluk.

Táluká. The Maráṭhi form of Táluk, but used in the Bombay presidency solely to denote the subdivision of a district or collectorate; a parganá. The Bombay zillah or collectorate consists on an average of eight tálukás; the average area of each táluká is about 500 square miles, and the population 92,000 (equal to that of Pembrokeshire, or half that of Cambridgeshire). At the chief town of each táluká reside the mámlatdár and the chief constable of the táluká ; and for each táluká or group of two or three tálukás there is a subordinate judge's court for the disposal of civil suits.

Tálukdár. [Persian *dár*, holder.] The holder of a táluk or estate; or the officer in charge of a táluk or the division of a zillah. The tálukdárs of upper India, since the settlement made after the mutiny, correspond to the zamindárs of Bengal. In the nizám's dominions the tálukdár is a revenue and judicial officer superior to the tahsildár.

Talwálá. [Hindi.] A fuel-seller.

Talwar. See Talawára.

Tamandár. The headman of a Biluch tribe.

Tamáshá. [Hindustáni, from the Arabic.] A spectacle, a show, an entertainment; any occurrence that attracts and amuses spectators.

Támbaṭ. [Maráṭhi, from the Sanskrit *támra*, copper.] The name of a caste ; they are coppersmiths.

Támbuli. [Sanskrit, from *támbula*, the piper betel.] The name of a high Śudra caste ; they were originally betel-growers, but many are now grain-merchants, land-holders, or money-lenders.

Tamburán. [Malayálam.] A prince, a lord ; the title of the ruler of Cochin.

Tamil. A Dravidian language spoken by about fifteen millions of persons in the southern part of the Madras presidency and the northern part of Ceylon. There are two dialects of it, the high and the low, called respectively Shen and Kodun, in both of which there is an extensive literature.

Tamila. [Tamil.] The name of a division of the Paraiyans ; they are usually merchants, and are regarded as men of some substance and respectability (*J. H. Nelson*).

Támli. Another form of Támbuli.

Támrapaṭ. [Maráṭhi, from the Sanskrit *támra*, copper, and *paṭṭa*, a tablet.] A copper plate on which a grant of land or of privileges is inscribed. Compare Śiláśásana.

Támraśásana. [Sanskrit *támra*, copper.] A śásana or grant inscribed on a copper plate or plates.

Tanam. A south of India coin worth about eightpence.

Tanḍu. [Malayálam.] An open palanquin.

Tangal. [Malayálam.] The name by which the Máppillas call their priests, for whom they have great reverence.

Tank. This word, as an Anglo-Indian term, designates what would in English be rather called a pond or pool, or even lake ; a tank is often of many acres in extent. The use of the word is curious, as the Indian *ṭánká*, like the English 'tank,' designates rather a cistern than a pond. See Taláo.

Tankha. The name given to Todar Mal's revenue settlement, under which each field was measured and the proportion of produce to be paid settled. See Settlement.

Tannah. See Thání.

Tánti. [Hindi, from the Sanskrit

tántra, a loom.] The name of a caste; they are weavers. Tántis are usually accorded middle Śudra rank, but in Dacca they are more and in Cuttack less esteemed.

Tantra. [Sanskrit.] Literally, a thread: thence the leading action of anything, ritual; the name of a class of works said to be founded on one of the upanishads. There are about sixty-four original tantras, and a large number of other tantric works, generally written in the form of a dialogue between Śiwa and his wife. Every tantra is supposed to treat of the creation, the destruction of the world, the worship of the gods, the attainment of objects, especially of the eight siddhis, and the four modes of union with the supreme spirit. But most of them are mere handbooks of a kind of witchcraft, giving collections of spells for making people enamoured, for destroying sight, for producing or preventing diseases, etc. Some explain the most effectual mode of worshipping the śaktis. The oldest tantras were written probably about the sixth century A.D. (*Monier Williams*).

Tantric. An adjective of English formation from tantra; pertaining to the tantras.

Tántrika. A follower of the doctrines of the tantras, a set of works inculcating mystical and impure rites in honour of Śiwa in his character of a free-living, jovial, dancing, and drinking god, and his consort Párwati.

Tapá. [Gujaráti, from the Sanskrit *tap*, to do penance.] The name of a sect of the Jains, generally in opposition to the Ḍhunḍiás. The greater asceticism of the latter having gained them more followers than their rivals, a new and stricter sect called the Śambigi has sprung up among the Tapás themselves (*A. K. Forbes*).

Tapá. [Hindi.] A group of villages, a subdivision of a parganah or táluk.

Tapádár. An officer in charge of a tapá. The tapádár in Sindh is subordinate to the mukhtyárkár as revenue officer, and he has (unlike the mahálkari of Bombay) no magisterial power. Also, in Sindh, an officer in charge of a forest.

Ṭappál. [Maráṭhi, from the Telugu *ṭappá*, a stage, a halting-place.] A post, a ḍák; thence, loosely, the letters delivered.

Tár. [Hindi, from the Sanskrit *tála.*] The palmyra or fan-palm, borassus flabelliformis, from which toddy is extracted. The name is sometimes applied also to the corypha and other palms.

Taraf. [Hindustáni.] Quarter, direction; a side, a part; a tract of country. A taraf is usually a subdivision of a parganah. The Báhmani rulers, however, divided their whole kingdom into four tarafs.

Tarafbánt. [Hindustáni.] The holding of several separate divisions of village lands by different branches of the community, the coparceners of one taraf having no interest in another, although included under the same village; the division may sometimes originate in difference of caste or religion, so that a village may have a Muhammadan and a Hindu taraf (*H. H. Wilson*).

Tarafdár. [Hindustáni, from *taraf*, q.v., and Persian *dár*, holder.] The officer administering a taraf or division of a parganah; the owner of a village taraf; the ruler over a taraf or province. The Adil Sháhi, Kutab Sháhi, Nizám Sháhi, Ahmad Sháhi, and Barid Sháhi dynasties were all founded by tarafdárs of the respective provinces of the Báhmani kingdom.

Taragan. [Malayálam.] A broker; a warehouse-keeper who receives goods from merchants and keeps them till they are sold, and who is sometimes employed himself to sell them.

Tarái. [Hindustáni, from the Persian *tar*, moist.] Marshy ground; especially the moist and jungly tract running along the foot of the first range of the Himálayas for several hundred miles, and varying in breadth from two to fifteen (*H. H. Wilson*).

Tárakeswar. [Hindi, from the Sanskrit *táraka*, who carries across, from *tára*, crossing; and *íswara*, q.v.] The god of salvation, who is supposed to whisper into the ear of a dying supplicant a mantra that will secure him future happiness. There is a temple to this god just above the masán on the bank of the Ganges at Benares.

Taram. [Tamil.] The name of a system of revenue assessment, under which the soils were classified according to their natures and capabilities, and each class separately assessed in each village (*J. H. Nelson*). Sometimes each class is called a taram.

Tari. [Maráṭhi.] Wet crop or rice-land, land which without artificial irrigation, but merely by means of a little bank round each plot, can be made to retain water enough for the cultivation of rice. Corresponding names are kyári, nanjey.

Tári. More commonly Toddy.

Táripatra. Another form of Tálipatra.

Tarkhán. The name of a dynasty that ruled for a few years in Sindh towards the close of the sixteenth century. It was followed by the Kalhora line.

Tarpan. [Sanskrit, from *trip*, to satisfy.] The presenting of libations to the soul of a deceased person or to pitris.

Taru. See Tháru.

Tasalmát. [Gujaráti.] The name of an operation in accounts, by which any outlay not provided for in the sanctioned budget is debited to a head called tasalmát; in the following budget, provision is made for such past expenditure, and the sums then debited to their proper heads, and the tasalmát cleared by corresponding credit items.

Tasar. [Hindi, from the Sanskrit *trasara*.] The name of a silk, the product of the larvæ of the moth antheræa paphia, found over nearly the whole of India. The caterpillars are about four inches long, green, with reddish spots and a reddish-yellow band running lengthways. They feed on several plants, including the teak, the baer, the sál, and simal trees, and the castor-oil plant. They hang their cocoons on the branches by thick hard cords of silky matter. Tasar is said to owe its peculiar glassy appearance to the fact that its fibre is flat and not round, as is that of ordinary silk.

Tasmahbázi. [Hindustáni *tasmah*, a strap, and *bázi*, playing.] A gambling game played with a leather strap and a stick.

Tat. An Anglo-Indian abbreviation of Taṭṭu.

Tattáma. [Bengali.] A weaver of tasar silk.

Tattán. A caste in Travancore; they are goldsmiths and jewellers.

Ṭaṭṭi. [Hindi.] A screen consisting of a frame filled in with khaskhas roots, which is set up at a door or window windward, and over which water is sprinkled so as to cool the air which passes through.

Taṭṭu. [Hindustáni.] A pony.

Taungya. The Burmese name of the jum or dahya system of cultivation, which consists of clearing a piece of forest, burning the fallen jungle, and then sowing.

Távit. [Panjábi.] A small casket made to contain a talisman, and worn on the arm or fastened round the neck.

Tavoy. The name of a branch of the Mrammá race.

Táyá. [Panjábi.] Properly an uncle, but used, like cháchá, to designate a father-in-law.

Táziah. [Arabic.] A model of Husain's shrine, a tábut.

Tázmin. [Persian.] A stanza of five lines, the first three of which are original, and the last two a quotation.

Teapoy. [From the Hindustáni *tín*, three, and *pái*, foot.] A small three-legged table. As to the formation of the word, compare Charpoy.

Tehsil. See Tahsil.

Tejaji. The name of a god much worshipped by the Játs; he is the dewa or spirit of a Ját cowherd who lived in the eleventh century, and is represented as a man on horseback with a drawn sword and a snake biting his tongue; the fable is that Tejaji had promised to offer himself as a victim to the snake, but got so wounded by a band of robbers that there was no whole part of his body but the tongue for the snake to bite (*J. D. La Touche*).

Teli. [Hindi, from *tel*, Sanskrit *taila*, oil, from *tila*, the sesamum seed.] The name of a caste; their hereditary profession is expressing and selling oil, which is deemed a base occupation, but in Bengal many Telis have raised themselves in the social scale, and are landholders, traders, and grain-merchants, and call themselves, not Telis, but Tilis (or sometimes Sháhás), to distinguish themselves from their former caste-fellows. Compare Ghánchi.

Telinga. A native of Telingana, or the Telugu country; also a sepoy or native soldier under European discipline, the first so enlisted having been from the Telugu country.

Telugu. [From *Telingana*, the name of the country, from *tri*, three, and *linga;* three linga temples having been its bounds.] A Dravidian language spoken by seventeen millions of persons in the northern parts of the Madras presidency and part of the nizám's territory. In extent of use it is the next language after Hindustáni (in its various forms) and Bengali.

Tene. The Tamil name of the Italian millet, or káng. See Millet.

Tengalai. [Tamil *ten*, the south.] The name of a division of the Vaishnawas of the peninsula of India who have a religious difference with an opposite party called Vaḍagalai. The two sides may eat together and intermarry.

Tengin. [Kanarese.] The name of a small agricultural caste.

Teor. See Tior.

Teppa. [Kanarese.] A raft formed of bamboos tied together.

Teppakulam. [Tamil.] A square stone tank for religious uses.

Ṭhag. More commonly Thug.

Ṭhákor. The Gujaráti form of Ṭhákur. It is the common title of Rájput chieftains not of sufficient rank to assume the title of ráwal.

Ṭhákorḍá. [Gujaráti.] This form of the word ṭhákur is chiefly used as the name of castes of mixed Rájput and Koli origin; their habits are mostly those of the Kolis, but they are finer-looking men, and call themselves by the name of the Rájput family, from which, on the father's side, they are descended, as Solanki, Ráṭhor, Chauhán.

Thakorine. An Anglicized form of Ṭhákuráin.

Ṭhákur. [Hindi, from the Sanskrit *ṭhakkura.*] A deity, an idol; every household that can afford it has a ṭhákur of its patron deity, which the purohit comes daily to worship. Ṭhákur is also an honorific title used after a name, whence it has become a surname under the corrupt form Tagore. The word is also used for chief, baron, or lord, especially among Rájputs, and sometimes as a synonym for Rájput.

Ṭhákur (the same word as the above). The name of a wild tribe found about Kalyán and Mátherán, and generally resembling the Warális. In the days of Mahmud Begada and other Muhammadan princes who used violence to convert the Hindus to islám, some of the ṭhákurs (barons) of Gujarát fled to the jungles with considerable numbers of Hindus of different tribes. The Jungle Ṭhákurs are the descendants of this mixed multitude. Their knowledge of Hinduism is very faint, and they shun the Bráhmans. They worship Pishunáth, the lord of cattle. They live by collecting firewood, carrying loads, etc. They also cultivate hill-lands, and are great shikáris (*J. Wilson*).

Ṭhákuráin, or Ṭhákuráni. Feminine forms of ṭhákur; a goddess or the wife of a Rájput chieftain.

Ṭhákurbári. [Bengali *bári*, a house.] The house, or chamber in a house, set apart for a family idol.

Ṭhákurdwára. [Hindi, Sanskrit *dwára*, a door.] An idol-house, a temple.

Thakurra. See Ṭhákorḍá.

Thal. [Panjábi.] A sandy tract or desert.

Thal. [Maráṭhi.] The actual admeasurement of a crop to separate the khot's share of the produce.

Thalkari. [Maráṭhi, from *thal*, Sanskrit *sthala*, a place, and the affix *kari*, q.v.] A landed proprietor as distinguished from an upari. Compare the Dravidian Ulkuḍi and Parakuḍi, the Hindi Khudkásht and Páikásht.

Thána. [Hindi, from the Sanskrit *sthána*, a place.] A station, especially the head-quarters of a táluk; also very commonly, a police-station. The term belongs properly to the times when military force was used both to preserve peace and to collect the revenue; the thána was the head-quarters of the troops maintained for those purposes in each division of a district. The word is often used to designate, not the station only, but the whole area subordinate to it. See Mulkgiri.

Thánádár. [Persian *dár*, holder.] An officer in charge of a thána. The name is now used chiefly in, or in connection with, native states. A thánádár in a native state is a revenue and magisterial officer corresponding generally with the mámlatdár or tahsildár of British India.

Thánádári. This is the name given to a system by which lands, belonging to petty native states under chiefs incapable of effective control, are formed into circles and placed under the magisterial jurisdiction of special thánádárs.

Thandalkára. [Tamil.] A village officer who collects the revenue from individual ryots, under the orders of the náṭṭánmaikára, and hands over the money to the noṭṭakára for inspection.

Ṭhánedár. The Maráṭhi form of Thánádár.

Tháni. [Hindi, from the Sanskrit *sthána*, a place.] Stationary, resident; a permanent as opposed to a páhi cultivator.

Ṭharáoband. [Maráṭhi, from *ṭharáv*, a settlement, and *band*, binding.] The document which records the annual revenue settlement of a village in the Bombay presidency; it is a general abstract of the other accounts, and deals with the village as a whole; it shows the total area and assessment of every kind of land and the total of every other head of revenue, and, deducting in every case what is not to be realized (whether on account of alienation, non-occupation, or remission) from the total, shows finally the amount which the village has to pay. By means of duplicate columns the accounts of the past year are compared throughout and the differences shown. See Táleband.

Thareli. See under Sindhi.

Tháru. The name of an aboriginal tribe numerous in Champáran; they are of Mongolian origin; they are excellent cultivators.

Ṭhaṭherá. [Hindi, perhaps formed from the sound of the brazier's work —*ṭha* in Sanskrit represents a noise as of a golden pitcher rolling down steps.] The name of a caste; they are an inferior division of the Kánsáris.

Thek. The Burmese form of Tsak or Chakmá.

Thiká. [Bengali.] An hereditary tenure under a zamindár. It is also a tenure terminable at will by either the occupant or the landholder (*W. W. Hunter*).

Ṭhikádár. [Hindustáni, from *ṭhiká*, hire, and *dár*, holder.] A contractor for work, a farmer of the revenue; a middle-man who receives rents from cultivators and pays a stipulated amount to the proprietor.

Thirty-six royal races. See Chattiskula.

Thlen. An imagined demon of the Khásias that takes the form of a gigantic snake and is appeased only by human blood.

Thori. [Hindustáni.] The name of a wandering tribe; they deal in bullocks and grain, and some are wood-cutters and make wooden combs and plates.

Thuar. [Hindustáni.] The cactus plant, euphorbia nerrifolia; that with the flat oval joints is called chithrá thuar or viláyati; the straight-jointed ḍanḍá thuar or deśi.

Thug. [Hindustáni *ṭhag*.] A cheat, a knave; the name of a class of murderers and robbers formerly very large and important, and not yet extinct; they were of different tribes and castes, Muhammadan as well as Hindu, and the profession was usually followed hereditarily; their victims were mostly travellers, to whom the thugs would present themselves as travellers also, and, when stopping to rest or eat, or at other favourable opportunity, the thugs would suddenly strangle each his victim by a handkerchief thrown round his neck from behind and twisted with some peculiar skill. Lately, such thugs as remain have taken to the use of poison instead of strangling, and a favourite plan is to hire a cart to take them to a particular town, poison the driver on the way, sell the cart and bullocks, and hire another.

Thuggee. [Hindustáni *ṭhagi*.] The profession of the thug.

Thugyi. [Burmese.] An officer placed in charge of a revenue circle.

Ticca. This word (a corruption of the Hindustáni *ṭhiká*, hire) is used in English as an adjective meaning hired, as ticca-gári, a hired carriage; ticca-cook, a cook engaged for a special occasion.

Tiffin. [Persian *tafan*.] A light repast of fruit, etc., eaten at midday; but the word is used in English as equivalent to luncheon.

Tigala. The name of a Tamil caste called also Palli; in Mysore they are chiefly market-gardeners; in Coorg they are labourers, and some have enlisted.

Tihan. The name of the subdivision of the Khatri caste to which Angad, the second Sikh guru, belonged; the name also of a denomination of Sikhs who specially revere Angad. See Behdi, Bhulle.

Ṭiká. Another name for Tilak.

Tikhur. A starchy substance obtained from the root of the curcuma angustifolia or Indian arrowroot.

Tikuti. See Trikuti.

Til. [Hindi, Sanskrit *tila*.] The sesamum indicum or orientale, from the seed of which oil is extracted. It is a kharif crop. See Gingelly.

Tilak. [Sanskrit *tilaka.*] The mark which a Hindu makes with coloured earths or unguents on his forehead to show to what sect he belongs, or for ornament. The tilak is made also on idols, and is sometimes used as the distinguishing mark of a sovereign. Also the name among some castes, as Rájputs and Káyasths, for the betrothal ceremony, when the girl's father pays an earnest of the dower, and the company are marked with tilaks. See Náma, Tripundra, Urdhwapundra.

Ṭiláyat. [Gujaráti, from *ṭilu*, the Sanskrit *tilaka.*] The lineal representative of the founder of a ruling family, so called as bearing the royal tilak on his forehead, and as distinguished from a phuṭáyá or cadet.

Tilgár. Another name for Tilvi.

Tili. [Bengali.] Another form of Teli, but now practically a distinct branch of that caste. The rájá of Dighá-patiyá is a Tili.

Tilvi. [Kanarese.] The name of an agricultural caste.

Timuride. A name sometimes given to the so-called Mogul dynasty, the founder of whom, Babar, was sixth in descent from Timur or Tamerlane. See Mogul.

Tindal. [Telugu *tanḍelu*, Gujaráti *ṭanḍel.*] The head of a body of men, especially of a gang of labourers or the crew of a ship. Thence tindal is the common name for the captain of a native vessel.

Tior. [Bengali.] The name of a low caste, perhaps a branch of the Kaibartta; they are fishermen, boatmen, cultivators, and domestic servants. Perhaps the same as the Tiyar.

Tipári. [Hindustáni.] The name of a fruit commonly called the Cape gooseberry.

Tipperah. [A corruption of the Sanskrit *tripura*, the name of a country.] The name of the principal tribe occupying the hills in the state called Hill Tipperah, which lies between 22° 59′ and 24° 31′ N. lat., and 91° 12′ and 92° 24′ E. long. The Tipperahs are divided into four classes: the pure Tipperahs, the class to which the reigning family belongs; the Jámáityás; the Nowattiás; and the Riangs. They worship the elements, and are very superstitious and timid. They have a language of their own, but no written character. They are very fond of drinking and dancing. Mr. Lewin names the four classes as Puran, Nowattiá, Osui, and Riang.

Tirmalli. [Maráṭhi.] A Śudra caste; they lead Nandi about and beg, and some are cultivators.

Tirtha. [Sanskrit, from *tri*, to cross over.] A holy place of pilgrimage, generally on the banks of a sacred river and particularly at the confluence of two streams. Some of the most famous are Puri in Orissa, where is the temple of Jagannáth; Haridwár, where the Ganges is supposed to take its rise; Chitrakot in Bundelkhand, where Ráma lived after his banishment; and Dwárká in Káṭhiáwár, which is sacred to Krishna. Tirtha is laxly extended to denote the officiating priest of a temple. See Pujári.

Tirthakar, or Tirthankar. [Sanskrit *tirtha*, q.v., and *kara*, making.] One who makes a passage through life.

Among Buddhists, an ascetic. Among Jains, an arhat, a jin. The Jain tirthakars are twenty-four in number, beginning with Ádináth or Rishabhdewa; of the rest those whose names chiefly occur are the last three, Nemináth, Párśwanáth, and Vira, Mahávira, or Wardhamán.

Tirvai. [Tamil.] The money assessment fixed on government lands and payable directly by those who hold them. Tirvai-jásti is the extra assessment realized after the jamábandi accounts have been made up (*J. H. Nelson*).

Tithi. [Sanskrit.] The thirtieth part of a lunation, a lunar day. The synodical month is divided into two parts, consisting of fifteen tithis each: the first fourteen tithis of each part are named after the numerals from one to fourteen; the last tithi of each part, that is, the fifteenth and thirtieth of the month, are called respectively purnimá and amáwasi, or amáwasi and purnimá, according as the śukladi or krishnadi method is followed. The tithi is less than the mean solar day by 22 min. 31 sec., but the tithis are kept in correspondence with the days by omitting every tithi on which the sun does not rise and repeating those on which it rises twice. See Month.

Tiyar. [Malayálam.] The name of a caste; they draw toddy from the baine-palm tree, and cultivate land. They are considered to have belonged originally to the island of Ceylon, and the name is said to be properly Tivan, from the Sanskrit *dvipa*, an island.

Tobra. [Hindustáni.] A leather bag used to feed horses; it is tied on the mouth by a thong which passes over the horse's head.

Toḍa. The name of an aboriginal tribe of the Nilgiri mountains. They surpass all the other tribes of that district in physique and dignity of bearing. Their features may best be described as European, with Roman noses and bright hazel eyes, good teeth, and an abundance of rather coarse but glossy black hair, which is worn in a crop by the men and in long thick ringlets by the women. The expression of their countenances is open, fearless, and agreeable. They are essentially a pastoral people and never make any attempt to cultivate their lands. They levy grain from the Baḍagas and Koṭas, and beyond that depend entirely upon their large herds of buffaloes for support. They allow polyandry, but it is now on the decline. Early betrothals are common. They burn their dead. Their exceedingly primitive worship is confined to one material object, the sacred buffalo-bell, which is hung round the neck of the best buffalo of the sacred herd. The Toḍa language is a dialect of old Kanarese, and closely allied to other Dravidian languages of the plains (*Grigg*). See Kedu, Mand, Pálál, Páltchi.

Ṭodágarás. [Gujaráti.] A cash allowance paid from the government treasury in lieu of former garás rights.

Toḍamand. See under Mand.

Toddy. [A corruption of the Maráṭhi *táḍi*, from *táḍ*, q.v.] Juice extracted from the palmyra, the date, or the cocoa palm. Toddy when first drawn is sweet and not intoxicating, but after fermentation it becomes a powerful spirit. See Máḍi, Nirá.

Todebandhi. The putting on of anklets, part of a marriage ceremony. See Lagan, Saptapadi.

Tofung. [Corrupt form.] An Afghán matchlock. Compare Juzail.

Togaṭaru. [Kanarese.] The name of a caste of weavers who manufacture the coarsest kinds of cloths. They are Vaishnawas.

Tol. [Bengali.] A college for the study of Sanskrit; the panḍit maintains himself and his pupils from such presents as he may receive.

Tolá. [Hindi.] A measure of weight. The standard tolá weighs 180 troy grains or one rupee. Eighty tolás make one Bengal or pakká ser.

Ṭolá. [Bengali.] A ward or quarter of a town, a wáḍá; also a suburb or outlying hamlet.

Tolliar. See Talári.

Tomar. The name of a Rájput dynasty, of which nineteen kings reigned at Delhi from 733 A.D. till the capture of Delhi by Visala Dewa, the Chauhán king of Ajmir, in 1151 A.D. The conqueror's son married the daughter of the Tomar king, and had issue Prithi Raj, the Chauhán king of Delhi. The Tomars next appear as a ruling family at Gwalior, where they reigned from 1375 to 1518 A.D. Only small communities of Tomars now remain, at Agra, in Budaon, Jaipur, and other places. The Tomars were esteemed as of the highest rank, and as they are not called either of the solar or lunar race, it is possible that they are of earlier date than the invention of that distinction. Vikramáditya, who established the samwat era, is supposed to have been a Tomar. Some Tomars have been converted to islám.

Tomaun. [Persian *tomán.*] A coin or sum equal to fifteen dollars and a half. Also a myriad, or 10,000 Arabic silver drachmas. Also a district (*C. P. Brown*). In Afghánistán a tomaun is reckoned equal to only twenty rupees.

Tom-tom. [Bengali *ṭanṭan.*] A small drum.

Toná. [Hindi.] Any performance in the nature of an incantation, or any act which, even without the use of any mantra, is intended to have a magical effect. Compare Jádu.

Tonda. [Tamil.] The name of a division of the Paraiyans; they are usually employed as cultivators and prædial slaves; but some are petty traders, some artisans, some domestic servants, some horse-keepers, and the like (*J. H. Nelson*).

Tonga. [Hindustáni *tángá.*] A two-wheeled, four-seated low carriage of strong construction for use in country where there are no made roads; it is drawn by a pair of ponies abreast, one in each of the ruts made by the wheels of country carts.

Toni. [Malayálam.] A long boat or coasting-sloop; also applied to a smaller vessel used for crossing rivers; a ferry-boat (*H. H. Wilson*).

Tonjon. [Hindustáni *támjhám.*] A kind of light open palanquin, or a chair with a pole projecting before and behind, by which it is carried on men's shoulders.

Toon. [Hindi *tun*, from the Sanskrit *tunna.*] The tree cedrela toona. It is a hardy tree, and has a strong stem and fine leafy head. The timber, reddish in colour, is much used for making furniture, and a yellow dye is obtained from the flower.

Topah. [Bengali.] The trade name of silk cocoons that will not wind.

Topas. [Portuguese *topaz*, perhaps from the Hindustáni *ṭopi*, a hat.] A native Christian sprung from a Portuguese father and Indian mother in the south of India; in the early history of the company these people were extensively enlisted as soldiers; hence the term came to be applied to the company's native soldiery generally in the peninsula; it is now obsolete (*H. H. Wilson*).

Topchi. [Hindustáni, from the Turkish.] A conductor of ordnance, an artillery officer (*H. H. Wilson*).

Tope. [A corruption of the Kanarese *topu.*] A clump or cluster of trees.

Tope. [A corruption of *stupa*, q.v.] A mound, a tumulus, a cairn. The word is widely used to include láṭs, minárs, and stambhas.

Topeewallah. See Ṭopiwálá.

Ṭopi. [Hindustáni.] A hat, a cap.

Ṭopiwálá. [See *wálá.*] One who wears a ṭopi and not a turban; a European. Also, in Bengal, a hat-maker, a milliner.

Topkhánah. [Hindustáni, from the Turkish *top*, a gun, and Persian *khánah*, house.] A foundry for cannon; an arsenal; also a battery of artillery.

Topper. [Corrupt form.] A kind of sedan made of basket-work used in the Khásiá hills.

Toran. [Panjábi.] A short stick, bearing a cross-arm, with five or seven uprights on it, each a few inches high, and rudely cut to imitate the human figure; it is stuck into the wall near the outer doorway on the occasion of a marriage, and the bridegroom on arrival strikes at it with a stick, and it is considered a good omen if he smashes it to bits (*W. Coldstream*). In Gujaráti toran (Sanskrit *torana*, a portal) means a cord, with mango and other leaves attached to it, hung from door-post to door-post or across a street, on festive occasions.

Tori. See Turi.

Tor Turin. The name of the tribe occupying Pishin.

Toshahkhánah. [Persian.] A store-room, a wardrobe; chambers in which objects of curiosity or value, not in daily request, are kept; especially the department for the disposal of darbár presents received by representatives of government.

Toṭa. [Kanarese.] A garden, garden-land, bágáit.

Toto. The name of a small, nearly extinct, hill tribe on the Bhutan frontier. They are very thin, with very flat noses, and lips projecting so as almost to suggest a Negritic origin. They have traditions which point to a retrogression from a higher scale of nations, and their belief is that from the time they became cow-eaters they became degraded; they are generally gloomy and fatalistic, and their language is unintelligible to other tribes. They bury their dead (*Dumont Beaghton*).

Toṭṭi. [Tamil.] The name of a division of the Paraiyans; they are the village scavengers and messengers; and a certain number of them are paid for their services by government (*J. H. Nelson*).

Tottiya. [Telugu.] The name of a caste; they are chiefly cultivators, but some are shepherds and some cowherds. They profess to be Vaishnawas, but do not employ Bráhmans, but have gurus of their own caste. They are much addicted to the practice of magic. The men wear brightly coloured handkerchiefs round their heads instead of turbans; the women wear several rows of red glass beads round their necks and a profusion of metal and earthenware bangles on their arms.

Toungjynya. [Arakanese.] The name of a branch of the Chakmá tribe.

Toungthá. [Arakanese, from *toung*, a hill, and *thá*, a son.] The children of the hills, a generic name for those of the tribes of the Chittagong hill tracts who live high on the hills. They are darker in colour and wilder than the Khyoungthá; their villages are generally situated in places difficult of access; they possess no written character; they worship the terrene elements. Captives taken in war become slaves, but slavery for debt is unknown except among the Mrus. The principal Toungthá tribes are the Tipperahs, Kumis, Mrus, Lusháis, and Shendus.

Tower of Silence. See Dokhmá.

Trágá. [Gujaráti.] A kind of importunity or extortion resembling dharná; particularly a Bháṭ's threat to destroy himself in order to enforce the fulfilment of an engagement for which he has pledged his personal surety. The wane of this superstition is noted by the political agent of Káṭhiáwár, who writes in 1842, 'I have known several instances of lives being taken and much blood shed without the least effect being produced, whereas, at the beginning of this century, a single life offered in trágá would have subdued the most stubborn landholder.'

Tretá. [Sanskrit, from *tri*, three.] The side of the die which marks three points, the name of the second yuga, or the silver age.

Trikuti. [Bengali, from *tri*, three.] A sub-tenure which gives the husbandman a third of the crop.

Trimurti. [Sanskrit, from *tri*, three, and *murti*, form.] The united form of the Hindu triad—Brahmá, Vishnu, and Śiwa. These gods, like the rest of the universe, are conceived of as emanations from or expansions of the eternal essence Brahma. But these three gods are considered the highest manifestations of that essence. They are typified by the three mystic letters *A*, *U*, and *M*, combined as *OM*, and are usually described as, respectively, the creator, the preserver, and the destroyer; but this description, Professor Monier Williams observes, is very inadequate, the functions of the three being interchangeable, and the whole idea of the trimurti having been one of gradual development. The complete idea is later than the time of Manu. It serves as a mark on the way of Hindu thought from pantheism to polytheism.

Tripiṭaka. [Sanskrit, from *tri*, three, and *piṭaka*, q.v.] The sacred writings of the Buddhists, which are divided into three parts, called the sutra, the vinaya, and the abhidharma piṭakas.

Tripundra. [Sanskrit, from *tri*, three, and *pundra*, line.] The mark which the Śaiwas make with coloured pigments on their foreheads. It consists of three horizontal lines covering the greater part of the forehead. See Náma, Tilak.

Triśanku swarga. The heaven of Triśanku, a proverbial name for the position of a man half-way between his original condition and that which he sought to attain, like Triśanku, who was raised to heaven by a sage, but thrown out by the gods, and remained hanging midway between the two worlds.

Triśula. [Sanskrit, from *tri*, three, and *śula*, a pike.] A trident, the weapon of Śiwa. Compare the Chakra of Vishnu, the Wajra of Indra.

Triveni. [Gujaráti.] The point of junction of three rivers.

Tsak, or **Tsakma.** See Chakmá.

Tughlak. The name of the third of the Ghori dynasties. It was established by a successful rebellion by Ghiyás-ud-din Tughlak in 1320, and lasted for nearly a century, with an interval caused by the invasion of Tamerlane in 1398.

Tughrá. [Arabic.] The imperial signature; also the name of an ornamental form of the Arabic character much used in architecture.

Tulábhára, or **Tuládána.** [Sanskrit *tulá*, a balance, *bhára*, a weight, *dána*, a gift.] The ceremony of weighing one's self against gold or silver, and presenting the sum to Bráhmans.

Tulam. [Malayálam, the Sanskrit *tulá*, a balance.] The month during which the sun is in Libra, coinciding most nearly with October and Áśvin (in Bengal, Kártik). See Month.

Tullatee. See Taláṭi.

Tulsi. [Sanskrit *tulasi.*] The shrub the ocymum sanctum, or holy basil. It is held sacred to Vishnu, and is fabled to have been produced from the hair of a nymph beloved by him in his incarnation as Krishna. The Vaishnawa rosaries are composed of 108 beads made of the wood.

Tulsidán. [Hindi.] A short pillar or stand on which a tulsi plant is grown.

Tulu. A Dravidian language much resembling Malayálam, and spoken by half a million people.

Tulwar. [Hindi, correctly *talwár*, from the Sanskrit *tarwári.*] A sword. A Rájput bridegroom sometimes sends his tulwar as his proxy at his wedding.

Tumár. [Arabic.] A roll, a record; but used especially as the name of official correspondence consisting of reports, references, and orders, all written each below the last and forwarded from office to office in original. See Bárnisi.

Tumbá. [Hindi, Sanskrit *tumba.*] The long gourd, lagenaria vulgaris; beggars use them to collect alms in.

Tunnus. The tree dalbergia oogeinensis; the wood is used in building, and for carts and ploughs.

Tur. [Hindi, from the Sanskrit *tuwari.*] The pulse cajanus indicus or cytisus cajan; it is both a kharif and a rabi crop; the green pods are used as vegetables, the beans are made into dál and much eaten with rice, and the dried stalks are reduced to charcoal to make gunpowder. Other names are arhar, kandi.

Turáhá. [Bengali.] The name of a low caste, a degraded branch of the Kahárs; they sell fish and vegetables, and carry palanquins.

Turanian. The use of this word is not always consistent; some writers use it as equivalent to or inclusive of Mongolian, and so make it embrace Kalmak and Chinese; but the better usage seems to be to confine it to that class of the Caucasian races and languages which is not Semitic and which is not Aryan. Taking Turanian in this sense, it includes the Scythian, Parthian, Turkish, Finnish, Hungarian, Tartar, Tibetan, Tai, Kolarian, Malay, and Dravidian races. And within India itself it is conveniently divided, with reference to the regions from which immigrants came, into Eastern (or Mongolian) Turanian and Western (or Scythian) Turanian. The first division includes the races commonly called aboriginal or Kolarian and the second the Dravidian races. In northern India, where the Dravidians are unknown, and where much later Turanian immigrants have settled, another classification of Turanian is current, namely, Early Turanian or the so-called aboriginal races which came before the Aryans; and Later Turanian, or those tribes like the Játs and Gujars, who are considered to have come later than the Aryans.

Turi. The name of a tribe occupying the western part of the Kuram valley, and having the Zymukhts as their neighbours on the east; they are Shiahs by religion, but subject to the amir of Kábul; they number about 6000 fighting men, but are less warlike and smaller men than the Waziris and Ghilzais.

Turi. [Bengali.] The name of a semi-Hinduised tribe in Bengal; in some parts, as Nadiyá and Jessor, they are musicians; in others, as Birbhum, they are cultivators and labourers. The Dheḍ minstrel is called Turi in Gujarát.

Tur-i-mau. See Mouse-deer.

Turiyá. [Gujaráti.] The name of a class of Musalmáns; they are tanners and leather-dyers.

Turk. This is a Tartar word, and means wanderer. As used in the Panjáb it means a native of Turkistán, but in other parts of India it is synonymous with Mogul or even with Musalmán.

Tusser, or **Tussore.** See Tasar.

Tuwar. The Gujaráti form of Tur.

Tuwari. The Telugu (and Sanskrit) form of Tur.

Twashtri. [Sanskrit, from *twaksh*, to work.] A carpenter, a builder; the name of a god who corresponds to the Latin Vulcan.

Twice-born. See Dvija.

Tyági. [Sanskrit, from *tyaj*, to leave, to give up.] One who has abandoned terrestrial objects and thoughts. The opposite word is sansári.

Tye. See Tai.

Tykhana. See Tahkhánah.

U.

Uarija. See Aorja.

Uḍaiyár. [Tamil.] A headman; the tribal title of the rájás of Coorg.

Udási. [Sanskrit, from *ud*, away, and *ás*, to sit.] One who sits apart and is indifferent, a stoic, a mendicant. Especially a particular order of mendicants founded by Śri Chandar, the son of Nának the first Sikh guru. They never shave, but tie up their hair like a turban, and they wear no clothes except a langoṭi, but rub their bodies with ashes. The Udásis were rejected by Amar Dás, the third guru, as not being genuine Sikhs.

Uddu. The Kanarese name for Black gram (q.v.). Two crops are grown in Mysore, called after their seasons, káruddu and hainuddu, or otherwise chikkuddu and doduddu, small and large uddu. The latter is reckoned the better. The flour made into cakes and fried in oil is a common article of food. The straw is considered to be pernicious to cattle.

Udgátri. [From the Sanskrit *udgai*, to chant.] The name of the second class of priests at a vedic sacrifice. The sáma-veda was for their use, and their chief duty was to chant hymns from it. The hymns were arranged in order in the sáma-veda-sanhita, and the bráhmana of the same veda prescribed their part in the ceremonial.

Udhaḍjamábandi. [Maráṭhi *udhaḍ*, in the lump.] A jamábandi or settlement made in the lump, the whole assessment being paid by one person or one joint body.

Ughrátdár. [Gujaráti, from *ughrát*, collection, and the Persian *dár*, holder, agent.] The title of the paṭel who collects the revenue, when that function is separated from the police paṭel's duties.

Ujbak. Another name of the káśa grass.

Ujli. [Gujaráti, from Sanskrit *ujjwala*, bright.] White; a name of the higher castes of cultivators as opposed to the káliparaj.

Ulanḍi. [Maráṭhi, from *ulanḍ*, to upset.] A balance-float consisting of a beam fastened, parallel to the side of a boat, and about eight feet from it, by two spars; the beam floats on the water, and prevents the boat from capsizing on the one side by its buoyancy, on the other by its weight.

Ulema. [Arabic, plural of *alim*, wise.] An assembly of alims.

Ulkuḍi. [Tamil, from *ul*, within, and *kuḍi*, an inhabitant.] A permanent resident tenant with hereditary rights, as distinguished from the parakuḍi. He corresponds to the khudkásht of northern India.

Ulladan. A hill tribe of Travancore; they are wild and timid, and without settled villages; they cultivate a little rági, but live chiefly on wild yams, arrowroot, and other esculents (*S. Mateer*).

Ullikhi. [Panjábi.] A star-shaped

tattoo mark made between the eyebrows.

Ulu. [Bengali.] The grass saccharum cylindricum; it is used for thatching.

Uluphá. [Telugu.] Supplies furnished gratuitously to great persons on a journey by the villages on their route (*H. H. Wilson*).

Umá. [Sanskrit.] A name of Párwati.

Umedwár. [Hindustáni, from the Arabic *umed*, hope.] An expectant, a candidate for employment; an unpaid probationer.

Umeen. See Amin.

Unalienated. As the English language supplies no positive term to express what is in India the normal political condition of land, this negative term is used for the purpose. It is equivalent to khálsá, and opposed to inámi, and denotes that the whole of the revenue according to the government assessment for the time being is payable to government. The ryot's right in the land, so long as this assessment is paid, is heritable and transferable; the government reserve the right of periodically revising the assessment and also of altering it if the land be applied to other than an agricultural purpose.

Unḍi. [Maráṭhi.] The tree calophyllum inophyllum; it grows only near the sea; it is a beautiful tree when in flower; a bitter oil is extracted from the seeds, and the trunks are scooped into canoes.

Unḍika. [Malayálam.] A bill of exchange, a hunḍi.

Untaj. See Antyaja.

Upádhyáya. [Sanskrit.] A subteacher who instructs only in a part of the veda, and is therefore inferior to the ácharya. Among the Jains, a religious instructor (but not a priest; the Jains have no priests).

Upákarma. [Sanskrit, from *upákri*, to begin.] The name of a ceremony performed by Bráhmans in the month Mágh. It used to be the practice for them to study the vedas for six months only, from Mágh to Sráwan, and this ceremony was performed at the commencement of that period.

Upanayana. [From the Sanskrit *upa*, below, and *ni*, to lead.] The ceremony of induction into the order of a twice-born man by investiture with the sacred cord called janeo. This rite is enjoined for a Bráhman in his eighth year, for a Kshatriya in his eleventh, and for a Vaiśya in his twelfth, but the time may be extended in each case. See Janeo.

Upanishad. [From the Sanskrit *upa*, below, *ni*, in, and *sad*, to sit—sitting at the feet of a teacher.] Mystical or secret doctrine. This is the name given to the third division of the veda. The upanishads were added, when the sacrificial ritual ceased to satisfy the people, with the object of investigating more definitely such abstruse problems as the origin of the universe, the nature of the deity and of the human soul, and the connection of spirit and matter. The upanishads were held to be integral parts of the veda and as much sruti as the mantras and bráhmanas. The upanishads, indeed, were held to be the highest part, the part meant for the select few capable of understanding the true doctrine, while the mantra and bráhmana parts were for the vast majority of persons unable to conceive of religion except as a process of laying up merit by prayers, sacrifices, rites, and ceremonies (*Monier Williams*).

Upapurán. [Sanskrit *upa*, under.] Secondary puráns. This name is given to eighteen works subordinate, one to each, to the eighteen puráns.

Upari. [Maráṭhi, from *upar*, above, beyond.] A cultivator not belonging originally to the village in which he occupies land; also a tenant as opposed to a thalkari, and especially a tenant-at-will.

Upásaka. [Sanskrit, from *upás*, to sit near to, to serve, to worship.] A worshipper; among Buddhists, a lay devotee bound by the aṭasil, as distinguished from a bhikshu who is bound by the dasasil.

Upavita. [Sanskrit.] Another name for the upanayana ceremony or for the janeo itself.

Uppáliga, or **Uppár.** [Kanarese, from *uppu*, salt.] The name of a caste; they are salt-makers, also gardeners, husbandmen, bricklayers, and builders.

Uppiliyan. The Tamil name of the Uppáliga caste.

Upurohit. See Purohit.

Ur. [Tamil.] A village, a town; often used in composition, as Vellur (commonly Vellore), Tanjaur (commonly Tanjore).

Urálan. [Malayálam.] The manager or guardian of a temple.

Uráli. [Malayálam.] A hill tribe of Travancore, formerly slaves to the Náirs; they cultivate on the jum system, and practise polyandry.

Uráon. The name of a Kolarian tribe belonging to Chutiá Nágpur; they are of dark complexion, short, and thick-set. They are an industrious race and are much employed as field-labourers.

Uras. [Hindustáni.] Offerings of food, incense, or lamps, made at Muhammadan shrines or tombs.

Urdhwabáhu. [Sanskrit *urdhwa*, erect, and *báhu*, arm.] An ascetic who holds his arm straight up in the air until the muscles have become rigid and the arm permanently fixed in that position.

Urdhwapundra. [*Urdhwa*, straight, and *pundra*, line.] The mark which the Vaishnawas make with coloured pigments on their foreheads. It consists of two perpendicular lines, about an inch apart, joined just above the nose by a curved line, and is supposed to represent the footprint of Vishnu. Another vertical line is added in the centre by some sects. See Tilak.

Urdu. A camp, a royal encampment; applied more commonly to the Hindustáni language as spoken at the courts of Delhi and Lucknow, and by the Muhammadans of India generally, being formed by a copious though not preponderating influx of Arabic, Persian, and Turkish words upon a basis of Hindi and Sanskrit, and following the grammatical inflexion of the former, occasionally slightly modified (*H. H. Wilson*).

Urf. [Hindustáni.] Known, known as; commonly used for alias.

Urhari. See under Karáo.

Urid. [Hindi.] The pulse phaseolus radiatus, or black gram. The name is also sometimes given to the phaseolus mungo, or green gram.

Uriya. The language of Orissa; it is an Aryan language of near affinity to Bengali, but with its own alphabet, grammar, and vocabulary. It is spoken by over six million people, and is thus the ninth language in order of extent of use in India.

Urzee. See Arzi.

Ushar. [Hindi.] A salt efflorescence that destroys the fertility of soil; it is more commonly called reh.

Ushas. [Sanskrit, from *was*, to shine.] The goddess of the dawn, one of the vedic deities.

Usoor. See Asura.

Utbandi. [Bengali, from *ut*, perhaps for *dut*, a plough, *bandi*, binding, settlement.] A term applied to land held for a season only, and usually on verbal permission.

Utbandijamá. [*Jamá*, amount, total.] A method of holding by which the cultivator pays each year for the land actually cultivated and not for the fallows.

Uṭhán. [Bengali.] The open rectangle round which a ryot's farm buildings stand. See Bhiṭi.

Uṭhánghát. [Bengali.] A landing-place, a wharf.

Uthman. [Pashṭo.] The name of a powerful independent Paṭhán tribe settled near the Amazais and to the north-east of the Momands.

Utkala. [Sanskrit.] The name of the fifth subdivision of the Gauḍa Bráhmans; those belonging originally to Orissa.

Utkar. [Bengali.] Land held by a tenant-at-will.

Utsab. [Bengali, Sanskrit *utsawa.*] A festival, a jubilee.

Utsarjana. [Sanskrit.] A ceremony to be performed on the conclusion of a period of study of the veda. Compare Upákarma.

Uttara. [Sanskrit *uttara*, last.] The Kanarese name for the krishnapaksh, or dark half of the month.

Uttára. [Kanarese.] Remission, deduction; land given at a reduced assessment or rent free, either for service or to a temple. See Dewasthán, Dewottara, Inám.

Uttaráyana. [Sanskrit, from *uttara*, high, and thence north, as the Himálayas are to the north; and *ayana*, going.] The passage of the sun to the north, or the period from his entering Capricorn to his leaving Taurus. See Dakshináyana.

Uttur. See Attar.

V.

Vaḍagalai. [Tamil *vaḍa*, the north.] The name of a division of the Vaishnawas opposed to another division called Tengalai (*C. P. Brown*).

Vadi, or Vadya. See Wadi.

Vaidika. [A Sanskrit adjective formed, by vriddhi, from *veda*, and equivalent, therefore, to the English form *vedic.*] Relating to the vedas, versed in the vedas; applied to some classes of Bráhmans held in repute as having lived according to the ordinances of the veda, in distinction from the Laukiks, who engage personally in agriculture and other forbidden professions. Also the special name of a branch of the Gauḍa (subdivision) Bráhmans.

Vaidu. [Sanskrit *vaidya*, a physician.] The name of a class of persons in the Konkan whose language resembles Telugu; they are doctors and especially employed to extract the guinea-worm. They wear clothes coloured with red ochre. The Hindi name is Baidya.

Vaikunṭha. [Sanskrit.] The heaven of Vishnu; the name was applied ironically to the disgusting ponds through which Hindu zamindárs were dragged for default of payment of revenue, under the nawáb of Bengal, early in the eighteenth century. Compare Kailása.

Vairágan. A female vairági, or a vairági's wife.

Vairági. [From *vi*, without, and *rág*, passion.] One who has forsaken all intercourse with the world, and meditates only on the deity and lives upon alms. The name is applied in particular to the Rámánandis.

Vaiśákh. [Sanskrit.] The name of the Hindu month most nearly corresponding with May; it is so called from *visákhá*, which means having branches, the name of the nakshatra (in Libra) in which the moon is at full in this month. See Month.

Vaiśeshika. [From the Sanskrit *visish*, to distinguish.] The name of one of the six darśans. It was founded by Kanáda (which means feeder on atoms) upon the nyáya system. It is called vaiśeshika from its distinguishing everything into nine elements each without cause and eternally distinct, namely, five atoms (of earth, water, fire, air, and mind) and four other entities, ether, time, space, and soul.

Vaishnawa. [Sanskrit.] A worshipper of the god Vishnu in any of his incarnations. The principal Vaishnawa sects are the Chaitanyas, Madhwácháryas, Rámánandis, Rámánujas, and Wallabhácháryas. See Vishnuvism.

Vaiśya. [Sanskrit, from *viś*, to enter into, to settle down on.] The third of the four divisions of Hindus according to Manu's code, and the last of those ranking as Dvija, or twice-born. The Vaiśya is described as the thigh of the creator, and his office was the accumulation of material wealth by the pursuits of agriculture and commerce. The Vaiśyas are now either extinct or partly represented by the great mercantile class of Banyás. There is also in the Deccan a caste claiming to be a remnant of the original Vaiśyas, and still called by that name; they are traders.

Vaitála. [Sanskrit.] One who is possessed by a vetála.

Vajragáre. [Kanarese, from *vajra*, hard, and *gáre*, q.v.] A mixture of plaster and stones for making floors.

Vakeel. See Wakil.

Valangei. See Walangai.

Valasa. [Telugu.] Flight of people

in a body from a village through fear of some calamity or exaction.

Valluva. [Telugu.] A man of a class of Pariahs considered somewhat superior, and held by the caste in the light of a family priest (*H. H. Wilson*).

Vandidád. The Pahlavi name of the twentieth book of the avastá. The term 'vandidád sáde' includes this and also other works called izashne and vispard (*Dosabhái Frámji*).

Vannia. Another name of the Palli caste.

Varahá. [Tamil.] The gold coin commonly called by Europeans pagoda.

Várakamu. [Telugu.] Advances made to cultivators, takávi.

Váriyan. [Malayálam.] A temple servant.

Veador. An appellate judge under the Portuguese government, who heard appeals from the ouvidors; also a land factor or overseer.

Veda. [Sanskrit, from *vid*, to see, to know.] Knowledge imagined to have issued like breath from the self-existent being called Brahma, and to have been perceived by rishis and by them orally transmitted, and eventually reduced into writing by Vyása. The term is now commonly applied to the writings. These works were at first three in number—the rig-veda, the yajur-veda, and the sáma-veda, and afterwards a fourth, the atharwa-veda, was added. They are spoken of collectively as the veda. The division of the veda into three was in accordance with the three classes of priests employed in the sacrifices, the rig-veda being for the Hotri priests, the yajur for the Adhwaryu, and the sáma for the Udgátri. The atharwa-veda was not used for sacrifices, but teaches only expiatory, preservative, or imprecatory rites. The oldest part of each of the three principal vedas consists of songs of prayer and praise; then follow precepts of ritual for the performance of sacrifices; and lastly philosophical treatises. See Áranyaka, Bráhmana, Mantra, and Upanishad.

Vedan. See Veḍar.

Vedánga. [Sanskrit, from *veda*, and *anga*, a limb.] A member of the veda. The four vedas are conceived as composing a body of which the six vedángas are limbs, *i.e.* the vedángas are auxiliary to the vedas. But the name (says Max Müller) does not imply the existence of six distinct books intimately connected with the vedas, but merely the admission of six subjects the study of which was necessary for using the vedas. The six doctrines are *śiksha*, pronunciation, and *chhandas*, metre; *vyákaran*, grammar, and *nirukta*, explanation of words; *jyotisha*, astronomy, and *kalpa*, ceremonial. The first two are considered necessary for reading the veda, the next two for understanding it, and the last two for employing it at sacrifices, the object of jyotisha being to fix the proper days and hours for sacrifices.

Vedánta. [Sanskrit *veda*, and *anta*, end.] One of the six darśans or systems of philosophy, so called from its being founded on the upanishads, which are the end of the veda. It is otherwise called the uttara mimánsá, and is attributed to Vyása. This is the non-dualistic system, which teaches that all souls are but part of the one eternal soul, and that all matter is mere illusion. There are passages in the vedic hymns also which at least approach the same notion, as, for instance, where all creatures are spoken of as constituting a quarter of god. See Advaita.

Veḍar. [The plural of the Tamil Vedan.] The name of a very wild aboriginal tribe in the south of India, and found also in Ceylon. They inhabit the hills and forests, and live by hunting. It seems possible that they and the Beḍars are one race.

Veddah. See Veḍar.

Vedic. Relating to the veda. Professor Max Müller divides the vedic age into four distinct periods, called the chhandas, the mantra, the bráhmana, and the sutra periods. The chhandas period (about 1200–1000 B.C.) is described as one of spontaneous song; the mantra period (about 1000–800 B.C.) as occupied at first in imitating previous works, and then collecting all works, old or new, to be handed down to posterity; the bráhmana period (about 800–600 B.C.) as spent in systematizing and interpreting the old works already become unintelligible and sacred; and the sutra period (about 600–200 B.C.) as devoted to the simplification of the complicated system of the theology and ceremonial of the previous period. Or the periods may, most or all of them, have been longer than the dates above. See also Vaidika.

Velama. [Telugu.] The name of a caste reckoned to be of high raṇk. They seem to correspond to the Náirs of Malabár.

Vellálan. [Tamil.] The name of an agricultural caste in southern India; they are landowners and farmers, and also enter the professions and trade. Many Vellálans passed over into Ceylon at a remote period; these are Buddhists, and hold no communication with the Hindu Vellálans.

Vellard. This word is said to be of Portuguese origin; otherwise the Maráṭhi *walháḍ*, to cross over, would supply a derivation, the more so as vellard may be met with under the form *walade*. The term is applied to the causeways built, between Bombay and the neighbouring islands, to serve both as moles to exclude water and as dry passages over the marshy land.

Veluttedan. The name of a caste in Travancore; they are washermen.

Verá. [Gujaráti.] A tax; especially a tax or impost in the nature of a licensing fee on trades and employments. Compare Muhtarafah.

Verakallu. See Virakallu.

Verandah. [Sanskrit *waranḍa*, from *wara*, surrounding.] The gallery or terrace, roofed, but without outer walls, which runs (wholly or partially) round an Indian house, both to protect it from the sun and to serve as a cooler resort than the house proper when the sun is down.

Vetá. [Gujaráti.] The name of the land, under the khátábandi system, upon which all the assessment was placed. The arrangement was made by the sharers among themselves, each of them paying the fixed rate on that small portion of his land which was assigned as vetá, and paying only nominal rates on his khoṭia land. It was part of the system that no person could give up vetá land, but if he took up fresh lands his vetá might be increased. See Settlement.

Vetála. [Sanskrit.] A ghost, a spirit; especially one that enters into a dead human body. Compare Bhut, Pret, Vira.

Veṭh. [Maráṭhi, from the Sanskrit *vishṭi.*] Forced labour, service exacted without payment; also the load carried by a person impressed. Compare Begári.

Veṭhiá. [Gujaráti, from *veṭh.*] A village servant; he is remunerated by a small holding of inám land; he attends at the chorá and generally assists the paṭel, and carries travellers' luggage as far as the next village.

Veṭṭiyán. [Tamil, from *veṭṭi*, a way.] The name of a division of the Paraiyans; they are tom-tom beaters, and act as undertakers at funerals, and some hawk goods. Some are village servants corresponding to the veṭhiás of Gujarát.

Vibhakta. [Sanskrit, from *vi*, apart, and *bhaj*, to assign.] Divided, separated; applied either to property divided or the sharer who has separated from his family.

Vichitra Náṭak. [Panjábi.] The wondrous tale, the name of a part of the Daswa Pádsháhká Granth; it was written by Govind Singh himself, and contains an account of his mission and his warfare.

Vidhátá. [Sanskrit, from *vi*, apart, and *dhá*, to fix, to place.] The disposer, a name of Brahmá, under which he is worshipped on the sixth day after the birth of a child, as he is then supposed to be recording its future fate.

Vighá. The Gujaráti form of Bighá. The vighá is divided into twenty wasás, and the wasá into twenty viswásis.

Vighoṭi. The Gujaráti form of Bighati. The name is often applied to the survey system introduced into the Bombay presidency in 1865, in contradistinction to previous systems in which, though assessment per vighá was part of some of them, the rates were fixed according to actual production (and not according merely to quality and position of the land), or else were on a portion only of each man's holding. But the vighá standard has since been replaced by the acre.

Vihára. [Sanskrit, from *vihri*, to walk about.] Walking about; a pleasure-garden; a place where Buddhist teachers met and walked about; a hall surrounded by cells for monks, with a verandah in front; a monastery. See Chaitya.

Viláyat. [Hindi, from the Arabic.] Native country. This seems to be the original meaning of the word, and, among Arabs, Paṭháns, and Sidis, those who have lately come from their native land are called viláyati as distinguished from the descendants of old settlers in India. But the word has come to be used especially of the Englishman's native country, and so to mean England or Europe.

Viláyati. Adjective from viláyat. English, European. The opposite word is Deshi.

Village. As a revenue term, this word denotes, not a group of houses, farmyards, etc., but a large or small area of land marked off by boundaries, known by one common name, and treated as a unit in the táluká accounts. The houses of the cultivators, the village servants, and others belonging to the village are usually grouped together in one spot, but sometimes there are two or three groups a mile or two apart, occupied generally by different castes; some of the wilder races do not build their houses in groups at all, but each lives by his own fields; there are villages again which have been permanently deserted, or which have had no residents within the memory of man, but which still bear each its separate name, and have each its separate servants and records, the cultivators living in one or more of the neighbouring villages.'

Village accountant. The title in English of an officer to be found, under one or other of the names given below, in almost every village of India. He is sometimes (as under the ryotwar system) a government servant, at others he is appointed and paid by a zamindár or jághirdár; he is in some places an hereditary officer remunerated by service land and permanently attached to his village; in others a stipendiary servant removable from place to place; he sometimes has charge of only one village, at others of a group of two or three. He is not merely an accountant, but a registrar also, keeping various statistical returns; he is also official scribe to the headman, and has to take an active part in the collection of the revenue. He is in different places variously called Berár, Bhoï, Kanakku-pillai, Kánungo, Karnam, Kaulige, Kauribhágiá, Kulkarni, Menon, Paṭwári, Shánbhog, Taláṭi.

Vimána. [Sanskrit.] A car or chariot of the gods, carrying them self-moving through the skies, and serving also as a seat or throne. Later, a temple. A Dravidian temple consists of four parts: the vimána, or actual temple, which is square in plan and surmounted by a pyramidal roof; the manṭapa, or porch; the gopura, or gateway towers; and the cháwaḍi, or pillared hall; the gopura is much higher than the temple proper. Compare the Aryan temple called Mandir.

Vinaya. [Sanskrit, from *vini*, to lead.] Leading, discipline; the name of one of the three piṭakas, that which treats of discipline for the order of bhikshus.

Vináyak. [Sanskrit, from *vi*, away, and *ni*, to lead.] Literally, the remover; a name of Ganeśa, also of Garuḍa.

Vindhya. [Sanskrit, perhaps from *bind*, to divide.] The name of the mountainous tract of country which runs across India from the province of Gujarát to that of Behar, and divides Hindustán from the Deccan. In explanation of the vast extent of this mountainous tract, contrasted with the small elevation of the hills, there is a legend relating that Vindhya, having prostrated himself before his guru, was ordered by him to remain in that position as a punishment for having emulated the lofty height of Himálaya and Meru.

Vira. [Sanskrit.] A departed spirit.

Vira. [Sanskrit, literally, bold, brave.] The name of the last arhat or jin of the Jains. See Tirthakar.

Virakallu. [Kanarese, from *vira*, a hero, and *kallu*, stone.] A sculptured stone erected in honour of a hero slain in battle; the slab generally consists of three compartments, the lowest representing the scene in which the hero fell; the middle one his triumphant ascent to the world of gods; and the top one the hero in the upper world seated before the divine linga (*L. Rice*). Compare Páliá.

Virbháv. [Bengali.] The name of a division of the Śákta sect.

Virchigam. [Malayálam, the Sanskrit *vriśchika*, a scorpion.] The month during which the sun is in Scorpio, corresponding most nearly to November and Kártik (in Bengal, Márgaśirsh). See Month.

Virla. See Irlá.

Vir Vaishnawa. Another name of the Madhwácharya sect.

Visa. [Hindi *vis*, twenty.] A term sometimes prefixed to the name of a caste to denote a branch of pure descent as opposed to a daśa branch.

Vishnu. [From *vish*, to pervade.] The second person of the Hindu triad—the preserver. See Trimurti. The name Vishnu occurs in the vedas as that of one of the twelve forms the sun takes in the course of the year, and Manu, in enumerating the various divine elements which the Bráhman may contemplate as existing in his body, says that in his power of motion he may perceive Vishnu. See Awatár, Hinduism, Vaishnawa, Wallabhácharya.

Vishnuvism. That form of Hinduism in which Vishnu is regarded as the principal god, usually in his awatár as Krishna. As compared with Śiwaism, it is a luxurious and sensuous religion, and it blended to some extent with Buddhism, while Śiwaism remained sharply antagonistic.

Vishnuvite. See Vaishnawa.

Viśishṭádvaita. [Sanskrit, from *viśishṭa*, distinct, and *advaita*, q.v.] The doctrine of the Rámánujas that purusha and prakriti, while distinct, are identical with Brahma.

Viswakarma. [Sanskrit, from *viswa*, everything, and *karma*, maker.] The name of a god, sometimes identical with Prajápati as the creator of all things, and sometimes with Twashtri as the architect of the gods. He presides over all manual labours and arts. From his five sons the Kanarese Páncháḷa claim descent, and the name is now applied particularly to one small subdivision of the Páncháḷa.

Viṭhobá, or **Viṭhṭhal.** [Maráṭhi.] The name of a god considered to be a form of Krishna. He is worshipped principally at Pandharpur, in the Deccan, and more especially by the mean and despised classes. A descriptive derivation has been invented for the name: *vit*, knowledge, *ṭha*, without, *la*, to take; the receiver of those without knowledge. His image is usually accompanied by that of his wife Rakhumai, each with the hands resting on the hips. The chief propagator of the worship of this god was the Maráṭhi poet Tukárám, who lived in the time of Śiwaji and Charles II., and was a follower of Chaitanya. See Wárkari.

Viyogi. [Sanskrit, from *vi*, apart, and *yoga*, junction.] One who is separated from society, as opposed to the Sanyogi.

Vizier. See Wazir.

Vorá. [Gujaráti, perhaps from the Sanskrit *vyawahára*, business.] The name of some large classes of Musalmáns in Gujarát converted from various Hindu castes. There are two main divisions of them, recognizing one another, but differing strangely in appearance: the first are the village Vorás, a fine manly race, devoted entirely to agriculture, but very quarrelsome among themselves, and utterly reckless in their animosity; the second are the city Vorás, who are engaged exclusively in trade. The village Vorás are Sunnis; the city Vorás, excepting only the Jáfari or Pátani sect, are all Shiahs of the Ismaili sect, Mustáli branch. The city Vorás are divided into the following classes: Daudi, Sulimáni, Alia, Nágoshi, and Jáfari.

Vriddhi. [Sanskrit, from *vridh*, to increase.] A grammatical term for the increase of vowels under certain conditions: by vriddhi *a* becomes *á*; *i* or *e* becomes *ai*; and *o* or *u* becomes *au*.

Vrihaspati. [Sanskrit, from *vrih*, to increase, and *pati*, lord.] The lord of increase, the name of the preceptor or purohit of the gods; also the planet Jupiter.

Vrindá. [Sanskrit.] The tulsi plant, the holy basil, personified also as a nymph beloved by Krishna.

Vrindáwan. A more classical form of Bindrában. Also a masonry stand or altar on which the tulsi is grown; a tulsidán.

Vritra. [Sanskrit.] A spirit of evil who imprisons the rain and causes drought.

Vyáhriti. [Sanskrit.] This word, which means literally utterance, is applied in particular to the three mystic words, *bhur*, *bhuwah*, and *swar*, or earth, the middle region, and heaven.

Vyási. The Tamil name of the solar month Eddavam, corresponding most nearly to May, Vaiśákh, and in Bengal to Jyeshṭh. See Month.

Vyawahára. [Sanskrit.] Worldly occupation and especially judicial procedure.

Vyetal. See Vetála.

Vyseea. See Vaiśya.

W.

Wáḍá. [Maráṭhi, from *wáḍ*, a hedge, from the Sanskrit *wáṭa*, enclosed, from *waṭ*, to surround.] An enclosure, the yard of a house; a large house with all its precincts; a ward or quarter of a town, as Khátkiwáḍá, the butchers' quarter. See Bári, Ṭolá, Wáḍi.

Waḍár. [Maráṭhi.] The name of a wild wandering tribe; they are stone-cutters and rat-catchers.

Waḍḍa. [Kanarese.] The name of a caste belonging originally to Orissa (Sanskrit *Oḍra*, whence the name); they are earth-workers, tank-diggers, well-sinkers, and some, distinguished as Kallu Waḍḍas, are stonemasons. They allow polygamy and the re-marriage of widows and divorced women. They are probably the same race as the Oḍs and Oṭṭas. They worship all the Hindu deities.

Waderu. [Sindhi.] The name of a village officer whose office has now fallen into disuse; he was probably originally the head of the village; in later times his duty was to summon the villagers for the annual clearance and repair of the canals and water-courses required for irrigation.

Wadi. [Sanskrit.] A term used after the name of a month to denote that the krishnapaksha or dark half is meant. See Month, Śudh, Tithi.

Wáḍi. This is the feminine form of Wáḍá. Its use is generally more literal than that of the masculine form. An enclosed field is a wáḍi rather than a wáḍá; a large house may be either; a country residence of which the garden is the main feature is a wáḍi; so is an enclosed hamlet distinct from the main village; the quarter of a town occupied by one caste is a wáḍá, though it have no ring fence; a rectangle of houses with the space enclosed is a wáḍi.

Wádi. A wandering tribe of Gujarát; they are conjurers, snake-charmers, and in particular dealers in the stone hand-mills used for grinding grain. Some have been converted to iślám.

Waduga. [Tamil, literally, north-man. Compare the Kanarese Badaga.] The name of a group of castes of Telugu origin; it includes the Kammawa, Káwarai, Reḍḍi, and Tottiya castes. They are mostly Vaishnawas, wear the sacred thread, and burn their dead. Also the name of a division of the Paraiyans, employed chiefly as palanquin-bearers.

Wáḍwal. [Maráṭhi.] The name of a small Hindu caste of the Konkan. They are gardeners, cultivating in particular the pán plant.

Waghair. The name of a tribe settled on the coast of the gulf of Cutch; they are fishermen and boatmen; those of Okhamánḍal are Hindus, but those of Hallar and of the opposite coast are Muhammadans. In the monsoon, when their boats are laid up, they take to cultivation.

Wághdewa. [Hindi *wágh*, a tiger, *dewa*, god.] The tiger regarded as a god and worshipped by some wild tribes.

Wághela. The name of a branch of the Chálukya Rájputs; they reigned at Anhilpur in Gujarát in the thirteenth century, and under the name Bhagel are still ruling in Rewa.

Wághnakh. [Maráṭhi, from *wágh*, tiger, and *nakh*, claw.] A tiger's claw, the name of a weapon used by the Maráṭhás.

Wághri. [Gujaráti, from the Sanskrit *wágura*, a net.] A class of persons whose occupation is the snaring of animals. They also sell vegetables and sticks, and some deal in cattle. They cultivate, too, but chiefly vegetables. Some bury and some burn their dead.

Wághyá. [Maráṭhi.] The tiger-god, Wághdewa. Some devotees of Khanḍobá call themselves by this name.

Wahábi. The name of a body of Musalmán reformers, so called after the name of their leader Shaikh Abdul Wahâb (born 1691 and died 1787 A.D.), but calling themselves Muwahaddin. During the eighteenth century they overran the greater part of Arabia, and in 1808 took Mecca and Medina. Their object was to sweep away all later innovations and return to the original religion of Muhammad and his companions. They rejected the Shiah heresy altogether and the four Sunni imáms, and all the caliphs but the first four. They also condemned the excessive reverence paid to the prophet himself, and disapproved of the decoration of temples and tombs; they threw down all minarets and distributed the treasures collected at Muhammad's tomb. This conduct caused a reaction to set in against them, and, with the aid of Turkish troops, they were driven out of the holy places, and their own capital, Deraiah, taken, and their leader put to death. The propagator of the reform in India was Saïd Ahmad, who was born at Rái Bareli in 1786, and was converted to Wahábism while making the haj.

Wáhan. [Sanskrit, from *wah*, to carry.] A vehicle, a chariot; any animal used in riding or draught, as the bull of Śiwa, or the rat of Ganeśa. Compare Rath.

Wahi. [Gujaráti.] An account-book; the merchant's wahis are worshipped at the diwáli. Also, the Bháṭ's record of genealogy and of births, marriages, and deaths among his clients.

Wahiwanchá. [Gujaráṭi *wánch*, to read.] An expounder of genealogies, a Bháṭ.

Wahiwáṭ. [Maráṭhi.] Administration, management; also enjoyment, use. Loosely used for practice, routine.

Wahiwáṭdár. [Persian *dár*, holder.] An administrator. In Baroda, the officer in charge of a mahál.

Wajra. [Sanskrit.] Literally, hard, adamantine; the name of the weapon of Indra, which is sometimes described as quoit-shaped like the chakra of Vishnu, and sometimes as consisting of two transverse bolts; a thunderbolt.

Wakálatnámah. [Persian *námah*, a document.] A letter appointing a wakil or representative, a power of attorney.

Wákátaka. The name of a Yawana dynasty that held part of Khándesh in the fifth or early in the sixth century A.D.

Wakf. See Waqf.

Wakil. [Arabic.] A person invested with authority to act for another, a representative, an ambassador, an agent; also, and especially, an attorney, a pleader authorized by sanad of a high court.

Wakliga. See Wokkaliga.

Wál. [Gujaráti.] The pulse dolichos lablab, or cow-gram; it is a rabi crop, and is often sown 'with the castor-oil plant. See Gram.

Wálá. This is a word of very common use in the vernaculars of India; it may be affixed to almost any noun or verb, and the word so formed then denotes a person connected in some way with the thing expressed by the first word; thus *gári-wálá* means cart-man, *ṭopi-wálá* one who wears a ṭopi, *Surat-wálá* one who lives in Surat, *ábru-wálá* a man of honour, *dene-wálá* a man in debt, *dudh-wálá* one who deals in milk; the connection may also be merely temporary, as *bolne-wálá* one who is speaking, *ṭopalá-wálá* a man with a basket in his hand. Wálá is often spelt *wallah* in English.

Wálá. [Maráṭhi.] The grass andropogon muricatum, the roots of which are fragrant and are used for making ṭaṭṭis; the Hindustáni khaskhas.

Wálá. The name of a dynasty that formerly ruled in Soreth; they were closely connected with, if not a division of, the Káṭhis.

Walad. [Arabic.] Son of; a prefix to a father's name. See Bin.

Wáland. [Gujaráti.] A barber, a hajám.

Walandez. [A corruption of *Hollandois.*] A Dutchman.

Walangai. The Tamil equivalent of Balagai. The principal members of the right-hand and left-hand factions are the same throughout the peninsula, but there are local variations both of caste and name. The Pariahs take the place of the Kanarese Holeyas. See Idangai, Left-hand.

Wále. [Kanarese.] Cadjan leaves used to write upon.

Wálekár. [Kanarese, from *wále*, q.v., and the Sanskrit *kára*, agent.] One who carries notes or messages, a harkára or peon.

Walgániá. [Gujaráti.] The name of a subdivision of the Dheḍs.

Wali. [Arabic.] A protector, guardian, or patron; also a master, a lord; a fakir who has attained to great sanctity.

Wáli. The Gujaráti form of Wali. Also a sponsor for an infant bride or bridegroom at a wedding.

Waliyan. [Tamil, from *walai*, a net.] The name of a low tribe; they snare animals, catch fish, smelt iron, or are employed as field-labourers or coolies.

Wálkala. [Sanskrit, from *wálka*, bark.] A dress made of the bark of trees, worn by ascetics.

Wallabhácharya. [Sanskrit.] The name of a Vaishnawa sect founded by Wallabha about the end of the fifteenth century. They worship the god Krishna as a youth, with his wives, the gopis, or cowherdesses. Their way of salvation is a corruption of the proper Vaishnawa *bhakti-márg*, and is called *pushṭi-márg*, or the way of enjoyment in a natural and carnal sense. Their spiritual chiefs, called mahárájas (whence the sect is also sometimes so called), dress and decorate themselves as gopis in order to commend themselves to Krishna, and to indicate that women united to them are joined only to the god Krishna. The Wallabhácháryas profess to dedicate their bodies, souls, and property to Krishna through the mahárájas. The sect is found in

Bombay, Gujarát, Cutch, and central and north-western India. Their tilak consists of two vertical lines, joined by a semicircle at the top of the nose, and a round red spot between them.

Wallabhi. The name of an era which began in samwat 375, or 319 A.D.

Wallah. [A corruption of *Wálá*, q.v.] This word, though properly only an affix, is sometimes used in English by itself; it then stands for *competition-wallah*, and denotes a member of the Indian civil service who has obtained his appointment by competition, as distinguished from those appointed under the previous system of nomination.

Wallamban. [Tamil.] The name of a caste, said to be the offspring of a Vellálan and a Waliyan woman; they are cultivators.

Wálmiki. [Sanskrit, from *walmika*, an ant-hill.] The name of the author of the Rámáyana, so called, according to some, because when immersed in thought he allowed himself to be overrun with ants like an ant-hill.

Wáman. [Sanskrit.] The dwarf, the fifth awatár of Vishnu. The legend is that a demon named Bali, or Balrájá, having obtained dominion over heaven, earth, and pátál, Vishnu took birth as a dwarf, and, appearing before him and obtaining as a boon as much land as he could stride over in three paces, stepped first over heaven, then over earth, and then refraining, in compassion, from a third step, left Bali still master of pátál; or, according to another version, there being no place for the third step, Bali offered his head and was trodden down to pátál and made its ruler. A festival in commemoration of this incarnation is held on the 12th Bhádrapad śudh.

Wán. [Hindi.] The tree salvadora oleoides; it grows commonly in waste lands, and especially in the saline tracts that border on the Indus and the Panjáb rivers; the leaves resemble those of the laurel, the flower is white and in shape like a violet, the fruit is the pilu.

Wánaprastha. [Sanskrit, from *wana*, a forest, and *prastha*, proceeding.] A Bráhman in his third áśrama or stage of life, a hermit, an anchoret. 'When the father of a family perceives his muscles become flaccid and his hair grey and sees the child of his child, let him then seek refuge in a forest' (*Manu*, vi. 2). This stage of life seems to have been meant as a period of preparation for the final sannyási stage. It was to be spent in the forest, where, with ever-increasing mortifications, the Bráhman was to dry up his bodily frame. The wánaprastha stage might indeed be omitted altogether, and the Bráhman proceed at once from householder to sannyási (*Manu*, vi. 38).

Wáni. [Maráṭhi, from the Sanskrit *wanij*, a merchant.] The name of a caste; they are corn-chandlers, retail-dealers, and money-lenders. The name is identical with Banyá, or Bunia, and is sometimes used, like that word, to denote the profession and not the caste. Some Wánis are Jains, some Vaishnawas, and some Lingáits. Some, as the Kudáli and Pátani Wánis, engage in agriculture as well as trade.

Wániá. The Gujaráti form of Wáni.

This caste in Gujarát is divided into the Daśa and Visa branches, and according to their religion into Mesaris and Śráwaks.

Wánikan. [Tamil.] The name of a low caste; they extract oil from various seeds, principally rape seed. As a rule, the Wánikan buys the seed from farmers, and himself sells the oil.

Wánjá. The name of a caste; they are silk-weavers.

Wanjárá, or **Wanjári.** Maráṭhi forms of Banjárá. Some Wanjárás have given up travelling, and have settled in the Konkan as resident traders and money-lenders.

Wannán. [Tamil.] The name of a caste; they are washermen. A division of them, called Potharawannáns, are the washermen for the Pariahs, Pallans, and other very low castes.

Wanniyan. [Tamil.] The name of a small and obscure agricultural caste. They formerly held a good position among the tribes of southern India.

Wanpayir. [Tamil.] Certain specially taxed products, viz. betel-vines, turmeric, plantains, chillies, and brinjals.

Wánṭá. [Gujaráti, from the Sanskrit *wanṭa*, a portion.] The alienated portion of the lands of a village, that is, the parts paying either no assessment or only a salámi. See Talpad.

Wáo. [Gujaráti, from the Sanskrit *wápi*, a large oblong pond.] A particular kind of well of elaborate structure; a long, straight passage, protected by side-walls and containing a flight of broad, easy steps, leads from the surface of the ground down to the water; portions of the passage are sometimes roofed over to form sheltered resting-places. The Hindi name is báoli.

Waoḍi. [Gujaráti.] A small wáo.

Waqf. [Arabic.] A bequest for religious or charitable purposes; an endowment.

Wara. See Wáḍá.

Waráḍi. Pertaining to Waráḍ or Berar; a term applied to a particular short-stapled cotton indigenous in Berar.

Waragu. The Tamil name of the common millet, paspalum frumentaceum. The Hindi name is kodra.

Waráh. [Sanskrit.] The boar, the name of the third awatár of Vishnu. In this form the god raised the earth from the water in which it was submerged. Some accounts say that a demon Hiranyaksh had carried the earth away to the bottom of the sea and that the boar rescued it.

Warát. [Maráṭhi.] A marriage procession, a barát; also an assignment on the revenue of a district.

Wardak. A tribe of Afghánistán. They are Saïds, and dwell in cultivated valleys bound on three sides by the Ghilzai country, and on the west by the Ghor mountains. They are comparatively quiet and obedient, and devoted to agriculture.

Wardhamán. See under Tirthakar.

Wárendriya. [Bengali, from the Sanskrit *wárendri*, the ancient name of the modern Rájsháhi.] The name of a branch of the Gauḍa (subdivision) Bráhmans.

Warghoḍá. [Maráṭhi, from *wara*, a bridegroom, and *ghodá*, a horse.] The procession of the bridegroom, or that of the bride and bridegroom; also the procession to the upanayana ceremony. Compare Barát.

Wari. [Maráṭhi.] The small millet, panicum miliaceum, or chenna; it is a warkas crop in the Deccan.

Wárkari. [Maráṭhi, from *wár*, a day, and *kari*, the active affix.] One who is dependent upon daily alms, or makes a daily pilgrimage; the name of a sect of Chaitanyas in the Deccan, whose favourite god is Viṭhṭhal of Pandharpur.

Warkas. [Maráṭhi.] Hilly land on which, in accordance with the mode of cultivation in use in the Konkan, the cultivators cut grass, brushwood, and branches of trees to be burned as manure (ráb) on their rice-fields. This, and not cultivation, is the use to which warkas land is ordinarily appropriated; but patches of such land are from time to time used for raising scanty crops of inferior grain, such as náchni, káng, and wari. The crops raised are also called warkas.

Wárli. The name of a tribe found in the jungly tracts of the coast tálukás of the Konkan. They wear long hair and beards generally untrimmed, are much given to drink, and rear many fowls but few cattle. They worship only Wághyá, the lord of tigers, whom they represent by a very rude figure of a tiger carved on a rough stone and set upright in any wild spot. They have no respect for Bráhmans, and their marriage ceremonies are performed by their own women. They eat monkeys as well as other animals (*A. K. Nairne*).

Warmálá. [Gujaráti, from the Sanskrit *wara*, a bridegroom, and *málá*, a garland.] The garland with which a maiden chose her husband at a swayamwara; the garland with which the bride and bridegroom are joined together at a modern marriage.

Warna. [Sanskrit.] A colour, a class, an order, a caste. The common name of the four divisions of Hindus, according to Manu, namely, Bráhmans, Kshatriyas, Vaiśyas, and Śudras. Hindu writers have always accepted this division as being as old as society, and represent each class as having sprung from a different member of Brahmá. The first division, Colebrooke suggests, was into freemen and slaves; and among the freemen two orders of nobility arose — the sacerdotal (or Bráhmans), who were the descendants of a few religious men, the austerity of whose lives earned for them the estimation of holiness, and the kingly (or Kshatriyas), who were the descendants of persons chosen to be rulers. The members of these two orders would in early times be few in number, and the bulk of the community would be the agricultural and trading classes (Vaiśyas) and the slaves (Śudras). See Caste.

Warra. See Wáḍá.

War-rájá. [Gujaráti, from the Sanskrit *wara*, a bridegroom, and *rájá*, a king.] The title of a bridegroom, who is treated for the time with royal state. In the north of India he is similarly called *naushâh*, or new king.

Warsha. [Sanskrit, literally, rain.] The season of the two solar months during which the sun is passing through the signs Cancer and Leo;

where the luni-solar year is observed the season is defined either as the two months Áshádh and Śráwan or as Śráwan and Bhádrapad. See Ritu, Year.

Warsháasan. [Maráṭhi, from *warsha*, a year.] An annual allowance or pension. Compare Sáliánah.

Wartaniá. [Gujaráti, perhaps from the Sanskrit *warttana*, means of subsistence, a derivation which would correspond with that of jiwáidár.] A village guard or watchman. Wartaniás constitute the village police, and are under the orders of the police paṭel. They are usually Kolis, Bhils, or Taláviás. They are remunerated either by rent-free land or a small cash allowance. Each one carries either a sword or a bow and arrow.

Waruna. [Sanskrit, from *vri*, to envelop.] The god of the sky, the all-enveloper. Waruna is one of the oldest vedic gods. He corresponds in name and partly in character to the Greek Ouranos. He is generally represented in fellowship with Mitra, and as presiding over the night as Mitra over the day. Yet he is also addressed as lord of all, as king of gods as well as of men. In particular he knows the whole order of nature and the future as well as the past. Waruna afterwards came to be a secondary deity and one of the ádityas, and again to be the god of the waters resting on the earth.

Waruni. The goddess of wine, regarded in the later mythology as the wife of Waruna.

Was. [Sinhalese, from Sanskrit *warsha*, rain.] The rainy season, during which Buddhist teachers are exempt from pilgrimage and allowed to settle in one place.

Wasá. [Gujaráti.] The twentieth part of a bighá.

Wasant. [Sanskrit, from *was*, to shine.] Properly the season during which the sun is in Pisces and Aries; but where the luni-solar year is observed this season is defined either as Phálgun and Chaitra or as Chaitra and Vaiśákh. See Ritu, Year.

Wasáwá. [Gujaráti.] A village watchman, a rakhwálá.

Wásilát. [Hindustáni.] The proceeds of an estate, the mesne profits of land.

Wástuśánti. [Maráṭhi, from the Sanskrit *wástu*, the foundation of a house, from *was*, to dwell; and *śánti*, tranquillity, from *śam*, to be pacified.] Particular ceremonies, including the employment of dancing-girls, towards the composing of evil spirits, observed on taking up residence in a new house.

Wásudewa. [Sanskrit.] An epithet of Krishna as the son of Wasudewa. Also the name of a class of mendicants in the Deccan.

Wásuki. [Sanskrit.] The name of the fabulous sovereign of the serpents; sometimes the same with, sometimes distinguished from, Śeshnág.

Waswáyá. [Gujaráti.] The village establishment of artisans in Gujarát, such as the carpenter, the smith, the oilman, the shoemaker, the tailor, the goldsmith, the potter, the barber. They usually enjoy pasáetá land. Compare Balutá.

Watan. [Arabic.] Native country; among the Maráṭhás it has come to mean an hereditary estate, a patrimony; and under the Bombay revenue system it means the duties, and the rights, and the property assigned in remuneration, of any hereditary office connected with the public revenue, the village police, or other matter of civil administration. The remuneration is most commonly in the form of pasáetá or wávlá land, but it may consist of cash payments or merely of a right to levy fees or perquisites in money or in kind. See Śáśwat.

Watandár. [Maráṭhi, Persian *dár*, holder.] The holder of a watan. The duties of some watandárs, such as deśáis, deśmukhs, deśpáṇḍes, pertained in former times to the táluká or parganah, but their services have been for the most part dispensed with, especially since 1863, when settlements were made with them by which, on payment of a quit-rent, their watan lands became private property. Village watandárs continue. Many páṭils and paṭels and kulkarnis (but no taláṭis) are watandárs. So also are lower village servants, as the Mahárs and Dheḍs, the jiwáidárs, wartaniás, and veṭhiás, who are classed as useful to government, and others useful to the village community, as the kumbhár, lohár, suthár, the kázi, ghámoṭ, guru, and joshi. The services of other village watandárs have been dispensed with as useless; among these were the potdár, mahájan, śikalgár, beldár, and chaudhri.

Water-rate. Under the native systems of settlement the government revenue was either a share of the actual crop or was calculated according to the actual production, and thus the government received its proper share of the benefit arising from the use of irrigation; under the English system (see Settlement), in order to secure the same result, water-rates are imposed. These are either fixed on the same principles as the soil-rates, and combined with them into one total assessment on each field, or, where the use of irrigation may be optional, are imposed separately.

Wávlá. [Gujaráti.] Land granted rent free or at a low rate as remuneration to village servants. See Chákarán, Inám.

Wáwá. The name of a caste in Cutch; they are grain-parchers.

Wáyu. [Sanskrit.] Wind, the god of the wind. He is one of the vedic gods. Hanumán the monkey-god and Bhima the Páṇḍawa were considered to be incarnations of him. He moves in a shining car drawn by purple horses.

Wazifah. [Arabic, from *waza*, deduction.] A pension, a stipend; also land granted either rent free or at a quit-rent by the Muhammadan government to kázis or other meritorious persons. See Inám.

Wazir. [Arabic.] The prime minister under a Muhammadan ruler.

Waziri. The name of a powerful and independent Paṭhán tribe, supposed to be descended from the Shoḍá Rájputs. In personal appearance they are very different from other Paṭhán tribes, and they retain many customs peculiar to themselves. They are settled beyond the Derá Ismail Khán frontier, with the Zymukhts on their north and the Ghilzais on the west. They number 20,000 fighting men and hold both sides of the Gomal pass.

Wilayat. See Viláyat.

Wodea. [From the Kanarese *odeya*, a lord.] The name of a caste of the Nilgiri hills, a division of the Badagas; they are a branch of the reigning family of Mysore, and are proud and poor. By religion they are Lingáits.

Wokkaliga. [Kanarese.] A cultivator, a farmer; the name of the agricultural caste of Mysore, of which there are some sixty subdivisions. Some are Vaishnawas and some Śaiwas, but all eat together without distinction, though they intermarry only in their tribes.

Woon. [Burmese.] Literally, burden; thence the burden of affairs, or the bearer of it, an official (*R. H. Pilcher*).

Woondouk. [Burmese.] An assistant to the Woongyee, a kind of under-secretary of state. In British Burma an assistant-commissioner.

Woongyee. [Burmese, from *woon*, q.v., and *gyee*, great.] A great official, the title of the officials of highest rank in the Burma kingdom; there are four of them; they are the chief members of the hlootdau.

Wordie Major. [Perhaps a corruption of the Kanarese *varadi*, information, a message, an order; *wardi* was also a title, and perhaps a military one, among the Rájputs.] A native adjutant. See under Risáldár.

Wotari. See Otári.

Wuḍḍar. [Telugu, from *voḍḍe* or *oḍḍe*, the old name of Orissa, the Sanskrit *oḍhra*.] The name of a caste; they are tank-diggers, and move about from place to place as they have work, and sometimes engage in the carrying trade. Compare Oḍ, Oṭṭa, Waḍḍa.

Wulfa. See Uluphá.

Wulsa. See Valasa.

Wye. See Wahi.

Wysnoo. See Vishnu.

Y.

Yabein. The name of a branch of the Mrammá race; they rear silkworms.

Yábu. The horse of the mountains near Kábul; it is a small breed, but heavy and very powerful.

Yád. [Persian.] Remembrance; a note, a memorandum. Native clerks in Bombay classify official letters as yáds, orders, and reports, the first being confined to communications between officers of similar rank.

Yádawa. [Sanskrit.] A descendant of Yadu, who was the son of Yayáti, a monarch of the lunar race. A line of Yádawa kings arose in the northern part of the old Chálukya kingdom at the end of the twelfth century. They overcame the Kalachuryas and became masters of all the western Deccan, having their capital at Dewagiri, the ancient Tagara, and now known as Daulatábád. The Yádawas had frequent struggles with the Hoysala Ballálas, till both were overthrown by the Musalmáns in the fourteenth century.

Yádi. Another form of Yád.

Yadu. The name of the most distinguished branch of the Chandrawansá, that in which both Krishna and the Buddha were born; it is now more generally known by the name Jádon or Jadubansi.

Yajamána. [Sanskrit, from *yaj*, to sacrifice.] One who institutes a sacrifice. The commoner vernacular form is Jajmán.

Yajmán. A vernacular form of Yajamána.

Yajmánvritti. [Hindi, from *yajamána*, and *vritti*, operation, function.] The duties of a patron, the obligation to support a family priest.

Yajnopavita. [Sanskrit, from *yajna*, sacrifice, and *upavita*.] The sacred cord worn by the dvija or twice-born classes as a mark of their second birth. 'The sacrificial thread of a Bráhman must be made of cotton, so as to be put on over his head in three strings; that of a Kshatriya, of hempen thread only; that of a Vaiśya of woollen thread' (*Manu*, ii. 44). See Janeo, Upanayana.

Yajur-veda. [Sanskrit, from *yajus*, sacrifice, and *vedu*, q.v.] The second veda; it is a collection of liturgical forms, or rather a sort of sacrificial prayer-book formed out of the rig-veda which had to be dissected and rearranged with additional texts for sacrificial purposes (*Monier Williams*).

Yajur-vedi. [Sanskrit.] Familiar with the yajur-veda; the name of a subdivision of the Mahárásh**ṭ**ra Bráhmans.

Yak. [Thibetan.] An animal of the ox kind—the pœphagus grunniens. It belonged originally to the mountains of Thibet. It has a long mane on the back, and the tail (of which chowries are made) is completely covered with long hairs like that of the horse.

Yaksha. [Sanskrit.] A mythical supernatural being or demigod. The yakshas attend on Kubera.

Yákula. [Kanarese.] The name of an agricultural caste in Mysore. Also the name of a division of the Golla caste.

Yama. [Sanskrit, literally, a rein or curb.] The god who presides over the spirits of the dead. In one place in the rig-veda he is spoken of as the first man that died, and thence as the guide to their home of later departed spirits. In post-vedic times he came to be considered as judge of the dead, sending each soul after trial either to swarga or narak.

Yamdut. [Hindi, from the Sanskrit *yama*, q.v., and *duta*, a messenger, from *du*, to go.] A messenger of death. The yamduts are supposed to seize and maltreat sinners at the time of death. Yamdut is a common nickname for a policeman.

Yanadi. [Telugu.] The name of a wild tribe of the Nellore district; they are employed in collecting forest produce and as agricultural labourers. They have adopted some Hindu customs, as wearing the boṭṭu, and call themselves Vaishnawas and Śaiwas. They bury their dead. Polygamy and widow remarriage are allowed.

Yati. [Sanskrit, from *yata*, restrained, from *yam*, to check.] A sage of subdued passions, an ascetic. The name is especially applied to the Jain ascetics in the north-west and south of India. Jain yatis are required to pluck out their hair or have it cut short, and to brush their seats and wear a cloth over their mouths lest they should crush or swallow any insect. See Ḍhunḍiá, Mohomati, Oghá.

Yátrá. The classical form of Játrá. Also a march or procession, or a dramatic representation.

Yaumiá. [Hindustáni, from the Arabic *yaum*, a day.] A daily pension. Compare Rozinah.

Yaw. The name of a branch of the Mrammá race; they are pedlars.

Yawana. [Sanskrit.] This name is first found as that of the Greeks, and is considered to be the Hindu form of Ionian; subsequently the Hindus applied it to any race approaching India from the west of Asia; and finally to Muhammadans of every description.

Year. The years principally used for the measurement of time in India are (1) the luni-solar year, or the interval between new moon in one sign of the zodiac and new moon in the same sign again; (2) the sidereal year, or the interval between the sun's entering any sign and its entering that same sign again; and (3) the lunar year, or the interval between any new moon and the twelfth new moon thereafter. The luni-solar year is used for the samwat and the śaka eras; the samwat beginning with the new moon in the sign Scorpio, that is, the first day of Kártik śudh; and the śaka with the new moon in Aries, that is the first day of Chaitra (śudh or wadi, according as the śukladi or krishnadi mode is followed). The sidereal year is used for the Bengali san and the Paraśuráma eras; the san beginning with the entrance of the sun into the sign Taurus, that is, the first day of Baiśákh; and the Paraśuráma year beginning with the sun's entrance of Virgo, that is, the first day of Kani. The lunar year is used for the hijra era; the Muharram is reckoned the first month, and as the year consists of only 354 days and a fraction, each one begins about eleven days earlier in the season than the preceding year did. See Month. The Pársi year consists of twelve months of thirty days each, with five extra days added to the last month; an adhika month is intercalated once in 120 years.

Yeḍagai. [Kanarese *yeḍa*, left, and *gai*, hand.] The left-hand castes; they consist of the Pánchála, Beri, Dewánga, Heggániga, some of the Golla, Beḍar, Yákula, Palli or Tigala, and the Mádiga. See Left-hand, Balagai.

Yendal. [Tamil.] A very small tank or reservoir, chiefly found in the Melur country.

Yerawa. The name of a wild tribe in the south of Mysore; they are said to have originally belonged to Wainád, where they were held in slavery by the Náirs. They resemble the African in features, having thick lips and compressed noses. They speak a language of their own, a dialect of Malayálam. They are distinguished as Panjara and Paniyara Yerawas; the former allow their fleecy hair to grow in dense uncombed masses; the latter appear more civilized (*L. Rice*).

Yerukala. [Telugu.] The name of a tribe who speak a dialect of Tamil, call themselves Kurru, and are probably allied to the Kurawas, whom they resemble in their wandering habits and their occupations. They are carriers of salt and grain, cutters of firewood, basket-makers, split-bamboo workers, fortune-tellers, and some work for hire; some also have settled down to agriculture. They are lighter in colour and of better physique than the Yanadis. They worship Hindu gods, but each gang carries about a tribal god of its own. The old men act as priests and settle disputes. Polygamy and the remarriage of widows are allowed.

Yetmaum. See Ihtimám.

Yoga. [Sanskrit, from *yuj*, to join, to yoke.] The name of one of the six darśans, so called from the practice which it prescribes of fixing the body in one position and concentrating the thoughts on one point as an aid to abstract meditation. The yoga is a branch of the sánkhya system, but differs from it in affirming the existence of a supreme being.'

Yogi. [Sanskrit.] Properly a follower of the yoga philosophy, but commonly applied to any ascetic.

Yogini. A female yogi. Also the name of a class of malicious female fiends.

Yuga. [Sanskrit, from *yuj*, to join.] An age of the world; there are four yugas, called (1) krita or satya, (2) tretá, (3) dwápara, and (4) kali, and they are named from the marks on dice, the best mark being four points and the worst one (*Monier Williams*).

Yunáni. A system of Indian medicine said, as suggested by the name, to be of Greek (Ionian) origin.

Yusufzai. Sons of Joseph, the name of a great Paṭhán tribe, consisting of many clans, belonging to the Afghán̄s proper. They occupy the plain (called after their name) to the north-east of Peshávar, and the mountains beyond, and Buner, and are the dominant tribe in Swát.

Z

Zabti. [Hindustáni, from *zabt*, seizure.] Sequestrated, attached; applied to rent-free lands resumed, or on which assessment has been imposed. Under Todar Mal's settlement the term was applied to that land in which the more valuable crops were grown, and the assessment of which had to be paid in cash; with regard to the land on which cereals were grown the cultivator could claim a division of the actual crop. See Japti.

Zahrnamáz. [Arabic *zahr*, midday, and Persian *namáz*, prayer.] Midday prayer.

Zai. [Persian.] Born of, a son; affixed to a man's name to denote his party or the clan sprung from him. Compare Khel.

Zaka. The name of one of the khels or clans of the Afridis.

Zakát. [Arabic.] The legal alms or tithe collected under the Musalmán system from all persons of substance for distribution among the poor. The name signifies purification, and is applied to this tax as the portion given sanctifies the use of the remainder.

Zamburká. [Hindi.] A weapon resembling a jinjál, but shorter and of larger calibre, a falconet.

Zamindár. [Hindustáni, from the Persian *zamin*, land, and *dár*, who has or possesses.] A landholder. Under the Muhammadan administration the zamindár was ordinarily considered as the responsible collector only of the revenues on behalf of government, and the chief authorities never hesitated to exercise the power, when they possessed it, of turning out a zamindár and putting another in his place. The zamindár was allowed a commission of ten per cent. on the total collections, besides which a portion of the land was exempted from assessment, and further deductions were allowed to cover various charges borne by the zamindár. Though in these respects the zamindár appears as a collector of the state revenue, yet the practice of hereditary succession, and the right to mortgage and sell, partook more of the tenure of ownership, and in the decline of the Muhammadan power the zamindárs assumed the state of chiefs and princes. By the perpetual settlement of 1793 the zamindárs of Bengal, Behar, and Orissa were recognized as enjoying their estates in absolute ownership as long as they paid the government revenue. In 1802 the same recognition was made in the case of the zamindárs of Madras (*H. H. Wilson*). In the Panjáb the term is used as equivalent to ryot.

Zamindári. The office and rights of a zamindár; also the tract of land he holds, his estate.

Zamorin. [Said to be a corruption of a Telugu word *samrát*, a sovereign; also said to be from *sumuri*, the crowing of a cock, the land granted having been so much as the crowing of a cock in a particular temple could be heard over.] The title of the ruler of Calicut.

Zanánah. [Persian, from *zan*, a woman.] Pertaining to women, the part of a house occupied by the women; the women of a family. The expression, 'zanánah system,' denotes the practice of keeping women secluded, and 'zanánah mission' the business of carrying education to women so secluded.

Zand. The word means commentary, but it has come to be the name of the language in which the sacred books of the Pársis are written. The Zand language is only separated by a short interval from that of one set of the cuneiform inscriptions, which again was closely followed by Pahlavi (*Monier Williams*).

Zand-Avastá. The popular name of the sacred writings of the Pársis. See Avastá. There is some confusion in the naming of these writings. The original name of the first scripture seems to have been avastá; on this a commentary or zand was written in the Pahlavi language, and then the name Zand was given to the language of the original. When the Pahlavi zand of the avastá became itself obsolete, it was underwritten in a more modern language, which received the name of Pázand.

Zarayet. See Ziráat.

Zemindar. See Zamindár.

Zhobwál. A native of the Zhob valley or country; they are chiefly of the Kákar tribe.

Zila. More commonly Zillah.

Ziárat. [Arabic.] Pilgrimage, going on pilgrimage to a Muhammadan shrine; also a place of pilgrimage, as Hazir Pir's Ziárat. See Haj.

Ziladár. [Hindustáni, Persian *dár*, holder.] The officer in charge of a zila or zillah; in the Delhi territory the title was given to the manager of a few villages.

Zilhijjah. [Arabic.] The last month of the Musalmán year.

Zilkadah. [Arabic.] The eleventh month of the Musalmán year, following Shawál.

Zillah. [A corruption of the Arabic *zila.*] A part, a division, a district; especially one of the main divisions into which the territory under one government is divided for the purposes of civil administration. The word is used sometimes as synonymous with collectorate, which denotes the territory in charge of a collector, and sometimes as denoting a judicial district which may comprise one or more collectorates.

Zimmah. [Arabic.] A deed of protection, an authorized assurance of immunity in life and property, such as may be granted to infidels under a Muhammadan government; also the corresponding obligation of subjection, fidelity, obedience; also trust, charge, custody; a tenure in trust, but which, by possession, came to signify a tenure in right in some places, in others an under-tenure or a subdivision of an estate, in which the holder is entitled to levy the revenue due by the cultivators, and pay it either to the zamindár, or sometimes direct to the government; a sub-tenure, part of a hawálá (*H. H. Wilson*).

Zimmahdár. [Persian *dár*, holder.] A trustee, a person in charge; also the holder of an under-tenure or portion of a zamindári.

Zimmahnámah. [Persian *námah*, a document.] A deed of trust, authority to have charge and make the collections of an estate.

Zimmi. [Arabic.] One who lives under protection; especially one who, being of another religion, pays tribute to live without molestation under a Musalmán government.

Zinda Pir. [Persian *zindagi*, life.] One who is accounted a saint even in his lifetime.

Ziráat. [Arabic.] Agriculture, cultivation, farming; a cultivated farm or field; sometimes land not artificially irrigated. See Jiráit. Also, in Bengal, lands subject to assessment.

Zohrak. [Sindhi *jaurak.*] The common cargo-boat of the Indus between Bukkur and Attock, drawing less water and sailing faster than the doondah, which takes its place lower down the river.

Zoolum. See Zulm.

Zoroastrian. The name now given to the religion of the Pársis, called after the founder Zoroaster (Zarathustra), who is supposed to have lived in the sixth century B.C. It was the religion of Persia till that country was converted to islám; meanwhile the Pársis had brought the creed with them to India. The religion is monotheistic: the principle of good is personified as Ahura Mazda or Hormazd, and symbolized by the sun or by fire; the opposing principle of evil is personified as Ahriman, and symbolized by darkness. The efficacy of prayer, a general resurrection, and a future heaven and hell, are other articles of belief. The Zoroastrian scriptures are called the avastá, which originally, as delivered by Zoroaster, consisted of twenty-one books in the Zand language, but the greater part of these have been lost; only the vandidád and a few other books or fragments of books remain. Repetitions from these works or their Pahlavi translations, which are not now understood, are to strangers the most prominent feature of the religion. There is a separate hereditary priestly class distinguished by their white turbans, but not all these actually serve as priests; some engage in trade or other business. There are three orders of priests, namely, dastur, mobed, and andhyáru.

Zulfakári. [Hindustáni, from the Arabic *zu-al-faqár*, or lord of the back-bone, the name of the sword of Ali.] The name of the currency of Hyderabad, which bears an impression of the sword of Ali, the prophet's son-in-law.

Zulm. [Arabic.] Tyranny, oppression, a heavier assessment than can be borne.

Zumbooruk. See Zamburká.

Zuptee. See Zabti.

Zymukht. A Paṭhán tribe occupying the country between the Arakzais on the north and the Waziris to the south. They are subjects of the Kábul government.

ADDENDA.

Arike. See under Millet.

Banṭi. See under Millet.

Bathi. See under Karáo.

Bero Gosain. The name of a god, said to be the sun, worshipped by some hill tribes.

Cholum. See under Millet.

Dátan. [Gujaráti, from the Sanskrit *danta*, a tooth.] A little stick cut from some tree, such as the bábul or neem, of which the juice has a cleansing property, and used by the natives of India in the place of a tooth-brush.

Hanumán. [Sanskrit, from *hanu*, the jaw.] Having (large) jaws; the name of a god who, according to some legends, is a son of Śiwa, but who is commonly conceived as one of the chiefs of the monkey armies that assisted Ráma in his war with Ráwana. See Rámáyana.

Hesaru. See under Mung.

Jadubansi. See under Yadu.

Jonna. See under Millet.

Korra. See under Millet.

Naushāh. See under War-rájá.

Oreng. The title of a god worshipped by the Mro tribe.

Sitá. [Sanskrit.] A furrow or husbandry personified as a goddess. Also the name of the wife of Ráma. See Rámáyana.

PRINTED BY WILLIAM CLOWES AND SONS, LIMITED, LONDON AND BECCLES.

A LIST OF

KEGAN PAUL, TRENCH, & CO.'S

PUBLICATIONS.

7,85

1 Paternoster Square, London.

A LIST OF

KEGAN PAUL, TRENCH, & CO.'S PUBLICATIONS.

CONTENTS.

A. K. H. B.—FROM A QUIET PLACE. A New Volume of Sermons. Crown 8vo. 5*s.*

ALLEN (Rev. R.) M.A.—ABRAHAM; HIS LIFE, TIMES, AND TRAVELS, 3,800 years ago. With Map. Second Edition. Post 8vo. 6*s.*

ALLIES (T. W.) M.A.—PER CRUCEM AD LUCEM. The Result of a Life. 2 vols. Demy 8vo. 25*s.*

A LIFE'S DECISION. Crown 8vo. 7*s.* 6*d.*

ALLNATT (F. J. B.) B.D.—THE WITNESS OF ST. MATTHEW. An Inquiry into the Sequence of Inspired Thought pervading the First Gospel, and into its Result of Unity, Symmetry, and Completeness, as a Perfect Portrait of the Perfect Man. Crown 8vo. 5*s.*

AMOS (Prof. Sheldon)—THE HISTORY AND PRINCIPLES OF THE CIVIL LAW OF ROME. An aid to the study of Scientific and Comparative Jurisprudence. Demy 8vo. 16*s.*

ANCIENT and MODERN BRITONS: a Retrospect. 2 vols. demy 8vo. 24*s.*

ANDERDON (Rev. W. H.)—FASTI APOSTOLICI. A Chronology of the Years between the Ascension of Our Lord and the Martyrdom of SS. Peter and Paul. Second Edition Enlarged. Square 8vo. 5*s.*

EVENINGS WITH THE SAINTS. Crown 8vo. 5*s.*

ANDERSON (David)—'SCENES' IN THE COMMONS. Crown 8vo. 5*s.*

ARMSTRONG (Richard A.) B.A.—LATTER-DAY TEACHERS. Six Lectures. Small crown 8vo. 2*s.* 6*d.*

AUBERTIN (J. J.)—A FLIGHT TO MEXICO. With 7 full-page Illustrations and a Railway Map of Mexico. Crown 8vo. 7*s.* 6*d.*

BADGER (George Percy) D.C.L.—AN ENGLISH-ARABIC LEXICON. In which the equivalents for English Words and Idiomatic Sentences are rendered into literary and colloquial Arabic. Royal 4to. 80*s.*

BAGEHOT (Walter)—THE ENGLISH CONSTITUTION. New and Revised Edition. Crown 8vo. 7*s*. 6*d*.

LOMBARD STREET. A Description of the Money Market. Eighth Edition. Crown 8vo. 7*s*. 6*d*.

ESSAYS ON PARLIAMENTARY REFORM. Crown 8vo. 5*s*.

SOME ARTICLES ON THE DEPRECIATION OF SILVER, AND TOPICS CONNECTED WITH IT. Demy 8vo. 5*s*.

BAGENAL (Philip H.)—THE AMERICAN-IRISH AND THEIR INFLUENCE ON IRISH POLITICS. Crown 8vo. 5*s*.

BAGOT (Alan) C.E.—ACCIDENTS IN MINES: Their Causes and Prevention. Crown 8vo. 6*s*.

THE PRINCIPLES OF COLLIERY VENTILATION. Second Edition, greatly enlarged, crown 8vo. 5*s*.

THE PRINCIPLES OF CIVIL ENGINEERING IN ESTATE MANAGEMENT. Crown 8vo. 7*s*. 6*d*.

BAKER (Sir Sherston, Bart.)—THE LAWS RELATING TO QUARANTINE. Crown 8vo. 12*s*. 6*d*.

BALDWIN (Capt. J. H.)—THE LARGE AND SMALL GAME OF BENGAL AND THE NORTH-WESTERN PROVINCES OF INDIA. Small 4to. With 20 Illustrations. New and Cheaper Edition. Small 4to. 10*s*. 6*d*.

BALLIN (Ada S. and F. L.)—A HEBREW GRAMMAR. With Exercises selected from the Bible. Crown 8vo. 7*s*. 6*d*.

BARCLAY (Edgar)—MOUNTAIN LIFE IN ALGERIA. Crown 4to. With numerous Illustrations by Photogravure. 16*s*.

BARLOW (J. W.) M.A.—THE ULTIMATUM OF PESSIMISM. An Ethical Study. Demy 8vo. 6*s*.

BARNES (William)—OUTLINES OF REDECRAFT (LOGIC). With English Wording. Crown 8vo. 3*s*.

BAUR (Ferdinand) Dr. Ph., Professor in Maulbronn.—A PHILOLOGICAL INTRODUCTION TO GREEK AND LATIN FOR STUDENTS. Translated and adapted from the German by C. KEGAN PAUL, M.A., and the Rev. E. D. STONE, M.A. Third Edition. Crown 8vo. 6*s*.

BELLARS (Rev. W.)—THE TESTIMONY OF CONSCIENCE TO THE TRUTH AND DIVINE ORIGIN OF THE CHRISTIAN REVELATION. Burney Prize Essay. Small crown 8vo. 3*s*. 6*d*.

BELLASIS (Edward)—THE MONEY JAR OF PLAUTUS AT THE ORATORY SCHOOL: An Account of the Recent Representation. With Appendix and 16 Illustrations. Small 4to. 2*s*.

BELLINGHAM (Henry) M.P.—SOCIAL ASPECTS OF CATHOLICISM AND PROTESTANTISM IN THEIR CIVIL BEARING UPON NATIONS. Translated and adapted from the French of M. le Baron de Haulleville. With a Preface by his Eminence Cardinal Manning. Second and Cheaper Edition. Crown 8vo. 3*s*. 6*d*.

BELLINGHAM (H. Belsches Graham)—UPS AND DOWNS OF SPANISH TRAVEL. Second Edition. Crown 8vo. 5*s*.

BENN (Alfred W.)—THE GREEK PHILOSOPHERS. 2 vols. Demy 8vo. 28*s*.

BENT (J. Theodore)—GENOA: How the Republic Rose and Fell. With 18 Illustrations. Demy 8vo. 18*s*.

BIBLE FOLK-LORE.—A STUDY IN COMPARATIVE MYTHOLOGY. Large crown 8vo. 10*s.* 6*d.*

BIRD (*Charles*) *F.G.S.*—HIGHER EDUCATION IN GERMANY AND ENGLAND: Being a Brief Practical Account of the Organisation and Curriculum of the German Higher Schools. With Critical Remarks and Suggestions with reference to those of England. Small crown 8vo. 2*s.* 6*d.*

BLACKLEY (*Rev. W. S.*)—ESSAYS ON PAUPERISM. 16mo. cloth, 1*s.* 6*d.*; sewed, 1*s.*

BLECKLY (*Henry*)—SOCRATES AND THE ATHENIANS: AN APOLOGY. Crown 8vo. 2*s.* 6*d.*

BLOOMFIELD (*The Lady*)—REMINISCENCES OF COURT AND DIPLOMATIC LIFE. New and Cheaper Edition. With Frontispiece. Crown 8vo. 6*s.*

BLUNT (*The Ven. Archdeacon*)—THE DIVINE PATRIOT, AND OTHER SERMONS, Preached in Scarborough and in Cannes. New and Cheaper Edition. Crown 8vo. 4*s.* 6*d.*

BLUNT (*Wilfrid S.*)—THE FUTURE OF ISLAM. Crown 8vo. 6*s.*

BODDY (*Alexander A.*)—TO KAIRWÂN the Holy. Scenes in Muhammedan Africa. With Route Map, and 8 Illustrations by A. F. JACASSEY. Crown 8vo. 6*s.*

BOOLE (*Mary*)—SYMBOLICAL METHODS OF STUDY. Crown 8vo. 5*s.*

BOUVERIE-PUSEY (*S. E. B.*)—PERMANENCE AND EVOLUTION. An Inquiry into the supposed Mutability of Animal Types. Crown 8vo. 5*s.*

BOWEN (*H. C.*) *M.A.*—STUDIES IN ENGLISH, for the use of Modern Schools. 7th Thousand. Small crown 8vo. 1*s.* 6*d.*

ENGLISH GRAMMAR FOR BEGINNERS. Fcp. 8vo. 1*s.*

SIMPLE ENGLISH POEMS. English Literature for Junior Classes. In Four Parts. Parts I., II., and III. 6*d.* each; Part IV. 1*s.*; complete, 3*s.*

BRADLEY (*F. H.*)—THE PRINCIPLES OF LOGIC. Demy 8vo. 16*s.*

BRIDGETT (*Rev. T. E.*)—HISTORY OF THE HOLY EUCHARIST IN GREAT BRITAIN. 2 vols. Demy 8vo. 18*s.*

BRODRICK (*The Hon. G. C.*)—POLITICAL STUDIES. Demy 8vo. 14*s.*

BROOKE (*Rev. S. A.*)—LIFE AND LETTERS OF THE LATE REV. F. W. ROBERTSON, M.A. Edited by.

I. Uniform with Robertson's Sermons. 2 vols. With Steel Portrait, 7*s.* 6*d.*
II. Library Edition. 8vo. With Portrait, 12*s.*
III. A Popular Edition. In 1 vol. 8vo. 6*s.*

THE FIGHT OF FAITH. Sermons preached on various occasions. Fifth Edition. Crown 8vo. 7*s.* 6*d.*

THE SPIRIT OF THE CHRISTIAN LIFE. Third Edition. Crown 8vo. 5*s.*

THEOLOGY IN THE ENGLISH POETS.—Cowper, Coleridge, Wordsworth, and Burns. Fifth Edition. Post 8vo. 5*s.*

CHRIST IN MODERN LIFE. Sixteenth Edition. Crown 8vo. 5*s.*

SERMONS. First Series. Thirteenth Edition. Crown 8vo. 5*s.*

SERMONS. Second Series. Sixth Edition. Crown 8vo. 5*s.*

BROWN (*Rev. J. Baldwin*) *B.A.*—THE HIGHER LIFE: its Reality, Experience, and Destiny. Sixth Edition. Crown 8vo. 5*s.*

DOCTRINE OF ANNIHILATION IN THE LIGHT OF THE GOSPEL OF LOVE. Five Discourses. Fourth Edition. Crown 8vo. 2*s.* 6*d.*

THE CHRISTIAN POLICY OF LIFE. A Book for Young Men of Business. Third Edition. Crown 8vo. 3*s.* 6*d.*

BROWN (*S. Borton*) *B.A.*—THE FIRE BAPTISM OF ALL FLESH; or, the Coming Spiritual Crisis of the Dispensation. Crown 8vo. 6*s.*

BROWN (*Horatio F.*)—LIFE ON THE LAGOONS. With two Illustrations and a Map. Crown 8vo. 6*s.*

BROWNBILL (*John*)—PRINCIPLES OF ENGLISH CANON LAW. Part I. General Introduction. Crown 8vo. 6*s.*

BROWNE (*W. R.*)—THE INSPIRATION OF THE NEW TESTAMENT. With a Preface by the Rev. J. P. NORRIS, D.D. Fcp. 8vo. 2*s.* 6*d.*

BURDETT (*Henry C.*)—HELP IN SICKNESS: Where to Go and What to Do. Crown 8vo. 1*s.* 6*d.*

HELPS TO HEALTH: The Habitation, The Nursery, The Schoolroom, and The Person. With a Chapter on Pleasure and Health Resorts. Crown 8vo. 1*s.* 6*d.*

BURTON (*Mrs. Richard*)—THE INNER LIFE OF SYRIA, PALESTINE, AND THE HOLY LAND. Post 8vo. 6*s.*

BUSBECQ (*Ogier Ghiselin de*)—HIS LIFE AND LETTERS. By CHARLES THORNTON FORSTER, M.A., and F. H. BLACKBURNE DANIELL, M.A. 2 vols. With Frontispieces. Demy 8vo. 24*s.*

CARPENTER (*W. B.*) *LL.D., M.D., F.R.S., &c.*—THE PRINCIPLES OF MENTAL PHYSIOLOGY. With their Applications to the Training and Discipline of the Mind, and the Study of its Morbid Conditions. Illustrated. Sixth Edition. 8vo. 12*s.*

CATHOLIC DICTIONARY—Containing some account of the Doctrine, Discipline, Rites, Ceremonies, Councils, and Religious Orders of the Catholic Church. By WILLIAM E. ADDIS and THOMAS ARNOLD, M.A. Second Edition, demy 8vo. 21*s.*

CERVANTES—JOURNEY TO PARNASSUS. Spanish Text, with Translation into English Tercets, Preface, and Illustrative Notes, by JAMES Y. GIBSON. Crown 8vo. 12*s.*

CHEYNE (*Rev. T. K.*)—THE PROPHECIES OF ISAIAH. Translated with Critical Notes and Dissertations. 2 vols. Third Edition. Demy 8vo. 25*s.*

CHICHELE (*Mary*)—DOING AND UNDOING. A Story. 1 vol. Crown 8vo.

CLAIRAUT—ELEMENTS OF GEOMETRY. Translated by Dr. KAINES. With 145 Figures. Crown 8vo. 4*s.* 6*d.*

CLARKE (*Rev. Henry James*) *A.K.C.*—THE FUNDAMENTAL SCIENCE. Demy 8vo. 10*s.* 6*d.*

CLAYDEN (*P. W.*)—SAMUEL SHARPE—EGYPTOLOGIST AND TRANSLATOR OF THE BIBLE. Crown 8vo. 6*s.*

CLIFFORD (*Samuel*)—WHAT THINK YE OF THE CHRIST? Crown 8vo. 6*s.*

CLODD (*Edward*) *F.R.A.S.*—THE CHILDHOOD OF THE WORLD: a Simple Account of Man in Early Times. Seventh Edition. Crown 8vo. 3*s.*
A Special Edition for Schools, 1*s.*

CLODD (*Edward*)—continued.

THE CHILDHOOD OF RELIGIONS. Including a Simple Account of the Birth and Growth of Myths and Legends. Eighth Thousand. Crown 8vo. 5*s.*

A Special Edition for Schools. 1*s.* 6*d.*

JESUS OF NAZARETH. With a brief sketch of Jewish History to the Time of His Birth. Small crown 8vo. 6*s.*

COGHLAN (*J. Cole*) *D.D.*—THE MODERN PHARISEE, AND OTHER SERMONS. Edited by the Very Rev. H. H. DICKINSON, D.D., Dean of Chapel Royal, Dublin. New and Cheaper Edition. Crown 8vo. 7*s.* 6*d.*

COLE (*George R. Fitz-Roy*)—THE PERUVIANS AT HOME. Crown 8vo. 6*s.*

COLERIDGE (*Sara*)—MEMOIR AND LETTERS OF SARA COLERIDGE. Edited by her Daughter. With Index. Cheap Edition. With one Portrait. 7*s.* 6*d.*

COLLECTS EXEMPLIFIED (*The*)—Being Illustrations from the Old and New Testaments of the Collects for the Sundays after Trinity. By the Author of 'A Commentary on the Epistles and Gospels.' Edited by the Rev. JOSEPH JACKSON. Crown 8vo. 5*s.*

CONNELL (*A. K.*)—DISCONTENT AND DANGER IN INDIA. Small crown 8vo. 3*s.* 6*d.*

THE ECONOMIC REVOLUTION OF INDIA. Crown 8vo. 4*s.* 6*d.*

CORY (*William*)—A GUIDE TO MODERN ENGLISH HISTORY. Part I.—MDCCCXV.-MDCCCXXX. Demy 8vo. 9*s.* Part II.—MDCCCXXX.-MDCCCXXXV. 15*s.*

COTTERILL (*H. B.*)—AN INTRODUCTION TO THE STUDY OF POETRY. Crown 8vo. 7*s.* 6*d.*

COUTTS (*Francis Burdett Money*)—THE TRAINING OF THE INSTINCT OF LOVE. With a Preface by the Rev. EDWARD THRING, M.A. Small crown 8vo. 2*s.* 6*d.*

COX (*Rev. Sir George W.*) *M.A., Bart.*—THE MYTHOLOGY OF THE ARYAN NATIONS. New Edition. Demy 8vo. 16*s.*

TALES OF ANCIENT GREECE. New Edition. Small crown 8vo. 6*s.*

A MANUAL OF MYTHOLOGY IN THE FORM OF QUESTION AND ANSWER. New Edition. Fcp. 8vo. 3*s.*

AN INTRODUCTION TO THE SCIENCE OF COMPARATIVE MYTHOLOGY AND FOLK-LORE. Second Edition. Crown 8vo. 7*s.* 6*d.*

COX (*Rev. Sir G. W.*) *M.A., Bart., and JONES* (*Eustace Hinton*)—POPULAR ROMANCES OF THE MIDDLE AGES. Third Edition, in 1 vol. Crown 8vo. 6*s.*

COX (*Rev. Samuel*) *D.D.*—A COMMENTARY ON THE BOOK OF JOB. With a Translation. Demy 8vo. 15*s.*

SALVATOR MUNDI; or, Is Christ the Saviour of all Men? Ninth Edition. Crown 8vo. 5*s.*

THE LARGER HOPE: a Sequel to 'SALVATOR MUNDI.' Second Edition. 16mo. 1*s.*

THE GENESIS OF EVIL, AND OTHER SERMONS, mainly expository. Third Edition. Crown 8vo. 6*s.*

COX (*Rev. Samuel*)—continued.

BALAAM: An Exposition and a Study. Crown 8vo. 5*s*.

MIRACLES. An Argument and a Challenge. Crown 8vo. 2*s*. 6*d*.

CRAVEN (*Mrs.*)—A YEAR'S MEDITATIONS. Crown 8vo. 6*s*.

CRAWFURD (*Oswald*)—PORTUGAL, OLD AND NEW. With Illustrations and Maps. New and Cheaper Edition. Crown 8vo. 6*s*.

CRIME OF CHRISTMAS DAY: A Tale of the Latin Quarter. By the Author of 'My Ducats and My Daughter.' 1*s*.

CROZIER (*John Beattie*) *M.B.*—THE RELIGION OF THE FUTURE. Crown 8vo. 6*s*.

DANIELL (*Clarmont*)—THE GOLD TREASURE OF INDIA: An Inquiry into its Amount, the Cause of its Accumulation, and the Proper Means of Using it as Money. Crown 8vo. 5*s*.

DANISH PARSONAGE. By an Angler. Crown 8vo. 6*s*.

DARKNESS AND DAWN. The Peaceful Birth of a New Age. Small crown 8vo. 2*s*. 6*d*.

DAVIDSON (*Rev. Samuel*) *D.D.*, *LL.D.*—CANON OF THE BIBLE: Its Formation, History, and Fluctuations. Third and revised Edition. Small crown 8vo. 5*s*.

THE DOCTRINE OF LAST THINGS, contained in the New Testament, compared with the Notions of the Jews and the Statements of Church Creeds. Small crown 8vo. 3*s*. 6*d*.

DAVIDSON (*Thomas*)—THE PARTHENON FRIEZE, and other Essays. Crown 8vo. 6*s*.

DAWSON (*Geo.*) *M.A.*—PRAYERS, WITH A DISCOURSE ON PRAYER. Edited by his Wife. First Series. Eighth Edition. Crown 8vo. 6*s*.

*** Also a New and Cheaper Edition. Crown 8vo. 3*s*. 6*d*.

PRAYERS, WITH A DISCOURSE ON PRAYER. Edited by GEORGE ST. CLAIR. Second Series. Crown 8vo. 6*s*.

SERMONS ON DISPUTED POINTS AND SPECIAL OCCASIONS. Edited by his Wife. Fourth Edition. Crown 8vo. 6*s*.

SERMONS ON DAILY LIFE AND DUTY. Edited by his Wife. Fourth Edition. Crown 8vo. 6*s*.

THE AUTHENTIC GOSPEL, and other Sermons. Edited by GEORGE ST. CLAIR. Third Edition. Crown 8vo. 6*s*.

THREE BOOKS OF GOD. Nature, History, and Scripture. Sermons, Edited by GEORGE ST. CLAIR. Crown 8vo. 6*s*.

DE JONCOURT (*Madame Marie*)—WHOLESOME COOKERY. Third Edition. Crown 8vo. 3*s*. 6*d*.

DE LONG (*Lieut.-Com. G. W.*)—THE VOYAGE OF THE 'JEANNETTE.' The Ship and Ice Journals of. Edited by his Wife, EMMA DE LONG. With Portraits, Maps, and many Illustrations on wood and stone. 2 vols. Demy 8vo. 36*s*.

DEMOCRACY IN THE OLD WORLD AND THE NEW. By the Author of 'The Suez Canal, the Eastern Question, and Abyssinia,' &c. Small crown 8vo. 2*s*. 6*d*.

DEVEREUX (*W. Cope*) *R.N.*, *F.R.G.S.*—FAIR ITALY, THE RIVIERA AND MONTE CARLO. Comprising a Tour through North and South Italy and Sicily, with a short account of Malta. Crown 8vo. 6*s*.

DOING AND UNDOING. A Story. By MARY CHICHELE. 1 vol. Crown 8vo.

DOWDEN (Edward) LL.D.—SHAKSPERE: a Critical Study of his Mind and Art. Seventh Edition. Post 8vo. 12*s.*

STUDIES IN LITERATURE, 1789–1877. Third Edition. Large post 8vo. 6*s.*

DUFFIELD (A. J.)—DON QUIXOTE: HIS CRITICS AND COMMENTATORS. With a brief account of the minor works of MIGUEL DE CERVANTES SAAVEDRA, and a statement of the aim and end of the greatest of them all. A handy book for general readers. Crown 8vo. 3*s.* 6*d.*

DU MONCEL (Count)—THE TELEPHONE, THE MICROPHONE, AND THE PHONOGRAPH. With 74 Illustrations. Second Edition. Small crown 8vo. 5*s.*

DURUY (Victor)—HISTORY OF ROME AND THE ROMAN PEOPLE. Edited by Professor MAHAFFY, with nearly 3,000 Illustrations. 4to. Vols. I., II., and III. in 6 Parts, 30*s.* each volume.

EDGEWORTH (F. Y.)—MATHEMATICAL PSYCHICS. An Essay on the Application of Mathematics to Social Science. Demy 8vo. 7*s.* 6*d.*

EDUCATIONAL CODE OF THE PRUSSIAN NATION, IN ITS PRESENT FORM. In accordance with the Decisions of the Common Provincial Law, and with those of Recent Legislation. Crown 8vo. 2*s.* 6*d.*

EDUCATION LIBRARY. Edited by PHILIP MAGNUS:—

AN INTRODUCTION TO THE HISTORY OF EDUCATIONAL THEORIES. By OSCAR BROWNING, M.A. Second Edition. 3*s.* 6*d.*

OLD GREEK EDUCATION. By the Rev. Prof. MAHAFFY, M.A. Second Edition. 3*s.* 6*d.*

SCHOOL MANAGEMENT; including a General View of the Work of Education, Organization, and Discipline. By JOSEPH LANDON. Third Edition. Crown 8vo. 6*s.*

ELSDALE (Henry)—STUDIES IN TENNYSON'S IDYLLS. Crown 8vo. 5*s.*

ELYOT (Sir Thomas)—THE BOKE NAMED THE GOUERNOUR. Edited from the First Edition of 1531 by HENRY HERBERT STEPHEN CROFT, M.A., Barrister-at-Law. 2 vols. Fcp. 4to. 50*s.*

EMERSON'S (Ralph Waldo) LIFE. By OLIVER WENDELL HOLMES. [English Copyright Edition.] With Portrait. Crown 8vo. 6*s.*

ENOCH, THE PROPHET. The Book of. Archbishop Laurence's Translation. With an Introduction by the Author of the 'Evolution of Christianity.' Crown 8vo. 5*s.*

ERANUS. A COLLECTION OF EXERCISES IN THE ALCAIC AND SAPPHIC METRES. Edited by F. W. CORNISH, Assistant Master at Eton. Second Edition. Crown 8vo. 2*s.*

EVANS (Mark)—THE STORY OF OUR FATHER'S LOVE, told to Children. Sixth and Cheaper Edition. With Four Illustrations. Fcp. 8vo. 1*s.* 6*d.*

'FAN KWAE' AT CANTON BEFORE TREATY DAYS, 1825–1844. By AN OLD RESIDENT. With Frontispiece. Crown 8vo. 5*s.*

FEIS (Jacob)—SHAKSPERE AND MONTAIGNE: An Endeavour to Explain the Tendency of Hamlet from Allusions in Contemporary Works. Crown 8vo. 5*s.*

FLECKER (Rev. Eliezer)—SCRIPTURE ONOMATOLOGY. Being Critical Notes on the Septuagint and other versions. Second Edition. Crown 8vo. 3*s.* 6*d.*

FLOREDICE (W. H.)—A MONTH AMONG THE MERE IRISH. Small crown 8vo. 5*s*.

FOWLE (Rev. T. W.)—THE DIVINE LEGATION OF CHRIST. Crown 8vo. 7*s*.

FRANK LEWARD. Edited by CHARLES BAMPTON. Crown 8vo. 7*s*. 6*d*.

FULLER (Rev. Morris)—THE LORD'S DAY; or, Christian Sunday. Its Unity, History, Philosophy, and Perpetual Obligation. Sermons. Demy 8vo. 10*s*. 6*d*.

GARDINER (Samuel R.) and J. BASS MULLINGER, M.A.—INTRODUCTION TO THE STUDY OF ENGLISH HISTORY. Second Edition. Large crown 8vo. 9*s*.

GARDNER (Dorsey)—QUATRE BRAS, LIGNY, AND WATERLOO. A Narrative of the Campaign in Belgium, 1815. With Maps and Plans. Demy 8vo. 16*s*.

GENESIS IN ADVANCE OF PRESENT SCIENCE. A Critical Investigation of Chapters I. to IX. By a Septuagenarian Beneficed Presbyter. Demy 8vo. 10*s*. 6*d*.

GENNA (E.)—IRRESPONSIBLE PHILANTHROPISTS. Being some Chapters on the Employment of Gentlewomen. Small crown 8vo. 2*s*. 6*d*.

GEORGE (Henry)—PROGRESS AND POVERTY: an Inquiry into the Causes of Industrial Depressions, and of Increase of Want with Increase of Wealth. The Remedy. Fifth Library Edition. Post 8vo. 7*s*. 6*d*. Cabinet Edition, crown 8vo. 2*s*. 6*d*.

*** Also a Cheap Edition, limp cloth, 1*s*. 6*d*.; paper covers, 1*s*.

SOCIAL PROBLEMS. Crown 8vo. 5*s*.

*** Also a Cheap Edition, paper covers, 1*s*.

GIBSON (James Y.)—JOURNEY TO PARNASSUS. Composed by MIGUEL DE CERVANTES SAAVEDRA. Spanish Text, with Translation into English Tercets, Preface, and Illustrative Notes by. Crown 8vo. 12*s*.

GLOSSARY OF TERMS AND PHRASES. Edited by the Rev. H. PERCY SMITH and others. Medium 8vo. 12*s*.

GLOVER (F.) M.A.—EXEMPLA LATINA. A First Construing Book, with Short Notes, Lexicon, and an Introduction to the Analysis of Sentences. Second Edition. Fcp. 8vo. 2*s*.

GOLDSMID (Sir Francis Henry) Bart., Q.C., M.P.—MEMOIR OF. Second Edition, revised. Crown 8vo. 6*s*.

GOODENOUGH (Commodore J. G.)—MEMOIR OF, with Extracts from his Letters and Journals. Edited by his Widow. With Steel Engraved Portrait. Third Edition. Crown 8vo. 5*s*.

GOSSE (Edmund)—STUDIES IN THE LITERATURE OF NORTHERN EUROPE. New Edition. Large post 8vo. 6*s*.

SEVENTEENTH CENTURY STUDIES. A Contribution to the History of English Poetry. Demy 8vo. 10*s*. 6*d*.

GOULD (Rev. S. Baring) M.A.—GERMANY, PRESENT AND PAST. New and Cheaper Edition. Large crown 8vo. 7*s*. 6*d*.

GOWAN (Major Walter E.)—A. IVANOFF'S RUSSIAN GRAMMAR. (16th Edition). Translated, enlarged, and arranged for use of Students of the Russian Language. Demy 8vo. 6*s*.

GOWER (Lord Ronald)—MY REMINISCENCES. Cheap Edition, with Portrait. Large crown 8vo. 7*s.* 6*d.*

GRAHAM (William) M.A.—THE CREED OF SCIENCE, Religious, Moral, and Social. Second Edition, revised. Crown 8vo. 6*s.*

GREY (Rowland).—IN SUNNY SWITZERLAND. A Tale of Six Weeks. Small crown 8vo. 5*s.*

GRIFFITH (Thomas) A.M.—THE GOSPEL OF THE DIVINE LIFE: a Study of the Fourth Evangelist. Demy 8vo. 14*s.*

GRIMLEY (Rev. H. N.) M.A.—TREMADOC SERMONS, CHIEFLY ON THE SPIRITUAL BODY, THE UNSEEN WORLD, AND THE DIVINE HUMANITY. Fourth Edition. Crown 8vo. 6*s.*

G. S. B.—A STUDY OF THE PROLOGUE AND EPILOGUE IN ENGLISH LITERATURE, from Shakespeare to Dryden. Crown 8vo. 5*s.*

GUSTAFSON (Axel)—THE FOUNDATION OF DEATH. A Study of the Drink Question. Third Edition. Crown 8vo. 5*s.*

HAECKEL (Prof. Ernst)—THE HISTORY OF CREATION. Translation revised by Professor E. RAY LANKESTER, M.A., F.R.S. With Coloured Plates and Genealogical Trees of the various groups of both plants and animals. 2 vols. Third Edition. Post 8vo. 32*s.*

THE HISTORY OF THE EVOLUTION OF MAN. With numerous Illustrations. 2 vols. Post 8vo. 32*s.*

A VISIT TO CEYLON. Post 8vo. 7*s.* 6*d.*

FREEDOM IN SCIENCE AND TEACHING. With a Prefatory Note by T. H. HUXLEY, F.R.S. Crown 8vo. 5*s.*

HALF-CROWN SERIES:—

A LOST LOVE. By ANNA C. OGLE (Ashford Owen).

SISTER DORA: a Biography. By MARGARET LONSDALE.

TRUE WORDS FOR BRAVE MEN: a Book for Soldiers and Sailors. By the late CHARLES KINGSLEY.

NOTES OF TRAVEL: being Extracts from the Journals of Count VON MOLTKE.

ENGLISH SONNETS. Collected and Arranged by J. DENNIS.

LONDON LYRICS. By F. LOCKER.

HOME SONGS FOR QUIET HOURS. By the Rev. Canon R. H. BAYNES.

HARRIS (William)—THE HISTORY OF THE RADICAL PARTY IN PARLIAMENT. Demy 8vo. 15*s.*

HARROP (Robert)—BOLINGBROKE. A Political Study and Criticism. Demy 8vo. 14*s.*

HART (Rev. J. W. T.)—AUTOBIOGRAPHY OF JUDAS ISCARIOT. A Character-Study. Crown 8vo. 3*s.* 6*d.*

HAWEIS (Rev. H. R.) M.A.—CURRENT COIN. Materialism—The Devil—Crime—Drunkenness—Pauperism—Emotion—Recreation—The Sabbath. Fifth Edition. Crown 8vo. 5*s.*

ARROWS IN THE AIR. Fifth Edition. Crown 8vo. 5*s.*

SPEECH IN SEASON. Fifth Edition. Crown 8vo. 5*s.*

THOUGHTS FOR THE TIMES. Thirteenth Edition. Crown 8vo. 5*s.*

UNSECTARIAN FAMILY PRAYERS. New Edition. Fcp. 8vo. 1*s.* 6*d.*

HAWKINS (Edwards Comerford)—SPIRIT AND FORM. Sermons preached in the Parish Church of Leatherhead. Crown 8vo. 6*s.*

HAWTHORNE (Nathaniel)—WORKS. Complete in 12 vols. Large post 8vo. each vol. 7*s.* 6*d.*

VOL. I. TWICE-TOLD TALES.
II. MOSSES FROM AN OLD MANSE.
III. THE HOUSE OF THE SEVEN GABLES, and THE SNOW IMAGE.
IV. THE WONDER BOOK, TANGLEWOOD TALES, and GRANDFATHER'S CHAIR.
V. THE SCARLET LETTER, and THE BLITHEDALE ROMANCE.
VI. THE MARBLE FAUN. (Transformation.)
VII. & VIII. OUR OLD HOME, and ENGLISH NOTE-BOOKS.
IX. AMERICAN NOTE-BOOKS.
X. FRENCH AND ITALIAN NOTE-BOOKS.
XI. SEPTIMIUS FELTON, THE DOLLIVER ROMANCE, FANSHAWE, and, in an appendix, THE ANCESTRAL FOOTSTEP.
XII. TALES AND ESSAYS, AND OTHER PAPERS, WITH A BIOGRAPHICAL SKETCH OF HAWTHORNE.

HAYES (A. A.) Jun.—NEW COLORADO AND THE SANTA FÉ TRAIL. With Map and 60 Illustrations. Square 8vo. 9*s.*

HENNESSY (Sir John Pope)—RALEGH IN IRELAND, WITH HIS LETTERS ON IRISH AFFAIRS AND SOME CONTEMPORARY DOCUMENTS. Large crown 8vo. printed on hand-made paper, parchment, 10*s.* 6*d.*

HENRY (Philip)—DIARIES AND LETTERS. Edited by MATTHEW HENRY LEE, M.A. Large crown 8vo. 7*s.* 6*d.*

HIDE (Albert)—THE AGE TO COME. Small crown 8vo. 2*s.* 6*d.*

HIME (Major H. W. L.) R.A.—WAGNERISM: a Protest. Crown 8vo. 2*s.* 6*d.*

HINTON (J.)—THE MYSTERY OF PAIN. New Edition. Fcp. 8vo. 1*s.*

LIFE AND LETTERS. With an Introduction by Sir W. W. GULL, Bart., and Portrait engraved on Steel by C. H. JEENS. Fifth Edition. Crown 8vo. 8*s.* 6*d.*

PHILOSOPHY AND RELIGION. Selections from the MSS. of the late JAMES HINTON. Edited by CAROLINE HADDON. Second Edition. Crown 8vo. 5*s.*

THE LAW BREAKER AND THE COMING OF THE LAW. Edited by MARGARET HINTON. Crown 8vo. 6*s.*

HODSON OF HODSON'S HORSE; or, Twelve Years of a Soldier's Life in India. Being Extracts from the Letters of the late Major W. S. R. Hodson. With a vindication from the attack of Mr. Bosworth Smith. Edited by his brother, G. H. HODSON, M.A. Fourth Edition. Large crown 8vo. 5*s.*

HOLTHAM (E. G.)—EIGHT YEARS IN JAPAN, 1873-1881. Work, Travel, and Recreation. With 3 Maps. Large crown 8vo. 9*s.*

HOMOLOGY OF ECONOMIC JUSTICE: An Essay by an EAST INDIA MERCHANT. Small crown 8vo. 5*s.*

HOOPER (Mary)—LITTLE DINNERS: HOW TO SERVE THEM WITH ELEGANCE AND ECONOMY. Eighteenth Edition. Crown 8vo. 2*s.* 6*d.*

COOKERY FOR INVALIDS, PERSONS OF DELICATE DIGESTION, AND CHILDREN. Fourth Edition. Crown 8vo. 2*s.* 6*d.*

EVERY-DAY MEALS. Being Economical and Wholesome Recipes for Breakfast, Luncheon, and Supper. Sixth Edition. Crown 8vo. 2*s.* 6*d.*

HOPKINS (Ellice)—WORK AMONGST WORKING MEN. Fifth Edition. Crown 8vo. 3*s*. 6*d*.

HOSPITALIER (E.)—THE MODERN APPLICATIONS OF ELECTRICITY. Translated and Enlarged by JULIUS MAIER, Ph.D. 2 vols. Second Edition, revised, with many additions and numerous Illustrations. Demy 8vo. 12*s*. 6*d*. each volume.

VOL. I.—Electric Generators, Electric Light.
II.—Telephone: Various Applications: Electrical Transmission of Energy.

HOUSEHOLD READINGS ON PROPHECY. By A LAYMAN. Small crown 8vo. 3*s*. 6*d*.

HUGHES (Henry)—THE REDEMPTION OF THE WORLD. Crown 8vo. 3*s*. 6*d*.

HUNTINGFORD (Rev. E.) D.C.L.—THE APOCALYPSE. With a Commentary and Introductory Essay. Demy 8vo. 9*s*.

HUTCHINSON (H.)—THOUGHT SYMBOLISM AND GRAMMATIC ILLUSIONS: Being a Treatise on the Nature, Purpose, and Material of Speech. Crown 8vo. 5*s*.

HUTTON (Rev. Charles F.)—UNCONSCIOUS TESTIMONY; OR, THE SILENT WITNESS OF THE HEBREW TO THE TRUTH OF THE HISTORICAL SCRIPTURES. Crown 8vo. 2*s*. 6*d*.

HYNDMAN (H. M.)—THE HISTORICAL BASIS OF SOCIALISM IN ENGLAND. Large crown 8vo. 8*s*. 6*d*.

IM THURN (Everard F.)—AMONG THE INDIANS OF GUIANA. Being Sketches, chiefly Anthropologic, from the Interior of British Guiana. With 53 Illustrations and a Map. Demy 8vo. 18*s*.

JACCOUD (Prof. S.)—THE CURABILITY AND TREATMENT OF PULMONARY PHTHISIS. Translated and Edited by MONTAGU LUBBOCK, M.D. Demy 8vo. 15*s*.

JAUNT IN A JUNK: A Ten Days' Cruise in Indian Seas. Large crown 8vo. 7*s*. 6*d*.

JENKINS (E.) and RAYMOND (J.)—THE ARCHITECT'S LEGAL HANDBOOK. Third Edition, Revised. Crown 8vo. 6*s*.

JENNINGS (Mrs. Vaughan)—RAHEL: Her Life and Letters. Large post 8vo. 7*s*. 6*d*.

JERVIS (Rev. W. Henley)—THE GALLICAN CHURCH AND THE REVOLUTION. A Sequel to the History of the Church of France, from the Concordat of Bologna to the Revolution. Demy 8vo. 18*s*.

JOEL (L.)—A CONSUL'S MANUAL AND SHIPOWNER'S AND SHIPMASTER'S PRACTICAL GUIDE IN THEIR TRANSACTIONS ABROAD. With Definitions of Nautical, Mercantile, and Legal Terms; a Glossary of Mercantile Terms in English, French, German, Italian, and Spanish; Tables of the Money, Weights, and Measures of the Principal Commercial Nations and their Equivalents in British Standards; and Forms of Consular and Notarial Acts. Demy 8vo. 12*s*.

JOHNSTONE (C. F.) M.A.—HISTORICAL ABSTRACTS: being Outlines of the History of some of the less known States of Europe. Crown 8vo. 7*s*. 6*d*.

JOLLY (William) F.R.S.E.—JOHN DUNCAN, Scotch Weaver and Botanist. With Sketches of his Friends and Notices of his Times. With Portrait. Second Edition. Large crown 8vo. 9*s.*

JONES (C. A.)—THE FOREIGN FREAKS OF FIVE FRIENDS. With 30 Illustrations. Crown 8vo. 6*s.*

JOYCE (P. W.) LL.D. &c.—OLD CELTIC ROMANCES. Translated from the Gaelic. Crown 8vo. 7*s.* 6*d.*

KAUFMANN (Rev. M.) B.A.—SOCIALISM: its Nature, its Dangers, and its Remedies considered. Crown 8vo. 7*s.* 6*d.*

UTOPIAS; or, Schemes of Social Improvement, from Sir Thomas More to Karl Marx. Crown 8vo. 5*s.*

KAY (David)—EDUCATION AND EDUCATORS. Crown 8vo. 7*s.* 6*d.*

KAY (Joseph)—FREE TRADE IN LAND. Edited by his Widow. With Preface by the Right Hon. JOHN BRIGHT, M.P. Seventh Edition. Crown 8vo. 5*s.*

KEMPIS (Thomas à)—OF THE IMITATION OF CHRIST. Parchment Library Edition, parchment or cloth, 6*s.*; vellum, 7*s.* 6*d.* The Red Line Edition, fcp. 8vo. red edges, 2*s.* 6*d.* The Cabinet Edition, small 8vo. cloth limp, 1*s.*; or cloth boards, red edges, 1*s.* 6*d.* The Miniature Edition, 32mo. red edges, 1*s.*

⁂ All the above Editions may be had in various extra bindings.

KENT (C.)—CORONA CATHOLICA AD PETRI SUCCESSORIS PEDES OBLATA. DE SUMMI PONTIFICIS LEONIS XIII. ASSUMPTIONE EPIGRAMMA. In Quinquaginta Linguis. Fcp. 4to. 15*s.*

KETTLEWELL (Rev. S.) M.A.—THOMAS À KEMPIS AND THE BROTHERS OF COMMON LIFE. 2 vols. With Frontispieces. Demy 8vo. 30*s.*

⁂ Also an Abridged Edition in 1 vol. With Portrait. Crown 8vo. 7*s.* 6*d.*

KIDD (Joseph) M.D.—THE LAWS OF THERAPEUTICS; or, the Science and Art of Medicine. Second Edition. Crown 8vo. 6*s.*

KINGSFORD (Anna) M.D.—THE PERFECT WAY IN DIET. A Treatise advocating a Return to the Natural and Ancient Food of Race. Small crown 8vo. 2*s.*

KINGSLEY (Charles) M.A.—LETTERS AND MEMORIES OF HIS LIFE. Edited by his WIFE. With Two Steel Engraved Portraits and Vignettes. Fifteenth Cabinet Edition, in 2 vols. Crown 8vo. 12*s.*

⁂ Also a People's Edition in 1 vol. With Portrait. Crown 8vo. 6*s.*

ALL SAINTS' DAY, and other Sermons. Edited by the Rev. W. HARRISON. Third Edition. Crown 8vo. 7*s.* 6*d.*

TRUE WORDS FOR BRAVE MEN. A Book for Soldiers' and Sailors' Libraries. Eleventh Edition. Crown 8vo. 2*s.* 6*d.*

KNOX (Alexander A.)—THE NEW PLAYGROUND; or, Wanderings in Algeria. New and Cheaper Edition. Large crown 8vo. 6*s.*

LANDON (Joseph)—SCHOOL MANAGEMENT; including a General View of the Work of Education, Organisation, and Discipline. Third Edition. Crown 8vo. 6*s.*

LAURIE (*S. S.*)—THE TRAINING OF TEACHERS, and other Educational Papers. Crown 8vo. 7*s*. 6*d*.

LEE (*Rev. F. G.*) *D.C.L.*—THE OTHER WORLD; or, Glimpses of the Supernatural. 2 vols. A New Edition. Crown 8vo. 15*s*.

LETTERS FROM AN UNKNOWN FRIEND. By the Author of 'Charles Lowder.' With a Preface by the Rev. W. H. Cleaver. Fcp. 8vo. 1*s*.

LETTERS FROM A YOUNG EMIGRANT IN MANITOBA. Second Edition. Small crown 8vo. 3*s*. 6*d*.

LEWARD (*Frank*)—Edited by CHAS. BAMPTON. Crown 8vo. 7*s*. 6*d*.

LEWIS (*Edward Dillon*)—A DRAFT CODE OF CRIMINAL LAW AND PROCEDURE. Demy 8vo. 21*s*.

LILLIE (*Arthur*) *M.R.A.S.*—THE POPULAR LIFE OF BUDDHA. Containing an Answer to the Hibbert Lectures of 1881. With Illustrations. Crown 8vo. 6*s*.

LLOYD (*Walter*)—THE HOPE OF THE WORLD: An Essay on Universal Redemption. Crown 8vo. 5*s*.

LONSDALE (*Margaret*)—SISTER DORA: a Biography. With Portrait. Cheap Edition. Crown 8vo. 2*s*. 6*d*.

LOUNSBURY (*Thomas R.*)—JAMES FENIMORE COOPER. With Portrait. Crown 8vo. 5*s*.

LOWDER (*Charles*)—A BIOGRAPHY. By the Author of 'St. Teresa.' New and Cheaper Edition. Crown 8vo. With Portrait. 3*s*. 6*d*.

LÜCKES (*Eva C. E.*)—LECTURES ON GENERAL NURSING, delivered to the Probationers of the London Hospital Training School for Nurses. Crown 8vo. 2*s*. 6*d*.

LYALL (*William Rowe*) *D.D.*—PROPÆDEIA PROPHETICA; or, The Use and Design of the Old Testament Examined. New Edition, with Notices by GEORGE C. PEARSON, M.A., Hon. Canon of Canterbury. Demy 8vo.

LYTTON (*Edward Bulwer, Lord*)—LIFE, LETTERS, AND LITERARY REMAINS. By his Son the EARL OF LYTTON. With Portraits, Illustrations, and Facsimiles. Demy 8vo. cloth. Vols. I. and II. 32*s*.

MACAULAY (*G. C.*)—FRANCIS BEAUMONT: A Critical Study. Crown 8vo. 5*s*.

MACCALLUM (*M. W.*)—STUDIES IN LOW GERMAN AND HIGH GERMAN LITERATURE. Crown 8vo. 6*s*.

MACHIAVELLI (*Niccolò*)—HIS LIFE AND TIMES. By Prof. VILLARI. Translated by LINDA VILLARI. 4 vols. Large post 8vo. 48*s*.

DISCOURSES ON THE FIRST DECADE OF TITUS LIVIUS. Translated from the Italian by NINIAN HILL THOMSON, M.A. Large crown 8vo. 12*s*.

THE PRINCE. Translated from the Italian by N. H. T. Small crown 8vo. printed on hand-made paper, bevelled boards, 6*s*.

MACKENZIE (*Alexander*)—HOW INDIA IS GOVERNED. Being an Account of England's work in India. Small crown 8vo. 2*s*.

MACNAUGHT (*Rev. John*)—CŒNA DOMINI: An Essay on the Lord's Supper, its Primitive Institution, Apostolic Uses, and Subsequent History. Demy 8vo. 14*s*.

MACWALTER (Rev. G. S.)—LIFE OF ANTONIO ROSMINI SERBATI (Founder of the Institute of Charity). 2 vols. Demy 8vo. [Vol. I. now ready, 12*s.*

MAGNUS (Mrs.)—ABOUT THE JEWS SINCE BIBLE TIMES. From the Babylonian Exile till the English Exodus. Small crown 8vo. 6*s.*

MAIR (R. S.) M.D., F.R.C.S.E.—THE MEDICAL GUIDE FOR ANGLO-INDIANS. Being a Compendium of Advice to Europeans in India, relating to the Preservation and Regulation of Health. With a Supplement on the Management of Children in India. Second Edition. Crown 8vo. 3*s.* 6*d.*

MALDEN (Henry Elliot)—VIENNA, 1683. The History and Consequences of the Defeat of the Turks before Vienna, September 12, 1683, by John Sobieski, King of Poland, and Charles Leopold, Duke of Lorraine. Crown 8vo. 4*s.* 6*d.*

MANY VOICES.—A Volume of Extracts from the Religious Writers of Christendom, from the First to the Sixteenth Century. With Biographical Sketches. Crown 8vo. cloth extra, red edges, 6*s.*

MARKHAM (Capt. Albert Hastings) R.N.—THE GREAT FROZEN SEA: a Personal Narrative of the Voyage of the *Alert* during the Arctic Expedition of 1875–6. With Six Full-page Illustrations, Two Maps, and Twenty-seven Woodcuts. Sixth and Cheaper Edition. Crown 8vo. 6*s.*

MARRIAGE AND MATERNITY; or, Scripture Wives and Mothers. Small crown 8vo. 4*s.* 6*d.*

MARTINEAU (Gertrude)—OUTLINE LESSONS ON MORALS. Small crown 8vo. 3*s.* 6*d.*

MAUDSLEY (H.) M.D.—BODY AND WILL. Being an Essay Concerning Will, in its Metaphysical, Physiological, and Pathological Aspects. 8vo. 12*s.*

McGRATH (Terence)—PICTURES FROM IRELAND. New and Cheaper Edition. Crown 8vo. 2*s.*

MEREDITH (M. A.)—THEOTOKOS, THE EXAMPLE FOR WOMAN. Dedicated, by permission, to Lady AGNES WOOD. Revised by the Venerable Archdeacon DENISON. 32mo. 1*s.* 6*d.*

MILLER (Edward)—THE HISTORY AND DOCTRINES OF IRVINGISM; or, the so-called Catholic and Apostolic Church. 2 vols. Large post 8vo. 25*s.*

THE CHURCH IN RELATION TO THE STATE. Large crown 8vo. 7*s.* 6*d.*

MINCHIN (J. G.)—BULGARIA SINCE THE WAR: Notes of a Tour in the Autumn of 1879. Small crown 8vo. 3*s.* 6*d.*

MITCHELL (Lucy M.)—A HISTORY OF ANCIENT SCULPTURE. With numerous Illustrations, including six Plates in Phototype. Super royal, 42*s.*

SELECTIONS FROM ANCIENT SCULPTURE. Being a Portfolio containing Reproductions in Phototype of 36 Masterpieces of Ancient Art, to illustrate Mrs. MITCHELL'S 'History of Ancient Sculpture.' 18*s.*

MITFORD (Bertram)—THROUGH THE ZULU COUNTRY. Its Battlefields and its People. With five Illustrations. Demy 8vo. 14*s.*

MOCKLER (E.)—A GRAMMAR OF THE BALOOCHEE LANGUAGE, as it is spoken in Makran (Ancient Gedrosia), in the Persia-Arabic and Roman characters. Fcp. 8vo. 5*s.*

MOLESWORTH (*W. Nassau*)—HISTORY OF THE CHURCH OF ENGLAND FROM 1660. Large crown 8vo. 7*s.* 6*d.*

MORELL (*J. R.*)—EUCLID SIMPLIFIED IN METHOD AND LANGUAGE. Being a Manual of Geometry. Compiled from the most important French Works, approved by the University of Paris and the Minister of Public Instruction. Fcp. 8vo. 2*s.* 6*d.*

MORRIS (*George*)—THE DUALITY OF ALL DIVINE TRUTH IN OUR LORD JESUS CHRIST: FOR GOD'S SELF-MANIFESTATION IN THE IMPARTATION OF THE DIVINE NATURE TO MAN. Large Crown 8vo. 7*s.* 6*d.*

MORSE (*E. S.*) *Ph.D.*—FIRST BOOK OF ZOOLOGY. With numerous Illustrations. New and Cheaper Edition. Crown 8vo. 2*s.* 6*d.*

MULL (*Matthias*)—PARADISE LOST. By JOHN MILTON. Books I.–VI. The Mutilations of the Text Emended, the Punctuation Revised, and all Collectively Presented, with Notes and Preface; also a Short Essay on the Intellectual Value of Milton's Works, &c. Demy 8vo. 6*s.*

MURPHY (*J. N.*)—THE CHAIR OF PETER; or, the Papacy Considered in its Institution, Development, and Organization, and in the Benefits which for over Eighteen Centuries it has conferred on Mankind. Demy 8vo. 18*s.*

NELSON (*J. H.*) *M.A.*—A PROSPECTUS OF THE SCIENTIFIC STUDY OF THE HINDÛ LAW. Demy 8vo. 9*s.*

NEWMAN (*Cardinal*)—CHARACTERISTICS FROM THE WRITINGS OF. Being Selections from his various Works. Arranged with the Author's personal Approval. Sixth Edition. With Portrait. Crown 8vo. 6*s.*

*** A Portrait of Cardinal Newman, mounted for framing, can be had, 2*s.* 6*d.*

NEWMAN (*Francis William*)—ESSAYS ON DIET. Small crown 8vo. 2*s.* 2*s.*

NEW TRUTH AND THE OLD FAITH: ARE THEY INCOMPATIBLE? By a Scientific Layman. Demy 8vo. 10*s.* 6*d.*

NEW WERTHER. By LOKI. Small crown 8vo. 2*s.* 6*d.*

NICHOLSON (*Edward Byron*)—THE GOSPEL ACCORDING TO THE HEBREWS. Its Fragments Translated and Annotated with a Critical Analysis of the External and Internal Evidence relating to it. Demy 8vo. 9*s.* 6*d.*

A NEW COMMENTARY ON THE GOSPEL ACCORDING TO MATTHEW. Demy 8vo. 12*s.*

NICOLS (*Arthur*) *F.G.S., F.R.G.S.*—CHAPTERS FROM THE PHYSICAL HISTORY OF THE EARTH: an Introduction to Geology and Palæontology With numerous Illustrations. Crown 8vo. 5*s.*

NOPS (*Marianne*)—CLASS LESSONS ON EUCLID. Part I. containing the First Two Books of the Elements. Crown 8vo. 2*s.* 6*a.*

NUCES: EXERCISES ON THE SYNTAX OF THE PUBLIC SCHOOL LATIN PRIMER. New Edition in Three Parts. Crown 8vo. each 1*s.*

*** The Three Parts can also be had bound together in cloth, 3*s.*

OATES (*Frank*) *F.R.G.S.*—MATABELE LAND AND THE VICTORIA FALLS. A Naturalist's Wanderings in the Interior of South Africa. Edited by C. G. OATES, B.A. With numerous Illustrations and 4 Maps. Demy 8vo. 21*s.*

OGLE (*W.*) *M.D., F.R.C.P.*—ARISTOTLE ON THE PARTS OF ANIMALS. Translated, with Introduction and Notes. Royal 8vo. 12*s.* 6*d.*

O'HAGAN (Lord) K.P.—OCCASIONAL PAPERS AND ADDRESSES. Large crown 8vo. 7*s.* 6*d.*

OKEN (Lorenz) Life of.—By ALEXANDER ECKER. With Explanatory Notes, Selections from Oken's Correspondence, and Portrait of the Professor. From the German by ALFRED TULK. Crown 8vo. 6*s.*

O'MEARA (Kathleen)—FREDERIC OZANAM, Professor of the Sorbonne: his Life and Work. Second Edition. Crown 8vo. 7*s.* 6*d.*

HENRI PERREYVE AND HIS COUNSELS TO THE SICK. Small crown 8vo. 5*s.*

OSBORNE (Rev. W. A.)—THE REVISED VERSION OF THE NEW TESTAMENT. A Critical Commentary, with Notes upon the Text. Crown 8vo. 5*s.*

OTTLEY (Henry Bickersteth)—THE GREAT DILEMMA: Christ His own Witness or His own Accuser. Six Lectures. Second Edition. Crown 8vo. 3*s.* 6*d.*

OUR PUBLIC SCHOOLS—ETON, HARROW, WINCHESTER, RUGBY, WESTMINSTER, MARLBOROUGH, THE CHARTERHOUSE. Crown 8vo. 6*s.*

OWEN (F. M.)—JOHN KEATS: a Study. Crown 8vo. 6*s.*

ACROSS THE HILLS. Small crown 8vo. 1*s.* 6*d.*

OWEN (Rev. Robert) B.D.—SANCTORALE CATHOLICUM; or, Book of Saints. With Notes, Critical, Exegetical, and Historical. Demy 8vo. 18*s.*

OXENHAM (Rev. F. Nutcombe)—WHAT IS THE TRUTH AS TO EVERLASTING PUNISHMENT? Part II. Being an Historical Enquiry into the Witness and Weight of certain Anti-Origenist Councils. Crown 8vo. 2*s.* 6*d.*

OXONIENSIS—ROMANISM, PROTESTANTISM, ANGLICANISM. Being a Layman's View of some Questions of the Day. Together with Remarks on Dr. Littledale's 'Plain Reasons against Joining the Church of Rome.' Small crown 8vo. 3*s.* 6*d.*

PALMER (the late William)—NOTES OF A VISIT TO RUSSIA IN 1840–41. Selected and arranged by JOHN H. CARDINAL NEWMAN. With Portrait. Crown 8vo. 8*s.* 6*d.*

EARLY CHRISTIAN SYMBOLISM. A series of Compositions from Fresco-Paintings, Glasses, and Sculptured Sarcophagi. Edited by the Rev. PROVOST NORTHCOTE, D.D., and the Rev. CANON BROWNLOW, M.A. With Coloured Plates, folio, 42*s.*; or with plain plates, folio, 25*s.*

PARCHMENT LIBRARY. Choicely printed on hand-made paper, limp parchment antique or cloth, 6*s.*; vellum, 7*s.* 6*d.* each volume.

SELECTIONS FROM THE PROSE WRITINGS OF JONATHAN SWIFT. With a Preface and Notes by STANLEY LANE-POOLE, and Portrait.

ENGLISH SACRED LYRICS.

SIR JOSHUA REYNOLDS' DISCOURSES. Edited by EDMUND GOSSE.

SELECTIONS FROM MILTON'S PROSE WRITINGS. Edited by ERNEST MYERS.

THE BOOK OF PSALMS. Translated by the Rev. T. K. CHEYNE, M.A.

THE VICAR OF WAKEFIELD. With Preface and Notes by AUSTIN DOBSON.

ENGLISH COMIC DRAMATISTS. Edited by OSWALD CRAWFURD.

ENGLISH LYRICS.

PARCHMENT LIBRARY—continued.

THE SONNETS OF JOHN MILTON. Edited by MARK PATTISON. With Portrait after Vertue.

FRENCH LYRICS. Selected and Annotated by GEORGE SAINTSBURY. With miniature Frontispiece, designed and etched by H. G. Glindoni.

FABLES by MR. JOHN GAY. With Memoir by AUSTIN DOBSON, and an etched Portrait from an unfinished Oil-sketch by Sir Godfrey Kneller.

SELECT LETTERS OF PERCY BYSSHE SHELLEY. Edited, with an Introtion, by RICHARD GARNETT.

THE CHRISTIAN YEAR; Thoughts in Verse for the Sundays and Holy Days throughout the Year. With etched Portrait of the Rev. J. Keble, after the Drawing by G. Richmond, R.A.

SHAKSPERE'S WORKS. Complete in Twelve Volumes.

EIGHTEENTH CENTURY ESSAYS. Selected and Edited by AUSTIN DOBSON. With a Miniature Frontispiece by R. Caldecott.

Q. HORATI FLACCI OPERA. Edited by F. A. CORNISH, Assistant Master at Eton. With a Frontispiece after a design by L. ALMA TADEMA. Etched by LEOPOLD LOWENSTAM.

EDGAR ALLAN POE'S POEMS. With an Essay on his Poetry by ANDREW LANG, and a Frontispiece by Linley Sambourne.

SHAKSPERE'S SONNETS. Edited by EDWARD DOWDEN. With a Frontispiece etched by Leopold Lowenstam, after the Death Mask.

ENGLISH ODES. Selected by EDMUND GOSSE. With Frontispiece on India paper by Hamo Thornycroft, A.R.A.

OF THE IMITATION OF CHRIST. By THOMAS À KEMPIS. A revised Translation. With Frontispiece on India paper, from a Design by W. B. Richmond.

POEMS: Selected from PERCY BYSSHE SHELLEY. Dedicated to Lady Shelley. With Preface by RICHARD GARNET and a Miniature Frontispiece.

*** The above Volumes may also be had in a variety of leather bindings.

PARSLOE (*Joseph*) — OUR RAILWAYS. Sketches, Historical and Descriptive. With Practical Information as to Fares and Rates, &c., and a Chapter on Railway Reform. Crown 8vo. 6*s*.

PASCAL (*Blaise*)—THE THOUGHTS OF. Translated from the Text of AUGUSTE MOLINIER by C. KEGAN PAUL. Large crown 8vo. with Frontispiece, printed on hand-made paper, parchment antique, or cloth, 12*s*.; vellum, 15*s*.

PAUL (*C. Kegan*)—BIOGRAPHICAL SKETCHES. Printed on hand-made paper, bound in buckram. Second Edition. Crown 8vo. 7*s*. 6*d*.

PAUL (*Alexander*)—SHORT PARLIAMENTS. A History of the National Demand for Frequent General Elections. Small crown 8vo. 3*s*. 6*d*.

PEARSON (*Rev. S.*)—WEEK-DAY LIVING. A Book for Young Men and Women. Second Edition. Crown 8vo. 5*s*.

PESCHEL (*Dr. Oscar*)—THE RACES OF MAN AND THEIR GEOGRAPHICAL DISTRIBUTION. Second Edition, large crown 8vo. 9*s*.

PETERS (*F. H.*)—THE NICOMACHEAN ETHICS OF ARISTOTLE. Translated by. Crown 8vo. 6*s*.

PHIPSON (*E.*)—THE ANIMAL LORE OF SHAKSPEARE'S TIME. Including Quadrupeds, Birds, Reptiles, Fish, and Insects. Large post 8vo. 9*s*.

PIDGEON (D.)—AN ENGINEER'S HOLIDAY; or, Notes of a Round Trip from Long. 0° to 0°. New and Cheaper Edition. Large crown 8vo. 7*s*. 6*d*.

OLD WORLD QUESTIONS AND NEW WORLD ANSWERS. Large crown 8vo. 7*s*. 6*d*.

PLAIN THOUGHTS FOR MEN. Eight Lectures delivered at the Foresters' Hall, Clerkenwell, during the London Mission, 1884. Crown 8vo. 1*s*. 6*d*.; paper covers, 1*s*.

POE (Edgar Allan)—WORKS OF. With an Introduction and a Memoir by RICHARD HENRY STODDARD. In 6 vols. with Frontispieces and Vignettes. Large crown 8vo. 6*s*. each vol.

POPE (J. Buckingham)—RAILWAY RATES AND RADICAL RULE. Trade Questions as Election Tests. Crown 8vo. 2*s*. 6*d*.

PRICE (Prof. Bonamy)—CHAPTERS ON PRACTICAL POLITICAL ECONOMY. Being the Substance of Lectures delivered before the University of Oxford. New and Cheaper Edition. Large post 8vo. 5*s*.

PULPIT COMMENTARY (THE). Old Testament Series. Edited by the Rev. J. S. EXELL and the Rev. Canon H. D. M. SPENCE.

GENESIS. By Rev. T. WHITELAW, M.A. With Homilies by the Very Rev. J. F. MONTGOMERY, D.D., Rev. Prof. R. A. REDFORD, M.A., LL.B., Rev. F. HASTINGS, Rev. W. ROBERTS, M.A.; an Introduction to the Study of the Old Testament by the Venerable Archdeacon FARRAR, D.D., F.R.S.; and Introductions to the Pentateuch by the Right Rev. H. COTTERILL, D.D., and Rev. T. WHITELAW, M.A. Eighth Edition. One vol. 15*s*.

EXODUS. By the Rev. Canon RAWLINSON. With Homilies by Rev. J. ORR, Rev. D. YOUNG, Rev. C. A. GOODHART, Rev. J. URQUHART, and Rev. H. T. ROBJOHNS. Fourth Edition. Two vols. 18*s*.

LEVITICUS. By the Rev. Prebendary MEYRICK, M.A. With Introductions by Rev. R. COLLINS, Rev. Professor A. CAVE, and Homilies by Rev. Prof. REDFORD, LL.B., Rev. J. A. MACDONALD, Rev. W. CLARKSON, Rev. S. R. ALDRIDGE, LL.B., and Rev. MCCHEYNE EDGAR. Fourth Edition. 15*s*.

NUMBERS. By the Rev R. WINTERBOTHAM, LL.B. With Homilies by the Rev. Professor W. BINNIE, D.D., Rev. E. S. PROUT, M.A., Rev. D. YOUNG, Rev. J. WAITE; and an Introduction by the Rev. THOMAS WHITELAW, M.A. Fourth Edition. 15*s*.

DEUTERONOMY. By Rev. W. L. ALEXANDER, D.D. With Homilies by Rev. D. DAVIES, M.A., Rev. C. CLEMANCE, D.D., Rev. J. ORR, B.D., and Rev. R. M. EDGAR, M.A. Third Edition. 15*s*.

JOSHUA. By Rev. J. J. LIAS, M.A. With Homilies by Rev. S. R. ALDRIDGE, LL.B., Rev. R. GLOVER, Rev. E. DE PRESSENSÉ, D.D., Rev. J. WAITE, B.A., Rev. F. W. ADENEY, M.A.; and an Introduction by the Rev. A. PLUMMER, M.A. Fifth Edition. 12*s*. 6*d*.

JUDGES AND RUTH. By the Bishop of Bath and Wells and Rev. J. MORISON, D.D. With Homilies by Rev. A. F. MUIR, M.A., Rev. F. W. ADENEY, M.A., Rev. W. M. STATHAM, and Rev. Professor J. THOMSON, M.A. Fourth Edition. 10*s*. 6*d*.

1 SAMUEL. By the Very Rev. R. P. SMITH, D.D. With Homilies by Rev. DONALD FRASER, D.D., Rev. Prof. CHAPMAN, and Rev. B. DALE. Sixth Edition. 15*s*.

PULPIT COMMENTARY (THE). Old Testament Series—continued.

I KINGS. By the Rev. JOSEPH HAMMOND, LL.B. With Homilies by the Rev. E DE PRESSENSÉ, D.D., Rev. J. WAITE, B.A., Rev. A. ROWLAND, LL.B., Rev. J. A. MACDONALD, and Rev. J. URQUHART. Fourth Edition. 15*s*.

I CHRONICLES. By the Rev. Prof. P. C. BARKER, M.A., LL.B. With Homilies by Rev. Prof. J. R. THOMSON, M.A., Rev. R. TUCK, B.A., Rev. W. CLARKSON, B.A., Rev. F. WHITFIELD, M A., and Rev. RICHARD GLOVER. 15*s*.

EZRA, NEHEMIAH, AND ESTHER. By Rev. Canon G. RAWLINSON, M.A. With Homilies by Rev. Prof. J. R. THOMSON, M.A., Rev. Prof. R. A. REDFORD, LL.B., M.A., Rev. W. S. LEWIS, M.A., Rev. J. A. MACDONALD, Rev. A. MACKENNAL, B.A., Rev. W. CLARKSON, B.A., Rev. F. HASTINGS, Rev. W. DINWIDDIE, LL.B., Rev. Prof. ROWLANDS, B.A., Rev. G. WOOD, B.A., Rev. Prof. P. C. BARKER, LL.B., M.A., and Rev. J. S. EXELL, M.A. Sixth Edition. One vol. 12*s*. 6*d*.

JEREMIAH (Vol. I.). By the Rev. T. K. CHEYNE, M.A. With Homilies by the Rev. F. W. ADENEY, M.A., Rev. A. F. MUIR, M.A., Rev. S. CONWAY, B.A., Rev. J. WAITE, B.A., and Rev. D. YOUNG, B.A. Second Edition. 15*s*.

JEREMIAH (Vol. II.), AND LAMENTATIONS. By Rev. T. K. CHEYNE, M.A. With Homilies by Rev. Prof. J. R. THOMSON, M.A., Rev. W. F. ADENEY, M.A., Rev. A. F. MUIR, M.A., Rev. S. CONWAY, B.A., Rev. D. YOUNG, B.A. 15*s*.

PULPIT COMMENTARY (THE). New Testament Series.

ST. MARK. By the Very Rev. E. BICKERSTETH, D.D., Dean of Lichfield. With Homilies by the Rev. Prof. THOMSON, M.A., Rev. Prof. GIVEN, M.A., Rev. Prof. JOHNSON, M.A., Rev. A. ROWLAND, LL.B., Rev. A. MUIR, M.A., and Rev. R. GREEN. Fourth Edition. 2 Vols. 21*s*.

THE ACTS OF THE APOSTLES. By the Bishop of BATH AND WELLS. With Homilies by Rev. Prof. P. C. BARKER, M.A., Rev. Prof. E. JOHNSON, M.A., Rev. Prof. R. A. REDFORD, M.A., Rev. R. TUCK, B.A., Rev. W. CLARKSON, B.A. Second Edition. Two vols. 21*s*.

I CORINTHIANS. By the Ven. Archdeacon FARRAR, D.D. With Homilies by Rev. Ex-Chancellor LIPSCOMB, LL.D., Rev. DAVID THOMAS, D.D., Rev. DONALD FRASER, D.D., Rev. Prof. J. R. THOMSON, M.A., Rev. R. TUCK, B.A., Rev. E. HURNDALL, M.A., Rev. J. WAITE, B.A., Rev. H. BREMNER, B.D. Second Edition. 15*s*.

PUSEY (*Dr.*)—SERMONS FOR THE CHURCH'S SEASONS FROM ADVENT TO TRINITY. Selected from the published Sermons of the late EDWARD BOUVERIE PUSEY, D.D. Crown 8vo. 5*s*.

RADCLIFFE (*Frank R. Y.*)—THE NEW POLITICUS. Small crown 8vo. 2*s*. 6*d*.

RANKE (*Leopold von*)—UNIVERSAL HISTORY. The Oldest Historical Group of Nations and the Greeks. Edited by G. W. PROTHERO. Demy 8vo. 16*s*.

REALITIES OF THE FUTURE LIFE. Small crown 8vo. 1*s*. 6*d*.

RENDELL (*J. M.*)—CONCISE HANDBOOK OF THE ISLAND OF MADEIRA. With Plan of Funchal and Map of the Island. Fcp. 8vo. 1*s*. 6*d*.

REYNOLDS (Rev. J. W.)—THE SUPERNATURAL IN NATURE. A Verification by Free Use of Science. Third Edition, revised and enlarged. Demy 8vo. 14*s.*

THE MYSTERY OF MIRACLES. Third and Enlarged Edition. Crown 8vo. 6*s.*

THE MYSTERY OF THE UNIVERSE: Our Common Faith. Demy 8vo. 14*s.*

RIBOT (Prof. Th.)—HEREDITY: a Psychological Study on its Phenomena, its Laws, its Causes, and its Consequences. Second Edition. Large crown 8vo. 9*s.*

RIMMER (William) M.D.—ART ANATOMY: A Portfolio of 81 Plates. Folio, 70*s.* nett.

ROBERTSON (The late Rev. F. W.) M.A.—LIFE AND LETTERS OF. Edited by the Rev. Stopford Brooke, M.A.

I. Two vols., uniform with the Sermons. With Steel Portrait. Crown 8vo. 7*s.* 6*d.*

II. Library Edition, in demy 8vo. with Portrait. 12*s.*

III. A Popular Edition, in 1 vol. Crown 8vo. 6*s.*

SERMONS. Four Series. Small crown 8vo. 3*s.* 6*d.*

THE HUMAN RACE, and other Sermons. Preached at Cheltenham, Oxford, and Brighton. New and Cheaper Edition. Small crown 8vo. 3*s.* 6*d.*

NOTES ON GENESIS. New and Cheaper Edition. Small crown 8vo. 3*s.* 6*d.*

EXPOSITORY LECTURES ON ST. PAUL'S EPISTLES TO THE CORINTHIANS. A New Edition. Small crown 8vo. 5*s.*

LECTURES AND ADDRESSES, with other Literary Remains. A New Edition. Small crown 8vo. 5*s.*

AN ANALYSIS OF TENNYSON'S 'IN MEMORIAM.' (Dedicated by Permission to the Poet-Laureate.) Fcp. 8vo. 2*s.*

THE EDUCATION OF THE HUMAN RACE. Translated from the German of Gotthold Ephraim Lessing. Fcp. 8vo. 2*s.* 6*d.*

The above Works can also be had bound in half-morocco.

*** A Portrait of the late Rev. F. W. Robertson, mounted for framing, can be had, 2*s.* 6*d.*

ROMANES (G. J.)—MENTAL EVOLUTION IN ANIMALS. With a Posthumous Essay on Instinct, by CHARLES DARWIN, F.R.S. Demy 8vo. 12*s.*

ROSMINI SERBATI (A.) Founder of the Institute of Charity—LIFE. By G. STUART MACWALTER. 2 vols. 8vo. [Vol. I. now ready, 12*s.*

ROSMINI'S ORIGIN OF IDEAS. Translated from the Fifth Italian Edition of the Nuovo Saggio. *Sull' origine delle idee.* 3 vols. Demy 8vo. 16*s* each.

ROSMINI'S PSYCHOLOGY. 3 vols. Demy 8vo. [Vol. I. now ready, 16*s.*

ROSMINI'S PHILOSOPHICAL SYSTEM. Translated, with a Sketch of the Author's Life, Bibliography, Introduction, and Notes, by THOMAS DAVIDSON. Demy 8vo. 16*s.*

RULE (Martin) M.A.—THE LIFE AND TIMES OF ST. ANSELM, ARCHBISHOP OF CANTERBURY AND PRIMATE OF THE BRITAINS. 2 vols. Demy 8vo. 32*s.*

SAMUEL (*Sydney M.*)—JEWISH LIFE IN THE EAST. Small crown 8vo. 3*s*. 6*d*.

SARTORIUS (*Ernestine*)—THREE MONTHS IN THE SOUDAN. With 11 Full-page Illustrations. Demy 8vo. 14*s*.

SAYCE (*Rev. Archibald Henry*)—INTRODUCTION TO THE SCIENCE OF LANGUAGE. 2 vols. Second Edition. Large post 8vo. 21*s*.

SCIENTIFIC LAYMAN. The New Truth and the Old Faith: are they Incompatible? Demy 8vo. 10*s*. 6*d*.

SCOONES (*W. Baptiste*)—FOUR CENTURIES OF ENGLISH LETTERS: A Selection of 350 Letters by 150 Writers, from the Period of the Paston Letters to the Present Time. Third Edition. Large crown 8vo. 6*s*.

SÉE (*Prof. Germain*)—BACILLARY PHTHISIS OF THE LUNGS. Translated and Edited for English Practitioners, by WILLIAM HENRY WEDDELL, M.R.C.S. Demy 8vo.

SHILLITO (*Rev. Joseph*)—WOMANHOOD: its Duties, Temptations, and Privileges. A Book for Young Women. Third Edition. Crown 8vo. 3*s*. 6*d*.

SHIPLEY (*Rev. Orby*) *M.A.*—PRINCIPLES OF THE FAITH IN RELATION TO SIN. Topics for Thought in Times of Retreat. Eleven Addresses delivered during a Retreat of Three Days to Persons living in the World. Demy 8vo. 12*s*.

SIDNEY (*Algernon*)—A REVIEW. By GERTRUDE M. IRELAND BLACKBURNE. Crown 8vo. 6*s*.

SISTER AUGUSTINE, Superior of the Sisters of Charity at the St. Johannis Hospital at Bonn. Authorised Translation by HANS THARAU, from the German 'Memorials of AMALIE VON LASAULX.' Cheap Edition. Large crown 8vo. 4*s*. 6*d*.

SKINNER (JAMES). A Memoir. By the Author of 'Charles Lowder.' With a Preface by the Rev. Canon CARTER, and Portrait. Large crown 8vo. 7*s*. 6*d*.

*** Also a Cheap Edition, with Portrait. Crown 8vo. 3*s*. 6*d*.

SMITH (*Edward*) *M.D., LL.B., F.R.S.*—TUBERCULAR CONSUMPTION IN ITS EARLY AND REMEDIABLE STAGES. Second Edition. Crown 8vo. 6*s*.

SPEDDING (*James*)—REVIEWS AND DISCUSSIONS, LITERARY, POLITICAL, AND HISTORICAL NOT RELATING TO BACON. Demy 8vo. 12*s*. 6*d*.

EVENINGS WITH A REVIEWER; or, Bacon and Macaulay. With a Prefatory Notice by G. S. VENABLES, Q.C. 2 vols. Demy 8vo. 18*s*.

STAPFER (*Paul*)—SHAKSPEARE AND CLASSICAL ANTIQUITY: Greek and Latin Antiquity as presented in Shakspeare's Plays. Translated by EMILY J. CAREY. Large post 8vo. 12*s*.

STATHAM (*F. Reginald*)—FREE THOUGHT AND TRUE THOUGHT. A Contribution to an Existing Argument. Crown 8vo. 6*s*.

STEVENSON (*Rev. W. F.*)—HYMNS FOR THE CHURCH AND HOME. Selected and Edited by the Rev. W. Fleming Stevenson.

The Hymn Book consists of Three Parts:—I. For Public Worship.—II. For Family and Private Worship.—III. For Children.

SMALL EDITION, cloth limp, 10*d*.; cloth boards, 1*s*.
LARGE TYPE EDITION, cloth limp, 1*s*. 3*d*.; cloth boards, 1*s*. 6*d*.

STRAY PAPERS ON EDUCATION AND SCENES FROM SCHOOL LIFE. By B. H. Second Edition. Small crown 8vo. 3*s*. 6*d*.

STREATFEILD (Rev. G. S.) M.A.—LINCOLNSHIRE AND THE DANES. Large crown 8vo. 7*s*. 6*d*.

STRECKER-WISLICENUS—ORGANIC CHEMISTRY. Translated and Edited, with Extensive Additions, by W. R. HODGKINSON, Ph.D., and A. J. GREENAWAY, F.I.C. Demy 8vo. 21*s*.

STUDY OF THE PROLOGUE AND EPILOGUE IN ENGLISH LITERATURE, FROM SHAKESPEARE TO DRYDEN. By G. S. B. Crown 8vo. 5*s*.

SULLY (James) M.A.—PESSIMISM: a History and a Criticism. Second Edition. Demy 8vo. 14*s*.

SUTHERST (Thomas).—DEATH AND DISEASE BEHIND THE COUNTER. Crown 8vo. 1*s*. 6*d*.; paper covers, 1*s*.

SWEDENBORG (Eman.)—DE CULTU ET AMORE DEI, UBI AGITUR DE TELLURIS ORTU, PARADISO ET VIVARIO, TUM DE PRIMOGENITI SEU ADAMI NATIVITATE, INFANTIA, ET AMORE. Crown 8vo. 6*s*.

SYME (David)—REPRESENTATIVE GOVERNMENT IN ENGLAND: its Faults and Failures. Second Edition. Large crown 8vo. 6*s*.

TACITUS'S AGRICOLA: A Translation. Small crown 8vo. 2*s*. 6*d*.

TAYLOR (Rev. Isaac)—THE ALPHABET. An Account of the Origin and Development of Letters. With numerous Tables and Facsimiles. 2 vols. Demy 8vo. 36*s*.

TAYLOR (Jeremy)—THE MARRIAGE RING. With Preface, Notes, and Appendices. Edited by FRANCIS BURDETT MONEY COUTTS. Small crown 8vo. 2*s*. 6*d*.

TAYLOR (Sedley)—PROFIT SHARING BETWEEN CAPITAL AND LABOUR. To which is added a Memorandum on the Industrial Partnership at the Whitwood Collieries, by ARCHIBALD and HENRY BRIGGS, with Remarks by SEDLEY TAYLOR. Crown 8vo. 2*s*. 6*d*.

THIRTY THOUSAND THOUGHTS. Edited by the Rev. Canon SPENCE, Rev. J. S. EXELL, and Rev. CHARLES NEIL. 6 vols. Super-royal 8vo.
[Vols. I., II., and III. now ready, 16*s*. each.

THOM (John Hamilton)—LAWS OF LIFE AFTER THE MIND OF CHRIST. Second Edition. Crown 8vo. 7*s*. 6*d*.

TIDMAN (Paul F.)—GOLD AND SILVER MONEY. Part I.—A Plain Statement. Part II.—Objections Answered. Third Edition. Crown 8vo. 1*s*.

TIPPLE (Rev. S. A.)—SUNDAY MORNINGS AT NORWOOD. Prayers and Sermons. Crown 8vo. 6*s*.

TODHUNTER (Dr. J.)—A STUDY OF SHELLEY. Crown 8vo. 7*s*.

TRANT (William)—TRADE UNIONS; Their Origin and Objects, Influence and Efficacy. Small crown 8vo. 1*s*. 6*d*.; paper covers, 1*s*.

TREMENHEERE (H. Seymour) C.B.—A MANUAL OF THE PRINCIPLES OF GOVERNMENT AS SET FORTH BY THE AUTHORITIES OF ANCIENT AND MODERN TIMES. New and enlarged Edition. Crown 8vo. 3*s*. 6*d*.

TUKE (Daniel Hack) M.D.—CHAPTERS IN THE HISTORY OF THE INSANE IN THE BRITISH ISLES. With Four Illustrations. Large crown 8vo. 12*s*.

TWINING (Louisa)—WORKHOUSE VISITING AND MANAGEMENT DURING TWENTY-FIVE YEARS. Small crown 8vo. 2*s*.

TYLER (*J.*)—The Mystery of Being; or, What Do We Know? Small crown 8vo. 3*s*. 6*d*.

UPTON (*Major R. D.*)—Gleanings from the Desert of Arabia. Large post 8vo. 10*s*. 6*d*.

VACUUS VIATOR—Flying South. Recollections of France and its Littoral. Small crown 8vo. 3*s*. 6*d*.

VAUGHAN (*H. Halford*)—New Readings and Renderings of Shakespeare's Tragedies. 2 vols. Demy 8vo. 25*s*.

VILLARI (*Professor*)—Niccolò Machiavelli and his Times. Translated by Linda Villari. 4 vols. Large crown 8vo. 48*s*.

VILLIERS (*The Right Hon. C. P.*)—Free Trade Speeches of. With Political Memoir. Edited by a Member of the Cobden Club. 2 vols. With Portrait. Demy 8vo. 25*s*.

*** Also a People's Edition, in 1 vol. crown 8vo. limp 2*s*. 6*d*.

VOGT (*Lieut.-Col. Hermann*)—The Egyptian War of 1882. A Translation. With Map and Plans. Large crown 8vo. 6*s*.

VOLCKXSOM (*E. W. v.*)—Catechism of Elementary Modern Chemistry. Small crown 8vo. 3*s*.

VYNER (*Lady Mary*)—Every Day a Portion. Adapted from the Bible and the Prayer Book, for the Private Devotions of those living in Widowhood. Collected and Edited by Lady Mary Vyner. Square crown 8vo. 5*s*.

WALDSTEIN (*Charles*) *Ph.D.*—The Balance of Emotion and Intellect; an Introductory Essay to the Study of Philosophy. Crown 8vo. 6*s*.

WALLER (*Rev. C. B.*)—The Apocalypse, reviewed under the Light of the Doctrine of the Unfolding Ages, and the Restitution of All Things. Demy 8vo. 12*s*.

WALPOLE (*Chas. George*)—A Short History of Ireland from the Earliest Times to the Union with Great Britain. With 5 Maps and Appendices. Second Edition. Crown 8vo. 6*s*.

WALSHE (*Walter Hayle*) *M.D.*—Dramatic Singing Physiologically Estimated. Crown 8vo. cloth, price 3*s*. 6*d*.

WARD (*William George*) *Ph.D.*—Essays on the Philosophy of Theism. Edited, with an Introduction, by Wilfrid Ward. 2 vols. demy 8vo. 21*s*.

WARD (*Wilfrid*)—The Wish to Believe: A Discussion concerning the Temper of Mind in which a reasonable Man should undertake Religious Inquiry. Small crown 8vo. 5*s*.

WEDDERBURN (*Sir David*) *Bart.*, *M.P.*—Life of. Compiled from his Journals and Writings by his Sister, Mrs. E. H. Percival. With etched Portrait, and facsimiles of Pencil Sketches. Demy 8vo. 14*s*.

WEDMORE (*Frederick*)—The Masters of Genre Painting. With Sixteen Illustrations. Post 8vo. 7*s*. 6*d*.

What to Do and How to Do It. A Manual of the Law affecting the Housing and Sanitary Condition of Londoners, with Special Reference to the Dwellings of the Poor. Issued by the Sanitary Laws Enforcement Society. Demy 8vo. 1*s*.

WHEWELL (William) D.D.—HIS LIFE AND SELECTIONS FROM HIS CORRESPONDENCE. By Mrs. STAIR DOUGLAS. With a Portrait from a Painting by SAMUEL LAURENCE. Demy 8vo. 21*s.*

WHITNEY (Prof. William Dwight)—ESSENTIALS OF ENGLISH GRAMMAR, for the Use of Schools. Second Edition, crown 8vo. 3*s.* 6*d.*

WILLIAMS (Rowland) D.D.—PSALMS, LITANIES, COUNSELS, AND COLLECTS FOR DEVOUT PERSONS. Edited by his Widow. New and Popular Edition. Crown 8vo. 3*s.* 6*d.*

STRAY THOUGHTS COLLECTED FROM THE WRITINGS OF THE LATE ROWLAND WILLIAMS, D.D. Edited by his Widow. Crown 8vo. 3*s.* 6*d.*

WILSON (Lieut.-Col. C. T.)—THE DUKE OF BERWICK, MARSHAL OF FRANCE, 1702–1734. Demy 8vo. 15*s.*

WILSON (Mrs. R. F.)—THE CHRISTIAN BROTHERS: THEIR ORIGIN AND WORK. With a Sketch of the Life of their Founder, the Ven. Jean Baptiste, de la Salle. Crown 8vo. 6*s.*

WOLTMANN (Dr. Alfred), and WOERMANN (Dr. Karl)—HISTORY OF PAINTING. Edited by Sidney Colvin. Vol. I. Painting in Antiquity and the Middle Ages. With numerous Illustrations. Medium 8vo. 28*s.*; bevelled boards, gilt leaves, 30*s.*

WORD WAS MADE FLESH. Short Family Readings on the Epistles for each Sunday of the Christian Year. Demy 8vo. 10*s.* 6*d.*

WREN (Sir Christopher)—HIS FAMILY AND HIS TIMES. With Original Letters, and a Discourse on Architecture hitherto unpublished. By LUCY PHILLIMORE. Demy 8vo. 10*s.* 6*d.*

YOUMANS (Eliza A.)—FIRST BOOK OF BOTANY. Designed to cultivate the Observing Powers of Children. With 300 Engravings. New and Cheaper Edition. Crown 8vo. 2*s.* 6*d.*

YOUMANS (Edward L.) M.D.—A CLASS BOOK OF CHEMISTRY, on the Basis of the New System. With 200 Illustrations. Crown 8vo. 5*s.*

THE INTERNATIONAL SCIENTIFIC SERIES.

I. FORMS OF WATER: a Familiar Exposition of the Origin and Phenomena of Glaciers. By J. Tyndall, LL.D., F.R.S. With 25 Illustrations. Eighth Edition. Crown 8vo. 5*s*.

II. PHYSICS AND POLITICS; or, Thoughts on the Application of the Principles of 'Natural Selection' and 'Inheritance' to Political Society. By Walter Bagehot. Sixth Edition. Crown 8vo. 4*s*.

III. FOODS. By Edward Smith, M.D., LL.B., F.R.S. With numerous Illustrations. Eighth Edition. Crown 8vo. 5*s*.

IV. MIND AND BODY: the Theories of their Relation. By Alexander Bain, LL.D. With Four Illustrations. Seventh Edition. Crown 8vo. 4*s*.

V. THE STUDY OF SOCIOLOGY. By Herbert Spencer. Eleventh Edition. Crown 8vo. 5*s*.

VI. ON THE CONSERVATION OF ENERGY. By Balfour Stewart, M.A., LL.D., F.R.S. With 14 Illustrations. Sixth Edition. Crown 8vo. 5*s*.

VII. ANIMAL LOCOMOTION; or, Walking, Swimming, and Flying. By J. B. Pettigrew, M.D., F.R.S., &c. With 130 Illustrations. Third Edition. Crown 8vo. 5*s*.

VIII. RESPONSIBILITY IN MENTAL DISEASE. By Henry Maudsley, M.D. Fourth Edition. Crown 8vo. 5*s*.

IX. THE NEW CHEMISTRY. By Professor J. P. Cooke. With 31 Illustrations. Eighth Edition, remodelled and enlarged. Crown 8vo. 5*s*.

X. THE SCIENCE OF LAW. By Professor Sheldon Amos. Fifth Edition. Crown 8vo. 5*s*.

XI. ANIMAL MECHANISM: a Treatise on Terrestrial and Aërial Locomotion. By Professor E. J. Marey. With 117 Illustrations. Third Edition. Crown 8vo. 5*s*.

XII. THE DOCTRINE OF DESCENT AND DARWINISM. By Professor Oscar Schmidt. With 26 Illustrations. Sixth Edition. Crown 8vo. 5*s*.

XIII. THE HISTORY OF THE CONFLICT BETWEEN RELIGION AND SCIENCE. By J. W. Draper, M.D., LL.D. Eighteenth Edition. Crown 8vo. 5*s*.

XIV. FUNGI: their Nature, Influences, Uses, &c. By M. C. Cooke, M.D., LL.D. Edited by the Rev. M. J. Berkeley, M.A., F.L.S. With numerous Illustrations. Third Edition. Crown 8vo. 5*s*.

XV. THE CHEMICAL EFFECTS OF LIGHT AND PHOTOGRAPHY. By Dr. Hermann Vogel. Translation thoroughly revised. With 100 Illustrations. Fourth Edition. Crown 8vo. 5*s*.

XVI. THE LIFE AND GROWTH OF LANGUAGE. By Professor William Dwight Whitney. Fourth Edition. Crown 8vo. 5*s*.

XVII. MONEY AND THE MECHANISM OF EXCHANGE. By W. Stanley Jevons, M.A., F.R.S. Sixth Edition. Crown 8vo. 5*s*.

XVIII. THE NATURE OF LIGHT. With a General Account of Physical Optics. By Dr. Eugene Lommel. With 188 Illustrations and a Table of Spectra in Chromo-lithography. Third Edit. Crown 8vo. 5*s*.

XIX. ANIMAL PARASITES AND MESSMATES. By P. J. Van Beneden. With 83 Illustrations. Third Edition. Crown 8vo. 5*s*.

XX. FERMENTATION. By Professor Schützenberger. With 28 Illustrations. Fourth Edition. Crown 8vo. 5*s*.

XXI. THE FIVE SENSES OF MAN. By Professor Bernstein. With 91 Illustrations. Fourth Edition. Crown 8vo. 5*s*.

XXII. THE THEORY OF SOUND IN ITS RELATION TO MUSIC. By Professor Pietro Blaserna. With numerous Illustrations. Third Edition. Crown 8vo. 5*s*.

XXIII. STUDIES IN SPECTRUM ANALYSIS. By J. Norman Lockyer, F.R.S. Third Edition. With six Photographic Illustrations of Spectra, and numerous Engravings on Wood. Crown 8vo. 6*s*. 6*d*.

XXIV. A History of the Growth of the Steam Engine. By Professor R. H. Thurston. With numerous Illustrations. Third Edition. Crown 8vo. 6*s*. 6*d*.

XXV. Education as a Science. By Alexander Bain, LL.D. Fourth Edition. Crown 8vo. 5*s*.

XXVI. The Human Species. By Prof. A. De Quatrefages. Third Edition. Crown 8vo. 5*s*.

XXVII. Modern Chromatics. With Applications to Art and Industry. By Ogden N. Rood. With 130 original Illustrations. Second Edition. Crown 8vo. 5*s*.

XXVIII. The Crayfish: an Introduction to the Study of Zoology. By Professor T. H. Huxley. With 82 Illustrations. Fourth Edition. Crown 8vo. 5*s*.

XXIX. The Brain as an Organ of Mind. By H. Charlton Bastian, M.D. With numerous Illustrations. Third Edition. Crown 8vo. 5*s*.

XXX. The Atomic Theory. By Prof. Wurtz. Translated by G. Cleminshaw, F.C.S. Third Edition. Crown 8vo. 5*s*.

XXXI. The Natural Conditions of Existence as they affect Animal Life. By Karl Semper. With 2 Maps and 106 Woodcuts. Third Edition. Crown 8vo. 5*s*.

XXXII. General Physiology of Muscles and Nerves. By Prof. J. Rosenthal. Third Edition. With Illustrations. Crown 8vo. 5*s*.

XXXIII. Sight: an Exposition of the Principles of Monocular and Binocular Vision. By Joseph Le Conte, LL.D. Second Edition. With 132 Illustrations. Crown 8vo. 5*s*.

XXXIV. Illusions: a Psychological Study. By James Sully. Second Edition. Crown 8vo. 5*s*.

XXXV. Volcanoes: what they are and what they teach. By Professor J. W. Judd, F.R.S. With 92 Illustrations on Wood. Third Edition. Crown 8vo. 5*s*.

XXXVI. Suicide: an Essay on Comparative Moral Statistics. By Prof. H. Morselli. Second Edition. With Diagrams. Crown 8vo. 5*s*.

XXXVII. The Brain and its Functions. By J. Luys. Second Edition. With Illustrations. Crown 8vo. 5*s*.

XXXVIII. Myth and Science: an Essay. By Tito Vignoli. Second Edition. Crown 8vo. 5*s*.

XXXIX. The Sun. By Professor Young. With Illustrations. Second Edition. Crown 8vo. 5*s*.

XL. Ants, Bees, and Wasps: a Record of Observations on the Habits of the Social Hymenoptera. By Sir John Lubbock, Bart., M.P. With 5 Chromolithographic Illustrations. Seventh Edition. Crown 8vo 5*s*.

XLI. Animal Intelligence. By G. J. Romanes, LL.D., F.R.S. Third Edition. Crown 8vo. 5*s*.

XLII. The Concepts and Theories of Modern Physics. By J. B. Stallo. Third Edition. Crown 8vo. 5*s*.

XLIII. Diseases of Memory: an Essay in the Positive Pyschology. By Prof. Th. Ribot. Second Edition. Crown 8vo. 5*s*.

XLIV. Man before Metals. By N. Joly. Third Edition. Crown 8vo. 5*s*.

XLV. The Science of Politics. By Prof. Sheldon Amos. Third Edit. Crown. 8vo. 5*s*.

XLVI. Elementary Meteorology. By Robert H. Scott. Third Edition. With numerous Illustrations. Crown 8vo. 5*s*.

XLVII. The Organs of Speech and their Application in the Formation of Articulate Sounds. By Georg Hermann von Meyer. With 47 Woodcuts. Crown 8vo. 5*s*.

XLVIII. Fallacies: a View of Logic from the Practical Side. By Alfred Sidgwick. Crown 8vo. 5*s*.

XLIX. Origin of Cultivated Plants. By Alphonse de Candolle. Crown 8vo. 5*s*.

L. Jelly Fish, Star Fish, and Sea Urchins. Being a Research on Primitive Nervous Systems. By G. J. Romanes. Crown 8vo. 5*s*.

MILITARY WORKS.

BARRINGTON (*Capt. J. T.*)—ENGLAND ON THE DEFENSIVE; or, the Problem of Invasion Critically Examined. Large crown 8vo. with Map, 7*s.* 6*d.*

BRACKENBURY (*Col. C. B.*) *R.A.* —MILITARY HANDBOOKS FOR REGIMENTAL OFFICERS:

I. MILITARY SKETCHING AND RECONNAISSANCE. By Colonel F. J. Hutchison and Major H. G. MacGregor. Fourth Edition. With 15 Plates. Small crown 8vo. 4*s.*

II. THE ELEMENTS OF MODERN TACTICS PRACTICALLY APPLIED TO ENGLISH FORMATIONS. By Lieut.-Col. Wilkinson Shaw. Fifth Edit. With 25 Plates and Maps. Small crown 8vo. 9*s.*

III. FIELD ARTILLERY: its Equipment, Organisation, and Tactics. By Major Sisson C. Pratt, R.A. With 12 Plates. Second Edition. Small crown 8vo. 6*s.*

IV. THE ELEMENTS OF MILITARY ADMINISTRATION. First Part: Permanent System of Administration. By Major J. W. Buxton. Small crown 8vo. 7*s.* 6*d.*

V. MILITARY LAW: its Procedure and Practice. By Major Sisson C. Pratt, R.A. Second Edition. Small crown 8vo. 4*s.* 6d.

VI. CAVALRY IN MODERN WAR. By Col. F. Chenevix Trench. Small crown 8vo. 6*s.*

VII. FIELD WORKS. Their Technical Construction and Tactical Application. By the Editor, Col. C. B. Brackenbury, R.A. Small crown 8vo.

BROOKE (*Major C. K.*)—A SYSTEM OF FIELD TRAINING. Small crown 8vo. 2*s.*

CLERY (*C.*) *Lieut.-Col.*—MINOR TACTICS. With 26 Maps and Plans. Sixth and cheaper Edition, revised. Crown 8vo. 9*s.*

COLVILE (*Lieut.-Col. C. F.*)—MILITARY TRIBUNALS. Sewed, 2*s.* 6*d.*

CRAUFURD (*Capt. H. J.*)—SUGGESTIONS FOR THE MILITARY TRAINING OF A COMPANY OF INFANTRY. Crown 8vo. 1*s.* 6*d.*

HARRISON (*Lieut.-Col. R.*) — THE OFFICER'S MEMORANDUM BOOK FOR PEACE AND WAR. Third Edition. Oblong 32mo. roan, with pencil, 3*s.* 6*d.*

NOTES ON CAVALRY TACTICS, ORGANISATION, &c. By a Cavalry Officer. With Diagrams. Demy 8vo. 12*s.*

PARR (*Capt. H. Hallam*) *C.M.G.*—THE DRESS, HORSES, AND EQUIPMENT OF INFANTRY AND STAFF OFFICERS. Crown 8vo. 1*s.*

SCHAW (*Col. H.*)—THE DEFENCE AND ATTACK OF POSITIONS AND LOCALITIES. Third Edition, revised and corrected. Crown 8vo. 3*s.* 6*d.*

WILKINSON (*H. Spenser*) *Capt. 20th Lancashire R.V.*—CITIZEN SOLDIERS. Essays towards the Improvement of the Volunteer Force. Crown 8vo. 2*s.* 6*d.*

POETRY.

ADAM OF ST. VICTOR—THE LITURGICAL POETRY OF ADAM OF ST. VICTOR. From the text of Gautier. With Translations into English in the Original Metres, and Short Explanatory Notes. By Digby S. Wrangham, M.A. 3 vols. Crown 8vo. printed on hand-made paper, boards, 21*s.*

AUCHMUTY (*A. C.*)—POEMS OF ENGLISH HEROISM: From Brunanburgh to Lucknow; from Athelstan to Albert. Small crown 8vo. 1*s.* 6*d.*

AVIA—THE ODYSSEY OF HOMER. Done into English Verse by. Fcp. 4to. 15*s.*

BARING (*T. C.*), *M.P.*—THE SCHEME OF EPICURUS. A Rendering into English Verse of the Unfinished Poem of Lucretius, entitled, 'De Rerum Naturâ.' Fcp. 4to. 7*s.*

BARNES (*William*)—POEMS OF RURAL LIFE, IN THE DORSET DIALECT. New Edition, complete in one vol. Crown 8vo. 8*s.* 6*d.*

BAYNES (*Rev. Canon H. R.*)—HOME SONGS FOR QUIET HOURS. Fourth and cheaper Edition. Fcp. 8vo. 2*s.* 6*d.*

BENDALL (*Gerard*)—MUSA SILVESTRIS. 16mo. 1*s.* 6*d.*

BEVINGTON (*L. S.*)—KEY NOTES. Small crown 8vo. 5*s.*

BILLSON (*C. J.*)—THE ACHARNIANS OF ARISTOPHANES. Crown 8vo. 3*s.* 6*d.*

BLUNT (*Wilfrid Scawen*)—THE WIND AND THE WHIRLWIND. Demy 8vo. 1*s.* 6*d.*

BOWEN (*H. C.*) *M.A.*—SIMPLE ENGLISH POEMS. English Literature for Junior Classes. In Four Parts. Parts I. II. and III. 6*d.* each, and Part IV. 1*s.*, complete 3*s.*

BRASHER (*Alfred*)—SOPHIA; or, the Viceroy of Valencia. A Comedy in Five Acts, Founded on a Story in Scarron. Small crown 8vo. 2*s.* 6*d.*

BRYANT (*W. C.*) — POEMS. Cheap Edition, with Frontispiece. Small crown 8vo. 3*s.* 6*d.*

BYRNNE (*E. Fairfax*)—MILICENT: a Poem. Small crown 8vo. 6*s.*

CAILLARD (*Emma Marie*) — CHARLOTTE CORDAY, and other Poems. Small crown 8vo. 3*s.* 6*d.*

CALDERON'S DRAMAS: the Wonder-working Magician—Life is a Dream—the Purgatory of St. Patrick. Translated by Denis Florence MacCarthy. Post 8vo. 10*s.*

CAMOENS LUSIADS. Portuguese Text with English Translation, by J. J. AUBERTIN. Second Edition. 2 vols. Crown 8vo. 12*s.*

CAMPBELL (*Lewis*)—SOPHOCLES. The Seven Plays in English Verse. Crown 8vo. 7*s.* 6*d.*

CASTILIAN BROTHERS (*The*)—CHATEAUBRIANT, WALDEMAR, THREE TRAGEDIES, AND THE ROSE OF SICILY. A Drama. By the Author of 'Ginevra,' &c. Crown 8vo. 6*s.*

CHRISTIAN (*Owen*)—POEMS. Small crown 8vo. 2*s.* 6*d.*

CHRONICLES OF CHRISTOPHER COLUMBUS: a Poem in Twelve Cantos. By M. D. C. Crown 8vo. 7*s.* 6*d.*

CLARKE (*Mary Cowden*)—HONEY FROM THE WEED. Verses. Crown 8vo. 7*s.*

COSMO DE MEDICI, The False One, Agramont and Beaumont, Three Tragedies, and The Deformed. A Dramatic Sketch. By the Author of 'Ginevra,' &c. Crown 8vo. 5*s.*

COXHEAD (*Ethel*)—BIRDS AND BABIES. Imp. 16mo. With 33 Illustrations. 2*s.* 6*d.*

DAVID RIZZIO, BOTHWELL, AND THE WITCH LADY. Three Tragedies. By the Author of 'Ginevra,' &c. Crown 8vo. 6*s.*

DAVIE (*G. S.*) *M.D.*—THE GARDEN OF FRAGRANCE. Being a complete Translation of the Bóstan of Sádi, from the original Persian into English Verse. Crown 8vo. 7*s.* 6*d.*

DAVIES (*T. Hart*)—CATULLUS. Translated into English Verse. Crown 8vo. 6*s.*

DENNIS (*J.*) — ENGLISH SONNETS. Collected and Arranged by. Small crown 8vo. 2*s.* 6*d.*

DE VERE (*Aubrey*)—POETICAL WORKS:

I. THE SEARCH AFTER PROSERPINE, &c. 6*s.*

II. THE LEGENDS OF ST. PATRICK, &c. 6*s.*

III. ALEXANDER THE GREAT, &c. 6*s.*

DE VERE (*Aubrey*)—continued.

THE FORAY OF QUEEN MEAVE, and other Legends of Ireland's Heroic Age. Small crown 8vo. 5*s*.

LEGENDS OF THE SAXON SAINTS. Small crown 8vo. 6*s*.

DILLON (*Arthur*)—RIVER SONGS and other Poems. With 13 Autotype Illustrations from designs by Margery May. Fcp. 4to. cloth extra, gilt leaves, 10*s*. 6*d*.

DOBELL (*Mrs. Horace*)—ETHELSTONE, EVELINE, and other Poems. Crown 8vo. 6*s*.

DOBSON (*Austin*)—OLD WORLD IDYLLS, and other Verses. Fourth Edition. 18mo. cloth extra, gilt tops, 6*s*.

DOMET (*Alfred*)—RANOLF AND AMOHIA: a Dream of Two Lives. New Edition revised. 2 vols. Crown 8vo. 12*s*.

DOROTHY: a Country Story in Elegiac Verse. With Preface. Demy 8vo. 5*s*.

DOWDEN (*Edward*) *LL.D.*—SHAKSPERE'S SONNETS. With Introduction and Notes. Large post 8vo. 7*s*. 6*d*.

DUTT (*Toru*)—A SHEAF GLEANED IN FRENCH FIELDS. New Edition. Demy 8vo. 10*s*. 6*d*.

EDMONDS (*E. M.*)—HESPERAS. Rhythm and Rhyme. Crown 8vo. 4*s*.

EDWARDS (*Miss Betham*)—POEMS. Small crown 8vo. 3*s*. 6*d*.

ELDRYTH (*Maud*)—MARGARET, and other Poems. Small crown 8vo. 3*s*. 6*d*.

ALL SOULS' EVE, 'NO GOD,' and other Poems. Fcp. 8vo. 3*s*. 6*d*.

ELLIOTT (*Ebenezer*), *The Corn Law Rhymer*—POEMS. Edited by his Son, the Rev. Edwin Elliott, of St. John's, Antigua. 2 vols. crown 8vo. 8*s*.

ENGLISH VERSE. Edited by W. J. LINTON and R. H. STODDARD. In 5 vols. Crown 8vo. each 5*s*.

1. CHAUCER TO BURNS.
2. TRANSLATIONS.
3. LYRICS OF THE NINETEENTH CENTURY.
4. DRAMATIC SCENES AND CHARACTERS.
5. BALLADS AND ROMANCES.

ENIS—GATHERED LEAVES. Small crown 8vo.

EVANS (*Anne*)—POEMS AND MUSIC. With Memorial Preface by ANN THACKERAY RITCHIE. Large crown 8vo. 7*s*.

FORSTER (*the late William*)—MIDAS. Crown 8vo. 5*s*.

GINNER (*Isaac B.*)—THE DEATH OF OTHO, and other Poems. Small crown 8vo. 5*s*.

GOODCHILD (*John A.*)—SOMNIA MEDICI. Small crown 8vo. 5*s*.

GOSSE (*Edmund W.*)—NEW POEMS. Crown 8vo. 7*s*. 6*d*.

GRAHAM (*William*)—TWO FANCIES, and other Poems. Crown 8vo. 5*s*.

GRINDROD (*Charles*)—PLAYS FROM ENGLISH HISTORY. Crown 8vo. 7*s*. 6*d*.

THE STRANGER'S STORY and his Poem, THE LAMENT OF LOVE: An Episode of the Malvern Hills. Small crown 8vo. 2*s*. 6*d*.

GURNEY (*Rev. Alfred*)—THE VISION OF THE EUCHARIST, and other Poems. Crown 8vo. 5*s*.

A CHRISTMAS FAGGOT. Small crown 8vo. 5*s*.

HELLON (*H. G.*)—DAPHNIS: a Pastoral Poem. Small crown 8vo. 3*s*. 6*d*.

HENRY (*Daniel*) *junr.*—UNDER A FOOL'S CAP. Songs. Crown 8vo. bevelled boards, 5*s*.

HERMAN WALDGRAVE: a Life's Drama. By the Author of 'Ginevra,' &c. Crown 8vo. 6*s*.

HEYWOOD (*J.C.*)—HERODIAS. A Dramatic Poem. New Edition revised. Small crown 8vo. 5*s*.

HICKEY (*E. H.*)—A SCULPTOR, and other Poems. Small crown 8vo. 5*s*.

HONEYWOOD (*Patty*)—POEMS. Dedicated, by permission, to Lord Wolseley, G.C.B., &c. Small crown 8vo. 2*s*. 6*d*.

JENKINS (*Rev. Canon*)—ALFONSO PETRUCCI, Cardinal and Conspirator: an Historical Tragedy in Five Acts. Small crown 8vo. 3*s.* 6*d.*

JOHNSON (*Ernle S. W.*)—ILARIA, and other Poems. Small crown 8vo. 3*s.* 6*d.*

KEATS (*John*)—POETICAL WORKS. Edited by W. T. ARNOLD. Large crown 8vo. choicely printed on hand-made paper, with Portrait in *eau forte*. Parchment, or cloth, 12*s.*; vellum, 15*s.*

KENNEDY (*Capt. Alexander W. M. Clark*)—ROBERT THE BRUCE. A Poem: Historical and Romantic. With 3 Illustrations by James Faed, Junr. Printed on hand-made paper, parchment, bevelled boards, crown 8vo. 10*s.* 6*d.*

KING (*Edward*)—ECHOES FROM THE ORIENT. With Miscellaneous Poems. Small crown 8vo. 3*s.* 6*d.*

KING (*Mrs. Hamilton*)—THE DISCIPLES. Sixth Edition, with Portrait and Notes. Crown 8vo. 5*s.*

A BOOK OF DREAMS. Crown 8vo. 3*s.* 6*d.*

KNOX (*The Hon. Mrs. O. N.*)—FOUR PICTURES FROM A LIFE, and other Poems. Small crown 8vo. 3*s.* 6*d.*

LANG (*A.*)—XXXII BALLADES IN BLUE CHINA. Elzevir 8vo. parchment, or cloth, 5*s.*

RHYMES À LA MODE. With Frontispiece by E. A. Abbey. 18mo. cloth extra, gilt tops, 5*s.*

LAWSON (*Right Hon. Mr. Justice*)—HYMNI USITATI LATINE REDDITI, with other Verses. Small 8vo. parchment, 5*s.*

LESSING'S NATHAN THE WISE. Translated by Eustace K. Corbett. Crown 8vo. 6*s.*

LIFE THOUGHTS. Small crown 8vo. 2*s.* 6*d.*

LIVING ENGLISH POETS. MDCCCLXXXII. With Frontispiece by Walter Crane. Second Edition. Large crown 8vo. printed on hand-made paper. Parchment, or cloth, 12*s.*; vellum, 15*s.*

LOCKER (*F.*)—LONDON LYRICS. New Edition, with Portrait. 18mo. cloth extra, gilt tops, 5*s.*

LOVE IN IDLENESS. A Volume of Poems. With an etching by W. B. Scott. Small crown 8vo. 5*s.*

LOVE SONNETS OF PROTEUS. With Frontispiece by the Author. Elzevir 8vo. 5*s.*

LUMSDEN (*Lieut.-Col. H. W.*)—BEOWULF: an Old English Poem. Translated into Modern Rhymes. Second and revised Edition. Small crown 8vo. 5*s.*

LYRE AND STAR. Poems by the Author of 'Ginevra,' &c. Crown 8vo. 5*s.*

MACGREGOR (*Duncan*)—CLOUDS AND SUNLIGHT. Poems. Small crown 8vo. 5*s.*

MAGNUSSON (*Eirikr*) *M.A.*, *and PALMER* (*E. H.*) *M.A.*—JOHAN LUDVIG RUNEBERG'S LYRICAL SONGS, IDYLLS, AND EPIGRAMS. Fcp. 8vo. 5*s.*

MDC. Chronicles of Christopher Columbus. A Poem in Twelve Cantos. Small crown 8vo. 7*s.* 6*d.*

MEREDITH (*Owen*) [*The Earl of Lytton*] LUCILE. New Edition. With 32 Illustrations. 16mo. 3*s.* 6*d.*; cloth extra, gilt edges, 4*s.* 6*d.*

MORRIS (*Lewis*)—POETICAL WORKS. New and Cheaper Editions, with Portrait, complete in 3 vols. 5*s.* each.

Vol. I. contains Songs of Two Worlds. Tenth Edition.

Vol. II. contains The Epic of Hades. Seventeenth Edition.

Vol. III. contains Gwen and the Ode of Life. Sixth Edition.

THE EPIC OF HADES. With 16 Autotype Illustrations after the drawings by the late George R. Chapman. 4to. cloth extra, gilt leaves, 21*s.*

THE EPIC OF HADES. Presentation Edition. 4to. cloth extra, gilt leaves, 10*s.* 6*d.*

SONGS UNSUNG. Fourth Edition. Fcp. 8vo. 6s.

THE LEWIS MORRIS BIRTHDAY BOOK. Edited by S. S. Copeman. With Frontispiece after a design by the late George R. Chapman. 32mo. cloth extra, gilt edges, 2*s.*; cloth limp, 1*s.* 6*d.*

MORSHEAD (*E. D. A.*)—THE HOUSE ATREUS. Being the Agamemnon, Libation-Bearers, and Furies of Æschylus. Translated into English Verse. Crown 8vo. 7*s.*

THE SUPPLIANT MAIDENS OF ÆSCHYLUS. Crown 8vo. 3*s.* 6*d.*

NADEN (*Constance W.*)—SONGS AND SONNETS OF SPRING TIME. Small crown 8vo. 5*s.*

NEWELL (*E. J.*)—THE SORROW OF SIMONA, and Lyrical Verses. Small crown 8vo. 3*s.* 6*d.*

NOEL (*The Hon. Roden*)—A LITTLE CHILD'S MONUMENT. Third Edition. Small crown 8vo. 3*s.* 6*d.*

THE RED FLAG, and other Poems. New Edition. Small crown 8vo. 6*s.*

O'HAGAN (*John*)—THE SONG OF ROLAND. Translated into English Verse. New and Cheaper Edition. Crown 8vo. 5*s.*

PFEIFFER (*Emily*)—THE RHYME OF THE LADY OF THE ROCK AND HOW IT GREW. Small crown 8vo. 3*s.* 6*d.*

GERARD'S MONUMENT, and other Poems. Second Edition. Crown 8vo. 6*s.*

UNDER THE ASPENS: Lyrical and Dramatic. With Portrait. Crown 8vo. 6*s.*

PIATT (*J. J.*)—IDYLS AND LYRICS OF THE OHIO VALLEY. Crown 8vo. 5*s.*

RAFFALOVICH (*Mark André*)—CYRIL AND LIONEL, and other Poems. A Volume of Sentimental Studies. Small crown 8vo. 3*s.* 6*d.*

RARE POEMS OF THE 16TH AND 17TH CENTURIES. Edited by W. J. Linton. Crown 8vo. 5*s.*

RHOADES (*James*)—THE GEORGICS OF VIRGIL. Translated into English Verse. Small crown 8vo. 5*s.*

ROBINSON (*A. Mary F.*)—A HANDFUL OF HONEYSUCKLE. Fcp. 8vo. 3*s.* 6*d.*

THE CROWNED HIPPOLYTUS. Translated from Euripides. With New Poems. Small crown 8vo. cloth, 5*s.*

ROUS (*Lieut.-Col.*)—CONRADIN. Small crown 8vo. 2*s.*

SCHILLER'S MARY STUART. German Text with English Translation on opposite page. By Leedham White. Crown 8vo. 6*s.*

SCOTT (*E. J. L.*)—THE ECLOGUES OF VIRGIL. Translated into English Verse. Small crown 8vo. 3*s.* 6*d.*

SCOTT (*George F. E.*)—THEODORA, and other Poems. Small crown 8vo. 3*s.* 6*d.*

SEAL (*W. H.*)—IONE, and other Poems. Second and cheaper edition, revised, crown 8vo. 3*s.* 6*d.*

SELKIRK (*J. B.*)—POEMS. Crown 8vo. 7*s.* 6*d.*

SHARP (*William*)—EUPHRENIA; or, The Test of Love. A Poem. Crown 8vo. 5*s.*

SKINNER (*H. J.*)—THE LILY OF THE LYN, and other Poems. Small crown 8vo. 3*s.* 6*d.*

SLADEN (*Douglas B. W.*)—FRITHJOF AND INGEBJORG, and other Poems. Small crown 8vo. 5*s.*

SMITH (*J. W. Gilbart*)—THE LOVES OF VANDYCK: a Tale of Genoa. Small crown 8vo. 2*s.* 6*d.*

THE LOG O' THE 'NORSEMAN,' Small crown 8vo. 5*s.*

SOPHOCLES: The Seven Plays in English Verse. Translated by Lewis Campbell. Crown 8vo. 7*s.* 6*d.*

SPICER (*Henry*)—HASKA: a Drama in Three Acts (as represented at the Theatre Royal, Drury Lane, March 10th, 1877). Third Edition, crown 8vo. 3*s.* 6*d.*

SYMONDS (*John Addington*)—VAGABUNDULI LIBELLUS. Crown 8vo. 6*s.*

TARES. Crown 8vo. 1*s.* 6*d.*

TASSO'S JERUSALEM DELIVERED. Translated by Sir John Kingston James, Bart. 2 vols. printed on hand-made paper, parchment, bevelled boards, large crown 8vo. 21*s.*

TAYLOR (*Sir H.*)—Works Complete in Five Volumes. Crown 8vo. 30*s.*

PHILIP VAN ARTEVELDE. Fcp. 8vo. 3*s.* 6*d.*

THE VIRGIN WIDOW, &c. Fcp. 8vo. 3*s.* 6*d.*

THE STATESMAN. Fcp. 8vo. 3*s.* 6*d.*

TAYLOR (*Augustus*)—POEMS. Fcp. 8vo. 5*s.*

TAYLOR (*Margaret Scott*) — 'BOYS TOGETHER,' and other Poems. Small crown 8vo. 6*s*.

THORNTON (*L. M.*)—THE SON OF SHELOMITH. Small crown 8vo. 3*s*. 6*d*.

TODHUNTER (*Dr. J.*) — LAURELLA, and other Poems. Crown 8vo. 6*s*. 6*d*.

FOREST SONGS. Small crown 8vo. 3*s*. 6*d*.

THE TRUE TRAGEDY OF RIENZI: a Drama. Crown 8vo. 3*s*. 6*d*.

ALCESTIS: a Dramatic Poem. Extra fcp. 8vo. 5*s*.

TYLER (*M. C.*) — ANNE BOLEYN: a Tragedy in Six Acts. Small crown 8vo. 2*s*. 6*d*.

WALTERS (*Sophia Lydia*) — A DREAMER'S SKETCH BOOK. With 21 Illustrations by Percival Skelton, R. P. Leitch, W. H. J. Boot, and T. R. Pritchett. Engraved by J. D. Cooper. Fcp. 4to. 12*s*. 6*d*.

WANDERING ECHOES. By J. E. D. G. In Four Parts. Small crown 8vo. 5*s*.

WATTS (*Alaric Alfred and Emma Mary Howitt*) — AURORA: a Medley of Verse. Fcp. 8vo. cloth, bevelled boards, 5*s*.

WEBSTER (*Augusta*)—IN A DAY: a Drama. Small crown 8vo. 2*s*. 6*d*.

DISGUISES: a Drama. Small crown 8vo. 5*s*.

WET DAYS. By a Farmer. Small crown 8vo. 6*s*.

WILLIAMS (*J.*)—A STORY OF THREE YEARS, and other Poems. Small crown 8vo. 3*s*. 6*d*.

WORDSWORTH BIRTHDAY BOOK, THE. Edited by ADELAIDE and VIOLET WORDSWORTH. 32mo. limp cloth, 1*s*. 6*d*.; cloth extra, 2*s*.

YOUNGMAN (*Thomas George*)—POEMS. Small crown 8vo. 5*s*.

YOUNGS (*Ella Sharpe*)—PAPHUS, and other Poems. Small crown 8vo. 3*s*. 6*d*.

A HEARTS LIFE, SARPEDON, and other Poems. Small crown 8vo. 3*s*. 6*d*.

WORKS OF FICTION IN ONE VOLUME.

BANKS (*Mrs. G. L.*)—GOD'S PROVIDENCE HOUSE. New Edition. Crown 8vo. 3*s*. 6*d*.

HUNTER (*Hay*)—CRIME OF CHRISTMAS DAY. A Tale of the Latin Quarter. By the Author of 'My Ducats and My Daughter.' 1*s*.

HUNTER (*Hay*) *and WHYTE* (*Walter*) MY DUCATS AND MY DAUGHTER. New and Cheaper Edition. With Frontispiece. Crown 8vo. 6*s*.

INGELOW (*Jean*)—OFF THE SKELLIGS. A Novel. With Frontispiece. Second Edition. Crown 8vo. 6*s*.

KIELLAND (*Alexander L.*)—GARMAN AND WORSE. A Norwegian Novel. Authorised Translation by W. W. Kettlewell. Crown 8vo. 6*s*.

MACDONALD (*G.*)—DONAL GRANT. A Novel. New and Cheap Edition, with Frontispiece. Crown 8vo. 6*s*.

CASTLE WARLOCK. A Novel. New and Cheaper Edition. Crown 8vo. 9*s*.

MALCOLM. With Portrait of the Author engraved on Steel. Sixth Edition. Crown 8vo. 6*s*.

THE MARQUIS OF LOSSIE. Fifth Edition. With Frontispiece. Crown 8vo. 6*s*.

ST. GEORGE AND ST. MICHAEL. Fourth Edition. With Frontispiece. Crown 8vo. 6*s*.

PALGRAVE (*W. Gifford*)—HERMANN AGHA: an Eastern Narrative. Third Edition. Crown 8vo. 6*s*.

SHAW (*Flora L.*)—CASTLE BLAIR; a Story of Youthful Days. New and Cheaper Edition. Crown 8vo. 3*s*. 6*d*.

STRETTON (*Hesba*) — THROUGH A NEEDLE'S EYE. A Story. New and Cheaper Edition, with Frontispiece. Crown 8vo. 6*s*.

TAYLOR (*Col. Meadows*) *C.S.I., M.R.I.A.*

SEETA. A Novel. New and Cheaper Edition. With Frontispiece. Crown 8vo. 6*s*.

TIPPOO SULTAUN: a Tale of the Mysore War. New Edition, with Frontispiece. Crown 8vo. 6*s*.

RALPH DARNELL. New and Cheaper Edition. With Frontispiece. Crown 8vo. 6*s*.

TAYLOR—continued.

A NOBLE QUEEN. New and Cheaper Edition. With Frontispiece. Crown 8vo. 6*s*.

THE CONFESSIONS OF A THUG. Crown 8vo. 6*s*.

TARA: a Mahratta Tale. Crown 8vo. 6*s*.

WITHIN SOUND OF THE SEA. New and Cheaper Edition, with Frontispiece. Crown 8vo. 6*s*.

BOOKS FOR THE YOUNG.

BRAVE MEN'S FOOTSTEPS. A Book of Example and Anecdote for Young People. By the Editor of 'Men who have Risen.' With Four Illustrations by C. Doyle. Eighth Edition. Crown 8vo. 3*s*. 6*d*.

COXHEAD (Ethel)—BIRDS AND BABIES. With 33 Illustrations. Imp. 16mo. cloth gilt, 2*s*. 6*d*.

DAVIES (G. Christopher) — RAMBLES AND ADVENTURES OF OUR SCHOOL FIELD CLUB. With Four Illustrations. New and Cheaper Edition. Crown 8vo. 3*s*. 6*d*.

EDMONDS (Herbert) — WELL-SPENT LIVES: a Series of Modern Biographies. New and Cheaper Edition. Crown 8vo. 3*s*. 6*d*.

EVANS (Mark)—THE STORY OF OUR FATHER'S LOVE, told to Children. Sixth and Cheaper Edition of Theology for Children. With Four Illustrations. Fcp. 8vo. 1*s*. 6*d*.

JOHNSON (Virginia W.)—THE CATSKILL FAIRIES. Illustrated by ALFRED FREDERICKS. 5*s*.

MAC KENNA (S. J.)—PLUCKY FELLOWS. A Book for Boys. With Six Illustrations. Fifth Edition. Crown 8vo. 3*s*. 6*d*.

REANEY (Mrs. G. S.)—WAKING AND WORKING; or, From Girlhood to Womanhood. New and Cheaper Edition. With a Frontispiece. Cr. 8vo. 3*s*. 6*d*.

BLESSING AND BLESSED: a Sketch of Girl Life. New and Cheaper Edition. Crown 8vo. 3*s*. 6*d*.

REANEY (Mrs. G. S.)—continued.

ROSE GURNEY'S DISCOVERY. A Book for Girls. Dedicated to their Mothers. Crown 8vo. 3*s*. 6*d*.

ENGLISH GIRLS: Their Place and Power. With Preface by the Rev. R. W. Dale. Fourth Edition. Fcp. 8vo. 2*s*. 6*d*.

JUST ANYONE, and other Stories. Three Illustrations. Royal 16mo. 1*s*. 6*d*.

SUNBEAM WILLIE, and other Stories. Three Illustrations. Royal 16mo. 1*s*. 6*d*.

SUNSHINE JENNY, and other Stories. Three Illustrations. Royal 16mo. 1*s*. 6*d*.

STOCKTON (Frank R.)—A JOLLY FELLOWSHIP. With 20 Illustrations. Crown 8vo. 5*s*.

STORR (Francis) and TURNER (Hawes). CANTERBURY CHIMES; or, Chaucer Tales Re-told to Children. With Six Illustrations from the Ellesmere MS. Third Edition. Fcp. 8vo. 3*s*. 6*d*.

STRETTON (Hesba)—DAVID LLOYD'S LAST WILL. With Four Illustrations. New Edition. Royal 16mo. 2*s*. 6*d*.

TALES FROM ARIOSTO RE-TOLD FOR CHILDREN. By a Lady. With Three Illustrations. Crown 8vo. 4*s*. 6*d*.

WHITAKER (Florence)—CHRISTY'S INHERITANCE: A London Story. Illustrated. Royal 16mo. 1*s*. 6*d*.